RICHARD SEVERO
and LEWIS MILFORD

SIMON AND SCHUSTER
New York London Toronto Sydney Tokyo

THE WAGES OF WAR

WHEN AMERICA'S SOLDIERS CAME HOME—FROM VALLEY FORGE TO VIETNAM

SIMON AND SCHUSTER
SIMON & SCHUSTER BUILDING
ROCKEFELLER CENTER
1230 AVENUE OF THE AMERICAS
NEW YORK, NEW YORK 10020

DESIGNED BY KAROLINA HARRIS
MANUFACTURED IN THE UNITED STATES OF AMERICA
10 9 8 7 6 5 4 3 2

LIBRARY OF CONGRESS CATALOGING-IN-PUBLICATION DATA

SEVERO, RICHARD.
    THE WAGES OF WAR.

    BIBLIOGRAPHY: P.
    INCLUDES INDEX.
    1. VETERANS—UNITED STATES—HISTORY.   I. MILFORD,
LEWIS.   II. TITLE.
UB357.S48   1989   355.1'15'0973   89–4299

ISBN 0–671–54325–3

This book is respectfully dedicated to Daniel Shays and to the forgotten men and women who fought by his side more than two hundred years ago; and to the men and women who served only yesterday in Korea and Vietnam, but who were quickly no less forgotten.

Contents

Prologue   9

PART ONE: AFTER THE REVOLUTION   19
  1 Lambs and Bees or Tigers and Wolves   21
  2 Half Pay, Full Taxes, and Engines of Vice   29
  3 Officer Princes and the Art of Living Happily Ever After   39
  4 Daniel Shays: From True Patriot to Counterfeit Public Enemy   51
  5 A Little Rebellion Now and Then   64

PART TWO: THE WAR OF 1812 AND THE MEXICAN WAR   81
  6 Like Sweet Poison on the Taste   83
  7 Just Debts and Common Sense   95
  8 St. Patrick Goes to Mexico   107

PART THREE: THE CIVIL WAR   119
  9 Nathaniel Hawthorne, Walt Whitman, and the Concussion of
    Young Men   121
  10 The Day That Michigan, Illinois, Pennsylvania, and Ohio
    Voted in Indiana   143
  11 Bounties and Blacks   160
  12 Palace of Pensions   169

PART FOUR: THE WAR WITH SPAIN AND THE PHILIPPINE INSURRECTION   187
  13 Embalmed Beef, Bad Water, Typhoid, and Five-Dollar
    Coffins at Montauk Point   189

14 Of Mutilations, Massacres, and McKinley   211

PART FIVE: AFTER THE FIRST WORLD WAR   229
15 When Italians Lacked the ''Conveniences for Thinking'' and Black Mothers Traveled Second Class   231
16 67,000 Quarts of Whiskey, Enough Floor Wax to Cover South Dakota, and ''to hell with the Central Office''   247
17 Mellon, du Pont, and the Chamber of Commerce: Fighting Is Its Own Reward   258
18 The Great Depression and the Ghost of Daniel Shays   264

PART SIX: AFTER THE SECOND WORLD WAR   281
19 Sweet Wine at Last   283
20 Forgotten Women, Failed Men   298

PART SEVEN: THE KOREAN WAR   315
21 The Scapegoats   317
22 The Scapegoaters   334

PART EIGHT: THE VIETNAM WAR AND THE AGENT ORANGE AFFAIR   345
23 The Red Carpet Leads to Rejection   347
24 When Not to Know Means Not to Pay   360
25 The VA and Dow versus the Christians   372
26 Avoid Politicians and Lawyers and Get a Good PR Man   382
27 The White House Suppresses a Report   397

Epilogue   419
Acknowledgments   427
Notes   431
Index   480

Prologue

Nothing had really changed in the last two hundred years. Or so it seemed. From Colrain to Amherst, we took back roads that slithered gray and yellow across calloused hills. Ancient red barns and pale white clapboard farmhouses clung to pastures fractured with dark rock, which only hinted at a land that was as hostile to growing crops as it was lovely in the scarlet of October.

But surely something must have changed in western Massachusetts since a Revolutionary War veteran and reluctant rebel named Daniel Shays had labored and suffered and inspired and then run for his very life. We made a long loop and came north on Route 202. Where 202 crossed Route 9, just opposite a little sandwich shop called Mike's Place, there was a sign announcing that from here on, Route 202 was now the "Daniel Shays Highway." Well, that was different. In 1786, when James Bowdoin was Governor, Boston was hardly predisposed to name a road after Daniel Shays. A debtor's cell maybe. Certainly not a state road that would be used by the God-fearing and law-abiding people of Massachusetts to further commerce and prosperity.

For Daniel Shays was an American dissident. He had a principled grievance against the British, and so he fought the British. But when he returned to his farm after the war, he found that he had a principled grievance against the new Government in Boston, too, the same American Government he had fought so hard to establish. The Government expected everyone—impoverished veterans and subsistence farmers included—to pay debts promptly with hard currency. Harsh and unyielding, Massachusetts law permitted creditors to exact retribution against debtors who could not pay, including the use of the court system to send them to prison. People certainly wanted to pay, but the hard currency of choice, which was British, not American, was in short supply. Many of the people Shays knew lost their farms and all else they owned. The debtors, Shays among them, were thus inexorably drawn into a confrontation with the bureaucrats and merchant princes of Boston. When mere protest failed, Shays and his friends tried to stop the courts from sitting, and that, in turn, brought an army of mercenary militiamen down on them. Those who were with Shays resisted the injustices of their Government just as hard, and with every bit as much courage and dignity as any Soviet or South African or Polish or Czech dissident of the twentieth century. But as we drove toward his hometown of Pelham and a celebration that would honor his memory, we realized that there were many Americans who had been taught that Shays was a rebel and an outlaw. And many more hadn't the faintest idea of who Daniel Shays was.

Daniel Shays Highway led directly up to Pelham. We passed nubs of stone walls that were young when Shays was old. Sometimes there were piles of cut wood piled neatly against the walls. The land around us rose to a wooded plateau in the east, then swooped down toward the valley that formed the watershed for the enormous Quabbin Reservoir, Boston's drinking-water supply. There were stands of hemlock everywhere, as there were in Shays' time, hemlock that Shays and his men sprigged for their hats; evergreen symbols of resistance to the conscienceless stiff-necked Government in Boston. The hemlock had been joined, a century after Shays disappeared, by elm and large oak and scrub oak, by balsam fir, maple, and scotch pine. The forest that now attended the Daniel Shays Highway may have been of interest to the leaf-seekers up from New York, but would not have been so comforting to Shays' rebels, who preferred solid hemlock to hide them from the thrusted bayonets of the privately financed army from Boston that hunted them, almost always cornered them, and sometimes killed them with musket and grapeshot.

The creation of the Quabbin in the 1930s had taken a third of Pelham, including the remains of Shays' house and his farm. His house was in the watershed but was not underwater, only out of bounds to anyone who might want to see it. It was deep in the woods and left unmarked, decidedly not promoted in Massachusetts tourism ads. We wondered, as we drove, what he would have said about the home he worked so hard for now within the eminent domain of Boston. The answer came quickly. "It was always in Boston's eminent domain," Shays would have told us. "It just took me a little while to figure that out. You have to expect that. After all, I'm only a farmer."

We continued driving obliquely toward Pelham; we felt the need to travel the roads that Shays had traveled. We passed Conkey's lumberyard, a prosperous-looking place. Two hundred years earlier, in 1786, a man named William Conkey was Shays' friend, ever-patient creditor, confidant, and favorite tavern keeper. We wondered if the present Conkey, David, a direct descendant of William, would do as much to help the likes of Shays as had his forebear, whose tavern lies as an unmarked ruin half a mile from Shays' place, also in the watershed of the Quabbin. There is no more left to either building than there is to ancient Troy. In a state where, it would seem, nothing has ever escaped the attention and protection of preservationists, the ruins of Shays' house and Conkey's tavern remain conspicuously inaccessible, known only to a few, destined to be forever viewed from afar. The Pelham Historical Commission had produced a map and directed people to a parking area on Daniel Shays Highway where, from a distance, they could see the barren hill that Shays tried to farm and know that Conkey's was not far off.

We reached Pelham early. We had to. It was a day for special doings. The people of Pelham were coming to the old Town Hall to commemorate the two hundredth anniversary of the event known desultorily in high school history books as Shays' Rebellion, though it did not belong to Shays and it most certainly was not a rebellion, even if the men and women who participated in it acted rebelliously. It takes more than rebelliousness to make a rebellion. Shays taught us that. There were only twenty-eight cars parked in a grassy area across the Daniel Shays Highway from Town Hall, but many more were due, and we wondered how many Pelham folk would actually come out to honor a man about whom there was so much misunderstanding so long ago, and not so long ago.

It was quite a brilliant October day, and in the searching white sunshine of autumn it seemed entirely appropriate to stir the phantom of Shays' Rebellion out of the stygian equivocality into which the Federalists had long ago consigned it. Many more people came, not just from Pelham, but from Amherst and Northampton and Springfield. They were coming quickly now. There was even one tall large man who had driven all the way from Utica, New York. He emerged from his car wearing a white tunic, a three-cornered hat, knickers, and the buckled shoes of Shays' time. His steely eyes were circled by old-fashioned steel-rimmed spectacles. He explained that he was something of a Revolutionary War buff and that whenever he heard of an appropriate event—and this was certainly appropriate—he packed his outfit and started driving. He patiently demonstrated the art of loading a musket and was disconcerted when the Pelham folk and their guests seemed not very interested in his considerable knowledge and expertise. Shays and his farmer friends, most of them veterans, had been little enough interested in muskets when they stood up to Government troops paid for by the merchants of Boston. What reason for Shays' friends to be any more concerned now?

They gathered on the green before the 1743 Town Hall, said to be the oldest town hall in continuous use in New England, and they bought Daniel Shays T-shirts, Daniel Shays coffee mugs, and Daniel Shays postcards. There were even plans to raffle off a newly designed Daniel Shays gold coin, which showed Shays standing at the ready with a bayonet affixed to his musket, superimposed over a likeness of the top of the Statue of Liberty. The coin bore the legend ''We the people . . .'' Daniel Shays, who began to care about money only when it was too late, when society insisted that he have it in order to survive, was now on a gold coin. Surely, he would have found that amusing.

It became quite impossible not to talk about Shays and what he stood for. Old friends had not forgotten him. A program distributed by the Pelham Historical Commission indicated that one of the many contributors to the observance was the Conkey Lumber Company, which donated the lumber onto which a narrative of Shays' Rebellion had been affixed. We were most pleased; no bond with the past had been broken. Shays was there, no doubt about it, and Conkey was still his friend. Within an hour after we arrived, there were many dozens of cars on the grass across from Town Hall and two hundred or three hundred people poked about, looking at exhibits, smiling, talking about Daniel Shays.

But why? Why would so many people in 1986 gather to commemorate such an abysmal failure? There was never any question that Shays had failed in his struggle with the merchants and Government in Boston, although perhaps he succeeded in making the Federalists a little less intractable. That is arguable. Suffice it to say here that Shays had thought that the Revolution he fought with so much valor against the British belonged to him as well as to the merchants, the professionals, and the Founding Father elite of Boston. When the war ended and it appeared that the Revolution had not been fought for the likes of Shays, he stood up to the sins of his Government, one of the very few Americans to do that after the British were ousted. To this day, the United States has not produced anyone quite like him; no doomed rebel who touches our hearts so, at least those few of us who know who Daniel Shays was. We like to lionize and idealize the dreamers who fight city hall in our novels and films. But few of us dare to be like them, and none of us has been like Shays. No other former soldier has gone to such lengths to correct a Government abuse.

Sins cannot be forgiven unless they are first acknowledged. The people who relaxed in the sun felt that some of those old sins still needed confirmation of a sort so that, perforce, the long-gone sinners who committed them could be absolved. The question of Shays' forgiveness was not an issue. He and his men had long ago been forgiven by Boston. But Boston had never really been forgiven by Pelham, neither for the witless way it created the problems that made great unrest and unhappiness inevitable, nor for the way it crushed the farmers' protest, nor for the way it rode roughshod over the countryside when it created the Quabbin watershed, a century and a half later.

The Pelham Historical Commission, apparently believing that the purging of shabby practices can be a cultural experience as well as a spiritual one, even published a poem outlining not only what Boston did to Shays but what it did to Pelham in this century. The poem was well received because there were new sins to talk about—mistakes made by Government since Shays' time, mistakes not having anything to do either with Shays or with the Quabbin, but mistakes having to do with all of us.

In Massachusetts, new mistakes always require new responses. Some of the people gathered on the Town Hall green talked about four veterans who were even then fasting on the steps of the Capitol in Washington. They had read about it that morning in New England newspapers, which carried many pictures. The veterans had fasted for forty days to protest American policy of aid to the Contras in Nicaragua. They had lost one hundred pounds among them. Other veterans, some of them women, had now joined the protest. Hurt and angry, they had returned to the Government medals they had won in World War II and Vietnam. There was a Congressional Medal of Honor, as well as a Silver Star, a Bronze Star, and quite a number of Purple Hearts and other medals. They just took off the medals they had been so pleased to receive and replaced them with "peace ribbons."

In Pelham, before the Town Hall in the sun, they talked about the protesters and liked to think that if Shays were still around, he might have been protesting in Washington, too. These were people who were trying to get in touch with their own Revolution, something Americans don't do that often.

The celebration of Shays' Rebellion "offers us a chance to honor the legacy we have in this town of standing up when things aren't right," said Barbara Jenkins, a member of the Pelham Historical Commission. "It is part of our heritage—part of our heritage that is dying. It is atrophying. It is reminding people that once we had a revolution. But when somebody else has a revolution," she added, "we become upset."

She said no more and moved around Town Hall, welcoming guests, handing them leaflets about the exhibit she had worked on for so long with her friends and neighbors. Four of the six people on the commission who did all the work were women—Ms. Jenkins, Peg Hepler, Ruth Gallagher, and Emma Weaver. It may have puzzled some outsiders that women would give so much of themselves to remember a movement so totally associated with men, but it did not surprise us. Notwithstanding their own underrated military service, it was women after our later wars, and especially after Vietnam, who would play a vital role in insisting that their veteran husbands and lovers demand their due from Government—and thus force it to remember. The compassion and persistence of such women were, at many times in our history, all that bridged the gap between the veterans' isolation and the Government.

Usually, farmers and veterans do not come up in the same conversation. It might be argued that they do not come up in enough conversations. But Shays was both a veteran and a farmer, and some of the people in Pelham that day drew comparisons between Daniel Shays and his friends and the beleaguered farmers of the Midwest, many of them veterans of the wars in Korea and Vietnam, who were leading their own protests, asking for Government assistance to prevent bank foreclosures and confiscation of their property because they were unable to pay off their debts. There was no Daniel Shays among these men.

There was a lot to consider in the two-day commemoration. It was clear by the second day that people were thinking not just about Shays but about the men and women driven to protest the injustices of their Government and a bicentennial of mistakes that had been made between the Revolution and the aftermath of Vietnam.

So, just as it was time to think differently about Daniel Shays, it was time to think differently about soldiers, all kinds of soldiers. It was time to make connections between what has happened to them and what has happened to everyone else. Because when one thinks about American veterans, one is confronted with American society in its broadest sense. They are our neighbors, friends, and lovers; our fathers and mothers; our husbands and wives; our sons and daughters.

The Government estimates that nearly 39 million Americans have served us in wartime since 1776. The Veterans Administration has estimated that more than a million of them have died doing that. It is a large number, but somehow, with all the violence that now surrounds us in less-than-global conflicts, the number seems as though it should be much, much higher. As of the 1980 census, more than 23 million Americans had served in a war and lived to tell about it. There were another 6 million survivors who had served in what we have come to call peacetime. And so, with time taking its toll, there are now nearly 28 million Americans among us who have served in the military, all because of war and our fears about war. Those 28 million have another 53 million who survive them or depend on them. *Thus, a third of our population has had a direct or indirect role in serving the military interests of this country.* In the face of their sheer number and the enormity of the debt we owe them, why have we ignored such people, scorned them, and wanted to forget about them? Why could the nation not have waited a bit longer for the veterans of Shays' time to pay their debts? Why was the indifference and the impatience accorded the Korea and Vietnam veterans upon their homecoming not all that different from what Shays experienced?

On that day in Pelham, we wondered about all the afterwards; how such young people had been treated after the ends of wars, police actions, skirmishes, and brief encounters—by politicians, merchants, corporations, families, neighbors, books, newspapers and magazines, and the clergy. And how, we also wondered, had our former soldiers regarded the people they fought so hard for? How did they regard each other?

Thus, this book is not only about soldiers. It is mostly about the people who have fought our wars over the past two centuries, the civilians who have surrendered their liberty and risked their lives to fight our wars, and how the people they returned to treated them. But in its truest sense, it is about those of us who stayed home and watched, too. Nor is this simply a book about the clichés of war. Stratagems and grand designs, crafty generals' brilliance flickering in softly lit war rooms, the valor under fire of the common foot soldier, are mentioned only in passing. No cannons regularly boom in these pages, no individual heroics with fixed bayonets on muddy battlefields are recounted, no enemy is vanquished.

Information about former soldiers is not abundant. To learn about their doings in the eighteenth and nineteenth centuries, we searched through old records—books, newspaper clippings, poems, sermons, ordinances, Government files—material all but unknown to most Americans. For the twentieth century, we did more of the same. To learn the truth about the Government's role in the Agent Orange tragedy, we combined historical research with the discipline of investigative reporting, using the Federal Freedom of Information Act to uncover thousands of pages of Government documents—some from the very highest levels of power—that had been kept from public view. We interviewed Government officials whose consciences mandated that they tell somebody what really happened, in the White House and elsewhere, when America decided it would use chemicals to deny crops and cover to the enemy in Vietnam, and not care very much about the effects, either on civilians or on its own soldiers.

We started with the years following the American Revolution and ended with the sad turmoil of the 1970s and 1980s, after the last battle involving American troops in Vietnam had been fought. The soldiers who had gone to battle in Vietnam appeared to be the loneliest of all Americans, scorned by their own Government as well as by civilians who thought they should have won a war that could not have been won and should not have been fought.

Vietnam was not the only unpopular war fought by the United States. As we looked at other postwar periods, we found that those veterans had been treated as badly by Government and society as were the veterans of Vietnam. It surprised us only because we, like so many other Americans, had nurtured special memories of the years following World War II. We had memories of homecoming soldiers welcomed as heroes who had defeated the armies of one of history's great madmen, then given opportunities to improve their lot through the provisions of the G.I. Bill. As we worked, we had reason, in due course, to wonder anew about our fond memories about the end of World War II. Was it the norm we had thought or was it really an anomaly in American history?

Throughout American history, even after "popular" wars, veterans have had to struggle against a Government that has mostly sought to limit its financial liability, more like a slippery insurance company than a polity rooted in the idea of justice and fair reward. Veterans have struggled, too, against a society that saw nothing wrong with patriotic civilians who amassed huge profits from wars, but saw something terribly wrong with civilian soldiers who tried to use military service to earn money and to obtain educational opportunities that might otherwise be denied them. There were times in American history, including recent history, when such soldiers were lured into service with offers of generous pay, bonuses, and benefits, only to be scorned as mercenaries and social parasites when they tried to collect their due.

We also found ominous efforts to deny or limit the soldier's right to vote or to cast doubt on its moderation with the suggestion that military service had somehow changed him and made him less sensitive to our Constitution's precepts; to pussyfoot, delay, or simply renege on promises to grant pensions, even when there was evidence that the applicant was deserving; to discriminate against former soldiers in the job market and in the press; to manipulate them as a group and induce them to vote for certain candidates;

to scrimp to the point of cheating on health care for veterans while functionaries in Government looted the Treasury; to secretly give LSD and other dangerous drugs to unsuspecting soldiers, then refuse to pay them a penny for the ruination of their lives; to misstate and misrepresent the effects of atomic radiation on soldiers exposed to it.

On that bright day in Pelham, when everyone was thinking about Daniel Shays—in his hometown they call him "the Captain"—it was time as well to think about women in the nineteenth century who were unjustly denied widows' pensions; about women in the twentieth century who served the war effort and yet were scorned, cheated and forgotten, and denied equal status with male veterans; about black soldiers during the Revolution who were distrusted and set apart; about black Union veterans abused in the South after the Civil War; about blacks set apart even as the armed services were desegregated in the twentieth century.

And what about the schism between veterans and so many intellectuals, the latter steadfast in believing they are capable of understanding everything— except, possibly, why they should care about former soldiers? That weekend in Pelham, four scholars from Amherst and Mount Holyoke colleges, Historic Deerfield, and Tufts University made it clear that they, at least, would like to close the gap. And although they spoke about Shays, they replicated the feelings of the rest of us, who wanted to think about Shays, the past, and the present, all at once.

Joseph Ellis, dean of Mount Holyoke College, praised Shays as a local hero, "full of life, not bigger than life." He thought that Shays would have understood much of what followed him—the populists of the nineteenth century, the farmers portrayed in Steinbeck's *Grapes of Wrath,* the veterans of Vietnam. "He would not, however, have been a fan of Rambo." As a rural rebel, he would have understood the failure of farms in the West, Ellis said, as well as how his own neighbors felt about the Quabbin.

With a glance at assembled officials, who included Congressman Silvio O. Conte, Republican of Pittsfield, Ellis also suggested that Shays would not have liked politicians, either. The politicians smiled faintly and rearranged themselves in their chairs.

"His values are still with us today, like the Red Sox fighting the good losing fight," Ellis said, as the Boston team prepared to lose yet another World Series, this time to the Mets. Shays, said Ellis, was committed to the values of "contemplation, quiet, and standing against bureaucracy . . . he had the courage of his own quaintness." But like the Pelham Historical Commission's Barbara Jenkins, he thought that whatever there was in the American character that had created Shays, we were losing it; losing it as we had lost the values of contemplation in a society that now seemed not to want to think about much of anything, except its material pleasures.

As all this was going on in the autumn of 1986, the Reagan Administration was curtailing health and other benefits for veterans—a year before America's second great stock market crash would make even further cuts an inevitability. Veterans old before their time and ailing from things that few in Government claimed to understand were finding the going tougher, and they could take little comfort from the news that privately financed monuments and memorials to the Vietnam dead were springing up all over the country. And the American Legion was informing its members that, much to its dismay, a third of all the homeless in America were veterans, half of them veterans of Vietnam.

We left Pelham with Daniel Shays very much on our minds. It was time to think about what really happened, way back when, to those who had fought the Revolution. It was also time, we sensed, to find out what had happened since, and what was really going on with our former soldiers now.

Richard Severo
Newburgh, New York

Lewis Milford
Montpelier, Vermont

December 1988

ONE
After
the
Revolution

An army of mercenaries fired upon Massachusetts farmers and Revolutionary War veterans in the uprising known as Shays' Rebellion. (*The Bettmann Archive*)

1

Lambs and Bees or Tigers and Wolves

Let the public only comply with their own promises, and the army will return to their respective homes the lambs and bees of the community. But if they should be disbanded previous to a settlement without knowing who to look to for an adjustment of accounts and a responsibility of payment, they will be so deeply stung by the injustice and ingratitude of their country so as to become its tigers and its wolves.
—Major-General Henry Knox, 1783

The soldiers who had been so hungry and wanting began to come home early in the summer of 1783. They came home slowly in the dust of summer's heat to the unforgiving fields and insatiable creditors they had left to take up the great struggle. They included Eliphalet Allen and Jeremiah Klumph and Jehu Grant and William Finnie and William Drew and John L. Schermerhorn and Cornelius Sauquayonk. Their service was honorable but their exploits and adventures had not attracted very much attention during the war. Famous or not, they were at last finished fighting the revolution that established the American republic. But their struggle for back pay, for pensions, for honorable treatment by the very Government they had helped create, was only beginning.

To marginal farms in the loam of the Carolinas or in the rocks of New England and Upstate New York, to small towns with pleasant village greens and white churches, the soldiers came home. They would soon do combat again, these unfamous veterans, armed with foolscap and scratchy quill pens; abetted by advising, persistent wives; impelled by lovable, hungry children; and they would be far less successful in this effort than they were in the war they had fought. Once their paper combat was over and lost, they would inevitably recede into the further anonymity of the inky flourishes that constituted Government's official record of their war—and of their efforts to get paid for fighting it.

Other veterans, hard-bitten New Englanders like Luke Day, Elijah Day, Asa Fisk, Aaron Jewett, Agrippa Wells, Luke Drury, Oliver Parker, Seth Murray, and most especially, Daniel Shays, were soldiers of another mind, another magnitude of desperation. They also had served well, if without much recognition, and were destined to earn some notoriety outside of Government ledgers kept by the War Office, although not the kind they had thought they would get when they volunteered to serve. Most certainly, not the kind they wanted. Not the kind they wanted to think about for the rest of their lives.

To New York, Boston, Baltimore, and Philadelphia the veterans came, eager to be civilians and to work as only they could. By late autumn and first snow they seemed to be everywhere in streets of cobbles and mud, lean and hungry, looking for work. But there was none for most of them. Sailmakers, blacksmiths, blockmakers, combmakers, tanners, coppersmiths, stonecutters, curriers, brewers, pewterers, silversmiths, chocolatemakers, carpenters, tanners, bakers, pot-bakers, ironmongers, clerks, liverymen, tobacconists, tallow chandlers, scriveners, chimney sweepers, hatters, coachmakers, staymakers, country lawyers, and common laborers: tradesmen without trade; artisans without commissions; workers without work. There was no work, and there was no money from the Government, either. At least, no money anybody could spend.

Paper money had been issued, toward the end of the war, by most of the states, in the form of bills of credit which generally promised to be "payable in Spanish milled dollars with 5 per cent interest." The promise of ownership of a coin minted in Spain was an elegant proposition but it was hardly the sort of cachet that would engender confidence in the ability of the United States to create its own hard currency. And so there was no confidence, especially after the Continental Congress debased American paper early on by allowing too much of it to be printed.

Virginia's finances, which were desperate, were a fair example of how much trouble the states were in. It had printed pound notes which were supposed to be redeemable at some future time at $1 specie (hard coin) for $40 in bills. Since hardly anybody thought that Virginia currency was worth that much, including the several state officials who personally signed each note, the ratio was changed in 1781 to $1 in specie for $1,000 in bills. All such bills bore the legend "Death to Counterfeit." Counterfeit or real, the notes all became worthless to whoever held them on October 1, 1792.

Ironically, the money's predictable downfall came just about a year after the British were so decisively drubbed at Yorktown. Its perceived value didn't reflect that rebel victory or the reality of Britain's doomed proprietorship of the colonies—only that Congress had overworked its printing presses to create a lot of new money to pay for a war it couldn't afford.

So, the victors returning to their home states found themselves with fancifully decorated pieces of paper that were greeted with contempt by merchants from Maine to Georgia. Creditors reproached the returning veterans sternly. How could they expect to pay for shoes or seed or livestock or anything with paper that everybody knew had no value? Give us coins, said the creditors. Specie was the way to the good life. Veterans had to learn that, just like everybody else. They simply had to adjust to the reality of civilian life, and the creditors hoped it wouldn't take forever.

But how appropriate was it to aspire to the good life? The veterans heard esteemed clergymen inveigh against the mammon pursued by the worldly people around them, resourceful landholders and burghers who, for the most part, had not been mere soldiers (although a few had been high-ranking officers) and who were crafty enough to survive in such disordered times. More than survive, they knew how to live well.

"If anything can be done by government to discourage prodigality and extravagance, vain and expensive amusements and fantastic foppery, and to encourage the opposite virtues, we hope it will not be neglected," preached the Rev. Simeon Howard, pastor of Boston's West Church. "We are ardently pursuing this world's riches, honors, powers, pleasures; let us possess them and then know that they are nothing, nothing, nothing," agreed Yale's president, the Rev. Ezra Stiles.

In their abject want, the former soldiers heard such sermons and they wondered—how could such admonition be for the likes of them? The preachers may have been talking about the merchant princes, like John Jacob Astor, John Murray, Isaac Moses, Theophylact Bache, or Joseph Alsop, who became the first president of the New York Chamber of Commerce after the war. Or, perhaps they were referring to land speculators like the Livingstons, the Schuylers, the Van Rensselaers. There were a few veterans who were doing well in speculation—Alexander Hamilton and Henry Knox, to name two. Most others did not fare so well.

And just where were all of life's pleasures? The Government had not paid them their promised due, and Army life had been an abomination. George

Washington had taken note of their penury over the years in various speeches and letters, including one to the Secretary of War in which he complained that his officers suffered "mortification" when they "cannot invite a French officer, a visiting friend, or a travelling acquaintance to a better repast than stinking whiskey (and not always that). . . ."

But when he thought of that part of American society that had stayed home and profited from the war, Washington agreed fully with the clergymen. He complained that "stockjobbing, dissipation, luxury and venality, with all their concomitants, are [too] deeply rooted . . . to yield to virtue and the common good." And he knew that the problems within his Army were not confined to the unavailability of good whiskey.

So did Joseph Plumb Martin, a private who served in the Army for seven years and was with Washington at Valley Forge. In 1783, he went home to Maine and told his neighbors that the condition of the troops was "pitiful and forlorn," that what little meat he had been given was "not many degrees above carion," and that the "six and two-thirds dollars" he had received for a single month—August of 1777—proved "scarcely enough to procure a man's dinner." Jeremiah Greenman, a regimental adjutant for Rhode Island troops, also served Washington well and believed in him but said of his fellow soldiers, as the war ended, "Some of them had not a Shoe or Stocking to their feet."

And in Boston, already beginning to think of itself as a wellspring of culture on the edge of the vast and barbaric American wilderness that included New York and Philadelphia, Samuel Adams wrote a letter to John Adams complaining that too many people there "are imitating the Britons in every idle amusement and expensive foppery which it is in [their] power to invent for the destruction of a young country. . . . You would be surprised to see the equipage, the furniture, the expensive living of too many, the pride and vanity of dress which pervades thro' every class, confounding the difference between the poor and the rich."

Only rarely did anyone mention the soldiers who had won the war, men now down on their luck.

A writer in the *Boston Gazette* was a partial exception, carrying the banner in a lighthearted way for those veterans who, at least, had money before the war. He mused on the *bon ton* of the time, which apparently favored rising at ten, breakfasting at eleven, and "rattling through our paved streets" at midnight, "to the great annoyance of the peaceful inhabitants." Then he asked: "How are our worthy patriots treated? Men who risked their lives and property, in the cause of freedom—lent their hard money to assist in the contest, and took securities or paper money for it, which now lie dormant in their desks, and they are obliged to pay specie for debts due to a set of vultures, who are now permitted to return. . . ."

If Lieutenant Joseph Bascomb had read the *Gazette* that day, he surely would have shaken his head sadly. Bascomb, who had been with the Minute Men at Concord, had all of $400 when he joined the Army, but was without a penny when he left it.

Major William Ballard, a veteran of Bunker Hill, had an estate when the war started. Now, as the men were coming home, he found himself a debtor. Even worse were the straits of Colonel Timothy Bigelow of Worcester, who had honorably served his country, but was destined to die soon, in debtor's prison. And there were countless others who had nothing when they joined and nothing when they got out. These were men whose fortunes were never lamented by the *Gazette* or any other newspaper musing about Boston's *bon ton*.

In the spring of 1782, when William Feltman decided to resign his lieutenancy in the 1st Pennsylvania Regiment, he asked General Nathaniel Greene for a "small some of money" so that he could get home. The general "very politely refused," and told Feltman that "he had not any money for those people who chose to return home at their own will." That was only part of the truth. In fact, General Greene had no money at all for any soldier who wanted to go home under anybody else's will, either, and he did not even have money for those who wanted to stay.

Later that same year, the war caught up to Major Samuel Shaw, who had enlisted in 1775 and remained in the Army for nine years. He wrote to his father bitterly late in 1782 that he would pay a particular debt: "I intend to pay it when it is due; though to do this I must contract another debt. It is no satisfaction to me to reflect that I am obliged to do this, notwithstanding the public owes me for nearly three years' service. . . ."

At the beginning of the war, Congress had passed a law that prohibited creditors from bringing lawsuits against those who enlisted. Soldiers were offered food, clothing, and land just for enlisting (one hundred acres for enlisted men and five hundred acres for officers—reflecting the constancy of history's class distinctions, even in a new country that tried not to have any). The offering of such inducements to men willing to do deadly combat did not seem extreme to those who were determined to get the British out. In fact, it looked like a bargain, as, indeed, it was. "Let us look upon freedom from the power of tyrants as a blessing that cannot be purchased too dear," the Rev. Samuel West had counseled when he appeared before the Honorable Council and the Honorable House of Representatives of the Colony of Massachusetts Bay in Boston.

Unfortunately, the eagerness and even the willingness to lavish material things on the nation's champions had evaporated in parsimony long before the war's meandering end. There had been mixed feelings about the war, and even the people who proudly waved goodbye to friends and neighbors who had volunteered felt a certain awkwardness at the homecoming of such poor men. For most soldiers, there were no homecoming parades, no flags flying nor bands playing, no smiles from many of the civilians whose fortunes had waxed with their liberties, whether they chose to acknowledge it or not. The veterans returned to a curious, chromatic world of indifference and even outright hostility; of gaunt privation and new-money opulence; of euphoria and bitterness; of former champions underemployed and assorted opportunists, charlatans, and thieves employed incessantly, it seemed.

There were few, if any, official welcomes. In Boston, for example, returning soldiers caused alarm among civilians. Indeed, the General Court there (the Massachusetts legislature) complained to Congress that needy veterans were creating problems for Bostonians since most of them came home without "a single month's pay" nor "so much as the means to carry them to their respective homes." But some of the same New Englanders complaining about penniless veterans with whom they were now forced to mingle had earlier condemned various plans to give the veterans pensions for life at half their wartime pay.

Probably nowhere was American life more eerie, more schizophrenic, than in the City of New York, a prize plum that the British had managed to dominate throughout the war.

Elkanah Watson was a member of the Continental Army that occupied New York on the 25th of November of 1783, after Englishmen under begrudging, laggard Sir Guy Carleton gave it up to George Washington, who found him tiresome but was determined to be ever polite and patient. Watson hardly felt like the conquering hero, for New York's physical and psychic state was clearly not the equal of the strategic value of its splendid harbor. "Close on the eve of an approaching winter," Watson wrote, "with a heterogeneous set of inhabitants, composed of almost ruined exiles, disbanded soldiery, mixed foreigners, disaffected Tories, and the refuse of a British army, we took possession of a ruined city."

Nearly a quarter of New York's settled area was rubble. The devastation from two major fires in 1776 and 1778 remained unremedied. Everywhere there was desolation. Roadways lay torn and treacherous, flanked by stumps of streetlamps; unrepaired wharves and docks lay moldering in Hudson's River; enormous heaps of rubbish and filth were everywhere. The city's population had dropped from its prewar high of nearly 22,000 to around

11,000. Those who remained were the targets of knaves and footpads, especially after the sun disappeared below the rim of the Palisades, across the river. The need for more police protection was a paramount concern among New Yorkers. The crimes most complained of were burglary, assault and battery, grand and petit larceny, the keeping of disorderly houses, gambling, arson, and dueling.

But within the squalor there was bounty. Fishmongers were everywhere, peddling the day's sweet and succulent catch. There was plenty of meat; cattle were driven into town for slaughter. There was produce from upstate. And in the markets, women sold hot coffee and chocolate and little cakes. The war, after all, was won. Those Americans with the means wanted to celebrate peace with the material things that had been so hard to get during the war. And so, as soldiers—some of them not paid in four years—moved through the rubble looking for work, they found tidy shops bursting with "pies, tarts, cakes, puddings, syllabubs, creams, flummery, jellies, giams and custards."

New York's merchants—and the merchants of the other cities—offered the whipped cream of peace, some of it sugared by the very nation the Americans had fought a war to be free of. There were lemons in boxes, apricots and peaches in brandy, candy for coughs, truffles in oil, vinegar in hand-blown bottles, sweetmeats in pots. There were mangoes from India and olive oil from Florence. There were Málaga raisins and Zandt currants; French dried morels, Italian macaroni and German vermicelli. There was even Tory salt from Turks Island.

Stores celebrating immoderation offered hogsheads of English nuts, peppermint and ginger comfits, puncheons of New York rum, pipes of Cognac, Madeira, claret, bohea tea, cinnamon, molasses, and port wine from Tenerife and Lisbon. Buyers with acceptable currency—that meant almost anything not endorsed by the irresolute Continental Congress in Philadelphia—could select from a wide assortment of cambricks and muslins, silk laces and edgings, callicoes, linens from Dublin, ladies' riding hats, corduroys, Seine twine, shallons and camblets and buttons made of fine mohair.

Once properly fed, warmed, coiffed, attired and decorated, the newly independent (and newly rich) could also buy something for the soul, like a book. Popular books of the day included *A View of Society and Manners in Italy, A View of Society and Manners in France*, a treatise on architecture by Langley, and other books by Chesterfield, Hawkesworth, and Raynal. It was all quite genteel if one were not set upon on the way home from the bookstore. In 1782, as the war was winding down, another book appeared in the shops, favored by wags who wanted to savor the sweetness of victory: *Advice to the Officers of the British Army,* which was advertised as trying to "restore the credit of the [British] army, by checking the still further progress of the abuses and irregularities that of late have so much sullied its honor, and diminished its importance. . . ." The book, a series of satirical essays, was popular in London bookstores; the losers did not forget how to laugh at themselves, even as they were losing. Upon its publication, *European Magazine* called it "one of the most laughable pieces of irony that has appeared since Swift provoked the risible muscles" and the *British Magazine and Review* said that soldiers should read it "once a week at every mess." But the author, taking no chances, did not insist that his name appear on his creation.

2
Half Pay, Full Taxes, and Engines of Vice

And he that cheats a soldier out of his little pay
May the devil take him on his back,
To hell with him straightaway.
　　　　　　　—Lyric written by a Revolutionary soldier

There were those who did not think the British Army was funny. Notable among them was George Washington, who was then ensconced in his headquarters at Newburgh, commanding a force of nine thousand men with around 550 officers. With him at his bivouac overlooking the Hudson, sixty miles north of Manhattan island, were three regiments of troops from Massachusetts, two from New York, and other contingents from New Jersey, New Hampshire, and Maryland. Despite his power and his record of achievement, Washington remained a worrier. He maintained an intense personal interest in the king's fumbling forces even before *Advice to the Officers of the British Army* was published. In Washington's view, the British Army's importance could never have been diminished enough. Hostilities had ceased, but the Treaty of Paris would not be signed until September, and he was fearful that the British, although defeated decisively more than a year before at Yorktown, would change their minds and start the messy business all over again.

Washington would have found it hard to smile at *Advice*'s chapter to be read by private soldiers, in which they were counseled to "consider all your officers as your natural enemies, with whom you are in a state of perpetual warfare . . . reflect that they are endeavoring to withhold from you all your past dues, and to impose on you every necessary hardship." The Government of the United States was withholding from its officers and men *their* past dues, and Washington, the man responsible for soldiers and to the Government, could find nothing humorous in 1783 in the notion of "perpetual warfare" with the veterans of an angry Army.

At this point, Washington lived with his wife, Martha, in an eleven-room fieldstone house built by a Dutchman named Rynders fifty-eight years before. The Army had rented it rather inexpensively for him from Jonathan Hasbrouck, its owner. When it was possible, and that was almost every day, he and Martha would have breakfast alone at a small table in their bedroom. It was the one meal they could be reasonably sure of having in private, and it was important to them. After breakfast, Washington would then go to a rather dark room, its one window facing west, away from the river, avoiding the mountains across the Hudson that he found so "rugged and dreary." His workroom looked out on a gentle hill rising westward. The house had a smashing view of the Hudson, but Washington had no time to assess it. It was not compatible with the contemplation of the problems he had just a stone's throw from his headquarters. When he looked up from his desk, beyond the muntin he could see the barracks, and the discontented men it held, less than a hundred yards away.

He worked in the Hasbrouck house longer than in any of the other 119 places he called "headquarters" during the war, for the sixteen months between April 1, 1782, and August 19, 1783. It was comfortable enough in its modesty, but Washington sorely missed Virginia's gentler climate. He was preoccupied, too, because the revolution he had directed with such skill had now reached a most awkward stage—not lost but not quite won, not threatening but not quite over, and certainly not nearly paid for.

Washington always expressed pride in his men and confidence in their ability to withstand anything. But the suggestion of a return to active war with the British, to anything like those dreary times at Valley Forge, six years earlier, was almost more than he could bear. He was tired of playing the stoic. "I must confess, I have my fears, that we shall be obliged to worry thro' another campaign, before we arrive at that happy period, which is to crown all our toils," he wrote to the president of Congress on March 19. And to Lafayette four days later he confided apprehensively, "Enemy posts have been strengthened."

He did not realize how strong his position was. In London, the king's Adjutant General called Britain's attempted reconquest of so huge an area "as wild an idea as ever controverted common sense." The king, mindful that many of his officers resigned their commissions rather than fight their own kind in the new world, had been ignominiously obliged to hire quite a number of Germans to uphold the crown's dignity (as Roman emperors had done to secure the dignity of their golden laurel wreaths twelve hundred years earlier), even though his aides knew that the City of New York contained so many Tories that more of them had enlisted in the king's army than in George Washington's. But news traveled slowly and with uncertainty, and Washington was much more aware of the pronounced indifference of his own people than he was about that of the British.

The winter of 1782–83 had been a most trying one for Washington. He had clearly outfoxed Cornwallis and the British Army. But now he was having problems of a more painful nature with his own melting Army. The privates and noncommissioned officers that Washington saw from his window were, understandably, not at all happy with not being paid. Still, they remained good soldiers, and there had been times, especially when hogsheads of rum were ample to best the night chill, that Washington could hear them put their own lyrics to "God Save the King":

> God save greate Washington
> Fair freedom's chosen son
> Long to command
> May every enemy
> Farr from his presence flee
> And see grim tyranny
> Bound by his hands.

The officers, however, were not singing as loudly. They were skeptical as to what the new order of things would hold for them. It was true that Washington's officers tended to come mostly from the upper, better-educated classes of colonial society. It was also true that even patricians who served tended to see military service as a way to advance themselves, just as their kind had done before, in other countries, and just as so many of those who followed them would do, over the next two centuries.

Early in the Revolution, in 1775 and 1776, many reasonably well-to-do men decided to join the struggle for what they assumed would be a short contest for victory. They had a sense of duty and honor (as well as of their own economic well-being), and a belief that they were fighting for a just cause, and they had not thought that the war would become so difficult for them. But the successful British offensives that were mounted at the end of 1776 had made them less optimistic. A sense of duty, it seemed, was not enough to overcome the professionalism and technical superiority of the British Army.

After 1776, more and more enlisted men and their officers were mindful that Congress was treating them most shabbily indeed. And they also became more representative of colonial society, with complements of "ne'er-do-wells, drifters, unemployed laborers, captured British soldiers and Hessians, indentured servants and slaves." Their ire was contained in another song of the day, one which still honored Washington but reflected disdain for the great bulk of American political and social thinking:

> What think you of a soldier that fights for liberty;
> Do you think he fights for money,
>   or to set his country free?
>
> I'd have you consider, and bear it on your mind,
> Lest you should want their help again
>   it might be hard to find.
>
> My time it has expired, my song is at an end,
> Here's health to General Washington
>   and every soldier's friend,
>
> And he that cheats a soldier out of his little pay
> May the devil take him on his back,
>   To hell with him straightaway.

The officers had pressed for a plan by which they could be retired on half pay for the rest of their lives. Washington at first was cool to such a notion. He thought it was too expensive and that it would "give a great disgust to the people." Later, he backed the half-pay scheme because, as the war progressed, ". . . no day nor scarce an hour passed without the offer of a resigned commission." Washington remained fearful, with justification, that large groups of officers might desert. In the seven months between August 1777 and March 1778, between two hundred and three hundred officers had resigned, and in a letter to the president of Congress, Washington reported that "many others were with great difficulty dissuaded from it." In the autumn of 1782, Washington said that he commanded "like a careful physician to prevent if possible the disorders getting to an incurable height."

The half-pay idea came from the system within the British Army. There, it had produced a professional caste of officers, presumably ready to serve competently in time of war, and receiving just half their regular pay during periods of peace, when they waited for the crown to become inevitably entangled somewhere in a situation that would require military force. The notion of half pay, however, had its opponents among the colonists, who saw the very existence of a permanent corps of officers as a potential threat to liberty, not the guardian of it.

The Boston Massacre on March 5, 1770, had only crystallized their thinking on the subject. The incident occurred when some British soldiers who had been pelted with snowballs somehow lost control of themselves (as armed officials are wont to do) and shot four Bostonians to death. The "Battle of King Street" stood as convincing evidence for the colonists in general that they could not continue their association with King George. It was the culmination of years of intimidating insults heaped upon Americans by Great Britain's vaunted standing army, led by regular officers. Americans were mindful of the fact that the very reason their taxes were so high was that King George had to find the money to pay his officers. Thus they did not trust standing armies, regarding them as "dangerous . . . the nursery of vice . . . engines of despotism . . . the grand engine of oppression." If permitted to thrive, thought the rebels, the standing army would become the "bane of freedom" that would "subvert the forms of government."

Early in 1778, Congress passed the half-pay proposal, more concerned about holding the Army together than about what might happen to social institutions later. But Congress had not yet given itself the power to tax Americans and therefore had no money to finance the scheme. As a result, the half-pay proposal was moribund by April. But in 1779, Congress again approved half pay for life, then immediately rescinded its own vote and voted instead that the states provide officers with "adequate compensation." It was, of course, an empty gesture. The states had money problems of their own.

In the autumn of 1780, Congress voted for half pay for officers who remained in service until the end of the war. The men whom it was intended to pacify knew that Congress still lacked the funds, and the means to get the funds, to make good on this latest promise. They knew that just the half-pay-for-life proposal was probably going to cost the Government between $400,000 and $500,000 a year. They also knew that during this period, the states contributed around $500,000 a year to the Federal treasury, which wasn't even enough to run a bare-bones government, let alone pay out pensions. Thus, with good reason, many officers had their doubts that Congress would ever make good on its promises—and half-promises, at that. Their discontentment was encouraged, directly, indirectly, and always discreetly, by nationalists, such as Congressman Alexander Hamilton and Robert Morris, Superintendent of Finance, who saw in it the means to institute tax schemes that, in their opinion, were imperative if America was to prosper and gain a respected international credit rating.

A national tax plan, irrevocably supported by all of the states, was obviously needed. The immense task of paying for the discomfiture of King George's army had simply overwhelmed a Congress that was powerless to force the states to contribute to the pot. In just the trying winter of 1777 at Valley Forge, the Continental Army had consumed 2,225,000 pounds of beef and 2,297,000 of flour. Yet, it was reported that the troops complained of hunger. They drank 500,000 gills (quarter pints) of rum and whiskey. Yet, Congress heard that soldiers were complaining of the cold. Congress was also mindful that in 1778 alone, it had to pay for the maintenance of Army horses that consumed more than 253,000 bushels of grain and 2,500,000 tons of hay. Quite aside from feeding men and horses, the hard-pressed Congress had to purchase wagons of raw materials for weapons, paid for by newly minted money.

Morris, a well-to-do Philadelphia merchant, had been appointed to his post by the Congress in 1781. He was quite efficient in eliminating some imprudent fiscal practices, and he had put the Government on as sound a financial footing as he could, given that the states had not yet come to terms with the concept of a national government's need of self-support. The brutal truth was that with all of Morris' fiscal maneuvers, specie circulated by French and British armies roaming about in America was of far greater value than anything printed by the Americans. By 1783, Morris, Hamilton, and other nationalists who had helped finance the war were now more than ever concerned about the new nation's image as a poor credit risk among foreign countries. They could think of no better way of establishing credit than paying the financiers of the Revolution, who included the French, the Spanish, some bankers in the Netherlands, and, of course, wealthy Americans who had large holdings of specie.

The propriety of paying bills to the people in America and Europe who had paid for the war was a theme not heard just in the secular halls of the Congress. Wherever one went, there were feelings that America must now work to get beyond its debtor status. There was a certain resentment about lingering war bills which threatened to stand in the way of a free nation's pursuit of its own dreams. "The present war being over, the future increase of population and property will in time enable us with convenience to discharge the heavy debt we have incurred in defence of our rights and liberties," preached Yale's Ezra Stiles. "Posterity may help to pay for the war which we have been obliged to fight out for them in our day."

When Congress considered that debt, it tended to think pragmatically, not ethically. Congressmen like Hamilton wanted to reward those who, in return, would spread the word that America was a good credit risk. Political leaders seemed less willing to factor in payment to the men who had fought the war, whose goodwill was not needed to establish national credit. Then, as in later wars, there were those who suggested that the soldiers were greatly honored simply by their participation in the war. To people concerned about commerce and credit, it seemed almost unpatriotic for the former soldiers to place a price tag on deeds that honored them so.

Veterans did not see it that way. The money that was owed to soldiers for their service continued to be unpaid, and resentment about it grew. In the fall of 1782, Major-General Henry Knox, Washington's Chief of Artillery, drafted a petition on the subject which was carried to Philadelphia by General Alexander McDougall and two colonels, John Brooks and Matthias Ogden.

McDougall was rather a good choice for such a mission. A broad-shouldered Scotsman who had a slight stammer, he nevertheless had a reputation for being very direct with people and institutions, no matter what the cost to himself. Before the Revolution had started, he had written two lively broadsides criticizing the Army and politics of the British. His pen contained none of the hesitancy of his speech. In one sheet, entitled "To the Betrayed Inhabitants of the City and Colony of New York," he asserted that British troops were "kept here not to protect but to enslave us." When called before the New York Assembly to answer for his words, which were considered seditious, McDougall said he thought that the procedure was unfair. He would sooner have his right hand cut off, he said, than "resign the rights and privileges of a British subject." In an outburst of emotion, he shook his fist at the Assembly. The nuance between temper and sedition was frequently lost in eighteenth-century America, and he was jailed for twelve weeks. In a second polemic, the undaunted McDougall offended the British Army's 16th Regiment by asking his fellow New Yorkers, "Is it not enough that you pay taxes for billeting money to support the soldiers, and a poor tax, to maintain many of their whores and bastards in the workhouse, without giving them the employment of the poor . . .?"

Quite aside from his loyalty to the Revolutionary cause, which was unquestioned, McDougall's finances were rendered a shambles by the war, and that made him an ideal advocate for the Army in Philadelphia. He had taken out a £1,000 personal loan to finance the formation of his own regiment. But in 1782, six years after the war started, he complained to New York's Governor, George Clinton, that he had been paid only twice in all that time. Like his fellow veterans, both officers and enlisted men, he also excoriated businessmen "who never risqued a scratch, or a shilling during the whole contest," but who bought interest-bearing certificates that had been paid to soldiers in lieu of hard currency. Many soldiers, desperate for cash to meet their bills, sold their certificates at a great discount to speculators who used them to acquire land.

McDougall and his party were to tell members of Congress "in the most express and positive terms" that unless something was done about the money owed the Army, Congress could expect "a convulsion of the most dreadful nature and fatal consequences." Their petition declared, "It would be criminal . . . to conceal the general dissatisfaction which prevails, and is gaining ground in the army. . . ."

At just about the time McDougall and his group reached Philadelphia, word was received there that Virginia had decided it was not, after all, in favor of the Impost of 1781 and repealed ratification. The impost had been strongly backed by Robert Morris and Hamilton as a means of raising revenue for a strong central government.

McDougall and his group met with Morris, who clearly saw possibilities in their discontent. Less than two weeks later, McDougall wrote to Knox his feeling that essentially the Army and Congress had a common interest in seeing to it that the central government had the power to tax. McDougall said in his letter that it would promise "ultimate security to the Army." Morris had made it clear that back pay and pensions for the Army were out of the question "until certain funds should be previously established."

Washington, still at his desk in Newburgh, knew well that trouble was brewing between the Army and Congress, but gave no indication he suspected anything might happen that would seriously question either his authority or the Government of the United States. But he, too, was gravely concerned about pay for the Army. On January 10, 1783, in a letter to Major-General John Armstrong, Sr., he wrote: "The Army, as usual, are without pay; and a great part of the Soldiery without Shirts; and tho the patience of them is equally thread bare, the States seem perfectly indifferent to their cries. In a word, if one was to hazard for them an opinion upon this subject, it would be that the Army had contracted such a habit of encountering distresses and difficulties, and of living without money, that it would be impolitic and injurious to introduce other customs to it."

Throughout the month of January 1783, Morris and McDougall continued to work for their respective, compatible goals with less than successful results. The nationalists suggested that perhaps the half-pay veterans' pension could be "commuted" into a one-time grant. But delegates from New Jersey, Connecticut, and Rhode Island voted it down.

At one point in all of this, Hamilton was heard to blurt out in Congress that perhaps the desires of the Army could be utilized to forge the taxation plans the nationalists wanted. James Madison, furiously taking notes on the proceedings, reported that members of Congress who supported states at odds with Hamilton over taxes "smiled at the disclosure" and "took notice in private that Mr. Hamilton had let out the secret." Madison said he thought that Hamilton's little slip was "imprudent and injurious to the cause which it was supposed to serve."

Hamilton presented a somewhat different face to Washington. In a letter, he advised Washington, ". . . the difficulty will be to keep a *complaining* and *suffering army* within the bounds of moderation." Hamilton advised Washington to "take direction of them" (the complaining soldiers) to keep their discontent moderate but cautioned that Washington "should not appear to do so. It is [of] moment to the public tranquility that Your Excellency should preserve the confidence of the army without losing that of the people."

It was the sort of advice that was bound not to sit well with Washington, who disliked subterfuge and who was every bit as direct as McDougall but without ever losing his reserve. When Washington replied three weeks later, he dryly told Hamilton, "I shall pursue the same steady line of conduct which has governed me hitherto," and added he had "no great apprehension of its [the army's discontent] exceeding the bounds of reason and moderation."

In the weeks that followed, there was a bit of a stink in Newburgh. Washington's officers conscripted one of their own, Major John Armstrong, to write a letter describing their unhappiness about not getting paid. Armstrong, one of Princeton's earlier dropouts, had a way with words—so much so that Washington thought some of his officers were planning a military takeover. The stimulus to Washington's temper came when Armstrong wrote: "Faith has its limits . . . that in a political event, the army has its alternative: If peace, that nothing shall separate you from your arms but death. . . ."

The Army has its alternative! That was quite an extraordinary thing for an American soldier to write in 1783. James Madison, who at thirty-two was still twenty-six years away from his own Presidency, wrote that the opposition in New England to officers' demands for money had "increased to such a degree to produce a general anarchy."

But Washington handled the matter with his typical dispatch. He called a meeting of his officers and caused some of them to weep when, in trying to read something, he told them, "Gentlemen, you must pardon me. I have grown gray in your service and now find myself growing blind." He assured his officers that Congress would "do it compleat justice" and warned them ''not to take any measures, which, when viewed in the calm light of reason, will lessen the dignity and sully the glory you have hitherto maintained.''

And so, nothing happened. The officers did not rebel—and they did not all get paid until well into the nineteenth century, when the Congress could more easily afford it. Their patience did not wear thin, and, contrary to what Armstrong had written, faith had no limits at all. But perhaps the officers could devise the means to obtain other kinds of rewards.

3
Officer Princes and the Art of Living Happily Ever After

Patriots and heroes may become different men when new and different prospects shall have altered their feelings and views.

—Samuel Adams, 1783

Henry Knox had started to think of the rewards that might be due a soldier long before anybody had an idea of how the Revolution would go. His thoughts were abundantly clear on a September's evening in 1776, when the British, with muskets at the ready, landed at a point in the Bronx they called Frog's Neck. Knox was not there, of course. As the British regulars landed, the man in charge of the Continental Army's artillery was enjoying himself in a tavern several miles away. It was neither imperative nor necessary for a man of Knox's importance to be so close to the enemy. Instead, he chatted and sipped and supped with John Adams, a fellow Bostonian and his good friend of many years' standing. Adams would later recall the conversation to an amused Thomas Jefferson, who recorded it thus:

They talked of antient history, of Fabius who used to raise the Romans from the dust, of the present contest &c. and Genl. Knox, in the course of the conversation, said he should wish for *some ribbon* to wear in his hat, or in his button hole, to be transmitted to his descendants as a badge and a proof that he had fought in defence of their liberties. He spoke of it in such precise terms as shewed he had revolved it in his mind before.

Knox desired more than a bit of ribbon; soldiers like Henry Knox never think purely in terms of ribbon. But at that moment, he may not have been sure of what sort of recognition he wanted for his war service and even less sure of how to explain it to a man like Adams. Surely it was rather taxing to even think properly about future desserts whilst coping with a main course as the king's soldiers sallied forth. Under such circumstances, even patriots with Knox's immoderate gift for conversation may be given to understatement. Seven years later, after he had further "revolved it in his mind," Knox would be able to say precisely what he wanted and get his bit of ribbon and then some. But in the process he learned that obtaining such trifles was not easy, for Americans would always insist upon their suspicions and disdain for anyone, especially soldiers, who attempted to win their official respect. They always preferred to give it unofficially. It was cheaper that way.

Thus was the Society of the Cincinnati born. With all of the animosity it aroused, it nevertheless survived. It lives to this day, although perhaps not quite the way Knox, its founder, envisioned it.

The Cincinnati was a complex thing from its birth, easily misunderstood. It sought esteem and honor for the officers who were its members. It also wanted land and money—compensation for the dreams and commerce that they felt had been taken from them by the war. But whatever the Cincinnati was or wanted to be, it cannot be truly understood without also understanding the man who thought it up. His vision and his values were typical of the aspiring eighteenth-century Army officer; his character left its mark on the society that endured its turbulent beginnings. And the occasion of the Cincinnati's founding, in turn, brought forth feelings about soldiers and their due in this country that would remain remarkably constant for the next two centuries.

There were times and places when it seemed there had been no American Revolution at all, and quite possibly not even a good reason to fight it. As in all things, it depended on where one stood. Knox had known the Revolution well, perhaps better than a man with his sensibilities might be expected to know it. He was not unlike many of his fellow officers who either had come from the upper class or actively sought to arrive in it (Knox was in the latter category). But he was better than most in understanding the economics of independence and what it would mean after the war was over.

He became one of George Washington's most trusted confidants and a major-general. He understood colonial ambivalence about the Britishers as well as colonial determination to fight them. Washington appreciated Knox's sophistication and his ability to deal with difficult situations and complex emotions, quite apart from dealing with trajectory and the positioning of cannon. Perhaps that is why he gave Knox difficult assignments. For example, during the most disheartening part of the war, when destitute Continental soldiers were in mutiny in Pennsylvania and New Jersey and it looked as though the British would win by default, if not military skill, Washington sent Knox on a tour of New England to spread alarums about the hungry, ill-clad Continentals.

It was an audacious assignment in more ways than one. Knox (a man destined to meet an untimely death from swallowing a chicken bone while engaged in the pursuit not of the British but of *haute cuisine*) never lost his appetite for grand lunches and dinners, even when he faced deadly combat. And so, as he left camp, he weighed an unseemly 280 pounds. And yet, the mission he received from Washington was ''to represent the suffering condition of the troops.'' It is a matter of some speculation how many dour New Englanders looked at the sheer bulk of Knox and wondered how hungry the troops really were. Washington may have been the only leader in world history with the dash to send so immense an emissary to represent a starving army. And who but a George Washington could have gotten away with it?

Whatever the New Englanders' feelings, Knox's tour was reasonably successful, thereby suggesting that his powers of persuasion were as formidable as he was. Despite the carping of Tories, who liked things as they were, and the indifference of many others, who disliked the capricious structure of England's taxes (but were afraid of the way things might be without the presence of the king's troops), the legislatures of Massachusetts and New Hampshire voted to send $24 in specie to each enlisted man and noncommissioned officer from those states serving in the Continental Army. By the standards of the day, it was no mean commitment.

For this and other valuable service, Washington's admiration for Knox grew. It grew so much that on November 25, 1783, when the rebel army occupied New York City—evacuated officially that same day by the British—Knox was given the conspicuous honor of entering the city just ahead of Washington and Governor George Clinton. Knox's proud officers from his encampment at West Point rode behind him, eight abreast. It was a rare moment; Knox, like other young, ambitious men of his century, had a sense of history, and he knew that his place in the new nation was assured, no less than his place in the old colonies would have been, had they remained colonies.

Readjustment to civilian life would not prove difficult to the veteran who was Henry Knox. He was a shrewd and successful man of commerce as well as a dedicated bibliophile, quite adaptable and implacably social. His future prospects were only enhanced by his wife, the former Lucy Flucker, who stood to inherit nearly 170,000 acres of land near Thomaston, Maine, whether the Revolution had been fought or not and no matter who won it. The land belonged to her maternal grandfather, General Samuel Waldo, and was called, appropriately enough, the Waldo Patent. The fetching Miss Lucy was blessed with a figure as generous as her material resources. Better yet, the materiality of Miss Lucy had been available to Knox without his having to undergo the rigors of war. Harrison Gray Otis, a friend of Knox's, described her as a "young lady of high intellectual endowments, very fond of books, especially the books sold by Knox" and said that their relationship was "destined to burn on the hymeneal altar" despite the opposition of her parents to the marriage. Otis was quite right, and so, with the war over, Knox was understandably anxious to return to her.

The war, for Knox, had been tiresome for reasons quite aside from his anticipation of the opportunities peace would bring. Among other things, war's end would bring about the altogether desirable objective of Knox's being able to have an occasional glass of sherry with his rich and powerful father-in-law without the occasion succumbing to a dreary argument over Whig and Tory politics. Knox was mindful that Thomas Flucker, scion of a French Huguenot family who had come to America by way of England, was an avowed Loyalist. Flucker was also the powerful secretary of the Province of Massachusetts Bay before the war started, and he and his kith and kin were regarded as "high-toned" aristocrats with "great family pretensions." With the class-conscious English gone, Knox could hope for a more tractable Flucker in a republic that aimed, however imperfectly, to retire class distinctions.

Flucker, his pretensions always at the ready, was so untaken with Knox or with the prospect of having him as a son-in-law that on March 7, 1774 (if not before), Knox was required to resort to secret correspondence in order to make clear his love for Miss Lucy and to press his desire for marriage: "What news? Have you spoken to your father or he to you, upon the subject? . . . I am in a state of anxiety heretofore unknown. My only consolation is in you . . . never distrust my affection for you without the most rational and convincing proof. . . . Don't distrust the sincerity of your Fidelio."

The American Revolution was hardly the sort of situation that would make so adept a man want to alter his universe so completely. But then Knox, who proved so good at defining life's complexities, was never himself so easily understandable.

Knox knew from personal experience that the British weren't all that bad, especially if one could somehow think about them as a people beyond and apart from the wooden indifference of George III to the vicissitudes of being a pink-skinned Anglo-Saxon in the wilderness of eighteenth-century America. Knox appreciated the pliant, appealing side of the British, unappreciated by most of his undereducated fellow rebels: the genteel side, the part of the English soul that loved belles lettres and beaux arts, good food and good drink and endless talk, provided there was some wit to it.

British officers and their Tory ladies had often visited his "London Book Store" soon after Knox opened it in 1771, opposite Williams' Court in Cornhill, Boston. They felt quite at home there, despite the fact that John Adams also visited the shop with some frequency and made no secret of his friendship with Knox. The English, ever mindful of the value of being at the right place at the right time, regarded the London Book Store as "a fashionable morning lounge," and Knox's selection of the name of his business would have made them feel welcome even if a closer examination of his politics would not.

Miss Lucy first met Knox in his bookstore, and, apparently charmed by his wares and intimidated by neither his size nor his politics, she felt no less welcome there, bobbing and smiling in the whispered Anglophilia and nervous pretensions of those whose task it was to follow the misguided king.

Thanks to Knox, the Britishers found many of the titles they would have found in the streets bordering Whitehall, had the Fates been kinder and posted them there—Dodd's *Sermons to Young Men*, *The Fool of Quality*, *The London Songster*, and Smollett's edition of *Don Quixote*. For those who weren't much interested in reading, not even in Fielding's bawdy *Tom Jones* (one of Knox's best-selling books), there were flutes made in Germany; a large assortment of bread baskets; a formidable array of telescopes; protractors by which schoolchildren could measure acute and obtuse angles for their geometry lessons; standishes for keeping quill pens and ink neatly in their proper places, where the British insisted that they, and all else, be; fancy playing cards, called moguls; stationery for the refined people who could use such stuff; and quite a number of gewgaws made out of paper that could be hung as decorations. Even then, booksellers apparently felt that they could not depend on the ever-chattering literati, even the fashionable ones, for survival.

Knox's own ledgers suggest that the Britishers occasionally stopped lounging and talking long enough actually to buy his books, including Armstrong's *Economy of Love*, which seems to have been one of his better sellers. The London Book Store's records indicate that between 1770 and 1772, Knox spent nearly £2,066 with the London bookseller Thomas Longman, who was his supplier. British taxes were a muddle and a nuisance and sometimes the British were an overbearing bore, but under their government, in peacetime, life had been passable for Knox, if not totally fulfilling. Others had done well enough, too, even those who chose to marry women who did not own thirty square miles of land. At least the world seemed to be ordered.

But as the years passed, Knox and many other men whose aspirations, if not social skills, rivaled his own were unable to be passive about talk of rebellion. John Locke had been born a century before Washington, but in his prose could be found fire for the crucible of the American Revolution, as well as the strong stuff of which sermons were made by New England preachers. The men who were the Revolution's intellectual underpinnings had either read Locke or been advised to embrace his ideas on liberty when they went to church on Sunday. An important premise of Locke's *Two Treatises on Government* was not lost on men like Henry Knox, to wit: "The great and chief end . . . of men's uniting into commonwealths, and putting themselves under government, *is the preservation of their own property.*"

Unfortunately for the British, it had become by no means certain to thinking men in the colonies that further submission to the rule of George III or those who might succeed him would preserve much of anything. London had become an eroding force in colonial economics, and it was mostly of the king's own doing. When he began, George had been conciliatory enough toward the colonists, but he approved a tax on tea that the Americans felt was punitively unfair. That led, in 1773, to the Boston Tea Party, which the king saw as an affront and served to make him less flexible about colonial policy. By his methods and levels of taxation, the king was making it ever more difficult for those laboring in his colonies to preserve their property. The Lockean axiom began to work—in reverse from London's point of view. Whatever appreciation men like Henry Knox had for the English way of life and English traditions had been rudely confronted by history and dunderheaded politics.

Knox, for one, had witnessed the unfortunate brawl of March 5, 1770, that came to be called the Boston Massacre. He also later shared Washington's humiliation of being chased by the British across the Jerseys with no power to counterattack, and was humbled further when he concluded that American troops really could not be asked to attack the British lines at Philadelphia because of "our entire want of clothing."

But the war had been won, and now, in the spring of 1783, Knox knew he and the others would soon be going home. He looked forward to his future with Miss Lucy, and this gave him a sense of financial security most of his fellow officers did not enjoy. But even so, he was more like them than not. In his desire to have not just the esteem of his fellow citizens, but some money, too, in recognition of the great victory just gained, Knox was a typical soldier.

What better reward, they thought, than land? Indeed, why not a whole state? The officers who were dissatisfied with the outcome of the Newburgh matter hit upon a scheme they thought would see them into civilian life.

Timothy Pickering, still disgruntled after the murky doings at Newburgh and still not above dallying in a bit of intrigue, came up with a scheme for the United States to buy property in what is now Ohio, then the country's western frontier. The land was to be divided among veterans, with major-generals getting eleven hundred acres each and privates one hundred acres. Those in between would get amounts commensurate with their rank or grade.

When Pickering was asked what he had in mind, he replied that it was "no less than the forming of a new state westward of Ohio." He found that at least 288 officers approved of his plan, which Washington also approved of, and which then went to Congress. It was rejected; Congress felt that if veterans got land, they would be less concerned with the financial stability of the nation. Money was the commodity that would make the new nation tick, said the Congress, not land.

Logically enough, the officers then said they wanted money. But the promises that Congress had made of a pension for life based on half their pay in active duty, and later talk of giving officers five years' pay instead of a lifetime pension, never materialized. Congress still lacked the power to tax. And so for the time being, the most tangible thing the officers had to talk about was the ceremonial side of their new society.

On March 12, 1783—ironically as the Newburgh Conspiracy was unfolding before George Washington—an obscure German periodical apparently had published some details for a proposed "Order of Liberty" that would be created in the United States. The article in the *Gazette des Deux Ponts* of Zweibrücken seemed to have been prepared in Philadelphia on the previous January 1 and it remained unclear who its author was or why the suggestion should have appeared first in Germany. There was speculation that it was Major-General Baron von Steuben, but this was by no means certain. Curiously, the proposed Order of Liberty (which was to have twenty-four "knights" uniformed in scarlet and blue who would carry a decoration made of gold, suspended on a ribbon carrying thirteen stripes) was not known to have been reported in an American newspaper.

Within a month after Washington confronted his own discontented officers at Newburgh, Knox had created eight pages of a document which he called an "Institution"—a constitution, really—for an organization of officers. A similar idea was being bandied about by other officers billeted in the Hudson Valley, but it was Knox's that carried the day. His Society of the Cincinnati was formed officially on May 13, 1783, at the Verplanck House, von Steuben's headquarters near Fish-kill Landing, on the east side of the Hudson, a few miles from Newburgh. It was immediately suspected by some to be the mechanism for making possible the coup that Washington and others had so recently feared, even though Washington himself would consent to become its first president. The critics included Thomas Jefferson, Benjamin Franklin, John Jay, and even John Adams, who recalled the society when it was just an innocent ribbon of small talk over dinner.

Jefferson thought the group's objectives were beneath Washington and that Washington should not join it. Franklin derided the group's eagle symbol, likening it to a turkey and saying that in any event eagles were cowardly. Jay was perhaps the most critical, saying that if the society made a go of it, he "would not care if the Revolutionary war had succeeded or not." And John Adams wrote that the society would be "the first step taken to deface the beauty of our temple of liberty."

In its trappings, the society reflected eighteenth-century America's interest in Roman history. The new organization was named by Knox for Lucius Quinctius Cincinnatus, who, the Romans were told, lived in humble circumstances but did not relate to others who also lived humbly and who were known as the plebeians. He resisted efforts in Rome to establish laws applicable equally to plebeians and Roman aristocrats, the patricians. Legend has it that he walked behind a plow at his farm, but left twice to run the country, and, in the bargain, defeated the pesky Aequians in a single day. And although he returned to Rome with much booty, the virtuous Cincinnatus left it all there and went back to his plow. Or so the Romans were told.

Knox may have picked the wrong Roman for whom to name this new group, for there was no evidence that Washington's officers were eager to live in the apparent penury that Cincinnatus knew. Certainly Knox himself did not embrace Cincinnatus' circumstances as those he wanted for himself. In any event, the founding language read, in part:

> It having pleased the Supreme Governor of the Universe, in the disposition of human affairs, to cause the separation of the Colonies of North America from the domination of Great Britain, and after a bloody conflict of eight years, to establish them free, independent and sovereign states, connected, by

alliances founded on reciprocal advantages, with some of the greatest princes and powers on earth.

To perpetuate, therefore, as well as remembrance of this vast event, as the mutual friendships which have been formed under the pressure of common danger, and in many instances cemented by the blood of the parties, the officers of the American Army do, hereby, in the most solemn manner, associate, constitute, and combine themselves into one SOCIETY OF FRIENDS, to endure as long as they shall endure, or any of their eldest male posterity, and in failure thereof, the collateral branches, who may be judged worthy of becoming its supporters and members.

The Cincinnati thereby initiated its controversial policy of primogeniture—an American military group was to determine its membership by the same method that had sustained the same British monarchy just overthrown by the colonials.

Americans were never shy in their criticism of self-honoring organizations, and the Cincinnati was no exception. They tended to see it as just another example of America's succumbing to the very things they had rejected in the English. "Many of the younger Class . . . are crying out for a monarchy and a standing army to support it. . . . These are joined by a whole class of Cincinnati who are panting for a nobility," complained Mrs. Mercy Warren, a historian and prominent Bostonian.

Of course, it wasn't only nobility that they wanted. They had never forgotten their interest in money and they still wanted their bonus of five years' pay.

One of the most vociferous critics of the Cincinnati and whatever they wanted was Judge Aedanus Burke, a local jurist in South Carolina. The judge enjoyed creating political pamphlets as much as he did issuing verdicts. He knew a thing or two about ancient Rome as well, and he signed his pamphlets not with his name but, in the style preferred by the educated of his day, with an appropriate name from Roman antiquity.

Burke had a special ire for Washington's officers which only grew after he had learned of the "Newburgh Conspiracy" and Knox's Society of the Cincinnati. He suspected, he said, that the homecoming officers had designs "planted in a fiery, hot ambition, and thirst for power," and that if they were not stopped, the United States would be disunited into "two ranks of men, the patricians, or nobles, and the rabble." All this, Burke said, "must give a thinking mind melancholy forebodings." Although thought to be the author of an earlier pamphlet supportive of Tories, Burke did not go so far in his Romanesque musings to suggest that Washington was actually a Caesar who would deserve what he got, but the ultimate unpleasantness of his message was clear enough in the assassin-patriot's name he used to sign his pamphlet: Cassius.

Burke's attack on the officers provoked a chuckle from Noah Webster, who was credited with creating this verse:

> Squire Burke, with signature of Cassius
> Thinks this society mean to lash us;
> Create a lineal race of Lords,
> And *nobly* bind our necks in cords;
> Engross all power, as sure as fate
> With neither office nor estate.
> Such views, which we judge no small bubble,
> Must give republicans much trouble.

Von Steuben, who was wholeheartedly in favor of the society from the beginning, began to tease his friend Knox over the Burke pamphlet: "Your pernicious designs are then unveiled,—you wish to introduce dukes and peers into our republic?" There was, however, more serious, more embarrassing criticism that flabbergasted Knox. General William Heath, who had been picked to be one of the society's principal organizers, decided not to join, feeling uneasy with the society's emphasis on primogeniture. And Pickering, who joined, said later he did so "absolutely and purely to avoid the reproach of singularity." He complained that the Society of the Cincinnati contained too much of Knox's values and "bore the marks of his pomposity."

If Knox was upset at the criticism, it did not deter him from his labor in behalf of the society. In his original language describing the group, he had spared no detail, including an elaboration of the "ribbon" he had talked to Adams about, something to "wear in his hat or in his buttonhole." Here are some of Knox's specifications, as he presented them in the founding papers:

The Society shall have an Order, by which its members shall be known and distinguished, which shall be a medal of gold, of a proper size to receive the emblems, and suspended by a deep blue ribbon, two inches wide, edged with white, descriptive of the union of America and France, viz:
"The principal figure
CINCINNATUS:
Three Senators presenting him with a sword and other military ensigns on a field in the back-ground, his wife standing at the door of their Cottage—near it

A PLOUGH AND IMPLEMENTS OF HUSBANDRY.

Round the whole,

OMNIA RELIQUITS ERVARER EMPUBLICAM.

On the reverse,

Sun rising—a city with open gates, and vessels entering the port—
Fame crowning CINCINNATUS with a wreath inscribed

VIRTUTIS PRÆMIUM.

Below,

HANDS JOINED, SUPPORTING A HEART,

With the motto,

ESTO PERPETUA.

Round the whole,

SOCIETAS CINCINNATORUM INSTITUTA,

A.D. 1783."

To make certain that all of this was rendered with taste and sensitivity, Knox prevailed upon one of Europe's most flamboyant and unreserved architects, planners, and military engineers—Pierre Charles L'Enfant, a Frenchman who had served in the American Revolutionary Army as a major. L'Enfant was then not thirty and still eight years away from creating the plans for the Capitol of the new nation he had just fought for, but the formidable object he created for Knox presaged the grandeur of Pennsylvania Avenue.

From the outset, Washington thought that the Society of the Cincinnati was a good idea, although he later said he was "most amazingly embarrassed" by the furor caused by Knox's primogeniture clause. On October 16, 1783, he wrote to Knox, "It was always my intention to present the Society with five hundred dollars." And just two weeks later, he sent $250 in banknotes to L'Enfant, with his request for "eight bald eagles."

Washington was an enormously popular man at that point, and Americans might have been expected to share his positive view of the Cincinnati. But they did not share it. They remained suspicious of the Cincinnati. In Massachusetts in particular, farmers, who were already headed for hard times with the state Government, made it clear they did not expect to see their tax dollars go for support of a leisure class of officers. They said it even though some of them had been officers themselves. Those Massachusetts farmers eligible to join the Cincinnati tended to stay away. Of the 442 officers of the Massachusetts line, a full quarter refused to have anything to do with the Cincinnati; and of the 226 Massachusetts men who had been in the Navy and Marines, only two actually joined the society.

Knox's ribbon remained a tiny ribbon; in Massachusetts, where times were hard for farmers and tempers were wearing thin, the soldiers who had fought the Revolution would soon find a sprig of hemlock a more suitable adornment for their hats.

4
Daniel Shays: From True Patriot to Counterfeit Public Enemy

Behold the Reign of Anarchy begun
And half the business of confusion done,
From Hell's dark caverns, Discord sounds alarms,
Blows her loud trumpet and calls my Shays to arms...
—Poem in *Connecticut Magazine*, 1787

Perhaps the Congress of the United States could not find the funds to pay its veterans of the Revolution. But that did not mean it was without the power to esteem them.

If order was the honor of the day—and the veterans were told repeatedly about the virtue of self-regulation—then honor was the order of the day. Government had a unique ability to honor people, an ability that could never be rivaled by organizations like the Cincinnati. Honor could be issued selectively, efficiently, inexpensively. Not the sort of honor that could be frittered away in a summer afternoon's homecoming parade before parents, proud of surviving sons, or before admiring young women, peeking out demurely from beneath fringed parasols at future prospects. Rather, formal tribute, intoned and inscribed, was the stuff of fond memories and strong loyalties.

In the eighteenth century, honor required ceremony. There could be ceremonies as only a century with grace the equal of its violence could produce them. There could be functions in which officers could see and be part of some pomp and circumstance. These could be pleasant events, chances to meet old comrades and speak of hard times and lean times over a fat dinner. If the cost was not unseemly, not an affront to American parsimony, there was no reason why Congress, or the states so reluctant to support a strong national treasury, could not find some way to honor officers, if not rank-and-file soldiers. There were so very many soldiers. Congress knew that veteran officers of the Army, the Navy, and the Marines deserved something that went beyond the Society of Cincinnati "eagles," which, after all, were recognition the society members gave themselves. Clearly, the Cincinnati could not be the only mechanism for honoring veterans. The Government had to play a role, however small. Honoring former soldiers was the least the public could do.

Newspapers frequently contained news of one event or another that was being planned for the heroes of the Revolution. "Col. Humphreys who lately arrived from France in the French packet, has brought with him a number of elegant swords, made agreeable to different resolves of the honorable Congress to be presented to a number of gentlemen who, by acts of heroism and valor, distinguished themselves in the late revolution," reported the *New York Daily Advertiser* on May 31, 1786.

The swords were eventually awarded by none other than Henry Knox, by then Secretary of War, a chubby-cheeked *bon vivant* who could always be counted on to enjoy thoroughly a little pomp and the dinner that went with it, especially if the chef was French. One of the swords went to Marinus Willet, the sheriff of New York, who had served the Revolution as an Army colonel. Willet simply called the recognition "a peculiar pleasure to me."

Seven other colonels also got swords, and so did a commodore and a captain. It was a most pleasant ceremony, and in the months that followed, swords and speeches were everywhere, making memories for men who were having difficulty adjusting to the present and preferred not to think about the future. Von Steuben, for example, whose personal finances reflected none of the splendid order he had been able to impose on his marching formations, received a special gold-filled sword to mark the "high sense Congress entertained of his character and services."

And yet, with all of it, certain realities were impinging on the euphoria of peace. People everywhere were mindful that in the new country, all was not well and that one of the biggest problems was all those veterans who had not adjusted to civilian life as well as they might have. No one was more troubled by that problem than James Bowdoin, the Governor of Massachusetts, a man who shared Knox's views that victory and peace would present Americans with unprecedented opportunities to prosper. But some Massachusetts veterans, especially those in the hinterlands, were not prospering and were becoming rather vociferous about the reasons for it. And so the Governor had mixed emotions about the quality of the peace that followed the conclusion of the American Revolution.

As founder of the Massachusetts First National Bank, Bowdoin knew that his dearest friends—men who were revered in the new republic—had found an abundance of ways for making money in the postwar period. He was not merely an observer of their good fortune. He had personally accumulated £1,000 worth of Continental securities, which, with some alacrity, he had purchased at great discount, mostly because so many former officers and soldiers who were down on their luck had to sell their Government paper at a fraction of its value. The public securities represented the pay the Army had clamored for, and speculators purchased them because they assumed the securities eventually would be worth more if the Congress, still trying to establish American credit, backed the paper with gold. But veterans had debts to pay and found they needed hard currency immediately for their creditors, not promise of profit tomorrow. Speculators may have wanted their paper; creditors did not. This was not a situation of Bowdoin's personal creation, and he and his friends saw no reason why the profit motive should not be pursued, in whatever thicket it might lie.

Men like Bowdoin felt strongly that investors should be properly rewarded for risk-taking and were outspokenly critical of those, like the veterans, who could not pay their debts in "real money"—coins made of silver or gold, which were commonly referred to as specie. The *Massachusetts Centinel*, one of many newspapers seeing only laudable and praiseworthy things in the ethics of speculation, carried a letter from North Carolina lamenting the plight of those who were owed for goods and services: "Still the wretched creditor is obliged to receive this paper trash for sterling debts, nay frequently happy to receive it as the only liquidation of accounts he can get, that have been standing for years."

Men of means, like Bowdoin, were not merely merchants walking a tightrope between customers and jobbers, but were in a position to play a waiting game with a speculative venture that was proving both interesting and profitable. Friends and acquaintances of the Governor's, such as Stephen Higginson, Rufus King, Benjamin Lincoln, Caleb Strong, Elbridge Gerry, Nathaniel Gorham, and even that man of great conscience Samuel Adams, were also doing very well, speculating with all manner of things, including paper purchased from veterans down on their luck.

In the suave and knowing Henry Knox, Bowdoin could see a model for what other veterans could be if only they had Knox's talent for perpetual motion in the interest of their own ambition. Knox, who apparently had no trouble switching from bookseller to Chief of the Continental Artillery, had shifted again just as effortlessly to become Secretary of War. The job kept him busy. But still he had found time to set up the Society of the Cincinnati, and managed, in addition, to remain an active member of Boston's estimable and glittering community of Founding Father speculators in public securities. By virtue of his brilliant marriage, however, Knox had pliantly decided to convert his speculative paper to speculative land, so that he could expand the possibilities offered by his beloved Lucy's massive holdings in Maine. Knox clearly knew how to manage the Flucker fortune.

But Bowdoin knew that almost all veterans, even the officers, were not of Henry Knox's resiliency, nor even of Marinus Willet's. He was also aware that there was considerable evidence, among the veterans, of wanting to put the war and the military behind them, of lingering bitterness about the way the Government had attempted to pay its debts to the soldiers. Feelings of indifference against the Government and the military were evident even among those who participated in the military. In Boston, for example, where efforts were under way to form a militia, residents were "repeatedly called upon, particularly on Wednesday, Thursday and Friday last, to meet and choose their officers; but they have unanimously declined to exercise the privilege, and consequently consider it a more eligible method to leave the choice of their officers to the will of the Supreme executive."

The indifference of Massachusetts militiamen was the least of Bowdoin's problems. Before the war, the Massachusetts debt was only £100,000. By the end of the war it had risen to £1,300,000, which did not include £250,000 it was supposed to pay to officers and noncommissioned soldiers who had fought the war in the belief that they were representing the will of the majority of people in Massachusetts. In 1784, the Massachusetts legislature decided that impost and excise taxes should be enacted to pay off £140,000 of the debt to veterans. It proved inadequate, and the legislators found that by 1786, another £100,000 was needed.

Tax delinquency was rampant. More than that, the state, reflecting attitudes elsewhere in the country, was sharply divided as to how to pay off its debts—and to maintain the way of life to which it had grown accustomed. The people of the maritime towns of eastern Massachusetts "relapsed into the voluptuousness" that stemmed from "the precarious wealth of naval adventures." But precarious or not, it was a wealth understood and cherished by sailors, merchants, lawyers, judges, shopkeepers, artisans, and others who lived in growing urban settlements such as Boston and Salem. It was a wealth measured in specie by the people who saw the accumulation of currency as their way to the good life. Governor Bowdoin understood such people. And so did most members of the Massachusetts General Court (the state legislature), many of them speculators in Federal securities.

Even in Boston, where everybody who was anybody seemed to be speculating in something, there were people who questioned the morality of this sort of approach to public securities. Massachusetts and other states had to struggle to meet their obligations, and even some of those who held traditional views about the value of coins wondered about the rightness in buying such paper at a fraction of its worth and making money on it. "It soon became a common observation," one observer of the period noted, "that the promise of a government could not, in equity, be extended to the man who was possessed of public notes for a partial consideration, to entitle him the payment of more than he gave. . . ."

The same thought was expressed by the writer of a letter to the *Massachusetts Centinel* which was published on February 18, 1786. The writer, who called himself "Plain Truth," took issue with those who offered apologias for speculation and warned that they should "TREMBLE for their cheap-bought wealth."

The judges who sat in various courts in Massachusetts could not see anything wrong with this sort of speculation, especially since they were involved in it themselves. But in western Massachusetts, feelings about money and its requirements ran in quite a different direction. There, the value system traditionally had been based not upon Spanish milled coins or pounds sterling but upon trust, the recognition that in the final analysis, humans needed each other more than anything else, and that the appropriate conduct in the new republic was one of self-reliance, firmly based on hard work.

This part of the state was the stronghold of the so-called yeoman, a kind of subsistence farmer who worked the land to grow enough to support himself and believed in helping his neighbor and in bartering what little extra he had for the few services he required. Before the Revolution, yeomen had had only marginal uses for money among themselves. Their wealth was in their ability to nurture themselves from the earth. After the war was over and the British gone, they, like everyone else in America, acquired some taste for manufactured goods. They remained mostly uninterested in accumulating wealth, however, and retained their strong desire to work the land and live simply.

The same could not be said of the merchants along the coast, who supplied the interior with manufactured items. The merchants found that although Americans might not have cared very much for the king's government, they had developed a certain taste for the way the king's subjects made things. The British, losers in war, were winners in the economics of peace. The English sensed an easy, lucrative market in the new world. The colonials may have outlasted the Redcoats, but to the British, the Americans remained largely a nation of bumpkins, busy fighting Indians, busy fighting over wilderness areas that seemed endless, busy squabbling among themselves as to what sort of country they were going to have. They were not a people who could compete with the sophisticated British in the marketplace, and there were merchants and manufacturers in Britain who doubted that they ever would.

The British wanted no part of what passed for American paper currency. Even the formidable likes of David Ricardo and Adam Smith could not say for sure what would happen to it. English businessmen demanded specie— not strange-looking paper whose value seemed to have endless downward mobility. And on the coast of New England, American merchants who savored the good life that grew out of the postwar spending spree were determined to provide it, to keep the goods coming.

The *Massachusetts Centinel* and other seaboard newspapers, owned and operated by men whose principal advertisers were the rich merchants, men in powdered wigs and velvet who spent much time counting their money, thought the insistence on specie was a jolly good idea. As befitting its New England station, the *Centinel* neatly preached against the evils of profligacy, but allowed that if Americans were going to be profligate, they shouldn't diminish the joyousness of self-indulgence by financing it with American paper, which, of necessity, would have to be issued by the states. That was money without a pedigree; surely nobody would take seriously any paper currency issued by the states or by the Federal Government. Alexander Hamilton's dream had not yet come true. From the *Centinel*'s vantage point, any paper money issued by any Government within the un-United States was a prospect that God-fearing creditors should be spared.

> Save us, we pray thee, Lord, for mercy's sake,
> From lux'ry's poison, and from moral evil.
> Should Rulers prove as dang'rous as the plague,
> And lawyers grow as wicked as the d—l,
> From what than these will prove a heavier curse,
> From *Paper Money*—Lord deliver us.

Yeomen could remember a time not so long before when they could barter the promise of a bushel of corn or a calf to satisfy a debt. The British wanted none of that. Bushels of corn and yearlings didn't travel all that well to London. Nor did importers on the eastern seaboard of the United States care to continue the barter tradition. For only with hard currency could the seaboard merchants continue to trade with jobbers in other nations. And it was currency that the Government of Massachusetts understood, too, and expected, in payment of its taxes.

New England tax collectors were as stridently insistent upon specie as were British exporters. The war debt had to be paid, and the Massachusetts legislature voted in a new scheme for directly taxing citizens. The taxes were based primarily on real estate. Merchants calculated their assets in the goods they had for sale, and so they were taxed comparatively little. But farmers, who earned their livings from the land they worked, were taxed at a much greater rate. In short, the people who were profiting most from postwar spending were paying the least taxes; those who profited least were taxed the most. And the commodity everyone wanted—coin—was in extremely short supply all over the state, but especially in the countryside, where it had never been all that important. America was a nation without a currency—it was still running on the money that had been left behind by the British. British soldiers might have been defeated, but not the pound sterling. So with tax collectors and coastal businessmen demanding something that was almost nonexistent in the farm country, Massachusetts was embarked on a collision course with itself.

Nowhere were the shortcomings of Massachusetts' policies of taxation and currency requirements more evident than in Pelham, a community in western Massachusetts, not far from Amherst. It wasn't much of a town by Boston standards. In 1786, it contained fewer than one thousand people, virtually all of them given to trying to eke out a living from soil that was rich only in rocks and in vast stands of fragrant hemlock. Their lives and their industry were conducted in 127 houses, ninety-eight barns, and two mills. There were also a tavern or two or three, an inn, and some stores selling the few essentials that could not be grown or made by the farmers.

Like other towns in Massachusetts and, indeed, in Europe, Pelham had a tradition of handing farmland down from parents to children. And as in the other towns observing the tradition, the size of divided farms grew smaller and smaller, the farmers more gaunt, the economy more desperate. In 1760, Pelham's average farm had 6.4 tilled acres; by 1771 it had fallen to 5.2 acres, and by 1784 it was down to only 2.3 acres. In that year, one-third of the adult men in Pelham owned no land at all. There simply wasn't any land for them to own.

Even in hard times, Pelham's tradition of democracy was as entrenched as was its austerity. Widows, provided they had some property, could vote at a time when women just about everywhere else could not, whatever their circumstances. It was also one of the relatively few places in Massachusetts where the voting age was only sixteen.

Pelham's economic problems did not start with the end of the American Revolution. Its poor land was always there, and those economics had long been coupled with a peculiar, feisty irreverence for authority figures. In 1762, for example, five men and four women, irked by the enforcement of a law they considered unjust, greeted a deputy sheriff sent up from Amherst "with axes, clubs, sticks, hot water and hot soap in a riotous and tumultuous manner." The nine were acquitted. It is not entirely clear precisely what they did or threatened to do to the deputy.

When the Revolution started, the people of Pelham were staunchly anti-Tory and understandably suspicious of big, remote government. Indeed, they may have felt more strongly against the British than did the patriots who won such great notoriety in Boston. At one point, a delegation of Pelham residents went to nearby Hatfield, kidnapped Israel Williams and his son, who were prominently pro-British, and confined them in a house in which the chimney had been clogged shut. A fire was set in the fireplace and the two were "smoked" overnight, like two pieces of New England bacon. The next morning they were induced to sign a statement that said they were opposed to Britain's Intolerable Acts. Then, and only then, were they let go.

After the war, Pelham's farmers, many of them veterans, had cause for a new grievance against authority when they saw their land confiscated for nonpayment of taxes, as did farmers elsewhere in western Massachusetts. Petitions were sent to the state legislature in Boston, asking for relief, asking for time, asking for the acceptance of paper money, asking for anything. The petitions were ignored, and Boston then began to assume the intransigent mantle that had been King George's. Or so it seemed to the farmers. But from Boston's point of view, bills were bills and they had to be paid.

Boston's mean spirit did not cause the people of Pelham to rise up as one in rebellion. They had just come through a war and they perceived the winning of that war as the end of something old and oppressive and the beginning of something new and promising. They were not predisposed to take up arms again; one revolution in a lifetime was quite enough.

But still, the way that Government and merchants on the seaboard treated them made the moment sour. American farmers in 1786, not unlike their counterparts two centuries later, felt abused both by the inexplicable myopia of urban-oriented Government and by business. Nowhere was the abuse greater than in Massachusetts, and nowhere did it engender more bitterness. As it happened, the farmer-veterans could not help but think that the justice they had fought for in the Revolution was being compromised. Perhaps the lessons they had learned during the Revolution could be applied to a post-Revolutionary problem.

Their view of the world was still not unlike John Locke's, who felt that "rebellion" was sinful but acknowledged that resistance might be necessary for those living under the power of unjust rulers. For if tyrants would not stop the tyrannizing, what can just and orderly people do but resist? "How they will be hindered from resisting illegal force used against them I cannot tell," Locke wrote in his *Second Treatise on Government*. "This is an inconvenience, I confess, that attends all governments whatsoever, when the governors have brought it to this pass, to be generally suspected of their people. . . ."

As the confiscations continued, Locke's description of "governors" could have been applied to James Bowdoin and the way he was viewed by the yeomen. In Worcester alone, from 1784 to 1786, the local jail was the destination of 145 of 169 persons unable to pay debts. Lest Bowdoin be viewed unfairly, it should be pointed out that in Connecticut at least five hundred farmers were seized in 1786 for nonpayment of taxes, and that in New Hampshire yeomen in forty-one towns joined fellow yeomen in seventy-three Massachusetts towns in sending petitions to the state legislature in Boston, seeking an end to seizure of farms and imprisonment of farmers for nonpayment of debts.

By late summer and early autumn of 1786, farmers had come to the conclusion that the state courts in general and lawyers and judges in particular were not just the agents of their agony, but quite possibly the root causes of it as well. On August 29, some fifteen hundred farmers led by Luke Day, a former captain in the Revolutionary Army, went into Northampton and stopped the Court of Common Pleas—the debtor court— from meeting. If it couldn't meet, foreclosures couldn't be ordered and life might go on as before.

Day's men called themselves "regulators," not insurgents or rebels. It was, after all, an effort to regulate—not destroy—a court that seemed out of control. It was never an effort to destroy the court. As they surrounded the courthouse, Day delivered a petition to the frightened judges, asking them to adjourn their sad and sorry business until the state legislature decided whether it could grant the farmers the relief they had sought earlier. At least seventy-three towns, representing a third of all those in the state, had petitioned the legislature to authorize the state's issuance of paper money, so that ordinary people could go about their business without having to ferret out British or French coins that had been floating around the countryside from before the war.

In the weeks to come, hundreds of farmers, following Day's example, stopped debtor courts from operating in Northampton, Concord, Taunton, and Great Barrington. There was similar action in Connecticut and Vermont. From most accounts, they stopped the courts in a decisive but nonviolent manner, and one militiaman said they carried out their missions "with military parade." But as frightening as the farmers may have appeared and alarming as they were, their pleas went unheeded. The legislature passed no reform measures, and debtor courts would certainly continue, if they could.

Quickly, the names of the leaders of the farmers became known, and all had served in the Continental Army. Luke Day of West Springfield was certainly one. Others, all of them former captains, included Thomas Grover of Montague, Joel Billings of Amherst, Asa Fisk of South Brimfield, and Aaron Jewett of Chesterfield. But one man perceived as a leader was a most reluctant one, indeed. His name was Daniel Shays.

Shays was born in Hopkinton, Massachusetts, in 1747, to poor Irish Protestant parents, who were not able to give him much formal education. He had worked on farms in Brookfield and Great Barrington and possibly elsewhere. He scraped enough money together to purchase some farmland in Shutesbury, but when the war started he enlisted as an ensign in a company of minutemen that was formed in Amherst by Captain Reuben Dickinson. The company served only eleven days, but a few months later, Dickinson started another one. Shays again volunteered, fought at Bunker Hill, was wounded, and was decorated for valor.

Subsequently he participated in the battle of Fort Ticonderoga, where Dickinson's company was part of a regiment under Colonel Ruggles Woodbridge. Then he joined Colonel Varnum's Rhode Island regiment, for which he recruited other soldiers before again going into combat. He witnessed the capture of General Burgoyne and was one of the rebels who fought and won at Stony Point. Again his valor was conspicuous, and the Marquis de Lafayette took note of it, presenting Shays with an ornamental sword.

Much to the chagrin of some of his fellow officers, especially those who were looking for status in the Cincinnati and wanted other officers to share their values, Shays did not treasure the sword nor look upon it as an artifact of honor that he could hand down to those who followed him. Instead, he sold it. He sold it because, as he explained, he already had a sword. He didn't need another, and so he sold it for a few dollars. With all his debts, he could dearly use the money.

"This excited the indignation of his company & the officers of his regiment," according to a staunch Federalist judge named Hinckley. "An outcry was made about his meanness in selling the gift of Lafayette. The officers refused to associate with him, and talked about trying him by a court martial for his base conduct, he resigned his office & came home, much incensed against the officers and even against Washington & the other patriots.''

The notion that Shays came home to sulk in his tent and to carry a personal grudge against George Washington did not square with accounts of him from other sources, who describe him as likable, down-to-earth, direct, and gregarious. Judge Hinckley's account may say more about him than it does about Shays, for Federalists later tried long and hard, with considerable success, to transform a Revolutionary hero who had protested an honest grievance into one that they, in the late eighteenth and early nineteenth centuries, considered disloyal and shameful.

Shays had returned to his Pelham farm after the war, wanting only to work the land and live in peace. But he was unable to come up with cash to pay small debts, and in 1784 a creditor named John Johnson took him to court because he failed to pay a debt of £12. He was back in court again a few months later, this time charged with failing to pay a debt of £3 to a merchant in nearby Brookfield. Shays was upset, but his problems were small compared to those of some other former soldiers of the Revolution, who ended up in debtors' prison.

At first, all that the farmers could do was talk about it. It was quite impossible for them not to air their grievances, as they saw their friends lose their farms and they felt threatened by their merchant and Government creditors. Bartenders may make decent listeners, and Shays confided in two of them. One was Oliver Clapp, who ran a tavern in Amherst that was well known for its flip, a most potent mixture he made of beer and spirits that was sweetened with sugar and heated with a hot iron. His wife brewed a passable beer, the locals said. Clapp, who was widely known as "Landlord Clapp," was married to Elizabeth Matoon, the sister of General Ebeneezer Matoon, and that may be one reason he was most discreet about his admiration for Shays and the sympathies he felt for struggling veterans who had come home to great debt. Clapp's tavern was several miles from Shays' house; Shays himself was not seen there frequently.

The innkeeper to whom Shays was closest was William Conkey, who ran a tavern in the east part of Pelham, only half a mile from Shays' house. As Shays and his farmer friends became more deeply mired in Boston's vindictive economics, they would come to Conkey's to commiserate. It was a natural meeting house for them, a two-story wooden building with a huge chimney separating its two first-floor rooms. A sign outside was painted with a picture of a man on horseback and on its reverse a picture of a horse with its groom. If Conkey meant to give the place a horse motif to go with a special name, it didn't work, for his place of business was always known simply as Conkey's tavern. There was a lean-to in back, and a great fireplace warmed the dining room. But the bar was the most comfortable room in Conkey's, also dominated by a huge fireplace and containing homey furniture, a fine room in which to wait out the bitterly cold New England days. Conkey did not rejoice at Clapp's reputation as a brewer and concocter, but in his own cellar were prodigious amounts of India rum, brandy, wine, and cordials. His walls were neither lathed nor plastered, but both the roof and the walls were well sheathed. Conkey himself provided the ultimate warmth from the elements with the good cheer and talk he provided. He made no secret of his friendship with Shays and the other farmer-veterans who gathered under his roof. Indeed, he lent Shays money with some frequency.

At the bar, the farmer-veterans were pretty much agreed that among all the foul creatures that prowled the earth, lawyers were the foulest; that lawyers—a word that when said in a certain way sounded dangerously close to "liars"—probably ought to be "annihilated" or, at the very least, abolished as a profession since they were little better than "savage beasts of prey"; that deputy sheriffs were quite useless as a group and almost as bad as lawyers. Judges, who were lawyers with even more power to make mischief, were the agents of the creditors.

Shays was looked up to by many of his fellow farmers, and as an older man who had been an officer, he was perceived as someone who knew something about administration. But from Governor Bowdoin's view, Shays was a most difficult man to relate to. Yes, he had served as an officer and he had served under Rufus Putnam, and Lafayette had personally honored him with the presentation of a sword. But he seemed to care more about farming than he did about money. He was never seen around the Bunch of Grapes or any other fashionable pub in Boston and clearly preferred to do his drinking with his unpretentious friends in Conkey's, a place Bowdoin would not have patronized, even if he had been extremely thirsty. Even worse, he had not even bothered to join the Society of the Cincinnati, although he qualified for membership. In a time when such memberships were precious, when they might enable someone from humble origins to ascend the social ladder, here was a man who seemed supremely uninterested in any of it. Such a man would have been perceived as a major troublemaker if for no other reason than that he did not share Bowdoin's value system. His likes tended to be ungovernable by the likes of men like James Bowdoin. Worse still, he was a man whom other debtors regarded as a leader.

Shays was not the only leader of the protest that was brewing in western Massachusetts. Among the other Revolutionary officers who joined with

Shays were more captains—Luke Day, Adam Wheeler, Luke Drury, Reuben Dickinson, Oliver Parker, John Nutting, William Smith, and Seth Murray. Former majors in the same cause included John Wiley and Jonathan Holman. Lieutenants included John Hubbard and Elijah Day. In the Massachusetts press, Drury was referred to as "one of the malcontents of Grafton."

Like Shays, most of these men were not known to be members of the Cincinnati, although Luke and Elijah Day were, for a time, before they were expelled as "particularly odious and obnoxious" to other members of the society. The *Massachusetts Centinel* carried a resolution of the Cincinnati that found Luke and Elijah Day so reprehensible for joining in rebellion that their membership dues were refunded and it was resolved, "they are not, and never have been considered as members of the Society."

Even as more farms were confiscated from impoverished veterans and as matters worsened, the members of the Society of the Cincinnati left no doubt as to where they stood. In July of 1786, at the society's annual meeting, one member offered the toast, "May the enemies of *public faith, public honor and public justice* hold no place in the Councils of America." The Cincinnati agreed that as long as "public faith and private credit" were the "sacred object of government," they would support the Government.

Pressure continued to build over the fall, and all manner of court proceedings were successfully interrupted by farmers led by former officers, while other former officers with different interests began to perceive the disruption as rebellion and agreed to put it down. Most of the officers in the latter group were members of the Society of the Cincinnati.

Bowdoin was not impressed with the fact that the men now disrupting the state's judiciary had only recently routed the British Army. By mid-January of 1787, as protest appeared to transform itself into insurgency, he complained of "a spirit of discontent, originating in unsupported grievances," which had "stimulated many of the citizens . . . to acts subversive of government." It was clear to him "that the object of the insurgents is to annihilate our present happy Constitution," and he announced that he would use the militia to put them down.

5

A Little Rebellion
Now and Then

> By the malign influence of the moon's eclipses, the
> United States of America will be troubled with intes-
> tine jars, and domestic quarrels, and contentions of
> every kind.
> —Prediction made by Samuel Ellsworth, an as-
> tronomer of Vermont, in the summer of 1786

> In former days my name was Shays
> In Pelham I did dwell, sir;
> But now I'm forced to leave that place
> Because I did rebel, sir.
>
> But in this state I lived till late:
> By Satan's foul invention;
> In Pluto's cause against the laws
> I raised an insurrection....
> —"The Confession of Captain Shays," a song
> of 1793

The New England press did not exactly cover itself with distinction in explaining the controversy surrounding the farmers who could not pay their taxes to Government and their bills to retailers. It was a moment in our history when the seacoast newspapers in particular could have seized their newfound freedom and asserted their ideological independence from the entrenched social and business groups that were their financial support. No reasonable person could have expected the press to condone or support civil unrest in the making; nor could anyone suggest that newspapers then had access to all the information that would enable them to make sophisticated judgments about breaking news events.

But even acknowledging the partisanship and primitive deficits of newsgathering in 1786, the problems caused by the newspapers were glaring and egregious. Perhaps there would never have been so much trouble between rural and urban dwellers had eastern Massachusetts newspapers done more to explain what the farmers were unhappy about. Perhaps they could have persuasively counseled Government and merchants alike not to be quite so fast to abandon the democratic principles that the farmers had fought for in the Revolution.

There would be times over the next two centuries when American journalists thought of themselves as the collective conscience of their society. There would be times when they were quite right to think so—usually in their ability to uncover corruption, wrongdoing, and ethical lapses among wielders of power, rather than in their more modest expertise in explaining dissent and dissenters. Journalists in eastern Massachusetts had nothing to crow about in the way they covered the events leading up to what became known as Shays' Rebellion, which was neither a rebellion nor the property of Daniel Shays.

The mere thought of fallen heroes in debtors' prison should have been a revulsion to reporters, editors, and publishers. But rather than explain and probe the problem, the press succumbed to vituperation. The pages of some newspapers were used not to explain a bad situation, but to fan the emotions of self-interested or assiduously noninformed readers. Most conspicuous in its abysmal lack of professionalism and its predilection for mischief is Benjamin Russell's *Massachusetts Centinel*, published in Boston. Here is a front-page editorial which purported to describe the most complicated and tragic circumstances leading up to the civil disobedience that then seemed to be erupting everywhere:

To the People
   How long will ye permit your rights and authorities to be invaded, and your laws and constitution to be trampled on, by the most desperate bankrupts, plotting knaves and ignorant madmen?
   . . . Do ye fear the desperate individuals who dare to tell you, as they have in the Hampshire Gazette of the 27th of December that no debts shall be collected in gold or silver; that there shall be a depreciating paper currency established by law. . . .
   . . . Let us sweep them from the land:—and since they do not know how to prize the blessing of equal law and liberty, let them be cut off, or exiled to those lands where no traitor can escape the punishment due his crimes.

A few days later, the *Centinel* printed an anonymous letter "to the printer of the *Centinel*" which purported to offer information from an unidentified

New Yorker who had served with Shays, whom the letter referred to as "the infamous and ignorant leader of the insurgents in the western counties." The unnamed New Yorker called Shays a "mushroom general" whose home had the "appearance of a den of brutes" and described Shays' associates as "enemies of mankind."

The *Centinel* was most certainly not alone in succumbing to excesses in expressing its elitist nonacceptance of Daniel Shays and its indifference to what was happening to the yeomen farmers who had been counted among the heroes of the Revolution. The *Essex Journal and New Hampshire Packet* said that Shays and his men were "traiterous opposition" (sic), "wicked and rebellious men," "unhappy and deluded offenders," and "thieves, debtors and other fugitives." Shays himself was called "a mere tool of faction," a "Mass. outlaw," and an "armed banditti" (sic), while he and his men were referred to as the "devil and his imps" and "children of the insolvent." The paper money whose adoption might have meant an end to the agony of the veterans and others in the postwar period was dismissed as "fraudulent currency."

With language like this, it is no wonder that Bostonians were frightened and alienated. Anti-Shays sentiment in Boston ran so high that "it is dangerous even to be silent," complained Boston lawyer James Sullivan in a letter. "A man is accused of rebellion if he does not loudly approve every measure as prudent, necessary, wise, and constitutional."

The following lyrics, which were supposed to be sung to the tune of a song called "Black Sloven," were printed first in the *Hampshire Chronicle* and then reprinted in the *Massachusetts Centinel* in 1787. It fairly represented much of Massachusetts journalism's curiously myopic view of the farmers' struggle. And it showed a hunger on the part of some editors and publishers for revenge, not compassion:

> HUZZA my joe-bunkers! No taxes we'll pay!
> Here's a pardon for *Wheeler*, *Shays*, *Parsons*, and *Day*:
> Fix green boughs in your hats and renew the old cause,
> Stop the courts in each county and bully the laws,
> Constitutions and oaths, sir, we mind not a rush,
> Such trifles must yield to us lads of the bush.

There were some, to be sure, who hazarded to take a broader view, as evidenced in this poem by Moses Leavitt Neal in the *Freeman's Oracle* of March 3, 1787:

Behold a country void of rule or law,
Rewards or punishments, or fear or awe;
Nor yet restraints, nor right, nor justice seen,
Extremes on ev'ry side, without a mean.
Equality's the cry, and just the sound
For equal all in poverty are found,
Equal in fraud, injustice and deceit
Is church, is law, is physic and is state. . . .

Governor Bowdoin thought he saw the worst coming and apparently felt he could do or wanted to do nothing to ameliorate the conditions of farmers. He held a secret meeting with Knox and sought his intervention to finance Federal troops to put down whatever might come up. With Knox's urging, Congress pledged $530,000 for a "special force" of 1,340 troops.

The public was given to believe the troops were to be dispatched to put down Indians. Congress, which had not been able to find the cash to pay Revolutionary soldiers their back wages, was now trying to find the funds necessary to pay a new army to defeat its creditors, the very men who had won the Revolution. Ultimately, the Congress proved just as unable to support the new army as it did the old; Virginia stubbornly rejected the $530,000 expenditure and the plan failed.

Bowdoin then suggested that Massachusetts create a privately financed army of 4,400 troops and placed General Benjamin Lincoln at the head of it. Lincoln, who had served during the Revolution and was the first president of the Cincinnati in Massachusetts, had no trouble raising funds for it among wealthy coastal merchants. Some of them even joined the army. Knox's good friend Harrison Gray Otis organized some Harvard students into a company of independent cadets to fight the farmers, should it become necessary. The army was called a "Government" force even though it was really a punitive expedition by and for the elite and paid for by private sources.

But who would the other soldiers for such an army be? Merchants, even if aided by Harvard students, would probably be unable to handle all the chores themselves. When Bowdoin looked around for volunteers, he was pleased to find that former soldiers of the Revolution, many of them Boston-area residents down on their luck, were willing to serve. Their pay was £2 a month—which was made possible through the generosity of such wealthy Boston merchants as Samuel Breck, Thomas Russell, Caleb Davis, and Joseph Barrell, who pledged around £4,000. Other wealthy residents added to that, so that in short order, Bowdoin found himself with a war chest of more than £6,000.

Bowdoin also found that he had allies in a group he had not counted on, a group that, historically, was even more abused and exploited than were the farmers of western Massachusetts. They were the blacks—hundreds of blacks who were residents of Boston. And their leader, whom Shays and his men probably had never heard of, now potentially appeared as a formidable adversary. His name was Prince Hall, and even though both men were veterans and both had a related interest—protecting from harm groups of people who had been badly hurt and exploited—his style was quite unlike that of Shays.

Shays was direct, earthy, and vociferous; if he had not wanted to be known as the leader of a movement that bore his name, he was always candid about where his feelings lay. Hall was astute, reserved, forever walking the tightrope that only an urban Negro in eighteenth-century America could understand. He fought as hard for his principles as Shays did for his.

Born in 1735, Hall was a veteran of the Revolutionary Army. He was one of the earliest black organizers and was a founder of Freemasonry among blacks in the United States. He had worked tirelessly before the Revolution for the termination of the slave trade and slavery itself. He had played an active role in the creation of petitions to the Government in 1773, 1774, 1777, and 1778.

After the Revolution, when slavery was ended officially in Massachusetts but its pernicious vestiges clung, there were still more petitions, and Hall was involved in framing and writing many of them. In the late 1780s, perhaps five thousand African-Americans lived in Massachusetts, most of them in the eastern counties. Perhaps one thousand lived in or near Boston. These blacks were free men and women, working as house servants, artisans, apprentices, factory workers, seamen, whalers, dock workers, and workers on fishing boats. A few hundred blacks had served in the American Revolution.

That any were permitted to join the Revolution was something of an accomplishment, since a series of laws dating back to the seventeenth century said that although a black might serve the military in some capacity, he would not be permitted to bear arms. But in 1774, the Massachusetts Committee of Safety decided that blacks would be permitted to serve in local detachments of minutemen. A year later, because Washington initially did not want blacks in the Army, they were barred from service. As a result, hundreds of blacks joined the British Army, and by the end of 1775, Washington authorized recruiters to accept black applicants for service. But many whites still remained uneasy about arming former slaves, even after blacks repeatedly proved their loyalty and their valor in battle. Indeed, records indicated that the first man to be shot in the Boston Massacre had been Crispus Attucks, who was black.

None of this explained why blacks would want to take up arms against farmers. Indeed, there is every reason to believe that they wanted to take up arms against no one. But late in 1786, Governor Bowdoin, in another response to sustained challenges brought by farmer-veterans to his authority, saw to it that a series of repressive measures were passed. The Militia Act held that any soldier involved in rebellious behavior would be subject to court-martial. The Riot Act which followed prohibited meetings of more than a dozen persons bearing arms. It specifically empowered sheriffs to kill rioters—an action that had been taken earlier by the British against the Americans in one of the events leading up to the Revolution. By November, Bowdoin was sufficiently alarmed to urge the state legislature to suspend habeas corpus so that people suspected of wrongdoing could be more easily (and capriciously) arrested and imprisoned.

In Boston, blacks watched all of this with much apprehension. They had long borne the brunt of racist distrust from white leaders. It seemed reasonable that Prince Hall wanted to make sure that none of Bowdoin's nervousness over farmers translated itself into still more oppression against the blacks. If lawyer James Sullivan, who was white, felt that in Boston "it was dangerous even to be silent," the potential ire of the Governor and the merchants was surely not lost on the blacks. Nor was talk—mostly from Secretary of War Knox—about a "special force" to wage war against the "Indians." Nor, especially, was the privately financed militia now at the disposal of Governor Bowdoin.

There were rumors that farmers would try to invade Boston around the first of November. None appeared. Since the troops had no one to fight, they were reviewed by Governor Bowdoin, who was accompanied by his staff and the president of Harvard. Tension continued to mount.

On November 26, 1786, after the suspension of habeas corpus had gone into effect, Hall wrote the Governor on behalf of the African Lodge of Masons, making an offer:

To His Excellency, James Bowdoin. We by the Providence of God, are members of a fraternity that not only enjoins us to be peaceable subjects to the Civil power where we reside, but it also forbids our having concern in any plot or conspiracies against the present state, and as the meanest of its members must feel that want of lawful and good government, and as we have been protected for many years under this once happy constitution, we do hope, by the blessing of God, we may enjoy that blessing: therefore, we though unworthy members of the Commonwealth are willing to help and support so far as our weak and feeble abilities become necessary in this time of trouble and confusion, as you in your wisdom shall direct us. That we may, under just and lawful authority, live peaceable lives in all godliness and honesty, is the hearty wish of your humble servants, the members of the African Lodge; and in their names I subscribe myself your most humble servant.

In short, Hall proposed that Bowdoin utilize the manpower available in Boston's African Lodge of Freemasons, which would have sent seven hundred black soldiers to confront the farmers of Daniel Shays.

Soon after the new year, Bowdoin turned down Hall's offer. The idea of arming that many blacks was disturbing to him. These, after all, had not been such passive folk, clamoring as they did, over the years, for such things as freedom, the right to keep their families intact, education, decent jobs, even the right to return to the Africa from which they had been taken. Memories are long; such people could not be useful in putting an end to whatever threat was posed by Shays and his farmer allies, Bowdoin concluded.

General Rufus Putnam, in whose command Shays had served in the late Revolution, wrote a rather remarkable letter to Governor Bowdoin on January 8, 1787. He told Bowdoin he had met Shays alone on the road as he had come through Pelham. Putnam's account of that meeting was quite detailed, almost as though he or someone else had taken notes furiously. But he explained to Bowdoin that the conversation, which he submitted almost in transcript form, was what he recollected. The conversation started with Shays inquiring as to whether a petition signed by farmers had gone to the Governor and Putnam responding, in effect, that it would not matter, since Bowdoin would not grant its request for relief.

"Then we must fight it out," Shays said.

"That as you please," Putnam replied, "but it's impossible you should succeed, and the event will be that you must either run your country or hang, unless you are fortunate enough to bleed."

"By God I'll never run my country," Shays said.

"Why not?" asked Putnam. "It's more honorable to fight in a bad cause and be the means of involving your country in a civil war; and that is bad cause; you have always owned to me; that is you owned to me . . . that it was wrong in the people ever to take up arms as they had."

"So I did, and so I say now, and I told you then and tell you now, that the sole motive with me in taking the command at Springfield was, as to prevent the shedding of blood, which absolutely would have been the case, if I had not; and I am so far from considering it a crime, that I look upon it that the government are indebted to me for what I did there.''

Putnam then asked Shays how he came ''to pursue the matter.''

''I did not pursue the matter,'' Shays said. ''It was noised about that the warrants were out after me, and I was determined not to be taken.''

Putnam pressed him. ''This won't do. How came you to write letters to several towns in the county of Hampshire, to choose officers and furnish themselves with arms and 60 rounds of ammunition?''

''I never did,'' Shays snapped. ''It was a cursed falsehood. . . . I never had any hand in the matter; it was done by a Committee, and Doctor Hunt and somebody else, who I don't know, put my name to the copy and sent it to the Governor and the Court.''

General Putnam asked Shays if it wasn't true that he had ordered a group of men to march on Shrewsbury, in order that they might go on and stop the court at Cambridge.

''I never ordered a man to march to Shrewsbury, nor anywhere else, except when I lay at Rutland. . . . You are deceived; I have never had half so much to do with the matter as you think . . .''

Shays added that he could not see ''why stopping that court was such a crime.'' He did not see that as insurgency; only an act of simple survival. And when Putnam referred to him as the ''head of the insurgents and the person who directs all their movements,'' Shays retorted: ''I at their head! I am not.''

The conversation ended with Putnam suggesting to Shays that he go to Boston immediately and ''throw yourself upon the mercy and under the protection of Government.'' But Shays had already had quite enough of being under the ''protection'' of Bowdoin's Government and told Putnam he wouldn't do it, ''unless I was first assured of a pardon.''

Shays was afraid to come in and the Government would not relent on the issue of foreclosure and the collection of debts, on the acceptability of paper money; on a host of things that concerned the farmers. The unrest continued, and clearly, Shays could not have stopped it if he tried. And now he was riding a tiger, made angry not by Shays, but by Bowdoin and company.

On January 19, Bowdoin's troops moved toward Worcester and Bowdoin issued arrest warrants for sixteen of the farmer leaders. The next day, the *Centinel* printed an interview that purported to quote Shays as saying that his men planned to march to Boston and plunder it. Given Shays' reticence to lead anything and the conversation reported by Putnam, the authenticity of this interview may be reasonably questioned. There never was any confirmation of the *Centinel*'s report. On January 24, 1787, someone in

Hampshire County was quoted as saying he saw "small bodies of men with green boughs in their hats" gathering under Luke Day.

It did not overly perturb Governor Bowdoin, who saw no problem in leaving Boston that day for Philadelphia, where he would be welcomed into the American Philosophical Society along with John Lowell of Boston, the Duke of Richmond, and John Jay, who was then Secretary for Foreign Affairs. On January 25, Daniel Shays, at the head of about twelve hundred men, marched on the Federal Arsenal at Springfield in what was to be the the most critical part of his movement. The arsenal, stocked with seven thousand muskets, thirteen hundred barrels of powder, and assorted military stores totaling 450 tons, was worth seizing, if only to deny its resources to the Boston merchants. But that tactic came a little late. Shays' plan apparently had been leaked to Major-General William Shepard, who had already occupied Springfield with a well-armed force of nine hundred men.

Indeed, on the same day, even as he prepared to confront the army of Massachusetts' merchant princes, if not that of all the Founding Fathers, Shays sent General Lincoln a letter. Its words were anything but those of one who wanted to "annihilate our present happy Constitution":

> Unwilling to be any way accessary to the shedding of blood, and greatly desirous of restoring peace and harmony to this convulsed commonwealth, we propose that all the troops on the part of the government be disbanded immediately, and that all and every person, who has been acting, or any way aiding or assisting in any of the late risings of the people, may be indemnified in their person and property, until the setting of the next General Court, respecting the matters of complaints of the people; and *that all matters rest* as they are. . . .
>
> . . . [We propose that] all persons that have been taken on the part of government be released without punishment. The above conditions to be made sure by proclamation, issued by His excellency, the Governeur: on which . . . condition, the people now in arms, in defence of their lives and liberties, will quietly return to their respective habitations, patiently waiting and hoping for constitutional relief from insupportable burdens they now labour under.

The confrontation between Shays' men and those dispatched by Governor Bowdoin started to unfold at four in the afternoon. Major-General Shepard, who was in charge of the Governor's army, sent two captains named Buffington and Woodbridge to ask Shays what he wanted. "His reply," said Shepard in a letter written to Bowdoin that very day, "was, he wanted barracks, and barracks he would have and stores. The answer was that he must purchase them dear. . . ."

Shays' men did not fire, but moved to about one hundred yards of the arsenal. The troops under Shepard fired first, over the heads of the approaching farmers. They continued to come. The Governor's artillery commander "directed his shot through the center of [Shays'] column. The fourth or fifth shot put their column into the utmost confusion." Shepard reported later that no musket was fired on either side.

When it was over and Shays' men had fled the scene, Shepard, himself a farmer and not so unsympathetic to Shays' cause, found three dead insurgents, with their muskets "all deeply loaded." Shays, who had been quoted as saying his men would invade and plunder Boston, had thus confronted the armed troops of Bowdoin—apparently without firing a single shot. At least no shot that hit anybody.

Bowdoin took no chances, however, and two days after the rout at the arsenal, General Benjamin Lincoln arrived with reinforcements, including four regiments from Suffolk, Essex, Middlesex, and Worcester, three companies of artillery, a corps of cavalry, and a group of extra volunteers. But Lincoln reported that when his men confronted those of Shays, the latter simply "made a little shew of force for a minute or two near the meeting house, and then retired in the utmost confusion and disorder." Lincoln was able to advise Bowdoin that no more men were required to quell Shays' rebellion and that "the state of our finances should be kept in view, and every unnecessary expence avoided."

While the forces of Lincoln and Shays took stock of each other, there were signs of civility and restraint not normally associated with rebellion. For example, Luke Day permitted Ensign Richard Edwards, a Government officer, to pass through his lines "as the gentleman and his men belong to the new raised troops for the Ohio service."

The only man reported wounded on Shepard's side in the ugly scene at the arsenal was a Sergeant Chaloner of Boston. He apparently stood between two of Shepard's cannon that were firing at Shays, became confused, and moved in front of a cannon about to be discharged, which cost him both his arms and his vision. The incident gave the *Centinel* yet another opportunity to dramatize the righteousness of Bowdoin, the merchants, and their army, and emphasize that it was not opposed to paying needy veterans their due when they proved their worth as clearly as Chaloner did:

> Although stone blind, as soon as he could speak, he eagerly inquired, whether the insurgents came on retreated, saying to those about him, "stand by our brave General, and so long as you have limbs, fight for the support of that Government which is able and willing to support all honest men."

This unlucky man has once before stood between us and danger, and almost ever since the peace kept a little school in the country. How can we recompence this man who can now neither fee nor feed himself?

After the confrontation at the arsenal, the rebels fled, and on January 29, most of them were in Pelham. Shays spent that evening in a room over Conkey's tavern. He went to sleep remembering better days and hoped there could be a truce. General Lincoln's men were camped at Hadley. Messages were exchanged between Shays and Lincoln—Shays wanting hostilities to cease until the legislature responded to his latest request for relief, Lincoln informing him that the only way to stop it was to disband.

The letter from the insurgents to the legislature, written at this time, was signed not by Shays, but by Francis Stone, who was appointed to be the signatory. The tone taken by the letter was anything but militant. It said that the rebels had "been in error" and that "we therefore heartily pray your honours, to overlook our failing."

They further said that "it appears to us, that the time is near approaching, when much human blood will be spilt, unless a reconciliation can immediately take place, which scene strikes us with horror. . . ." The farmers agreed to lay down their arms "and repair to our respective homes, in a peaceable and quiet manner; and so remain, provided your honours will grant to your petitioners . . . a general pardon for their past offences."

The legislature rejected the petition. One of the reasons given was that the petitioners made themselves appear the equal of the legislature, "by proposing 'a reconciliation.' " As important as anything else in this sad business was the drawing of class distinctions by the rich and the powerful in Boston.

Only a decade had passed since Americans had issued their Declaration of Independence which spoke to the dignity of humankind and the equal value of individuals under law; it had been only a scant three years since the winning of the war; and yet, Boston's powerful would not agree to anything that suggested that they and the farmers might be equals. Some of these same people had participated in writing the Declaration. The farmers seemed to have a better recollection of it than did the Federalists who espoused its principles. Issues of ethics and short memories aside, the legislature knew the farmers were not in a position of strength, and so it decided to remain firm. The rebels were to be pursued, the rebellion to be put down.

On February 3, Shays and his men moved to Petersham after he treated them to some libations, not at his friend Conkey's, but at Dr. Nehemiah Hinds' tavern on Pelham East Hill. He thought he was well ahead of his pursuers, but Lincoln force-marched Bowdoin's mercenaries thirty miles through Amherst, Shutesbury, and New Salem, in bitterly cold weather and through deep snow, surprised the Shays force at Petersham, and sent it scattering.

As the insurrection that never was fell apart, the legislature sat in Boston and denounced the farmers' actions as "open, unnatural, unprovoked and wicked rebellion," and gave Bowdoin the power to do pretty much what he wanted to put it down. The denunciation was accompanied by passage of yet another law to intimidate dissidents—the Disqualification Act, which made it illegal for the rebels to hold public office, teach in public schools, run taverns, or vote in a public election. Bowdoin nevertheless offered pardons to all but Shays and the other leaders if they would return to the fold.

In mid-February, before it was finally over, thirty more rebels were killed at Sheffield, as were three of Bowdoin's soldiers. And there was ample spite on the rebel side. General Shepard's woodlands were burned and some of his horses were mutilated.

There were holdouts. Eli Parsons, a rebel leader who had fled to Vermont, advised his fellow farmers: "Will you now tamely suffer your arms to be taken from you, your estates to be confiscated, and even swear to support a constitution and form of government . . . which common sense and your conscience declare to be iniquitous and cruel?"

That was precisely what the farmers did. By March, they began to return home. There was spring planting to be done, Government or not.

In April of 1787, Massachusetts elected John Hancock as Governor, and he was not predisposed to follow his predecessor's harsh example. Sam Adams, who most certainly did not like the rebels, became president of the state senate, but there was no wave of oppression. Even so, some of the farmers who had taken part in the rebellion left Massachusetts and settled in Vermont and New York. For a time, it looked as though their leaders, if caught, would go to the gallows. But pardons were issued, nobody was hanged, and in the years that followed, many former rebels married into nonrebel families.

Daniel Shays and the men who agreed with him that the system wasn't working for a great many people after the war, including most of those who fought it, were too knowledgable about warfare to think they could ever win a true rebellion. Indeed, the uprising was really a prolonged form of rough-hewn protest in which almost all the violence was produced by

Bowdoin's army, not that of the dissident farmers. Soldiers hunted the farmers for months thereafter, even though towns in western Massachusetts petitioned both the Governor and Lincoln to cease the use of military force against Shays' men. Many townspeople feared civil war. The farmers, in turn, raided the properties of the merchants who had demanded specie of them in western Massachusetts. As for Shays himself, by early summer, neither his followers nor his pursuers were sure where he was.

Shays, who was a good soldier and an honorable man, if a desperate one, was judged most harshly by his contemporaries, and their evaluation of what he did tarnished his name in history. Six months after the protest movement called Shays' Rebellion was over, both the *Albany Gazette* and the *Massachusetts Centinel* printed this letter "from a gentleman in Washington County to his friend in Albany":

> Where is Shays? Is he in Canada, Vermont, or White Creek? I have been asked these questions a thousand times, and a thousand times I declared myself unable to gratify the curiosity of the inquirers.
>
> But what in the name of common sense is this *Shays?* A mere tool of faction—a puppet which some political mountebank has play'd off upon the populace—an idol, void of intrinsic merit, to which a thoughtless multitude have bent the knee: Supposing that he was taken and gibbetted [sent to the gallows] today, how soon would the prevailing rage of excessive democracy— this fashionable contempt for government—of public and private faith, raise up another *Shays*, as mad and as audacious as the present!

The question that nagged was what, if anything, the thing called Shays' Rebellion might have accomplished. Traditional wisdom has it that the uprising galvanized the Federalists to forge a more perfect union and prompted George Washington to come out of retirement and become the nation's first President. But Federalism was born before the rebellion. Washington, Hamilton, and Madison were working hard for its implementation long before they ever heard of Daniel Shays.

Rebellion may have caused the Federalists to work a mite harder, however. In Massachusetts, as in other states, those who wanted a strong Federal Government were merchants, lawyers, large landowners, and clergymen. Anti-Federalists, those who were suspicious of granting much power to a central Government, included small farmers. When, in short order, the Massachusetts towns voted on ratification of the United States Constitution, support for it was not overwhelming; the vote was 187 for to 168 against. The vote cannot be easily explained. Were they voting mostly against a strong Federal Government or simply against anything they knew Bowdoin favored?

There is no question that the Founding Fathers were aware of the farmers' movement that was called a rebellion, and not all the Federalists looked upon Shays as did Bowdoin and Sam Adams. "The spirit of resistance to government is so valuable, on certain occasions, that I wish it to be always kept alive," Thomas Jefferson wrote to Abigail Adams in February of 1787 from Paris. "It will often be exercised when wrong but better so than not to be exercised at all. I like a little rebellion now and then. It is like a storm in the atmosphere. . . ."

The correspondence of Madison and Jefferson in 1787 mentions the farmers, with Madison more concerned than Jefferson. Madison informed Jefferson on March 19, 1787, "The expedition under General Lincoln against the insurgents has efectually succeeded in dispersing them. Whether the calm which he has restored will be durable or not is uncertain. . . ."

Jefferson, who was minister to France, responded to Madison on June 20, making no mention of the unrest but thanking Madison for a package of pecans that Madison had sent to Paris in March. Jefferson said nothing about the uprising to Madison until the following December 20. His words were memorable, starkly contrasting Jefferson's approach to Bowdoin's:

> I own I am not a friend to very energetic government. It is always oppressive. The late rebellion in Massachusetts has given more alarm than I think it should have done. Calculate that one rebellion in 13 states in the course of 11 years is but one for each state in a century and a half. No country should be so long without one.
>
> I think our governments will remain virtuous for many centuries; as long as they are chiefly agricultural; and this will be as long as there shall be vacant lands in any part of America. When they get piled upon one another in large cities, as in Europe, they will become corrupt as in Europe.

Resisting Government certainly did nothing for Shays personally. It merely assured his poverty. The man who really didn't want to lead a movement that was doomed to fail by the collective indifference and callousness of merchants, speculators, Government, and a largely mindless press never again worked his farm at Pelham, nor did he ever feel he could again live there permanently. He remained a fugitive for a time, although Massachusetts granted him a pardon in 1788. After hostilities ended, he moved about, living first in Bennington County, Vermont, then in a town of

Massachusetts exiles called Sandgate, which was near Salem, in New York
State. Neither he nor his former comrades-in-arms prospered there, in their
hamlet of fifteen or eighteen houses, a store, a school, a tavern, all clustered
about a green. He remained there only until his pardon from Massachusetts
came through, then moved on. His less fortunate neighbors stayed on, but
many were killed by an epidemic in 1813 and the town ceased to exist.

Shays visited Pelham one more time, then moved to other locations in
Upstate New York, but his fortunes did not change. In 1799, Shays and his
son were sued for failing to do so some work they had promised to do and
were fined $32.10. He finally moved to Livingston County, in central New
York State. In 1818, twenty-five years after the Revolution, Shays applied
for the pension that was due him for his honorable service in the American
Revolution. It was approved and Shays purchased twelve acres of land near
Scottsburgh, New York, on which he built a log cabin and a frame barn. It
was there that a young Millard Fillmore met him and described him as
"short, stout, talkative and sprightly." He drank no more nor less than he
had at Conkey's, but always held his liquor well, was good to be with, and,
it was said, "never kept low company." When he entertained his friends,
he took pride in seeing to it that despite his circumstances, they received
good drink and good food.

It remains a matter of some speculation whether Shays made a lasting
impression on Fillmore. But after his election to the New York State
legislature, Fillmore sponsored an "Act to Abolish Imprisonment for
Debt." It gave him recognition, not among the inheritors of Bowdoin's
tradition, but among enough others so that his political career was given a
boost toward his becoming the thirteenth President of the United States.

Shays died in 1825 at the age of eighty-four. There is no evidence to
suggest that, despite his bad luck of being a farmer in post-Revolutionary
Massachusetts, he was ever bitter. He was buried at Conesus, New York,
but the rough stone that marked his grave was inscribed only with a
jackknife. Not until the 1930s was a proper headstone put into place there.

As for the Shays farm in Pelham, its ninety-five acres eventually became
part of the watershed for the 412-billion-gallon Quabbin Reservoir, which
was created in the 1930s to serve the needs of Boston—the city whose
original interests had proved so disastrous to Shays and the other western
Massachusetts farmers who had served in the Revolution. The house itself
long ago ceased to exist. Only its foundation remains, and it bears no
marker. Only history buffs and the people of Pelham know where it is.

Conkey's tavern is also in the clutches of the Quabbin. It was burned down in 1883. Its foundation remains, also without a marker. Since both house and tavern are in a reservoir area, Massachusetts officialdom has never been anxious to make them tourist attractions. And so, although Shays' farm and Conkey's tavern are not underwater, they are among the lost towns of the Quabbin.

The people of Pelham understand Boston's need to keep its drinking water pure, although some of them wonder, at times, if the lack of a marker and the unwillingness of the state to let a few hardy visitors hike to the site of Shays' farm are, in fact, the ultimate contempt that the Federalist tradition harbors for the likes of Daniel Shays. To make matters worse, from Pelham's point of view, the Quabbin water delivery system leaks badly— estimates are that from 7 to 25 percent of the water from the reservoir is lost long before it reaches Boston. It is the sort of thing Shays himself might have protested, to the delight of Thomas Jefferson, but to the embarrassment of the politicians in Boston.

As for Shays' comrades-in-arms, many of them stayed in various places in Vermont and in New York State. Pelham, Shays' home base, lost half of its population permanently. Of those who stayed, some did well enough. Adam Johnson, for example, left $4,000 to something called the Collegiate Charity Institution in Amherst, which became Amherst College. The Johnson Chapel still stands there, made of stone that was quarried in Pelham.

Ultimately, Shays' Rebellion was nervously laughed into the dark side of history by the people who most feared what it represented. And so to Benjamin Russell, the publisher of the *Centinel*, and a journalist who had never adequately explained what the farmers' movement was all about, it was entirely appropriate to print this sniping little *morceau* in January, as soldiers-become-farmers-become-soldiers-again began the final stage of their resistance:

> [To the tune of "Yankee Doodle"]
>
> Insurgents all what will ye say?
>   Come—is this not a griper?
> That when your hopes are danced away,
>   'Tis you must pay the piper.

TWO
The War of 1812
and the
Mexican War

VOLUNTEERS!

Men of the Granite State!
Men of Old Rockingham!! the
strawberry-bed of patriotism, renowned for bravery and
devotion to Country, rally at this call. Santa Anna, reek-
ing with the generous confidence and magnanimity of your
countrymen, is in arms, eager to plunge his traitor-dagger
in their bosoms. To arms, then, and rush to the standard
of the fearless and gallant CUSHING---put to the blush
the dastardly meanness and rank toryism of Massachusetts. Let the half civilized Mexicans hear the crack of
the unerring New Hampshire rifleman, and illustrate on
the plains of San Luis Potosi, the fierce, determined, and
undaunted bravery that has always characterized her
sons.
    Col. THEODORE F. ROWE, at No. 31 Daniel-street,
is authorized and will enlist men this week for the Massachusetts Regiment of Volunteers. The compensation is
$10 per month---$30 in advance. Congress will grant
a handsome bounty in money and ONE HUNDRED
AND SIXTY ACRES OF LAND.
    Portsmouth, Feb. 2. 1847.

A recruiting poster for the
Mexican-American War
promised New Hampshire
volunteers land and money.
(*The Bettman Archive*)

6

Like Sweet Poison on the Taste

Americans! Then rejoice! Thank your warriors who
have given you Glory, and your ministers who have
given you Peace! Be virtuous and happy! Abuse not
the benefits which a good Providence has showered
upon your heads!
—*Richmond Enquirer,* February 22, 1815

All the despotisms in Europe have had their foundations in a claim to military merit.... And when we are
gone to rest posterity will writhe beneath the yoke,
borne down by hearth money, excises, and taxes to
support pensions and places—the curse of a nation.
This will be the beginning of a military pension system
that posterity will regret.
—Senator William Smith of Virginia in a
debate in the Senate, January 29, 1818

It was only reasonable that President James Monroe seemed in a giving
mood in his message to Congress of December 1817. The Treasury had
taken in $24.5 million that year and, in a conjunction of prosperity and
parsimony that would be the envy of many future Governments, actually had
$2.7 million left.

It was a time of peace and plenty. And of pride, too. The War of 1812 was
over and the British had been beaten again—and again the combatants on the
American side had been an army in tatters, distressingly not unlike the one
that had fought the Revolution. During the War of 1812, both Government
inspectors and civilians saw soldiers who were ragged and destitute, some
with "no trousers and no coats." In enlisting, these men were motivated as

much by future visions of bounties and land grants as by patriotism, even though the best-informed among them surely knew that no such largess had ever been lavished on those who had suffered through Valley Forge.

In some quarters, such men could do no right. In 1812, the Rev. Brown Emerson, the father of Ralph Waldo Emerson, had preached a sermon at Salem and expressed his concern over the "profaneness, blasphemy, debauchery" that, in his mind, were associated with soldiers, whatever the cause. To him, soldiers, by virtue of their service, lost "every spark of kindness and mercy" whenever they became "accustomed to rapine and blood."

The soldiers would see a measure of bloodletting before the War of 1812 was over. It had not been a war the insecure Americans wanted. But when the British began to kidnap American sailors off their ships on the high seas and force them to serve in the British Navy, America could not tolerate it and declared war. It was really nothing less than a second Declaration of Independence, the reaffirmation of America's right to exist free of Britain, and of its competence to handle its own destiny.

Like the Revolution itself, the war had been marked by many defeats and much humiliation for the Americans, not the least of which was the burning of Washington, and the ruination of what might have been one of Dolley Madison's better dinner parties. Even this disaster was not without its auspicious moments: Mrs. Madison had the presence to save her silverware before the British arrived with their torches.

But finally the Americans achieved a stunning victory in the Battle of New Orleans when the British, who committed a force of some six thousand frontally against Andrew Jackson's well-protected force of thirty-five hundred, suffered two thousand casualties. The Americans reported they had lost only thirteen dead and counted fifty-eight wounded. The fact that all of this was largely irrelevant—it occurred after peace had been secured by the Treaty of Ghent—was unknown by combatants on either side. It did not deter the public from acclaiming Andrew Jackson as a hero in a new country that needed heroes.

By 1817, the Americans and the British had begun to tolerate if not actually like each other; some of the wounds caused by the War of 1812 had been healed in the three years since hostilities ceased. For example, both sides had agreed to reduce their naval forces on the Great Lakes, even though some Americans still harbored desire for the corpus of Canada and some British thought fondly of the good old days when Boston, now growing more genteel by the hour, was their colonial city. And although other problems remained with the British, such as the right of American fishermen to "take and cure fish" in Canadian waters, Monroe clearly felt and expressed the public euphoria of his time.

Relations with the Indians were better, he thought; the $15 million Louisiana Purchase he had helped to negotiate fourteen years earlier would be paid for in only two more years, thus adding 827,192 square miles of land to the United States at a bargain price; and in the rutted streets of Washington, he could see the Capitol under construction, even though the city radiant that L'Enfant envisioned was still mired in mud, a place that Abigail Adams had called "a wild wilderness." In his message to Congress, the President said, "At no period of our political existence had we so much cause to felicitate ourselves at the prosperous and happy condition of our country. The abundant fruits of the earth have filled it with plenty." He thought so much of his own words that he ordered two thousand copies of the speech to be printed.

As the Congress heard Monroe, Christmas was only twenty-three days away and the Panic of 1819 would not bring calamity down on the heads of the unsuspecting for another two years. And so why not think of people and times other Americans had forgotten, namely, the men who had fought the American Revolution thirty-five years earlier? "In contemplating the happy situation of the United States," Monroe told the Congress, "our attention is drawn, with peculiar interest, to the surviving officers and soldiers of our Revolutionary Army, who so eminently contributed, by their services, to lay its foundation."

Monroe noted that many of them had already "paid the debt of nature and gone to repose," but that "among the survivors, there are some not provided for by existing laws, who are reduced to indigence, and even to real distress." The country would honor itself "to provide for them," the President added, warning that with the passage of a few years more "the opportunity will be forever lost." In short, James Monroe sought a "great and important change," in the very concept of providing veterans' benefits.

His feeling was that indigent and infirm veterans, including those who had never been injured in the war, deserved to be paid something by their Government. This was in contrast to the traditional American wisdom about military pensions, which held that such money should go only to those who had been wounded, not simply those who had served and now found themselves on hard times. What is more, Monroe proposed that the more liberal pension arrangement should be for all destitute veterans, including those from the War of 1812, and for those who, before that, had spent the better part of three fruitful years with Meriwether Lewis and William Clark, trying to find a suitable land route westward and learn more about the Indians who lived beyond the frontier.

Not that the Lewis and Clark troopers had been shortchanged. When, in 1806, the expedition had returned to St. Louis to a great public welcome, President Jefferson recommended that each expeditionary soldier (all had Army rank, even if they had not been traditional soldiers previously) receive a bonus of 320 acres of land, while Lewis and Clark got 1,500 acres each. The soldiers also got double pay for the time they had spent on the expedition, along with five brand-new uniforms adorned with gold braid and brass buttons. But the Lewis and Clark expedition had consisted of only thirty-two soldiers and ten Indians; such magnanimity was not encumbering to the people of the United States.

But there were thousands of veterans of the Revolution and the War of 1812, and the Fates, not to mention the Treasury, would never ordain gold braid and brass buttons for so many. These men were caught in something of a postwar limbo. The surviving Revolutionary veterans, now quite gray, stood romanticized if not rewarded; the younger men, the ones who had fought "Jemmy Madison's war," had overcome that conflict's initial unpopularity as the nation decided, finally, that it really had been worth something. But just what had not yet been made clear to them.

Americans who first were reluctant to fight the war had grown to become resentful about what they heard of Britain's support of Indian uprisings and British trade restrictions. From Henry Clay's view, the War of 1812 had succeeded in achieving "the firm establishment of the American character." The *National Advocate* ran an editorial that went even further. "Cold and unfeeling must be that man who thinks we have gained nothing by the present war. If there exists such an animal in the bosom of our country, suspect him—he is fit for strategems, spoils and treasons."

The *Advocate* concluded that the War of 1812 had "awakened a patriotic flame, and called forth, in volunteers, in the field of battle, the friends of the country, and its government. . . . We have thus proved ourselves worthy of the rich inheritance, freedom and independence, bequeathed us by our fathers; and for 'our children we have preserved it unsullied.' "

Clearly, it was a good time to crow. Winning one against the British might have been just luck. Winning two meant that like it or not, other nations had to take America seriously. All the more reason for America to take itself seriously and for Monroe to want to pay tribute to all the soldiers who had made it possible. His pension suggestion appears to have been the first ever in this nation to give Government funds to help the poor. It began a debate on the Government's role in fighting poverty that would continue into our own times.

Monroe not only started the dialogue about the "first principles" that justify all military benefits from the Government. He also raised fundamental questions about war's sacrifices and selfishness, the inevitable and unrelenting dichotomy between those who thought first of a citizen's duty to his country and those who preferred to think about a civilized nation's presumed concern and compassion for its own who were ill clothed and ill fed. Further, Monroe sparked the quarrel between those who felt that the veterans who had risked their very lives for America were owed something as a debt of honor, and those who said that the financial solvency of the nation was more important—that pensions for veterans would sap its strength and put its future solvency in question. One such critic was Senator Nathaniel Macon of North Carolina, who felt that military pensions would work "like sweet poison on the taste; it pleases at first, but kills at last."

When Monroe's idea came before the House of Representatives, the issue was the cost of it, not the lofty ideals behind it. And the way the cost issue was put to rest demonstrated that finessing numbers in order to meet a budget objective was invented long before the twentieth century produced legendary budget jousters.

On December 19, only seventeen days after Monroe's pension ideas were released to the Congress, Representative Joseph Bloomfield of New Jersey introduced them in bill form. He knew the proposal would at least have to look cheap to his colleagues in the House, and the best way to do that, he thought, was to convince them that when all was said and done, very few Revolutionary soldiers would seek benefits because there simply weren't very many of them around.

Bloomfield devised a most unusual statistical analysis to support his salesmanship. Using what he said was "personal knowledge," he said that of the original 160 officers of the Jersey Brigade, only twenty had survived, as of the last Fourth of July. This information, he said, could be taken as a "guide" to determine the "proportion of survivors" for the rest of the Revolutionary Army. According to Bloomfield this meant that of the 2,720 officers who were alive at the end of the Revolution, only 340, or about one-eighth, would have survived until 1817. Of these, he estimated that only one-tenth, or thirty-four, would apply for pensions.

Enlisted men would similarly not prove to be a burden, Bloomfield claimed. He reasoned that enlisted men would not live as long as the officers, "being generally not of as regular habits as officers." He further estimated that although officers would live longer, fewer of them would apply for pensions, so that when it was all worked out, an equal number of officers and enlisted men would receive a monthly payment from the Government.

Finally, he calculated that it would cost only $34,376 a year to provide all surviving officers and enlisted men with pensions—officers were to receive $17 a month, and enlisted men $8. His bill was immediately amended to increase the officers' share to $20 and keep the enlisted men's at $8. The projected cost of the entire program, taking into account that Revolutionary veterans were a rapidly declining class of men, was thus put at around $500,000.

The debate that followed contained arguments that would become a fixture in American political rhetoric and define a part of our particular national schizophrenia. From the very beginning, we thought of ourselves as a generous and compassionate people but invariably fell to judging harshly the objects of our compassion and generosity. We urged our best young men to fight hard for us, even if we did not always believe in what the fight was all about. We venerated patriotism but found something pesky in the expense vouchers of our patriots.

That attitude had an impact upon the famous and the not-so-famous. Thirty-four years before Monroe's proposition was first advanced, George Washington himself was shortchanged at least £1,000 in expense money when he left the Army. Washington had accepted no pay during the war and only billed the Government £8,422.16.4 after it was over. The Government seems not to have paid him for six round trips and part of a seventh that Martha took between Mount Vernon and where the Army was. Washington, ever the diplomat, speculated that he had probably forgotten to charge the Government enough "through hurry, I suppose, and the perplexity of business (for I know not how else to account for the deficiency). . . ."

Could Monroe's pension suggestions become law in a land that would not pay George Washington? There were objections to the proposal from those who feared it would be abused by those not really entitled to pensions, who were, in fact, too lazy to work or, perhaps, too old.

The more compassionate Representative Edward Colston of Virginia said he would object to any qualification of indigence. "Let not the soldier by whose bravery and sufferings we are entitled to hold seats on this floor, be required to expose his poverty to the world, and exhibit the proof of it, to entitle him to relief," Colston said. He thought the incorporation of such a requirement would be "degrading" to the House. He said he hoped that "a liberal spirit" would prevail in the House and that "for the short remnant of their lives a pension would be given to all who survived of the soldiers of the Revolution.''

Representative William Henry Harrison of Ohio avowed his ''high respect for the survivors of the Revolution,'' but said he felt the bill as proposed went too far in that it would ''embrace everyone who had shouldered a musket, even for an hour. . . . Persons . . . covered with scars and borne down by the length of service in those days ought not to be confounded with those who had been called out for an hour or a day.'' He said most emphatically that the bill should benefit only those who had served six months or more.

Representative Samuel L. Southard, one of Bloomfield's colleagues from New Jersey, objected to the use of the word ''shall'' as applied to those who would receive pensions because it made the bill compulsory, giving it to the wealthy as well as the poor. He disagreed with Colston's position that the pensions should go to all, regardless of means. He pointed out that some of those who survived the war had been made rich by the war. In some instances, he was sorry to note, ''unbounded wealth'' had been acquired by those who had speculated on the paper given to soldiers at the end of the Revolution.

While members of the House engaged in desultory debate about the specter of the rich and one-hour veterans on the pension rolls, the Senate had its eye on the poor in general. ''Are you prepared to put all your poor on the pension list?'' cried out Senator William Smith of Virginia.

Smith was irked because at one point, there had been talk of resurrecting an old issue and restricting the benefits to half pay for officers and not grant pensions to anyone else. ''The tide of pity swells as high for the sufferings of the indigent and necessitous soldier, as it can do for the indigent and necessitous officer, if we are really governed by pity,'' he said. The proposed pension, he said, ''will be as sweet to the one as it is to the other.'' He also noted that while many officers in the Continental Army had been honorable men, ''yet it is a fact not to be denied, that many of them enriched themselves by speculating, in their turn, on the poor soldiers, in buying their certificates and land warrants at very reduced prices.'' Smith wondered if Americans wanted their tax money to go to former officers, and, in an early reference to what was to become a major issue a century and a half later, he added, ''There are thousands of poor who are unable to work and demand your attention in an equal degree.''

The most intriguing and controversial point Smith raised was whether soldiers had actually made more sacrifices than ordinary citizens during the

Revolution. "No particular merit could be ascribed to any particular portion of the people of the United States, for services rendered during the Revolutionary war, in exclusion to any portion who espoused that cause," he said. The Army and the citizenry were equally responsible and "one could not have been as well dispensed with as the other. . . . This was a war that brought the enemy to every man's door and in which every man was obliged to take an active part in some shape or other. Yet every man could not be in the army. This was a war of a different character from all other wars. It was a war for liberty and independence, in which every soul was engaged and in which every one contributed. . . ."

Senator Smith also reflected a legitimate grievance shared by many Americans who had fought the British at Cape Fear and Charleston and elsewhere but not as members of the Continental Army and were thus not eligible for pensions. Many of these men were in the South. In an early complaint that presaged the schism that would become civil war in another half century, Smith noted that Southern "volunteers and patriots" had been ignored. He was content to let the bill die in the Senate.

As the debate over pensions went on, aged paupers could be seen from the windows of the new Capitol. How could the senators, Senator David L. Morril asked, "see the warworn soldier of the Revolution hovering around their dwellings, round this Capitol, asking for a pittance, and not manifest a disposition to afford them that pecuniary assistance necessary to supply to cravings of nature, and repair their shattered garments? This is the only tribunal to which they can apply. Shall they seek in vain? . . . It is to the indigent that I would extend the hand of liberality."

At this point, North Carolina's Senator Macon, who was strongly opposed to the bill, likened pensioners to "flatterers and sycophants of kings and despots" who "live sumptuously on their folly or wickedness or both. . . . The opinion is founded in idleness and hatred to free Governments, where every man ought to live by the sweat of his own brow—where no man ought to be paid to do nothing." As for who should be lauded from the Revolution, Macon said that "no class of men in the nation had more merit for the Revolution than the lawyers."

Macon would not be alone in his complaints about the perils of idleness. In the next two decades, Americans would become increasingly judgmental about those within their society who could not succeed financially, and great attention would be given to "indulging" vagrants. Nevertheless, the bill President Monroe wanted was passed in March 1818, without a requirement that veterans prove poverty in order to qualify for a pension. In the next two years, however, demands for pensions grew far more than Congressman

Bloomfield ever dreamed, and some suspected that there were more pensioners than could possibly have survived since the Revolution.

From the moment the bill was enacted, Monroe's wishes were compromised. Late in the summer of 1818, the quasi-official *Intelligencer* advised that "the number of applicants for pensions after the last session has been so great, that it has not been possible, with every exertion, to act upon them so fast as they come in." At least some of the delay was attributed to the loss of many Revolutionary War records through a fire in the War Office in 1801. To add to the crush of applications, the Panic of 1819 may have forced many to seek pensions, and the same panic put pressure on Government to reduce its expenditures. That year the program for veterans was sharply reduced under the measures adopted to reduce Federal spending.

When Monroe made his speech, there was no Federally financed home for soldiers anywhere in the United States, although the Naval Home in Philadelphia had been established by the Secretary of the Navy in 1811 as a "permanent asylum for disabled and decrepit navy officers, seamen and marines." Not until 1851 would the nation open its first home for soldiers.

As the years passed after Monroe's initial appeal for compassion, whatever mood there was for giving within the Congress, and the taxpaying voters, changed, and not in favor of veterans' benefits. By the panic year of 1819, an article in *Niles Register* complained that the benefits enacted by Government "had almost been wholly perverted to the profit of speculators and knaves." One reason some editors and their readers might have felt that way went back to Congressman Bloomfield's original calculations as to how many would apply, which were disastrously inaccurate. Instead of the $500,000 in costs that Bloomfield had predicted, the law had cost the taxpayers more than six times that amount.

According to *Niles Register*, "persons supposed to be worth from 10 to 20,000 dollars have made themselves out to be paupers, to receive the benefits of it; and it was lately announced in a New York paper, that a certain pensioner had deposited the whole amount of this pension in the savings bank!" The same publication reported that in Philadelphia, "Eighteen hundred persons applied at the bank of the United States" for their pension money and that "they almost literally blocked up the court leading to the bank."

The cast of other stories wasn't so mean. In Boston, a newspaper, excerpted in *Niles Register*, reported with empathy the scene when two veterans of the American Revolution, both of them past seventy, met after not having seen each other for forty years. They borrowed a drum and fife and "played the reveille and other airs, which recalled to their minds the ardor which inspired their bosoms in the trying scenes of the revolution, the pride of which was not then extinct, and gave delight to the numerous persons who witnessed the interesting scene."

But overall, the rural, rawboned America of the Revolution was vanishing, becoming urban and complicated, its citizens ever more influenced by the ups and downs of the economic enterprises that cities fostered. As it did after the Revolution, Britain dumped its manufactured goods on America and Americans bought them with borrowed cash, amassing a debt which was largely responsible for the Panic of 1819. It was not a way of life Daniel Shays would have fought for; it was an arena that only entrepreneurs found rewarding.

In 1820, Congress passed a law requiring veterans to make a statement of indigency before they could qualify for pensions. The law also authorized the Secretary of War to strike veterans already on the rolls if they did not have proof of poverty. Secretary of War John C. Calhoun told John Adams that the law required him to wield a "scythe of retrenchment" against pensioners. He reported that veterans on the rolls fell from 18,880 when the law was passed to 12,331 just two years later. Even the reduced number was fifteen times greater than Bloomfield had anticipated. But by 1823, times were good again and Congress took note of the fact that many veterans in need were improperly pushed off the rolls by zealous Government clerks. Legislation was passed on March 1 restoring those who had been dropped improperly.

More soldiers of the Revolution died of old age, and in 1829, President Jackson proposed to increase the pensions of those who survived. He encountered strong resistance from Senator Robert Hayne of South Carolina, who said the measure would compensate "mere sunshine and holiday soldiers, the hangers-on of the camp, men of straw, substitutes, who never enlisted until after the preliminaries of peace were signed." The President's bill was defeated.

By 1833, another wave of generosity toward veterans was stirring the Congress. This time, the recipients were to be the men who had fought Indians on the American frontier after the Revolution. Among the opponents of such a proposal was Congressman Thomas T. Bouldin, who raised a question that would become a rallying point for those opposed to a variety of social programs in the United States for the next century and a half. He asked Congress to conduct an inquiry "into the moral and political effect of the pension laws of the United States." Like many proponents of Government investigations who would come after him, Bouldin made it quite clear what he expected to find even before he began to look.

The "practical effects" of America's pension system thus far, he said, had been to "discourage private industry, and lead a large portion of the people of the United States to look to the Treasury as the unfailing spring from which they were to receive every good." Bouldin thought that the poor ex-soldier, like the poor civilian, was the province of state and local governments, not the Federal establishment. His motion to conduct an investigation was tabled. His ideas lived on in an age and in a nation where small Government was a virtue and success was thought of in terms of individual effort in the wildness of laissez-faire capitalism. Indeed, by the time Charles Dickens journeyed through America in the early 1840s, he was struck with Americans "as a trading people" who so wanted to make money that "healthful amusements, cheerful means of recreation, and wholesome fancies, must fade before the stern utilitarian joys of trade."

Amid all the the pious assertions about the value of hard work in the decade of the 1830s, America saw a proliferation of what a later historian would call "a wide variety of swindles, frauds, forgeries, counterfeiting activities and other confidence games." Pension funds proved to be an irresistible lure for schemers in this area. On one occasion, Robert Temple, the president of the Bank of Vermont in Rutland, pulled off what *Niles Register* called a "magnificent fraud . . . practiced upon the government" when he bilked the newly created Pensions Office of thousands of dollars that had been earmarked for veterans. Temple did it by filing claims for people who did not exist, a trick that would reassert itself more than once in American history. The House Committee on Revolutionary Pensions said that the "recent developments in Vermont had astonished the most incredulous" and that there were at least two hundred instances of fraud there.

Temple proved a volatile swindler. When he learned that the Federal Government was planning to release the names of all persons receiving pensions, so as to smoke out the ghosts on the rolls, he went to Washington and threatened to shoot one clerk who was compiling the list and tried to bribe another clerk, "so as to conceal his fraud." Back in Vermont, when he learned of his impending arrest, Temple "retired to his stable and shot himself through the heart," according to *Niles Register*. His heirs promised to make good on what he had stolen.

There were so many frauds involving pension money for veterans that the House Committee on Revolutionary Pensions studied the situation and issued a report on December 8, 1834, and charged that, "Men in the highest walks of life, of the most honorable pretensions, and in whom the greatest confidence was reposed, are among those who have largely participated in drawing money from the Treasury, by means of false papers, the grossest acts of forgery, and the most wilful and corrupt perjury. To what extent these frauds have been practised, or how much money has been drawn from the Treasury by fraudulent means, it is not now fully known, and perhaps never will be fully ascertained.'' However, the committee estimated that the veterans' benefits fund had lost between $50,000 and $100,000 to fraud in Vermont, New York, Virginia, Kentucky, and Ohio.

The proliferation of fraud cast doubt over the validity of every veteran's claim. Congress noted that in 1832, fifteen years after the original Bloomfield calculations, it had been estimated that ten thousand veterans who survived the Revolution would probably apply for assistance under the law. "The number of applicants at the Pension Office, under this law, already exceeds thirty-two thousand nine hundred," said the report. "The mind is forced to make the inquiry, 'Can so many revolutionary officers and soldiers be now living?' Fifty-two years have nearly passed away since the peace of 1783. Every soldier who entered at the age of sixteen, in that year of the war, must now be, if living, at least sixty-eight years old: those who entered the service the first year of the revolution, in 1775, at the same age, must be, at the present period, if still living, at least seventy-five years of age. The question again presents itself—Are there forty thousand of these old revolutionary soldiers still living?''

The study concluded, rather hopefully, "They are all rapidly approaching the grave. A few years will number them with the dead. . . . The country will soon be released from every pecuniary obligation which it now owes them. . . .''

Congress never did make an inquiry into the real or imagined moral deficits of the pension system. It became too apparent that the system was being abused not by impoverished men who had borne arms for their country, but by the more privileged—or clever—members of American society who never saw a day of combat.

7
Just Debts and Common Sense

After so many years of service, my heart grows cold towards America.
—Tom Paine, March 1808

A great American truth, perhaps an eternal one, since it has never shown any sign of becoming untrue, bloomed in the years after the Revolution and the War of 1812: People who fight wars, be they volunteers or conscripts, expect to be paid, pensioned, and nurtured for their sacrifices. The people married to them expect it, too, as do some of their descendants. But people who do not fight wars—even wars they approve of and perhaps even encouraged—tend to believe that those who do should perform deeds of combat as an act of patriotism. Noncombatants, it would seem, feel that soldiers should not trivialize their patriotism in a sea of complaints about old wounds suffered in battles long forgotten. Also true is that frequently patriots who join to fight only for the good of the cause eventually come to feel that, well, yes, the cause was worthy enough, but now that it's over, a little money wouldn't hurt, either.

This last notion was there when the Congress received the claim of John Paulding in January of 1817. Paulding was one of three men who had arrested Major John André, an important British spy who had had dealings with Benedict Arnold in connection with Arnold's intention to betray West Point. George Washington had commended Paulding and the Congress approved an annuity of $200 for Paulding and the other two as well. But as he grew old and infirm, Paulding found that he could not support his large family on the annuity, nor could he withstand the rigors of hard labor. He asked that the annuity be increased or that Congress "grant him such further assistance as faithful and patriotic services, and his infirmity and advanced age, may demand."

The House Committee on Pensions and Revolutionary Claims turned him down with these words:

> The petitioner did his duty faithfully, and for it he has been liberally rewarded. However, he did nothing more than his duty; the country expects this much, at least, from everyone, and yet it is not expected that she is to support all who have done so.

Applications for pensions were submitted to the American Government almost as soon as it began to exist, certainly well before laws were enacted to provide such funds, or the bureaucracy established to administer them. Initially, the relationship between claimants and Government was not bad, even when the claim was denied. For example, on February 5, 1790, when the second session of the First Congress heard the first claim on "invalid pensions," Henry Knox, then Secretary of War, personally dictated a one-thousand-word letter explaining why the Government could give no money to Ruth Roberts, whose husband had been a lieutenant in the Connecticut Militia but who had served only twenty-three days during the Revolution. Knox was straightforward and not acrimonious when he gave his opinion rejecting the Roberts claim, even though the language he used presaged some of the argument that would surround the Agent Orange controversy, nearly two centuries later:

> . . . the judges of the Superior court have given certificates to disabled officers and soldiers but few instances except such as have been wounded in service, and in no case but such wherein it appeared that the disability *was the immediate effect of some exertion or suffering in the line of duty*.

And in March of 1790, in a moment of early enlightenment about war's effect on the mind, Knox recommended that Congress pay a pension of $5 a month to Jeremiah Ryan, who had served in the Revolutionary Army from 1775 to 1780. While in service, Knox said, Ryan suffered "under a debility of nerves, which has continued ever since in such a degree as utterly to incapacitate him from obtaining a livelihood by his labor." Knox noted that Ryan had not filed his papers when he was supposed to but that his "faithful services are explicit and honorable."

There is no evidence to suggest Knox did not mean what he said. There was goodwill in the Secretary of War, by then quite wealthy and secure, when he suggested that Congress "grant the prayers of several invalids, [that] they might be comprehended in one general act to be passed towards the close of each session; which would save the perplexity arising from a multiplicity of acts of the same nature."

Cases came to the Treasury Department, too, but when Secretary Hamilton considered most claimants, his rejection of them reflected his priggishness as well as his brevet wit. For example, in March of 1790, when an officer named William Mumford of Portsmouth, Massachusetts, claimed he was entitled to pay for the time it took him to settle his account with the Government, Hamilton dismissed him summarily, saying that honoring Mumford's claim would only lead to "inconvenient consequences." He also told the Congress that no interest should be paid on the lingering claims of some officers from North Carolina:

> The past situation of public affairs has unavoidably given too much occasion for complaints of individual hardships, but in most instances, they are rather to be regretted than redressed.

Later, Knox's generosity was tempered with a bit of Hamilton's brand of pragmatism, perhaps more expressive of the soul of the survivor-achiever that was Henry Knox. He recommended to the House that it reject a request for half pay for the artillery officers of one regiment since, logically enough, it had turned them down before:

> . . . when the abilities, integrity and liberality of the former Congresses be considered, it may be justly presumed that individuals experienced the fairest investigation of their claims, and that upright decisions were formed thereon.

But not all veterans were treated the same way, and in the case of a claimant named Frederick William Augustus Henry Ferdinand Steuben, more simply known as Baron von Steuben, America showed there were times when it could overlook little technicalities to help the needy veteran. The baron appears to have been one of those patriots who wanted nothing when the war started, but needed more than that when victory was achieved. He was a general who fell upon hard times after the war, not unlike many of the enlisted men who had learned formation marching under his exacting command. His treatment at the hands of Government, however, was markedly different from that of most other veterans.

According to a report issued by Secretary of the Treasury Hamilton in 1790, a year in which von Steuben was quite broke, the baron originally seemed not to have any intention "to accept any rank or pay," wishing only to "join the army as a volunteer, and to render such services as the commander-in-chief should think him capable of. . . ." A letter from von Steuben to the Continental Congress, dated December 6, 1777, had made his intentions clear. It said, in part:

The honor of serving a respectable nation, engaged in the noble enterprise of defending its rights and liberty, is the only motive that brought me over to this continent. I ask neither riches nor titles; I am come here from the remotest end of Germany at my own expense, and have given up an honorable and lucrative rank; I have made no condition with your deputies in France, nor shall I make any with you. My only ambition is to serve you as a volunteer, to desire to the confidence of your general-in-chief, and to follow him in all his operations, as I have done during seven campaigns with the King of Prussia; two-and-twenty years passed at such a school seem to give me a right of thinking myself in the number of experienced officers; and if I am possessor of some talents in the art of war, they should be much dearer to me if I could employ them in the service of a republic, such as I hope soon to see America. I should willingly purchase at my whole blood's expense the honor of seeing my name after those defenders of your liberty. Your gracious acceptance will be sufficient for me, and I ask no other favor than to be received among your officers.

After five years of service, in December of 1782, with the war winding down and the Americans looking more like victor than vanquished, von Steuben wrote another letter to the Congress. The altruism he possessed earlier was still intact, but his expectations (and debts) were rising, and so he altered the sentiments expressed in his original declaration, moving back a bit from his willingness to fight only for "honor" and to do so at his "whole blood's expense," if need be. There were things that not even blood could buy.

. . . I was determined not to ask a favor or reward previous to having deserved it; that, however, I expected from the generosity of Congress that, in imitation of all European Powers, they would defray my expenses, although a volunteer, according to the rank which I held in Europe, as well for myself as my aides and servants.

Some members of Congress might have been perplexed. They knew that when von Steuben arrived, he met at Yorktown and chatted in French with some of Washington's aides, who, in turn, had never reported before 1790 that he had asked them to defray his expenses and those of his subordinates and servants. Had some nuance been lost in translation? The people he had met at Yorktown, who included John Witherspoon, Elbridge Gerry, Francis Lightfoot Lee, and William Duer, backed up von Steuben's assertion that no matter what he said in that 1777 letter, he had always expected that Congress "make . . . amends," as Lee put it.

Von Steuben enlightened those who may have continued to harbor doubts, despite the testimonials from Gerry, Witherspoon, Duer, and Lee. Why did he say he did not want money when, in fact, he expected it? He recalled his motives to Alexander Hamilton in a letter of January 27, 1790, explaining that, first of all, he wanted his skills as a military leader to be used by the United States "without exciting the dissatisfaction and jealousy of the officers of your army." Von Steuben said he thought that if he had plainly stated that he expected something, it might have proved counterproductive.

But why, he asked, would anyone think the United States would really have to pay nothing for his services, even though he had offered to work for free?

> I would ask, sir, in what light would such a proposition have been received by so enlightened a body as the Congress of the United States. To me it appears that common sense would have declared the author of such a proposition to be either a lunatic or a traitor. The former, for his coming from another part of the globe to serve a nation unknown to him; at the same time, renouncing all his possessions for a cause to which he was an utter stranger, without having in view the gratification of ambition or the advancement of interest.

It was quite preposterous that anyone would have taken his original offer seriously since, according to von Steuben, it was "dictated by no other motive than to facilitate my reception into your army." As for those he had confided in at Yorktown, he said he told them he would ask for "indemnification" for his "sacrifices and disbursements," and for "such other marks of acknowledgement and generosity as in the justice of Congress should be deemed adequate" to his services. It didn't surprise him that Gerry and the others had never mentioned this condition to anyone.

> The Congress were besieged by a crowd of foreign officers, who were as little satisfied as the national troops which was a circumstance, that, probably, induced some respectable persons, then members of Congress (in whom I

place the greatest confidence,) to advise me to pass over in silence all that
related to a former contract and to rest my pretensions solely on the merit of
my services, and the generosity of the United States.

The baron added, in his plea to Hamilton: "All I ask of you is, to
accelerate the decision; no event can render my situation more unhappy—in
fact, it is insupportable."

Hamilton and the Congress agreed that this was all very reasonable, and
so Hamilton proposed that von Steuben receive from the Treasury "the sum
of seven thousand dollars, in addition to former grants"; that he be given a
gold-hilted sword (not much different from the one Lafayette had given to
Daniel Shays) "as a mark of the high sense [that] Congress entertain of his
character and services"; that he receive another $2,400 for past expenses;
and that he further be credited with 580 guineas a year from the time he left
Europe to make his sacrifice for American freedom and the sum be paid to
him for the rest of his life. Hamilton also suggested Congress give him land,
which it did, in Upstate New York.

The money authorized did not totally solve von Steuben's problems, but
they ended with his life. Four years later, in 1794, he died on the land given
him by the Government.

Hamilton's and the Congress's attitude toward this debt of honor
contrasted with their attitude about other debts to veterans no less honorable
and no less dedicated than von Steuben. Perhaps because Hamilton could
find it much easier to understand the plight of a European patrician without
funds than he could the less glittering homegrown ranks of the Continental
Army, the graciousness that attended von Steuben's bailout was not visited
upon many others.

Hamilton's treatment of William Finnie, about a month later, was more
typical of the way he viewed the claims of veterans, even veterans who were
of high rank. Finnie, a deputy quartermaster who held the rank of colonel in
the Continental Army, sought compensation for the loss he suffered when,
of apparent necessity, he sold a certificate issued him by Congress after the
war, just as did so many of his fellow officers and enlisted men. Like the
already rejected William Mumford, Finnie wanted to be reimbursed for
the money he spent while pleading with the Government to settle his accounts, and he thought that he should get land, since he had held high rank.

In a tart letter dated April 10, 1790, Hamilton summarily dismissed
Finnie's claim, saying he had been unable "to discover sufficient and
unexceptional ground upon which, in his opinion, any part of the prayer of
the petitioner may be granted." As to the possibility of Finnie's receiving

land, as von Steuben did, Hamilton said, "it does not appear to be warranted either by the resolutions of Congress respecting bounties of land to officers and soldiers or by the practice upon these resolutions."

If Hamilton's attitude tended to imbue the new Government with an aura of officiousness, the trait was ultimately visited upon his own family. His widow, Elizabeth Hamilton, was herself subjected to a measure of it after he was killed in his duel with Aaron Burr in 1804. Mrs. Hamilton, the mother of seven children, was hardly accorded the kind of courtesy that Hamilton might have expected, given his contributions to the founding of the nation. She made her petition for financial assistance in January of 1810, but a Congressional committee concluded that "the prayer of the petition ought not to be granted" because the statute of limitations had run out.

In February of 1816, still in need of funds, Mrs. Hamilton pressed her effort again, insisting that her husband was entitled to five years' full pay as a lieutenant colonel. She said he had never received the pay to which he was entitled and that "if he ever relinquished his claim to said pay . . . it was from the delicate motive of divesting himself of all interest upon the subject of making provision for the disbanded officers of the revolutionary army. . . ."

The Committee on Pensions and Revolutionary Claims replied that it had no knowledge that Hamilton relinquished his claim to the money, and in any event, "to reject the claim under the peculiar circumstances by which it is characterized, would not comport with that honorable sense of justice and magnanimous policy which ought ever to distinguish the legislative proceedings of a virtuous and enlightened nation." And so the committee finally prepared a bill to grant Mrs. Hamilton the money she sought, but only after she had been subjected to the petty humiliation known to other veterans and their widows.

Tom Paine, the author of *Common Sense* and the recipient of land from New York State and money from Congress, suffered the same indifference from the Committee on Claims when he attempted to press for more money that he felt was owed him. "I know not who the Committee of Claims are," Paine wrote in March of 1808, "but if they are men of younger standing than 'the times that try men's souls,' and consequently, too young to know what the condition of the country was at the time I published *Common Sense,* (for I do not believe independence would have been declared had it not been for the effect of that work,) they are not capable of judging the whole of the services of Thomas Paine. . . . If my memorial [claim application] was referred to the Committee of Claims, for the purpose of losing it, it is unmanly policy. After so many years of service my heart grows cold towards America.'' The issue remained unresolved to Paine's satisfaction when he died a year later.

As the years passed, there were scandals about whatever money reached veterans, and there were judgments about those scandals, spelled out in many words in Government documents, which caused the Government to grow wary of the very men who had made its founding possible. For example, Jacob A. Young, of Herkimer County, had borne arms against the British during the Revolution, as had others among his stubborn neighbors in the rolling hills of Upstate New York. But in the words of the Government, he fought only ''for self-defence, without military authority of a public character.'' So, as the nineteenth century became middle-aged and Young grew old, he could not participate in the pension programs set up for veterans of the Revolutionary War. Claim denied.

Nor did the Government dispute that Cornelius Sauquayonk, a chief of the Oneida Indians in New York State, was opposed to the British and helped the Colonials. But like Young, ''he did not serve in any regularly organized corps, nor by virtue of any competent authority,'' according to the Government. Claim denied. It must have been an especially galling rejection for Chief Sauquayonk, who supported the Colonials when many of his brothers were inclined to think it might be better to stick with the British.

Aaron Keeler of Skaneateles, New York, served in the Continental Army and thus had all the military authority of a public character that Jacob Young and Cornelius Sauquayonk did not have. His youth was his undoing. He was ''under age—only twelve years old when he entered the service.'' The Government decided it could not lavish pension benefits upon twelve-year-olds who fancied themselves patriots and talked themselves into war service. Claim denied.

John L. Schermerhorn, who lived near Albany, New York, served in the Continental Army, and unlike Keeler, he was no boy when he joined. The Army he served in was recognized and nobody suggested he fought for only his own selfish pleasure. But when he applied for a pension, the Government discovered that Schermerhorn did not share in the precise suffering of his fellow soldiers and that, even worse, he may have actually *enjoyed* his Revolutionary service. ''He was taken prisoner by the Indians,'' said a Government report, ''and a squaw adopted him as her son, and his constructive service ceased from that time, which reduces his service below six months.'' Men who served less than six months were not entitled to pensions. Men who were comforted by squaws while being held captive by Indians could not be regarded as in the service of their country. Claim denied.

Thomas Miller of Charlestown, Massachusetts, served as an ensign in a recognized outfit, was of the right age, and was not captured by Indians or adopted by a squaw or anyone else. But someone forgot to take note of how long he had served, and he was unable to prove his length of service. Claim denied.

Nobody doubted that James Nonemacher of East Penn Township, Pennsylvania, fought the British and that he suffered long and hard and conspicuously, just like everybody else. But he made the mistake of doing it with the French Army. The Government certainly appreciated the assistance offered by French troops, but if the French were going to get mixed up in an American war, they would have to take care of their own pensioners. Claim denied.

The Government also denied benefits to William Brown, who waited nearly half a century for them but expired before the Pension Law of 1832 was enacted; to Jehu Grant because, as the cannon belched, he served only as a waiter; and to Jeremiah Klumph, who, it turned out, was an express rider and not a real soldier at all. As for William Drew, he served the cause as only a blacksmith, and in the eyes of the Government, that wasn't any better than being an express rider.

If the rejections of these New York Staters which were made between the 1830s and 1850 seemed a little arbitrary, the Government rejected many others for what may have appeared to be good reasons at the time. For by then, the dwindling ranks of the Revolutionary veterans were swelled by those who had fought the War of 1812. The Government had to save money, and from the Government's point of view, there was ample reason to believe that some veterans were applying for benefits they did not deserve, thus draining the Treasury needlessly.

Eliphalet Allen of Chautauqua, New York, for one, was classified as a deserter. There were many good soldiers who were deserters because they could not continue to fight for no pay and little food. If they had all been treated like Allen, the pension rolls would have been very small, indeed. And then there was Jesse Miles. He was suspect because he insisted that he had served at Bunker Hill, which, in the years following the war, was a battle that stirred patriotic juices everywhere. But Miles was from Brooklyn Township, Pennsylvania, and a Government investigator suspended his pension payments because ''there were no Pennsylvania troops at the Battle of Bunker Hill.'' The investigator didn't believe Miles' story that he was an exception.

The women of the Revolution found a harbinger of equality in their treatment at the hands of the Government, in that they were treated as badly as were the men. Catharine Beatty of Trenton, New Jersey, was married to John Beatty, a Revolutionary veteran, and as such she would have been entitled to a widow's pension after his death. But she didn't marry him until after the war was over, and her payments were ordered suspended. The logic of why a widow's needs would be more modest if she married after 1783 rather than before remained a mystery.

Two other suspensions were ordered for Polly Davidson and Abiah Bumpas, both of Massachusetts. Mrs. Davidson's marriage to her husband, Benjamin, was adjudged to be "incomplete" under an act passed on July 4, 1836. Maybe her nuptials were not recorded properly or perhaps the person who joined Polly and Benjamin in holy matrimony wasn't qualified to conduct such a service. Quite possibly Polly and Benjamin lived together as man and wife for all those years without bothering to get anyone actually to pronounce them as married. Such things were and are not unheard of. In any event, payments to her were suspended and placed in jeopardy over the question of the "legality" of her marriage.

As for Mrs. Bumpas, the widow of the Joseph Bumpas, the Government decided to suspend her pension because "three . . . soldiers of the same name makes it difficult to identify claimant's service without more perfect details." It was the ultimate weapon of a clerk in the nascent bureaucracy, since no claimant could possibly be as perfect as the Government might want him to be.

As the Congress grappled with the veterans of the Revolution or those who survived them, the soldiers from the War of 1812 began to make their presence felt. One was Joseph Wescott of Penobscot, Hancock County, Massachusetts, who had commanded a company of volunteers in 1813. According to his petition, he went to Portland, Maine, in March of that year to obtain the wages of his men personally, since he had no paymaster. He received $1,374.35 and boarded the sloop *Harriet* to make the return voyage to where his men were. It was while at sea, Wescott claimed, that "a bundle of paper," which constituted everything he had obtained in Portland, except for $24.35, "dropped from a pocket in the left breast of his coat into the water, and that, in consequence of the violence of the wind and the difficulty of stopping the vessel immediately, the bundle containing the money was lost. . . ." The Committee on Claims said it had two affidavits from individuals who said they saw *"something like* a bundle of paper, but could not say positively whether it was or not, floating on the water." Claim denied.

A recruiting officer, Captain John A. Thomas, complained to Congress that in 1814, while trying to win enlistees in New Haven, somebody picked his pocket of the $650 he was carrying as inducement money. The Government withheld it from his pay "as a settlement of his account." The Committee on Claims recommended he not be given the money lest the Government be "always subject to imposition and fraud."

In 1815, a British cannonball fired during the Battle of New Orleans killed a slave who worked for Basil Shaw, and in 1818, Shaw asked the Government to reimburse him the $500 he paid the slave's owner. (He was only using the slave as a personal servant, he said, while he was assistant adjutant general in the Tennessee Militia.) The Committee on Claims felt the Government was not liable.

Quite possibly the most curious of the petitioners was Archibald W. Hamilton (no kin to Alexander), who served as a captain during the War of 1812—not in the America's Navy, but in Britain's. Hamilton sent his entreaty to a committee of the House of Representatives on March 2, 1818, explaining that he was a native New Yorker who assumed that Britain and the United States would be friends forever and that the messy business in the years following 1776 would never be repeated. With this confidence, he had become a British ensign in 1809 and was assigned to various ships and stations in the Caribbean. But as soon as Hamilton learned that America and Britain were at each other again, he said, he did what any decent American chap would do in the British Navy and "tendered his resignation; and refused from that moment to perform a tour of duty."

The British, who well remembered the massive indifference that native Englishmen felt toward the original American insurrection, surely had no hope that this American Anglo-Saxon would be of any use. But the War of 1812 was on and the British understandably felt they were under orders to fight the war and accept Hamilton's resignation later. That was probably a mistake. The British decided to invade New Orleans, only to be told by Hamilton that he "positively refused to accompany them, representing to [his] commanding officer that he was an American by birth and sentiment. . . ." But according to Hamilton, the British refused to accept his resignation and explained to him that they were only trying to invade New Orleans, not abet him in his patriotism.

In the papers he later submitted to Congress, Hamilton said he was "resolute in his determination not to serve against his country." It must have been quite tiresome for his commanding officer, who ordered him confined, with the result that Hamilton, the American patriot in British uniform, "suffered hardships and indignities which devotion to country alone could have supported." The British, who were tired of listening to him, finally accepted his resignation and, logically enough, discontinued his pay.

Hamilton returned to the United States (precisely where the British landed him is unclear) and said that he had tried to enlist in the American Army so that he could fight the very British he had just served. The Americans explained that they did not need him, since the war had ended and they had won it without him. This left Hamilton out quite a piece of change. He had earned 12 shillings eight pence a day in the British Navy and figured that now the war was over, the British owed him £137.5.6 sterling. The British refused—resigning from their Navy had been his idea, not theirs. Clearly, Hamilton concluded, his was a hardship case. And so he asked the U.S. Congress to pay him.

Said a Congressional committee:

> Putting the evidence entirely out of view, the Committee feels no hesitation in saying his claim is utterly inadmissible upon principle. That the Congress of the United States should be called upon to compensate for the loss complained of by the petitioner, who was actually in the ranks of the enemy throughout the late war, appears to be a pretension as extravagant as it is unprecedented.

The committee further said it suspected Hamilton was "aiding and abetting the enemy" while drifting from one tropical isle to the next. Nor was Congress surprised that the British balked at receiving Hamilton's resignation. The Congress issued language that showed some empathy with what the British Navy must have had to put up with. "No Government . . . would accept a resignation in the hour of battle, or at the moment of undertaking a hazardous enterprise." The Battle of New Orleans was surely that. Congress criticized Hamilton for not resigning the instant war began and resolved that he "have leave to withdraw his petition and documents."

8
St. Patrick Goes to Mexico

> Now these men have tasted the idleness, the intemperance, the debauchery of a camp—tasted of its riot, tasted of its blood! They will come home before long, hirelings of murder; what will their influence be as fathers, husbands?
> —The Rev. Theodore Parker, pastor of the 28th Congregational Church, Boston, June 25, 1848

> ... great reliance is not placed upon the present privates in the Army (they for the most part composed of those wretched Dutch and Irish immigrants).
> —Lieutenant George B. McClellan, May 19, 1848

Perhaps it didn't always seem that way, but there really was an American Army after the War of 1812. Even as veterans of 1812 and of the Revolution maneuvered for a taste of the tender meat of pensions and other slivers of the elusive Government banquet, there were others who elected to remain in peacetime service, if the next four or five expansionist decades may be called times of peace. There were veterans who, for one reason or another, found little that was attractive in the prospect of returning to civilian life. Over the years, they were joined by recruits who were new arrivals in the United States. The recruits had been treated so shabbily by Americans of some of the nation's older families that they felt they could not compete at all as civilians.

From the end of the War of 1812 to the War Between the States, the American military more resembled a public works gang than it did a well-disciplined fighting force, despite the experience of its veterans and the training given its newcomers. Even the advent of the sixteen-month war with Mexico in 1846 did little to transform an institution Americans came to regard as decidedly *déclassé*. To be sure, the Army did some of the things that one might expect an army to do. It patrolled the frontier of the 827,192 square miles of land acquired by the Louisiana Purchase of 1803. It manned new forts. It rousted Indians from lands the whites invariably and insatiably coveted. It also policed raw and rowdy frontier towns. It acted as frequent revenue agent, sometime road builder, and part-time explorer. But mostly, aside from the occasional forays to see America's unsullied beauty and to meet its largely trusting indigenous peoples, the Army was a singular place to be housed poorly, fed badly, paid closefistedly, and bored constantly.

The boredom was accompanied by bedeviling loneliness. There was explicit boredom in assignment to lonely boondocks posts, many hundreds of miles away from the East Coast, where a young soldier might not see an eligible woman nor taste the sweetness of urban life for months at a time. The tedium was made worse by the knowledge that wherever a soldier went, he would have precious few of his own kind to talk to. In 1821, the Congress reduced the size of the Army to no more than a paltry six thousand; camaraderie was thus hard to come by.

The few were hardly the proud; the core of understrappers who made up this Army made no claim to elitism. Indeed, prospects of the new recruits were so bleak and their current straits so hapless that claiming elitism did not have a priority for them. The Army came to be filled with what established society saw as its own dark dregs; men who aspired to be not heroes, only survivors. These included the Irish, who came to America, in the eyes of their detractors, only because their beloved potato was blighted to short supply; and the Germans, who said unkind things about both political parties and who drank the beer they brewed incessantly, even on the Sabbath. To the Americans who saw the new immigrants this way, the Army had ceased to be an American institution. The Surgeon General referred to recruits as "newly arrived immigrants . . . broken down by bad habits and dissipation."

In less than a century, novels would be written about the life and times of the soldier in the first five decades of the nineteenth century and filmmakers would use this same period as the backdrop for cinema filled with dashing and gallant officers who forever met fragrant young women in need of attention; graceful women presenting just the right mingling of helpless decorum and décolletage. But the soldiers of the 1830s and 1840s saw little romance in what they were doing. The tasks they were asked to perform seemed so transparently unattractive to the public that ambitious men who might have enlisted were not so sure the Army would provide them the opportunities that it seemed to have provided in the past.

"All classes of labourers in America can do better than being shot at for one shilling a day," said one observer of the period. He wasn't totally correct. The Irish, the Germans, the Poles, and other new arrivals were a class of laborer who did not think they could do better than what the Army offered. From the Anglo-Protestant perspective, their immigrant status made them hard to train and their Roman Catholicism made them near impossible to trust.

Protestants listened to Catholics and did not like what they heard. The stated reasons among Catholics for enlisting were hardly in what Protestant Americans liked to think of as the highest traditions of patriotism, even though the Army had always been a magnet not only for patriots but for men—even Protestant men—who needed jobs. One Army surgeon who claimed to have conducted something of a survey to determine why the fifty-five men in one company had enlisted in such an enterprise wrote that "nine-tenths enlisted on account of some female difficulty; thirteen of them had changed their names, and forty-three were either drunk, or partially so, at the time of their enlistment."

It was a most disturbing trend when viewed by Americans who had always thought of their country as a Protestant place, run by God-fearing men who had come to represent all that was native and good about the United States. The newcomers may have feared God, but they weren't doing it properly, the nativists said. The country had been founded without the scapular and the rosary and could prosper onward and upward without them. Their feelings were reinforced by citizens they respected. The Rev. Lyman Beecher, pastor of the Park Street Church in Boston, regularly held forth on the perils of Catholicism in the 1830s, seeking to prove that the ideals of the Church of Rome and those of the U.S. Constitution were incompatible. Popery, he said bluntly, was dangerous to the health of the Government.

Americans did not even need to go to Protestant churches to hear about the evil within Catholicism. They could hear about it from the Protestant Reformation Society, which vowed to "convert the Papists to Christianity"; read about it in the *American Protestant Vindicator,* which was in effect the society's house organ; and discover it in even the finest bookstores. In the 1830s, Maria Monk's best-selling *Awful Disclosures of the Hotel Dieu Nunnery of Montreal* disclosed the misfortunes of a woman who claimed she entered a convent with the highest intentions, only to be forced to have "criminal intercourse" with priests. Babies born out of such unions were strangled by priests immediately after they were baptized, she claimed.

Most readers did not notice, and perhaps did not care, that Maria Monk's mother, a Protestant, said that Maria had never been in the Hotel Dieu Nunnery and that her daughter was a bit daft.

The Monk book was first offered to the publishing house of the Harper Brothers. James Harper, who was of the Methodist persuasion, was known to be alarmed about what he saw as the growing Catholic peril. But Harper Brothers, intent on building a quality publishing house, turned the manuscript down. However, it permitted two of its employees to set up a dummy publishing house called Howe and Bates, and it was this front that published Maria Monk's book.

For the first time since its creation as a nation independent of Great Britain, America felt the need to define itself in terms of its own Founding Father roots. The largely homogeneous society that had founded the country did not always agree with itself, but at least it had functioned without the obeisance to Rome that the newcomers favored. Catholics, with an allegiance to an ancient, symbol-laden church headquartered in an earthy and presumably corrupt Latin city, had to be suspect. They were more than suspect; they were detested. In the third and fourth decades of the nineteenth century, Protestants found it impossible to contain their feelings that they were losing their country to foreigners, and there were bloody anti-Catholic incidents in New York, Philadelphia, Boston, Baltimore, Providence, Hartford, New Orleans, St. Louis, Cincinnati, Louisville, and San Francisco. There were ugly scenes even in the smaller, ordinarily sleepy towns where, aside from Catholic-baiting and Catholic-bashing, nothing ever seemed to happen.

The incidents were too violent not to be taken seriously. In Boston, Irish Catholics were pelted with stones for three days in 1829 by Protestants who had recently come from a revivalist meeting. Four years later, Irish who were reportedly drunk beat a Protestant to death in Charlestown, Massachusetts. The very next night, five hundred Protestants converged on Charlestown's Irish quarter and burned houses down. The police stood by and largely did nothing.

The struggle to keep America for the Americans knew no bounds. An Ursuline convent was burned in Charlestown in 1834. In Cambridge, worried Harvard students took to patrolling their Yard, fearful that Irish Catholics, seeking revenge, might try to attack the college. In Philadelphia, in the summer of 1844, mobs of angry Protestants invaded Irish neighborhoods and thirty Irish homes were burned before the militia arrived to restore some semblance of order.

Years passed and feelings of nativism grew stronger. The parties that had been known as Whig and Democratic no longer seemed to serve adequately as the expression of national politics. In their place came splinter groups known as American Republicans, Free Soilers, City Reformers, Native Americans, Liberty Party, Anti-Catholics, Nativists, the Supreme Order of the Star-Spangled Banner, and the Know-Nothings. Sworn to secrecy about their ritual, the Know-Nothings got their name because when they were asked what they were about, their rules required them to reply, "I know nothing." These groups did not always agree as to what was right and wrong with the United States, except that Catholics should be kept out of public office, or, if possible, any office.

Protestant America also thought that Catholics could not even do justice to common soldiering. There were so many Catholics in the Army that the Army found it difficult to recruit people who were not Catholic. Soldiering thus became an even more disreputable occupation than it had been before. The common soldier "feels that the country has placed on him a seal of abasement," observed Secretary of War Eaton in 1830, "and sinks dispirited under its withering influence."

Adult recruits proved so untrustworthy that for a time, the Government seriously considered enlisting teenage boys, and the House of Representatives passed a bill to achieve this. Boys, thought some in Government, "will elevate the moral condition of the soldier generally."

The Army did not want to continue admitting all those Irish and German Catholics, but that's what so many of the new recruits seemed to be. In the 1830s, 540,000 immigrants arrived in the United States, four times the number that had come to America a decade earlier. The identity crisis worsened appreciably in 1846–47, when potato disease invaded Irish fields, pushing a million acres of potato-growing land out of cultivation and about an equal number of Irish nationals out of Ireland.

Between 1847 and 1854, some 1.2 million Irish emigrated to the United States, constituting nearly half of all immigrants. Only the Germans came close to rivaling them in sheer numbers. The Army was not pleased to have so many of them as enlistees, and for a while it prohibited all foreigners with a directive barring them "without special permission from head-quarters." The prohibition was dropped in 1847, since it succeeded in barring the Europeans but had not succeeded in attracting the "preferred" type of soldier, as in days of yore. The regulations after 1847 still stated that the inductees had to have knowledge of English, however. The Germans and Poles clearly had deficits on that score. It was quite apparent that the Army did not view these Europeans as it had Baron von Steuben, Thaddeus Kosciusko, and the Marquis de Lafayette, sixty years earlier. Indeed,

Colonel Enos Cutler, recruiting superintendent for the Army in the Eastern states, found the immigrants "of turbulent character and intemperate habits," although his recruit-seeking counterpart in the West, Major William Davenport, found the foreigners no worse than the Americans who were born in the States.

If Davenport was right, it did not speak well of either immigrant or native-born soldiers. As America moved toward its war with Mexico, peacetime desertions were becoming a serious problem. In 1823, 25 percent of all the men who enlisted deserted before the year was up. Three years later, half of the enlistees for the year were classified as deserters. In 1830, twelve hundred of the five thousand men under arms had deserted. It was a problem that would plague the Army for the rest of the century.

Deserters would come and go, but no deserter commanded quite the attention or generated the lore of John Riley. It seems not to have been very clear to most of his contemporaries who he was or where he came from. Certainly he was an Irishman, and nobody disputed that. But what was his name? Various records gave it as "Riley," "Reilly," and "O'Reilly." Where did he come from? It was said that he served, and deserted from, the 66th Regiment of the British Army, from which he reportedly fled when the regiment was stationed in Canada. For a while, he worked on a farm in Michigan, and Charles M. O'Malley, the Irish-American farmer who hired him, would later recall him as "always at variance with everyone he had anything to do with." Farm work was not for Riley, and he enlisted as a regular in the American Army on September 4, 1845.

Riley may have been difficult, but he proved a good soldier wherever he was sent, which included a recruiting station in New York City and West Point, where he was a formidable drill instructor. He was promoted to sergeant. As the United States prepared to make war against Mexico, Riley was a sergeant in Company K of the 5th U.S. Infantry, stationed in the valley of the Rio Grande. One day, after he had been reprimanded by his captain, Riley asked for permission to attend Mass. That was the last the American Army would see of John Riley in an American uniform.

The United States soon went to war against Mexico, a war it would win, enabling it to gain more than a million square miles of territory and thus doubling its size. President James Polk sent his war message to Congress on May 11, 1846, and said he needed fifty thousand volunteers. He got pretty much what he wanted; the war was as unabashedly popular as it was nakedly rapacious.

But it was not without its critics. "What a mercy it is that we have the Atlantic on the east, and the Pacific on the west," lamented the Rev. Milton

P. Braman, pastor of the First Church in Danvers, Massachusetts, "for if these oceans were land, it would not be long before a scheme would be devised for annexing all mankind to the United States." The Reverend Mr. Braman made clear in his sermon that he was no pacifist, but that the war with the Mexicans, or, indeed, any Catholic country, might result in the country being inundated with "a vast catholic, ignorant, vicious population, to threaten mischief to our free institutions."

With so much being said publicly betraying the low status of American Catholics, the Mexicans logically wondered if America's Catholic soldiers resented Anglo-Protestant scorn as much as did the Mexicans themselves. The Mexicans decided to appeal to them to resist American aggression, defect to Mexico, and promised all those who wanted it an expense-paid trip to Mexico. The appeal was written in English and widely distributed along the Rio Grande. A few weeks later the Mexicans issued another proclamation, which sweetened the offer considerably. Not only would there be a trip to Mexico City, but if Americans who shared the Mexican disdain for the gringos would fight for Mexico, they would be rewarded with at least 320 acres of land and Mexican citizenship. That offer was for mere privates; commissioned and noncommissioned officers would get even more. These first entreaties made no mention of religion, although later flyers did.

Hostilities had not yet started, although they were clearly in the offing. The Mexican enticements apparently sounded good to Riley, who defected across the Rio Grande and was commissioned a lieutenant in the Mexican Army. Dozens of other disaffected soldiers soon joined him south of the Rio Grande. In short order, this disaffection caused the creation of a new unit in the Mexican Army, the Batallón San Patricio, which the Mexicans also called the Foreign Legion and, on occasion, the Red Company. This latter sobriquet was not an allusion to the activities of Karl Marx, whose publication with Friedrich Engels of *The Communist Manifesto* was still two years away. The Mexicans saw red not in the politics of the deserters but in their whiskers and ruddy complexions.

From the beginning, the Battalion of St. Patrick was thought of as a largely Irish group, and it is true that its ranks contained names such as Matthew Doyle, Patrick Mahoney, Patrick Casey, Kerr Delaney, James Kelly, John Lynch, Thomas O'Connor, William O'Connor, Peter O'Brien, and others from the old sod. But it also contained such Nordic names as William Fischer, Parian Fritz, Henry Logenhamer, Henry Octker, Herman Schmidt, and John Vader, and others with Scottish and English names whose fondness for Ireland or Catholicism was open to serious question.

Although Riley was not the commander of the battalion, he quickly became a colonel and one of its more influential officers. The battalion's flag—which showed St. Patrick, the harp of Erin, and the shamrock upon a green field—apparently reflected something of his taste. Nobody ever suspected that the likes of Herman Schmidt or Henry Logenhamer would have designed such a flag. Indeed, some of the Germans found themselves at a loss in both English and Spanish; flag design was not a priority for any of them. Because of Riley, the battalion took on an Irish patina, even though it was not predominantly Irish.

The battalion was thus formed in 1846 with a contingent of about one hundred men. The *San Patricios* were first seen in battle that September, when they helped defend Monterrey. The Mexicans then dispatched the battalion southward to Mexico City so that others of foreign birth living in the capital might join. These Mexico City enlistees were in no sense deserters from anything. As residents or citizens of Mexico, they were dedicated to preserving their way of life against the onslaught of the Anglos.

The St. Patricks were seen again in February of 1847 by Americans who had been taken prisoner by Santa Anna, the Mexican general. Shortly thereafter, they served as artillerymen in the Battle of Buena Vista. Although they reportedly fought well, the Mexicans lost and Santa Anna fell back toward Mexico City.

That spring, it apparently occurred to Santa Anna that perhaps he could win over even more men from Winfield Scott's army if he reworked the original appeal. The result was his promise of a bonus of $10 and two hundred acres of land to every soldier who would defect to the Mexican side. Officers would receive more and were promised rank in the Mexican Army equal to what they had in the U.S. Army. More important than the offer was the supplement that came with it. It was called "From the Mexican Nation to the Catholic Irishmen," and for the first time, it explicitly appealed to them on religious grounds: "Can you fight by the side of those who put fire to your temples in Boston and Philadelphia? Come over to us! . . . May Mexicans and Irishmen, united by the sacred tie of religion and benevolence, form only one people."

There were more defections, but nothing like the three thousand that Santa Anna had hoped for. Indeed, there probably weren't more than two hundred. Other soldiers deserted, of course, but not to the Mexican side—only to escape the war. Ten percent of Winfield Scott's army deserted, with most of the unfaithful coming from the old Regular Army. Fourteen percent of all desertions—2,247 men—were old regulars; 6.2 percent of the newer regulars deserted, while the heavily immigrant Catholic volunteer group, so frequently accused of untrustworthiness, accounted for only 5.3 percent. Most deserters, if caught, were hanged.

Whatever their number, the battalion appeared again late in the summer of 1847, when General Scott and the Mexicans marshaled their armies at Churubusco. The American deserters, knowing what would happen to them if they lost, fought fiercely. On three separate occasions, the Mexican commander, General Rincón, wanted to surrender to avert what he saw as useless bloodshed. But the American deserters kept pulling down the white flag that Rincón's men raised. Scott won the day, and sixty-five of the *San Patricios,* including Riley, were captured. Many others were killed or escaped.

The court-martial of some of the captured men was conducted by Colonel Bennet Riley, who was not related to John Riley, but who was one of the Army's relatively new Roman Catholic officers. The word "tokenism" was not used in those days, and Bennet Riley was seen as an example of what could happen to an Irish-Catholic who showed a little respect to Anglo-Protestants and learned "American" ways.

The twin issue of religious and ethnic discrimination that must have been felt by the soldiers willing to abandon an adopted country was not mentioned in the court-martial. That was not surprising. Even though their oppression at the hands of Protestants undoubtedly played a role in their decision to desert, that would have been a highly improbable and risky defense to offer in 1847. Of course there was discrimination against foreigners and Catholics! But surely that was no reason to desert the Army.

Six of the defendants apparently felt there was nothing better to do than accept the inevitable, and they simply pleaded guilty to the charges against them. In a vain effort to save their skins, some of the others said that they had been captured. Thirty of them claimed that they were drunk when the Mexicans caught them. It did not soften the attitudes of their American captors. All thirty were to be hanged as soon as the battle for Chapultepec was won, but when the prisoners were brought out to be fitted for their nooses, only twenty-nine were present and accounted for.

Colonel William Selby Harney, a man not blessed with an enormous excess of appropriateness, was in charge of some of the executions. He demanded to know where the missing deserter was. Somebody told him that one of the men scheduled to die had been wounded at Churubusco, had lost both legs in the fighting, and would die soon anyhow. "Bring the damned son of a bitch out!" Harney bellowed. "My order is to hang thirty and by God I'll do it!"

Harney delayed the hanging only long enough so that the condemned men could see Chapultepec fall to U.S. troops. The American attack began at eight o'clock on the morning of September 13, 1847. The Mexicans fought hard, and asked Santa Anna to send them reinforcements. Santa Anna, ever the pragmatist, refused. Within an hour and a half, the fortress had fallen and the American flag was raised over the castle. The condemned men cheered when that happened, perhaps forgetting that they had nothing to cheer about. Moments later, the traps were snapped and they were gone. Twenty other of the *San Patricio* deserters were executed at another location.

Riley was not among them. He pleaded that hc had cooperated with the Mexicans only to help fellow Americans who were also being coerced into fighting against their own side. A skeptical court-martial found him guilty and sentenced him to be executed, but General-in-Chief Scott spared him. Scott said that Riley had deserted in April of 1846, weeks before the war with Mexico actually began. According to the Articles of War, the worst that Riley and four of his cohorts could receive was a lashing and a branding with the letter D, for "deserter." It was unknown whether Scott was the least bit influenced by a petition he received, which had been signed by twenty-one persons, including the Archbishop of Mexico and a number of prominent Mexican women. The women said that Riley had concealed and protected "banished Americans" hiding in Mexico City after the war started. "We believe him to have a generous heart admitting all his errors," wrote the petitioners. They referred to Riley as "O'Reilly," and they pleaded for the lives of all the deserters, but Riley's in particular.

Riley was given fifty lashes, branded with a D on his cheek, and subjected to months at hard labor. Indeed, he was branded twice. The Americans applied the first D upside down and happily did it again, to make it conform to rules and regulations. It angered Riley (for years there were rumors he tried to sue the U.S. Government for his branding, but no court records to that effect were ever found) but scarcely detracted from his power to charm, which was as great as his power to be contentious. Another rumor, more persistent and quite possibly more true, was that he married a wealthy Mexican woman and remained in Mexico after the war, there to raise a family.

George Ballentine, a Scottish soldier in the American Army and not one of the deserters, saw some of the punishment meted out. He called the branding of deserters a "gross refinement of the cruelty which we might expect to find among Indian tribes, but to which it would be difficult to find a parallel among the transactions of civilized nations."

News of the executions also shocked many in the United States and brought forth some defenses of desertion. "Why should they not?" asked the Rev. Theodore Parker, a well-known antiwar activist. "If it were right to kill Mexicans for a few dollars a month, why was it not right also to kill Americans, especially when it pays the most? Perhaps it is not an American habit to inquire into the justice of war, only into the profit it may bring."

But then, what could be expected of Government? "Government is at best but an expedient; but most governments are usually, and all governments are sometimes, inexpedient," wrote Henry David Thoreau in his essay "Civil Disobedience." But not unlike the Rev. Milton Braman, Thoreau directed his ire at the vast unwashed, the people who were caught up in war and did the bidding of Government because they did not know what else to do. "Law never made men a whit more just," Thoreau wrote, "and by means of their respect for it, even the well-disposed are daily made the agents of injustice. A common and natural result of an undue respect for law is, that you may see a file of soldiers . . . marching in admirable order over the hill and dale to the wars, against their wills, aye, against their common sense and consciences, which makes it very steep marching indeed. . . ."

The Mexican War saw 1,500 Americans die in battle and another 10,800 succumb to disease. In terms of the numbers of men involved, it was one of the costliest wars America had ever fought, claiming 153.5 dead for every 1,000 participants per year. The Civil War, lying just ahead, would claim only 98 per 1,000 participants.

When the war ended, its soldiers were given enthusiastic homecomings. But the Government soon forgot that thousands came home with diseases and fevers contracted in Mexico, illnesses that would kill them if left untreated. And nobody paid much attention to the plight of veterans down on their luck, who sold 160-acre land grants for less than $50 in the streets of New Orleans.

Winfield Scott was the winning general, but he was not to carry his victory into civilian life, when he was nominated for the Presidency by the Whigs in 1852. One of his deficits was that, unlike his Democratic opponent, Franklin Pierce, who had risen from private to brigadier general in the war, Scott had not gone to Bowdoin College with Nathaniel Hawthorne. Hawthorne's slender election-campaign biography of Pierce, containing extensive excerpts from Pierce's own account of the war, made it almost seem that Pierce had been the general in charge, rather than Scott.

Hawthorne's prose contained much enthusiasm for the war. "There is nothing in any other country similar to what we see in our own, when the blast of the trumpet at once converts men of peaceful pursuits into warriors. . . . The valor that wins our battles is not the trained hardihood of veterans, but a native and spontaneous fire; and there is surely a chivalrous beauty in the devotion of the citizen soldier in his country's cause.''

The war and the Army seemed ''to create a spirit of romantic adventure which more than supplies the place of disciplined courage,'' Hawthorne said, adding, ''There never was a more gallant body of officers than those came from civil life into the army on occasion of the Mexican War. All of them, from the rank of general downward, appear to have been animated by the spirit of young knights, in times of chivalry, when fighting for their spurs.''

With a writer such as Hawthorne doing his election-year puffery for him, Pierce was undoubtedly aided, although it is difficult to assess how much. He was also aided by the simple fact that it was Scott who had ordered the grotesque executions of the *San Patricios* and other deserters, not Pierce. At least there were Catholics who took some comfort in thinking that in 1852, after the returns were in. Pierce won the election handily, and Scott's decision to spare Riley was somehow lost in the shouting.

Bloody as it was, the Mexican War was quickly forgotten by the Americans, perhaps because the Civil War overtook them so quickly and overcame them so totally. It quite overcame Nathaniel Hawthorne, too. Never again would he seem so uncritically praiseful about armed conflict; never again would he write about American soldiers in terms of knighthood and chivalry.

THREE
The
Civil War

Black veterans of the Civil War won their freedom but little else. (*The Metropolitan Museum of Art, Gift of Charles Stewart Smith, 1884*)

9
Nathaniel Hawthorne, Walt Whitman, and the Concussion of Young Men

... to care for him who should have borne the battle, and for his widow and orphan.
—Abraham Lincoln, Second Inaugural Address, March 4, 1865

It had not been an auspicious moment to return to United States, at least not for the likes of Nathaniel Hawthorne. He had always regarded himself as an orderly man, a self-regulating man; indeed, he found it impossible to be otherwise. But now the United States were neither united nor stately, and Hawthorne, who had spent the last seven years abroad, was required to bear witness to the illogic and the wildfire disorder of civil war. In June of 1860, he established himself in Concord, one of the wellsprings of the Revolution, and, from a distance, watched the destruction of the dreams that the Revolution had nurtured.

After the Confederate States of America were set up, early in 1861, followed by the fall of Fort Sumter in April, Hawthorne, who was then fifty-six years old, felt unusually combative. "If I were younger," he earnestly wrote to his publisher, William D. Ticknor, "I would volunteer." At about the same time and apparently in the same gladiatorial spirit, he wrote to fellow writer Horatio Bridge and said, "I regret . . . I am too old to shoulder a musket myself."

Two months later, in the warming relief of a New England July, he got word that the Confederate Army had repelled Union forces at Bull Run. Once again he burned with uncommon anger. He wrote to James Russell Lowell, "If last evening's news puts all of us into the same grim and bloody humor that it does me, the South had better have suffered ten defeats than won this victory.''

He could not see the war, nor could he hear it, but the very idea of the brutal events that were unfolding five hundred miles away filled him with anger and fear. He was working on a novel called *Septimius Felton* about then, a novel he would never finish. It was set not in his time but during the Revolution that had ended seventy-nine years earlier. In its pages were Hawthorne's feelings about his own war:

> In times of revolution and public disturbance . . . the measure of calm sense, the habits, the orderly decency, are partially lost. . . . Offences against public morality, female license, are more numerous; suicides, murders, all ungovernable outbreaks of men's thoughts, embodying themselves in wild acts, take place more frequently and with less horror to the lookers-on.

And yet, as the war reviled him, it inevitably possessed him, too. Hawthorne was, after all, a writer, a chronicler of his times and of all times, one of the finest his country would ever produce. The utter waste and devastation of such madness have always fascinated writers, even if they be given to pacifism, ambivalence, or a mix of the two. And so, early in 1862, he decided to write about some of his feelings for *The Atlantic Monthly*. Called ''Chiefly About War-Matters by a Peaceable Man,'' it was a stylish *divertissement* written with grace in time of national dysphoria, and it covered Hawthorne's winter journey from the sanctuary of Boston to Washington, not too distant from the front. Not surprisingly, it remains fresh and literate to this day.

And yet, coming when it did, at the bloody beginning of a bloody war whose outcome was then very much in doubt, it was a most curious piece, indeed. For here was the man who said that he wanted to volunteer, who regretted that he was too old to fight, who snarled with anger at Bull Run's loss, now using his wit to claw at the people running and serving in the Army that, as an instrument designed to save the Union and force the abolition of slavery, represented the very moral indignation he had expressed.

In this article—his musings on how it would be when the boys came home—Hawthorne adopted an attitude that nobody would have thought anything of in peacetime but that almost everybody would notice in a country at war with itself and in imminent danger of extinction. Perhaps only in America, with its innate intolerance of anything different tempered and thwarted by the First Amendment to its own Constitution, could a mere writer have gotten away with it.

"Will the time ever come again in America," Hawthorne asked, "when we may live half a score of years without once seeing the likeness of a soldier, except it be in the fatal march of a company on its summer tour? Not in this generation, I fear, nor in the next, nor till the Millennium; and even that blessed epoch, as the prophecies seem to intimate, will advance to the sound of the trumpet."

Hawthorne suspected that even if the war should end tomorrow, "and the army melt into the mass of the population within the next year, what an incalculable preponderance there will be of military titles and pretensions for at least half a century to come! Every country neighborhood will have its general or two, its three or four colonels, half a dozen majors, and captains without end. . . . One bullet-headed general will succeed another in the Presidential chair; and veterans will hold the offices at home and abroad and sit in Congress and the State legislatures, and fill in all the avenues of public life."

Thus spoke Hawthorne, not after victory was secure and Americans could laugh again, but at war's start, when they doubted they would ever laugh again. It presaged the feelings he would have when the veterans started to come home. Hawthorne emphasized he was not trying to deprecate the military, "but it behooves civilians to consider their wretched prospects in the future, and assume the military button before it is too late." Dark humor in a country already draped in deep black. Was anyone really expected to laugh?

Here was Nathaniel Hawthorne, a year after Sumter's fall, pondering not the defeated South's future, if the South was, in fact, to be defeated; nor the prospects for freed slaves, if the slaves were, in fact, to be freed; but what it would be like for the noncombatants when the combatants came home. A loss by the North would have rendered the Union extinct and the Emancipation Proclamation impotent. Who would have worried about the military button then?

As for the young men who were engaged in killing each other by the tens of thousands to determine if Hawthorne's New England abolitionist friends would prevail, he committed these rather incredible thoughts to paper: ". . . it seemed to me that the war had brought good fortune to the Youth of this epoch. . . . They now make it their daily business to ride a horse and handle a sword, instead of lounging listlessly through the duties, occupations, pleasures . . . to which the artificial state of society limits a peaceful generation." This was other than a philosopher-writer's lament over peace lost.

One historian would later suggest that Hawthorne wrote "Chiefly About

War-Matters'' as he did in part because he was ''oppressed by the ebb of his creative imagination,'' in part because he sensed the ''feverish intrigue'' in Washington, then filled with ''politically ambitious Union officers.'' But the piece was nonfiction, not the stuff of which *The Scarlet Letter* was wrought. Feverish intrigue among officers would hardly intimidate a writer of Hawthorne's measure. Such intrigue was the seed corn of the gothic novel. And the quality of his prose, if not his sensibility, does not bear the telltale signs of the burned-out writer, even though a burned-out Hawthorne would be more than a match for other writers in their best fettle. But burnout was not the thing here. Quite to the contrary. ''Chiefly About War-Matters'' revealed one very special Northerner taking the initial steps toward adopting attitudes about the blacks held by many Northerners who were not so special—whites who thought that Lincoln's intentions were, at best, foolish and not worth all the bloodshed.

Hawthorne could never have actively condoned slavery. But the war had caused him to conclude privately that nothing could be done about it—certainly no war should be fought over it—and that slavery would ultimately go away by itself. His position was not so different from that adopted by American conservatives over apartheid in South Africa, a century and a quarter later. Hawthorne had felt this way even before the war. In his campaign biography of his friend Franklin Pierce, he wrote that when all slavery's uses ''have been fulfilled, it causes to vanish like a dream.''

He felt his own sense of apartness from the blacks. On his trip to Washington for *The Atlantic,* he saw some runaway slaves and wrote, ''I felt most kindly towards these poor fugitives, but knew not precisely what to wish in their behalf.'' His mind about the war roller-coasted between one writing and another, between one conversation and another. ''If compelled to choose,'' he said at one point, ''I go for the North.'' But he also told friends in September of 1862, just a year or so after he had regretted that he was too old to fight, that perhaps it would be better for the North and South not to try to live as a nation and that ''amputation seems the better plan . . . the North and the South were two distinct nations in opinion and had better not try to live under the same institutions.''

As brother fought brother and the fatalities were counted at Chancellorsville, Gettysburg, and Lookout Mountain, Hawthorne never lost sight of the truly important things in his Transcendentalist universe—a universe of symbols and ideas and the power and beauty of language, where there was no room for anything but good thoughts. He was quite in the clutches of his own milieu as he confided in his wife, Sophia, his fear that ''when the soldiers returned the quiet rural life of the New England villages would be spoiled and coarsened.''

If he had so spoken or written during the Vietnam War he might well have expressed the same protective concerns about veterans wandering into the Hamptons. For in the Civil War, as in Vietnam, it was the youth of the poor and the working classes who dominated the ranks, constituted its cannon fodder, and produced the survivors who would sully the quiet of Concord. Neither Civil War nor Vietnam saw the depth and breadth of American society represented, as was the case, for example, in the two world wars. But given all that he said in ''Chiefly About War-Matters,'' it is quite conceivable that had he lived in the twentieth century, he might have taken the same position a year after the Germans marched into Poland or the Japanese attack on Pearl Harbor. In all his eloquence, would he have felt that Hitler or the Japanese warlords would ''vanish like a dream,'' without some prompting from the Allies?

In truth, for Hawthorne and others like him, the War Between the States was tiresome. Even worse to contemplate from his perspective was that peace might be just as tiresome. In his wonderment, he thus expressed the thinking person's unthinking disdain for anything soldierly, even though the cause be just, the very future of the nation at stake, and the war as much wrapped in ethics as in economics. But soldiers submit to barracks discipline, accept a loss of privacy and of freedom, and, as paid agents of Government, are practitioners of a frequently disagreeable occupation that may leave a mark on them. Even if he had fought with them, instead of only observing them, the reclusive, introspective novelist would have found it difficult to relate to men who bore arms or who had borne arms.

The Atlantic Monthly published ''Chiefly About War-Matters'' with some reluctance, and its editor, James T. Fields, actually purged some things Hawthorne had to say about Lincoln that were adjudged especially unflattering, although Lincoln surely was used to such things if he read certain newspapers. In any event, *The Atlantic* printed the expurgated material nine years later.

Hawthorne was not alone among the literati in having such feelings about the Civil War. Henry David Thoreau, another of the Transcendentalist group, similarly did not approve of slavery and the exploitation of blacks, even though clearly he felt an aloofness from people who were not a part of his group, his upper-class lineage. He had nothing but scorn for another minority group of his time, the Scots-Irish, and with all of his insights, there is no indication he ever made the connection between those who were slaves and those who were a new breed of serf in America—the immigrants employed by his family's pencil and graphite business. Thoreau said he never knew of a slave who had been mistreated, and doubtless he would also have been hard pressed to find an Irishman who had been wronged.

In any event, the war and the men who fought it could be of no moment to him because he deplored the use of firearms and found the war immoral. Later, Thoreau somehow found John Brown a personal hero, however. The reasons are not entirely clear, but Alfred Kazin would surmise that "Brown represented in the most convulsively personal way the hatred of injustice that was Thoreau's most significant political passion—and this was literally a *hatred,* more so than he could acknowledge to himself, a hatred of anyone as well as anything that marred the perfect design of his moral principles."

And there were others with their own insights about the Civil War and the men who fought it: James Russell Lowell mused that war always brings up the dregs in society; former Speaker of the House Robert C. Winthrop feared that gallantry in battle would supplant obeisance to the Bible; and Dwight Moody, the shoe salesman and evangelist tirelessly concerned with souls as well as soles, feared that the war might cause Christians to stray from their faith. He buttonholed strangers on trains and boats and demanded to know, "Are *you* a Christian?"

These men, although of primary importance in their fields, did not speak for all those who wrote the books, delivered the orations, and preached the sermons of the day. Whatever their feelings about the war, writers such as Whittier, Longfellow, Emerson, and Harriet Beecher Stowe were steadfast in their support of Lincoln and his cause. And there was Walt Whitman.

Whitman did not simply cover the war as any observant writer would. His descriptions of war were as erotic as they were rhapsodic: ". . . the beautiful young men, in wholesale death & agony, everything sometimes as if blood color, & dripping blood." He immersed himself in the war's misery and, at one point, likened it to the Trojan War in the effect it would have as a stimulator of American culture. "Our land and history are so full of spinal subjects," he wrote. "To take only one siege—what the ancient war of Ilium and the respective Greek and Trojan warriors proved to Hellenic poetry and art, and onward indeed to all poetry and art since, so it has been predicted by more than one shrewd thinker and prophet, will prove the War of Attempted Secession of 1861–5 to the future of esthetic United States."

Thus, rather than regard them as beings he could not associate with, Whitman saw soldiers as progenitors of high culture as well as bearers of deadly force. He cared so much about them, he even helped them write letters home. "The real war will never get in the books," he wrote. "The actual soldier of 1862–'65, North and South, with all his ways, his incredible dauntlessness, habits, practices, tastes, language, his fierce friendship, his appetite, rankness, his superb strength and animality, lawless gait, and a hundred unnamed lights and shades of camp, I say, will never be written—perhaps must not and should not be.''

For Whitman, war was the ''concussion of young men on each other.'' He cut through the scream of brazen war horns to the deadly sound of war on each man in his age of anarchy where people had become as numerous as leaves of grass. And so they were as easy to ignore as leaves of grass. But to Whitman, soldiers ''were of more significance even than the political interests involved.'' For him, they could never disrupt the quiet of peace.

As it turned out, Hawthorne need not have worried about the noise of the homecoming, because he expired before the war did. But the end of the war brought all the huzzahs he dreaded and the soldiers expected—at least for a while. The Union feted its homecoming victors, and quite possibly nothing like it had been seen since cheering Romans lined the Appian Way, trying to pierce Caesar's skepticism about them, after his defeat of Vercingetorix.

Ulysses S. Grant was no Caesar, Mark Twain's enthusiasm for him notwithstanding. But in Robert E. Lee and in Johnny Reb, that collective Southern enlisted man cloned from Lee's formidable image, there was a reasonable Vercingetorix and maybe even something more, something of Hektor—at once dashing and despised, doomed but valiant, a man who could remain chivalrous even in the face of his own mortality.

To best such an attractive foe was a victory the North could be proud of, a victory deserving of the extravagance of the welcoming parades that would presage the extravagance of the Gilded Age later in the nineteenth century. When the 15th New York Artillery returned, it marched along Lower Broadway and the men enjoyed libations at the Liberty Garden, in the Bowery. Many other fighting outfits received similar welcomes in New York. The Romans would have loved it.

Indeed, there were parades in cities all over the country, cannon thundering out over village greens, flags flying everywhere. In Washington, one parade—the grand review of the armies—lasted two full days, and President Andrew Johnson and his Cabinet watched it go by.

So did a jubilant Whitman, in the rutted streets of a city trying to put its swampy origins behind it, a Washington still trying to consummate L'Enfant's grand design. Whitman found the returning armies ''a magnificent sight. . . . In their ranks stretching clear across the Avenue, I watch them march or ride along, at a brisk pace, through two whole days— infantry, cavalry, artillery—some 200,000 men.'' Leaves of grass, indeed.

Although not mentioned by Whitman, an enormous strip of canvas was stretched across the Capitol during the event, on which was printed, "The only national debt we can never pay is the debt we owe the victorious Union soldiers." Vigilant reporters for both the *New York Herald* and *The New York Times* noticed it and reported it without comment in their dispatches.

The veterans knew they had the esteem of their fellow Americans. Could love be far behind? There was no question about it, thought the *New York Herald*. "The gallant conquerors of many hard fought field are going home to share the blessings they have won for the nation," the *Herald* chimed. It further predicted that those who fought would participate in the nation's bounty. "They are not only heroes, but they are heroes of the sublimist conflict in all history. . . . From one end of the world to the other, the people thank our soldiers for having conquered in the people's cause. . . . Their remaining years may be passed in quiet usefulness at their homes. . . ."

Americans loved parades, seeming to lose their ardor only occasionally. When the all-black 52nd Pennsylvania Regiment arrived in New York, it left immediately for Philadelphia without parading. There was no parade reported for them in Philadelphia, either. The men were simply mustered out of the service. No explanation was offered, and perhaps the reasons lay in a cause other than the contempt in which blacks were held by so many Northerners. Other black soldiers paraded, however, especially when they returned home to all-black communities, and for the most part, the celebrations and the hyperbole about soldiers in the public press belied the notion that anything could be sour, either in relations between whites and those newly freed, or between those who stayed behind and those who fought the war.

Civil War veterans, at least those on the Union side of it, had every reason to believe that they were going to benefit materially from their service, that the debt the public said was owed them would, in fact, be paid. It would have been hard for anyone to predict that the message on the Capitol canvas was not an expression of earnest intent but rather the stark statement of an unbeautiful American truth. The soldiers who enlisted to fight the Civil War did not think very much about what happened to soldiers who fought earlier wars. And so the victorious veterans thought money and other good things would come their way. In this they were little different from the men who had fought the Revolution or the War of 1812 or, for that matter, the foot soldiers who had done Caesar's bidding and saw the military as a way to serve nation and self.

As it turned out, the average Union veteran received around $250 upon discharge. It represented pay he had not drawn while on active duty and, perhaps, the bounty promised him when he enlisted but left unpaid during the war years. By the standards of the day it was something, but not very much for "him who should have borne the battle, and for his widow and orphan." There were a considerable number of such people who knew too well the truth in Walt Whitman's observation that the war had turned the nation into "one vast central hospital." If they were not patients in that hospital they knew family or friends who were.

Spring turned to summer, the triumphal parades seemed interminable, and Northern editorial writers continued to lavish praise on the heroes who had saved the Union. But the men they were praising were fast becoming desperate. At first, their desperation went unnoticed by the press. Then, on August 5, 1865, the *New York Herald* published this letter from a disgruntled cavalryman:

> What are the returned soldiers who volunteered to fight for their country and were mustered out honorably from the service to do for employment? Are our wives and children to starve? All are willing to work, I am sure, if they can find employment. If a soldier asks for a situation, the response, generally is, "we are full," or "we engaged a clerk this morning."

By then, there was ample evidence that the cavalryman wasn't alone, wasn't just one bitter man who could not take care of himself. The want ads of big-city papers were filled with announcements placed by veterans seeking work. Indeed, in that very first summer after the end of the war, the *Herald* and other newspapers contained "situation wanted" advertisements that, although less eloquent, starkly described the straits of those who had fought. One example:

> Wanted—By A YOUNG MAN WHO SERVED IN the army for three years, at anything he can make an honest living. Call 356 7th Avenue.

It is impossible to say precisely how many "Situation Wanted" ads were placed by former soldiers, since some men did not identify themselves as veterans, fearing that their military service might be held against them. One would be safer to say he was a German or an Irish *Protestant* if he wanted a job—which is precisely the "qualification" some of the ads emphasized.

Clearly, unemployed veterans needed advice, and there was much of that. *The Army and Navy Journal* advised veteran-applicants in 1865 "not to slump and become a dirty loafer 'who has been in the army' " and that if mutilated by war, "teach yourself the strategy of new muscular habits." In Chicago, Governor Richard James Oglesby appeared at a reception supposed to honor returning veterans and advised them that they had to help themselves and not expect to be given "soup . . . with a silver spoon." From the pulpit, the Rev. John Ware advised, "The soldier is made at the expense of the man," and newspapers and magazines advised that if a man wanted a job, he ought to go to a rural area where there wasn't much competition.

The suggestion to look for jobs in rural areas was initially not taken very seriously, although ultimately veterans became numerous among those who sought new lives on the frontier. But in the first few months after the end of the war, veterans, still wearing the uniforms they wore at Vicksburg and Antietam, were frequently seen as organ grinders on the streets of Boston, New York, and Philadelphia. Someone in Boston wrote in the spring of 1868 that most people "pass coldly by . . . or quiet their consciences with dropping five or ten cents in the soldier's box."

By the barrenness of late autumn, the "Situation Wanted" advertisements diminished, perhaps because some veterans found work and others did, in fact, start looking in the hinterlands. But those who remained in the cities faced a winter without shelter. Governor Reuben E. Fenton said that in New York alone, homeless veterans "are numbered by the thousands, and are altogether beyond the power of Executive and Legislative Relief. Their needs cannot be postponed." He called upon charitable New Yorkers to help.

Discharged soldiers without homes in big cities were more than a national disgrace—they were an enticement to the Americans who ran the scams of the day. *The Soldier's Friend,* a monthly, reported the stories of soldiers who lost their money to check cashers and to crooks who put knockout drops in their beer. Chicago swarmed with "blacklegs, burglars, garroters and harlots (male and female) who have congregated to rob the soldiers . . . of their hard-earned wages," warned the *Chicago Tribune.*

In Detroit, "scores" of soldiers were said to have been set upon by thugs loafing around barracks and saloons. One man reportedly lost $600 at dice and another veteran lost the $80 his wife had sewn into his pocket—the thief simply cut the pocket out of his pants while the veteran was still wearing them.

At its height, demobilization of Civil War soldiers was sending 300,000 men a month looking for work in a society that did not feel it really needed them, now that the war was over. By January of 1866, nearly a million of them had received the last pay they would ever receive as soldiers and were sent back to their homes.

President Johnson may not have felt he could do anything about the problem, but it wasn't for lack of knowing. Just after the Christmas of 1865, he received a letter from Jane H. Todd, the mother of two veterans who could not find work. Mrs. Todd said she wished that Congress would "for an hour drop the eternal Negro question and devote that time for the interest of the suffering soldiers." Among the soldiers of the North, there was much antagonism toward the blacks, on whom they blamed a goodly measure of their desperation.

As postwar unemployment problems grew, so did a spirit of vindictive-ness between conqueror and conquered. It manifested itself in badgering little ways; for example, the disposition of dead bodies. The question of what to do with the bodies of Confederates was first raised by Union troops in 1862, as they were winning the Battle of Antietam. They complained that dead Confederate soldiers were getting in the way. Rebel bodies had been dumped efficiently and quickly by the Yankees into shallow trenches so that the battle could continue unimpeded. But Union soldiers reported that hogs, either wild or escaped from some derelict farm, wandered into the battle zone and rooted up the corpses. The corpses lay exposed and rotting in the fields, they said. In the hills of Maryland that warm September, the crops that survived the fight ripened amidst decaying flesh. Union soldiers said they then decided to give the Southerners deeper, more permanent burials. If the reports of Union soldiers were accurate and not just nasty wartime bragging, then it would seem that the Northerners felt that the dead Southerners were more dangerous to their health than they had been when they were alive.

Seven years later, on a pleasant spring day in Virginia, dead rebels were becoming a problem again, even though the war they had fought had been over for four years. This time, the bodies were buried properly enough, and there were no hogs in the Arlington Heights Churchyard. But it was Memorial Day, a holiday that had been born in the South at the end of the war. Southern families took it seriously, and they insisted on casting flowers upon the graves of their dead, even though the Washington-area chapters of the Grand Army of the Republic, a new and growing association of Union veterans, had resolved that this should not be permitted. In its resolution, the Grand Army said that "to throw flowers on Confederate graves would be a desecration of the graves of loyal Union soldiers."

Despite the warning, publicly made, the Southerners had the temerity to persist in honoring their dead with their prayers and their flowers. Women concealed flowers in the billows of their skirts, men hid flowers in the sleeves and breast pockets of their jackets, and when they thought no one was looking, they dropped fragrant blossoms on the earth covering their dead.

Grand Army members were appalled. Ever vigilant, they notified the Government. Quickly, orders came down the line from someone, somewhere, to a Marine lieutenant. The lieutenant promptly appeared at the Confederate gravesite with six enlisted men, armed and under orders to prevent any further desecrations offensive to the Government of the United States or its Union veterans.

The *New York Herald* reported the incident, describing the lieutenant as "fierce-looking." James Gordon Bennett, the unrestrained proprietor of the *Herald,* had tepidly supported the Union side, even though he had strong reservations about the abolitionist notions held by some of his more liberal readers, notions that Negroes, once freed, would ultimately become citizens as good in every way as were the whites. His paper never missed an opportunity to print unfavorable stories about blacks, even if the dateline was many hundreds of miles away from New York. But his mixed feelings about the end of slavery apparently were more than overridden by his personal disdain for Jefferson Davis. Whatever his private thoughts, he could not regard the encounter in the Arlington cemetery as the Marines' finest hour.

"Is this really true?" grieved the *Herald* in an editorial on May 31. "The men on both sides were born under one flag. . . . In an unhappy moment, they were estranged by the machinations of selfish politicians; family disunion, even to the death ensued; but who attempts to continue this division after death? Did General Grant know of the order given to the Marines in Arlington?" The next day, the *Herald,* to its credit, lamented the incident again: "shame on the zeal that pursues a quarrel beyond the grave."

The aspect of a nation at war with its mourners only hinted at the anguish that persisted after Appomattox. Veterans bore much of this pain as they came home to communities that offered them unemployment and even a lack of acceptance. The war was over, but families and neighborhoods and communities remained divided over the issues that had caused the war in the first place, even in the victorious North.

Veterans were out of step not only with the civilians they returned to, but also with the regular Army and Navy officers with whom they had served. It was a division not always perceived by those who saw veterans as essentially members of a preening, acquisitive military subculture sharing a single view of what the world should be like. But the regulars—as opposed to the civilians who had temporarily given up their freedom and risked their lives to fight for a cause as well as for whatever enlistment bounties might have enticed them—did not necessarily share with veterans their priorities. Some of the professional soldiers felt a brotherhood with the men they had fought with and were genuinely concerned about what happened to them afterward. But more often than not, the professionals who remained in the Union Army were now far more interested in the enemies they perceived before the war—the Cheyenne, Sioux, Apache, and other stubborn Indian nations—and they simply assumed that society back East would be orderly, prosperous, and productive. They also assumed that the voices of soldiers, whether professionals or those returned to civilian life, would always be heard.

The publications they read reinforced their view of the world. "It is clear that the soldier element, Northern and Southern, will be a powerful one in American politics, society, institutions and laws," predicted the *Army and Navy Journal* in 1869, a scant five months after the incident in Arlington Heights Churchyard. "Military influence will be seen in our legislation, national and local, in our manners and customs, in our local usages, and in our choice of rulers," bubbled the *Journal*. ". . . It is easy to see that the great body of citizen-soldiers have melted back into the great body of the people, their leaven has 'leavened the whole lump.' "

The leavening process lasted longer than the *Journal* apparently wanted to acknowledge. The relatively few professional soldiers who cared about veterans were frustrated in their efforts to induce the private sector to support the creation of a Soldiers' and Sailors' Home, then proposed for Philadelphia. The city had more than its share of wounded soldiers, and some women had established a home for them there at the corner of Crown and Race streets. They and others felt that much more should be done, and thus a glittering fund-raiser was held on an October evening in 1865. No less than George G. Meade, one of the North's most able generals, was the principal speaker, and those in attendance included General Ulysses S. Grant and Admiral David G. Farragut.

"The Government is slow to move," complained Meade. "A few days ago I had to go to Washington. I am a member of an institution whose object is to establish a national home for soldiers and sailors. A hundred gentlemen are appointed as corporators, and over fifty must be present before anything can be done on this subject. Three times I have been to Washington, but not once were fifty collected. . . . These poor fellows [wounded veterans] cannot wait. . . .'' He warned that if his efforts failed, ''our alms houses will soon be filled with the disabled.''

There were many public officials who vigorously disagreed with Meade, one of them Governor Alexander Hamilton Bullock of Massachusetts. He denounced the notion of a home in a speech to the legislature and said that no soldiers ''should be consigned to a public 'home' or separated from their friends, or removed from the town of their residence, unless mental or moral obliquity should demand it.'' Bullock, using language not totally unfamiliar to anyone who knew about the early debates on pensions for Revolutionary War soldiers, said, ''. . . there is a feeling against adding another to our large permanent institutions on the twofold ground that it would tend to pauperize the soldier, and that the money which should be expended for his benefit would be absorbed by the necessary salaries and incidentals of a great establishment.''

It would not be until 1898 and the war with Spain that the national Government would assume its proper responsibility for the care of Confederate graves. In the interim, the bodies of veterans continued to be grist for political tempests that were as ugly as they were petty. Peace was only a technicality. The special quality of national mindlessness about the war dead was not confined to Northerners, nor was it limited to members of the Grand Army. In 1871, the Democrats, who had constituted the Lincoln Administration's opposition during the war, proposed exhuming the remains of seventeen thousand Northern soldiers and carting them to another resting spot so that Mary Lee, Robert E. Lee's widow, could reclaim and reoccupy the Custis-Lee estate at Arlington. Elsewhere there were only a few glimmers of compassion and forgiveness in those early years, as when some women in Mississippi placed flowers over the graves of all the soldiers, regardless of whether their uniforms were of blue or of gray.

As for those who survived, there was much uncaring. Neither on the state nor on the Federal level had any commitment been made for the creation of hospitals for American soldiers. There was nothing, save for something popularly called the U.S. Sanitary Commission, or, more accurately, the Commission of Inquiry and Advice in Respect to the Sanitary Interests of the United States Forces.

The commission, a creation of the quasi-governmental variety, had been established by the Secretary of War because of demands made by private citizens, most notably the Rev. Henry W. Bellows, minister of the Church of All Souls in New York. Its executive officer was Frederick Law

Olmstead, the brilliant landscape architect and writer who was a vigorous leader if an eccentric one: He reportedly was at his most creative when he worked until four o'clock in the morning, sleeping in his clothes and arising to breakfast on coffee and pickles.

The commission did good work—Allan Nevins would one day praise its "sturdy common sense" and its "consecrated devotion to a great aim"— and it raised funds to improve the health of combat soldiers by improving their hygiene in the field and in hospitals. But after the end of the war, the commission became rather quiescent. In its own pronouncements, it reflected the popular biases of the day. It advised the public that the Government did not think it could pay for all the medical treatment veterans needed and that the civil sector had, as a result, a special responsibility.

The Rev. Mr. Bellows had made it clear he did not believe in coddling soldiers after the war, saying that local governments ought "to discourage all favor to mendacity" among the disabled. He warned, "You . . . know how easily loose, indulgent and destructive notions creep into communities, under the name and purpose of humanity, and what temptations of a sentimental kind there will be to favor a policy which will undermine self-respect, self-support, and the true American pride of personal independence."

The Sanitary Commission "excogitated" three guiding principles for caring for veterans. First, there should be little "outside interference" with "natural laws" that would deprive the wounded veteran of his dignity. In short, if he looked as if he was going to fail anyhow, there was no point in prolonging the agony. Second, veterans should be induced to strengthen "natural reliances" with their own families, which could help them in their time of need. And third, there should be the "utmost endeavor to promote the healthy absorption of the invalid class into the homes and into the ordinary industry of the country."

These were the commission's guidelines and this was the way most Americans seemed to feel about veterans. This, even though the nation had just come through a war of unprecedented violence, in which a total of between three million and four million Northerners and Southerners had been involved, in which nearly half a million had died, and in which many thousands were maimed for life. Of those who bore no physical marks, many would pay the emotional cost of the conflict for the rest of their lives. It was, indeed, the first "modern war," in terms of the method and magnitude of killing, the violent years that Robert Penn Warren would call the "secret school" for the First and Second World Wars that lay ahead.

The payments to Union veterans for serious injuries were modest, even by the standards of the day. They were entitled to $75 from the Government if they lost a leg and $50 if they lost an arm, or, if they preferred, they could forgo the payment and the Government would provide an artificial limb. Makers thus hawked their wares aggressively; this advertisement in the *Army and Navy Journal* advised:

> LEGS AND ARMS
> Just patented by John Condell. Furnished, *warranted five years,* at the same prices of unwarranted limbs of the other styles.
> Generals Dix and Hooker say that for amputations either above or below the knee, or above or below the elbow, they are the best they ever saw.
> Send for a circular, addressing A.F. Williams, General Agent
> 24 Bible House, New York City

Veterans were entitled to a new artificial limb every three years, along with transportation to and from the place where they selected it. Ultimately, the Government would report that most took money rather than artificial limbs.

If the policy seemed a bit modest, it was only because the Government, like the people, was unprepared philosophically for the suggestion that it take care of the men who had served it in war. The Government was, in fact, unable to think about its possible role as a provider for citizens in difficulty on any level. The national inclination toward those suffering from misfortune, including those whose problems were created during service to the Government, remained as it had always been. Simply put, soldiers were expected to take care of themselves after the end of war, Lincoln's concerns to the contrary.

Americans meant no disrespect to the wishes of their martyred President. But Lincoln's sense of responsibility for those who had served was ahead of its time. Especially in the North, there was a feeling that a properly motivated individual could help himself, whatever the scope of his problems. The feeling was reflected in the popular literature of the day. Shortly after the war ended, an obscure young man named Horatio Alger abandoned the ministry, came to New York, and began to write stories and novels that carried the message that hard work was always rewarded. The quintessential Alger bootstrapper could pull himself out of poverty by dint of his own efforts, no matter what misfortunes overtook him. The Horatio Alger fictions were successful because Americans wanted to believe they were true. Broken men never were the stuff of which dreams were made.

As the war faded from memory, so did the sacrifices of those men who had fought it. Said one, "I would have felt better to have met at least one person who would have given me a hearty handshake and said he was glad to see me home, safe from the war.'' He added, ''It almost seemed, sometimes, as if I had been away only a day or two, and had just taken up where I had left off.''

On the West Coast, far from where most of the war had been fought, a veteran named W. C. Morris spoke of his homecoming in San Francisco: ''If there had been a single instance of public recognition, I am not aware of it. . . . After years of toil, privation and hardship, you are turned out to graze on short feed like a broken down mustang.''

A less ebullient, less euphoric America also quickly came to the conclusion that in evaluating candidates for jobs, soldiers were perhaps not the best prospects. In fact, the Civil War soldier suffered discrimination simply because he had gone to war. He was seen as unstable, untutored, unmanageable—a bad risk. Some soldiers succeeded in getting employment at the Post Office, but when they tried to get the clerk and messenger jobs that reportedly existed at the Treasury Department in Washington, the department issued a starchy communiqué advising them that ''no vacancies exist.''

The Soldier's Friend saw discrimination against the veteran as such a serious issue that it advised men not to disclose their military service. After so many rejections, ''They strive to conceal the fact of their having been in the army,'' the journal said. ''One man, who had lost both arms, making an appeal for aid, was told by a man at that time in government service, with an oath, 'he was a —— fool for going to the war.' ''

In June of 1866, *The Soldier's Friend* reported, ''There is no disguising it boys; the people are afraid of us! . . . Hearing that soldiers gambled, swore, visited low dives, these men now ask, 'Shall we admit them into our families, and allow them to mingle with our friends, our little ones?' ''

A month before his assassination, Lincoln had assured all that he was ready to ''recognize the paramount claims of the soldiers of the nation in disposition of public trusts.'' But after the war was over, George Bliss, a Rhode Island volunteer, bitterly complained, ''When peace came and our services were no longer necessary, we found not only the offices were filled by those who remained at home, but also that an old soldier was looked upon with some suspicion. Many thought that a soldier's life was evil.''

Some even blamed America's growing drug abuse problem on the Union and Confederate soldiers who fought each other. The hypodermic syringe had been introduced into the United States in 1856, and reportedly more than two thousand of them were issued to Union doctors. Morphine, a derivative of opium and arguably the most effective natural painkiller ever discovered, was injected into wounded soldiers by doctors who had no alternatives. Where needles were lacking, morphine was simply dusted on wounds. An estimated ten million opium pills were issued to the Union Army, along with more than 2,841,000 ounces of other opiates, "including powdered opium, powdered opium with ipecac, laudanum and paregoric." In many instances, soldiers also received opiates to take orally in order to stop the symptoms of dysentery, which they did, most effectively. In short, Army doctors gave to soldiers the same thing they would have given to civilians and did give to civilians before the war.

Soldiers thus became addicts, as would many civilians who were given morphine frequently. In 1879, a U.S. Army surgeon named Joseph Janvier Woodward expressed his concern about addiction to opiates: "I confess, the more I learn of the behavior of such cases under treatment, the more I am inclined to advise that opiates should be as far as possible avoided." But it was already too late; he estimated that at least 45,000 veterans were either addicted or well on the way to becoming addicted.

By the end of the century, scientists had learned how to buffer morphine into a substance called heroin, and heroin and morphine addiction became known as "soldiers disease" or the "army disease." The Civil War soldier, like his Vietnam counterpart a century later, thus came to be linked in an accusing way to drug abuse, even though it was by no means clear whether the addiction was started as soldier or civilian, or whether it started before the war, during it, or in the years following.

In the case of the Civil War veteran, the insensitive links to drug abuse were made not only by the officials of the very Government that induced morphine dependency, but also by a society that did not question the Government's role. Although hard numbers were lacking, there was a widespread belief that the problem of addiction was worst not in New York City, as it was a century later, but in the South, where it was attributed to the "population's rurality and tendency to brood over the Civil War and Reconstruction."

By the turn of the century, various studies placed the number of American addicts at over a quarter of a million. It was a time when morphine derivatives were frequently being used in the preparation of over-the-counter medicines designed to ease the pain of teething (paregoric) or of neuralgia (Gross's Neuralgia Pills). Even so, the resulting addiction continued to be called "army disease." One druggist of the day summed up the problem and said, "Veteran soldiers, as a class, are addicted to it [opium]." The war was a convenient target on which to blame America's drug ambience, which it still has not lost. Surely the war was a contributing factor; just as surely were veterans made the scapegoats for a society that could not learn to solve its drug abuse problems.

The nation also went through something of a crime wave between the end of the war and 1870, although there were differences of opinion about how severe it was. But in a way consistent with what would happen after other wars, there were publicly expressed feelings that much of whatever crime there was was due to homecoming veterans. For example, the Eastern Penitentiary of Pennsylvania reported that nine-tenths of the men in prison

> had been more or less incapacitated and demoralized by an apprenticeship to the trade of war. . . . That this disbandment of large bodies of troops should produce the effect not only of increasing the amount of crime, but also of the grave character of the offenses committed is a fact so severely felt by the community that it may be freely stated without disparagement to the many thousands who from patriotic and other motives have served faithfully and since the close of the war have returned to their customary peaceful avocation.

The same prison also reported an unprecedented increase in its population and told the public that "by the subsidence of this great national convulsion this penitentiary, in common with all other institutions in this country, has indirectly received, at least, its share of shattered mortality."

There were similar reports elsewhere. In 1866, the overcrowded prison at Charlestown, Massachusetts, attributed its rapid rise in population to "the rapid development of crime since the war ended" and noted that of 327 people committed in the year ending October 1, 1866, 215 were veterans of service in the Army or Navy for the Union. The warden issued a report and explained:

> The great majority of these were good soldiers and sailors; they are young men who entered the service before they had learned a trade, and before their principles were firmly fixed; and on their discharge they were unable to find employment, or had learned the vices of the camp, and so fell readily into crime.

In the Midwest, the State Prison Commission of Wisconsin reported in 1866 that "many of the prisoners who served in the army were physically in a very lamentable condition, being unfit for any manual labor. . . ." And in Chicago at one point, most of the 112 inmates of the county jail were veterans of the late war and their veteran status was duly noted by Jeremiah Willits, a Quaker who worked for the Philadelphia Society for Alleviating the Miseries of Public Prisons. He also found that two-thirds of the more recent admissions to the prison at Jackson, Michigan, had been soldiers and that the veteran population of the Ohio penitentiary was three-quarters of the total. In Kansas, 97 of the 126 men who were prisoners in the state penitentiary in 1867 were either Union or Confederate soldiers, and a physician who checked them over concluded, "They have come to us with constitutions shattered by wounds, disease or intemperance."

Although reliable national figures were lacking, the *North American Review* estimated in 1866 that between five thousand and six thousand Union soldiers and sailors were incarcerated in various state prisons but this did not count thousands more in local jails. Moralizing was inevitable: "Absence from home, exciting circumstances of the war, the false idea that jayhawking [stealing] was not a crime, and the ever baneful influence of intoxicating drink were the causes of all the crimes which sent the convicts to prison," read the explanation of the situation in Kansas.

There was also no doubt that some of the soldiers who enlisted had been convicts before the war started, and so it was probably unwise to argue the cause-and-effect relationship between war and crime. Men convicted of both misdemeanors and felonies were paroled during the war and permitted to serve in the military, a precursor of the practice later made famous by the French Foreign Legion.

A certain Judge Hill of Massachusetts told a state senate committee there that when accused offenders came before him during the war he always asked them if they wanted to enlist, and if they said they would rather not, he'd tell them that they ought to. A sheriff told the New York legislature in 1867 that the punishment for crime was "to enlist in the army and get a large bounty."

The prospect of so many convict-veterans was not so disturbing to some. Prison inspectors in New York found it helped in making contracts for prison labor if one could point to a work force of young and presumably able-bodied young men. In 1865, the *New York Report* noted that "since the close of the war . . . contracts recently let are at a higher price than formerly paid. . . . There is reason to believe that the prisons may possibly become nearly or quite self-sustaining."

It also proved easy to blame veterans for crimes they had nothing to do with. In June of 1866, three men robbed a bank in Bowdoinham, Maine, and told the cashier, "We do not want your lives. We have been in this bloody war, and it's money we want." When they were caught four months later in New York City, it turned out that the three had spent the Civil War not fighting the Confederate Army, but as languishing convicts in a forty-five-acre prison called Sing Sing, conveniently upriver from New York City.

In any event, the spectacle of so many former soldiers in jail was greeted with a loud I-told-you-so by those Americans who had opposed the war and who had waited it out in Europe. The expatriates thought the disbanded men would hardly submit to civilized rule at the end of the war and would, instead, roam about "with arms in their hands, flushed with intoxicating victory, led by officers schooled in battle."

If many Americans seemed judgmental about the veterans and their wicked ways, some also saw the moment as one for promoting prison reform. The *North American Review* made this plea in January of 1866:

> Now that our prisons are filling up at an enormous rate . . . and drawing into their fatal contamination thousands of returning soldiers and neglected children, it is the duty of every community to take serious thought for the welfare of these persons, remembering how and by whom it was said, "Inasmuch as ye did it not to one of the least of these, ye did it not to me."

Discrimination against veterans of the Civil War is not something that has emerged with the scholar's assessment of events of the day. It was apparent then and taken note of at the time. *Leslie's Illustrated Newspaper* reported in 1865 that there were too many men who could not make a living, and offered its reason why:

> At this moment, in the City of New York, there are many thousands of stalwart and educated men wandering the streets, utterly unable to procure employment. This arises mainly from the vast influx of labor suddenly let loose upon the community by the mustering-out of our armies, and by the hard but truthful fact that there is a prejudice in the minds of employers against the returned soldiers. . . . While we must blame the employer very much, we must also blame the soldier. He has, as a soldier, been pleased to encourage a belief in his recklessness. He has felt somewhat proud to hear tales told of his whisky-drinking abilities and foraging operations, in which the laws of *meum* and *tuum* are set at utter defiance. They have encouraged in the minds of citizens the belief that the army has acted as a school of demoralization and they are suffering the results.

Leslie's thus acknowledged the discrimination. But the cause of it was found to be not in the lack of national conscience, rather in the soldier's own braggart behavior. So, they had come full circle, heroes fallen to braggarts and deserving of all they got. With sentiments such as this appearing in the press, the time was ripe for the creation of organizations that would unite the fallen heroes and enable them to obtain collectively what they had failed so miserably to get as individuals.

10
The Day That Michigan, Illinois, Pennsylvania, and Ohio Voted in Indiana

Decoration Day ... is a day that can never become national.... It is an occasion for heaping epithets of infamy upon one set of graves while piling flowers upon another set—for reviving the bitter memories of conflict....
—*New York Times,* editorial, June 3, 1869

Better to have 500 maimed veterans stumping about the towns and villages of Massachusetts, living partly by their pension and partly by their work, than shut up in the costliest and best structures that art could plan or money could build.
—Second Annual Report of the Massachusetts Board of State Charities, 1866

There never was a time when anyone could accuse soldiers and politics of being alien to each other, neither in American history nor in the history of any other nation on earth. And yet, the two in tandem have at times suffered some awkwardness. This was apparent as the Civil War entered its final phase and politicians at every level of Government began to think about what they would need in the peace to come.

The Union's leading generals were mostly registered Democrats. This did not go unnoticed by the Republicans, who were then not the Grand Old Party at all, but more like a Trifling Newfangled Party, barely a decade old, largely untried, inexperienced, and understandably very nervous about getting and retaining power. Democrats traced their roots all the way back to Thomas Jefferson. As poised as they were, they struggled with the heavy burden of trying to oppose Abraham Lincoln and simultaneously appear loyal to the Union.

As the Republicans surveyed their prospects, they saw in Lincoln a President whom they did not champion as especially couth, and who did not enjoy enormous support among voters, despite his sagacity (or perhaps because of it); they saw a war that was pointedly unpopular in the North, still stunned by what Herman Melville called "the atheistic roar of riot" among those who were to be conscripted; they saw the general lack of enthusiasm among the young, especially those with means and education, for soldiering; and they were mindful that many thousands of voters agreed with Nathaniel Hawthorne's private sometime thinking that perhaps the South ought to be permitted to go its own way, as Jefferson Davis had strongly suggested.

It would complicate the war if conscripts, most of them from modest backgrounds and not nearly as sophisticated as those who bought their way out of the war, were to believe some of the things they read in leading Northern newspapers—whose editors and publishers were doubtful that the war would achieve anything. Republicans came to believe that Democrats were engineering some bizarre newspaper distribution to soldiers in the field that was not helping the Union cause. On February 16, 1863, the *New York World* ran a brief item with a Washington dateline on page 1 that carped, "No newspapers are to be forwarded to the army until further notice. . . . It must not be inferred from the absence of interesting news from the Rappahannock that the army is in a condition of idleness."

The decision to curtail newspaper delivery was encouraged by Radical Republicans. They claimed that soldiers saw copies of the Lincoln-baiting *New York Herald* and *New York World* through Democratic chicanery, but did not see journals more favorable to the Lincoln Administration. Such journals were of the "Copperhead" persuasion. The word was applied to individuals and institutions who were loyal to the Union, but believed that the war should be ended and that the South should be permitted to retain its way of life, including slavery. The Republicans met in secret caucus, fumed about it, and decided to contain such sentiments. Thus did the Government come to forbid the forwarding of all newspapers to Union troops.

As the soldiers learned less about the way things were back home, so did back home learn less about the fortunes of war. This did not displease some of Lincoln's generals. "The paucity of news from the army at this time in Northern papers is most satisfactory to me," wrote General William Tecumseh Sherman to his wife, adding: "The press caused the war, the press gives it point and bitterness and as long as the press . . . is allowed to fan the flames of discord, so long must the war last."

The *World* grumbled on its editorial page that the news embargo was a "very strange movement" which would be "very difficult to justify before the country" and complained that there was "universal dissatisfaction" in the nation "with the negro policy the [Republican] radicals are forcing upon government. . . . It is not the newspapers that are responsible for the state of feeling throughout the country and in the army; Mr. Lincoln's advisors are responsible for that. . . . The absence of newspapers will increase and embitter the feelings of the soldiers, who will learn all the government wishes they would not learn from their private correspondence and by report."

In 1864, as the Civil War was about to be won by a skeptical and malcontented North, still disbelieving in itself, smarting from brilliant Southern victories earlier in the war, General George B. McClellan received the Democratic nomination for President. That really should not have surprised anyone. McClellan had never been in favor of the war, although his loyalty to the Union was unquestioned. He had been a competent enough general—indeed, Robert E. Lee would say after the war that McClellan was the most able of his opponents "by all odds." But Lincoln felt that McClellan had "the slows"—he was laggard in committing troops to battle—and some of his fellow generals, including Sherman, were not all that impressed with him. "He never manifested the simple courage and manliness of Grant," Sherman wrote his wife, "and he had too much staff, too many toadies."

Perhaps all that staff and all those toadies were the reason that McClellan was perceived as indecisive during the Peninsular Campaign. His reluctance to commit his troops to battle was starkly unpopular in Washington after the Battle of Antietam, when it was felt that had he only attacked Lee, the war could have been ended then and there. Lincoln relieved him of his command of the Army of the Potomac, and so his emergence as a candidate was hardly a surprise to the Republicans.

Much of the war's beginning had gone disastrously for the North. It had become fashionable to denigrate the effort. The Democrats decided to be in high fashion when they made public their national platform. The model for the fashion was a resolution adopted in August of 1864, drafted by Ohio's controversial candidate for Governor, Clement L. Vallandigham, a most coppery Copperhead indeed, with strong emotional and personal ties to the Confederacy. It was a nomination he received after he took up residence first in the Confederacy, then in Canada (Lincoln was said to be amused by his moves), since the Union Army made it clear that a man with his feelings toward the South belonged not in public office but in jail. The Democrats finessed that by calling him a "peace candidate."

Vallandigham's resolution asserted that after four years of a war that was not won, "justice, humanity, liberty and the public welfare demand that immediate efforts be made for a cessation of hostilities" and expressed the hope that peace could be restored "on the basis of the Federal Union of the States." Stop the war now—the Democrats thought that surely this would prove a popular stand to take.

The Vallandigham resolution would not prove as fashionable as the Democrats hoped. In fact, the timing of its language could not have been worse. No doubt it would have had more appeal a year or so before, when the bumbling North looked like a sure loser. But between the Democratic embrace of Vallandigham's assuaging prose and the November election lay important wins for the North at Cedar Creek and in the Shenandoah Valley. There is no high like winning, and many skeptical Northerners came to feel quickly that maybe the war wasn't as bad as they had thought.

How to feel about the general who sought peace before victory was won? Although McClellan did not personally embrace Vallandigham's resolution, he embraced the party that did, much to his detriment. Vallandigham himself was to lose the vote of soldiers—men who were winning did not want to be told their war was a failure. His prominent identification as a Democrat would not do McClellan any good.

There was no doubt that Democrats and Republicans alike perceived a "soldier's vote," during the late stages of the war and just after it, and the way they dealt with it would significantly alter the relationship between American politics and the American military. For the courting process that was now to begin had never occurred before in American history, at least not with this intensity. From the Democratic point of view, whatever esteem soldiers held for McClellan's unwillingness to commit his troops to battle might just be offset by Republican success in painting McClellan's party as one flirting with sedition, if not permanently engaged to it. The Democrats decided to take no chances with the soldiers. Party regulars wanted to minimize "military influence" at the polls.

Nobody could deny the vote to soldiers just because they were soldiers. That would not have been legal, however desirable it might appear to the Democrats. But under the Constitution, specific voting regulations were left to the states, and when the war started, there was no legislation anywhere that would enable a soldier to vote outside his district. Soldiers, like anyone else, were required to obey the voting regulations of the states where they lived. Of the twenty-five states remaining in the Union for the election of 1864, only fourteen had passed legislation permitting soldiers to vote in the field. Democrats wondered if voting in the field was a good idea, and in some of the states, they managed to stop enabling legislation. Thus they tried to make it difficult, if not impossible, for combat troops to vote.

On the surface, it seemed transparently ludicrous. In most countries in the throes of civil war, armies would not be given time off from battle to vote. But Republicans would not permit themselves to succumb to such senseless prudence, and so they embarked on a plan to give the soldiers that which the Democrats thought they could not possibly give—voting furloughs.

Indiana's Governor, Oliver P. Morton, one of the craftier of the Republicans, was especially resourceful in arranging such things. A man who felt vulnerability keenly, especially when he appeared before his Democratically controlled legislature, he found it abominably frightening even to contemplate the thought of Union soldiers marching toward Confederates on election day instead of to the state's voting booths, where he felt they belonged. The very prospect of the absence of soldiers on election day was most discomfitting to Morton, who had attended innumerable rallies and receptions for them, and suffered the inevitable heartburn therefrom, as though he were a soldier himself. Morton was as much a fixture on such occasions as the red-white-and-blue bunting that invariably adorned their meeting places. Surely such a friend of the soldier could not be faulted if he sought their aid at election time. He thus went to Washington and personally advised Lincoln's War Secretary, Edwin Stanton, that the Republicans might lose the day without the support of the state's fifteen thousand soldiers. Would it be possible to let Indiana troops come home to vote if they appeared to be wounded or sick?

Of course it was possible. Anything was possible. Lincoln personally endorsed the effort in a letter to William Tecumseh Sherman in September, which makes no mention of "sick" soldiers but leaves no doubt of the election's importance:

> Indiana is the only important State voting in October, whose soldiers cannot vote in the field. Anything you can do to let her soldiers, or any part of them, go home and vote at the State election will be greatly in point. . . . This is in no sense an order, but is merely intended to impress you with the importance, to the army itself, of your doing all you safely can, yourself being the judge of what you can safely do.

More soldiers going home in the middle of a war? Sherman was tired of the very concept of furloughs, especially when he was fearful he would be overwhelmed at any moment by the rebels. His was not an idle concern. The previous April, he had complained to his wife that he would have twenty thousand fewer men than he had anticipated for an upcoming campaign because of furloughs, and these had not even been asked for by Lincoln. ". . . when men get home they forget their comrades here. . . . Our armies are now weaker than at any point in the war."

Dutiful officer that he was, General Sherman complied with his commander-in-chief's request but distinctly felt that he was in charge of an evaporating Army. "Our armies vanish before our eyes and it is useless to complain," he wrote to his wife, "because the election is more important than the war. Our armies are merely paper armies. I have 40,000 cavalry on paper but less than 5,000 in fact. Mr. Lincoln will be [elected], but I hope it will be done quick, that voters may come to their regiments and not give the rebels [that which] they know so well to take." The soldiers themselves were rather amused at all the "sick leave" they got, and one of them wrote that "Indiana troops seemed to be rather sickly."

The furloughs or sick leaves or whatever they were rankled the Democrats at least as much as the front-line circulation of the *New York Herald* and *New York World* had bothered Republicans. The fact that soldiers on leave in some areas took the time to vandalize the offices of newspapers friendly to the Democrats made their visits all the more burdensome. Even worse, from the Democrats' point of view, was evidence that voting soldiers were made so enthusiastic by their furloughs that they voted where they weren't supposed to, and perhaps more than once in the same election. Morton said he needed fifteen thousand, not a paltry nine thousand. The Republicans may have obliged, since Democrats alleged afterward that Michigan troops had voted in the Indiana election. It might have been argued that they simply got off the train too early. But how to explain the six thousand Massachusetts men who also voted in Indiana? Or the thousands more from Illinois, Pennsylvania, and Ohio?

There were questions about the election of 1864 as to whether soldiers would relate strongly to one of their own, George McClellan, and see it as a chance to vindicate him after Lincoln's removal of him from top commands. The Democrats hoped that they would, but as it turned out, they woefully underestimated Lincoln's ability to get votes from the very same people he had sent to war. After his removal of McClellan, Lincoln had first moved to make clear that he did not approve of the indifference he saw toward the maimed and wounded men who got early discharges and who came to the cities. For example, he wrote to Postmaster General Montgomery Blair regarding the preference he would give veterans or their survivors who applied for jobs:

Yesterday little endorsements of mine were sent to you in two cases of postmasterships sought for widows whose husbands have fallen in battles of this war. These cases . . . brought me to reflect more attentively than I had before done, as to what is fairly due from us here in the dispensing of patronage toward the men who, by fighting our battles, bear the chief burden of saving our country. My conclusion is that, other claims and qualifications being equal, they have the better right, and this is especially applicable to the disabled soldier and the deceased soldier's family.

Lincoln approached soldiers personally, undoubtedly because he believed in what he had asked them to do, but also because he wanted to be reelected and he knew their votes might be important. "Old Abe was up here a few days ago and saw for himself the state of things," wrote soldier Felix Brannigan to his sister. "He, we are all convinced, is the soldier's friend, and the man alone above all in the right place. We feel that he takes an interest in us and that he has done what not one of ten thousand in a similar position would have brains enough to think of doing i.e. to take nobody's word, or reports got up for effect. He came and saw for himself."

When the election of 1864 was over, it seemed that maybe both the Democrats and the Republicans had doted excessively on the soldier vote, because it wasn't even close. Soldiers voted for Lincoln, 78 percent, as opposed to General McClellan's 22 percent. Clearly, it was the civilians who were more narrowly divided and who should have been more intensively courted, although it probably would not have changed the final outcome—McClellan was not that strong a candidate. In terms of total votes, Lincoln received 2,216,067 as opposed to General McClellan's 1,808,725, a spread of only 407,342 in a total vote of roughly four million. Of all votes cast, Lincoln had 55.06 percent of the popular vote to McClellan's 44.04 percent. Lincoln carried the electoral vote handily, however, with 212 to McClellan's 21.

After it was over, a relieved Lincoln said that the election "has demonstrated that a people's government can sustain a national election in the midst of a great civil war." Whatever else it demonstrated, the election put the lie to those who tended to see the soldier vote as some sort of threat to civilian rule in the United States.

Given the courtship, censorship, stroking, and shuttlecock political furloughing to which they had been exposed, one might have expected soldiers to return home just a little vexed and chafing to share in the political power which they had created by saving the Union. This was not the case. For a golden moment, there seemed to be a self-satisfied passivity among the

Union veterans after the war ended. Perhaps it was just the euphoria of winning. The cliché of euphoria is said to visit humankind after every period of warmaking, and if that is so, maybe the spring and summer of 1865 saw this kind of psycholepsy, a belief that there had been a graduation of sorts, that the Union was saved and that the nation would never be divided again and, even more, that there would be no more war. Humans want to believe in such success even if the politicians who lead them more predictably plan for failure.

Whatever it was in those initial months after Appomattox, it lasted only a few months and it was not totally appreciated at the time. The indifference of veterans to things political was there well into the summer, even in the face of massive unemployment and their realization that they were being discriminated against. Perhaps it was this way because even though they had shared the burden of a great struggle, they could not become the monolith the rest of the people feared they would become. They could not take the quick, decisive steps necessary to become a military elite, any more than the soldiers of the Revolution could. The bonds that were forged in combat were not strong enough in those first few months to transform the veterans into a cohesive, savvy group.

Despite expressed fears throughout American history of military power politics and even a coup, most of the people who have fought our wars have remained respectful of the Constitution and largely behaved as our Founding Fathers hoped they would. Civil War veterans were no exception. They were, after all, citizen soldiers—civilians who had been soldiers only briefly. Citizenship in a nation given to individual freedom is seductive stuff, even if the freedom be only the freedom to be unemployed. The veterans' perceived right to be individuals in a free society was far more powerful a force than whatever they thought they might gain by collective action as veterans. And so they remained divided among themselves, as civilians are wont to do, as to their expectations and how to go about achieving those expectations.

And yet, a kind of anger was contained within their passivity. They wanted something. *Something!* Some recognition that had been lost in the triumphal parades; something more tangible than having a beer in a downtown Manhattan garden, no matter how well tended the greenery. For example, a job. If there had been jobs, or if Americans and their elected officials had not been quite so given to squeaky preachifying about the work ethic, the men who fought the war might have melted back into society as those who feared their potential power wanted them to. But such sermons only reflected secular values. If any minister or public official had preached preference, or even tolerance of the soldier come home, he would not have been in character for that time. Alger's novels, like all pulp produced before and after, were popular only because he was expressing something that American society wanted to believe in. The virtuous society believed in every man for himself. And so it was.

The beginning of the end of the passive Civil War veteran started innocently enough. In August of 1865, some veterans held a mass meeting and marched around New York City "with a view to enlisting the sympathy of our merchants and others." Before the month was up, the New York veterans were complaining to the press that although they were "making the most laudable efforts to resume their former occupations . . . the great number of them have not succeeded in getting employment and cannot support their families." They formed something called the United States Soldiers and Sailors Protective Society, and the press reported that all they wanted was "the amelioration of their condition and the benefit of the country." In a phrase that seems to have come out of the goodness of Horace Greeley's cockeyed optimism rather than the reality of what might be revealed in a more clinical inspection of what was going on, the *Tribune* told its readers the veterans had "no political purpose."

The *Tribune* had a right to its observations, but this one must have caused a few to chuckle. In Indiana, for example, Governor Oliver Morton, who owed favors not only to veterans of his state but to those from Illinois, Pennsylvania, Ohio, and Massachusetts as well, continued to find time in his busy schedule to address veterans' groups and emphasize his belief, no doubt sincerely felt, that in his state, at least, veterans' organizations ought to be strengthened. In peace as in war, Morton regarded the men who had borne arms as essential to his political strength, which was estimable; he was destined to be elected to the United States Senate. Politicians in Massachusetts, Wisconsin, Illinois, and elsewhere also seemed to take pleasure in telling veterans how proud everyone was of them; how everyone who was anyone totally supported their views.

Seven months passed. The nonpolitical purpose of the veterans noted by the *Tribune* was not holding up well under the springtime sun, and the press began to notice it, even though the early signs came not in the *Tribune* but in the trade press. One hint appeared in the parochial *Army and Navy Journal,* which carried a small notice that there had been a meeting of veterans of the Army and Navy in New York and that they had formed a union of sorts, "for mutual confidence and mutual help." There was no suggestion in this article that veterans were as nonpolitical as choirboys. Precisely what did they mean by "mutual confidence and mutual help"?

The New York veterans had, in fact, adopted a position platform, which they called an "address," even though nobody bothered to deliver it but which, in any event, they made public. It said, in part, that "while soldiers and sailors in union perpetuate the patriotism which led them to battle, it is deemed fitting that they should remind one another of certain obligations of gratitude, imposed through their services, upon the nation at large."

In other towns and other states, veterans of the Civil War seemed to be doing much the same thing. But no national organizational efforts were apparent from reading the newspapers. However, not all the press was as deludable as Horace Greeley's fine *New York Tribune* proved to be in this instance. The *Chicago Times,* for one, told its readers that this new creation was, in fact, partisan in nature. The *Chicago Times'* perceptiveness came nearly a year after the *Tribune* made its observation. More important, Chicago was a lot closer to Decatur than was New York, and Decatur was where the organizing action was.

Early in the spring of 1866, less than a year after Appomattox, Dr. Benjamin Stephenson, a Decatur obstetrician who had served nonobstetrically in the Union Army, made up his mind to form a "national soldiers' mutual benefit society" whose name would be the Grand Army of the Republic and which would be completely secret, down to the handshake and reverently whispered password. With the birth of the Grand Army, Dr. Stephenson made his most prominent delivery, a bawling child whose precocity would be remembered long after its timely demise. Within the G.A.R.'s extraordinary machinations over the next half century, veterans would achieve collective power unprecedented before and unmatched since in American history.

At first glance, New York City might have been expected to become the locus for an aggressive national organization of dissatisfied veterans. Certainly other dissatisfied Americans with all kinds of causes felt at home there, before and after the Civil War. But Illinois was especially fertile ground for such a development. Lincoln's assassination a year earlier had left its politics in a muddle. Republicans there (and elsewhere) wanted to wrest control of the party away from President Johnson, who, without Lincoln's stature, was trying to follow Lincoln's plan for peace. It would prove ruinous; his impeachment ordeal lay only two years away.

As political predators circled each other, looking for voters who would support them, somebody took note of Stephenson's effort. It would have been difficult not to, for the good doctor had a very clear idea of what he wanted to do, and wasn't bashful about telling politicians and veterans what it was, even though most of the press that covered the Grand Army at the time gave the impression that it did not understand the organization's motives. And for reasons unclear, the doctor went down in many history books as a man who was manipulated by politicians, whereas the evidence at hand suggests that he was as good a puppeteer as he was a puppet.

The full scope of his intent and the single-mindedness with which he pursued his objectives did not become widely known publicly until years later, when his remaining letters were referred to by his daughter in her *Memoir of Dr. Stephenson.* ". . . whatever views we may have as an order," the doctor said in one letter written shortly after the G.A.R.'s founding, "we, as an order, have nothing to do with politics. We are free, untrammeled; free to take whatever side appears to be for the interest of the soldier."

Most of Dr. Stephenson's letters were burned by his wife ("she was ignorant of their value," dryly explained daughter Mary). But those remaining clearly showed that from the outset, he was determined to involve veterans deeply in the political process and change the way they had been treated in the months following the war. He complained that soldiers "can't even get employment as a day-laborer, provided the people can get somebody else cheaper. . . . The offices, promised to the soldiers, have been few and far between," he wrote. "The citizens are generally very careful about allowing a soldier to run for office, unless it is some party that is greatly in the minority." And on another occasion: "The order is destined to be the power in the land and stay-at-home politicians are beginning to tremble in their boots, and are more willing to feed and clothe the poor widows and orphans of our noble dead soldiers. . . . The pioneers in this order will not be forgotten."

The style and the purpose of the Grand Army were all developed by Stephenson, who, according to his daughter, all but lost his practice in trying to get the cause off the ground. It was widely supposed at the time that Stephenson was aided and abetted by the Rev. William Rutledge, who during the war had served as chaplain with the 14th Illinois Infantry and who said that he and the doctor dreamed up the Grand Army one evening over the camp fire. Stephenson's daughter later disputed this. Her father and her father alone, she claimed, founded the Grand Army of the Republic.

However laudatory Stephenson's feelings may have been about ending discrimination against veterans, and whatever influence the Reverend Mr. Rutledge may have had on the new organization in the way of imbuing it with Christian charity and forgiveness, the ritual developed for new members somehow lacked Lincolnesque compassion and Lincoln's desire to heal the wounds of war. The new members, called "recruits," were hooded so that they could not see, then marched around the meeting room, which the G.A.R. called an "encampment." At one point they kneeled before an altar and an open coffin, symbolizing the soldiers who were killed by the rebels. They were also brought before a mock firing squad—a gentle reminder of what would happen to them if they ever told anyone any of the secrets of the ritual—and were reminded by the senior vice-commander, ". . . remember, ever, that Traitors shall be punished!"

"The Penalty of Treason Is Death!" sang out the membership. After this interlude, the new members were given the secret password—"McPherson"—and told the secret handshake, which was interlocking pinkies.

To those then known as Radical Republicans, such stuff, however un-Christian it might be, was yeast for the baking—or at least the half-baking—of political ideas. With Radical Republican help, the G.A.R. spread first around Illinois, then into Indiana (where it held its first national convention on November 20, 1866), then to Ohio, Wisconsin, Missouri, Iowa, Arkansas, and Kentucky. In the East, early chapters were formed in Philadelphia, Camden, New York City, and Rochester, although initially there didn't seem to be as much interest in the East as there was in the Midwest. Where interest sagged, as was the case temporarily in the East, the same Republicans planted Grand Army seeds with existing veterans' groups, among them the Soldiers' and Sailors' National Union League, the Boys in Blue clubs and, logically enough, the Republican Veteran Union clubs.

"The order is growing with superhuman strides in the East, and they threaten to beat us," warned Stephenson in one of his letters that escaped his wife's torch. He exhorted his followers, "We must not let them. We are glad to see the work going ahead. It is bound to be the great power, and those who take the lead will not be forgotten." The suggestion that loyalty would not be forgotten and that those who consistently helped the Grand Army might themselves be helped was alluded to in his letters more than once.

In Massachusetts, at least, the local organizing of veterans—unrelated to what Stephenson was trying to hatch in Decatur—was finally beginning to be watched. A few seemed to realize what the soldiers' union movement represented. The nation, by its indifference to the problems of the unemployed and dispirited men who had fought the war, had created a problem that need not have existed.

In September of 1865, while the veterans' groups were still regarded as benign and several months before Stephenson had finalized his own thoughts on the Grand Army, a letter appeared in the *Boston Advertiser* from someone who thought he could see where the veterans were going and felt compelled to warn the public that they should be given their due. Without such consideration, the writer predicted forebodingly,

> . . . we shall generate a faction, a political power, to be known as the soldiers' vote. . . . I wonder if our state politicians remember that 17,000 men can give an election to either party. . . . Unless some action is immediately taken, we shall, in a few years, have the whole country engaged in an endeavor to suppress and destroy an evil which a proper sense of justice and gratitude exhibited now would have prevented.

The letter writer was not a lone prophet. As he knew that veterans-become-civilians could not be expected to remain indifferent to their own destruction, so did the Sanitary Commission. Early in 1865, before the war ended, the commission had written to President Lincoln expressing its concern about the prospect of rising unemployment among returning soldiers. It urged that the Government set an example for prejudiced employers in the private sector by giving preference to veterans for Government jobs. Lincoln probably would have seen that suggestion through to fruition—he was too wise not to—but his assassination threw the Government into such disarray that problems facing veterans were eclipsed by other issues.

Indeed, there were portions of Government that did not even see veterans as needing jobs as much as a little charity and a lot of sympathy. The order of the day was more accurately stated not by the Sanitary Commission, but by the Massachusetts Board of State Charities. This august body issued a report in January of 1866 showing that its understanding of the condition of veterans was matched only by the ease with which it inserted poetry into its prose:

> There is, indeed, danger at this very moment that the earnest desire of the people to show their gratitude to those who carried the country triumphantly through the war, may lead to the formation of institutions upon unsound principles, which may prove to be nuisances, and cumber the field of charity in the next generation. . . . Better the poorest hut in a retired hamlet, with its single family gathered round the hearthstone, where,
>
> > the broken soldier, kindly bade to stay
> > sits by the fire and talks the night away,

than a showy building, set upon a hill, with its corps of officials, its parade of charity, its clock-work and steam for doing domestic work so thoroughly that it is robbed of all its old and endearing associations.

. . . the natural desire of the deserving soldier, disabled in war is . . . to be at or near his old home and among his old associates . . . wearing his orders of merit—his honorable scars—to keep alive in their hearts the feelings of patriotism and gratitude.

Not until April of 1866 did President Johnson pledge his cooperation to help those soldiers who wanted something more than spending the evening in the poorest hut in town, and who were able and willing to work. Washington politicians were flooded with requests from job seekers, but most of them, unlike Indiana's Governor Morton and some others, saw no reason to replace party faithful with those of uncertain conviction. Even if they had seen the problem for what it was, it was too late, by the spring of 1866, to thwart the Grand Army. Stephenson had too much energy and too many legitimate issues for that to happen.

The Grand Army organized itself not along clear-cut military lines, as might have been expected of a group calling itself an army, but along lines similar to state political parties. Precinct clubs were called posts, and these were supervised by a state organization known as a department. For a time, there were also county units as well, but they withered from lack of interest. All in all, however, there was much interest, and most of it accrued to the Radical Republicans, who were out gunning for Democrats. Indeed, the Grand Army momentum so pleased the Republican National Committee that it endorsed a plan for the creation of musical groups known as the Singing Boys in Blue, who appeared at political gatherings all around the country to render the lyrics of war songs and somehow preserve the Government from what Republicans saw as the seemingly interminable seditious behavior of the Democrats.

In the fall of 1866, while the Singing Boys in Blue were still in good voice, five veterans showed up in Washington and issued a proclamation of sorts, strongly urging fellow veterans to establish an army in order to protect the "loyal majority"—Republicans, of course—who had just been elected to Congress. The five—Messrs. Curtis, Hinton, Bennett, Morse, and Dudley—said such an army was necessary "to show how stern loyalty can rebuke treason," and, according to the *New York Tribune*, "to prove that the threats of a treacherous executive against the legislative branch of government cannot intimidate a free people."

The *Tribune*'s response to this doomed-to-fail proposal could not have endeared the newspaper to women readers, even though Greeley supported women's rights and women were used to hearing this sort of thing: "Let us be calm. Let us, in such a tremendous emergency, leave hysteria to the naturally hysterical sex. . . . What reason is there for apprehending that any considerable number of our returned soldiers will be betrayed into acts of folly and of crime?" The paper was correct, however, in its opinion of the proclamation, although there were some who saw it as evidence of too much Radical Republican influence on veterans, and possibly the prelude to developments that could lead to a military coup or another major conflict.

There never was the threat of a coup by soldiers nor of a war following a war by the defeated Southerners. As the Macon, Georgia, *Journal and Messenger* put it in 1867, "We had much rather raise corn, meat and cotton, and do what we can to repair our dilapidated fortunes, than to take a hand in any new revolution." But within two years of the end of the war, President Johnson's reconciliatory efforts to make the United States a reality again were coming under heavy attack. During this trying time, the Grand Army did little to disabuse the skeptics who thought that organized veterans were trouble. The G.A.R. offered scant evidence that the Union troops who had won the war were now in the vanguard of those trying to keep the peace and the stability of duly elected Government. Grand Army brass wanted no part of Johnson's moves toward reconciliation and seemed to feel that any move away from harsh punishment of the South was in itself a kind of treason.

"No thinking man can examine the acts of the President, his dissertion of the party who [elected] him to office, his affiliation with the rebels since that time, and taking council with the [vilest] of traitors . . ." complained a letter written by F. M. Thomas, adjutant of Post No. 1, Grand Army of the District of Washington of the Department of the Potomac. ". . . he almost defies Congress to try to impeach him. . . . I lost one foot while fighting for my Country and think the cause for which I fought [too] sacred to be [sacrificed] to the will of any man even if he is the President of this Great Republic."

When Ulysses S. Grant took office in 1868 as the eighteenth President, Grand Army vinegar was transformed into wine, at least temporarily. After all, the man who accepted Lee's surrender at Appomattox was now in the White House. The indisposition that persisted during President Johnson's tenure—a furuncle he did not cause but which he could not lance—was, for veterans, thus soothed. Even though they could remember the discrimination they suffered after war's end, the veterans themselves were tired of the ranting of their own organization and they turned, finally, to their own prospects in time of peace.

Their born-again mellowness was not to last. But for now, it was welcome to America-at-large. For if veterans had become bored with Grand Army posturing, no less had other Americans grown tired of the same thing. When, in 1869, the Grand Army proved instrumental in introducing Memorial Day as national holiday in the North, the event was looked upon with a mixture of hope and apprehension by *The New York Times:*

> National anniversaries in all countries are apt to be wearisome nuisances; and if we may so say without heresy to the popular gods, they are particularly stale, flat and unprofitable here in America. . . . [But] to honor those who have died for the Union; the memories it awakens—not vindictive but tender and grateful: the cordial ceremony of the day—to bedeck the hallowed grounds where heroes sleep with the freshest flowers of Spring; all these combine to make it a memorial day as useful and suggestive to the living as it is significant and grateful to the dead.

That editorial was clearly prepared before Memorial Day had actually been observed—newspapers routinely did and do such things—and certainly before anyone at the *Times* knew about the ugly scene at Arlington Heights Churchyard, in which Marines prevented Southerners from placing flowers on the graves of rebels.

After it had a chance to review the articles written by its own reporters and correspondents, as well as the *Herald*'s coverage of events at the churchyard, the *Times* ran another editorial, titled "Shall the Hatchet Ever Be Buried?" It left no doubt that as far as the newspaper was concerned, its worst fears about Memorial Day had been realized. The editorial was written without specific mention of what happened at Arlington, which had been reported in another newspaper, but the *Times'* anger was palpable:

> The North and West have had their Decoration Day and published reports lead to the conclusion that it has not been a great success. In this City it was a conspicuous failure, and we see no reason for believing that it was anywhere much else. As a military display it challenged no particular notice. As an attempt to organize and consecrate a new national ceremony—to dedicate a day to the memory of the dead, in the name of the cause for which they died—it commanded little support.
>
>   . . . it is apparent that the movement did not commend itself to the judgment or feeling of the country. . . . Decoration Day, as it has been inaugurated, is a day that can never become national. It is an appeal to the patriotism of one section at the expense of the pride and feeling due the other section. . . . It is a method of reminding the North that it is a conqueror, and

the South that it is conquered. It is an attempt to convert even the graves of the dead into testimony affecting the history of millions who are living. As managed by reverend gentlemen here and at Washington, and elsewhere, it is an occasion for heaping epithets of infamy upon one set of graves while piling flowers upon another set—for reviving the bitter memories of conflict, scattering afresh the seeds of hate, and, under the pretense of glorifying Union heroes, invoking curses upon the misguided but scarcely less heroic Confederate dead. . . .

Concentric circles. Patterns in abstract geometry that would prove endless. It did not really matter how the aftermath of such a war was contemplated by the likes of Nathaniel Hawthorne before it ended or by the *Times* or the *Herald* after it ended. The veterans, who had either been ignored or discriminated against, had now acted in their own behalf. But they remained an underclass to the intellectuals, who found them a bit of a bore; an embarrassment to the businessmen, who refused to hire them; a convenience to the politicians, who used them; and something apart to the civilians, who could not understand what soldiers-come-home really wanted or why they felt they had to have a secret handshake.

For Americans, talk about the real or imagined problems faced by veterans was like talking about the war itself, and nobody wanted to do that. This was a war the likes of which Americans had never seen before, and, God willing, would never see again. They wanted to put the divisions of nationhood behind them. And so, of necessity, they put the reminders of those divisions behind them, too.

11
Bounties and Blacks

Soldiers, I tell you, you can well afford to wait; for the time is coming, and is not far distant, when those who enslaved you, shall be forced to acknowledge, that to have been a colored soldier, is to be a citizen, and to have been an advocate of slavery, is but another name for traitor.
—Farewell of Colonel T. H. Barrett to the officers and men of the 62nd U.S. Colored Infantry, January 4, 1866

I am about to be mustered out without any bounty. . . . I have no space to live. After serving the U.S.A. almost three years then to put me out without anything. I am sorry to know that.
—Letter written in the first person singular but signed by two Louisiana black corporals to the Secretary of War, January 31, 1867

The very idea of bounties, extra pay, for those who enlisted to fight for the North in the Civil War never did sit well with Americans. The war—at least as the abstraction for a few if not the reality for everyone—was a principled struggle to save the Union. Inducing a man to fight for such principles by offering him common money tended to sully the idealism of the enterprise, or so thought many of the civilians who watched the war from afar. The reverent novels of Horatio Alger, ever-spewing of all manner of virtue, preached that hard work and goodness would be rewarded. But he was talking about civilian work and civilian rewards. Civilian Americans found it hard to believe that soldiers who had killed and maimed and destroyed would want the same thing. It was understandable that soldiers would defend capitalism, but those whose interests they had represented could not comprehend how the warriors in such a noble struggle might want to enjoy the material rewards of the society they had helped preserve.

The men who were promised such money upon enlisting were viewed with a certain scorn after the war was over and even before it was over. The Union soldier never had been imbued with the unqualified confidence of those he fought for. Indeed, even before the guns were silenced, *Harper's* complained that the ranks were "swelled with idiots, blind men, [and] paralytics," and blamed the Army's personnel problems on the examining doctors who let them in. *The New York Times* was even more unflattering and charged that soldier brokers, boards of enrollments, and doctors had given the Army "cripples from birth; men potentially blind; idiots from town farms; people with hernia of long standing; puny boys of fourteen or fifteen; men being constantly claimed as subjects of other governments; graduates from the Five Points of New York; escaped prisoners from the Dry Tortugas; rebel adventurers from Canada and elsewhere . . . and hundreds of others who cannot understand one word of the English language." The *Times* also said that the Army was literally filled with "unprincipled adventurers and vagabonds" as well as "limping imbeciles." Hardly the sort who would be deserving of bounties, even if they managed to win.

And then there were men of even more dubious rectitude, who had taken bounties and failed to fight in a manly way. Or, even worse in some instances, to show up for the war. Bounty jumpers in the East were mired in despicability, not perceived with any more charity than were horse thieves in the West.

As the war neared an end, the soldiers who fought it started to think, as they kicked the mud off their boots and bunked down in their bare-floor shantytown barracks and wind-shuddering tents, about how they would spend the money that was owed them. But in the towns and cities to which they planned to return, there was a feeling of uncongeniality about them and what they stood for. To those who waited at home, the Army appeared filled with men who sought rank lucre for their spilled blood instead of the pure, unabashed, everlasting thanks of a grateful nation, as the signs along parade routes had so generously offered. And so the Army had to be purged "of the villainous distemper with which it has been so wickedly and willfully inoculated," maintained a feisty *New York Times* correspondent named J. R. Hamilton.

Reporter Hamilton, one of those who covered the war for a fourteen-year-old newspaper that Lincoln rather liked, complained in one dispatch that "dearly purchased men in buckram" had cost the Government $1,000 each even "before they have lifted a finger in battle." Some of them, Hamilton maintained, were nothing more than "deserters from the rebel army" who were joining the Union cause not because they believed in it but for money.

Given all the bluster about those who had received or were going to receive bounties, it was inevitable that men who had enlisted without receiving so much as an extra penny would come to hunger for battle money. The soldiers who were nonbountied had wounds that hurt as much as those who were bountied; the time and liberty they lost while in service was just as precious to them; their need for grubstakes to fight the peace was the same as that of the civilians they had left safely behind. And so using their newly founded veterans' groups, they pushed for parity.

Early in 1866, a smart new magazine called *The Nation*—then only a scant half-year old—found the yearning for bounties among soldiers something to complain about, for in soldierly interest in material things, the editors apparently thought, lay the seeds of national insolvency.

> There is a scheme on foot to equalize the bounty of all volunteers who served during the war. It appears there has been already paid in bounties upwards of three hundred millions of dollars, or nearly one-tenth of the national debt. If each man who served were paid as [the scheme] proposed . . . three hundred millions more would be necessary, making in all one-fifth of the national debt. . . . The whole bounty system was one of the most frightful sources of corruption ever opened on an afflicted people. An attempt to equalize the bounties would open another almost as bad. . . . What Congress ought to be doing instead of considering such preposterous schemes as this, is forming a good militia law, which would give us a trained army of the bone and the sinew of the country whenever we wanted it, on short notice.

It would not have been unlikely for a *Nation* reader also to have read *Harper's Weekly,* and so it must have been rather galling for those who had read in *Harper's,* just six months earlier, that a soldiers' home had been established on Howard Street in New York City, and that it offered military men in transit "a good number of sleeping rooms, a dining hall and an excellent library." The place was run by Colonel Vincent Colyer and his wife, who, according to *Harper's,* spent a great deal of time distributing fruit and berries to soldiers and were, perforce, deserving of financial support from the magazine's readers. But why would anyone want to help the colonel and his good wife when veterans were trying to equalize bounties and drive the nation even deeper into debt? If fruit and berries weren't enough for the Union's warriors, perhaps the Revolution's ministers had been right to warn against profligacy as they did after the first civil war, eighty years earlier. Or so thought the fiscal conservatives who dug in their heels as the veterans pressed for more.

Despite its wit and erudition, *The Nation* did not dwell on how people would be induced to join the rawboned ever-ready militia of its dreams and fight on cue, without succumbing to the soldier's classic consideration about his pay, or what he, personally, would get from the struggle. For there were and would always be soldiers who wanted much more than the Colyers' kindnesses, and this, in the eyes of much of the press, was something to lament.

The Nation had an unlikely kindred spirit in the *Army and Navy Journal,* which never pretended to be witty and erudite and proved it each time a new issue came out. The *Journal* catered mostly to the interests of career soldiers, and it was not especially sensitive to the needs and wants of the men the professionals called ''sunshine soldiers''—civilians who bore arms, perhaps with great valor, but really only wanted to survive so that they could become civilians again. When the quest for bounty by such civilians seemed as though it would never end, the *Journal* printed this item, which essentially advocated paying no attention to the citizen soldiers who had fought the war:

> A number of discharged soldiers who enlisted in the Regular Army before the breaking out of the rebellion, and served during the war, have . . . petitioned Congress to be put on the same footing as to bounty with soldiers who enlisted during the war. . . . No attention has been paid to them heretofore and it is not likely that Congress, in these times of economy and retrenchment, will be seized with any spasm of liberality that will cause the adoption of a new policy toward these soldiers.

Certainly nobody in the postwar era wanted to be accused of being spastically liberal. The war had been spastic enough; peace was a time to be very certain about the right things. It was far more important to make certain that the South be reminded, from time to time, who won the war and that the men who achieved the victory not be coddled.

The slowness of Government to pay many promised bounties made homecoming difficult for all Union soldiers, but none more so than the approximately 200,000 who were black. Black soldiers certainly had the lofty goal of ending slavery in their minds when they enlisted to fight. But they sought promises of bounties, too, because as America's wretched underclass, abused, cheated, and barred wherever they went, they had virtually no chance to amass the capital necessary to improve themselves. Thus their bounties were vitally important to them as they came home, especially if that home was in the South, which was filled with defeated, disgruntled veterans of the Confederate Army.

If Northern veterans felt alienated and despised, their Southern counterparts felt even worse, for they were not only soldiers, but losers. In aimless poverty, in listless cities, and on farms fallen to ruin, they would have become mean under the best of circumstances. Under ham-handed Reconstructionists, they became meaner.

Six veterans in such straits met in Pulaski, Tennessee, and formed a fraternity of sorts which derived its name from *kuklos,* the Greek word for "circle." The fraternity was called the Ku Klux Klan, and it was invented in December of 1865—just in time for Christmas. The Klan said it wanted to "protect the weak, the innocent and defenseless," to "protect and defend the Constitution of the United States," and "to protect the people from unlawful seizure."

The Klansmen had an odd way of living up to their high-sounding purpose. They sometimes worked at night, roaming the countryside cloaked in white sheets which, they led blacks to believe, were the ghosts of slain rebel soldiers who had risen up from their graves to punish not only men and women of color, who had no business being free, but also the whites responsible for the undoing of the South. The Klan owed its existence not just to racism but to Radical Reconstructionism, which was quite vindictive in Tennessee. And although former Confederate soldiers were the Klan's founders, its ranks came to be filled with equally disaffected and vindictive civilians.

The Klan, and other secret societies that sprang up in the South during this period, reminded the homecoming blacks that they had an imperative to take care of themselves quickly and effectively. The promised bounties, slow in coming though they may have been, seemed a reasonable way to do that. Bounties were first approved to black soldiers who were free before the beginning of the war or who had enlisted in the draft that President Lincoln announced in October 1863. The program was later expanded to blacks who enlisted after July 1864, in order to induce more of them to join. Slaves who enlisted before 1864 received no such consideration. The Government took the position that the freedom they received was adequate reward.

The bounties, uneven though they were in their scope and administration, did something to ameliorate the discrimination blacks had suffered during the war when they were paid less than whites. Moreover, they had been as discriminated against in the service as when, free or slave, they had civilian status. Even though they repeatedly proved themselves in battle, as they had in wars before, black privates went through most of the war receiving $10 a month and $3 more for clothing, while their white counterparts received $13 plus a $3.50 clothing allowance. This, even though Lincoln had personally praised their valor and no less than the *New York Tribune* took note of their sacrifice in an editorial that said, "The Negro gave one in three of his number to the cause of freedom. Did we with our valor do half as well?"

When the bounties seemed slow in arriving, blacks and whites alike pressed the issue and both races used claims agents as intermediaries. But the blacks, especially vulnerable and unable to fend for themselves, fell prey to unscrupulous claims agents, who cheated them. In the South, where so many lived, they also fell prey to the Klan, and the bounties promised to black soldiers in many instances went uncollected.

Veterans were encouraged to look to the Grand Army of the Republic for support in their efforts to get bounty money still owed them and to deal with the many other problems they had in readjusting to civilian life. But black veterans who had served the Union found their problems only became even more complicated when they approached the G.A.R. The Grand Army was certainly aware that blacks had acquitted themselves well in the war. It was known that some 38,000 black troops had lost their lives fighting for the Union. In terms of their number in the Army, their mortality rate was fully a third higher than that of white troops, even though they entered the war late. As was the case in other wars, before and after the War Between the States, blacks served in high-risk areas. But as the Klan was unable to live up to the letter of its stated purposes, so was the Grand Army unable to fulfill Dr. Stephenson's pledge to help the Union soldier—if he happened to be black.

The G.A.R.'s power waxed and waned as the remaining decades of the nineteenth century passed, but it underwent a distinct resurgence in the 1880s. Civil War veterans had grown older and were thus more vulnerable; they looked to the nation's most important veterans' organization with hope, and no more so than in the South, which was still trying to regain the vitality it had lost at Appomattox. By the early 1890s, there were some three hundred G.A.R. posts in the old states of the Confederacy, offering the 110,000 Union veterans who lived there assistance, comradeship, and the succor reasonably owed to aging soldiers. But in most cases, those soldiers were white, not black, despite the conspicuous contributions blacks had made to the Union victory.

Louisiana was where the issue first came to a head. Grand Army members had quietly refused to admit Negroes. There was nothing publicly said about the admissions policy until 1889, when the Louisiana state commander, Jacob Gray, authorized the formation of some colored posts. His reasons for so doing may have been his respect for his fellow veterans and his disregard of their color. But to his opponents in the Grand Army, he did it out of spite and drunkenness. They alleged that when Jefferson Davis died, Gray respectfully decided to go to the funeral and, in fact, acted as a pallbearer. As he helped carry the mortal remains of the Confederacy's first and last president to the cemetery, his G.A.R. badge was on his lapel, there for all the world to see, much to the dismay of some Grand Army folk. So fond was Gray of Davis, said Gray's critics, that he ordered Louisiana's Grand Army members to attend the funeral.

It was a gesture of which Lincoln might well have approved. But Lincoln had been gone for nearly a quarter of a century, and there was nothing remotely like him in the White House presence of Benjamin Harrison. If it was true that former rebel and Union soldiers had already paraded together at Independence Day celebrations—that had happened in Philadelphia at the Centennial Celebration of July 4, 1876—it was also true that the South was not even close to forgetting its humiliation nor the Yankee efforts to crush the vestiges of its antebellum customs.

Grand Army posts passed resolutions condemning Jacob Gray, who, it was alleged, was so angry at those who had failed to honor Davis that he saw to it that seven hundred black former Union soldiers became part of the Grand Army in Louisiana in the course of a single week. White Grand Army members said that the black veterans were "aggressive and insolent in manner" and Gray's successor as commander (the incident had not left Gray with much of a future as a leader of the Grand Army) claimed that Gray admitted them in an act of "fraud and most flagrant rascality, and all done from a spirit of revenge."

A great many G.A.R. members in Louisiana seemed to agree that although they, as Union soldiers, had fought a war in the nominal interests of egalitarianism, there was little point in stirring the pot further. A Louisiana delegate to the twenty-fifth national encampment said, ". . . we live in a country that we have chosen as our homes. We have made up our minds to live there. Our children are growing up there. They marry. It is right that we should conform to the social laws and rules that surround us." Indeed, the assistant quartermaster general of the Louisiana G.A.R. warned that if black veterans became G.A.R. members in that state, white veterans would probably quit. The commander of the Tennessee G.A.R., William J. Ramage, said he did not see how the G.A.R. could invite blacks to form "colored posts" because men of color would not know how to run them. White Northerners would not behave any better than their Southern counterparts. Was the social mixing of the two races why the War Between the States was fought? Not really, said leading members of the G.A.R., who, despite all the praise of black valor in the New York press, continued to feel that black soldiers weren't soldiers in the sense that the white men had been. "When I enlisted in April, 1861, with thousands of others, the black was never taken into consideration at all," said A. S. Graham, the commander of a G.A.R. department. "I went to defend the flag. My comrades went to do the same thing."

Not all the white veterans of the Union Army felt this way. In Virginia, Junior Vice-Commander Edgar Allen came out squarely against segregation and said he would "rather shake hands with the blackest nigger in the land if he was a true, honest man, than with a traitor." And in West Virginia, R. S. Northcott said he was willing to have blacks come into his post as full members. "I have plowed many a day beside a nigger boy when I was a boy, and in the evening we would go swimming together, and I am willing to meet him upon an equality in our Post."

There were few Northerners who showed as much simple dignity as did Northcott, despite his use of language. In fact, as time went on, it was clear that blacks were better treated in some border states than they were in either the deep South or the North. Early on, the North began to express beliefs that the blacks and their Southern oppressors would ultimately come to agree were just as preachingly restrictive as anything said by out-and-out segregationists, and much more hypocritical. The hypocrisy was apparent not just in the spoken words of Northerners who had only recently been so pious about the need to end slavery. It was in some of the North's leading newspapers, as well.

Not surprisingly, the *New York Herald* was one. The *Herald* had never thought all that much of Negroes, and on August 10, 1891, it asked the questions that Northerners were asking with increased frequency: ". . . should these races, which are not at present on a social equality, be forced to mingle? . . . Can you condemn a minority of white men for their unwillingness to submit to a majority of colored men?"

The *New York Tribune,* which had never earned the sobriquet of Copperhead and was still three decades away from its unlikely merger with the *Herald,* echoed the *Herald*'s sentiment: "In the South . . . it seems that nobody can live long without bowing to Southern bias, and while this by no means condones the general illiberality, it at least illumines the situation."

The problem was by no means limited to relations between male veterans.

The G.A.R.'s auxiliary, the Women's Relief Corps, with a membership of well over 100,000 as the century neared its end, was unable to say what should be done with the wives of black veterans. "As a Massachusetts woman, no one will accuse me of drawing the color line," said Mrs. Harriet Reed of Dorchester, a former national secretary of the Women's Relief Corps, in a speech given in 1897. But she pointed out that the branch in Maryland, for example, which had originally attracted "some of the very best women in the city of Baltimore," was in danger of losing them because of Baltimore's "peculiar conditions." From all that she had heard, Mrs. Reed concluded that "there can never be in our day a Department of white and colored Corps working together harmoniously."

In short, among both former Union soldiers and their wives, there was a feeling that they could not fight the South's pattern of segregation and should, in fact, accept it, if they were going to live in Southern states. Involvement of black veterans in the G.A.R. chapters in the South was carried out only at the distinct risk of incurring the displeasure not only of Southerners, but of the Northerners living in the South.

And what of the blacks who remained in the Army? Or, more to the point, aspired to it and saw it as a means of upward mobility, just as so many whites had found it to be? Between 1870 and 1899, twelve blacks entered West Point. Most of them dropped out after a semester or so. But Henry O. Flipper persevered despite four years of what Flipper would later call "these little tortures—the sneer, the shrug of the shoulder, the epithet." An uncommon man, he learned to withstand the meanness directed at him. In 1877, he was the first black to graduate. From all accounts, he won the hearts of many of his white classmates, who applauded him when he got his diploma.

But in 1882, Flipper was court-martialed because of the way he kept his accounts as head of the commissary at Fort Davis. Instead of being confined to his quarters, as would be customary for any white officer charged with such an infraction, he was slapped in the guardhouse. He was convicted of making false reports, and although white officers had been convicted of the same thing and let off with just a reprimand, Flipper was dismissed from the Army.

Flipper, who lived until 1940, was successful enough in the thing West Point trained him for—engineering. Not to the credit of the Army, his successes came to him only in civilian life.

12
Palace of Pensions

If Mr. Flood's brain was blown into the eye of a
mosquito, it would not make the mosquito wink.
—Comment about New York Congressman
Thomas S. Flood, attributed to James Tanner,
Commissioner of Pensions, 1889

As things are, gentlemen, one cannot tell whether a
pensioner of the United States received an honorable
wound in battle or contracted a chronic catarrh
twenty years after the war.
—Charles Eliot, president of Harvard, 1889

As the G.A.R.'s men and their fair ladies fretted and chattered about shades
of brown and black, the major issue facing former soldiers had a distinctly
green tinge. Soldiers continued to want and expect the Congress to pass two
kinds of pension bills. The bills were known loosely as ''arrears'' and
''bounty equalization.''

''Bounty equalization'' referred to the desire on the part of many who
fought on the Union side to have the inequality among various bounties
ended. The ''arrears'' bill sought to satisfy veterans who wanted to file
disability claims—even though the five-year cutoff for such applications had
long been passed. The debates over these issues seemed interminable and
agonizingly complex in the 1870s. And the central figures in both were not
the men who had fought the war, but rather the lawyers who wanted to
represent them.

If the coverage of Shays' Rebellion by the seacoast newspapers of
Massachusetts was not the brightest chapter in American journalism, so the

predatory behavior of lawyers acting as claims agents for former soldiers, black and white alike, did not exactly bestow luster upon the legal profession. As the debate droned on in Washington, there were more than a few who, in short order, ranked lawyers a wee mite lower than horse thieves and bounty jumpers.

The debates started, stayed with, and ended with the cost—the perceived need of Government to protect itself and the Treasury against the veterans of the Union Army. Senator John J. Ingalls of Kansas, sponsor of the arrears bill, was of the opinion that to pay the arrears already allowed, the Government would have to ante up between $18 million and $20 million, but he had no precise figure. When pressed to be more specific, Ingalls abruptly declined: "What would be required . . . could no more be calculated or estimated than one could calculate the number of birds that will fly through the air next year."

It was a most unsettling statement to taxpayers and journalists, one that only engendered bigger and more grandiose projections. For example, Secretary of the Treasury John Sherman estimated that because of the difficulty in assessing how many Union veterans would make claims against the Government in the future, as much as $150 million might be needed. On January 20, 1879, the *New York Tribune* predicted that nothing but a Presidential veto could prevent "a grand scramble by a horde of hungry claims agents to get their hands upon vast unearned portions of the national treasury." One of the few major papers to support the legislation was *The Washington Post,* which defended the arrears bill as a simple act of needed justice. The *Post* also felt that the predictions as to how much money would be needed to pay for arrears had been grossly exaggerated.

Five days later, President Rutherford B. Hayes signed the bill, and still later he made it clear that he, at least, felt the country had to spend some money to meet its commitments to its former soldiers and that unscrupulous claims agents were no reason to stop it. "That act was required by good faith," Hayes would later write. The soldiers had the pledge of the Government and the people. Congress, state legislatures, the press—everybody assured the soldier that if disabled in the line of duty he would be pensioned. The failure of Government to protect itself against frauds was no reason for evading just obligations. "It is said the amount to be paid is larger than was anticipated. That is no reason for repudiating the obligation. The amount is small compared with other war expenditure and debt. And the frauds and hardships upon Government are less than in many other items of unquestioned obligation. We can't make fish of one and flesh of another creditor. *I would do it again.*" But Hayes hastily added, ". . . I will keep silent and don't want to be quoted." Clearly, he was aware of the resentment against the bill on the part of the public, which was reminded of it by the press.

Some in Washington felt the legislation that Hayes signed with an apparent sense of duty to soldiers was more the work of claims agents than of veterans. Claims agents had scoured the countryside looking for men who might be likely applicants for pensions. Some were more aggressive than others, and by 1880, one observer estimated that about six-sevenths of matters pending before the Pension Bureau were controlled by less than one hundred lawyers. The Arrears Act itself attempted to assure the public that it was for veterans and not lawyers, by the inclusion of language that forbade agents from charging veterans for making benefits applications.

A law frequently cited in 1879—one that would remain on the books for more than a century—precluded lawyers from charging former soldiers more than $10 in cases against the Government. In 1862, ostensibly to protect soldiers against unscrupulous lawyers, but probably as much to protect Government from hungry and angry veterans, the Congress passed a law authorizing a fee of no more than $5 for attorneys assisting soldiers in obtaining pensions or bounties. It provided for the possible payment of an extra $1.50 for each affidavit required. In 1864, the law was amended, enabling lawyers to get a fee of $10, but only if they were successful in pursuing a pension claim.

Both laws loomed over lawyers who sought to make money out of the Arrears Act, but there were loopholes in it enabling lawyers who successfully pursued arrears claims to receive high premiums. The machinations were complex, but the fact was that soldiers filing late for pension money got it retroactively, and that might amount to $1,000 or more in a single payment. There was thus ample opportunity for pension agents to take a healthy cut.

Much tedious jawboning and moralizing preceded and followed passage of the Arrears Act. "I would promptly repeal [it]," said Senator James B. Beck of Kentucky, as Hayes' signature lay fresh upon the legislation. "It was conceived in sin and brought forth in iniquity. It is a fraud upon the American people, and a standing monument to the ignorance, selfishness and cowardice of the American Congress." General Joseph Hawley, whom some regarded as a spokesman for the former Union soldiers, said, "I believe that the mass of the soldiers did not ask for this act; they did not expect it; they were as much surprised by it as anybody; they did not enlist with a chief view to the awards in money; nor would they unduly burden the country they offered their lives to save."

The general wasn't really correct. The soldiers did want pensions. If they had been uninterested in the beginning, they surely changed their minds if they read the *National Tribune,* which was the official organ of the Grand Army and was owned and edited by George E. Lemon. By coincidence, he happened to be the head of the largest firm of pension lawyers scurrying around the District of Columbia. The Grand Army most certainly did not agree with General Hawley. Their members had won the war, the banner over the Capitol had told them how much the country owed them, and nobody raised any question about the investors who had purchased Union bonds and were now enjoying the promised interest.

The Nation maintained its fiscal conservatism, at least when it thought about former Union soldiers. In 1882, the expenditures of the Pension Bureau probably approximated $200 million. Seven years later, the magazine noted, expenditures for pensions exceeded what the budget of the entire nation had been before the war. Until the new laws were passed, few Civil War veterans had filed claims against the Government. But the number of claims climbed rapidly after Hayes signed the legislation in 1879. In 1878 there were only 25,904 new claims. In 1879, new claims totaled 47,416; and in 1880, 138,195—most of them brought by a relatively small number of attorneys.

The Union Army had used about 2.25 million men at one time or another during the war, although probably not more than a million at a time. Of those who served, 250,000 were killed, a third of them by bombs and bullets, two-thirds from various diseases. Neither the Grand Army of the Republic nor its numerous critics were satisfied with the way survivors had been treated, even as the rate of new claims rose. In 1880–81, the Grand Army counted among its members no more than 61,000 of the roughly 1.5 million men who had served in the Union Army during the Civil War and still lived to tell about it. But the influence it was able to bring to bear through George Lemon's *National Tribune* made it formidable, indeed. Politicians feared it and pandered to it, and even those veterans who hadn't the remotest intention of joining its ranks were impressed by what they thought it stood for.

And just about everybody else was impressed with the Government's plan for a Pension Building, to be constructed in downtown Washington. For if the nation was to have bigger and better pensions, as the Grand Army wanted, it logically needed a bigger and better Pension Building, and there was nobody better to design it, in 1882, than General Montgomery C. Meigs, who had been quartermaster of the Union Army, and the designer of the iron dome on the Capitol, a man of action who had already proved he could cope with the city radiant wrought from Pierre L'Enfant's dream by providing it with a water delivery system. L'Enfant had long since died, but surely this galumphant building was the equal of the symphony of urban diagonals that L'Enfant had envisioned rising out of Maryland and Virginia swampland.

The Pension Building was, and remains, 15.5 million bricks in search of an identity, and arguably, such a Tutankhamenesque creation could have been built only in nineteenth-century America (or, perhaps, in twentieth-century Moscow). It dutifully reflected the taste of its designer. Meigs, a man of considerable perspicacity, adored Corinthian columns, especially as they had been rendered by architects working for the emperor Diocletian in Rome, in the second century after Christ. Thus there are soaring Corinthian columns inside the Pension Building, seventy-five feet high, larger than anything that Diocletian ever envisioned for Rome and larger than Corinthian columns that exist anywhere else in the world, including Corinth.

Meigs, a most civilized soldier with a sense of history, was most fond of the Farnese Palace in Rome. And so the building sort of resembles the Farnese, or, at least, what the Farnese would have looked like had da Sangallo, Michelangelo, and della Porta tried to build a red brick barn for a wealthy farmer instead of a palazzo for a wealthier cardinal. Meigs, who was possessed of sensitivity to the decorative arts, had a certain weakness for urns, as did many refined people of his day, and not just undertakers. The Pension Building had a stock of 244 of them on display atop tiers of arcades, each with its own lion-headed handle. Meigs, consistent with the majesty of his high rank, was inspired by great halls. The Pension Building had one that was 316 feet long and 116 feet wide. It was so enormous that long after it ceased to be a drafty workplace for pension clerks, it was sought for the inaugural balls of American Presidents. Meigs, surely no stranger to Philip of Macedon and Alexander the Great and to the formidable culture that inspired them, turned to the Parthenon for inspiration and wondered about the form of the frieze. He wanted to explore its possible adaptability to other kinds of structures. The Pension Building was thus given a terra-cotta frieze that certainly outdid the Parthenon's for size, if not originality of sculpture, running the entire quarter of a mile around the building and offering, in bas-relief, cohorts of little soldiers and sailors modeled after real people who worked in the Boston quartermaster depot that Meigs knew and loved so well. All this cost $886,614.04.

When it was finished, Meigs' fellow officer General William Tecumseh Sherman, who had ordered the burning down of a goodly number of things while marching through the South during the war, said he was sorry that this building was fireproof. And Meigs, whose sense of humor did not match the titanic mass of this most consequential edifice, was offended when someone suggested that money could be made simply by selling wool socks and underwear in the drafty lobby.

The Pension Building was constructed to ensilage the fifteen hundred clerks (shivering in wintertime, even when the building's four boilers were going full tilt) who paid out the money that many in the country did not want them to pay out, in offices that had no doors, because Meigs wisely concluded that in the pension business, affairs would better be conducted in a place which looked as if it had no secrets. Whatever its other attributes, the Pension Building had no secrets.

With a veritable palace of pensions growing out of the corner of 5th and F streets in northwest Washington, it was reasonable to ask if the power of soldiers was finally more real than perceived. Had they finally become a power unto themselves, and were they shaping the sum and substance of American politics?

In 1884, as the building neared completion, Colonel W. W. Dudley, chief of the Pension Bureau, saw absolutely nothing wrong in taking two months off from his job in Washington to go to Ohio to campaign for Republicans. In order that no voter be left unwooed, he brought with him a retinue of assorted clerks and examiners from the bureau so that the "soldier vote" could be neatly delivered to the Republicans, who were in a state of sublime salivation at the thought of all those veterans in voting booths.

The hapless target of this concerted attack was Democratic Congressman William Warner, who, as chairman of the House Committee on Pensions, Bounty, and Back Pay, did not do precisely what the G.A.R. wanted him to do on a piece of legislation. "Gentlemen like Mr. Warner must be taught that it is not to prove safe to play with soldiers' interests in the committee-rooms and on the floor of the house," wrote James Tanner, then an ascendant star in the G.A.R. hierarchy. "Every old soldier in that Congressional district owes it to the large number of his needy and suffering comrades in the country at large who look to us for assistance to make an example of WARNER and terminate his congressional career now." Warner, who in fact was defeated, credited the Grand Army with his undoing. Dudley, who had lost a leg in the Battle of Gettysburg, apparently lost no mobility to his handicap, for as soon as he had destroyed Warner, he moved quickly on to Indiana and did much the same thing to two other Democrats.

By the time Grover Cleveland was inaugurated as the nation's twenty-second President in March of 1885, the G.A.R. had ballooned to nearly

270,000 members—an increase of 209,000 in only four years. Fifteen years had passed since Appomattox, and Civil War soldiers were older in more ways than one; perhaps they had a right to feel more vulnerable. They had seen Jay Gould and Jim Fisk attempt to corner the gold market by manipulating the President and thus causing the "Black Friday" panic of 1869, in which thousands were ruined.

They had watched in awe as the great robber barons grew rich, men like Gould, Fisk, Daniel Drew, J. P. Morgan, and John D. Rockefeller, Andrew Carnegie, Cornelius Vanderbilt, and others, hobnailing over the backs of little men like them and richer men than they, men whose positions they had admired. They saw the beginning of rapacious exploitation of American timberland and other precious natural resources. They had also been stung by the more generalized Panic of 1873 and the five years of depression that followed it; they had watched the shenanigans of William Marcy Tweed in New York City and a dozen rascals not so unlike him in as many other cities in America. They were neither ahead of their time nor behind it, neither worse nor better than their fellow Americans. They were of their time, and they embraced its political morality, understood that theirs was a Government that could be manipulated and was manipulated by others, richer and more powerful than they, every day. They wanted *theirs*.

Cleveland, who at the age of forty-seven could easily understand what the veterans were going through, was not insensitive to their needs. Of the survivors of the men who fought the war, some 520,000 had already received pensions of some sort. The others had either been rejected or had not bothered to apply. Of those who had been rejected, an increasing number, encouraged by the G.A.R. and the *National Tribune,* hired claims agents to obtain what were essentially private pensions—pensions that skirted ordinary rules and requirements set up by the Government. Cleveland signed 1,453 such bills, a number that exceeded by two-thirds those signed by all previous Presidents since the Civil War. That alone should have made him popular with all veterans, even the more vociferous members of the Grand Army. But in 1887, Cleveland vetoed something called the Dependent Pension Bill, which was supposed to grant pensions to all former soldiers suffering from disabilities, whether their ailments originated with their military service or not. The G.A.R. then determined that his days as President should and would be numbered, as, indeed, they were. He lost the election the very next year to Benjamin Harrison, thanks in no small measure to the vote of veterans. "They have vetoed the great vetoer everywhere," sniped George Lemon's *National Tribune,* which said the defeat was "unquestionably due to the veterans. . . ."

Pensions for soldiers now appeared as the largest single item in the Government's budget, and one source estimated that in 1885, pensions constituted 18 percent of the total budget. With an esteemed former brevet brigadier general as President of the Republic, and committed to more generous benefits for those who fought the late war, former soldiers now seemed to be doing what they had never been able to do before in the United States. If they were taking their lead from the Grand Army, perhaps it was because the Grand Army had produced its own "Little Corporal" in James Tanner. Tanner was widely regarded in his day as a Brooklynite (the place was then associated with a certain flamboyance), but in reality, he had been born in 1844 near the small town of Richmondville in Schoharie County, about 150 miles north of New York City. He was the son of a farmer of modest means but rather took to book learning. At the age of seventeen, he was teaching in the school from which he had only recently been graduated.

When the war started, Tanner enlisted in Company C of the 87th New York Volunteer Infantry and went immediately to the front, where he saw action in the Peninsular Campaign, the siege of Yorktown, and the Battle of Malvern Hill. His outfit also fought at Bull Run, and it was there, on August 30, 1862, that a shell burst near Tanner, badly injuring both legs. Field surgeons quickly amputated his legs four inches below the knee, and to the utter surprise of his doctors, Tanner survived.

After his discharge, he returned to Schoharie County, was fitted with artificial limbs and, in short order, got himself appointed Deputy Doorkeeper of the New York State Assembly in Albany. That Tanner was a politician with the power to manipulate people was never in doubt. By 1864, he had wrangled a clerkship in the Department of War, then run by Secretary Edwin M. Stanton. As it happened, he took his Washington rooms in the house adjoining the Peterson House, where a mortally wounded President Lincoln was brought after being shot in Ford's Theater by John Wilkes Booth. Known as someone who used a form of shorthand, he was pressed into service, sitting in the very house where Lincoln lay dying, taking notes from those who had been at the theater and saw the assassination and who gathered that night in the parlor.

Tanner quit the War Department in 1865, returned to Richmondville, became a lawyer by reading with a judge, as was common practice in those days, and was admitted to the bar in 1869. He then moved to Brooklyn, where he worked in the Brooklyn Custom House and soon maneuvered his way into another job—deputy tax collector, later tax collector for Brooklyn. An efficient sort, he increased Brooklyn's tax receipts, which was no easy task. He knew the right people, had a way with oratory, and in 1876 was elected commander of the Grand Army's New York Department. It gave him a power base and a place from which to speak out on his firmly held belief that veterans' benefits had been at best a disappointment and ought to be improved. He was also a vociferous and effervescent member of the Grand Army's pension committee, the unit that recommended G.A.R. policy on pensions—recommendations that were heeded by national officers.

Tanner's strong feelings for veterans as a group did not extend to other men in other groups, veteran and nonveteran, who were trying to better their lot through the nascent American labor union movement. In 1877, when there were strikes in New York, he generously offered the Governor of New York the services of Grand Army members in putting strikes down—seemingly insensitive to the prospect of pitting one exploited group against another. "All over the land," Tanner said in a speech, "was witnessed the spectacle of men, to whom the handling of arms . . . had been a memory of the past, spring into the breach and holding at bay the aroused, unreasoning physical forces of our land."

Tanner remained in New York for the next ten years, and his voice was listened to throughout the Grand Army and wherever politicians thought they could use the "soldier vote." He was by then referred to as "The Corporal," affectionately by some, derisively by many others. In 1888, The Corporal went to Indiana, a state that was no stranger to exhortations by and for soldiers, and campaigned vigorously for Alvin P. Hovey, who was running for Governor, and for Benjamin Harrison, the Republican candidate for President against Grover Cleveland. Tanner said he "plastered Indiana with promises"—promises to veterans that if Harrison became President, the lot of the men who had won the Union's war would change for the better.

After it was over, and Harrison was looking for someone to run his Pension Bureau, Tanner seemed an attractive candidate. His strong advocacy for veterans did not put the President off at all. Tanner was popular with veterans and veterans were popular with Republicans. And since Harrison had been elected in no small measure because of Cleveland's unpopularity with veterans, it seemed almost mandatory that he appoint a Pension Commissioner who would be perceived as unquestionably representing the veterans. There was nothing about Tanner that would cause a man of Harrison's background any alarm. The great-grandson of a signer of the Declaration of Independence and the son of the ninth President of the United States, Harrison had served in the Civil War as a colonel and brevet brigadier general, leading volunteers. He was quite used to spirited enlisted men.

And so when he offered the job to The Corporal and The Corporal accepted, Harrison reportedly told him, "Be liberal with the boys." The instructions could not have made Tanner any happier. "I will drive a six-mule team through the Treasury," he reportedly replied, to conspicuous notices in a press that would never be able to overcome its feelings of distrust toward him.

Tanner unquestionably intended to keep the promises made to veterans in the Republican platform—something neither elected nor appointed officials do very often—and soon after his appointment, on March 26, 1889, he made an impression on Washington that it would not soon forget. He was invited to attend a "Scotch-Irish Convention" at Columbia, Tennessee, and told the assorted happy Celts that he would call up the cases of 33,871 Civil War veterans who were receiving less than $3.75 a month. In talking about those cases, Tanner uttered four words which sent fear and fire into the refrigerated hearts of America's fiscal pooh-bahs: "God help the surplus." The phrase would be repeated again and again in the months to come as the press and the Congress came to view The Corporal with growing concern.

But the phrase was not nearly the threat it was made out to be, when read in the context in which it was given that day in Tennessee. What Tanner had promised to do was to take the cases "and reissue them on the basis of the truth, that no man ought to be down on the pension roll of the United States for less than the miserable pittance of one dollar per week, though I may wring from the hearts of some the prayer, 'God help the surplus.' " And so it wasn't Tanner at all who was saying "God help the surplus." It was what he said he thought others would say when they found that he did not approve of giving veterans pensions of $1 a week. In the age of the robber barons, who stole hundreds of millions of dollars for themselves, and thus established their own nouveau aristocracy in a nation that expected its aristocrats to have fat wallets if not noble lineage, it would later seem a rather modest thing to seek for one's constituency.

But Tanner was not a man in whom the press looked for nuance. He was larger than life, even by American standards, a portrait in black and white with the grays left out, a strange causative bureaucrat-activist who never lived in the conditional subjunctive of the ordinary Washington politician. He was a man to be watched—and perhaps to fear.

Most Republican politicians were pleased when Tanner brought his oratory to the state of Indiana to campaign for Harrison but were aghast when he came back East and said that he expected the Republicans to keep the promises to veterans he had made in Indiana. Many of them had never considered the possibility of someone in high office who would take election promises seriously.

So, when *The Nation* took stock of Tanner's appointment in its issue of May 30, 1889, it was not a happy prospect, for Tanner had begun to keep what he regarded as his commitment to the veterans. Pension expenditures for 1889 were over $88.4 million and were estimated for 1890 to go to $95 million. "This is a greater amount than the cost of the entire military establishment of Germany, under which the people of that nation groan so loudly," said the magazine, emphasizing that what the country didn't need was somebody who thought those numbers were somehow warranted.

For the most important, responsible, and delicate office of Commissioner, General Harrison picked out—no, that is not the proper expression; he allowed to be shoved upon him—a loud-mouthed Grand Army stump speaker.

The Nation's rebuke was apparently anchored in fears that soldiers might lose their marvelous image as patriots, if they continued to be so concerned about obtaining money from the Government. Said *The Nation:*

The regular expenditures of the Pension Bureau now far exceed the total cost of the whole Federal Government before the war.

Every right-minded man desires that the volunteer's reputation for self-sacrificing devotion shall never be tarnished. The Commissioner of Pensions wields more influence than any other officer of Government in deciding whether the Union soldier shall go down in history as a patriot, or as a mercenary who apparently entered the army chiefly to see how much he could make out of it. For some years there has been a strong tendency on the part of many old soldiers to convert their supposed patriotism into a club for securing undeserved pensions.

As for the Grand Army of the Republic, *The Nation* called it a "money-making machine" that had "drifted into politics and was now 'bulldozing' officials" into making concessions to veterans. Tanner, said *The Nation*, did not have the power "he egotistically claims to possess" but "has the Grand Army machine behind him and he can threat its displeasure upon any politician who ventures a protest."

The Nation was surely not alone in its condemnation of Tanner. The *Philadelphia Press* complained, "He would apparently like to pension everybody and everything." The *Philadelphia Bulletin* agreed. "In encouraging this order of claimants," said the *Bulletin,* "Commissioner Tanner not only destroys the value of the pension list as a roll of honor in the eyes of the Grand Army of the Republic, and, indeed, of all good citizens, but he fosters, no matter how good his intentions may be, the arts and tricks of the tribe of pension shysters who are always ready to corrupt and demoralize this branch of the public service.''

It was not just what Tanner did, but what he said when he did it. Congressman Thomas S. Flood of New York was said to be rather restrained about Tanner because Tanner, displeased with Flood's reticence on pension questions, publicly stated that if "Flood's brain was blown into the eye of a mosquito, it would not make the mosquito wink." In Chicago, he frightened more political conservatives when he said, "I tell you frankly that I am for 'the old flag and an appropriation' for every old comrade who needs it. . . . I know I have the support of the President and the Cabinet on this line—a pension for every old soldier who needs one."

Corporal Tanner's concern was not limited to those who had been on the Union side, and he openly lamented that Southern troops had so little to hope for, even though they had fought honorably. "We of the North had the coffers of the Treasury to draw upon for our pensions; we had honor among the nations of the earth, but I stated that the man who followed the fortunes of the Confederacy . . . sat in the solitude of his wrecked and ruined home and contemplated, possibly, loss of limb and saw his wife in rags and his child in hunger. . . .''

At one point, Tanner actively raised money to build a home for former Confederate soldiers in Virginia and enlisted the aid of no less than the Rev. Henry Ward Beecher, who gave a speech at the Academy of Music in Brooklyn, an event that raised $1,600. After the home was built, Tanner served as one of its trustees.

The Republicans did not know quite what to do with The Corporal. "If Tanner does not go soon," said one party regular, "the surplus will—and the Republican party after it." Major George S. Merrill, a commander-in-chief of the G.A.R. who had served on the Pension Committee with Tanner and who admired him, observed, "Tanner's worst enemy has always been his tongue. What could have been more indiscreet than the style in which he mounted the housetops and summoned the people of the United States to watch him while he made the wheels go round, or while he pulled a string and dangled the Secretary of the Interior at the other end."

Tanner's ability to get bigger and better Civil War pensions out of the Republican majority so incensed Charles William Eliot, the president of Harvard, that he ventured forth from Cambridge and spoke about it at the Bay State Club in Boston:

I hold it to be a hideous wrong inflicted upon the republic that the pension system instituted for the benefit of the soldiers and sailors of the United States has been prostituted and degraded by the whole series of Republican administrations. As things are, gentlemen, one cannot tell whether a pensioner of the United States received an honorable wound in battle or contracted a chronic catarrh twenty years after the war. . . .

President Eliot meant what he said. And to underscore the intensity of his disapproval of what was going on, he took the ultimate rash step for a registered Republican—he became a Democrat. He would not be the last Republican in the Harvard administration to convert, although perhaps his total immersion was the most public and his reasons for it the most wide-reaching. He objected not only to the way the Republicans had managed veterans' pensions, but also to the way they handled tariffs and the civil service generally. The irrepressible Tanner paid all this no heed. He said it was the "bounden duty of this great Republic of ours to see to it that no man who wore the blue and laid it off in honor, shall . . . be permitted to crawl under the roof of an almshouse for shelter."

It was hard to find a journal that had a kind thing to say about his zeal for securing pensions for veterans. It was harder still to find anyone who suggested that Tanner himself profited from all the work he did for veterans, a phenomenon that would not always be observable with pension chiefs in years to come. Tanner, in the final analysis, was basically an honest man. Not always right, not always prudent, but honest.

With such energy and such commitment to what he thought the Republicans had promised, it was inevitable that Corporal Tanner should have a short tenure. After six months of service, during which he was frequently depicted in the press as a man out to loot the Treasury, and with mounting difficulties with the Secretary of the Interior, to whom he was supposed to report but didn't, Tanner sent a letter of resignation to President Harrison.

The difference which exists between the Secretary of the Interior and myself as to policy to be pursued in the administration of the Pension Bureau has reached a stage which threatens to embarrass you to an extent which I feel I should not call upon you to suffer. . . . I hereby place my resignation in your hands, to take effect at your pleasure, to the end that you may be relieved of any further embarrassment in the matters.

Harrison accepted it promptly. Even in his relief to be rid of such a feisty, controversially vocal aside, he had the presence of mind to take care to note that Tanner's honesty had never been questioned. "I beg to renew the expression of my personal good will," he said. There was never even the hint of an investigation of Tanner, and even the most hostile press coverage did not suggest that he had somehow gained personally from his time in office. However, he was accused of nepotism by the press after reporters learned that he gave Pension Bureau jobs to his daughters. "If he had been a man who could understand that the party's promises in its platforms and on the stump are not at all which the party intends to carry out, he would have been in office today," wistfully observed the *Boston Globe.*

How close did Tanner really come to compromising the solvency of the United States? For the fiscal year ending June 30, 1889, which included three months of Tanner as head of the Pension Bureau, pension costs totaled $89,131,768. This was an increase of about $9.5 million over the year before, but it was only a wee bit more than the average annual increase for the 1886–90 half-decade. As for the fiscal year ending June 30, 1890, which included the last three months of The Corporal's administration, the increase was over $17 million. But this included nine months of the work of the next Pension Commissioner, Green B. Raum.

Raum, also a veteran (he had been wounded in the Battle of Missionary Ridge), was welcomed warmly by the press, which seemed to feel that anybody other than Tanner would be an improvement. The press was wrong. In contrast to Tanner, the shifty Raum apparently did skulk about in his own interest, and was soon investigated by Congress for alleged wrongdoing in office.

Specifically, it was charged that some of Raum's subordinates owned stock in his refrigeration company; that he had an inappropriate financial relationship with George Lemon, the newspaper publisher and pension agent promoter; and that his twenty-three-year-old son, Green B. Raum, Jr., whom he named as the unlikely head of the Appointment Division of the Pension Bureau, was either careless with funds or willfully misappropriated them. However, Raum was much less candid and more diplomatic with the press, not so outspoken about getting money for veterans, and so he was not drummed out of office the way his predecessor was. It almost seemed as though Raum's cynicism and duplicity were more predictable and less threatening. Since he seemed to stand for nothing more than the enrichment of his own wallet, he was easier for official Washington and its journalists to understand.

On June 27, 1890, the Congress passed the Dependent Pension Act of 1890. It went further than any other act of its kind had done before. Before this, Civil War benefits were given only for death or disability occurring while in service. The new law held that any veteran who had served at least ninety days and who for any reason could not earn a living by his own labor could receive a pension. The law made no distinction between rich and poor veterans and no distinction between ninety-day veterans and those who had served for years. The widows of such men were also eligible.

"These wholesale pension schemes . . . threaten to ruin the reputation of the Union soldier," moaned the *The Nation,* a few weeks before the bill headed toward its final approval. "While the soldier who served in the Confederate army represents the best element in Southern society—the men who have built up a new prosperity on the ruins of the old by working hard and depending on themselves—the ex-Union soldier is coming to stand in the public mind for a helpless and greedy sort of person, who says that he is not able to support himself, and whines that other people ought to do it for him."

"The hero covered with honorable wounds, the faithful and courageous soldier who served long and bore the brunt of battle, is now no better than the deserter, the straggler, the bounty-jumper and the coward," protested William M. Sloane, writing in *The Century.*

It is for the sake of his [the honest soldier's] honor, to preserve unfading his hard-earned laurels that we protest against the shame of legislation which in his name depletes our purse in the interest of pension brokers, and against the undiscriminating lavishness which draws no distinction between suffering heroes and those who should be content with the honor, which pales before no other, of having saved their country in the hour of her greatest need.

In the North during the war, Confederate soldiers had been described in terms of their "savagery" because they "bayonetted our wounded." The rhetoric was not unlike that used to describe Indians. But within a few years, the savagery that Yankees said they could never forgive was all but forgotten in the North. Maybe Johnny Reb had been quick, on occasion, to bayonet intruding Union troops, but his rates for doing so were reasonable. In fact, it became rather fashionable to compare the nobility of the losing, long-suffering Confederate veteran with the avarice of his winning Union counterpart.

The hatred that Northerners originally had for the rebel had become admiration for his ability to muddle through. The sentiment had its genesis not in what happened at Appomattox, but in the Government's ledger sheets. By the end of 1893, one million Union veterans were taking nearly $150 million in pension money. But in the South, only 26,538 persons, including widows, were receiving just over $1 million. An article in *The Forum* magazine estimated that a typical Northerner was receiving around

$165 in Government money each year, while his Southern counterpart got only $38.50. *The Forum* noted that in addition to all the pension money being lavished on the Northerners, the Government was also supporting "seven National Soldiers' Homes with 14,193 inmates and twenty State Union Soldiers' homes, with 5,325 inmates."

Counting pennies when it came to pensions did not carry over to other Americans adjudged to be dependent on some form of "charity." "In works of active beneficence no country has surpassed, perhaps none has equalled the United States," proudly wrote James Bryce in 1888. Americans were unbegrudgingly giving to the charities of Presbyterians, Baptists, Methodists, and Episcopalians. Voluntary giving to Protestant denominations actually rose during the Panic of 1873. The $3.3 million raised in the 1860s climbed to $5.2 million in the 1870s and further increased to $7 million in the 1880s. Giving to churches and their good works ameliorated "the perils of abounding wealth" that might otherwise cause the country to falter in its moral course. But this outpouring of Christian charity did not discern the Union veteran as a worthy sharer in the national largess.

While the North was busy complimenting Confederate soldiers for losing the war so inexpensively, the former Confederates were doing everything they could to end the bargain prices they had paid their soldiers. They were not nearly so happy with the penurious condition of the men who had fought for them. Southern newspapers, whose Northern counterparts wanted the Government to spend less, took the position that the various states of the old Confederacy should be doing more, much more. Georgia was criticized when its legislature balked at providing support for a soldiers' home in Atlanta. "It is a lamentable sight to see a battle-scarred soldier of the Confederacy in a poor-house," editorialized the *Richmond Dispatch*. "It is well-calculated to arouse the suspicion that there is more buncombe than heartfelt sympathy in the often-heard praise of the men who fought our battles. . . . It is disgraceful that any worthy veteran of the Confederate army should be forced to live the life of a pauper. . . ."

But up North, it was as though these sentiments were not being heard at all. "Did loyal citizens volunteer for pay?" asked Allen R. Foote, a writer and an untypical veteran who contributed an article to *The Forum*. "If you did," he wrote, "you have no right to pose as loyal defenders of your country, or to share the gratitude of the nation. You are mercenaries. You have your price: let it be paid, and your names be stricken from the roll of honorable men." The article even suggested that pension-grubbing veterans in the North were little better than the rebels they had defeated: "Such as you have disgraced the old flag with a stain that traitors' hands had no power to place upon it. Do you not know that loyalty, honor, and honesty are qualities of character that cannot be bought and sold?'' Indeed, *The Forum* took pains to point out that when the Dependent Pension Act of 1890 went into effect, there was so much money to be made that ''dozens of clerks quitted the [Pension] Bureau to set themselves up in practice as solicitors of claims.''

Perhaps it was inevitable that, given the intensity of feeling expressed in the press, some soldiers would finally want to disassociate themselves from the Grand Army's success in playing power politics with the Republicans. When the disaffection came, it came from within the Grand Army itself. On March 8, 1893, the Grand Army's Noah L. Farnham Post of New York City met and passed a series of resolutions to the effect that pensions should not be paid to veterans whose disabilities did not originate in the service, and further, that veterans who took such pensions ''are guilty of conduct calculated to injure old soldiers who take the higher ground.''Clearly, members of Farnham were afraid that continued liberal dispensation of pensions would put the whole pension system in jeopardy, such was the resentment against it at that point. Not only did they disassociate themselves from the pension policy, but they suggested that other posts might want to do the same thing.

The New York Department was shocked and angry and, from its headquarters in Albany, informed Farnham's commander, John J. Finn, that what his post had done violated the rules of the Grand Army, so that it was in contempt. The State G.A.R. demanded that the resolutions be rescinded. Farnham refused. The State G.A.R. told Farnham that it was suspended.

On April 12, Commander Finn wrote to P. J. O'Connor, Assistant Adjutant General of the New York Department: ''I have the honor to inform you that it is the opinion of this Post that if it is the desire of the Grand Army of the Republic to pay pensions to people who have not incurred their disabilities in the service of the country and to those who do not need them, then this Post does not desire to remain in the Grand Army of the Republic.''

Weeks after the dispute erupted, Farnham's charter was annulled. The gory details were gleefully taken note of by Mr. Foote, who had tried unsuccessfully to organize a Society of Loyal Volunteers who would not look upon pensions so covetously. Finn made the correspondence available to Foote and Foote saw to it that it was all made public in *The Forum* in July 1893, under the byline of Finn.

There is no evidence that any other Grand Army post even considered adopting Farnham's position. Memories of the pension fights in the decades following the Civil War remained moist, foul, and dark, like a robber baron's twisty cheroot from the night before. Life went on, the country survived, and events led to a most curious and dirty little war against Spain. The contentiousness over the size of pensions for the soldiers of the Civil War slowly evaporated, as did the soldiers themselves.

FOUR
The War with Spain and the Philippine Insurrection

Sent to Camp Wikoff on Long Island, hundreds of Spanish-American War veterans died from disease and shortages of food, water and medical supplies. (*Vassar Library / Harper's Weekly*)

13
Embalmed Beef, Bad Water, Typhoid, and Five-Dollar Coffins at Montauk Point

> The talk about the soldiers suffering for want of food at the camp is bosh. There are 75,000 rations already on the field, and the store houses filled.
> —*East-Hampton* (Long Island) *Star,* editorial, August 12, 1898

> There must be a screw loose somewhere when Uncle Sam's soldiers, backed by a country of unlimited resources, are allowed to starve on transports and compelled to depend upon charity for food when they land upon our shores.
> —*East-Hampton Star,* editorial, August 26, 1898

By the time America reached the last few years of the nineteenth century, it was quite ready for another war. More than thirty years had passed since Appomattox; the blood had dried and memories of how the stain got there had faded. There was a new generation of young men, many of them not even alive during the Civil War nor any American war. Some of them were not all that different from Henry Knox more than a century before; they looked upon military service as a means of achieving status and security. Still others, like soldiers before them everywhere, sought adventure, the dash of wearing a uniform, and the chance to demonstrate their patriotism through individual heroics on the battlefield.

But there was no battlefield. To some, the persistence of peace and the lack of a national shooting gallery were not a source of satisfaction but a cause for concern. A number of the starchier Civil War veterans, picking their way jauntily through their middle years, saw the lack of war as detrimental to the creation of praiseworthy national character. One such man was Oliver Wendell Holmes, Jr., still seven years away from his appointment to the United States Supreme Court. He had the astuteness required of jurists, but he was nevertheless a man of his times. He had put behind him his own severe chest wounds, inflicted at the Battle of Ball's Bluff in the Civil War. His memories of those awful days had been overtaken by his convictions about the value gained by going into combat.

As associate justice of the Massachusetts supreme court, Holmes addressed a graduating class at Harvard on Memorial Day of 1895 and lamented that war was now "out of fashion." He proclaimed that "the faith is true and adorable which leads a soldier to throw away his life in obedience to a blindly accepted duty, in a cause which he little understands . . . under tactics of which he does not see the use." Three years later, quite a number of soldiers would be given the opportunity to throw away their lives for a war as popular as it was incomprehensible.

The Spanish-American War started in the spring of 1898 to the popular tune "There'll Be a Hot Time in the Old Town Tonight." The Cuban campaign involved only one day's fighting of any consequence, but hostilities were recorded on paper for one hundred days. The Philippine Insurrection that grew out of the victory in Cuba seemed to linger interminably. What really caused America's involvement in its sad, strange war with Spain would be the cause of much discussion. There would be talk of American concern for the way the Spanish were treating the Cubans who wanted to be free of Spain (the phrase "human rights" was never used but it easily could have been). There also would be consideration of American economic interests in Cuba; of the anti-Spanish bellicosity that developed after the battleship *Maine* was destroyed at anchor in Havana harbor, to which it had ostensibly come on a "peaceful" visit; of the resulting jingoism contained in the lively prose of such papers as William Randolph Hearst's *Journal* and Joseph Pulitzer's *World,* both of them situated in New York; and of some undiplomatic things that the Spanish ambassador in Washington said about President William McKinley, blown out of all proportion by the *Journal*.

It was a war from which soldiers came home—indeed, had to come home—before victory was achieved. Their circumstances caused some to question the accuracy of John Hay's observation that it was a "splendid little war, begun with the highest motives, carried on with magnificent intelligence and spirit. . . ."

The soldiers came home suffering from yellow fever, malaria, dysentery, and malnutrition. Some of it was picked up because of their unsuspecting exposure to the parasites, viruses, and bacteria that flourished in the tropics, illnesses then not fully understood by medical science; some of it was the result of a war that the United States entered without adequate preparation or, apparently, without even a rudimentary awareness of what the consequences of such an adventure might be. But they were home, nevertheless, not to do battle again.

The Spanish-American War was backed by influential people and persuasive newspaper editors. Indeed, it was as favored as the Vietnam War would be disfavored. And yet, there were striking parallels between it and Vietnam. For with both wars, there would be questions about how the United States became involved; whether its troops fought ethically, honorably, and well; and how, in turn, they were treated when they came home in view of the conduct of the campaigns and how Americans came to be there. The only difference was the order in which the questions were asked and the importance given to the answers.

America's interest was engaged in 1895, when a small group of Cuban-Americans landed secretly on the island to foment an armed revolution against Spain. Spain responded with predictable force to protect what it saw as its legitimate interests. Accounts of atrocities reportedly committed by the Spanish against their Cuban subjects were given prominent display in Hearst and Pulitzer newspapers. The *New York Herald,* the *New York Tribune,* and the *Evening Post* conducted themselves either with restraint or outright resistance to the war. *The New York Times* may have been enamored of Imperial America but it did not share quite the exuberance of the Hearstian view. It did not matter; the circulation of antiwar or lukewarm-to-war newspapers was quite modest. In contrast, the Pulitzer papers sold more than 800,000 and Hearst's morning and evening *Journal* sold around 700,000 copies daily. New York newspapers that supported the war thus sold around 1.5 million; those that opposed the war only 225,000.

An extreme form of patriotism nurtured itself throughout the United States. There were large anti-Spanish rallies, organized by a determined if somewhat enervated Grand Army of the Republic, aided and abetted by guileful Republicans, who saw in the Cuban doings a chance to regain some of the power they had lost in the campaign of 1892, which led to the reelection of Democrat Grover Cleveland. The fact that Cleveland, in 1884, had been the only Democrat to occupy the White House since James Buchanan won it in 1856 did not, for the Republicans, mitigate four more years of Cleveland.

When William McKinley handily defeated William Jennings Bryan in the election of November 1896, the Republicans, who had grown used to running the country, looked around for issues that would keep the White House in their hands. It did not take them long to find Cuba. When McKinley was inaugurated the following March, he and the party regulars were mindful of all the sabers that were being rattled around them. And so when he learned ten months later that Spanish Army officers had ordered the attacking of the offices of some anti-Spanish newspapers, he sent the battleship *Maine* on a "friendly visit" to Havana. The idea of such a cruise was enormously popular in the United States, although Democratic Senator Mark Hanna sourly observed, "Sending the *Maine* to Havana is like waving a match in an oil well for fun."

The ship exploded while riding at anchor in Havana harbor on February 15, 1898, killing 252 of the 350 men aboard. There were exuberant, persistent calls for war with Spain. The character-building exercise that Oliver Wendell Holmes had recommended to the Harvards was thus at hand.

The war began in April of 1898 with a formal declaration by Congress. But the country, for all of its prowar sentiment, was unprepared. It was America's first war ever against an "enemy" who was not within or contiguous to its borders. Since ninety miles of Caribbean Sea intervened between American troops and the mainland, it required a level of planning that had not been necessary when the United States fought Mexico, fifty years before. Unfortunately, that planning was not present when McKinley pressed into service 275,000 regulars and volunteers.

The Government had a stockpile of supplies that might have been adequate for a force of forty thousand—not one that was nearly seven times larger. Thus, at the outset, soldiers were short on such things as uniforms, shoes, socks, and underwear. Even if the supplies had been available, the Government could not have sent them quickly to Tampa, then a sleepy city of 25,000. Despite its lack of facilities, it somehow became the chief staging area for the invasion. Tampa was serviced by a single-track railroad that, like many other American single-track railroads, was not a model of efficiency. At one point, while troops waited for basic supplies, fifteen carloads of uniforms and ammunition were sidetracked a mere twenty-five miles away.

The experienced core of the American Army—the regulars—was confident and well trained, mostly from forays against Indians in the years after the Civil War. The volunteers lacked expertise, but they had great spirit and contemplated battle with the exhilaration that comes only to those who have never been in such doings. If shoes and khaki had been the only things withheld from the soldiers, the war with Spain might have gone better.

Spain surrendered soon enough, but Cuba's diseases proved much more resistant and decimated even the Rough Riders, an elite group of cavalry founded by Theodore Roosevelt and Leonard Wood. Colonel Roosevelt informed General William R. Shafter, who was in command of a large contingent, that within Roosevelt's division alone there were fifteen hundred cases of malaria. Roosevelt was thus appalled when he learned that the War Department, whose minions viewed the Cuban campaign from the sticky comfort of Washington, had decided to keep the troops on the island as an army of occupation.

The move "will simply involve the destruction of thousands," an alarmed Roosevelt wrote to Shafter, neatly making sure that the Associated Press got a copy of his letter. "The whole command is so weakened and shattered as to be ripe for dying like rotten sheep when a real yellow fever epidemic . . . strikes us and it is bound to if we stay here," he warned. Roosevelt thought that things would be so much better if only his men could get out of Cuba and spend six weeks "on the north Maine coast . . . or elsewhere where the yellow fever germ cannot propagate." He was backed up by other officers, and it all received wide circulation.

The War Department relented and began to move men from Cuba. It was also the beginning of one of the worst disasters in the annals of American military medicine.

Typhoid, yellow fever and malaria were beginning to be reported in Cuba, but Surgeon General George Miller Sternberg said the fevers were of a "mild" type that would not require a convalescent period of more than ten days. General Sternberg was an unlikely physician to misread a developing public health problem. A graduate of the College of Physicians and Surgeons at Columbia University, Sternberg had a strong interest in bacteriology and had written the acclaimed *Textbook on Bacteriology,* which was published three years before the war. He was regarded as an authority on typhoid.

But curiously, when he was told about health conditions in Cuba, the words he used in public were not those of a learned physician, but rather those of a political appointee who was trying to minimize the situation for an unsuspecting public, still happy with America's successful righteousness in fighting the Spaniards. Whatever his motive, Sternberg was wrong about the "mildness" of the fevers that had begun to spread in Cuba, where troops suffered without adequate nursing care, since the Surgeon General, easily as much a man of his times as Holmes was, would not permit female nurses of the Red Cross to attend troops in the field. When the *Concho* and the *Alamo,* the first two troop ships to leave Cuba, reached Hampton Roads, Virginia, it seemed that the fevers were not mild at all. The *Concho* was rife with typhoid, malaria, dysentery, and yellow fever. Of the 190 passengers on board, at least 157 were sick. Twenty-five reportedly suffered from both malaria and yellow fever, although the problems were by no means confined to those illnesses. Soldiers John Koch died of what was described as "hemorrhages," Charles C. Le Reviere from overeating after not having eaten for too long, and Frederick Denner from blood poisoning that developed after he received an Army vaccination. Others had died at sea, but that was attributed in the press to nothing more "than the inadequacy of proper food and facilities for treating them."

"Inadequacy" was a kind word to use in describing the food and facilities. Dr. A. Monae Lesser, a surgeon working for the Red Cross who made the voyage, complained, "There was no food for the men on the *Concho*. The food given the sick men would have sickened well men." Lesser was not the least bit timid about telling reporters what he saw. Among other things, he charged that sick men had been transported without medicine, disinfectant, ice, fresh water, mattresses, and, in some cases, clothing. That wasn't totally accurate. There was a bit of medicine—some quinine, as well as camphor and sulfur. A little quinine, camphor, and sulfur had never stopped typhoid before and it would not stop it now.

There was plenty of corroboration of Lesser's appraisal. An officer, who wanted anonymity, told the *Tribune* that "many of the men were actually worse physically than when they left Cuba." Samuel McMillan, a former Commissioner of Parks in New York City who had gone to Cuba looking for his wounded son, a member of Roosevelt's Rough Riders, was one of the civilian passengers on the *Concho,* and he told what it was like to be aboard under a hot summer sky as the *Concho* wallowed northward. "For thirty-eight hours before we reached Hampton Roads the bodies of three men lay uncovered right under the saloon," he said, "and the stench was terrible. . . . The men who sewed the bodies up in canvas were dosed with brandy before they were able to handle the bodies. I never saw such blundering in my life from beginning to end and I believe that with proper food all the men might have been saved." McMillan's ordeal was especially painful. Having gone all the way to Cuba to bring his fever-stricken son home, he was told that his son had already been transported to New York.

The *Concho*'s skipper, Captain Samuel Risk, had wanted to lay over in Kingston, Jamaica, before heading north, so that he could take on fresh water and get other essential provisions. His wireless request was denied by General Shafter. Once in Hampton Roads, with the condition of passengers deteriorating rapidly, Risk wired Washington as to what was happening. He waited a full three days without receiving a clear-cut directive. As the

Concho waited, more soldiers died. When orders came, they obliged him to put to sea immediately so that the *Concho* could bury its dead. And when the funeral service was held, the pallbearers were tipsy under the influence of the captain's brandy. The sweet smell of rotting flesh filled the ship. Finally, the ship was ordered to sail on to New York. "Thank God we are going to New York!" exclaimed Captain Risk. "They will know how to treat us there." He would soon be proved even more wrong than was General Sternberg.

As the ship moved on to New York, its passengers became sicker by the day. Weak and desperately ill with high fevers, unclean, malnourished men sprawled on the *Concho*'s decks, sometimes lying in their own waste, waiting to be attended. Volunteer Red Cross nurses poured seawater on the brows of those burning up with fever. Soon the nurses became ill, too.

The *Concho* anchored in New York harbor off the Battery, and efforts were made to disinfect and fumigate it as its passengers were removed to Hoffman's Island. Captain Risk may have taken solace in New York City's reputation for excellent hospitals. Apparently, he did not know of the city's equally formidable reputation for bureaucratic detachment. Dr. Alvah H. Doty, health officer for the Port of New York, surveyed the situation and decided that reports of the poor health of the *Concho*'s passengers had been exaggerated. But he added that if they had contracted some illness in Cuba, it did not come within his province to determine precisely what it was.

The question of medical responsibility was raised by many of the doctors involved, even though they already knew the answers. Asking the obvious and answering disingenuously became as epidemic among doctors as the fevers were among the soldiers. Surgeon General Sternberg said that whatever was wrong with the men on the *Concho*, it certainly wasn't the responsibility of authorities under his command at Santiago, Cuba.

"The men are worn out and suffering from great mental and physical depression," said John H. Sloan, regimental surgeon of the 16th Infantry, in a reasonably candid interview with a correspondent from the *New York Herald*. "I think that with the approach of the bad fever months the mortality will be awful. . . . Tell your paper that if there is no military reason for our retention to try to get the men out." On the day of the interview, August 3, the Army reported there were 4,104 soldiers ill, 3,212 of them with some sort of fever.

There was no agreement as to what was happening, neither in New York nor back in Cuba. Clara Barton was in Cuba, seemed impelled to put the best face on it, and cabled the Red Cross, "Don't be alarmed by reports. All's well." All was *not* well.

Soon, the questioning syndrome spread from Army doctors to Army officers and thence to the Government itself. Everyone wanted to know why the soldiers had been allowed to become so sick. President McKinley wanted to know. He ordered an investigation. It was most tiresome for his Republican colleagues. They could now see political peril in what had promised to be the benefits of an easy war. Fortunately for the Republicans, McKinley was in a position to allow the War Department to investigate itself, which it promptly did.

It was an especially difficult situation for Secretary of War Russell A. Alger, who had served well as a colonel of a Michigan regiment during the Civil War, then made a fortune in the lumber business and found time to serve a term as Governor of Michigan. The Republicans loved him, of course, and at one point they thought that Alger's timber might be Presidential. That was not the case, but his business acumen was formidable, and McKinley thought he might make a suitable member of the Cabinet. As a vigorous sixty-year-old, Alger had been appointed Secretary of War in March of 1897. The War Department he was asked to run was truly an American antique, populated by bureaucrats who rejoiced in red tape, jealousy, and inefficiency. But Alger did not bring the same vigor to Government that he had brought to the lumber business. And now, he sensed, he was in imminent danger of becoming the goat.

Alger had not left the comfort of Michigan for this, and so he made the first of a number of statements in which he placed the blame not on the doctors in Santiago, not on the Surgeon General, not on the Navy, not on the Army brass, but on the soldiers who were sick. In Alger's considered opinion, it was the soldiers who boarded when they shouldn't have. That situation was made worse by other passengers of the transport ships, who, in Alger's view, may not have been thinking enough about the needs of the soldiers.

"At the time they left Santiago," Alger said, "the general desire of the convalescents to come home doubtless overcrowded both ships. . . . Then, also, a large number of civilians rushed aboard to get away and they occupied many staterooms that should have been given over to the soldiers." The "civilians," in this case, were personnel of the Red Cross, among them Dr. Lesser, who had already been publicly critical of the way the soldiers had been treated. The others included the women under Lesser's supervision who volunteered as nurses and whose extraordinary dedication thus was ignored.

The press, even in remote, stoical sections of the country not ordinarily quick to question the wisdom of Washington, was not satisfied with Alger's explanation. "Men who go to war, and especially men of the class who compose our Army, do not expect feather beds, with battlefields on shaded grass plots," editorialized the Boise, Idaho, *Sentinel*. "Neither do they anticipate Delmonico fare. But they do expect, and they have a right to expect, that the ordinary Army provisions for their comfort and health will be carried out. This was not done before they sailed; if it has been done since it will be a great surprise."

The War Department said the situation on board the *Concho* was much ado about nothing. Major Charles H. Heyl of the Inspector General's office exonerated the Army for what happened and said that Captain Risk was at fault for not explicitly telling the Army he needed water. "Had [he] done so, it would have been provided," said Heyl's report, which was released by the War Department. The Army even suggested that the *Concho*'s conditions had not been all that bad. Major John W. Summerhayes of the Army Quartermaster Corps went on board the *Concho*, anchored in New York, took a sip and sniff of its water, and declared it to be potable. Its foulness was exaggerated, he said.

The *Concho* wasn't the only source of embarrassment to the Government. Another ship, the *Santiago*, also laden with sick men from Cuba, landed in the Florida Keys. The men were happy when they sighted land, but nobody told the Army camp at Egmont Key that the ship was coming. "The station keepers at Egmont Key knew no more of our whereabouts than if we had been making a voyage of the upper reaches of the Congo," said one eyewitness aboard the ship, Stanhope Sams. "There was not even a hospital steward at the station—absolutely no one to look after the ship. . . ."

When this situation became known, *The New York Times* editorialized, "It is Alger and not Pitt who is entitled to the historical distinction of 'the most profuse and incapable of War Ministers.' "

But the worst events of all took place neither in Virginia, nor in New York City, nor in the Florida Keys.

In early June, the Army announced that it would create a camp at the eastern tip of Long Island where sick soldiers, homebound from Cuba, would be quarantined and treated. Montauk Point was selected, said the Army, because it had good drainage, was free of swampy ground, and was otherwise good for the health. The camp there was to be called Wikoff, after Charles A. Wikoff, an officer who had perished in the war.

Montauk was an unlikely place for a military reservation of any kind. The site selected was close to East Hampton, which was then in the early stages of becoming a colony for New York residents who wanted to escape the oppressiveness of summer in the city. Indeed, the local newspaper was most anxious that regular East Hampton residents be on their best behavior so as to favorably impress the visitors from Manhattan and Brooklyn, a notoriously demanding bunch. The paper urged homeowners to "keep lawns mowed . . . walks trimmed . . . yards clean. Everyone should do all in his or her power to make East Hampton, which is attracting new comers every year, appear so well that the very first impression the stranger receives shall be a good one."

It was an age of gentility, especially if war or its aftermath was not concerned. It was important for Americans to surround themselves with refinement. As East Hampton wondered what effect all those soldiers (sometimes given to using strong language) would have on its environment, the New York City Board of Aldermen debated an anti-swearing ordinance. Up in Greenwich, Connecticut, where such an ordinance had already been passed, Theodore Newton was fined $2, plus $13 in court costs, because he used the word "damn" to express his exasperation when he found Mr. and Mrs. Paul Putnam on board his yacht, even though Mr. Newton explained to the judge that he really hadn't been angry. If he had, he said, he would have simply chucked the Putnams overboard.

The *East-Hampton Star,* while never overtly hostile to the new Army camp, certainly did not want rough talk or rough lawns developing on Long Island. As the Army was deciding what should go where at Montauk, and a cataclysm was in the making, East Hamptonites concerned themselves with the vicissitudes of rural life. Betsey Beanstalk, said to be a resident of East Hampton, was advising the editor and the power structure of the truly important things in East Hampton's universe, among them a town clock that was not running ("a little whale oil would limber up its joints," she said) and the town's plans to move sand dunes so that "some parties [owning] land down there can sell building lots close up the ocean." Betsey Beanstalk did not think that was a good idea, since one could never tell when the Spanish fleet might show up and the sand dunes were "all we have to depend on. . . . They ought not to be touched." East Hampton thus evidenced its fear of the Spanish menace.

For reasons that collided with rational planning, the War Department ordered troops in Santiago, Cuba, to leave for Montauk, *at the very same time* that it ordered Army personnel in Montauk to build a camp hospital. How the generals thought that the Montauk setup was all going to be completed in time for the first arrivals was not spelled out anywhere. In deference, perhaps, to East Hampton's self-vision as a scrumptious new tourist area, the Department assured the village that the soldiers to be staying at Montauk would not carry any diseases that might be contagious. Surgeon

General Sternberg, outdoing his own fantasies in a single sentence, said he had been "reliably informed that they have not been exposed to fever infection." Even more assuring was his assertion that if any soldier was found to have anything that seemed to be contagious, he would "be left behind at the hospitals in the field."

But the promise was one that General Sternberg could not have kept, even if the public and the Government were totally impervious to considerations of common decency toward the veterans of the war. His plans for Montauk were being revealed at the same time that Roosevelt's letter, complaining of poor health conditions in Cuba, was released to the press. Roosevelt was a shrewd, powerful, and charismatic figure. There was no question about it now; troops would not be left behind in Cuba to make the world safer for the good people of East Hampton and Montauk. General Sternberg was then forced to admit that he said what he said because he did not know the true condition of troops in the field.

As the plight of soldiers in Cuba became more widely known to the public, the officials responsible for running the Army produced some explanations that were bizarre, even by the generous standards of the closing years of the nineteenth century. Maybe the soldiers didn't have real diseases at all, said an Adjutant General named Corbin. Maybe the thing that was making everybody sick was really "homesickness" and "nostalgia." "I think I could believe that the disease that is affecting so many of the men who are not reported by the doctors but who are said to be disabled from the performance of duty, is homesickness," Corbin said. He hastened to assure the public that such things seldom proved fatal and that out on Long Island people could breathe easier. Nostalgia wasn't the least bit contagious.

Ships laden with seriously ill and dying soldiers were on their way from Cuba, but as of August 7, a week after orders had been given to the carpenters to build the hospital, they had not built a hospital or anything else. There were one hundred of them, but they had not done any work. The reasons for their inactivity were not clear. There were no complaints from the carpenters; Montauk is very pleasant in August. And so in the grand tradition of the Army, they waited.

Not all workers at Montauk were inactive. The commander of the nonexistent camp was Brigadier General S.B.M. Young, who wisely decided that wells should be dug, so that soldiers would have fresh water. Well diggers were pressed into service, and they found water easily; four wells were dug that were only twelve feet deep and another went down to thirty feet. One well produced bad water within a few days, and the others produced water irregularly because of faulty pumps. Ultimately, bottled water was sent to the badly dehydrated soldiers who soon started to arrive, but much of it never reached them. Where it all went was unclear, but some of it was consumed by contract physicians who had been sent to Montauk's Camp Wikoff to tend the sick. Within a month, it would be reported that soldiers were rationed to a cup of water a day and that some, in desperation, were taking water from a stagnant pond. But "contract physicians are not depriving themselves of comforts," complained the *New York Herald,* after observing the doctors on duty.

Although there was no hospital in the commonly accepted sense of the word, General Young thought he could house the sick men in Barnum-sized tents—one of them big enough to shelter twenty thousand. It would be a field hospital to end all field hospitals. His circusian call went out from the Army that tents all over the country were to be sent to Montauk. Unfortunately, he envisioned the need for only five hundred beds. He apparently thought that many of the sick would get better before they even reached Montauk. It would prove a tragic miscalculation.

If the press had been alarmed at some of the things it had learned about the state of health among Americans in Cuba, it did not initially carry its justifiable skepticism to Montauk. And although the Government would later criticize the press for frightening the public about the health of soldiers, much of the press reported what it saw at Wikoff with restraint and gave the Army the benefit of the doubt.

"Every breeze is cool and every wind is laden with health and strength from the surrounding waters," reported a hopeful *New York Times* in a descriptive piece about Montauk, published on August 6. "The point should be an ideal one for sick and weary soldiers, exhausted by the fevers and burning heats of the tropics." Apparently, the *Times* believed, or wanted to believe, Colonel Roosevelt when he said that what the men needed was a bracing climate. It wasn't Maine, but Montauk was closer to Maine than it was to Cuba. Army doctors, who surely knew that it would take more than a pleasant day on eastern Long Island to cure malaria, yellow fever, and dysentery, remained silent. The people at Wikoff must have been somewhat alarmed at what they had heard about another camp—this one named, antemortem, after Secretary Alger—that had been receiving the sick in northern Virginia. Camp Alger was described as a "nursery of typhoid," and its modest amenities were severely compromised when the Army dug wells for drinking water next to the garbage dump. Well-digging, it seemed, was not the Army's strong point.

Meanwhile, work, such as it was, gained in momentum at Wikoff. The Army quartermaster reported that he shipped to it 150,000 pounds of oats,

150,000 pounds of hay, 50 cords of wood, and 250,000 pounds of straw. That promised to make it livable for the horses of officers. As for the incoming soldiers, the Army readied five carloads of tents that it had received from Philadelphia.

In the way that the tents were situated, troops would be treated to a marvelous view of the Atlantic—much the same one that New Yorkers, ensconced down the road in East Hampton, were paying considerable sums of money for. All in all, from the Army's perch, Camp Wikoff was shaping up as an almost recreational conclusion to the "splendid little war" in Cuba. Indeed, Army planners were so sure that just the trip by sea would be so pleasant and health-giving that it cut back on its orders not only for cots, but for medicine and clothing as well. It had not yet arranged for food, but was planning to accept bids from private companies. *The New York Times* said, ". . . it is feared that there will be a deplorable lack of accommodations, and that the wounded and sick will on their arrival find the conditions anything but enviable."

Meanwhile, transport ships moved closer to Montauk. The *Grande Duchesse*'s facilities were horribly taxed, and conditions seemed as bad as they had been on the *Concho*. Troops had no water, food was bad, no one tended the sick, and those who were ambulatory moved about on deck in a vain effort to stay out of the same sun that was tanning the tourists on shore. The men were relieved to see Montauk Point. But when the first troops—six hundred cavalrymen—arrived on August 9, there still was no hospital of any kind, no supply of fresh water for drinking or bathing, no suitable food, no suitable sanitary facilities. The view, however, was quite magnificent, and one officer, a Colonel Forwood, "was of the opinion that in most cases the change in air and scenery would work the cure of the sick."

The change in air and scenery did not help the sick. It began to rain. Most soldiers had no shelter. The soldiers pulled blankets and ponchos over themselves for protection as they huddled in the mud. The typhoid the men brought with them began to spread through the camp. There was still no fresh water because lost fittings for the recently installed well pumps had not yet been found; and the one hundred ready, willing, and able carpenters, who presumably could have helped and who had been on the scene only two weeks before, had vanished, leaving only two of their number behind.

The situation worsened. Dr. Frederick A. Castle, a former assistant surgeon in the Navy, visited Montauk and said that no large body of men should have been placed there because the site would not yield fresh water in sufficient quantity. He warned Surgeon General Sternberg by letter that more sickness was on the way. His letter made clear that he was aware of the Government's evasive comments on the health of the soldiers. He complained that he had written to the Army but had received no reply. "Orders have been issued without regard to their consequences, and the soldiers have had to suffer on account of thoughtlessness or incompetence," he said. Another officer, who apparently did not want to be identified, told the press that troops "were sent before the camp was in shape to receive them." His understatement was not contradicted.

East Hampton was not initially aware of what was happening at Camp Wikoff. A reader of the *East-Hampton Star,* who apparently expected Wikoff and its environs to be the scene of some sort of triumphal parade, wrote a poem in anticipation of that happy day.

> Strike the cymbals! Strike the cymbals!
>   Let joy bells ring out,
> And flags float in triumph o'er cottage and
>   dome;
>
> Strike the cymbals exhumant,
> With echoing shout;
>   Welcome home gallant heroes, welcome home,
>   welcome home . . .

The very same day the poem appeared, the *Star* ran an editorial, which asserted, "The talk about soldiers suffering for want of food at the camp is bosh. There are 75,000 rations already on the field, and the store houses filled." The source for the statement was not identified.

As soldiers continued to deteriorate, the *Star* wanted to make sure that all the rumors it was hearing about the soldiers would not ruin summer business. It reprinted an article from the *Brooklyn Eagle* which said, "The fears of the people in the villages . . . that the camp will drive away the families who are spending the summer there, are groundless. The camp is far enough away from the villages to prevent the soldiers from wandering into them and disturbing people. . . ."

But by late August, even the *Star* put the commercial interests of its own community to one side and acknowledged the problem in an abrupt change from its earlier editorial: "There must be a screw loose somewhere when Uncle Sam's soldiers, backed by a country of unlimited resources, are allowed to starve on transports and compelled to depend upon charity for food when they land upon our shores."

It would have been quite impossible for the *Star* to do otherwise. If there had been a Chamber of Commerce patina on its earlier prose, such considerations were not appreciated by its fashionable readers, who began to take a real interest in the unfashionable conditions at the camp and made considerable efforts to help the soldiers survive what was clearly an appalling mess.

One East Hampton woman named Chadwick wrote a letter to the editor and asked: "These starving men whom we are feeding, who are so reduced that they come to me and beg, and who burst out crying when they get more than they can eat, who are they? Paupers reduced to want through their own fault? No! but the members of one of the finest armies the world ever saw . . . the victors of Santiago, come home to die for want of food."

Meanwhile, General Sternberg was doing his damaged credibility no good at all by suggesting that the spread of typhoid could be controlled by filtering contaminated water. Still more troops arrived. The camp was overflowing with sick men, and the newcomers, also sick, were sent home. They hung about the camp for a time, hungry, confused, not knowing quite what to do, and were given plates of bread and butter by daughters of officers. Enlisted men were little better than beggars.

The question of nourishment was a puzzle. Charles E. Eagen, who was head of the Army's Subsistence Department, provided hardtack, salted pork, and a little bacon, the food soldiers had been used to in war. The hardtack arrived in wooden crates. It was filled with worms. He bought no fruit, although it was available in abundance. He also bought seven million pounds of canned boiled beef. It was so bad that even starving soldiers could not eat it. They called it "embalmed beef."

At the time soldiers could not find enough decent food at Montauk, Secretary Alger said he was under the impression they had more than enough, since reports that crossed his desk showed, among other things, that the Army had sent to the camp 54,860 gallons of milk, 3,000 pounds of halibut, 47,047 pounds of lima beans, 250 pounds of tea, 6,020 three-pound cans of apples, 1,774 gallon cans of apples, 14,500 pounds of apricots, 34,799 pounds of butter, 53,070 dozen fresh eggs, 300 crates of oranges, 13,889 cans of canned corn, 19,927 pounds of sugar-cured ham, and many thousands of cans of peaches, peas, beef soup, and chicken soup. There were even 7,100 gallons of pickles. Where did it all go? Nobody could say.

Alger even claimed that the Army hired "the best chefs that could be found in New York and Boston" to feed the soldiers, and perhaps such chefs did do the honors and used all that food. No one was sure except for Alger and his colleagues in Government. The only thing certain was that sick soldiers seemed, to the reporters who watched them, hungry all the time.

Moreover, many alert and well-intentioned residents of East Hampton put their own comfort aside and started regularly visiting the sick men with food and reassurances.

The camp hospital, jerry-built and teetering, was dangerously over-crowded with men sleeping on blankets on the floor. Most men had no blankets and there weren't enough tents. Some sick men, sensing their vulnerability if they continued to remain at Wikoff, somehow made it to New York City, where they were seen on street corners and in the city's hospitals, in desperate condition. But the more seriously ill were too weak to leave, and typhoid began to kill them. Wikoff became more of a killing ground than any battlefield in Cuba.

At one point, New York's Governor, Frank S. Black, became so concerned about reports of typhoid in the camp that he threatened to declare Wikoff quarantined from the rest of the state. General Young promptly responded that if the Governor did that, he would not recognize the quarantine. The standoff was resolved when the Army agreed to move the typhoid cases to established hospitals in New York.

When the Rough Riders arrived at Wikoff, crowds who may not have been totally aware of the seriousness of the health situation showed up to welcome them. The health of most of the Rough Riders had also suffered. One exception was their robust leader, Colonel Roosevelt, who told his admirers that he was "disgracefully healthy" and that, while in Cuba, his men had put up a "bully fight" and had a "bully time" from start to finish. Roosevelt, still wearing his brown service uniform, strode off the boat with General Joe Wheeler, who would soon be placed in charge of the camp by McKinley. Roosevelt was promptly given leave to visit his home in nearby Oyster Bay, where fifteen hundred people turned out to greet him.

But not all the Rough Riders had found Cuba as invigorating an experience as had the colonel. The *Tribune* reported that the Rough Riders and the 1st Battalion of the 71st New York that followed them had a "death-like pallor" on their faces. Within a week, three Rough Riders spent the night in a police station on East 35th Street in Manhattan, because they hadn't the money for a hotel room. On the same day, Rough Rider Lieutenant William Tiffany, son of the well-known Manhattan jeweler, died in Boston of "exposure and starvation." To the dismay of the Army, the circumstances of his death were reported fully by the New York press. The *Journal* put it on page one.

On August 22, with thousands of sick encamped at Wikoff, forty new typhoid cases were reported. It is not clear how many there were, but the disease was infecting scores of men, and deaths from the disease occurred every day. The situation was grim for all of them, but it may have been worst of all for the members of the Regular Army. Volunteers had enlisted in state units, and within those states, volunteer relief organizations tried to get food and medicine to them. Regular troops had no such benefactors, and to make matters worse, the Army was running out of its staple ration of hardtack and coffee for them. The rations that were on hand were reported to be moldy and rancid.

In Washington, Alger inured himself to present vicissitudes and kept the big picture in mind. He knew that this unfortunate incident would eventually pass. He wanted to make certain that in future years, nobody taking cues from the post–Civil War period tried to abuse the pension system because of the problems that allegedly existed at Wikoff and camps like it. The War Department thus issued an order mandating a physical for every soldier mustered out, so that if soldiers hungered for pensions as they did after the Civil War, the Government would be in a better position to deal with unjust claims.

Finally, in late August, Alger decided to visit Wikoff himself. Whatever he had heard since the first troops had arrived, he had not seen the situation firsthand. Perhaps he could not send the clothing, food, and medicine that the soldiers needed if they were to survive. But he could show them that he cared by sending himself. He came to New York City, checked into the Fifth Avenue Hotel, just north of Washington Square, and told a reporter from the *Herald:* "I shall . . . stay one, two or three days if necessary to make a complete investigation of the facts. If I can make one soldier a little more comfortable, I shall feel repaid."

Although mindful that Wikoff was a serious problem and that he was in New York for very serious business, Alger did not lose sight of the conduct expected of a public official of his high rank. He ventured to Montauk the next morning on a special train from Long Island City, and somehow the Army found sixteen men who were not especially sick to form an honor guard so that the Secretary's carriage would not be unaccompanied as it transported him from the station to lunch with Army officers. Alger, magnanimous as he rose to the occasion, said he wanted no special treatment and that, in fact, he would sleep in a tent, rather than in the snug cottage that the Army had provided. But it rained, and when Alger looked at the muddy disorder that was Camp Wikoff, he decided that he could empathize with the plight of his soldiers just as easily from the private car of the president of the Long Island Rail Road, and that was where he spent the night. Three more sick soldiers died overnight, their condition made worse by the rain and their own total lack of shelter.

Alger toured the camp and he was treated to a parade of sorts—"every man well enough was paraded in the best clothes he had." But as he toured, he spied a soldier who did not look well to him. Alger approached the soldier and asked, "Are you feeling pretty sick?"

"Yes sir, I am, rather, I do not feel at all well."

"He is quite sick, sir," said the soldier's father, who had come to Wikoff in a largely futile effort to take care of his son, "and I do not think he can get well very fast here. I have been trying to get him a furlough for several days so that he can go home to be taken care of, but I have not yet succeeded."

Alger offered him a furlough immediately. And so, by his standards, he was repaid for his trouble in coming to Wikoff. He had indisputably made one soldier a little more comfortable.

Then Alger faced reporters, who wanted to know what his impressions were. "I am very agreeably surprised at the conditions I find here," he told them. "The sick seem to be very cheerful."

There was a question as to whether Alger's review was thorough. A reporter for the *Herald* accompanied Alger on tour and included in the story he wired back to New York: "All the time I was with him I did not see him even look in the direction of a company kitchen." Apparently Alger also did not see Wikoff's contingent of coffin makers, who had steady work. Nor did he know, it would seem, that some of his soldiers had not been paid in three months and in order to save themselves from starvation, took to hanging around the luncheon counter at the railroad station, picking up fragments of sandwiches left behind by paying customers.

Alger, mindful that the approximately thirteen thousand troops present at Wikoff were a burden the camp's facilities could not carry, ruled that volunteers who were free of quarantine should be given furloughs and encouraged to make their way home on their own. When asked if he could find any substance to all the complaints that had surfaced about conditions at Wikoff, Alger snapped, "None." Alger felt the whole thing was the creation of the press and would later write that the "record of Camp Wikoff conclusively proves that most of the charges against it were without cause or reason." Indeed, he must have been delighted when Corporal Edward G. Stanton of the 2nd Volunteer Engineers later testified in a hearing that he personally had nothing to complain of at Camp Wikoff, but that civilians wrote to him expressing their concern because of what they had read in newspapers. "The *New York Journal* was responsible for a good deal," Stanton said.

Perhaps Alger saw nothing untoward, but New Yorkers, 125 miles away, did. The tragedy began to move to Manhattan. Sergeant Thomas Brennan, furloughed although stricken with malaria and malnutrition, collapsed at the corner of Bowery and Grand Street and was rushed to Governor's Island for treatment; Peter Baxter was found ill on 14th Street and taken to Bellevue Hospital, where his malaria was treated; and two other malaria victims, Edward Smith and Samuel T. Jones, were hospitalized in Manhattan. Private E. Percy McKeever's father went to Wikoff and whisked his son off to the Mount Sinai Hospital, but too late; young McKeever died of typhoid. "We were treated like dogs," he told his parents at his deathbed.

The news of what was happening to veterans of the Cuban campaign was greeted with sympathy. But the sympathy was not endless. For example, as the Wikoff debacle unfolded, officials of New Rochelle, New York, a fashionable community just north of New York City, sold the home of Edward Findley at 14 Warren Street at public auction for $1,800, because Findley, who had enlisted in the Army, was unable to pay the taxes with the wages he earned as a soldier. Where his wife and four children would go remained a question.

The New York Times had been covering the tragedy assiduously, with a restrained thoroughness. But with more and more evidence at hand that the War Department had bungled things badly, the *Times* grew bolder, asking President McKinley to dismiss Alger and demanding, "What kindness of heart is that which lets brave soldiers who have served their country well die of maltreatment and neglect . . . ?"

Even if the press had not been aggressive in its reporting, Manhattan residents would have become aware of the situation by themselves. Wikoff's furloughed troops were given train tickets to Long Island City, just across the East River from Manhattan, then somehow made it on their own to Whitehall Street, in Lower Manhattan, where, at the Quartermaster's Building, they would pick up pay and transportation money so that they could make it home. The trains would arrive invariably late in Long Island City, sick soldiers in cars at one end, the bodies of dead soldiers at the other, in the baggage compartment. It was a sight that New Yorkers would not soon forget.

Since Alger's visit to Camp Wikoff had placated neither press nor public, President McKinley decided to see it for himself. It was a long journey for McKinley. As he moved toward Montauk Point by rail, his train became mired in other rail traffic bearing sick soldiers, who were said to be "shrunken and ghastly white, and their faces told a terrible tale of suffering and hardship.'' At one point, McKinley entered a Red Cross hospital crammed with soldiers just in from Montauk and asked, ''Well, boys, how are you?'' There was no reply.

Sternberg, meanwhile, was emulating Alger's tendency to blame others for the mess created by the Government at Montauk. He said that the Red Cross had to share the responsibility, since it had had authority to send supplies since early June. Unfortunately for Sternberg's credibility, his accusation was made public a day after the Red Cross sent to Montauk ''twenty-five dozen suits of underwear, one case of sheets, fifty dozen towels, 200 pairs of slippers, three dozen napkins, fifty dozen pairs of socks, ten dozen belts, ten dozen pairs of suspenders, five cases of soups,'' as well as pipes and smoking tobacco.

The Army, finally acknowledging that Wikoff was, in fact, filled with yellow fever, began to furlough men furiously and, at the same time, remain silent on the scope of the health problems, apparently in an effort to keep it all secret. It kept no records of who was admitted and who was discharged. The ploy served only to confuse families who wanted to know where their sons were.

On August 20, New Yorkers enjoyed a naval review. It was a perfect Saturday afternoon as a huge throng gathered at Grant's Tomb to watch U.S. warships cruise up the Hudson River. The faces of the sailors on board could not be seen, but from all reports, sailors emerged from the Cuban campaign in reasonably good condition. The event was so successful that as the month ended, someone thought that it would be appropriate to honor foot soldiers. It was a parade the likes of which New York had not seen before. The men parading were ''pathetic . . . emaciated, hollow-eyed and enfeebled,'' all of them members of New York's 71st Regiment, refugees from Wikoff, numbering only 348. Those watching were in the thousands and gave them cheering ovations as they made their way from the Battery in Lower Manhattan to 34th Street.

At Wikoff, meanwhile, so many were dying so quickly that the Army was unable to notify next of kin. A man named Farnum brought a bag of delicacies for his son, who, he thought, was convalescing at Wikoff. He found his son's body in a coffin near the graveyard, waiting to be buried.

''Where will our patriots be found should another [war] come upon us after this terrible crime of our Nation in the name of humanity?'' asked Flora Adams Darling, founder general of the Daughters' Auxiliary League, in a letter to President McKinley. On August 30, the day her letter was published in the *Times,* the paper had a missive of its own for McKinley: ''Does the President know that the lives of American soldiers sacrificed in peaceful camps at home outnumber those lost on the fields of battle in Cuba and Manila?''

Perhaps McKinley did know. Within two weeks, Washington ordered that the men at Wikoff be moved out as quickly as possible. Indeed, Wikoff had already begun turning men away; it simply could not accommodate them. In a belated effort to contain the damage, McKinley appointed General Grenville M. Dodge, a close friend of Alger's, to head a commission to investigate the conduct of the War Department. It became known as the Dodge Commission. Its other members were Dr. Phineas T. Connor of Ohio and a former Governor of Vermont, Urban A. Woodbury.

As the Dodge Commission began its formation, two soldiers kept at Camp Hamilton, another Wikoff-like facility in Lexington, Kentucky, wagered 50 cents on who would die first. Albert Fish of New York and James Mitchell of Illinois both died on September 9—Fish at one in the afternoon, Mitchell fifty minutes later.

Wikoff was dismantled, and the only problem that remained, really, was the disposal of dead bodies. Even in this, the Army did not do well. The bodies were placed in pine coffins that cost less than $5 each. But many coffins were too small; the limbs of corpses were bent so that they could be crammed in. Many of the dead were buried not in their uniforms, but in nightshirts or, in some cases, in nothing at all.

In Washington, Secretary Alger lost none of his expertise in putting the blame where he thought it belonged. ''The whole trouble,'' he said, ''has been in the volunteer troops not knowing how to care for themselves and carelessness in warding off disease. The Regular Army men have not been troubled as the volunteers have. . . . Their general health has been good. . . .'' Alger issued that assessment shortly before going to visit Brigadier General Duffield, Regular Army, who was recuperating from an illness he had contracted in Cuba. Alger held some criticism in reserve for officers. Several days later, he said that the reports from officers had been generally good ''and if they are not well cared for and if the hospital and sanitary conditions are bad, the commanding officers must answer for it.''

Wherever the blame, the Dodge Commission studied the War Office and, not surprisingly, eventually commended Alger for his performance. The investigators said that the soldiers received bad beef and suggested that it was the beef, not Alger, that was at the root of the problem.

Thus, the Cuban campaign ended and the officers who managed it said that its aftermath might have been much better had it not been for the press. Major-General Adna R. Chaffee complained of the ''baneful and pernicious effect'' upon soldiers from ''careless and exaggerated newspaper statements.'' In a report of 1901 to the War Department, Chaffee noted, ''Soldiers do not like sympathy; sympathy is for women and children.''

The safeguards put into place by Alger to make certain that soldiers did not cheat on pension claims worked effectively. For example, James Fitch of Troop F, 1st Regiment, Illinois Volunteer Company, was rejected in 1914 for a pension because the Government told him he had not proved he got ''malarial poisoning, disease of the stomach and diarrhea'' while in the Spanish-American War. Fitch, whose home was in Muncie, Indiana, was apparently convinced that he could not have contracted malaria there. Fitch's widow, Lula, kept applying for war benefits into the early 1960s, when she died.

14
Of Mutilations, Massacres, and McKinley

A wounded enemy is a guest. A prisoner is a guest. That is the doctrine of military courtesy.
—General Arthur MacArthur, to the U.S. Senate Committee on the Philippines, 1901

We had no friends among the inhabitants.
—First Lieutenant Julien E. Gaujot, in explaining why he ordered the water torture of three Roman Catholic priests in the Philippines in 1902

We have invited our clean young men to shoulder a discredited musket and do bandits' work under a flag which bandits have been accustomed to fear, not to follow; we have debauched America's honor and blackened her face before the world....
—Mark Twain, "To the Person Sitting in Darkness" (1901)

Brigadier General Jacob H. Smith was both tired and impatient. He had come to the Philippines with hopes that the war there against native insurgents would be won as quickly and decisively as it had been against the Spanish in Cuba. That was not an unreasonable wish for a career Army officer who had only recently been promoted from colonel and whose direct, decisive manner had earned him the nickname "Hell Roaring Jake." The United States had, after all, paid Spain $20 million for the roughly seven thousand islands that composed the Philippine archipelago, even though the Americans, as victors, could have simply seized it as a spoil of war. In 1898, victors with the grace to buy a nation they already thought they owned did not expect to court violent rebellion by inhabitants who could not understand why Imperial America felt it was a better uncle than Imperial Spain had been. As Mark Twain put it, not just for the Filipinos but for all those subjugated by colonialism, "They have become suspicious of the blessings of civilization." But Smith's hopes for a quick end to the war were not to be realized, even though his superior, General E. S. Otis, had assured Americans publicly that he could put the rebels down in a matter of weeks.

In response to Spanish colonialism, native Filipinos had already rallied around Emilio Aguinaldo, who felt that they—not Spaniards—should run the Philippines. Now that the Spanish were gone, Aguinaldo continued to feel that logically, if unrealistically, his people should not be subjected to yet another foreign power, the $20 million notwithstanding. He was not impressed with the Americans and their desire to "improve" the Philippines, by planting the seeds of American democracy and the Protestant-Christian–tinged work ethic that many Protestants (if not so many of their Catholic and Jewish brethren) felt had worked so well in the United States. Nor was he attracted to President McKinley's assurances that American soldiers were in the Philippines not "as invaders or conquerors, but as friends to protect the natives in their homes, in their businesses, and in their personal or religious liberty." Filipinos felt they could do all that themselves, if only outsiders would leave them alone. And so the first clash between Aguinaldo's insurgents and the Americans took place in February of 1899.

Two years later, the war was still on, and Americans had come to regard the Filipinos as ungrateful primitives who simply did not understand what goodness would accrue to them if they accepted American values. Smith and his fellow officers were being asked to fight an enemy that forever lurked deep in thick forests and insisted on conducting guerrilla forays that cost many American lives. There was no front. Only the guerrillas. Among the incidents called to Smith's attention: insurgents reportedly "mutilated" dead Americans; they burned the face and head of one officer that they captured; they filled a gaping wound across the face of a young lieutenant with jam; an enlisted man "had his abdomen cut open and codfish flour had been put in the wound"; a sentinel was "stabbed full of holes."

It did not seem to matter very much that there were now thirty thousand American soldiers in the Philippines. What seemed to matter was that there were seven million Filipinos, and the Americans were not entirely certain that any of them could be trusted, whether they wore a soldier's uniform or not. One lieutenant complained that he found Filipinos "treacherous and cruel . . . what I consider savages." Another lieutenant was upset because he had encountered insurgents as young as twelve years of age but that as guerrilla fighters, they were "just as good" as those who were twenty.

Ambushes continued. Rifle fire came from unexpected places. On one Sunday morning in September of 1901, fifty-nine American soldiers were killed and twenty-three were wounded in a guerrilla attack at Balangiga. The guerrillas had disguised themselves as women. Although Balangiga was the single worst American rout, it was by no means the only one. Knives and bayonets took their toll everywhere. It was not a war that the Americans really knew how to fight, and the guerrillas were as implacable as the jungle itself.

There finally came a day when Smith, commander of the 6th Separate Brigade, could stand it no more. He summoned one of his subordinates, Major Littleton W. T. Waller of the Marines, and told him: "I want no prisoners. I wish you to kill and burn—the more you kill and burn the better you will please me." He also told Waller that "the interior of the Samar must be made a howling wilderness."

Waller, a veteran of much combat who well knew the rules of war, was stunned by the order. He asked Smith to clarify what he meant by taking *no* prisoners. What age would be the cutoff for summary execution? Waller demanded to know. What age would determine who would live and who would die?

Smith designated the limit as ten years of age. Anybody over that, he said, could be considered an "enemy" and killed.

Waller was too effective an officer not to insist on a clarification. He had to be sure that Smith had said what he thought Smith had said. And so he asked Smith, once again, if he had really told him to regard anyone over the age of ten years as a potential enemy who could be subject to summary execution. Smith replied, in a voice that was as loud as Smith was short, that this was precisely what he had said.

Obediently, Waller led a detachment of fifty-four enlisted men, two guides and thirty-three *cargadores* (porters) in search of insurgents in the Samar, which was one of the larger of the Philippine islands, south of Luzon. The march was not an easy one, not even for Marines. It rained incessantly, there were no roads, the jungle and its quagmires were unforgiving, and the Americans began to get ill. Their shoes were worn away, many were stricken with fever, leeches attacked their open wounds, and the soldiers ran out of food. They ran out of medicine, too. For days, they subsisted on roots and tropical berries. It was maddening. The enemy was everywhere, or so it seemed. "Even the women carried arms," Waller

observed. Gradually, the people of the Samar, who had never been held in
very high esteem by the Americans, seemed something less than human.
One of Waller's officers, a Lieutenant Baines, considered the people of
Samar as being "very low in intelligence" and having "no feeling, either
for their families or for anybody else." It did not bode well for what
Americans liked to think of as their leading role in practicing "civilized"
warfare.

Waller's officers grew weak, then angry, then nasty. Waller himself
became ill. And when they all suspected that the porters "did not efficiently
respond" to the cries for more food, and may, in fact, have been engaged
in hostile or violent acts against the Marines, Waller had eleven of them
executed by the very Marines they were trying to serve. There was no trial.
No charges were filed before a judge. There was none of the due process that
the Americans cherished in their own Constitution. So beneath the contempt
of Americans were the Filipino people that the names of the dead Filipinos
were not even recorded. All those shot were unarmed and technically in the
employ of the U.S. Government.

Waller's men were relieved of their duties on Samar on February 26,
1902, and as the Army came in and the Marines pulled out, Smith took stock
of the executions and told Waller's men, "You are as fine a group of
soldiers as has ever served under my command and I have been an officer for
forty years."

But in the inevitable court-martial that followed, Smith was only ordered
to be "admonished." Secretary of War Elihu Root wrote to President
Roosevelt that Smith's orders were "justified by the history and conditions
of the warfare with the cruel and treacherous savages who inhabited the
island" and that Smith had shown "high courage" in many earlier battles.
Root thought Smith simply ought to be retired from the Army. President
Roosevelt, who had succeeded the assassinated McKinley, agreed; Smith
got a polite letter from the Army advising him to "repair to his home." No
courageous U.S. Army officer would ever need fear that he did not have the
support of Teddy Roosevelt, whether in the baptism of fire on San Juan Hill
or in soldier politics on Capitol Hill.

Waller, who by following Smith's orders earned the sobriquet "Butcher
of Samar," was court-martialed, too. General Smith, for all his courage, did
not stand by the men he only recently had thought so highly of. Indeed, he
appeared as a prosecution witness and testified that Waller had no order from
him to execute the eleven. Waller had tried to go through his trial without
hurting Smith. The court-martial found, "In this instance there was no
overwhelming necessity, no impending danger, no imperative interests,

and, on the part of the natives, no overt acts to justify the summary course pursued.'' But Waller was nevertheless acquitted and returned to active duty. The court cited his ''mental attitude'' in making its decision.

The press gave prominent play to the Samar incident, and that, in turn, helped America's antiwar faction, which contained such outspoken men as Senator George F. Hoar, Republican of Massachusetts; Charles Eliot Norton, president of Harvard; and Andrew Carnegie, the industrialist. If the invasion of Cuba had been a ''splendid little war,'' there was no similar feeling about the War of the Philippine Insurgency.

There were other incidents. Although none was as bloody as the Samar executions, they said much about what the Americans were doing in the Philippines and they hinted at a homecoming that could be somewhat marred, certainly less than was expected at the beginning of such a war. They would also give evidence that if some American soldiers were succumbing to shoddy behavior as soldiers, other soldiers were able to acknowledge that behavior and did not hesitate to share their feelings with friends and family back home. Among the incidents:

• First Lieutenant Preston Brown, 2nd U.S. Infantry, shot an unarmed, unresisting Filipino prisoner in the back of the head shortly before Christmas of 1900, after the prisoner reportedly said *''No sabe''* to one of Brown's questions. Brown had suspected the man of being an *insurrecto*. At Brown's court-martial, Private Chester Rhodes said he saw Brown pistol-whip the Filipino shortly before killing him. Brown was unclear as to why he shot the man; he testified he had actually planned to hire him as a guide. The court-martial did not clarify how the Filipino made the rapid descent from guide to enemy in Brown's eyes. He was given a five-year prison sentence, but when President Roosevelt learned of the sentence, he decided it was too harsh and, instead, suspended Brown and fined him half his pay for nine months.

• Major Edwin F. Glenn was court-martialed and found guilty of applying the ''water cure'' to Toneniano Ealdama, a Filipino from whom he wanted to obtain information about possible insurgents. Ealdama, who was president of the town of Igbarras, testified that Glenn made him lie down on some rocks, put a faucet in his mouth, and poured water into him until his stomach hurt. ''I thought I was going to die,'' he said. Glenn's sentence was suspension from command for a month and a fine of $50.

• First Lieutenant Julien E. Gaujot, 10th Regiment of Cavalry, was court-martialed because he applied the water cure to three priests who he suspected were sympathetic to or knowledgeable about the insurgents. "We had no friends among the inhabitants," Gaujot said in his own defense. He pleaded guilty, was suspended for three months, and fined $150.

• Captain James A. Ryan, 15th Cavalry, ordered the water cure on Uvaldo Abing, president, and Luis Gineño, vice-president, of the pueblo of Jiminez on Mindanao Island. Abing's hands were tied behind his back and his head was held underwater in a galvanized bucket. In a rather creative defense of Ryan, Army medical officer Major P. R. Egan compared Abing's immersion to "bobbing for apples in a tub of water at Hallowe'en." As for Gineño, Second Lieutenant Charles Burnett noted that Ryan showed "no animus" toward him and that "clear water" was used for the cure, as though that would somehow make it seem less savage. Burnett testified that he became curious about the effects of the water cure and put his own head underwater. He found it to be "without any disagreeable sensations," although he did not liken it to bobbing for apples. Ryan said he needed an acquittal so that it would send a supportive message to other officers and enlisted men in the future. He was acquitted.

• Captain Cornelius M. Brownell subjected the Rev. Augustine de la Peña to the water cure, after the priest denied that he sympathized with the insurgents or knew the whereabouts of their money. The priest died after treatments in which soldiers were told by their sergeant to "dose the nigger again." He also suffered from days of underfeeding. He was buried not in a cemetery, but in the field where the Americans played baseball. His grave was not marked. Brownell said in his defense that he was told that de la Peña was "not a regularly admitted priest" and that the priest became "insolent." Brownell said he did not believe that the water cure was "cruel or barbarous in any manner" and he added that in selecting soldiers to administer the water cure, he always insisted on men who were "intelligent, careful and humane." Indeed, the Army seemed to feel that de la Peña may have been at least partly to blame for his own death. The Army said that he died of a heart attack and cited his obesity as a contributory cause. First Sergeant Alonzo Woodside said he had always understood that the cause of the priest's death was "fatty degeneration of the heart." The implication was that if de la Peña had been more restrained at dinner, he might have been in better condition to take the cure. However, Walter Snow, an enlisted man, described Brownell's method of applying the water cure to the priest, which suggested that even men in much better condition than de la Peña might have succumbed:

. . . Captain Brownell tried to get some information out of him and he would not give it. There were three or four men got him and put him down and held him down, took a stick and pried his mouth open. Then we went out and got a bucket of water and kept pouring it into his mouth, but he would not tell. Then they let him up. We then held him down again, poured more in him, and the captain says, "I will fix him." He takes out a rifle—a six-shooter—and he says to one of the lads, to Moran of the same company, "When I fire this pistol you hit him on the head, not very hard, with a stone, a little stone that just cut his head," and the nigger when he heard the pistol shot thought he was shot and he told him that if they left him up he would show them some rifles.

As this sorry business unfolded in the Philippines, letters from enlisted men describing American conduct in the war began to be received by friends and relatives at home. Many of them wound up in newspapers or were published by the Anti-Imperialist League in Boston, whose vociferous members were opposed to the war and the transformation of America into a colonial power. As the letters became public knowledge, the image of the American warrior on an overseas adventure changed; the messages made some Americans think again about the war they had supported so uncritically. For in these letters, the very decency of the country seemed to be evaporating. Soldiers admitted that they had stolen, murdered innocent men, women, and children, and otherwise acted as American soldiers were not supposed to act, at least in popular lore. Americans who wanted to believe so much in their own goodness were now being told by their own troops that they were no better than anyone else.

"We burned hundreds of houses and looted hundreds more," wrote E. D. Furnham of the Washington Regiment. "Some of the boys made good hauls of jewelry and clothing. . . . We have horses and carriages, and bull-carts galore, and enough furniture and other plunder to load a steamer."

Anthony Michea of the 3rd Artillery wrote home, "We bombarded a place called Malabon, and then we went in and killed every native we met, men, women and children. It was a dreadful sight, the killing of the poor creatures. The natives captured some of them Americans and literally hacked them to pieces, so we got orders to spare no one."

One unidentified soldier at Manila wrote to his father, "Talk about Spanish cruelty: they are not in with the Yank. Even the Spanish are shocked. Of course I don't expect to have war without death and destruction, but I do expect that when an enemy gets down on his knees and begs for his life that he won't be shot in cold blood. But it is a fact that the order was not to take a prisoner, and I have seen enough to almost make me ashamed to call myself an American."

With the reports of American barbarity in the Philippines, revealed in the letters of the soldiers who in some instances were committing the acts, the war became less popular. People in Meadville, Pennsylvania, for example, actually assaulted some young men who were trying to enlist in the Army there so that they could fight in the Philippines. There were also reports that some American enlisted men actually defected to Aguinaldo and likened him to George Washington.

"I am not afraid and I am always ready to do my duty," wrote Sergeant Arthur H. Vickers of the 1st Nebraska Regiment, "but I would like some one to tell me what we are fighting for." The sergeant's officers couldn't tell him. "I deprecate this war, this slaughter of our own boys and of the Filipinos," wrote General Felix A. Reeve, who had served as a colonel in the 13th Minnesota Regiment, "because it seems to me that we are doing something that is contrary to our principles. . . . Certainly we are doing something that we should have shrunk from not so very long ago."

Even after such letters were printed, some Americans could not bring themselves to believe them. *The New York Times,* for example, charged that some anti-imperialists had used "forged or distorted documents in support of their arguments" about American conduct of the war. The *Times* said it felt that the charges of atrocities committed by Americans were "so grotesque and uncharacteristic as to carry, for most of us, clear proof of falsity or inaccuracy."

Just as disturbing as reports of the American atrocities themselves was ample evidence that bigotry was apparent in the campaign against the *insurrectos.* Americans were having a difficult time, as usual, in understanding their own developing national ethos. With the exception of the Indians, whom they had only recently defeated, they were a nation of immigrants. The insecurity associated with immigrant status made it difficult for some of them to understand or accept people who were not cast in the nation's dominant Anglo-Saxon mold.

Only a decade and a half earlier, Americans had taken comfort in the passage of the Chinese Exclusion Act of 1882, which barred the importation of Chinese laborers into the United States for ten years. There was a feeling that such people, no matter how hard they worked, could not really be American. Now that America had acquired the Philippines, Americans feared that the Filipinos would create some of the same problems that the Chinese Exclusion Act had gotten rid of. "With the danger from the invasion of the Chinese laborers still fresh in our memories, there are those who favor annexing to this union nine millions of people inferior in every respect to the Chinese, and who will then become a perpetual menace to every wage earner in this country," warned Congressman Claude A.

Swanson of Virginia, who was strongly against ratifying the treaty to acquire the Philippines.

American apprehensions about the national identity were not confined to Asians or blacks. At the turn of the century, Americans could not count on Washington to even admit the right kind of immigrant from Europe. The Irish who had come over sixty years earlier had been trouble enough. But they seemed almost nice when compared to some of the newer immigrants, who not only arrived unable to speak English but could not even be counted on to emulate the fair complexion of the people who had become Americans earlier. "Without any prejudice, express or implied," said *The New York Times,* "it is clear from experience that the immigrants coming to us from the East of Europe and from Southern Italy are of less benefit to the country and are more likely to be a burden than those coming from the races of Western Europe, the British Isles, Germany, France and Scandinavia."

Already exasperated because of the attributes of Chinese, Italian, and Eastern European immigrants, Americans who agreed with the message of the editorial were in no mood to be indulgent with the Filipinos. But to a few thinking people back in the States, what was happening to Americans in relation to the Filipinos was a blot on national honor and the cause for profound concern. Their feelings only intensified when some of the worst expressions of racism appeared in letters home from soldiers and were printed in local newspapers. Indeed, there were times when it seemed that the Filipino peril and the southern European peril were interchangeable, at least in the common talk the soldiers knew.

"We can lick them, but it will take us a long time, because there are about 150,000 of the dagos back in the hills, and as soon as one of them gets killed or wounded there is a man to take his place at once," complained Martin P. Olson of the 14th Regulars.

Frank M. Erb of the Pennsylvania Regiment reported, "We have been in this nigger-fighting for twenty-three days, and have been under fire for the greater part of that time. The niggers shoot over one another's heads or any old way. Even while I am writing this the black boys are banging away at our outposts, but they very seldom hit anybody. The morning of the 6th a burying detail from our regiment buried forty-nine nigger enlisted men and two nigger officers. . . . We will, no doubt, start home as we get these niggers rounded up."

An unidentified private of Company H of the 1st Regiment, Washington State Volunteers, complained, "The weather is intensely hot, and we are all tired, dirty, and hungry, so we have to kill niggers whenever we have a chance, to get even for all our trouble."

"I am probably growing hard-hearted," wrote A. A. Barnes, Battery G, 3rd U.S. Artillery, "for I am in my glory when I can sight my gun on some dark skin and pull the trigger. . . . Tell all my inquiring friends that I am doing everything I can for Old Glory and for America I love so well."

The racism expressed by white American soldiers was not lost on the blacks who also served in the Philippines. "I have not had any fighting to do since I have been here and don't care to do any," wrote Sergeant Patrick Mason to the *Cleveland Gazette*. "I feel sorry for these people and all that have come under the control of the United States. . . . The first thing in the morning is the 'Nigger' and the last thing at night is the 'Nigger.' " Mason was a light-skinned black man who apparently passed for white among many of his fellow soldiers. "I love to hear them [white Americans] talk that I may know how they feel," he wrote. "The poor whites don't believe that anyone has the right to live but the white American. . . ."

Some blacks thought that the intensity of the insurrection itself was due to American racism. "All this never would have occurred if the army of occupation would have treated them as people," complained an unidentified black soldier in a letter to the *Wisconsin Weekly Advocate*. "The Spaniards, even if their laws were hard, were polite and treated them with some consideration; but the Americans . . . began to apply home treatment for colored peoples: cursed them as damned niggers, steal [from] and ravish them, rob them on the street of their small change, take from the fruit vendors whatever suited their fancy, and kick the poor unfortunate if he complained, desecrate their church property, and after fighting began, looted everything in sight, burning, robbing the graves. . . . I want to say right here that if it were not for the sake of 10,000,000 black people in the United States, God alone knows on which side of the subject I would be."

A few blacks were so distraught that they deserted to the Filipino side, although the overwhelming majority were loyal and served well, even in the face of the oppressive discrimination they faced at the hands of their white compatriots. "We are now arrayed to meet what we consider a common foe, men of our own hue and color," wrote M. W. Saddler, a sergeant with the 25th Infantry, in a letter to the *Freeman* of Indianapolis. "Whether it is right to reduce these people to submission is not a question for the soldier to decide."

The nature of American patriotism may have been becoming an intense embarrassment to the people who had been opposed to the Spanish-American War in the first place, such as those in the Anti-Imperialist League in New England, but many others did not seem to notice a problem. As Americans began to send more troops into the Philippines, Oliver Wendell

Holmes, Jr., confided to a friend, "I confess to pleasure in hearing some rattling jingo talk after the self-righteous and preaching discourse which has prevailed to some extent at Harvard College and elsewhere."

Two years went by. The end of the war was not in sight. As questions surfaced about American conduct in the Philippines, demand grew for a Congressional investigation. Herbert Welsh, a supporter of the Anti-Imperialist League and one of those incensed at the war and its effect on the country, tracked down returning soldiers and induced them to tell him their stories about the atrocities. It was not unlike the Winter Soldier investigations that would be held by the veterans of the Vietnam War, some seventy years later.

The Senate initiated the investigation in early 1902 and selected a supporter of the war, Henry Cabot Lodge of Massachusetts, to chair it. From Lodge's point of view, it could not have been a very auspicious moment to look at such a war closely: Seven soldiers had just signed a proclamation openly inviting their fellows to desert and join the Filipino army.

Lodge attempted to rebuff the Army's critics. In a speech before the Senate, he emphasized the good things about the Army: ". . . these soldiers are our own. They are flesh and blood, bone of our bone, flesh of our flesh. They are men drawn from our American communities . . . graduates of West Point, graduates of Harvard and Yale. . . . They are not saints; no, and they are not devils, either."

With feelings such as these, Lodge had no other choice but to try to put the best face on a bad situation. He certainly got that from his first witness, William Howard Taft, who was the civilian Governor of the Philippines and had been resident there for two years. Taft was a sort of tour guide, skipping around in his testimony to such peaceable oddments as what sort of grass was consumed, or at least preferred, by Filipino cows. He also observed that the Filipinos had a good ear for music. "I have never met a Filipino who was not a musician, who could not carry an air with a remarkable memory; and everywhere you go you find Filipino bands." And he added, "I think I may say that we have had chiefly in mind always the good of the Filipino people. Of course, it is said that this is an Oriental people; that this is a people that loves siestas; that seizes every occasion to have joyful gathering. . . ."

Taft credited the American Army with putting a stop to guerrilla activity, which he characterized as a "system of terrorism." When he was asked about American use of the water cure, he initially sidestepped the question, but he did address himself to the stresses felt by American soldiers. ". . . that [guerrilla] system of warfare kept troops on a nervous strain," he said, suggesting that he regarded guerrilla warfare as ''hardly within the laws of war.'' Taft acknowledged that American soldiers might have been a little harsh at times, but that was only in retaliation for the constant guerrilla actions directed against them. Taft also agreed with Senator Thomas M. Patterson that in any war the ''superior race'' will succumb to ''inhuman conduct'' if the superior race is waging war against an enemy considered ''inferior in the scale of civilization.''

If Senator Lodge hoped to take the edge off criticism of the war with the hearing, it did not work that way. If anything, the public revelations emanating from the hearing room got Americans more stirred up than they had been before. For example, the people who supported the war hoped that when General Robert P. Hughes testified, he would exhibit the decorum, dignity, and restraint that Americans associated with a senior military commander. Hughes had been commander of Manila. But there was nothing decorous to be found in his words. He admitted to the most extreme kinds of war crimes and did it without blinking an eye.

At one point, he was asked by Senator Joseph Rawlins about the burning of towns filled with civilians and what purpose there was in it.

''The destruction was as punishment,'' Hughes said.

Rawlins pressed the matter. Weren't the towns filled mostly with women and children?

''The women and children are part of the family, and where you wish to inflict punishment you can punish the man probably worse in that way than in any other,'' Hughes replied.

''But is that within the ordinary rules of civilized warfare?''

''These people are not civilized,'' Hughes said.

''Then I understand you to say it is not civilized warfare?''

''No; I think it is not,'' the general said.

''Are they not like all Latin races,'' asked Senator Fred T. Dubois, ''or all people who come under the domination of the Spaniards, indolent; and if they do not go to a bullfight, will they not go to a cockfight? Will they not go off for two or three days if they get two or three dollars? Can you depend upon them as laborers, even if they had the physical ability?''

''They are lazy,'' Hughes said, ''. . . they want to go to cockfights, and they want to gamble, and they want to whet up their bolos.''

''They want to play,'' concluded Senator Dubois.

Hughes went on to say he favored using American Negro troops in the Philippines. ''The darky troops . . . sent to Samar mixed with the natives at once. Wherever they came together they became great friends. When I withdrew the darky company from Santa Rita I was told that the natives even shed tears over their going away. I know they begged me to leave them.''

As for the water cure, Hughes at first testified, ''I never heard anything about it.'' When pressed, he conceded, ''I heard of but one case of that character.''

Until the Senate hearings, the official line from the Government was that no war crimes of any kind had ever been committed by American troops in the Philippines. But Elihu Root, Secretary of War, thought that in light of the disclosures, perhaps it might be better to own up to them and punish those responsible in a very public way. He thus issued a report called ''Letter from the Secretary of War Relative to the Reports and Charges in the Public Press of Cruelty and Oppression Exercised by Our Soldiers Toward Natives of the Philippines.'' Root, who was a political novice, disclosed more than he should have. Rather than smooth over public concern about the conduct of American troops, he got people riled up even more.

The most disturbing aspect of Root's report was his detailing of forty-four military trials which culminated in convictions for rape, murder, the burning of villages, and assorted assaults. Such detail, much of which had not been known to the American public at large, made the testimony of Taft and Hughes seem tepid. Root blamed the atrocities not on the American soldiers or on the Government that sent them on their Philippine adventure, but on the Filipino troops, who, he said, ''have frequently fired upon our men from under protection of flags of truce, tortured to death American prisoners . . . buried alive both Americans and friendly natives, and horribly mutilated the bodies of American dead.''

Soldiers who had written letters alluded to by Root in his report curiously began to retract what they had written. Sometimes their officers did it for them. Second Lieutenant P. M. Kessler, for example, said that Edward Gard, who had been a private in his command, did not mean what he wrote home about the killing of wounded Filipino prisoners. It was not unusual for enlisted men ''to boast of what they had done,'' the lieutenant wrote. As for Gard, he now alleged that what he had written his mother earlier was ''an exaggeration.''

Exaggeration or not, between August of 1898 and March of 1901, ten officers and thirty-six soldiers and scouts were brought to trial ''for cruelty of natives and for violations of the laws of war.'' The sentences were generally light: Lieutenant Bissell Thomas paid a $300 fine and was reprimanded following his conviction for applying ''acute torture'' to a prisoner; Joseph Faust had to pay $60 for ''kicking native woman in face.'' Two officers were charged with torturing natives by causing them ''to be hung by neck for ten seconds'' but they were acquitted with no explanation.

When pressured by their officers to recant the letters they had written home, some of the soldiers refused. Perhaps the most conspicuous of these was Charles Riley, a feisty and stubborn plumber from Northampton, Massachusetts. There was no question that Riley was a good soldier—he had risen from private to first sergeant in only eighteen months. And there was also no question that Riley would not be budged from his determination to tell the truth about what he had seen in the Philippines.

Appearing before the Senate committee, he gave an account of a water cure he had witnessed in the town of Igbaras on November 27, 1900. "He [the prisoner] was stripped to the waist; he had nothing on but a pair of white trousers and his hands were tied behind him," Riley said. He recalled there was also a one-hundred-gallon tank in the room that had been used for catching rainwater. It was on a raised platform.

> He was then taken and placed under the tank, and the faucet was opened and a stream of water was forced down or allowed to run down his throat; his throat was held so that he could not prevent swallowing the water, so that he had to allow the water to run into his stomach. . . . When he was filled with water, it was forced out of him by pressing a foot on his stomach or else with their hands . . . from five to fifteen minutes. There was a native interpreter that stood directly over the man. . . . He practically kept talking to him all the time, kept saying some one word which I should judge meant "confess" or "answer."

The following colloquy then took place between Riley and two senators:

> Q. At the conclusion, what was then done?
> A. After he was willing to answer he was allowed to partly sit up, and kind of rolled on his side, and then he answered the questions put to him by the officer through the interpreter.
> Q. Where did they take him?
> A. They took him downstairs outside the building, and he stood in front of the building, waiting for his horse. He was to guide the expedition up into the mountains.
> Q. While standing on the sidewalk, what took place?
> A. More information was sought for; and [when] he refused to answer a second treatment was ordered. . . . They started to take him inside the building and Captain Glenn said, "Don't take him inside, right here is good enough." One of the men from the Eighteenth Infantry went to his saddle and took a syringe from the saddlebag, and another man was sent for a can of water, what we call a kerosene can, holding about five gallons. He brought

this can of water down from upstairs, and then a syringe was inserted, one end in the water and the other end in his mouth. This time he was not bound, but he was held by four or five men and the water was forced into his mouth from the can, through the syringe. . . . The syringe did not seem to have the desired effect, and the doctor ordered a second one. The man got a second syringe, and that was inserted in his nose. Then the doctor ordered some salt, and a handful of salt was procured and thrown into the water. Two syringes were then in operation. The interpreter stood over him in the meantime asking for this second information that was desired. Finally he gave in and gave the information that they sought, and he was allowed to rise.

Q. May I ask the name of the doctor.

A. Dr. Lyons, the contract surgeon.

Q. An American?

A. Yes sir.

Riley then went on to describe the burning of a town, and Senator Albert J. Beveridge tried to puncture his testimony by asking him why, in his letter home on the water cure, he did not also mention the "outrages committed by the natives upon the Americans."

"I was not comparing the case at all," Riley answered, unruffled. "I was simply stating this fact."

Senator Julius Caesar Burrows then had another joust at Riley in an effort to show, as had been intimated by some officers, that the water cure was not a disagreeable experience at all, and that perhaps Lieutenant Burnett had not been so far off when he likened it to bobbing for apples.

Q. You never had the water cure administered to you?

A. No, sir.

Q. Should you judge from the actions of the person to whom it was administered that it was a pleasant operation?

A. No, sir.

Q. Painful?

A. Yes, sir.

Q. What makes you think so?

A. From the way he would struggle and try to get up, and of course he could not holler or make any noise, any loud noise.

Q. Why not?

A. On account of the water being in his mouth. He could gurgle, and he would struggle and try to get up. . . .

Riley could not be budged, and his testimony was powerful and powerfully uncomfortable to the members of the United States Senate who heard it. How could they not believe such straightforwardness? More to the point, how could they square Riley's testimony in even a remote way with what they had been told by officers and high Government officials? General Arthur MacArthur, Governor of the Philippines in 1900–01, had told the senators that the Army was "planting the best characteristics of American-ism in such a way that they never can be removed from that soil." But Sergeant Riley told them that they had planted the worst excesses of imperialism, excesses that even the simplest natives would never forget.

By the turn of the century, the United States had fought six wars or punitive campaigns. Not until the Philippine Insurrection did the Govern-ment formally question, after the fact, the reason for making war and why it was that the children of a nation that prided itself on its own goodness went to war and committed the crimes of war. Their deeds would be remembered long after the war itself, which was eminently forgettable.

Was this because those earlier wars were of a calling so virtuous that no questions had to be asked? Quite to the contrary. The acts against the Indians in the nineteenth century surely did not possess the Revolution's luster; the clarity and the rapacity of the land-acquisition motive for the Mexican War could not be compared to the probity of the War of 1812, when the nation had to repulse the British once again, just to retain freedoms won earlier. The Civil War was an abysmal failure of all Americans to resolve a myriad of differences of their own invention.

But those wars ended and there was only silence. Nobody formed commissions to question the way they had been fought or the moral purpose of their cause. Americans already thought they knew the answers to those questions, whether they had been soldiers or not. And if they did not know all the answers, questions about the ethics of war were better left to philosophers and historians, who had the time to think about such things. War's morality had never been the province of American Government or its ordinary people. But in 1901, it suddenly seemed to be.

There was ample reason to think about it, and Mark Twain spoke for the best in the American people when he summed up the Philippine Insurrection:

> . . . we have crushed a deceived and confiding people; we have turned against the weak and the friendless who trusted us; we have stamped out a just and intelligent and well-ordered republic; we have stabbed an ally in the back and slapped the face of a guest; we have bought a Shadow from an enemy that hadn't it to sell; we have robbed a trusting friend of his land and his liberty;

we have invited our clean young men to shoulder a discredited musket and do bandits' work under a flag which bandits have been accustomed to fear, not to follow; we have debauched America's honor and blackened her face before the world. . . .

What American could possibly suggest in 1901 that soldiers were responsible not just for fighting wars but also for the morality of the cause as well? If Oliver Wendell Holmes, Jr., had been right—and many Americans tended to think he was—that soldiers achieved a kind of nobility by simply following orders and doing the nation's killing, even though they might not understand the whys of it, then nobody could expect them to say if one variety of bloodletting was more civilized than another, or if one cause was noble and another an exercise in greed and jingoism.

And yet, that is precisely what soldiers did—after the Philippine Insurrection. It was they who committed the war crimes. It was also they who revealed what they did. Such duty would not be called for again until the war in Vietnam.

FIVE

After the First World War

In 1932, troops commanded by General Douglas MacArthur, bayonets fixed, advanced through tear gas against the unarmed World War I veterans of the Bonus March on Washington. (*The Bettman Archive*)

15
When Italians Lacked the "Conveniences for Thinking" and Black Mothers Traveled Second Class

If the time has come for Negroes and dagoes to be officers in the regular army, it is time for the white man to step out.
—Colonel I. C. Jenks, U.S. Army, 1918

From the earliest days of the nation, well before slavery was abolished, blacks had always been eager to volunteer for military service. In 1787, when Prince Hall asked Governor Bowdoin to permit the blacks to help in putting down Shays' Rebellion, the eagerness was born of the fear of slavery that still existed around them, and a desire to please the white power structure that held them down and back and judged them harshly. In 1917, as the United States moved closer to entering World War I, blacks were still trying to please the whites. Blacks were free—free to be unemployed, to be shunned, to be left out of most avenues of advancement in America. They saw the war as a way to prove to whites that they were not only trustworthy, but of such merit that, at long last, they deserved equal treatment. In 1918 in particular, blacks thought that their time had come; that somehow, if they now did what they had done so well in wars past—fight for their country—they would finally be accepted into the nation's economic life, if not its high society.

It was a time to put aside temporarily just grievances of long standing, a time not just to fight the Germans, but to fight for a better twentieth century, for the very survival of blacks in the United States. For no thinking black person felt that things could continue as they were. "We make no ordinary sacrifice," wrote W.E.B. Du Bois in the June 1918 issue of *The Crisis*, "but we make it gladly and willingly with our eyes lifted to the hills."

Most blacks agreed with him, and they were thus represented in great number at induction centers among the ranks of volunteers. They were even less welcome as volunteers than the Irish and the German Catholics had been seventy years earlier. The Marines, pride of America's warrior class, refused to accept any of them; the Navy took only 5,328 of them, most for mess duty or other menial jobs, none as officers; and the Army, that vast khaki repository of men unwanted or unnoticed by the other services, took 367,000 of them only reluctantly, and assigned as many as possible to Graves Registration—the difficult and most disagreeable collection and identification of battlefield dead. Only about 42,000 blacks got the combat assignments that they had enlisted for.

Perhaps the events that were about to overtake blacks just before and after World War I are better understood not in the light of the first two decades of the twentieth century, but rather in that of an incident that occurred a century earlier, in 1814. It was in September of 1814 that Andrew Jackson, then a military commander still fourteen years away from his Presidency, decided that blacks would be able to play an important role in the defense of New Orleans against the attacking British. He wrote to Louisiana's Governor William C. C. Claiborne telling him, "Our country has been invaded and threatened with destruction. The free men of colour in your city are inured to the Southern Climate and would make excellent soldiers. . . . Distrust them, and you make them your enemies." To all blacks volunteering, Jackson said he would offer "the same bounty and money and lands now received by the white soldiers of the United States"—$124 in cash and 160 acres of land. That was certainly a manifestation of equality that the blacks were still waiting for one hundred years later.

Blacks in Jackson's time were willing to help, just as they had been during the Revolution. But Governor Claiborne didn't want their help. Claiborne was as much a man of his times as Jackson was a man for all times. "I must not disguise from you," he wrote back to his friend Jackson, "that many excellent citizens will disapprove the policy you wish to observe towards free people of color," and he predicted that when the war was over, "colored men" who had been armed "would prove dangerous."

Jackson at first seemed to acquiesce. He wrote again to Claiborne, suggesting that when the British came, perhaps blacks might "be moved in the rear to some point where they will be kept from doing us an injury." Unwilling to retreat entirely before Claiborne's intransigence, he added, "If their pride and merit entitle them to confidence, they can be employed against the enemy. If not they can be kept from uniting with him."

Neither Claiborne nor the "excellent citizens" to whom he referred could take comfort from Jackson's letter that the reassuring status quo would be maintained. Two black battalions were quickly formed, and one of the first things Jackson did was to review them. When one Louisiana official questioned the wisdom of placing blacks into military service, Jackson advised him to "keep to yourself your opinions upon the policy of making payments of the troops with the necessary muster rolls without inquiring whether the troops are white, black or tea."

After the War of 1812 was over, Jackson's aide-de-camp saluted the "noble enthusiasm" of the blacks who fought the British and he promised them that "the voice of the representatives of the American nation shall applaud your honor." The applause died quickly, and in the years that followed, not all that much changed for men of color contemplating military service. At first, whites said they did not want to arm blacks, for fear that they might turn their guns against the class of ruling whites. In later years, possessed by many of the same persistent fears and prejudices, whites suggested that it was not a very good idea to train blacks for combat because they weren't bright enough nor dedicated enough to fight. "As fighting troops the Negro must be rated as second-class material; this is due primarily to his inferior intelligence and lack of mental and moral qualifications," said the commander of the 367th Infantry as the country plunged into the Great War.

There was no Jackson to override the commander's attitude in 1918— certainly Woodrow Wilson was not about to do it. Despite his learning and erudition in so many things, he rather agreed with the prevailing white attitude about blacks. Nor was relief forthcoming from the commander of the American Expeditionary Forces, General John J. Pershing, who complained that black troops were beset by "tuberculosis, old fractures, extreme flat feet, hernia, venerial [sic] diseases" and who fretted that black soldiers lusted after French women. Matters only grew worse. This time around, the Negrophobes were aided and abetted by the new science of psychology.

Intelligence testing had been given considerable impetus by the work of Alfred Binet, a Frenchman, although there were some who doubted the accuracy of his tests. New York State Supreme Court Justice John W. Goff, ruling in one case, said that "standardizing the mind is as futile as standardizing electricity." But testing programs quickly grew popular and the military was greatly influenced by the work of Harvard's Robert M. Yerkes, who developed a test for inductees in 1917 and announced it on December 24.

"Psychology," Yerkes said, without succumbing to undue modesty, "has achieved a position which will enable it to substantially help win the war and shorten the necessary period of conflict.'' How a mere test was going to do this was unclear. The so-called beta test was not so much an intelligence test as a test of specific knowledge. At least half of the whites and 90 percent of the blacks who took it were adjudged to have a mental age of no more than thirteen.

By 1918 the Army had revised the test, and blacks, many of whom had not been given written tests for anything before, were at a distinct disadvantage. Still, literate Negroes from some Northern states did better than did literate whites from some Southern states. The worst scores for Northern whites and blacks alike were recorded in Delaware and New Jersey, which had stingy budgets for schools and were generally not known for their enlightened educational programs. And yet, when the scores were in, no less than Carl C. Brigham of Princeton University suggested that the reason Northern blacks did better than expected was that the many blacks in the South had lowered the intelligence of whites, while Northern blacks, who were smarter to begin with (the demonstration of their brightness was their leaving Dixie, he said), were further blessed by being mixed racially with more intelligent white folk. Whatever the reason, if blacks were not fit to be Marines, draft boards nevertheless found most of them suitable for less elite service, placing about half of all the blacks who registered in Class I, whereas only a third of whites who were examined were so classified. The blacks constituted only 9 percent of the American population, but they constituted 13 percent of all those who were drafted in World War I.

But the hopes that Du Bois had for blacks were not to be realized by anything that happened during the war. Blacks and whites were inducted separately and stayed that way through training; black officers generally remained at junior levels; black enlisted men, who lived in conditions that were inferior to those of their white counterparts, found themselves harassed, severely punished, and sometimes summarily executed during training on specious charges. And when blacks went home in uniform, they were abused by whites who thought that the uniform was somehow degraded because a Negro wore it. Indeed, on at least one occasion, blacks were issued vintage uniforms that had been made to the specifications that had existed during the Civil War. Whites seemed determined to make them the clowns, whatever they did and however hard they tried.

The results could have been predicted. ''The country is alarmed over the rioting of Negro soldiers,'' said an editorial in *The Messenger*. ''We are not surprised or alarmed. . . .[Negro soldiers] have restrained themselves well under the taunts, insults and abuses so unsparingly heaped upon them. The Negro is probably the best and most loyal soldier in the United States . . .

but the Government has failed too often to do its duty by the Negro soldier.''

During the war, the Germans attempted to capitalize on American racism much as the Mexicans had earlier tried to capitalize on American anti-Catholicism. The Germans produced a motion picture called *Black Shame,* which depicted blacks as rapists and war criminals. Although the blacks tended to get along very well indeed with the French, the Army made it clear it did not want fraternization. ''The men will not be permitted to wander aimlessly around the country,'' ruled Colonel Greer of the 93rd Division, ''but efforts will be made to have games, sports and other amusements.''

Indeed, black men were sometimes not permitted to wander even if the purpose was well focused. When the Allies marched in victory in Paris, American blacks were not present in the American ranks, although men of color who were the colonials of France and Britain were permitted to march with the armies of those nations. Not until they got back to New York City were American blacks permitted to parade smartly in triumph— on Lincoln's Birthday of 1919. New Yorkers were quite taken with their phalanx marching, which the blacks had been taught by the French, with whom they had served.

The blacks were by no means alone as a despised class. For example, the Italians, only recently arrived from Europe in great number to constitute nearly 12 percent of the country's foreign-born population, were feeling much the same kind of discrimination. The Italians were, after all, the first south-of-the-Alps group to enter the country in great number. They were Latin, much to the dismay of America's Latinophobes within the power structure; and they were only nominally Catholic, to the equal dismay of the Irish, who had suffered quite enough because of their own Catholicism for the past seventy years. The Irish had worked hard to present themselves properly to the Americans of English stock, and they wanted no part of this people whom they regarded as too emotional, possessed of easy virtue, and exhibiting a rather cavalier attitude toward the teachings of Mother Church. The Italians reflected badly on the church and thus on the Irish, the Irish thought. ''The Italians are not a sensitive people like our own,'' complained the Rev. B. J. Reilly to New York's John Cardinal Farley. ''When they are told that they are about the worst Catholics that ever came to this country they don't resent it or deny it. . . . The Italians are callous as regards religion.''

In those days, Italians were widely regarded as nonwhite, or, perhaps, subwhite. They were routinely called ''wops'' and ''dagos'' and told that it took two or three of them to do the job of a ''white man.'' Their intellectual abilities were not more highly regarded than those of blacks. ''The Slavic and Latin countries show a marked contrast in intelligence with the Western and Northern European group,'' said one advocate of mental tests for immigrants. ''It is largely from this source that the stream of intelligent citizenship is polluted. . . . We need immigrants. Our fields are hungry for cultivation . . . [but] we do not need the ignorant, the mentally feeble, the moron. . . .''

''Steerage passengers from a Naples boat show a distressing frequency of low foreheads, open mouths, weak chins, poor features, skew faces, small or knobby crania and backless heads,'' wrote Prof. Edward Ross in *The Century*. ''Such people lack the power to take rational care of themselves. . . . While they take to drawing and music, they are poor in spelling and language and very weak in abstract mathematics. In the words of one [school] superintendent, 'they lack the conveniences for thinking.' They are below even the Portuguese and the Poles, while at the other extremity stand the children of the Scandinavians and the Hebrews.''

Although most of the Italians remained in the Northern states, there were substantial numbers of them in the South by the time the war ended. They were 35 percent of the foreign-born population in Louisiana and 22 percent of the foreigners in Mississippi. As violence stalked the blacks, so did it visit itself upon the Italians. They were the victims of violence in Arkansas, Louisiana, Mississippi, Colorado, Pennsylvania, and Illinois. There were lynchings of Italians every year from 1874 to the beginning of World War I. The lynchings occurred in Vicksburg, Mississippi; New Orleans; Denver; Hahnville, Louisiana; Tampa; and Johnson City, Illinois. Italians were so unpopular in Altoona, Pennsylvania, that two hundred of them were driven out of the city by residents who found them unacceptable either as neighbors or as humans deserving of a place in town. In West Frankfort, Illinois, ''race warfare'' was reported between Italians and non-Italians. A mob invaded an Italian neighborhood and, despite the presence of 720 Illinois State Guardsmen, the mob killed one man in his home as his wife and children stood watching, and looted the homes of Italian-speaking residents.

The Italians got uneven protection, at best, from the Catholic church. ''They [Italians] did not belong to the Church in a real sense when they landed on our shores,'' complained a cleric in the Catholic magazine *America*. ''By no stretch of the imagination can they be styled as Catholics as Catholics are counted in the United States. . . . They never or seldom go to mass or receive the sacraments; and they do not know what loyalty to the church means, intellectually, financially or morally.''

In one limited sense, Anglo-Americans were more apprehensive about the Italians than they were about the blacks. Blacks, they felt, could always be identified. But there were Italians who did not "look" Italian. The devils seemed to be everywhere, and many of them even had blue eyes and fair skin. In his *The Passing of the Great Race,* which was published during the World War, Madison Grant warned that immigrants from southern and eastern Europe were streaming into the country, marrying Anglo-Saxons who ought to know better, and thus "mongrelizing good old American stock."

Like the blacks, Italians saw World War I as an opportunity to win the acceptance that had eluded them. Indeed, their acceptance would be quite tangible, since they knew they would win automatic citizenship if they enlisted. Various estimates place the number of Italians in the American military service at between 245,000 and 400,000. Although by no means trusted, they were not stigmatized quite as much as were the blacks and thus probably saw more combat. Eighty native-born Italians won Distinguished Service Crosses and another twenty men of Italian descent won the same honor. Many more received Purple Hearts, as did the blacks, and in many instances, the medals were given posthumously.

After the war ended, both blacks and Italians came home, the Italians with the cherished citizenship that they had earned by enlisting, the blacks with fond memories of what it meant to be treated as equals by the French. They soon learned that their military service did not earn for them the esteem of their fellow Americans. Italians and blacks alike were still seen as an unattractive people who were mentally defective. ". . . there is not one in a thousand from Naples or Sicily that is not a burden on America," said David Starr Jordan, the president of Stanford University, in a letter to the Committee on Immigration of the House of Representatives on April 5, 1922. "Our social perils do not rise from the rapacity of the strong, but from the incapacity of these hereditarily weak." Starr said that the Italians and others from southern and eastern Europe were "biologically incapable of rising either now or through their descendants above the mentality of a 12-year-old child. . . ."

Blacks returned not just to charges that they were inferior but to unrelenting violence. The lynchings that had begun before the war had continued. The Ku Klux Klan had been revived in 1915, and its members seemed especially offended at the thought of a black man in the uniform of his country or who had recently worn such a uniform. In 1918, sixty-two Americans were lynched, fifty-eight of them black men. After one lynching, a photograph of it was taken and transformed into a picture postcard, which Klan members and their allies sent to friends and relatives around the country. The lynchings continued unabated the next year. In Bogalusa,

Louisiana, Lucius McCarty, a black who had only recently been honorably discharged from the Army, was accused by a white woman of having attacked her. He was trailed by bloodhounds, caught, and, without a trial, lynched before a mob of a thousand men. After he was dead, his body was tied to an automobile and dragged around the streets of Bogalusa. It was finally burned in front of the home of the woman who claimed she was his victim.

That same year, at least ten of the black lynch victims were veterans, and some of them were killed while they were still wearing the uniforms in which they had served. The summer of that year was called "Red Summer" because of the bloodshed. There was violence between blacks and whites in Chicago, Washington, Omaha, Charleston, New York City, Knoxville, Norfolk, and elsewhere. Returning black veterans were insisting upon the rights they had fought for, and whites were clearly not prepared to give in to them. Paul Filton, a black veteran, said, "We are not asking favors. We are demanding our rights. If the bigots are counting upon still relegating us to the back door of public hostelries, hat in hand, they are reckoning without their host. If that modern 'Ku Klux Klan' thinks that these hard fighting, straight-shooting veterans of the World War are the same timid field hands, crouching in terror, they have another 'think' coming." "We helped carry 'Democracy' to France," said the Rev. W. S. Carpenter, another black veteran. "On the return trip home Negro officers were not allowed to eat in the same places with the officers in their regiment."

W.E.B. Du Bois was most distraught by such mistreatment. He had counseled his people to take the high road and prove to whites that blacks were good Americans. His people had complied. Those wages were won and had to be paid by white America. Now he joined with A. Philip Randolph and Chandler Owen in insisting that things change. He had no tolerance for blacks who were afraid and thus content to let their unequal treatment continue. "We are cowards and jackasses if now that the war is over, we do not marshal every ounce of our brain and brawn to fight a sterner, longer, more unbending battle against the forces of hell in our own land," Du Bois wrote. ". . . lynching is barbarism of a degree of contemptible nastiness unparalleled in human history. Yet, for fifty years, we have lynched two Negroes a week and have kept this up right through the war. . . . A dominant minority does not want Negroes educated. It wants servants, dogs, whores and monkeys."

Du Bois wrote powerfully and passionately of the country that had acted so dishonorably and had so totally disappointed him. "It organizes industry to cheat us. It cheats us out of our land; it cheats us out of our labor. It confiscates our savings. It reduces our wages. It raises our rent. It steals our profit. It taxes us without representation. It keeps us consistently and universally poor, and then feeds us on charity and derides our property.''

So persistent were the malicious rumors spread by white Americans that black soldiers had behaved badly in France that an angry Du Bois took it upon himself to write to the twenty-one French mayors whose towns were near bases that had been used by blacks, asking them to tell him if blacks had done anything wrong. To the ignominy of the whites who had spread the rumors, Du Bois dutifully printed the responses of the mayors in his magazine, *The Crisis*. The French people had no complaints about American blacks, the mayors wrote back. At one point, the French came under much pressure from white Americans to stay away from black Americans. Some French restaurants that had never had problems with blacks began to segregate them, and the French people—who had their own colored colonials—found themselves in wonderment of the white Americans who went to so much trouble to put down their fellow soldiers who were black.

As a moral America tried to deal with uppity blacks and their protesting brethren, the Italians, the nation thought it perceived a postwar crime wave. Whether it was or not, or whether it was as large as Americans thought it was, remained a subject of speculation. It was true that the roaring twenties were upon America, that Al Capone and Dion O'Bannion and Arthur Flegenheimer (Dutch Schultz) were galloping about Chicago and New York; and speakeasies everywhere were unambiguously violating the Volstead Act, which America had enacted but which Americans did not want. Indeed, the Italians received special attention from other Americans when Italian criminals challenged the hegemony, in bootlegging, at least, of non-Italians. ''To try to explain the theory of prohibition to a group of Italian workmen is very much like trying to explain to you, the reader, that in Siberia people walk on their ears,'' said one critic.

There was undoubtedly a great deal of bootlegging all over the country. And yet, the crime data available for Chicago in the 1920s suggested that robberies and burglaries were fewer in the twenties than they had been in the teens; the national homicide rate was hardly above what it had been in the teens; and in Cicero, Illinois, which was supposed to be quite wicked, the murder rate was comparable to that which existed in the small Connecticut city which is home to Yale University.

Few periodicals ever questioned the prevailing view. One exception, in 1921, was *The New Republic*. ''If newspaper accounts of the 'crime wave' lead people to think that it is abnormal and temporary, they are grossly misleading,'' said the magazine. The United States, it explained, ''is in a perpetual crime wave.'' *The New Republic* presented data to show, for example, that in 1916, long before the ''crime wave'' was believed to have started, London, with a population of 7.25 million, reported nine premeditated murders in a year, while Chicago, with a population of only 2.4 million, reported 105 such crimes.

But police either did not read *The New Republic* or did not believe it. Everywhere, police said there was a crime wave, the press picked up their characterizations uncritically (what the police said, after all, was ''news''), and even the novelist Arthur Conan Doyle, who stopped Sherlocking long enough to visit the United States, believed the crime wave to be a fact. And so there was a ''crime wave'' cachet to the decade of the 1920s that would remain a part of its lore.

Whatever its nature, it put a great many former soldiers in jail. In Wisconsin, in the early 1920s, for example, fully 25 percent of all prisoners in the state prison system were former soldiers, and in 20 percent of those cases, the crime was attributable in some way to military life. A study showed that 70 percent of all the veterans in jail were there for actions concerning money or property, mostly seizing food or funds to buy food so that they could feed themselves or their families.

One soldier who had lost his right arm in France and had suffered massive injuries to his right leg was imprisoned because he violated the Volstead Act and sold whiskey to support his wife and family. Yet another veteran, who had been unable to find work after his discharge and who was literally begging for food, got a ninety-day sentence for vagrancy. A third soldier who went joy-riding in the car of an acquaintance without asking that person for permission was sentenced to four years. These three and many others were pardoned by Wisconsin's Governor John James Blaine, who called the sentences ''excessive'' and who thought that the soldiers were not hardened criminals and were, in fact, redeemable. ''When I can pluck a thistle and plant a flower when I think a flower will grow, I am going to do it,'' Blaine said to the critics who howled for stiffer jail sentences in order to restore law and order to Wisconsin.

A study was done for Blaine on the prison situation in Wisconsin by W. F. Lorenz, director of the Wisconsin Psychiatric Laboratory, who had been a major during the war, and Dr. W. S. Middleton, another veteran who was a member of the clinical staff of the University of Wisconsin. When the two made their final report, they noted, ''Nothing in war is uplifting, at least not for the humbler participants.'' Their feelings were in sharp contrast to those of Oliver Wendell Holmes, who thought it was quite beautiful to see a soldier "throw away his life" out of duty to his country, even if he did not understand what it was all about.

Although the fact of a crime wave was by no means certain, it was acknowledged as a fact by W.E.B. Du Bois in *The Crisis,* perhaps because he, too, believed what the police told him through newspaper accounts. His resulting editorials could only have made whites even more irrational on the subject of homecoming Negro soldiers. "Karl Marx was right when he said that 'capitalism contains the seeds of its own destruction,' " Du Bois wrote. ". . . Discontent will grow among the soldiers, both white and black. Negro soldiers, especially, are asking, 'How are things going to be with us now?' This, of course, is dreadful for we know that things will not only not be any better, but they will unquestionably be worse."

A few months later, Du Bois wrote, ". . . hungry soldiers roam the streets of the cities without money or work. They discuss the four billion dollars coined by the big business of the United States last year. They read from the Federal Income Tax reports that the millionaires have increased by 22,000 in the U.S. since the war began. They read that the packing industry made 300 percent profits, that a certain textile company made 700 percent. All this was done while the soldier boys were risking their lives on the fields of Flanders. And yet, there is wonder at social unrest."

Black writers were no less despairing over at *The Crisis'* competitor, *The Messenger.* William Colson, who had been a black officer, wrote a number of articles in which he said that in view of what white Americans were doing to the blacks, he thought it had been a mistake for the Negroes to be so patriotic and supportive of the war effort. "The Negroes' greatest opportunity since emancipation to bargain collectively was lost" when they so readily volunteered and submitted to the draft, he said. Negroes, he added, were "beginning to learn that [their] loyalty has been of little avail."

This sort of talk did not sit well with the American populace, which was then obsessed with nuances of patriotism, superlatives of patriotism, or any form of patriotism and was quite hostile about criticism of the nation, most of which was adjudged to be not only unpatriotic but possibly seditious. Absolutely scared stiff of Bolsheviks and anarchists, Americans got the two mixed up with considerable regularity, and suspected that somehow one or the other was going to take over the country. The "Red Scare" of 1919 would have a profound impact on former soldiers, how they felt about their country and its diverse minorities, and how their country would feel about them.

After the war ended, the United States found itself beset, not surprisingly, by high unemployment and runaway inflation. The former condition was exacerbated when the Government decided to discharge 600,000 soldiers soon after the Armistice was signed on November 11, 1918, and another 3.4 million in the next year and a half. As the war economy slowed down, prices went up. By the end of 1919, the dollar had lost 55 cents of the buying power it had had six years before. The cost of food had climbed by 84 percent and clothing was up 114.5 percent. The overall cost of living in 1919 was nearly 100 percent higher than it had been only five years earlier.

Former soldiers, many of them unsuccessfully seeking jobs, were hit hard by such economics, and many of them, white and black alike, quickly became disillusioned about what their role would be in an America at peace. Those who were employed were hardly less sanguine—during the year more than four million American workers were engaged in some thirty-six hundred strikes, most of them unsuccessful. Some workers turned to socialism and communism. There were two communist parties in existence by autumn of 1919 with small but vociferous memberships closely watched by the press, the police, and the Government. The radicals were, for a time, implicated in the bombings and attempted bombings of prominent Government officials.

The old Socialist Labor Party that had been formed before the war had increased its membership tenfold to 100,000 by the time the war started in Europe. But it had opposed American involvement in the war and had fallen out of favor. Thus, the cause of social reformers and have-nots became associated, in the public's mind, with a measure of disloyalty. Complicating America's thinking about the left was the fact that a large contingent of American soldiers had been sent to Russia after hostilities with Germany had ceased and there were fears that many of them would become contaminated by the precepts of Bolshevism.

The fear of radicalism was too easily translated into a fear of minority groups. Blacks, Italian Catholics, and Jews were high on the list of people to be watched. Individuals and groups outdid themselves to make certain that Americans were committed to their country. Among the groups were the National Security League, the American Defense Society, and the National Civic Federation. Among the individuals speaking in support of such groups were Nicholas Murray Butler, the president of Columbia University; Alton Brooks Parker, a liberal who had been the Democratic candidate for President in 1904; and Albert Bushnell Hart, professor of American history and government at Harvard. The cause of patriotism was also firmly endorsed by the Boy Scouts and the Sons and Daughters of the American Revolution. In short, all the best people were doing it. No wonder that the veterans themselves felt justified in taking the same strong posture when they founded the American Legion in the spring of 1919.

"It is unfortunate to put the American Legion in comparison with political parties," warned Brigadier General William G. Price, a member of the founding executive committee that met in Paris a month before the St. Louis founding, "but it will uphold what is right so firmly and forcefully that whatever party is wrong will learn to fear it." General John J. Pershing heard this, and perhaps mindful of the problems that the G.A.R. had created for itself, benignly warned the new group not to become "a political tool in the hands of political aspirants."

The Legion did not originate attitudes about the nature of American society that were embraced by the country. Rather, it embraced attitudes that were already there and truly reflected the society of which it was a part: It was suspicious of aliens, condemning of dissident liberals, and quite unforgiving of anyone who had, through subterfuge, evaded military service in the late war. It was so imbued with its founding pledge to work for "100 percent Americanism" that it even disdained and discouraged those who would listen to German opera or speak the German language.

White veterans flocked to the new organization. Within months after its founding, its membership stood at 650,000. But black veterans complained they found no brotherhood in Legion halls. The Legion, always a part of its time, did not want blacks and whites mixing at the same posts, a move it knew would offend some of its Southern white members, just as the question of integration had offended some Southern members of the Grand Army of the Republic before it.

The Legion was "mobbish" and "preoccupied in reviling the German-American and the Irish-American," complained William Colson, now sorrier than ever that he was one of the few blacks to serve as an Army officer. Others denounced it for being opposed to Negroes in general and the National Association for the Advancement of Colored People in particular, as well as to foreigners and the Japanese. *The Messenger* referred to it as "simply another Ku Klux Klan but national in scope" and accused the Legion of being antilabor as well, especially after Legion members involved themselves in forays against the Industrial Workers of the World, a militant, antiwar labor union, and helped break the 1919 police strike in Boston. *The Messenger* suggested that black veterans might have to form "Race Defense Legions" to protect the NAACP from Legion animus. It would take years for black suspicions of the Legion to begin to subside, even though much of what the Legion stood for was embraced by Americans who were never singled out for criticism. For example, one of the other active strikebreakers in the Boston police dispute was the student body of Harvard, whose president, Abbott L. Lowell, assured those who volunteered for police duty that they would not be penalized in the grading process.

What the blacks loathed the newspapers loved, at least initially. The Legion's founding was hailed by the press, which could see that, among other things, the Legion would be a force to keep veterans on the straight and narrow and away from the radicalism that the nation feared might grow in almost any direction. The *New York World* was representative of the press when it hailed the Legion's founding and commented, ". . . what a power this organization can exert throughout the length and breadth of the land to keep all postwar changes safe and sane." The Legion's presumed hostility to organized labor did not appear to bother any newspaper publishers.

It was not a decade that black and Italian veterans would look back on with unlimited satisfaction. Italians had served in the military and won their citizenship. But they were still not accepted, more remembered for their fascination with *anarchismo* and their suspicions about Government than for the discipline and dignity they showed in the face of discrimination, in and out of the armed services. The war built up no collective goodwill for them. When, in 1927, two Italian anarchists named Nicola Sacco and Bartolomeo Vanzetti were executed in Massachusetts in connection with a 1920 robbery and murder in South Braintree, it did not seem to matter very much to the people of Massachusetts that so many Italians had fought in the Great War. Of more importance was the fact that Sacco and Vanzetti had evaded the draft by fleeing to Mexico. The trial made much of this. It had to, really, for there was virtually no evidence to prove that Sacco and Vanzetti did the things they were accused of.

When Vanzetti made his last statement to the court on April 9, 1927, after having spent seven years in jail, Italian veterans wondered what, in fact, they had fought for:

> What I say is that I am innocent. . . . I have never killed and I have never spilled blood. That is what I want to say. . . . I will say that even a dog that killed chickens would not have found an American jury to convict it with the proof that the Commonwealth produced against us. . . . I would not wish to a dog or to a snake, to the most low and misfortunate creature of the earth—would not wish to any of them what I have had to suffer for things that I am not guilty of. But my conviction is that I have suffered for things that I am guilty of. I am suffering because I am a radical and indeed I am a radical; I have suffered because I was an Italian, and indeed I am an Italian. . . . I am so convinced to be right that if you could execute me two times, and I could be reborn two other times, I would live again to do what I have done already.

As for the blacks, perhaps they had been the bravest soldiers of all. They wanted to be knights-errant for a country in error. They wanted to fight the Hun and the nation told them to tend dead bodies instead. They wanted to volunteer but the nation took only four thousand of them as volunteers, and meanly conscripted the rest, treating extraordinary motivation as ordinary service. Their valor went mostly unrecorded, unreported, and unacknowledged. Even so, the all-black 369th Infantry, which saw action at Maison-en-Champagne, received the Croix de Guerre for its gallantry and was cited by the French eleven times. Another black outfit, the 8th Infantry of Illinois, was also extensively decorated for its conduct during combat. With all of it, the blacks acquitted themselves well, as they always had in the past. The Germans, having failed to diminish the blacks in battle, called them the "Hell Fighters."

As the decade ended, and Ku Klux Klan night-riding continued, some blacks thought they could see progress anyhow. It was there, they thought, early in 1930 when the Government decided that it would invite the wives and mothers of servicemen killed and buried in Europe to go to Europe as guests of the Government, to visit the graves of their dead. The bodies of more than thirty thousand Americans were buried in France. The Government said it would spend $840 on each of the 5,640 women who accepted the invitations and that it would devote more than $5 million to their "travel and entertainment." The *Times* said that the average age of mothers going was sixty-five, with many well over eighty.

"Every Gold Star mother in the nation, however humble, dwelling however obscurely, of whatever racial origin . . . can take this journey," reported *The New York Times*. And they would all go first class. Thousands of black women all over the nation felt good about that. And 450 of them decided to take the trip. It seemed to them that the Great War had achieved something after all. But when they accepted, they were told they could travel only with other black women. And when some of them attempted to travel, they found that they were not going first class at all. Boardinghouses took the place of fashionable hotels.

And so even in pilgrimage, the National Association for the Advancement of Colored People had to do battle to protect the widows and mothers of the men who died. It devised a petition and offered it to black women to send to the Government. Most of them used it. "Twelve years after the Armistice, the high principles of 1918 seem to have been forgotten," said the petition from black women. ". . . we . . . who are colored are insulted by the implication that we are not fit persons to travel with other bereaved ones."

Most black women then dropped out, but fifty-eight retained their reservations. They were given something of a lift when they were feted at New York City Hall on July 11, 1930, and they heard Major William F. Deegan, the tenement house commissioner, say that in New York, at least, blacks and whites would be treated the same. A very good concert band from the Sanitation Department—composed almost totally of Italian garbage collectors and street sweepers—played for them.

A spokesman for the War Department said that in making arrangements, it wanted to relieve the "strain" of the journey, "but not disturbing the normal contacts of individual pilgrims. It would seem natural to assume that these mothers and widows would prefer to seek solace in their grief from companions of their own race."

Among black women, most of the remaining reservations were canceled. Very few of them ever went to France.

16
67,000 Quarts of Whiskey, Enough Floor Wax to Cover South Dakota, and "to Hell with the Central Office"

We could clean up enough on this one job to retire
for life.
—Attributed during a Senate corruption hearing in
1923 to Charles R. Forbes, director of the
Veterans' Bureau

After so much neglect of its former soldiers, the Government began to acknowledge, following the Great War, that it was time to provide veterans with a conspicuous plan that would care for the sick and wounded. What President Warren G. Harding actually provided was more spectacular than conspicuous. But it did nothing to help veterans. In fact, it made their situation much worse.

Perhaps only in America, with its unshakable belief in its own goodness, could a hopefully rehabilitated deserter from the United States Army be named to head a new invention of the bureaucracy called the Veterans' Bureau. But that is precisely what Harding did when, in 1921, he appointed Colonel Charles R. Forbes to be the $10,000-a-year executive director of the bureau. This inauspicious, unlikely appointee was given the task of bringing together the nonservices that had been provided by the Bureau of War Risk Insurance, the Public Health Service, and the Federal Board for Vocational Rehabilitation.

For all his extroversion and bluster, Forbes was something of a man of mystery in 1921. There was some confusion as to what his name really was and questions were raised as to whether he had ever altered it to avoid public attention. It was said that he had been born in Scotland, but some insisted it was Wales; it was said he had been educated at Columbia, M.I.T., and the

Cooper Institute, but others suspected that Forbes had never gone to college and certainly had no degree. His friends in Government proudly noted that his credentials as a patriot were made impressive by his having enlisted in the Marines at age twelve to be a drummer boy; but his detractors claimed that his record was sullied when, as an enlisted man in the Army in 1900, he deserted just two months after taking the oath to serve his country.

But his desertion had not bothered the Army very much, and so why should it inconvenience the Harding Administration, in which standards of conduct were not nearly as high? After the wayward Forbes was caught, the Army had reinstated him without a trial and sent him off to the Philippines, where his campfire politicking quickly won him sergeant's stripes and the fond if inexact nickname ''Willie off the pickle boat'' among his peers.

For the next dozen years Forbes may have stayed out of serious trouble, although given his uncanny ability to cloak his official record in innocence, this was by no means certain. In 1912, he was assigned to Pearl Harbor Naval Station, which was then under construction. It was there that he met an up-and-coming young Republican named Warren Gamaliel Harding, an Ohio farmer's son and newspaperman, whose gifts for oratory were never challenged by his sense of discretion or his ability to perceive honesty or its lack in the people he contemplated as friends or public servants. Harding was quite taken with Forbes and, as he did whenever he met people he liked, suggested to Forbes that if he ever chanced to be in the vicinity of Marion, Ohio, he should not hesitate to stop by for a friendly chat. Harding apparently made that offer to quite a number of rather odd people.

After Harding was picked to nominate William Howard Taft at the Republican Convention of 1912 and was elected a U.S. senator in 1914, it was an invitation that Forbes was not likely to forget. He was a major when the World War started and served in France, rising to the rank of lieutenant colonel and winning a Croix de Guerre in the bargain. In 1921, with the mistakes of his youth behind him and Harding's friendship assured, Forbes lobbied for high office in Washington, at one point with a reported interest in becoming Secretary of the Interior. But Harding saved that honor for an equally inappropriate candidate named Albert Fall and instead appointed Forbes chief of the War Risk Insurance Bureau. When War Risk became the Veterans' Bureau, Forbes hung on and found himself at the top.

It was quite a swatch of the bureaucracy to be in control of. In March of 1919, Congress had voted an initial $9,050,000 for the creation of hospitals and rehabilitation camps for the 200,000 U.S. veterans who had survived the war but were left damaged by it; then followed up that appropriation with a new allotment of $18.6 million. Aside from the special appropriations for new hospitals, the new agency was given an annual operating budget of $450 million, and its contingent of clerks and minor officials quickly approached the size of a small city, with the better part of thirty thousand largely indifferent bureaucrats convening every day at bureau headquarters in downtown Washington.

The new bureau must be seen in light of what had come just before. A Federal Bureau for Vocational Rehabilitation, created shortly after the end of the war, had done largely nothing to help former soldiers and had, in fact, placed enormous burdens on them to prove they were ailing because of the war. In the first nineteen months of its existence, the bureau had only about 24,000 men of an estimated eligible 110,000 in some sort of training, not an enviable record for an agency that was supposed to deal with the homecoming soldier. Veterans could not stand its ineptitude, and at least 30 percent of those approved for some sort of training program dropped out in disgust because of all the delays to which they had been subjected. As the decade of the twenties began, the bureau reported that a mere 217 men in the entire country had been retrained, although it had at least one clerk for every ten soldiers.

The case of Joseph Furphy of East Newark, New Jersey, was a typical example of the bureau's work. He had seen action at Belleau Wood and Soissons, where he was wounded. His wounds required three separate surgical procedures. Back home, he applied to become an accountant. First he was kept waiting, then the bureau required huge amounts of documentation from him, as though it did not trust him. "The Board is undecided," it told him in a needlessly priggish letter, "if the facts are as reported, as to whether you can be awarded the training you desired, under the terms of the Vocational Act." Literally thousands of other former soldiers were given the same shabby runaround. Then late in 1920, the records of soldiers were scrapped when the bureau said it was undergoing "reorganization." Nobody seemed to know what to do. Disabled veterans were given jobs pulling weeds at the Brooklyn Botanical Garden, and the bureau seemed to think that was all right.

The bureau smacked of corruption. Late in 1919 it reported it had paid out $386,807 in salaries—but only $139,335 in tuition for soldiers who had come home trying to readjust. In short, the Vocational Act was a joke and the bureau that was supposed to implement that act was a bad joke. By the time the Veterans' Bureau was finally formed, the men it was designed to help were quite desperate and prayed that Forbes would be an able administrator. They hoped that he could do more in the next year and a half than had the Federal Board for Vocational Rehabilitation. They hoped in vain.

Forbes started his Washington stewardship with Charles Cramer, who might be described as a legal adviser but who was widely known at the time as Forbes' "shadow." Cramer, another ascending star in the Republican Party, helped Forbes take charge with the alacrity if not the substance needed to obtain results. In eighteen months, Forbes would zoom through all of $33 million on new hospital construction but would add only two hundred beds—all of them in Memphis, Tennessee.

The siting and acquisition of hospital land was clearly of more interest to Forbes than construction, and it was in this activity that his true colors emerged—colors which enabled him to take the United States Government on a hayride it had not known since Jay Gould and Jim Fisk had the ear of the gullible Ulysses S. Grant. There were wounded veterans all over the country, and so it was reasonable to locate hospitals regionally. Forbes inspected the sites himself, frequently in the company of another friend, Elias H. Mortimer, a representative of the Thompson-Black Construction Company of St. Louis. It was a firm that had every reason to be nice to Forbes, since it coveted any contract he might care to let. It was, to say the least, the beginning of a very bizarre relationship.

Mortimer and his wife maintained an apartment at the Wardman Park Hotel, and Forbes and his wife soon took their own suite there. Mrs. Mortimer was an important person to Forbes in more ways than one: She was a close friend of President Harding's sister, Mrs. Herbert Votaw. The Wardman Park did not exactly exude unbounded goodness and morality; even by the standards of Washington hotels, its quiet hallways harbored a most unusual collection of collusive predators. Its other guests included Interior Secretary Albert Fall and oilman Harry F. Sinclair, who met in secret and hatched the particulars of what would soon become the Teapot Dome scandal; Harry Micajah Daugherty, Harding's Attorney General, who was shortly to be tried and acquitted of charges stemming from alleged wrongdoing in the Alien Property Custodian's Office; and Jess Smith, whose main claim to fame was that he was a friend of Daugherty's and that he also ran one of Washington's better-known card parlors. This enterprise doubled as a speakeasy and center for the offering and accepting of bribes. With such attributes, Smith's place understandably became famous as a cozy spot for all manner of assignations, especially for those persons without a suite at the Wardman Park.

The Forbeses and the Mortimers would dine in great style together, frequently at the Wardman Park, and it did not seem to bother Forbes that his relationship with Mortimer was a conflict of interest most naked. Mortimer quickly became Forbes' flunky, clown, and part-time bag man. Forbes found Mortimer handy to have along on all of his "business" trips—for it was Mortimer who paid the bills.

It would appear that much of the business was of the monkey variety, and the bills Mortimer happily paid showed that clearly. Among his formidable expenses were a four-day booze-and-floozy-filled party at the Traymore Hotel in Atlantic City, even though Prohibition was on and the Government had told its citizens that drinking was against the law; another drinking party in Philadephia's Ritz-Carlton; and yet another drinking party in Manhattan using an apartment at 200 West 59th Street as well as the facilities of the Ambassador Hotel.

Mortimer was a witness to much of what Forbes did. It was Mortimer who watched (in disgust, he said) when an especially exuberant Forbes and an unidentified woman inexplicably jumped into Hayden Lake in the state of Washington while fully clothed. Forbes was then on one of his Government missions to Spokane. And Mortimer was a central player when he delivered a $5,000 "loan" from Thompson-Black to Forbes in a bathroom at Chicago's Drake Hotel. The money was presented in an unusual way for a loan—ten $500 bills, fresh from the bank, and not an IOU in sight. It was occasioned when Forbes told Mortimer that he was "very hard up for money" because his wife had gone abroad. Mortimer, team player that he was, asked not why Mrs. Forbes' vacation meant that Thompson-Black should have to make an emergency loan. He delivered the money promptly, as any good errand boy would.

But he was a most knowledgeable errand boy. He was one of the select stalwarts who knew a code devised by Forbes so that all the grafters could protect their privacy when they communicated with each other telegraphically. In code parlance, Forbes was "McAdoo" and Mortimer was "Moxey," according to Mortimer. Loyal both to his company and to Forbes (the distinction between the two became ever harder to discern), Mortimer even remained silent when one day he found his wife and Forbes shooting craps on a bed in Chicago's Drake Hotel. (Forbes took her for $220, Mortimer claimed, but he was never able to say if Mrs. Mortimer paid up, perhaps because he and his wife soon split up.)

Mortimer also bore witness to Forbes' skills as an administrator and planner, which manifested themselves in the creation of a most unusual veterans' hospital, perhaps even a unique one, in Excelsior Springs, Missouri. It was literally planned and executed *without a kitchen* and without an explanation of how the sick veterans who entered it were supposed to get their sustenance. It would not, however, lack for floor wax and soap. Forbes did not simply buy these two items; he amassed them with the pharaohesque abandon previously associated in the United States only with William Randolph Hearst's accumulation of *objets d'art* for his six castles. On one occasion, although the Veterans' Bureau already had thousands of gallons of floor wax on hand, he acquired a shipment for which the Government paid $70,944.45 to the Continental Chemical Corporation— enough to last the Veterans' Bureau for one hundred years, the wags said, enough wax to wax a floor the size of South Dakota. He also bought 45,045 gallons of soap at 87 cents a gallon, which a Government expert later said was worth only 1.8 cents a gallon.

The very idea of Prohibition must have seemed especially implausible to a man with Forbes' appetites. The unlawful drinking parties that accompanied hospital siting tours "would start in the afternoon and end up early in the morning," according to Mortimer. Forbes' appetite for liquor was as unquenchable as his interest in large sums of money. There was one afternoon when he polished off a bottle of gin by himself. Then there was the Christmas when Forbes actually gave a bottle of scotch to Frank R. Chambers, a mechanical engineer. But Chambers was not to enjoy the gift. "On the day after Christmas," he said, "he [Forbes] called on me and drank most of it up."

Nobody was surprised, therefore, that Forbes was elated to learn that there were 67,000 quarts of bourbon, rye, and gin stored in a warehouse at Perryville, Maryland. The liquor apparently had been purchased for medicinal purposes by the Government for possible use during World War I. But the Armistice had been signed with the liquor unquaffed. Prohibition intervened, and somehow the intrepid Government agents who were paid to destroy bottles of liquor when the Volstead Act became law neglected to look in the Perryville warehouse. It was all to the good as far as Forbes was concerned. But he had no intention of trying to drink it. Rather, he thought he might sell it.

"Now, here, Mort," he told Mortimer. "I have got up at Perryville about 67,000 quarts of liquor. I have changed all the old men there and I have got men in there that I can trust. If you can find a market for it, while I will have to make some return to the Government, we can fix that part of it all right." Ever the entrepreneur, he also tried to find a market for the $5 million in morphine, cocaine, and codeine also found in the warehouse. Forbes told Mortimer, "We could clean up enough on this one job to retire for life."

Forbes may have been right, for the largess in Perryville was quite incredible; it filled 126 railroad cars, to the great delight of the Thompson-Kelly Company, a related company to Thompson-Black, which got it. Included in this sale of all sales were 754,680 new bath towels, which cost the Government 54 cents each but which were sold for a tad over 3 cents; 84,000 best-quality pequot bedsheets, worth $1.03½, sold to Thompson-Kelly for 17 cents; 98,995 pairs of winter pajamas, homemade for soldiers by the women of America and donated to the Red Cross, 30 cents each; 5,387 pounds of oiled paper that cost the Government 60 cents a pound, sold for 5 cents a pound; and thousands of other items at bargain-basement prices. Basically, Thompson-Kelly got the lot for about 8⅔ cents on the dollar, with the result that goods worth nearly $7 million were sold for $600,000.

Forbes cleaned out the Perryville warehouse so quickly that some new sheets that were being delivered to the Government for $1.03½ each were inadvertently trucked across the warehouse floor, out the back door, and into waiting railroad cars, a virtual gift to Thompson-Kelly from the taxpayers of America. When President Harding questioned Forbes about the Perryville sales, Forbes assured him the materials were not in good condition. In fact, they were in very good condition, virtually new and pristine in their original packaging.

If morale was not very good among former soldiers who could find no Government treatment for old wounds, morale was very good among employees of the Veterans' Bureau, some of whom were quick to learn to love Forbes' life-style as much as he did. "You are missing the *real old times*," wrote an exuberant bureau employee named Tripp to a colleague back in Washington from one of his out-of-town assignments. "Hunting season is on—rabbit dinners, pheasant suppers, wines, beers, and booze—and by God we haven't missed a one yet. Collins and I get invitations to 'em all. Last Wed. I was soused to the gills on rabbit, etc. Last Sat. wines—Oh, Boy! . . . We eat and wine with the mayor, the sheriff, the prosecuting atty. To hell with the Central Office and the work. And the fun is in the field—'tis all the work I want—just travel around."

Apparently it had been Tripp's assignment to survey the safety of the grounds around a veterans' hospital. He wrote: "Fire hazards, say, if Forbes could only see the 'lovely' high (3') grass & if fire comes—boom! up she goes." Most of the rest of Tripp's letter isn't understandable, although at one point, he alluded to having bested some Jews: ". . . then the Jews—Oh, my, how they weep: 'I got stung.' Let me know when Forbes is going to sell by sealed proposals, then when I get a Rolls Royce. Got a good drink coming, so here's back to you. Respectfully, Tripp."

Morale may have been good among certain prospective employees, too. A young man named Tulladge, for example, had been working for a pittance driving a cream truck somewhere in Pennsylvania. He aspired to work for the Veterans' Bureau. Forbes gave him a job as a hospital inspector. It paid $3,500 a year, which was not bad money in those days. By coincidence, Tulladge was Mortimer's brother-in-law. Morale also may have been at acceptable levels among certain dentists. In 1921, Forbes' agency paid dentists $5,627,851.54 for fixing the teeth of former soldiers. Later, it was suggested that teeth were fixed even if they did not need fixing and that the Government was being charged for gold fillings by dentists who used copper, nickel, and brass.

Even by the modest standards of probity within the Harding Administration, it was inevitable that somebody somewhere would demand an investigation of all of this. Both the American Legion and the Disabled American Veterans made it known that they were most unhappy with Forbes' record. Forbes sensed trouble coming and left for Europe, saying that he needed a vacation to improve his health. He was in Europe when he resigned in February 1923. Cramer, who remained in Washington, resigned at about the same time.

On March 2, the Senate passed a resolution calling for an investigation of the Veterans' Bureau. Before it went to term in the nine months of its existence, the investigation would receive the services of 1,350 eager volunteers, so that the senators would be able to check out every complaint that had been lodged against Forbes' operation. Aiding the Senate were 600 volunteer lawyers, 550 doctors, and 200 other experts in various fields. It was an inquiry almost worthy of the world-class grafters who had looted the Treasury.

Cramer, like Forbes, knew that there was trouble of tragic proportions headed his way, and he wanted no part of it. On March 14, he locked himself in the bathroom of his home and shot himself in the head. His body was found in his bathtub. On his dresser, police noticed a poem about death that he had clipped from a newspaper. Forbes, of course, was not the least bit suicidal. Nor was he contrite. He returned home filled with his usual supply of vigor and vinegar and, on the following November 13, testified before the Senate committee. He charged that he was the victim of a "conspiracy" by Mortimer and others, the purpose of which was to "encompass my destruction by means of perjury . . . and the suppression of material facts and documents. . . ."

Forbes grew defiant. "I now deny generally, and shall hereafter deny specifically and in detail, the utterly false and groundless charges of official and personal neglect, dishonesty, graft, liquor drinking, loose conduct and any and every other dereliction of duty, official or personal, which has been ascribed to me . . . or charged against me by the counsel of this committee.''

But wasn't it true that when he left office, there were 200,000 pieces of mail that hadn't been answered? Didn't that say something about his competence as an administrator?

There were 200,000 unanswered letters, Forbes said, but the cause of it was that "very frequently, you would find ten people writing about the same claimant." In other words, the veterans and their supporters were to blame for the logjam; in their zeal, they had simply overwhelmed the very agency that was trying so hard to help them. The senators were trying to comprehend the likes of an agency that had one employee for every 6.6 letters received.

What about that drinking party at the Ritz-Carlton in Philadelphia? Forbes said it was really Mortimer's party and that he, Forbes, had only attended it for five minutes "and then I got up and went to my room and went to bed."

What about that especially naughty party at the Traymore Hotel in Atlantic City? Wasn't it true that two "actresses from New York" joined Forbes, who was traveling without his wife, and Mr. and Mrs. Mortimer? Yes, Forbes said, but the actresses stayed only one night and left the next morning. He was not asked, nor did he volunteer, to explain what they had to do with the business of the Veterans' Bureau.

Was it true that he had had a secret meeting in the Wardman Park Hotel with Mr. Thompson and Mr. Black, construction company officials? "I never had a confidential meeting with Thompson and Black in my life," Forbes replied with the earnestness of a new choirboy.

Was Mortimer telling the truth when he said he had slipped Forbes a $5,000 loan in the bathroom of a Chicago hotel? "It is false," Forbes told the senators.

What about all the drinking that he was supposed to have done?

Forbes maintained that the only thing he remembered was having a large gin fizz just before breakfast once during a trip to Stockton, California. "That is the only drinking I know about."

At one point, the senators tried to find out if Forbes' name was Charles R. Forbes, Charles F. Forbes, or simply Charles Forbes. Forbes explained he liked to use the initial R because he was fond of his Uncle Robert. He never changed his name to avoid publicity or detection, he said.

How about the story that while in Spokane, he and a woman had jumped into the water with their clothes on? That was easy to explain, Forbes said.

He told the senators that he loved to fish and that when he checked into his room, he found a fishing pole, apparently placed there by friends and admirers. "They called it a rod, I always call it a pole," Forbes volunteered. Anyhow, he continued, he went fishing on a wharf near where he had dinner, somebody suggested he ought to go swimming, and before he knew it, he had jumped into the water with his overalls on. He added that "a friend" also jumped in with him. "That's all there was to it," he said.

What about the 67,000 quarts of liquor and the $5 million in morphine, cocaine, and codeine sold from the Perryville warehouse? Did Forbes ever tell Mortimer that "we could clean up enough on this one job to retire for life"?

"I never made such a statement," Forbes said. "It is absolutely false."

What about all the education Forbes was supposed to have had at Columbia, M.I.T., and the Cooper Institute? Was Forbes really an engineer? He insisted he was, indeed, an engineer, had a lot of practical experience in it, and could apply for a license "in any state in the union," whatever that meant. Forbes said he studied "privately," although still insisting that he had done "special work at Columbia."

And what about Mortimer's assertion that there was a secret code among Forbes and his cronies? Had Forbes ever heard of it? "No," he said, "I never did."

Was it true that Mortimer found Forbes and Mortimer's wife together in an apartment in the Wardman Park Hotel on Labor Day of 1922? (The senators didn't ask him the details of the crap game with Mrs. Mortimer on the bed in Chicago.) Yes, Forbes said, he was visiting Mrs. Mortimer but "with the doors wide open." As for Mortimer, he said, he was nothing but a boozer and a wife-beater. But he added that Mortimer had been "highly recommended" to him and so he continued the relationship.

"Did it not occur to you," asked Major-General John O'Ryan, counsel for the committee, "that it was an improper thing to take this man whose business you know so little about clear across the continent, in and out of hospitals, and sitting around where you were transacting all this important business?"

"It might have been a little indiscreet," Forbes conceded.

And what did Forbes accomplish during his eighteen months in office after spending all that money? What hospitals were constructed? "Didn't construct any," Forbes said, although he proudly noted that the two hundred beds he added came with an existing hospital that he ordered purchased in Memphis. He called it "a very wonderful institution."

About the only thing on which the Senate agreed with Forbes was that he had been indiscreet. Charles Forbes was eventually tried along with construction man John W. Thompson on charges of conspiracy to defraud the United States Government. Both were convicted. Thompson was never incarcerated. His heart was ailing and he died in St. Louis on May 23, 1926. Forbes, who was much more robust, appealed his case unsuccessfully to the Supreme Court, served twenty months in Leavenworth, was fined a mere $10,000, and was released on November 26, 1927. When he left prison he vowed to clear the muddied name of his friend and benefactor President Harding, who died in 1923; and to make certain that the world came to know that his cellmate in Leavenworth, Dr. Frederick Cook, had reached the North Pole before Robert E. Peary. He was less than successful in both efforts. Harding's place in history was assured as a President who presided over one of the most corrupt administrations in American history; Cook's name would remain eclipsed by Peary's, even though questions would persist about Peary's claim.

Somehow Forbes had been able to squirrel away a coin or two from his Government service, and for the next twenty-five years he divided his time between his comfortable homes in Washington, D.C., and Florida. When he died in 1952 at the age of seventy-four, the lead of his obituary in *The New York Times* referred to him as a "retired soldier and politician." To this day, nobody knows how much money he may have realized from his dealings. However, conservative estimates suggested that during his tenure, the waste and graft in the Veterans' Bureau was well over $225 million—perhaps two-thirds of the Government's total surplus.

Mortimer, the Government's star witness against Forbes, was divorced by his wife in June of 1925. Her dim view of him was shared by the Government that had used him as a witness. He was called "a crook and a fixer" by Assistant Attorney General John W. H. Crim, the prosecutor, but was not indicted for any of the activities in which he had engaged with Forbes. That did not stop him from getting indicted for other offenses, however. In May of 1923 he was accused of bootlegging. Fortunately for Mortimer, he had the wit to hire Thomas B. Felder as his lawyer. Felder was rather able and had the advantage of being a friend and associate of Attorney General Daugherty. And so the indictment was quashed.

The America that had entrusted the Veterans' Bureau to a former deserter was no less generous with Mortimer the accused bootlegger. No sooner had his bootlegging charge been dropped than he was appointed a special agent in the Department of Justice—with the responsibility of investigating violations of the Volstead Act.

17
Mellon, du Pont, and the Chamber of Commerce: Fighting Is Its Own Reward

Congress little realizes that its creature, the Veterans'
Bureau, has probably made wrecks of more men
since the war than the war itself took in dead and
maimed.
—William Edler in *The American Mercury*, 1925

The abysmal failure and egregious waste that was the Veterans' Bureau had a devastating effect upon the soldiers who had fought the World War. The Senate investigation of Forbes and company found that "thousands of worthy claims for compensation had been disallowed by the Bureau or its predecessor agencies" and that the veterans were put off by the "attitude of indifference." Contrary to the impression conveyed by Forbes that his agency was overwhelmed by letters from veterans and their insistent, aggressive families and friends, the evidence strongly suggested that once turned down, claimants simply did not pursue their claims vigorously. They were defeated in a way that they never had been in the war.

Hardest hit were those seriously wounded. The Senate report concluded that there was "complete indifference on the part of examiners concerning the origin of claimants' disabilities." Such numbness would not visit itself again upon ex-soldiers for fifty years, when the Veterans Administration, successor to the Veterans' Bureau, attempted to deal with the Agent Orange issue.

Public officials and private citizens who had been among the most vociferous, moist-eyed flag-wavers before the war now succumbed to assiduous silence when evaluating the wounds of the men who had fought the war. As Forbes gamboled about the country, drinking, womanizing, and, it would seem, swimming in his overalls, his loyal minions fell back upon the ultimate refuge of the uncaring bureaucrat—''technical'' considerations and endless queries to determine who might be eligible to get what. Whether Government lines be for soup, disaster relief, or a driver's license, there could be nothing more maddening than the fine lines drawn by an official inquisitor.

''Neither Congress nor the people of the country intended that bureau employees should split hairs when the claimants affected are men who were wounded in actual battle,'' snapped the Senate's report. And yet, through the early 1920s, endless delay was precisely what the Government engaged in with its war veterans. Its motives were clearly not to help soldiers heal their wounds, but to limit Government's liability to them for their part in the war.

The investigating committee concluded that ''no American'' could read the testimony relating to the bureau under Forbes ''without a feeling of disgust for the manner in which the great work of aiding the disabled was prostituted for self-aggrandizement and greed.'' The committee was wrong. A great many Americans read accounts of what the Veterans' Bureau had done to former soldiers. There was no national feeling of disgust. The press was not bursting with righteous editorials demanding justice for the nation's heroes; pulpits were not filled with passionately moral clergymen explaining in quavering tones to their flocks how important a trust this was; liberals and Democrats, who liked to think of themselves as the caretakers of the human condition, did not emerge as the champions of sick and wounded men. And so, conservative, self-indulgent Republicans who never pretended to care about much of anything except themselves were permitted to dawdle away most of the decade. Some senators and congressmen were undoubtedly very much concerned about what was happening. But they were not in sufficient number to motivate either their colleagues or their constituents, who were intent on pursuing peacetime activities and putting the late war out of their minds.

''Congress little realizes that its creature, the Veterans' Bureau, has probably made wrecks of more men since the war than the war itself took in dead and maimed,'' bemoaned William Edler in *The American Mercury* in mid-decade. It was one of the relatively few statements that made it into print suggesting somebody somewhere thought about the men who had given so much of themselves in the war.

⁻Some curious statistics came out of this epoch of national incompetence. For example, the Veterans' Bureau allowed 49,000 claims for diseases that the veterans had—but there were only 47,000 claims allowed for combat injuries. The statistic was striking in light of the unassailable fact that more than 300,000 men were wounded in combat against the Germans. What was happening to those whose claims were not allowed? Where were those men whose wounds still hurt and whose minds had not yet healed from the blood-letting they had seen and been engaged in?

The wounded soldiers waited as wounded soldiers had always waited. The nation, in contrast, was very much on the move. But where was it going? For critic Edmund Wilson, it was engaged in the "liquidation of genteel culture," although some Americans may not have been quite as successful as Wilson in finding the gentility in the raw early years of the twentieth century.

But the vulgarization of America was hardly confined to what then passed for its culture, and the Forbes affair that was so crucial to former soldiers was only a small part of the national malady. As in the years after the Civil War, political corruption was ubiquitous. Huge sums of money were being made illegally and flagrantly; respect for America's professed interest in being a nation of law was hard to find. Above all was the nation's overriding materialism. Money lust fluxed out of the unlikeliest people and institutions —even from what Americans had come to regard as the national pastime. Baseball was a part of the goodness America so much wanted for itself. It was a "clean straight game," President Taft had declared in 1910, a game that "summons to presence everybody who enjoys clean, straight athletics." But in 1919, eight members of the Chicago White Sox baseball team, not nearly as clean and straight as Taft had supposed, fixed the World Series so that the Cincinnati Reds would win it. The players received bribes of either $5,000 or $10,000 from gamblers to throw the games, and the White Sox shocked the nation to become the Black Sox in the indignant national press. The twenties were indeed roaring—except for the men whose wounds had never been properly tended to, who never seemed to get back on the track after the armed services were demobilized.

It was inevitable that ex-soldiers, who had earned $1 a day for the dubious privilege of being shot at and who were now unable to feed themselves and their families, would want *theirs* and thus come to share in the real national pastime of acquiring money. The soldiers had not forgotten that they had received $60 as mustering-out pay on discharge. But they also had not forgotten that civilians who had carried the banner of patriotism in hometown factories had received much larger bonuses to keep up wartime production. Pugilist Jack Dempsey, for example, who served his country by working in a shipyard, received a bonus of around $14 a day for his services—and nobody shot at him. The men who had been targets for the

Germans wondered why it was patriotic to produce the goods of war and to be rewarded for them with cash bonuses or more fat contracts, but somehow less patriotic to use the goods of war in deadly combat and expect a pinch of indemnification. The people who had been civilians were not so interested in discussing such impenetrable stuff. They, and the large companies that employed them, were more interested in lowering taxes. That, in essence, was what Harding was talking about when he ventured to Boston and said that what America needed was "not heroics but healing; not nostrums but normalcy." In short, he wanted the nation to forget, which it was most happy to do.

Even some of the veterans themselves were unsure what they were entitled to. Within the American Legion there was considerable reluctance to pursue material rewards for fighting. The Legion knew that many veterans believed that patriotism was its own reward and that it was somehow wrong for soldiers to seek money. Finally, though, the Legion came around to supporting the idea of a "bonus" for the soldiers. It really had to. The condition of many of its members gave its leadership no choice.

In 1920, Secretary of the Treasury Andrew Mellon, who was then one of the richest men in the nation, held forth against the bonus, asserting that it would cause "renewed inflation, increased commodity prices and unsettled business conditions." Mellon, like so many others, thought that the soldiers should be content with the reward of having served with so much distinction, since that was "the highest duty of citizenship," not the acquisition of money. The Secretary was not especially beloved—one reporter suggested that if Mellon were accused of a serious crime "he would hang himself by appearing in his own defense"—and yet the Harding Administration was prepared to listen to him. His word was gospel, even though in 1923, he estimated that there would be a deficit of $650 million, when in fact there was a surplus of $310 million. How a financial wizard could make such a miscalculation was never explained.

Early in the decade, the squalor of the Harding Administration's various delinquencies was not yet visible. And so the President had no problem in mustering the audacity to appear personally before the Senate to use his considerable powers of persuasion to speak against a proposed bill to pay veterans a bonus, which the public tended to favor, especially when not thinking about the cost of it. Harding told the senators that he regarded a bonus bill as a "disaster to the nation's finances" unless there was a way to pay for it. Later, after the Senate and House produced a bonus bill they could agree on, Harding vetoed it.

Whatever veterans felt about Harding in the early 1920s was considerably modified in short order by the Forbes and Teapot Dome scandals, which promptly blossomed. The President died in 1923, leaving the White House with the President's legacy not only of a lot of questions unanswered, but also of a tradition for drinking when it was against the law to drink; gambling in violation of the Protestant ethic if not that of the District of Columbia; assorted corrupt aides; and a Cleveland brokerage house with an unpaid bill of $180,000. The brokerage bill represented Harding's stock transactions, which were both fanciful and unsuccessful; a prelude, of sorts, to the end of the decade, when everyone else's stock speculations would prove just as fanciful and even less successful.

But no bonus bill appeared for several years after Harding's veto, and many thousands of veterans watched a decade prosper without their participation. Foreign nations were extended credit, not veterans; huge loans went to railroads and other corporations, not to veterans; the stock market soared from a volume of $3.2 billion in 1923 to $10 billion just a few years later, but there were precious few former enlisted men among the temporarily happy speculators. Again the veterans began to think of the bonus that never was, and through veterans' organizations such as the American Legion they began to clamor for it, one more time.

Whatever tolerance Americans had for the idea of a bonus in the months following the Armistice had vanished by mid-decade. The president of the Chamber of Commerce, Julius H. Barnes, said that passage of a bonus bill would hurt "business activity, full employment and agricultural revival." George Eastman, who was building a better camera, warned that a bonus would make "mercenaries out of our patriotic boys." And Pierre S. du Pont, who shared in the golden splendor of Mellon's credit rating, especially after his company made so much money with its war contracts, said that as far as he was concerned, veterans needed no bonus. They were already "the most favored class in the United States," he asserted, apparently forgetting, for the moment, about politicians and the crafty entrepreneurs who had supplied munitions for all of America's wars.

The American Legion found it was no easy going representing its constituents. One of them, Brigadier General Lincoln Andrews, resigned from the Legion over the bonus issue. Retired high-ranking officers clearly did not have the same needs as former enlisted men. In quitting, Andrews used a ploy the veterans had never learned to cope with in years past and could not cope with now: guilt. "We performed splendidly in the war," he said, "and returned filled with the highest ideals of service. It is not our fault that political expediency buried this idealism neath a mass of selfish materialism, nor should we now allow ourselves to become a party to it."

The Legion, trying to be a bulwark of selfless patriotism, was stung when it heard such harsh judgments. It had not only its own fierce pride and pangs of conscience to deal with, but the judgments of rival veterans' groups, some of them created just to defeat the bonus issue and to bait the Legion in the process. When Andrews quit the Legion, his sanctimony was attended by Captain Knowlton Durham, president of the Ex-Servicemen's Anti-Bonus League. Durham also quit the Legion and attacked it, saying that he and his friends could "no longer consistently square their ideals of service and soldiers with membership in the American Legion so long as its principal activity is an attempt to add from two to five billion dollars to the war debt in payment of the bonus."

Still, the bonus idea remained popular with those veterans who were desperate. In 1924, Calvin Coolidge used some of the same rhetoric as his predecessors when he observed that the nation could not pay soldiers for a sacred duty. He said the "service they rendered was of such a nature that it cannot be recompensed to them by the payment of money." Indeed, Coolidge asserted, "Patriotism which is bought and paid for is not patriotism." *The Wall Street Journal,* whose editorial pages were hardly a wellspring of liberalism, went even further, calling bonus advocates "panhandlers" who were after an "unearned and undefensible dole."

Coolidge's veto of the bonus bill was quick, but the measure, such as it was, passed anyhow in 1924. It was a treasure trove of promises, not money. It offered veterans a wait of twenty-one years—until 1945—to get anything out of it. Its sponsors thought that the help would be useful then, because the men who fought the World War would be past their primes and probably in need of insurance. The veterans themselves already felt past their primes. They needed something more immediate. But as it did after the Revolution, the Government told its veterans only to be patient.

18

The Great Depression and the Ghost of Daniel Shays

We ain't gonna ever get a bonus. What the hell use is a veteran to the Government after the war's over, buddy?
—Unidentified bonus marcher as he marched into Washington in May 1932

No person because he wore a uniform, must there-after be placed in a special class of beneficiaries over and above all other citizens.
—President Franklin D. Roosevelt in a speech to the American Legion, October 1933

As the years passed, the patience urged upon veterans by Government was harder for them to maintain. The effects of the 1929 crash were soon pervasive and devastating, especially for those who had never shared in the fleeting prosperity of the twenties. The veterans' hospitals that had finally been built (no thanks to Charles Forbes) were filled with men who were not so old and should have been comparatively healthy. Yet in November and December of 1930, there were more than 32,000 patients in veterans' hospitals and another 23,000 in soldiers' homes—far more than there had been at any time since the war. The Government offered no explanation, but perhaps no explanation was needed. The Depression had taken from them whatever homes and security they had. The hospitals set aside for them in time of sickness were now becoming sanctuaries against times of economic hardship. In a sense, the way former soldiers looked to Government for aid, as the Depression hit, presaged the demands other Americans would make upon the New Deal of the thirties. But the country had not yet written that social contract and the lexicon of charity had not changed all that much since the nineteenth century.

There were some in Government who thought that the veterans ought to get a bonus, provided payment of it could be withheld until 1945. As the enormity of America's financial crisis became clearer and more frightening, veterans in the worst straits began to renew their demands for something that would see them through the bleak present. Former soldiers represented a special problem, even for those who wished them well, people who thought they should have received something from the Government years earlier. For now, almost everyone was in trouble. The question became whether the Government could single out veterans for special treatment—and not do precisely the same thing for other unemployed Americans who were no less needy and no less deserving.

The American Legion advocated that a bonus be paid to veterans, but even within the Legion's public statements, the reason was broadened and moderated to emphasize that although the Legion was representing veterans, what it advocated was for the good of the nation at large. A bonus, said the Legion, would "materially assist in the relief of present distressful economic conditions and put new life into American business."

The Legion was strongly anticommunist and a firm believer in the wisdom that it believed was residing within the noggins of American industry. It hoped that its exalted friends in the cathedral of capitalism would understand that what veterans wanted was reasonable. Clearly, the Legion's friends did not understand. The board of governors of the Investment Bankers of America warned their clients that the bonus was a menace that might cause the "disorganization" of the money market, the depression of the values of stocks, and the retardation of business prosperity. The chairman of the board of the powerful National City Bank of New York predicted that bonuses for veterans would mean "hundreds and hundreds of bank failures, small bank failures, throughout the United States." How and why this would happen was never made entirely clear. But the specter of bank failures caused by payment of bonuses to veterans became a slogan that many accepted. National City banker Charles E. Mitchell told a Senate committee, "A cash bonus will later do more evil than it will do good now. It is like a hypodermic of strychnine given to a sick person."

Congress listened to all of this, its sympathy for veterans modified by its fears that the moguls might know what they were talking about, even though a goodly number of them had proved conclusively in 1929 that in actuality they had very little idea of what they were talking about, especially when it came to investing money. The result was a compromise bill that would allow veterans to take out loans based on 50 percent of the face value of bonus certificates. They would be expected to pay interest on their loans at the rate of 4½ percent, which was high enough in those days. But President Herbert Hoover promptly vetoed the measure, saying that it was local communities, not the Federal Government, that had the responsibility of caring for needy men. What's more, he did not feel that there were all that many of them. "Inquiry indicates . . . that the number of veterans in need of such relief is a minor percentage of the whole," he said in his veto message. The Congress was not impressed with Hoover's research and overrode his veto in a scant forty-three minutes, which was said to be something of a record.

While all this was going on, the American Legion found itself carped at by the people it normally looked to for understanding. From the Legion's point of view, it was bad enough not to have the esteem of the princelings of business and industry, who essentially felt the Legion was pushing for something veterans shouldn't have. It was even worse when Wright Patman, a Democrat only recently elected from Texas and a strong believer in providing the veterans with an immediate cash bonus, criticized the Legion for not doing enough. Patman specifically and publicly criticized John Thomas Taylor, the Legion's chief Washington lobbyist, for going along with the 1945 payout and for failing to go after immediate cash, which was what many veterans wanted. Taylor, charged Patman, "has refused to turn his hand for justice" for the veteran and his actions were "part of the scheme of the predatory interests to deny the veterans of the World War the payment of a just debt." The Legion was thus sandbagged on two sides.

In any event, the bonus loan bill became law, and to the dismay of thousands of nonveteran unemployed Americans who had their own serious problems in making do, veterans said it wasn't enough. They needed money immediately, not in 1945. One such veteran was Walter W. Waters, and what he and others then did about their predicament culminated in the ugliest, most violent and heart-wrenching confrontation between veterans and Government since the crushing of Shays' Rebellion, nearly a century and a half before.

Born in Oregon in 1898, Waters enlisted in the Idaho National Guard in 1917 and served during the war as a sergeant, winning his honorable discharge in 1919. He had serious problems of readjustment when he returned home and spent time in several private hospitals (there were no Government institutions to help him). He was twenty-one years old with his life in front of him, but from his perspective, he had nowhere to go, "no occupation or profession to resume." He drifted about, working as a garage mechanic, automobile salesman, farmhand, and baker. He was engaging, outgoing, and not unmotivated. Yet he failed at all of the jobs he was given, or, at the very least, remained unfulfilled by them. He lived in Idaho for a time, then in 1925 moved to the state of Washington, where he again became a farmhand. He even took a new name—Bill Kinkaid—and simply stopped communicating with the people he had known before. Finally, he went to Oregon and got a job in a cannery in Portland, and from his point of view, he began to do something that he liked. He regarded himself as assistant superintendent, although others said he was only a worker.

Whatever the job, he lost it in 1930, a victim not of his lack of performance, but of the Depression. He, his wife, and their two children moved into a small, shabby apartment in Portland. First they used up the $1,000 they had saved, then they pawned their belongings, and finally, they took charity wherever they could find it, as he looked everywhere for a job, without success. By March of 1932 Waters and his family were quite destitute. He began to move around, talking to bitter, impoverished veterans whose experiences were not unlike his own. "Newspapers, which can always be picked out of trash cans in the parks and public places, published stories of extensions of credit to foreign nations," Waters would write of his own disaffection. "Headlines told of loans to railroads and to large corporations. . . . The 'Bonus' in men's minds became a substitute or symbol for that long dreamt of new start, a job. These men had nothing to which to look forward except to the shiny shoulders of the man in front of them in the breadline."

Waters began giving impromptu speeches, which were not well received by the veterans. But he kept talking and his speeches got better. Veterans began to listen to him. Within a relatively short time, he found himself regarded as something of a leader.

The thing that became the Bonus March started in the Portland, Oregon, business district in early May of 1932. At that point, it was nothing more than a local demonstration, and it was not the invention of Walter Waters. There was initially no plan to launch a national movement. The marchers had no money, no prospects, and no backers. Washington was more than three thousand miles away. But the notion of going to Washington to press their demands upon the Congress began to grow, in part out of desperation, in part, perhaps, because of some instigation that probably will never be fully explained. Critics of the march, including President Hoover and Secretary of War Patrick J. Hurley, would later claim, without documentation, that there were men among the marchers more interested in

promoting communism than the cause of veterans in need. They underestimated the spontaneity of the thing. They underestimated a great many
things in those days.

Hopping slow, foul-smelling freights and hitching rides with sympathetic
truckers and motorists, Waters and his friends from Oregon began to move
toward Washington, and somehow, other veterans around the country heard
of their move and made plans to join them. Waters' group was on the road
for eighteen days, much of it in filthy cattle cars. There were fine moments,
as when three hundred men all volunteered to give blood to a little girl who
was going to have an operation in Council Bluffs, Iowa; there was despair,
too, as in Idaho, where Waters and his men were told that a state leader of
the marchers had collected money for the trip to Washington but now
claimed not to have any of it left.

At two points, there were confrontations of sorts between marchers and
employees of the railroads, first the Wabash at Council Bluffs, then the
Baltimore & Ohio at East St. Louis. The railroads were not comfortable with
the prospect of granting free rides to unemployed men who were going to
Washington to pressure the Government. It was a replay of what had
happened with Coxey's Army thirty-eight years earlier. After the panic of
1893, Jacob S. Coxey led some 20,000 unemployed men to Washington to
urge the Government to use public works as a catalyst to provide
employment. At the request of the Governor of Montana, President Grover
Cleveland sent troops to prevent Coxey's men from riding freights. In 1932,
Hoover may have wanted to do the same thing, but he decided not to
interfere with the movement of the bonus marchers on the road. Baltimore
& Ohio employees were not about to relent as the Wabash officials had, but
the Missouri State Guard and private citizens got the marchers to the state
line in cars and trucks, and more hitchhiking and freight hopping continued
without interference.

At first, much of the nation paid little attention to the marchers. The tense
situation at East St. Louis made headlines, however, and the press was on
hand when Waters said, ''I don't know when we'll get to Washington but
we're going to stay there until the bonus bill is passed if it takes until 1945.''
But even then, it was hardly news of transcendent interest, at least not when
compared to the other major stories of the day, such as the deepening
Depression and the kidnapping of the Lindbergh baby.

Waters' group arrived in the District of Columbia on May 29, pleased and
rather surprised to see that other contingents were pouring in, too. Indeed,
about one thousand ex-soldiers had preceded them to town. It had the
bearing of a real mass movement. Before it was over, the Bonus March

would involve anywhere from 25,000 to 40,000 veterans. A cause of such magnitude had to have a name, and so they named it: the Bonus Expeditionary Force, or B.E.F., taken from the American Expeditionary Forces, or A.E.F., that had served fourteen years earlier in France.

It was something to see. Men in white shirts, sleeves rolled up to reveal hardened arms with no work to do. No manual work, at least. The ex-soldiers had a far more formidable job, that of persuading Congress to part with public money. Black veterans were much in evidence, one of the few times in the history of veterans' movements in the United States when the two races lived and worked easily together. These were bony, hungry-looking men, weathered from days and weeks on the road. A few wore the uniforms they had worn when they were in the A.E.F., but many more came wearing the dark caps and dark, baggy work trousers that were common in those days. They were a sea of stains and wrinkled pants and wrinkled shirts smelling from many days of no showers or laundry facilities to use. Some of them walked with the aid of canes. They milled about Washington, most finally alighting, dusty, parched, and hungry, in the flats of Anacostia, an orphaned and isolated portion of Southeast Washington, separated from the rest of the city by an undernourished river, also called the Anacostia. There was a drawbridge over it at 11th Street which could be raised and lowered at the whim of the District of Columbia authorities.

That the men were able to locate themselves in Anacostia was largely the work of Washington's remarkable police chief, Pelham Glassford, who interceded on behalf of the veterans with Ulysses S. Grant III, the Director of Public Buildings and Grounds. Glassford was as sophisticated as the nabobs he represented were not. He had been a career Army officer before his retirement in 1932. A West Point graduate, he was an officer of considerable perception who had an unusual tolerance for individualism, including his own, which manifested itself, in part, in the motorcycle on which he liked to wheel around town. Glassford's father had also been a soldier, and perhaps that is part of the reason that Glassford felt easy with military responsibility. He had held the rank of brigadier general at the age of thirty-five, the youngest officer of such rank in the A.E.F. Aloof, tall, and imposing, always every inch the professional officer he was trained to be, Glassford also had a sense of humor (he had worked for a circus and for a newspaper during Army furloughs) and compassion for the men who had served in the war but had been so little served by the peace that followed. He was no ideologue, but from the outset, it was clear he was not going to permit the provincial officials who ran the District of Columbia's inordinately backward, creaky Government to make mischief where there need be none. Given the way Washington was in those days, Glassford knew that the District would regard the soldiers as little more than drifters and deal with them harshly. This he was determined to prevent.

It would be no easy task. When Glassford asked Secretary of War Hurley to permit the marchers to use such surplus military equipment as tents, cots, and bedsacks, Hurley refused and said that the Federal Government "could not recognize the invasion. . . ." Glassford knew that increased discomfort could mean increased edginess between District officials and the men, and so he involved himself totally in the business of seeing to it that the veterans' encampment was run as well as it could be, under the circumstances. In a sharp departure from the way most police officials look upon the crowds they are asked to control, he literally became the B.E.F.'s treasurer and helped the veterans raise money. He even donated $120 of his own money.

The men were there to demonstrate in support of their own grievances, and demonstrate they did. The first show was in early June, when five thousand veterans marched down Pennsylvania Avenue to the cadence of what Waters called a "borrowed drum corps," passing before spectators who did not cheer them. And unlike the triumphal paraders just after the war, these soldiers did not jest in the ranks.

Thanks mostly to Glassford's abilities, the ex-soldiers got along quite well with the police, so much so that they named their Anacostia encampment Camp Marks, for a captain on Glassford's staff, S. J. Marks. Marks and all the other police officers assigned to work with the veterans were veterans themselves; Glassford saw to that. The veterans began to make the Anacostia flats their own, filling it with the flotsam of the wanderer's housing—shacks, wooden boxes, cardboard piano boxes, oilcloth, canvas, bricks, the lumber of dumps and abandoned buildings. To Waters, Anacostia began to resemble a "cross between a Congo village, a trash pile, a picnic ground and a tourist camp." It had its compensations, however. "No landlords came daily threatening eviction. No bill collectors came. There was no need to fear the imperious ring of the door bell. The absence of gas and electricity had at least the compensating comfort that neither could be cut off for non-payment of bills," Waters would write.

There were nevertheless tensions. The men would frequently be seen with empty bean cans strapped to their belts. The cans were precious—used for carrying water—and the ex-soldiers sometimes appropriated the cans even from men whom they regarded as their friends. President Hoover appreciated neither the resilience of the men nor Glassford's ability to induce them to remain orderly and self-regulating. What Glassford saw as a basic civilized gesture that one human might make to another, Hoover saw as an action that would only make it easier for the marchers to stay in Washington, which is precisely what he did not want. Nor would Hoover meet with the veterans and their representatives. The put-down was underscored when the President who had no time for such business met with a group of Boy Scouts and an aviatrix.

The number of veterans swelled. But Congress was not about to accommodate their demands for a cash bill. The conservatives remained opposed to anything resembling a cohesive national policy on social welfare; the liberals preferred to think about legislation that would ease unemployment problems for everyone, not just veterans. In mid-June, some three weeks after their arrival in Washington and only a few days after their march down Pennsylvania Avenue, about eight thousand veterans arranged themselves undecorously on the steps of the Capitol. There they parked in the hot sun, looking even more unwashed than they had when they arrived, lobbying in tatters the congressmen who might try to scurry past them.

The bill they wanted came up in the Congress, but it was voted down. The veterans greeted their defeat with stony silence. One journalist, apparently just a little intimidated by the moment, likened the veterans to the "mobs of the French Revolution; the crash of the Kerensky Government," but in truth, the only response Congress heard from the veterans that day was when they broke into the singing of "America, the Beautiful."

It wasn't only reporters who overreacted. Senator Hiram Johnson, a Republican of California, saw it all happen and thought that it was "ominous." To his way of thinking, "if the farmers of this nation, who are suffering united, as these men have united, and with the same abandon, started a march upon the Capitol, and joined ranks with those of the city whose souls have been seared with misery during the past few years, it would not be difficult for a real revolution to start in this country."

Everywhere, there were reports that the veterans had been organized and led to Washington by communists, and the rumors were picked up by the press, which lacked either the interest or the ability to check out the rumors. *The Washington Post* declared that the Bonus March was the work of reds who had "double-crossed the nation." Charges of subversion amused Waters, even though he was probably as opposed to communism as was the Legion: "Until very recently the average American in small town and city knew little about Communism. . . . Karl Marx, in his mind, was probably one of the four Marx brothers, the one with the beard." Subversion from the far left was not the only charge. The Catholic magazine *Commonweal*, then a publication not to miss out on any prevailing national hysteria, felt that such a massive gathering of veterans spoke more of fascism.

Even though chances for passage of a bill were not good, some veterans, sparked by militants from Los Angeles, threw a picket line around the Capitol in mid-July and slept there for three days. They would awaken and walk slowly around the Capitol—they called what they were doing a "Death March." It greatly alarmed those in Washington who were already predisposed to be alarmed. Whatever faith the Hoover Administration had in Chief Glassford to keep the peace was seriously eroded, so much so that Vice-President Charles Curtis, otherwise an eminently forgettable man, called out the Marines. There might have been serious trouble right then and there had it not been for Glassford, who intervened and persuaded Admiral Henry V. Butler to recall them, even though they had already boarded a trolley bound for the Capitol, with orders to disperse the veterans. The working relationship between Curtis and Chief Glassford further deteriorated as a result.

Rumors grew that President Hoover would soon move against the veterans and drive them from the city. "I hope that rumor is not true," said Congressman Patman. "There are men here who do not have a home." Because of official concern about what the veterans might do, the White House was effectively isolated from the rest of Washington at one point by the cordoning power of more than a hundred police. Tension built within Government; it could not go on much longer. Some of the veterans, seeing the futility of their situation and sensing trouble, left town. But many thousands remained.

On July 25, there were a series of fights in the streets between police and veterans who wanted to picket the White House. Among those arrested were John Pace of Detroit, who police suggested might be a communist; and George Represas, a Spanish-born dishwasher. Police said he gave no address "except the communist camp at Twelfth and B streets, southwest." Pace, Represas, and several others were charged with disorderly conduct, even though Pace insisted, "We were just out for a walk, that's all."

While all this was going on, the newly formed Veterans Administration took to itself a curious role, saying that only 3,500 veterans remained in town and that between five hundred and eight hundred of them were not even war veterans. At that point, the number of bonus marchers in Washington was closer to eleven thousand. And almost all of them were veterans. Hoover hung back for a time, fearful that if he did anything against the veterans in Washington it might galvanize thousands of other veterans throughout the country into rash action against the Government.

Waters, who was reasonably good at reading between the lines of Washington newspapers, suspected that some within the Federal Government were indulging in a bit of red-baiting, trying to make it seem as though the veterans were not really what they said they were. "You and your bonus army have no business in Washington," Secretary Hurley told Waters and other marchers in a meeting. "We are not in sympathy with your being here. We will not cooperate in any way with your remaining here. We are interested only in getting you out of the District. . . ."

Waters didn't know it then, but a secret Army intelligence report confirmed his suspicions about red-baiting. The report, bizarre even for Army intelligence, stated that "the first bloodshed by the Bonus Army at Washington is to be the signal for a communist uprising in all large cities thus initiating a revolution. The entire movement is stated to be under communist control, with branches rapidly developed in commercial centers."

The Government reaction to the veteran problem seemed awfully well tailored. Apparently, it benefited from considerable coordination. The message was that even veterans who were not communists were a burden to the rest of the country. As the Hoover Administration beat the red drum in Washington, Army Major-General James O. Harbord told the "first annual meeting" of the National Economics League in New York City that by 1945, payments to veterans and their families would reach $2 billion. The league sought to eliminate at least $450 million a year in payments to Spanish-American and World War veterans "who suffered no disability in war service." The same day that it reported Harbord's speech, the *Washington Evening Star* editorialized that "the real design of those who are now using the bonus plea as an excuse for agitation is to attract attention, even at the cost of a possible riot at the Capitol."

Troublemakers were everywhere, if Washingtonians believed what they read in their newspapers. On July 27, a wire service story datelined Pontiac, Michigan, reported that police were looking for a "radical" group which was making uncomplimentary statements about the nation's banks. It was fanciful to suggest that any rumors circulated by radicals would make banks more distrusted than they were already, but such was the way of it in Pontiac and Detroit. That set it up rather nicely: communists or maybe fascists were running the veterans' Bonus March and those veterans who were not communists or fascists were greedy and, worse still, were even bank-haters.

On July 28, time and patience ran out. Police and Treasury agents tried to evict veterans from the partially demolished old National Guard Armory at 3rd and Pennsylvania, three blocks from the Capitol and half a mile from the White House. The reason for the eviction, said the Government, was that the building had to be demolished so that new Government buildings could

be constructed. Why demolition had to proceed just then in the heat of a
Washington summer was unclear. Some of the police clubbed the veterans.
Later that day, not far from the Armory, there was another incident and two
veterans were shot in a confrontation with the police. Both died; one
immediately, the other somewhat later. A twelve-week-old baby was also
gassed and died later, although the cause of his death was never attributed
by officials to his gassing. One policeman suffered a fractured skull. And
Chief Glassford, who waded into the middle of it all to try to quiet the
veterans down, had his badge ripped off. After the deaths, Glassford, whose
influence had already been waning, was unable to use his good offices to
control either the veterans or the irrationality of Government.

There is some question as to who precisely called upon Federal troops to
remove the veterans. The task fell to General Douglas MacArthur, who was
then Army Chief of Staff. Not everything that happened then is clear, but
Hoover would later claim that he only wanted MacArthur to move the
veterans out of the business district and back to their camps. That is not what
MacArthur did.

MacArthur first pressed his aide, Major Dwight D. Eisenhower, into
service. Eisenhower was not enthusiastic about MacArthur's mindset, for
MacArthur believed the reports he had heard and thought that the veterans
were actually going to engage in an attempt to overthrow the U.S.
Government, implausible though it seemed. Indeed, he thought that Waters
was assembling a supply of machine guns to use for the occasion. Thus,
expulsion of the veterans from Washington became MacArthur's solution.
Eisenhower would later say that he argued with MacArthur not to take such
drastic action. But MacArthur would hear none of it. The hour was at hand
to save the nation from its supposed usurpers.

MacArthur assembled six hundred troops, which included two hundred
mounted cavalry and more than three hundred infantry, carrying rifles and
bayonets. There were also five tanks and a special machine-gun unit.
Hundreds of other troops were alerted in Federal installations in Maryland
and Virginia. On a hot summer evening, MacArthur advanced upon the
bonus marchers not far from the Capitol, his tear gas preceding him, the
bayonets of his men fixed. The marchers threw bricks and swore, but
MacArthur was undeterred. At one point, the cavalry under the direction of
Major George S. Patton became angry at the veterans and jostled them as
well as some hapless civilian onlookers. One of the veterans Patton would
roust before the day was through was Joe Angelo, who was credited with
having saved his life during the war. Indeed, before it was over a great many
people would be rousted, including some civilians. Among them would be

a book salesman, an employee of a wallpaper company coming home from a dance, and an off-duty member of the District of Columbia National Guard.

At about half-past six in the afternoon, MacArthur paused. He wanted his men to have supper before moving against the big camp in Anacostia. The advance soon continued, and at a little after nine o'clock, MacArthur's troops crossed the 11th Street Bridge and moved toward the camp. As they approached, the veterans who were supposed to be so disloyal sang "My Country 'Tis of Thee."

By ten o'clock, the camp at Anacostia was burning. Eisenhower said that the veterans fired their own huts. The wives and children of the fleeing veterans stood on a little hillside, watching their shacks burn and weeping. Dressed in rags, they contrasted with the middle-class Washington residents who stood beside them in fresh summer linen. One veteran's wife refused to leave the area, which was becoming uncomfortable from the tear gas and perhaps even dangerous. "If he's going to be killed, I'm going to stay here and be killed with him," she said.

Soon after, MacArthur held a press conference and said extraordinary things as only he could make them extraordinary. He claimed that only one out of ten of those evicted was a "real" war veteran. The rest, he said, were "insurrectionists." He was supported by the press. "The misguided men have refused to listen to persuasion," said *The New York Times*. "Now they must submit to compulsion." Not until much later was a survey conducted by the Veterans Administration, which showed that 94 percent of those who had made the Bonus March were, in fact, veterans, that 67 percent had served overseas, and that 20 percent had suffered some sort of disability. There were relatively few men there who might be classified as trouble-makers.

Next day the expelled and bedraggled veterans trudged the roads leading from the Capitol, relying on sympathetic motorists for rides. The Baltimore & Ohio Railroad offered to give them rides but insisted that somebody would have to pay for it. "Railroads are not permitted to carry passengers without charge," said a railroad spokesperson, who seemed uncommonly observant of the rules of the Interstate Commmerce Commission. In Washington, the Army congratulated itself for doing such a splendid job and MacArthur was declared the "man of the hour" by Secretary Hurley.

Out in Las Vegas, as he made his way to the opening of the 1932 Olympics in Los Angeles, Vice-President Curtis was rudely reminded that he was a long way from his friends in Washington. He got into a shouting match with hecklers who denounced MacArthur and praised Franklin

Delano Roosevelt, Hoover's chief political opponent. "You cowards, I'm not afraid of you," Curtis yelled, the decorum of his high office eluding him. "If you wait for [Roosevelt] to be elected, you'll be an old man." Curtis was mistaken; his hecklers were to wait less than four months.

The grotesque spectacle of the rousting of ex-servicemen clearly caught the leaders of the veterans' movement off guard. In Washington, one exception to the weak reponse was the newly elected district commander of the American Legion, Norman Landreau, who had the presence of mind to attack the military eviction of the bonus marchers as "unwarranted and un-American." He criticized Hoover and his aides for having "no sympathy in their hearts for the American people, no desire to aid the common man, but their whole aim is to care for Wall Street. . . ." But the Legion's national commander, Henry Stevenson, Jr., reached in Spokane, said lamely that he could not comment on what had happened and that he believed the Legion wasn't even insisting on the bonus. Richard O. Melton, national commander of the Disabled American Veterans, said, "The bonus march has in no way been sponsored or encouraged by the D.A.V.," and Oscar Hollingsworth, deputy commander of the Veterans of Foreign Wars, said he thought the B.E.F. "is doing all veterans all over the country a great harm." The Government had again succeeded in making veterans feel guilty about asking for help.

President Hoover, encouraged by a press that largely backed what MacArthur had done and by his friends in the Cabinet, then compounded MacArthur's mistake by saying, "Government cannot be coerced by mob rule." By the time he issued his statement, most of the fleeing unarmed veterans, who had not thought of themselves as coercive when they saw MacArthur's tanks and smelled his tear gas, were in Maryland, headed north. They had a place to go, thanks to a former prize fighter named Eddie McCloskey who had become mayor of Johnstown, Pennsylvania, in 1931 by advocating some curious anti-Depression measures, such as building sidewalks from Maine to California in order to provide jobs for those who had none.

McCloskey had come to Anacostia in the middle of July and told Waters that if the veterans ever needed a place to go, Johnstown should be their destination. On the morning of July 29, they had a need, and Johnstown was thus about to experience its second inundation since 1889. The city's population was only 67,000, and when some six thousand decidedly underfinanced veterans showed up, it put a strain on everyone. The local press described the men as "thieves" and "degenerates," even though neither stealing nor degeneracy had marked their stay in Washington.

The veterans were put up at an amusement park just ouside of Johnstown, and life was unpleasant. Water supplies were uncertain, toilet facilities woefully overtaxed, and food scarce. And yet, given what they had wherever they had come from, the veterans were in no particular hurry to leave. Pennsylvania's Governor Gifford Pinchot assigned state troopers to see to it that the gathering remained lawful and peaceful, and the state made no move to evict the men.

The District of Columbia, glad to be rid of the bonus marchers, was not nearly so benign. Hoover, who showed signs of possessing limitless ineptitude, asked a grand jury to investigate whether "subversive influences" had control of the veterans remaining in Washington, and, predictably, the judge heading the inquiry concluded, without taking any evidence, that the veterans who were left were composed "mainly of Communists and other disorderly persons." Hoover said publicly that many of those remaining "are not veterans, many are communists and persons with criminal records." Then he headed for his retreat in the Virginia mountains, apparently feeling for the moment that it was a job well done.

Waters, who had left Washington and was with the men in Johnstown, tried to create a kind of organization out of something which had no form. He called on the veterans to start a "khaki shirts" movement for economic justice and told the men encamped at Johnstown that perhaps they ought to be permanently encamped at Laurel, Maryland, about twenty miles from the Capitol. His words caused *The New York Times* to suggest that he seemed to want an organization "molded, outwardly at least, along the lines of the Nazis of Germany." So while Hoover's minions searched for communists in Washington, New York journalism thought it could see evidence of the far right at work. Waters was not about to win a popularity contest.

In the days to come, as the enormity of the MacArthur debacle was comprehended by the nation, Hoover seemed even more defensive. He refused to see a delegation of writers, led by Sherwood Anderson, who visited Washington in August to protest what had happened to the veterans. Hoover shunted them off to a press officer, but no amount of Government public relations could stop the writers from issuing a critical release, which said, in part: "During the past week destitute, unarmed men were shot down by the police, and *by your personal order* defenseless men and women were harried through the streets of Washington by soldiers with bayonets, saber and gas. . . ." MacArthur had had his way, but it would clearly be Herbert Hoover who would pay the political price.

The Administration got off another weak salvo in September, shortly before the American Legion was to hold its convention, when it issued a report on the bonus marchers prepared by the Attorney General. The report suggested that in all probability, "the Bonus Army brought to the city of Washington the largest aggregation of criminals that had ever assembled in the city at any one time." Coming so soon after Teapot Dome and the Veterans' Bureau under Forbes, that was quite something for the Government to say. Nobody bought it. H. L. Mencken, writing in *The American Mercury,* explained, "Hoover had to defame the poor idiots he had gassed."

Mencken's sentiments were usually not those of most newspaper editors, and this was no exception. Most papers supported Hoover. "Whether these men are really communists or not is immaterial; they are agitators and their object is to foment trouble and make headlines," said the *New York Herald Tribune.* "The obvious duty of the authorities at Washington is to maintain order at whatever cost" was the opinion of the *Plain Dealer* of Cleveland. The *Memphis Evening Appeal* said, "At a time when grubs of revolution and degenerative social upheaval are gnawing at the very foundations of American governmental order, it [expulsion] may have a salutary effect. . . . Let those who dare assail the basic structure of the American governmental system take heed." The most disturbing editorial of all ran in Washington's own *Evening Star* on July 30, 1932, for the *Star* made it clear it no longer wanted any sort of demonstrations to take place in Washington: "The end of tolerant dealing with itinerant tramps and idlers, as well as bonus marchers, has come."

American voters may not have taken to heart what they read in their newspapers, because Hoover's (really MacArthur's) folly cost Hoover the November election. But the veterans could take little solace in the political philosophy of Franklin Delano Roosevelt as it then existed. He regarded the idea of a bonus for World War veterans as nothing less than a raid on the Treasury, and he wanted no part of it. Although Roosevelt would go down in history as a President who tried to use Government programs to stimulate employment in a weak economy, in those early years his motive was to energize the economy by cutting Government spending. Indeed, he systematically went about eliminating most of what Congress had provided veterans in the past with his Economy Act of 1933, which among other things cut allowances for service-related disabilities by 25 percent.

A second bonus march quickly developed, smaller in size, and more expertly handled by Roosevelt, who had his Veterans Administrator, Frank Hines, establish a camp for the veterans at Fort Hunt, fifteen miles from Washington. No veterans were allowed to loiter in Washington parks, and neither MacArthur nor any other general was given an opportunity to cause mischief. The second march, like the first, proved fruitless to the veterans and passed without serious problems for the Government.

In a speech to the American Legion, Roosevelt explained his opposition to the bonus by asserting, "No person because he wore a uniform, must thereafter be placed in a special class of beneficiaries over and above all other citizens." Roosevelt's convictions notwithstanding, the Congress would soon pass a cash bonus—over his veto.

As it was with Shays' Rebellion, nobody held grudges when the Bonus March finally came to its ignominious end. Forgiveness was always the American way. The veterans eventually went home, or at least left Washington so that the District Commissioners would not have to worry about them anymore. The B.E.F. was gone for good. Walter Waters, no longer the commandant of anything, disappeared again and went to work first as an attendant in a Kansas City gasoline station, then as a cement worker on the San Francisco–Oakland bridge. He found the time to write a book about the Bonus March.

MacArthur may have thought that Waters and his men were a threat to the very survival of the republic, but within three years he was all forgiveness. He was able to banish his little misgivings by early in 1935. For it was then that MacArthur hired Waters—to work as a clerk in the War Department, which he ran. Waters' salary was $1,500 a year. And MacArthur seemed not the least bit concerned that Waters might say or do something subversive in that most sensitive of places, the War Department.

Within a few years, America would have a new war to fight—the most monstrous war in all history. MacArthur, of course, would be a hero again. As the United States drifted closer to that war, the veterans of the Great War—expelled from Washington by the very Government they had fought for—were not only forgiven. They were forgotten.

SIX

After the
Second
World War

with Pride and
Patriotism

NAVY

Women who answered the call to
serve in World War II were later
told they could not be considered
veterans. (*The Bettman Archive*)

19
Sweet Wine
at Last

If we give special status to veterans today, we are
faced with the problem of special consideration for
minority groups tomorrow.
—Warning issued in 1945 by Robert J. Watt,
international representative of the American
Federation of Labor

Americans had two great basic concerns as they struggled through World
War II. The first, of course, was winning it. This the civilians (if not always
the generals) thought their country could do handily. In the past, even in
wars whose contributions to the national honor were questionable, Americans had been generally steadfast. With this war, the rightness of the cause
brought the country together as it had never been before; the Americans truly
were indomitable. It was to be their finest hour and they knew it.

The second concern was far more complicated and harder to deal with.
Many Americans were quite convinced that there would be a depression
when the war was over. This was a problem that had nothing to do with the
justice of the conflict, and about it they were not nearly so confident. A big
part of the problem, from the civilian perspective, was the soldiers—the
very people who gave civilians cause for optimism about winning. There
were more than sixteen million of them, who with their families constituted
a quarter of the population. Most of the military men and women were
anxious to resume being civilians. The people who were civilians already
wondered what would happen to the economy when they all came home.

Of the civilian work force approaching sixty million, roughly a third were
women, many of them in the workplace for the first time, doing well and

enjoying it. At least, Americans were so led to believe from their newsreels and newspapers, which sang the praises of smiling young females whose hair was tucked up in the turbans of factory fashion, wielding riveting machines in a most authoritative and productive way. Always dependable workers, they constituted 10 percent of the labor that made the vital steel mills go. Even though it was still an age when a woman's place was supposed to be in the home, nobody could say for sure how many of them would want to remain in a traditionally male workplace—if not in steel, then perhaps somewhere else—and nobody could say how many an American economy at peace could absorb, nor how quickly.

The national worry about the U.S. economy's future performance had its genesis in the decade before Pearl Harbor, which was dominated by an economic catastrophe so profound and hurtful that many Americans, including those who claimed to be sophisticated about economics, doubted that the average citizen would ever see good times again. More to the point, they doubted that the nation could have gotten itself out of the Depression without the stimulus that another world war had provided to its economy.

It was a syndrome that John Kenneth Galbraith would call ''the Depression Psychosis,'' literally a gut feeling that the Depression never really ended and that after the fighting stopped, the conditions of the thirties would return and remain for good. It was knowledge derived of common wisdom and therefore so unassailably true, so imbedded in the national psyche, that fathers and mothers passed it on to their children, so that they would not expect too much out of life. If Americans could have won the war and somehow kept a war economy going afterward, they probably would have elected to do so. They did not believe they had an alternative, if most were to partake of life's banquet. And so, as the war was about to end, there were dire and frightening predictions about the peace to come.

The Department of Labor, which certainly had no cause to accentuate the negative, predicted that when it ended, between twelve million and fifteen million workers would be unemployed. *The New Republic,* a distinguished and responsible journal, predicted that there would be a ''Pearl Harbor of peace'' because Congress was ''not making adequate advance plans for demobilization and full employment.'' And a poll by George Gallup's well-regarded organization found that 24 percent of those polled thought that postwar unemployment would be massive—seven million to ten million; 11 percent thought it would be eleven to nineteen million; and another 8 percent were even more pessimistic, predicting at least twenty million.

The soldiers themselves were hardly more hopeful. As the war was winding down, a Government survey indicated that fully 56 percent of them

anticipated a widespread depression after the war, 15 percent were undecided, and only 29 percent thought the nation would avoid a depression.
Indeed, learned, Harvard-educated economist Stuart Chase shared their
biases. He predicted in 1943 that when D-Day finally came, everyone would
have "a shout in his heart," but even he succumbed to the national mania
and wondered if returning soldiers would be "glad to sell apples in the
street."

The Government, *The New Republic*, the soldiers, Gallup, and Chase
were all dead wrong. Returning soldiers had no intention of selling apples
in the street, and nobody was going to ask them to. Peace yielded not the
resumption of the Great Depression that everyone feared, but a sustained
boom, fueled in large measure by fat wartime savings and a people aching
to spend their money on something other than used clunkers and war bonds.
Within two years after victory, President Harry S. Truman could tell the
Congress that the soldiers whose demobilization had been so feared had
joined with wartime civilian workers to find gainful employment "in the
swiftest change-over that any nation has ever made from war to peace."
Unemployment in 1945 totaled only 1.9 percent, and for the next two years
it remained under 4 percent. By 1948, the inevitable inflation occurred and
unregulated retail prices of food were rising at an annual rate of 15 percent,
textiles at 12 percent, fuel and lighting at 36 percent. The economy fizzled
in 1949, a recession year, when unemployment soared to 5.9 percent (not so
bad when compared to other years), and Truman braced himself and the
country for bad times. But they never came; the outbreak of the Korean War
in 1950 provided a powerful economic stimulus. And even if there had been
no Korea, no Great Depression was indisputably in view.

There was no way Franklin Delano Roosevelt could have known what
was coming. During the war, he had shared the apprehensions of everyone
else. But he had too much of a sense of history to permit the events
following World War I to repeat themselves; he started preparing for peace
even before America formally entered World War II. In 1940, a year before
Pearl Harbor, he signed the Selective Service Act. Among other things, the
law sought to assure those drafted that, within certain limitations, they could
regain the jobs they had when they returned to civilian status.

In 1942, the Government again considered the problems that might have
to be overcome to win the peace. On this occasion, it was barely a year after
the Japanese attack on Pearl Harbor, when the Axis Powers were still very
strong and the outcome of the war uncertain. But General George C.
Marshall, who was then Army Chief of Staff, began to consider the problem
of demobilization anyhow and directed some of his subordinates to begin

planning for it. Most Americans may have put the Bonus March out of their minds. They may have forgotten the indifference and abysmal lack of planning that had attended the end of the First World War, thereby creating the conditions that caused the Bonus March. But Marshall was not one of them, nor was his boss, the President.

Marshall's colleagues did their peace-thinking quietly, and appropriately so. The whole country was in deadly combat against a tyrant who was arguably the craziest and meanest ever, and it was not a propitious moment to consider social legislation that would have been welcome a few years before. As President Roosevelt put it, "Dr. New Deal" had outlived his usefulness and was being replaced by "Dr. Win-the-War."

Writers and others outside of Government felt much freer to talk about peace planning. In 1943, there was such a spate of speeches and books dealing with a presumed victory and the peace that would follow that book reviewer R. M. MacIver, after laboring through Rudolph Flesch's treatise *Towards an Abiding Peace,* complained of reconstruction as "the daily fare of ad writers and platform speakers."

But the frequent and open discussion of peacetime planning was not something that the President felt very comfortable with. He was sensitive that the more conservative members of Government would be critical if he appeared to care too much about social concerns in such a time. Critics like Representative Bertrand W. Gearhart, a Republican of California, were on guard to make certain that Roosevelt and his liberal friends did not use the postwar period to enact yet more New Deal legislation, even if it was ostensibly designed to help veterans. Gearhart's early role as a founding father of the American Legion did not make him any more amenable to Roosevelt-style social legislation for soldiers.

But the conservative whose wrath the liberals most wanted to avoid was Congressman John E. Rankin of Mississippi, who was chairman of the House Veterans Committee. He was clearly in a position to do violence, if he chose, to any and all legislation aimed at helping veterans. Mr. Rankin was not the most farsighted politician the South had ever produced, although in his day, he was probably one of the House's better character actors. At a time when a new South was emerging and when it had begun to send to Washington resourceful men who could put the past in its place and look to the future in a constructive way, Rankin remained inflexibly dedicated to infusing, resuscitating, and retaining some of the more unfortunate aspects of ancient North-South relations.

Rankin, a nominal Democrat, regarded himself as a patriot and so he might have been expected to be understanding of the needs of veterans. But he also saw himself as a conservative guardian of taxpayer funds, forever on the lookout for more New Deal legislation or communists who might want to pervert the mission of the Government to their own nefarious purposes. With arms flailing and voice wailing, Rankin was a formidable weapon against those who might propose social legislation for any reason. He thought that any Government social program, even for veterans, might reasonably be suspected of having been inspired by communists, whom he suspected were under every rock. And he suspected that communists were inspired, organized, and otherwise manipulated by Jews, whom he saw as bitter, treasonous, and conspiratorial. His distaste for Jews and communists was surpassed only by his disdain for blacks, who, he was convinced, were inherently incapable of taking care of themselves. Such a man was naturally restrained about almost any suggestion that might come from Franklin Delano Roosevelt.

Rankin made it clear early on that he thought of veterans' benefits as a boon to the unmotivated. He also viewed the prospect of exposing untutored veterans to the educational process as dangerous and even unpatriotic, since it would bring them in contact with college instructors, whom he viewed at best as excessively liberal, at worst the dupes and apologists of those ubiquitous Jews and communists. "I would rather send my child to a red schoolhouse than to a red school teacher," Rankin said. Even worse, from his perspective, was the idea of educating blacks, which would be included in the provisions of a veterans' bill then under consideration. He felt that blacks were largely incapable of benefiting from the process. "We have 50,000 negroes in the service from our State, and in my opinion, if the bill should pass in its present form, a vast majority of them would remain unemployed for at least a year, and a great many white men would do the same thing."

Roosevelt wanted results, not confrontation, and he knew that if he appeared too forthcoming, it would work against his plans. Even so, in July of 1943, in one of his "fireside chats" on the radio, he mentioned the need to plan for the returning soldier when he told his audience, "While concentrating on military victory, we are not neglecting the planning of things to come. . . . Among other things, we are . . . laying plans for the return to civilian life of our gallant men and women of the armed services. They must not be demobilized into an environment of inflation and unemployment. . . ."

The following October, Roosevelt presented to Congress a proposal for funding honorably discharged veterans to study for one calendar year, with the suggestion that perhaps a much smaller group of veterans—those with "exceptional ability and skill"—might be able to study for three years at Government expense. He had already moved well away from the anti-bonus position he had taken eleven years earlier. Politically, it was a well-timed decision. A Presidential election was near at hand, and he knew that congressmen, even those intimidated by Rankin and others like him, would be more inclined to make concessions to soldiers under such circumstances.

People skeptical of Roosevelt's education measure were by no means confined to the Congress. Robert M. Hutchins, the president of the University of Chicago, said he was afraid that "colleges and universities will find themselves converted into educational hobo jungles. And veterans unable to get work and equally unable to resist putting pressure on the colleges and universities, will find themselves educational hoboes."

In any event, in these early maneuvers, Roosevelt skillfully softened up the foes of liberal veterans' legislation. The seeds he planted would eventually become the Serviceman's Readjustment Act of 1944—better known as the G.I. Bill of Rights.

In November of 1943, Roosevelt continued his careful courting of Congress in the interests of soldiers:

> All of us are concentrating now on the one primary objective of winning this war. But even as we devote our energy and resources to that purpose, we cannot neglect to plan for things to come after victory is won. . . . Members of the armed forces have been compelled to make greater economic sacrifice and every other kind of sacrifice than the rest of us, and are entitled to definite action to help take care of their special problems. . . . What our service men and women want, more than anything else, is the assurance of satisfactory employment upon their return to civil life. The first task after the war is to provide employment for them and for our demobilized war workers.

But when Roosevelt's uncle, Frederic A. Delano, the chairman of the National Resources Planning Board, suggested that an interagency conference on postwar planning might be a good idea, Roosevelt wrote to him, "I finally decided that this is no time for a public interest in or discussion of post-war problems—on the broad ground that there will not be any post-war problems if we lose the war. This includes the danger of diverting people's attention from the winning of the war."

David Lilienthal, then head of the Tennessee Valley Authority, was clearly in agreement and sought to make his liberal friends understand that the concerns they had during the 1930s had to be put aside now. "Progressives should understand that programs which do not forward the war must be given up or drastically curtailed," he said. "Where a social service doesn't help to beat Hitler, it may have to be sacrificed."

Such talk was disheartening to liberals, who wanted to win the war no less than conservatives but wondered what damage it was doing to the national conscience. "Liberals meet in Washington these days, if they meet at all," said Archibald MacLeish, "to discuss the tragic outlook for all liberal proposals, the collapse of all liberal leadership and the inevitable defeat of all liberal aims."

But liberal aims were being furthered by one of the unlikeliest of sources—the American Legion. The Legion had always been cool to social programs. But Harry W. Colmery of Topeka, Kansas, a former national commander of the Legion and a former Republican national chairman, knew that without proper planning, soldiers would return to the same savagely indifferent homecoming they had known after World War I. Thus, he took it upon himself to write specific recommendations which outlined a broad program for veterans. Its purposes were to give the soldier a chance to reach the status he would have enjoyed if he had not served in the military, and to establish a benefits program to see veterans through the "troublous times which are ahead."

The prospect of the G.I. Bill was not greeted warmly on all fronts, and there were efforts to soften it. Congressman Rankin and other conservatives tried to force Roosevelt to remove certain parts of the bill—actions that would narrow the scope of the educational component. Roosevelt signed it into law on June 22, 1944, as Americans fought in Europe to capture Cherbourg, and in the Pacific in the Philippines. Roosevelt used ten pens to sign the legislation. Rankin, who knew he had to relent and did, got one of them. But the first pen went to Representative Edith Nourse Rogers of Massachusetts, a consistently strong advocate of veterans' rights and benefits.

As finally passed, the measure authorized veterans to receive up to fifty-two weeks of unemployment compensation at the rate of $20 a week (this came to be called the "52-20 Club" by the more than eight million veterans who had to use its provisions for weeks or months during the four years it was on the books). The G.I. Bill also guaranteed half of any loan up to $2,000 at an interest rate of no more than 4 percent to veterans who wanted to establish homes or businesses. It further sought to help veterans find employment and, for those who wanted more training and education, granted allowances of $500 a year for as much as four years. Single veterans received subsistence pay of $50 a month and married veterans received $75.

In the years ahead, veterans would complain that the G.I. Bill did not go far enough, especially in the financing of the housing that returning veterans needed, and that it did not provide nearly enough for education. And yet, the G.I. Bill caused the Government to spend at least $50 billion on veterans in the next several years. It backed veterans in their efforts to buy homes, get into business, finish high school, and get a college education. Despite the warnings from the University of Chicago's Hutchins, the G.I.s became anything but educational hoboes, nor did most institutions regard them that way. Between 1945 and '46, college enrollment in the United States increased by more than 45 percent; between 1946 and '47, by 24 percent. In 1945 there were only 400,000 veterans in college. A year later, the campuses held 1.5 million. Whatever its shortcomings, the G.I. Bill emerged as one of the most enlightened and significant pieces of social legislation ever written in this country, and it produced a generation of well-educated professionals, businessmen, and homeowners who became the basis for a greatly strengthened American middle class.

Even after the bill was passed and operative, there were Americans who complained that veterans were getting too much. The Roosevelt Administration remained firm. Vice-President Harry S. Truman, ever direct, took the offensive in 1945. Just four days before Roosevelt's death, Truman gave the Grover Cleveland dinner speech to the Erie County Democratic Committee in Buffalo. He discounted fears that veterans would flood the labor market and ruin everything for everybody. America, he told his $25-a-plate audience, "will never again permit the callous indifference, the economic and political ineptitude of the late twenties and early thirties to return to political power. No depression will be allowed to grow, like a Frankenstein monster, ultimately threatening our entire social structure."

Quite apart from being apprehensive about what the nation's unemployed heroes would do to its breadlines, Americans, especially members of the clergy, fretted about the readjustment from military to civilian life and what effect the returning veterans would have on the morality of the nation. The Rev. Bernard Iddings Bell, an Episcopalian, warned in 1944 that returning soldiers would "take command over this country which they sacrificed themselves to save . . . for good or ill." He said, "It was veterans who put over every political and economic revolution in Europe between 1919 and 1939; in Russia first, then in Italy, in Germany, in Spain. These countries all went totalitarian during those post-war years because the democratic leaders were not revolutionary enough, daring enough, to satisfy the veteran type of mind."

Others among the clergy worried about the loss of old-fashioned virtue and suggested that veterans of the war might spread their sinful ways to civilians who had not been so contaminated by the war. The end of the war "will surely bring a slump of morals and morale," predicted J. Gordon Chamberlin in his 1945 book *The Church and Demobilization.* "The grass may cover war's scars on earth; but the spirits of men, once blighted by war, will pass on that blight." Mr. Chamberlin said that the veterans would recall their "days of action" when "to be a soldier was *something.* . . . They will not forget when girls were always glad to go out with a serviceman and it did not make much difference what one did, since tomorrow might be the end."

In academia, they wondered if, given the way the United States had treated its soldiers in the past, the G.I.s could handle their military service without doing damage to themselves or to the country they had served. In 1944, Professor Willard Waller of Barnard College, Columbia University, took stock of the situation and warned that veterans were "our gravest social problem." Waller said that since the time of Daniel Shays, America had wrongly relied on a policy "of paying on account of veterans' claims too much, too late, in the wrong way, and to the wrong person." Waller felt, "The veteran who comes home is a social problem, and certainly the major social problem of the next few years. . . . Unless and until he can be renaturalized into his native land, the veteran is a threat to society."

It seemed almost as though Waller felt that soldiers had a collective conscience about their past mistreatment and that now, after this bloodiest of all wars, they might seek collective redress, at long last. But this was impossible. Few veterans had either Waller's perspective or his passion growing out of what had happened to soldiers after wars in the past:

> Our traditional policy has been to neglect our veterans for a period of years after the end of a major war. During this period of neglect, uninjured veterans take up the broken threads of their lives as best they can, struggle against discouragements to compete successfully, force their way into economic, social and political life, while the injured, the maimed, gassed, tubercular, and mentally unbalanced contrive to live by such little jobs as their conditions permit, learn to beg on the streets, and become paupers, steal and are sent to prison, or else just starve and are forgotten together with their widows and dependents. Then, after some years, the veterans suddenly emerge as a powerful political force. Still burning with resentment over their wrongs, they see to it that ample provision is made for the unfortunate veterans. But it is too late then to do justice, too late to help many who have died or been ruined beyond hope of reclamation.

The notion that the soldier had somehow become a different sort of person who could return to the civilian life he left behind only with great and difficult effort was repeated in the press and in books. It wasn't only that a soldier might have been wounded in battle or emotionally damaged by what he had seen and done. Soldiers were perceived almost as members of a monolith. They would think alike, vote alike, and act in certain prescribed patterns, the experts wrote. "If the Presidential election were being held at this time, the outcome would . . . be determined by the soldier vote," announced the Gallup poll visionarily in late 1943. That should have cheered Roosevelt; Gallup said 61 percent of soldiers favored the President for reelection. It vexed the Republicans, who already suspected that the soldiers were radical Democrats. Republicans found themselves in much the same position that Democrats had been in during the Civil War, and they did not like it.

So worried was the Government about what the soldier monolith was thinking that when legislation was enacted enabling states to permit soldiers to vote for President by using the Federal mail ballot, the law contained a provision prohibiting the Army and Navy from distributing any news or books "containing political argument or political propaganda of any kind designed or calculated to affect the result of [a Federal] election." Such a preposterous law deserved to be obeyed in a preposterous manner, and the military did not miss the spirit of the thing. No sooner was it passed than the Army somehow banned *The Republic* of Plato, a harmless biography of Oliver Wendell Holmes, and Charles A. Beard's dialogues on American constitutional government.

"A civilian can be licked into shape as a soldier by the manual of arms and a drillmaster," wrote Dixon Wecter, a sort of rival of Waller's in the uncertain art of veteran-watching, "but no manual has ever been written for changing him back into a civilian." These two veteran-watchers by no means agreed as to what they observed. Wecter accused Waller of romanticizing the veteran and of overdoing the need for a special science of the veteran, which, in Wecter's view, would "combine the worst vices of Columbia Teachers College with those of Yale's Institute of Human Relations." What was wrong with Waller, Wecter argued, was that he forgot about the ordinary soldier who wanted only "his girl, his job and a little home." Wecter was convinced that the World War II G.I. would return as he left: "friendly, generous, easy-going, brave, the citizen-soldier of America."

As for Waller, he was quite astonished that Wecter would be retained by so respected a journal as the *Saturday Review of Literature* to review his book, since Wecter was "the author of the only competing book . . . who is committed by his book to a point of view opposed to my own." Waller accused Wecter of "sheer callousness" and further charged that Wecter's ideas were "wanting in humanity." Thus went the acetic literary war as the real war of bombs and bayonets became history.

The advent of the end of World War II and the prospect of returning, job-seeking soldiers created a rather awkward moment for the American labor movement. The CIO had been warned as early as 1943 by Vice-President Henry A. Wallace that the Roosevelt Administration expected labor not to clamor for a "balanced budget" when the war ended if this meant Government would be thus rendered powerless to help the homecoming veteran. Wallace said that unless "our energies, our great affection, our wisdom, plan now for jobs and health and security and full production," the postwar nation would be filled with "roving bands seeking food where there is no food, seeking jobs where there are no jobs, seeking shelter where there is no shelter."

It did not matter that one out of every six soldiers had been a member of a labor union before the war or that organized labor had helped create and endorsed the reemployment provisions of the Selective Service Act of 1940. The middle-aged civilians who stayed behind—many of them veterans of World War I—saw the returning soldiers as a threat to their security. The thought of young soldiers grabbing their jobs, coupled with what they assumed would be depressionlike conditions anyhow, was enough to drive older workers to distraction.

They found that peace could be frightening. There was the lightning-strike day in August of 1945, right after the surrender of the Japanese, when Boeing laid off 21,200 of 29,000 workers in its two West Coast plants. Peace was not even three days old when the Army sent sixty thousand form letters to defense contractors, instantly terminating about $7.3 billion in business. And in less than a month, the Government had canceled war contracts worth $15 billion. The workers wondered where it would all end.

For them, it had not been a bad war, all things considered. America had not been bombed and its citizens had been denied little, save their insatiable appetite for new cars. Some of their neighbors had been killed or wounded (battles had killed 292,131, noncombat deaths totaled 115,185, and another 670,846 had been wounded). But on the home front, the factories making armaments lost nearly 300,000 workers to fatal accidents and another million who were permanently disabled. Civilian workers knew that what they did was not entirely safe, and they were proud of the productivity they had been able to maintain. Their labor had been well rewarded; the war was won and, in the bargain, nearly 50 million Americans out of 140 million were now paying income taxes.

A society that might have identified strongly with the plight of the Joads a decade earlier had in four short years become new-money middle-class; the income of the average worker had doubled since 1939 and now stood at $3,000 a year. What's more, the national wealth was now more evenly distributed. The gross national product had gone from a paltry $90 billion in 1939 to a more respectable $213 billion. The wealthiest 5 percent of American society now controlled 16.8 percent of the take, whereas in 1939 the same privileged few controlled 23.7 percent. That was worth something, workers thought. Now the country had to return to peacetime pursuits. But just how quickly could the country turn from making tanks to making Chevies, and who would be the casualties in the bargain?

The tension was natural enough, and it did not get out of hand, which was remarkable, given the nature of indelicate pronouncements by public officials, industry leaders, and scare headlines in publications that should have known better. In New York, for example, in an untypically inappropriate statement, Mayor La Guardia warned that a million unemployed workers might migrate there from the war-boom towns in New Jersey, Pennsylvania, and Connecticut. New York would get a lot of such workers, said the mayor, because it has the "reputation for being big-hearted." *The New York Times* only made matters worse when it headlined its report just as untypically: "POST-WAR JOBLESS SEEN INVADING CITY."

Workers all over the country were hardly reassured about their future when industrialist Paul G. Hoffman, chairman of the Committee of Economic Development was quoted in an N.A.M. pamphlet as saying, "I don't believe it is even socially desirable to have jobs for every man or woman who may want a job." They were probably not heartened when they heard that a *Wall Street Journal* story labeled efforts toward full employment a "halfway house to socialism," nor when they were told that the Atlantic Elevator Company of Philadelphia had applied to the Regional War Labor Board to modify its contract with the United Electrical Workers to permit the company to hire veterans without requiring them to join the union. The company explained that many veterans had little sympathy for civilian workers, some of whom had struck for higher wages during the war. Nor did it help relations between veterans and civilian workers when Representative Paul Stewart, Democrat of Oklahoma, gave a speech to his colleagues in the House in which he urged that veterans be permitted to find employment without organized labor forcing them to "pay union dues, fees and tribute." After he spoke, veterans in the chamber hollered their approval so loudly that Speaker of the House Sam Rayburn had to reprimand them.

Former President Herbert Hoover agreed with Congressman Stewart. The men coming home "must have the free right to join the union or, alternately, we must have complete open shop and no fooling," he wrote in 1944. Hoover did not predict a depression but he said the most important thing to keep in mind was that whatever happened, "organized labor and employers alike have a mutual interest in keeping the government out of business and preventing it from dictating to business." If hard times should come, Hoover felt the Government would have little or no role in taking care of anybody who might become unemployed. He thought Americans should put their trust in business.

"Our business associations through their national committees are making a great contribution in organization to take care of this marginal group," Hoover said, adding that he felt the Government could not find jobs for many people after the war, "unless it is going to transform industry into a full socialized state." Hoover thought the best thing to do was "repair many moral standards" that had fallen away during the war and "restore faith" in America. His position was consistent with that advanced by the National Association of Manufacturers, which spent a great deal of time and money, as the war was ending, to assure all that "the public is turning again with confidence to business leaders" who had stood discredited and distrusted through much of the thirties.

Americans were not so sure Hoover and the manufacturers were right. The Depression was still too vivid a memory in the minds of adults. All of this and similar developments led *The New Republic* to conclude, "Plans are far advanced for a big-business drive to break the back of organized labor as soon as the war in Europe ends." It was more than Robert J. Watt could stand. Watt was international representative of the American Federation of Labor and was invited to attend a conference in Washington sponsored by the American Legion. The theme was reemployment for veterans. A good many veterans appreciated neither his philosophy nor his gift of prophecy. "If we give special status to veterans today," Watt told them, "we are faced with the problem of special consideration for minority groups tomorrow. There will be other special claims—those of women workers against men, single women against married women, and married men against single men."

With all of the rhetoric, and as much as they were concerned about keeping the good life for themselves, Americans nevertheless gave ample evidence of wanting to share what the country had to offer with the men and women who had been in the military. The *Philadelphia Bulletin* conducted a survey and found that people there favored giving veterans a bonus by fourteen to one. That was even greater than the ratio in favor of the bonus among veterans themselves, who favored it ten to one. The spirit of giving was there—as long as nobody had to surrender his job.

The war ended as it should have. On that warm night in August, after it was announced that the Japanese had agreed to unconditional surrender, all America became a small town going to a football game at the high school. Church bells began to peal and people poured out of their homes and strolled about their streets, laughing, singing, waving to each other, as though to reclaim the streets, at long last, from the grouchy air raid wardens who had oppressed them so. The steel-hatted wardens, many of them veterans of World War I, had insisted that even the flare of a match needed to light a cigarette could be seen from two miles up in the air by German bombers that never came. Even though no smoker believed them, they had to abstain, an early example of what smokers came to regard as their twentieth-century burden. In reality, air raid drills had probably been good for their health.

In New York on that magic night, trains from the boroughs and the boonies, their air horns blaring, brought more than two million hot and happy people to Times Square, which was much happier and safer and more crowded than it had been on any New Year's Eve. In many cases, conductors charged no fares; it seemed wrong to charge for anything. The merrymakers stayed up all night, tooting horns, throwing confetti. Peace had come, for good, they thought, and stranger kissed stranger.

In San Francisco, a couple of curvy, naked blondes danced in front of city hall. In Salt Lake City it rained but Utahans didn't mind and snake-danced, fully clothed, through the puddles. In Newburgh, New York, where 162 years earlier George Washington had wondered if his angry unpaid officers were conspiring to take over the country, young men of draft age bounded up on the terraced lawn of a grade school a mile or so from Washington's Headquarters and tore down the wooden sign that described the school's secondary role as headquarters for Draft Board Local 15. The young men had been drinking, and one of them urinated on what was left of the signpost. Police watched and smiled at them. To the police on V-J night, the young men were no more delinquent than effusive fans who would knock down uprights after the big Thanksgiving Day game.

It had been one gigantic football game after all, although Local 15, with absolutely no regard for the ceremonial micturition, remained very much in business. Within a week, a new sign, larger and more permanent-looking than that which had been ripped down, would be erected precisely where the old one had been. Forgotten that night were fears of depression and unemployment. Every American was indestructible. They were launched into a euphoria that years later they would remember wistfully, as their economy suffered not a jot from homecoming veterans, but from the self-indulgence born of victory in war and from goods made better and more cheaply by the very nations whose defeat they had celebrated.

It was a time for the Judy Garland–like girl next door to marry the eager, skinny Frank Sinatra–like sailor from the next block and give him the stability he needed, even though nearly a third of the marriages were ending in divorce; a time for everyone to go to college, to study *something,* to work for a boss who would surely be nice, to be comfortable, to move to fragrant, blossom-covered suburbs doomed to be Levitized, and watch skylarks in flight at eventide, for skylarks would never be intimidated by the likes of William Levitt and his imitators; to buy a little Ford and a big refrigerator and dance to Hoagy Carmichael and Johnny Mercer and Richard Rodgers in church basements on gentle Saturday evenings in spring; to go to air-conditioned movies and see Bing Crosby Smile Right Back at the Sun; to eat chicken every Sunday and not worry about anything more serious than the fate of last night's pot roast or next spring's tulips. There really were porch swings and green rocking chairs and girls in calico and Virginia creeper and homemade lemonade and Tuesday-night band concerts in July and August in the park and streets so peaceful, even in the great cities, that you could sleep on them all night in safety if not comfort.

No country had ever known such sweet wine but, for a moment, Americans, at least white, new-middle-class Americans, tasted it. Nothing bad could ever happen to them again, they thought. Half a decade would streak by like fifteen minutes, and neither they nor anyone else on earth would ever know anything quite like it again. It would end and they would not want it to end. For once in America's history, it was so good that neither veterans nor anyone else would be able to remember it accurately. It was so good that their children and grandchildren would not believe them that it was ever that way or ever could be that way.

Forgotten Women,
Failed Men

> In most cases, women cannot receive gynecological care from the VA, although this is the most elemental health care need of a woman veteran.... In some cases, women veterans have been subjected to [gynecological] exams in full view of men passing through the exam area.
> —Lynda M. Van Devanter, national women's director, Vietnam Veterans of America

Doris "Dorie" Miller was not exactly what the United States Navy preferred to think of when it considered its typical World War II hero. He was not white but black. He was not a highly trained, combat-oriented sailor but, like so many other blacks who had been admitted to the Navy with that service's traditional reservations about people of color, a lowly mess attendant, second class. He was assigned to the USS *West Virginia*. On December 7, 1941, the mess he was attending was both inside and outside his kitchen at a once-lovely spot in Hawaii called Pearl Harbor, which is where the *West Virginia* was moored. When the conflagration that attended the massive Japanese attack was over, one of the few things clear in an otherwise dismal day was that Dorie Miller was a most unusual man. Because in a decidedly un-mess-attendant way, he had laid down the pots and pans he was trained to use, run up to the bridge, dragged the *West Virginia*'s badly wounded captain to relative safety, then taken up a machine gun that had been dropped by a wounded sailor and shot down four marauding Japanese warplanes. Hollywood, which was ever on the alert for heroes, never celebrated Dorie Miller's feat; "The Dorie Miller Story" was not the stuff of which movies were made in the 1940s. But the Navy took stock of itself, goaded by both whites and blacks active in the civil rights movement, wisely decided that he was, in fact, a hero, and awarded him the Navy Cross. The award, which acknowledged Miller's "distinguished devotion to duty, extraordinary courage and disregard for his own personal safety," was not given until a year passed, at which time Miller was promoted to mess attendant, first class. Three years later, Dorie Miller—still assigned to mess duty—was killed when the *Liscombe Bay,* the aircraft carrier to which he had been assigned, was sunk by a Japanese submarine.

Certain changes flowed rather quickly after Miller's feat became known, although it would not be until the early 1970s that the Navy would get around to naming a destroyer for Miller. Whether the changes that began during World War II came in recognition of Miller's contribution or the desperate needs of war, or whether the ideas articulated so eloquently a quarter of a century earlier by W.E.B. Du Bois, A. Philip Randolph, and other black leaders finally permeated the Government's universe, remains a question. Whatever the case, some wondrous things began to happen to blacks before V-E Day. The Navy started to accept more of them as volunteers and many were not shunted into kitchen service. The Marines, that prideful subgroup within the Navy which during World War I wanted no part of blacks, now became convinced that blacks were loyal and patriotic and could fight and thus accepted around twenty thousand recruits.

The Army and the Coast Guard also began to accept them. For the first time ever, blacks began to be taken into the military in a number that was more consistent with their presence in the population. The Selective Service, which had been passing over black draftees to get white ones (much to the dismay of whites), changed that policy. Even the Coast Guard, whose image was represented in 1940s late-afternoon radio serials by dashing Lieutenant Commander Don Winslow (the quintessential white, Anglo-Saxon role model, rivaling radio's Tom Mix and Hop Harrigan in his popularity), would find itself in 1945 with four thousand black enlisted men and seven hundred black officers. What Du Bois and Randolph prayed would happen was finally happening. If blacks were finally being accepted, truly accepted, as warriors, it had to mean they also stood a pretty good chance of being accepted later on as real people. Blacks, who had not been trusted to bear arms for the United States since the days of the Revolution, were now being invited to play a significant role in the mightiest struggle the earth had ever seen.

Given the relentlessly backward, virulent racism that would attend the homecoming of blacks, it would seem that the armed services were probably ahead of the civil standards of American society, not behind them. For there was progress. But the military showed no comparable imagination with another large group of Americans that it had long ignored—women. The place of women in America was never clearer than in the way the Government treated women who volunteered for military service during the war.

Women were hardly strangers to the wars that the United States had fought throughout its history. Their "official" participation, however, did not begin until 1901, when the Army Nurse Corps was founded. This was followed, seven years later, by its Navy counterpart. These were no more important than the efforts women had made before. What made them official was that somebody somewhere kept a record of who was serving.

Women had served much earlier as nurses in the Revolution and also as scouts, messengers, and the effective defenders of lonely, isolated settlements when men were away. Their efforts went unrecorded and largely unrewarded. During the Civil War, seven thousand women served as nurses, most of them for the Union side. It is believed that around four hundred women actually fought in the war, disguised as men. Some wanted to be with husbands and lovers; others were there because they believed in the cause. It was during this period that Dr. Elizabeth Blackwell established the Women's Central Relief Organization in the North; Clara Barton worked assiduously, supplying medicine to the Union forces.

Women also nursed soldiers wounded in combat (sometimes at great danger to themselves) as well as those afflicted with typhoid, malaria, and yellow fever in both the Spanish-American War and in the Philippine Insurrection. The need for nurses was great during the Spanish-American War, but the men who ran the Government could not bring themselves to admit women formally into the military service. A civilian nurse corps was established, and the women who joined it were paid as independent contract workers, not regular employees of the Army. Thus they remained unprotected by the normal pension and insurance provisions, such as they were, that existed for soldiers.

Even after the creation of the nurse corps for the Army and Navy, women had no clear-cut roles, no specific rank or grade in the military—no assurances of much of anything. Their status remained unclear throughout World War I, but not their achievements. Women participated in war as they never before had in American history, with 22,000 serving as Army nurses and 1,400 providing their nursing skills to the Navy. Some three hundred of them died from disease, others were gassed and received wounds, and still others were captured by the Germans and imprisoned. But because the status of the nurses was unclear, the Government later decided that it could not pay them for the time during which they were imprisoned.

There were other women during World War I who sought to join the military not as nurses, but in areas that had previously been the sole province of men. There were twelve thousand Navy "Yeomanettes," as well as 305 women who served in the Marines as "Marinettes." The Marines in particular distinguished themselves in this brief period by conspicuously treating women pretty much as they treated men, with the result that women Marines received rights to Government insurance, a $60 bonus, and hospitalization for any disability received while in service.

What was good enough for the Marines, however, was not totally acceptable to the Army. Women who had any association with the Army found that after the war it was difficult if not impossible for them to prove that they had any rights at all to whatever benefits were due soldiers. The Army made it clear: It wanted no women either in its ranks or in its civilian employ. An exception of sorts was made when General John J. Pershing, head of the American Expeditionary Forces, said he needed two hundred women who spoke French to act as telephone operators in France. The women who volunteered were called "Hello Girls," wore lieutenant's bars, and were paid for their time at the lieutenant rate of $60 a month. But nobody had to salute them. Despite their rather stylish uniforms, the Hello Girls were regarded as civilians and received absolutely none of the benefits or protections due soldiers, even though they worked near the front lines and were subject to military discipline. Other women who worked for the Army as volunteers found they were treated much the same way.

In 1920, Congress passed the Army Reorganization Act. Its murky purposes reportedly included clarification of the role of nurses in the military, if not all women who might serve. It did not totally succeed. By virtue of the "clarification," Army nurses could wear the insignia of "relative rank." But nobody had to accord them the privileges of rank. That meant they were not eligible to dine at officers' clubs. And it meant that enlisted men were thus not absolutely required to salute Army nurses who looked like officers.

Initially, it was not all that much better for the women who wanted to serve in World War II. By this time, the Government had more clearly defined non-nursing duties that women might perform. But again, the Army did not really want them. The Women's Army Auxiliary Corps (WAAC) was founded in 1942, but the very language that founded it perpetuated prior ambiguity: "The corps shall not be a part of the army but it shall be the only women's organization authorized to service the army exclusive of the Army

Nurse Corps.'' Thus women were invited to wear uniforms and march in formation—but they would not really be soldiers, and not really be in the Army, however lofty their ideals and motivation.

It was too confusing for even those wizards of obfuscation in the War Department, who decided in 1943—nudged by Congresswoman Edith Nourse Rogers of Massachusetts—that the WAACs should be invited to become a regular part of the Army. For reasons that are not entirely clear, this meant disbanding the WAACs and creating a new group called simply the Women's Army Corps (WAC).

More confusion ensued. Since the WAACs were being disbanded, its members were logically enough discharged. Some enlisted in the WACs. But many others never understood that the WACs were going to be formed and simply became civilians. As civilians who thought they had been in the Army, they were more than a little mystified when they were told that they were not veterans at all. It took the Government more than thirty years to determine that the WAACs had indeed experienced military service and were entitled to status as veterans.

Other women who served the military, sometimes at great risk, also learned as veterans of the experience that as far as the Government was concerned, they had not been in the military. Among them were the WASPs—Women's Air Force Service Pilots. As members of this organization, women ferried warplanes from factories to Air Force bases, including, on occasion, large bombers. They also served as flight instructors to men. They flew more than sixty million miles with a splendid safety record. None of this was surprising; women had a long and distinguished career in aviation. Their record persisted through the most adverse conditions, even when they were asked to tow target sleeves behind their aircraft so that fighter planes, operated by men only, could practice with real bullets on something that was moving.

The WASPs apparently had the admiration of the men with whom they served, although male pilots did not want the use of women to go too far. The Army had never mentioned them in its requests for money. So, although the Secretary of War was in favor of granting full Army Air Force commissions to women pilots, the WASPs were disbanded. It happened in December of 1944, with the end of the war seven months away. The WASPs then learned that despite their achievements, the Government had no intention of ever declaring them a bona fide military organization. The Government said that the WASPs had never really been ''militarized.'' Not until 1977 did the WASPs get veteran status, far too late to give them access to the provisions of the G.I. Bill. Nor did WASP time count for higher pay when some of them served the military again during the Korean War.

After the war, even women who were recognized as real members of the military establishment found that when they went to hospitals run by the Veterans Administration, they could not find the services they needed. By the early 1980s, although there were at least 1.2 million women veterans, VA hospitals essentially discouraged their using veterans' facilities—they employed only seven full-time gynecologists, according to June A. Willenz, executive director of the American Veterans Committee. There were private doctors that the VA could direct women to, but waits of up to four months for gynecological examinations were reported. Most VA hospitals lacked the ability to do Pap smears and competent breast examinations.

Lynda M. Van Devanter, national women's director of the Vietnam Veterans of America, would complain in 1983, "In most cases, women cannot receive gynecological care from the VA, although this is the most elemental health care need of a woman veteran." She was talking about all women veterans, not just those from World War II. But because of their age, it was those older women who would clearly need more medical services.

Van Devanter testified before the U.S. Senate Committee on Veterans' Affairs that some of the women had been examined "in full view of men passing through the exam area" and that there was a general lack of privacy in VA hospitals. "Qualified gynecologists are not available and older, retired physicians are doing the exams instead," she said. Van Devanter further suggested that the Government had never really cared to find out what the stresses of war had been on women who had served in battle zones during World War II. "Some sixty-five women were held prisoners of war on Corregidor for the duration of WW II," she said. "Where are studies of those women?"

And yet, in the years following World War II, there was evidence that military service and even unrecognized military service, unpleasant and rigorous though it may have been at times, proved a positive experience for many women. For example, one study of two hundred women who served in World War II indicated that 27 percent of them made the military a career. Twenty-seven percent of WACs, WAVEs (Navy), and SPARs (Coast Guard), and 45 percent of all nurses never married, as compared to 5 percent of the other women of their generation. Many of them looked back on their war experiences as positive—a time when they were independent and made important decisions. Almost all of those surveyed retained more positive than negative memories of World War II, despite all the battlefield suffering they saw.

After the war, the overwhelming majority of those who returned to civilian status did volunteer work. If the studies were at all indicative, 95 percent of the women who had served in the Army or Navy were engaged in volunteerism for at least one group and more than 60 percent were active in three groups. Among American women in general, about half were active in volunteer work.

Men and women may have felt differently about their roles in the war, but it was clear to President Roosevelt that they might well share many of the same concerns as they became veterans in need of help. Republicans sensed the value in needling Roosevelt that, although the G.I. Bill was now law and geared to help the homecoming, much more was needed. In 1945, Roosevelt needed no prodding to realize that the country needed someone to coordinate all the policies pertaining to the reemployment of veterans and war workers, but even his admirers were not entirely sure he picked the right man for the job: Brigadier General Frank T. Hines, who had run the Veterans Administration since 1923, the year that Charles Forbes got into difficulty.

Hines had been nothing like Forbes; there were no strange meetings in the bedrooms and bathrooms of the nation's hostelries, no loans that never had to be returned, no missing money, no Government merchandise mysteriously turning up in private warehouses. But neither had there been any indication that Hines was an independently creative administrator who could handle such a complex job, nor that he was passionate enough to handle the needs of veterans after World War II. *The New Republic* called Hines "an old-line bureaucrat of Harding's day, who is hostile to the New Deal and the sort of Government aid that will be needed to cushion the shock of transfer from war to peace economy." And I. F. Stone, never a man to mince words, charged that the appointment of Hines "makes the job a cruel joke."

The press began to suggest that Hines, although personally honest, had succumbed to bureaucratic indifference. Columnist Marquis Childs, writing in *The Washington Post,* complained that the Veterans Administration under Hines was "enmeshed in red tape," that the American Legion had too much to say about who got care in VA hospitals, and that the VA's medical staff was not all that good.

The liabilities for Hines began to pile up considerably as a few published articles suggested that the VA during his tenure was not really doing the job. One such article came in the form of an exposé in *Cosmopolitan* by Albert Q. Maisel. He found the battlefield care the soldiers had received to be praiseworthy. But once those soldiers became veterans, Maisel wrote, they were "suffering needlessly and, all too often, dying needlessly. . . ." In his investigation, Maisel found the VA hospitals overcrowded and its doctors hopelessly overloaded. He documented his charges by citing case studies and printing letters written by veterans. He reported, for example, that one veteran had died in a VA hospital because nobody had bothered to aspirate the fluid that was in his lungs.

The veterans themselves were vocal in quite a number of forums about what they saw as shoddy treatment from the VA, and writers and reporters around the country began to listen. *The New Republic* said the veterans it had listened to complained that "attendants are sometimes brutal, food inedible, surroundings frequently unsanitary, medical treatment often perfunctory or incomplete." *The New York Times* quoted another veteran's complaint: "I would much rather be on Iwo Jima Island with our Marines, than be in a veterans' hospital under the experiences I have had. I could certainly fight back there, but here you cannot."

Congressman Rankin heard all of the dissent with disbelief. His opinion of writers was no higher than his opinion of college instructors, blacks, and Jews. He sensed that something disrespectful if not disloyal was being perpetrated on the people of the United States by its journalists. In one aspect of his behavior, Rankin was not unlike General George S. Patton: When in doubt, he attacked. Rankin thus lunged after Albert Deutsch, a writer for the short-lived New York City newspaper *PM*. Rankin said he thought that Deutsch ought to be held in contempt for some of the things he had written about the VA and strongly suspected that Deutsch was nothing more than a communist agitator. Unfortunately for Rankin, the members of his Committee of World War Veterans' Legislation wanted no part of that approach and it did not succeed. In short order, the House Rules Committee reported out a Rankin resolution calling for a "limited" investigation of VA facilities. Representative Philip J. Philbin, a Democrat from Massachusetts, predicted that if anyone took a good look at the hospitals for veterans, it would create "a national scandal that will shake the country to its roots."

Philbin overstated the matter. The country could hardly be shaken with mere disclosures about the Veterans Administration; not with newspaper headlines advising them that the Allies were storming across the Rhine River at four different locations and that Russians were chasing the ragged but still dangerous Germans deep inside Hungary. But back in Washington, a tired Frank Hines knew he was in trouble. He testified before the committee and said he had requested that an internal investigation of his agency be conducted by his own personnel. He denied that the medicine practiced in VA hospitals was "third rate."

Roosevelt was fading fast at that point, far too ill to do much of anything. He died on April 12, leaving the matter to his successor, Harry Truman.

Less than a month after Roosevelt's passing, Truman held a press conference
and with his usual vigor announced his intention to "modernize" the agency
that had been under Hines' leadership for twenty-two years. And less than
a month after that, Hines was gone.

Truman was almost mild-mannered when he permitted the blade to fall.
"As a World War I soldier," he said, "I wouldn't have been happy to have
the Spanish-American War veterans running the Veterans Administration,
and I don't think the new veterans would. I think they would much rather
have a general of their own war in the place. And General Hines thought so,
too—after we discussed it." Truman smiled, and the reporters who covered
his news conference that day laughed on cue.

As the new director of the VA, Truman named General Omar N. Bradley,
who reported for work on August 15, the day after the Japanese surrendered
and the struggle known as World War II was over. "I don't think there's any
job in the country I'd sooner not have nor any job in the world I'd like to do
better," said Bradley, who knew he would be trying to take care of no less
than twenty million men and women who had survived America's world
wars, as well as the Spanish-American War and Philippine Insurrection and
some of its nineteenth-century wars against the Indians. In 1945, there were
even a handful of survivors from the Civil War. Fully 43 percent of the
nation's men were going to be counted as veterans, and Bradley would have
a command befitting his military experience—a civilian army of 65,000
employees who constituted the largest single agency in the whole bureaucracy.

Bradley had much going for him. He may not have possessed Eisenhower's ability to charm the American populace at large, but neither did he have
MacArthur's reputation for being manipulative and egomaniacal. Tall,
athletic (he was once courted as a professional baseball player), and vital,
yet given to modesty and understatement, he had been enormously popular
with his soldiers. As a man who had given much of himself during the war,
presumably he would have no credibility problem with any veteran. When
he spoke, he seemed to express the common soldier's point of view, directly
and without being overbearing. "We've got to look on veterans as
individual problems, not as numbers in a file," he told his VA staff soon
after taking office. "Our job is to give the veterans service. And we must not
forget that the service we give them they have earned by sweat and blood.
It is a service they have paid for. We must realize that it is not a charity
service."

Some members of the VA staff had, like Hines, been there since the
agency started its work. They could remember the Bonus March and the

countless times they got the distinct impression that veterans were viewed as a group to whom the Government wanted to limit its liability. Some of them must have wondered how long the likes of Omar Bradley would last in their midst. But the support of the press, at least, was clearly there. Ernest K. Lindley, then an influential columnist with *Newsweek,* expressed the view of many when he said that the VA under Hines had been guilty of "medical old fogyism."

At first, it went well enough for Bradley, who made an unprecedented good-faith effort to help the former soldiers. He increased his staff more than threefold to 200,000, and the quality of medicine practiced in the VA hospitals was reported to improve. Changes in policy were considerable. And to make certain that those changes were aggressively presented to the veterans and to the general public, Bradley also expanded the VA's public relations department to three hundred people, who spread the good word. But what might have looked good to many veterans was not viewed quite the same way by some, although not all, of the top officials of the most powerful of all veterans' organizations, the American Legion. The Legion had always been in favor of better care for war veterans. But it wanted things done the Legion way, the way it had become used to. It did not want to lose the influence that it had gained in the VA since the agency's founding. Under Hines, many of the top posts in the VA were held by Legionnaires, and when VA hospitals looked for new workers, members of the Legion received special consideration.

Under Hines, the Legion had assumed a position as broker for veterans that was as creative as it was powerful. It had been the Legion's Harry Colmery, not Hines, who had drafted the G.I. Bill, thus telling the world what the veterans wanted. And the chief Washington lobbyist for the Legion, John T. Taylor, had a formidable reputation for successfully dealing with officials. It was said that Taylor had "rammed 630 bills through Congress, forced three Presidents to their knees and obtained $13,000,000,000 worth of benefits for ex-servicemen." Could things be as good under any new leader?

Within months after Bradley's tenure began, the Legion was uncomfortable with the new order. The VA advised its employees that they should not become involved with any veterans' service organization "to the point where they might be charged with favoritism in their official acts toward any particular organization." And they were pointedly told that it was "bad judgment for an employee of the VA to hold elective or appointive office in a service organization. . . ."

In 1945, the Legion selected John Stelle as its national commander. Stelle had served briefly as Governor of Illinois. He was used to wielding power and having his power respected. The stage was thus set for a tiff between the Legion and Omar Bradley. Bradley had wanted to suspend the VA hospitalization privileges of veterans who had not been injured in the war, as long as beds were still needed by those who had been disabled in combat. It was not an especially enlightened proposal from an otherwise enlightened general. It was strongly suspected that even soldiers not wounded in combat could become seriously ill from the stresses of combat. To favor only those who had suffered visible wounds was unrealistic. Stelle assessed the situation and said there had been a "tragic breakdown" in the VA. He publicly complained that the VA needed a good businessman to run it, not a soldier, "however good a soldier he may be."

The issues between Stelle and Bradley went well beyond their divergent views as to how veterans ought to be treated. Stelle had wanted a VA hospital constructed in Decatur, Illinois, his hometown. Bradley refused, relations deteriorated, and before anyone could calm the waters, Stelle demanded the resignation of Omar Bradley.

"It sounds like communism to me" was the initial reaction of Mississippi's Congressman Rankin, who in his support of Bradley suddenly saw a chance to transmogrify his intense dislike for communists and writers into a new art form. The Legion was stunned. Since the very day of its founding, it had steadfastly been strongly opposed to anything that smacked of Bolshevism. None of its members had ever indicated they wanted it any other way, let alone one whom it had honored with the national commander designation.

Stelle was not the least bit intimidated. The "ranting of Rankin," he said, "recalls to mind that Tupelo, Mississippi, is immediately getting a [VA] hospital." The unfortunate business rumbled downhill from there. Stelle charged that under Bradley's VA, between 300,000 and 500,000 veterans suffering from war-caused disabilities had received no money from the Government because the VA had failed to retain the medical records of those who served. He also charged that the VA still lacked competent medical help and—shades of Forbes!—that there were at least 270,000 letters lying unanswered in VA offices around the country.

But Bradley had many friends, both in and out of the Legion. President Truman, who was also a Legionnaire, said he backed Bradley "to the hilt" and charged that Stelle was not speaking for most of the Legion. General Dwight D. Eisenhower, the most popular of all the nation's military leaders, also issued kind words about Bradley.

Other veterans' groups backed away from Stelle's position. The Veterans of Foreign Wars said that Bradley should be given the time to prove himself, and the Disabled American Veterans said it felt that Bradley had been trying to do the job. Amvets, a much smaller group, said it felt the Legion had attacked Bradley because with the departure of Hines, it had lost some of its clout in the VA.

The nation's newspapers quickly lined up behind Bradley. "We see little merit to the Legion's charges," editorialized *The New York Times,* adding that it did not want either Bradley's removal or a congressional investigation of the VA. "Commander Stelle and the Legion are playing with dynamite. They are doing a disservice to the veteran instead of helping him." At one point, Bradley and Stelle had a heated telephone exchange, and when pressed by reporters as to what was said, Bradley replied, "Well, I never lost *my* temper."

Stelle found himself with eroding support. He was not surprised when members of rival veterans' groups supported Bradley, but he was stung when men in his own organization turned on him. Legionnaires in Ohio were so upset by the spectacle of one of the nation's leading patriotic groups feuding with a popular general that the state commander sent Stelle a telegram. Two Ohio posts in the formative stages said they wanted their charter applications held up until the executive committee met. The matter ended in a whimper, as it deserved to, and Bradley, after a year, headed back into the Army. Soldiers, he decided, were much easier to deal with than veterans.

A new group was also engaging in Legion-watching—the American Veterans Committee. The committee had no particular clout with the VA; nor did it have any particular grievance against Hines before his departure. Charles G. Bolte, one of the committee's founders, regarded Hines as "a man of irreproachable character, honesty and integrity, an efficient administrator within certain limits." If there was anything wrong with the VA—and Bolte thought that perhaps there was—he could blame it on the tradition of indifference that persisted in the agency from the Forbes years, not because of anything Hines had or had not done.

The American Veterans Committee was a departure from the mold of traditional veterans' organizations. Bolte, a Dartmouth graduate who had served in both the British and American armies, lost a leg at El Alamein, and was now writing a column for the *New York Herald Tribune.* He was joined in founding the group by Gilbert Harrison, who had been educated at the University of California at Los Angeles and who had served with both the Royal Air Force and the U.S. Army Air Corps. These two represented a generation of veterans who felt that the American Legion's values were stuck in the 1920s and that the veterans of World War II needed a new organization. In this, they were not so different from the World War I veterans who thought that their own times and their war had required an organization quite separate from that of the Grand Army of the Republic or the groups that represented Spanish-American War veterans.

Typical of the kind of veteran the new group attracted was Sergeant Bill Caldwell of the Army Air Force, who had written to Bolte, "We need a new organization. . . . The old organizations, despite their success with the bonus, didn't do much about peace, jobs and freedom—which are a hell of a lot more important." Other veterans criticized the Legion more pointedly. "The American Legion in my mind is associated with decadence and symbolizes the many mistakes associated with World War I and the debauched postwar era that cast us all into the present conflict," complained Second Lieutenant Keith D. Skelton in a wartime letter to *Yank.*

The American Veterans Committee took a markedly different approach from that taken by the American Legion when it had set its goals. There were no militant stands against communism. The expressions of patriotism that had so been identified with the Legion were missing from anything issued by the American Veterans Committee. In their place were the feelings of soldiers trying to understand themselves and the nightmare of a war that they had come through. If the Legion had been ebullient to the point of boisterousness, these new veterans were introspective to the point of un-common gentleness, a trait that most Americans did not associate with their warriors.

". . . we had an uncertain world to live in," Bolte wrote, "we had to watch the war grow—in its causes, in its long and nerve-racking prelude of depression and chaos, in its agonizing bloody course, in its indefinite fearful future. We grew up to the dying strains of the jazz age, in the bitter years when there were maybe no jobs for our fathers. . . ." But if they seemed gentle, they made it equally clear that like their brothers in the Legion, they had demands to make. "We look forward to becoming civilians; making a decent living, raising a family, and living in freedom from the threat of another war," Bolte wrote. ". . . veterans should be restored to the status in life they would have held if they had not gone to war."

In addition to wanting the financial help they thought every veteran was entitled to, the AVC emphasized tolerance and freedom of speech, press, worship, assembly, and ballot, and, in considerable contrast to the Legion's suspicions about international bodies, supported the concept of the United Nations.

It was probably inevitable that an organization of former soldiers who espoused such lofty ideals would get into trouble in a country that had always regarded such people as nascent rightists, whose goals could predictably be measured materially—not ethically or spiritually. Suspicions about what the AVC was really up to came fast and early. Within a year after the war, the American Legion, Catholic War Veterans, and the Veterans of Foreign Wars, joined by some powerful elements in the press, all expressed their concern publicly that the American Veterans Committee had been infiltrated by communists. Robert Patterson, the Legion's former New York County commander, said that the AVC was under "communist influences" and he warned that veterans should "keep constantly alert for such influences" in the other organizations serving their needs.

Westbrook Pegler, a columnist for the Hearst newspapers who rivaled Congressman Rankin's ability to divine the communist menace, wrote at least three columns early in 1946 questioning the AVC's loyalty to the American way of life. Bill Mauldin, World War II's leading cartoonist-chronicler and an AVC member, responded with a defense which was printed in New York City's *PM*. Franklin D. Roosevelt, Jr., another member, also joined the joust, saying, "I am proud to be one of the officials of AVC and to help in its work of pressing for common-sense forward-looking solutions to the problems veterans face today." One veteran wrote to the *Cincinnati Inquirer,* one of the papers that had printed Pegler's columns, accusing both the paper and Pegler of "the shabbiest kind of journalism . . . used to besmirch the reputation of men who fought for, among other things, your privilege to run a free paper."

But the doubts persisted and the criticisms continued. Louis E. Starr, national vice-commander of the Veterans of Foreign Wars, made serious charges during a Wisconsin state convention, calling the AVC a "red front organization." He charged that the top officers of the AVC had affiliations of some sort with the Communist Party. Gilbert Harrison tartly replied that the communists were advising party members not to join the AVC but "one of the major established veterans' organizations." The President's son again responded, voicing his support. Starr, he said, was worried about the future of the VFW because of the AVC's rapidly growing popularity.

Even though the foes that had just been defeated were fascists, it was communists who commanded the nation's concern, just as they had after World War I, when the Russian Revolution was still fresh in the public's mind. The nation was moving to the cusp of a new round of red-baiting. The feeling among most AVC members that the United States and the Soviet Union should learn to coexist peacefully was not an especially popular sentiment. And so it did not seem to matter very much to the American

Veterans Committee's detractors that, in addition to Mauldin and Roosevelt, the AVC's membership rolls contained the names of such solid citizens as former U.S. senator Henry Cabot Lodge, who had only recently been discharged from the Army; Leverett Saltonstall, former Governor of Massachusetts and a new U.S. senator; Audie Murphy, much decorated war hero soon to become an actor; former Vice-President Henry Wallace, his Presidential aspirations still intact in the Progressive Party; Interior Secretary J. A. Krug; Senator Paul Douglas of Illinois; Michigan Governor G. Mennen "Soapy" Williams; United Auto Workers president Walter Reuther; Dwight David Eisenhower; and a liberal Hollywood celebrity named Ronald Reagan. These people met and communicated with each other at AVC meetings and conventions as well as in the pages of the *AVC Bulletin*. The red-baiters were not impressed. Indeed, the Legion's national commander, James O'Neill, said he thought that Wallace's backers were merely "loud speakers for the Communist Party in this country."

Reagan, who had been a captain in the Army Air Force, attacked fascism and hate groups in a column for the *AVC Bulletin* in 1946. "I think the AVC can be a key organization in the preservation of democracy for which 300,000 Americans died," he wrote, "and because I have attacked the extreme right does not mean I am ignorant of the menace of the extreme left. They, too, want to force something unwanted on the American people, and the fact that many of them go along with those of us who are liberal means nothing because they are only hitching a ride as far as we go, hoping that they can use us as a vehicle for their own program."

Reagan's approach was not so much a portent of the political metamorphosis he would undergo in years to come, but rather his realization that communists were joining veterans' groups, so that anyone who would defend such a group had to make an obligatory preemptive strike at the red-baiters. In those days, the baiters stood ready to attack anyone who would describe himself as a liberal, as Reagan did. The late forties were a time when protecting one's backside was essential to survival. Nothing and nobody was safe. At one point, Senator Robert A. Taft, Republican of Ohio, said that the Truman Administration had asked Congress to pass legislation that was close to communism and "essentially totalitarian."

The American Veterans Committee was seen as uppity, elitist, too intellectual. It only angered the Legion and the traditional veterans' organizations when Mauldin, mindful that the G.I. Bill was law but that the social needs of many others went untended, took pen in hand and wrote that the attitude of other veterans'organizations "seemed to be to grab everything they could for the veterans, and to hell with the rest of the country."

The AVC may have been intellectual, but it did not have the compleat intellectual's self-confidence—it fretted about the "liberal image" it had with its detractors. Its concerns led it into trouble in 1948, when it decided to publicly purge a communist from its ranks. The veteran was John Gates. When Gates joined the American Veterans Committee, he had signed the AVC's preamble, without telling the AVC that he was a veteran not only of the war but also of the Communist Party and the *Communist Daily Worker,* of which he was editor. Jittery AVC officials accused him of essentially joining the organization under false pretenses, and charged he was "guilty of perjury and should, therefore, be expelled."

What to do about Gates? Left-of-center Americans watched the AVC closely. They wanted to trust the new group to live up to its own pronouncements on tolerance, political and otherwise. The conservatives were no less interested. If Gates was permitted to stay, it would reinforce their feelings that the AVC was too far to the left to be of any use to veterans.

It would have been awkward enough just to drum Gates out. But the AVC's leadership, in what can only be described as a supreme act of self-flagellation, decided to conduct a hearing about the matter. Its National Administrative Committee, with no one dissenting, ordered a "fact-finding board to determine whether or not Mr. Gates is a member of the Communist Party"—even though Gates had already proudly admitted that.

The hearing—really a mock trial with evocations of both Salem in 1692 and of the contemporary Kremlin—was conducted on a sticky August evening in New York City, with some 250 spectators jamming a room in the Hotel Whitehall to watch it happen. AVC members sat in judgment of Gates and the rest of the nation sat in judgment of the AVC. As Gates' fate was being decided, the Hiss-Chambers case was heating up and the House Un-American Activities Committee was deciding who should be tried for perjury—Alger Hiss or Whittaker Chambers. And a Federal jury in New York was trying to decide the fate of twelve communists who had been indicted on charges of conspiracy to overthrow the Government by force. It was not a propitious moment to try to be charitable.

And so nobody was charitable. Those who judged Gates recommended by a vote of sixteen to one, with one abstention, that he be expelled from the AVC, even though he was a veteran of World War II and it was not against the law to be a member of the Communist Party. At the time of the expulsion, the AVC reaffirmed its 1947 resolution against communism, which also called for "vigorous enforcement of civil rights statutes."

The liberals were appalled; the communists were delighted. Indeed, the

Communist Daily Worker carried Gates' version of the story. The communists knew they had caught the AVC with its civil liberties down. The *Worker* attacked in a manner that was calm, cold, and devastating. "The planning committee's contention that no communist in good faith could subscribe to the preamble of the AVC is almost too childish to answer. Communists hold membership in social, economic and civic groups whose programs do not go beyond the framework of free enterprise capitalism. Under this ruling members of the Socialist Party would be barred from membership in AVC."

Gates, playing well to the balcony, accused the AVC of red-baiting. "Rather than join the witch-hunt against me and other communists who are members," he wrote, "it would be far better that the present leadership stopped aping the methods of the American Legion and devoted themselves to uniting veterans for housing, the bonus and progressive legislation."

Shortly thereafter, the purgative effort continued, with AVC officials suspending the charter of their freewheeling New York City chapter because another individual had allegedly used the chapter for political purposes. In expelling Gates, the AVC made an extraordinary and most unfortunate departure from the precepts of tolerance it had been preaching. Under fire, the AVC lacked fidelity to its own principles. It failed a crucial test of its own liberal convictions and thus lost support among liberals. It did not gain support among those on the right, who found the American Legion and other traditional veterans' organizations more to their liking.

In the years to come, as Wisconsin's Senator Joseph R. McCarthy gave his name to a punishing epoch in American history, the Legion would attract considerable attention for its work in exposing communists in American society. The Legion's sometimes controversial policies adopted in opposition to the far left would all but obliterate the fact that the Legion's official position against Nazism and fascism, dating from 1935, was just as strong.

The AVC incident made it clear, in the years following the defeat of the Nazis and fascists of World War II, that nobody, not even the veterans of that victory, was immune to the hysteria about the communists.

SEVEN
The Korean War

American soldiers imprisoned and tortured during the Korean War were unjustly accused of collaborating with the enemy. (*Life Picture Service*)

The Scapegoats

> How would you feel if you fought for your country
> and were captured and wounded and then flew
> 10,000 miles to a hospital to find you were being
> labeled a possible communist?
> —Major James Campbell, Public Information
> Officer, Valley Forge Hospital, May 2, 1953

Someone had to be blamed for the mess of the 1950s. The facts of the mess were clear enough to some: America, which had destroyed the powers of fascism, was losing the war against communism. Or so it seemed to many in public life and the military, who began to dwell on the menace and supposed prowess of communism with an intensity that the country had not seen since the 1920s. Were they correct in suggesting that the nation was, in fact, losing?

If there was any value in corroboration, they convinced themselves that they were indeed correct. Senators Joseph R. McCarthy and Robert A. Taft feared the advancing specter and blamed its virulence on namby-pambies in the State Department; Richard Nixon, soon to be Vice-President, blamed it on Harry Truman; Major-General Lewis B. Hershey, who ran the Selective Service System, blamed it on soft, spoiled, self-indulgent young men who did not want to surrender their freedom to Army discipline; John F. Kennedy, a promising young congressman from Massachusetts, blamed it on past diplomats and past Presidents; the American Legion suspected that much of the fault reposed with the American Civil Liberties Union, which it saw as a front for sneaky communists; General Douglas MacArthur suggested it might be certain politicians in Washington, who shackled him instead of letting him do what he knew was right for the country; the State of Indiana thought that liberal college professors might be a cause and concluded that they ought to be required to take loyalty oaths; and the State of Ohio, never to be outdone by Indiana, was so convinced that communists were winning that it ruled that in the event any of them became unemployed while in Ohio, they would not get unemployment insurance benefits.

With so many scapegoaters, the United States of America was clearly in need of a scapegoat. The United States Army was pleased to provide one: its former soldiers. For it was soldiers who had fought the nonwar in Korea that Harry Truman had insisted upon calling a mere police action; it was soldiers who had failed to win that nonwar—the first time in American history that an American army was not decisively victorious. Neither generals nor their civilian leaders wanted to be held accountable for such lackluster doings. They were like little boys after a bad Hallowe'en prank. They had all convinced themselves that the war and its loss were not their fault. So the answer had to lie with the soldiers—the young men who lacked the resolve to win.

Even more important in determining culpability, from the Army's point of view, was that these soldiers had also forgotten what no earlier American soldier had ever forgotten—the etiquette of how a real man is supposed to act when he is being starved and tortured and his brains are being scrambled with alien slogans, as was the case when the North Koreans and the Chinese took Americans prisoner. Before the fifties were over, the nation's military leaders would, in effect, tell Americans that their sons had comported themselves as collaborators and traitors. If returning soldiers did not know what it meant to be an American, then it followed that communists would have the upper hand, the scapegoaters declared. Such was the nature of America after Korea.

The World War II victor's orgasm of euphoria had ended on June 25, 1950, when the North Koreans crossed the 38th parallel in a move against the South. And even the memories of that euphoria faded after American troops began to return home at war's end, in 1953. Americans had come through two decades of harsh reality. First the Depression, then the war. They were ill prepared to deal with the psychodrama of the post-Korea years.

That psychodrama took many forms: accusations of disloyalty that were as vicious as they were theatrical; the posturing of patriots who aspired to high office; and that fair day in May of 1950 when the American Legion decided to dramatize the red peril. On May Day, the traditional time for communists to kick up their heels, Legionnaires went to Mosinee, in north-central Wisconsin (Senator McCarthy's home state), dressed themselves as Russian soldiers, and staged a mock takeover of the town in order to show all doubters what it would be like if the communists were in control. With the cooperation of townsfolk, Legionnaires plucked Mosinee's mayor from his home in his nightclothes, businesses were declared "nationalized," and local restaurants put potato soup and dark bread on their menus. The make-believe Russians said that the only people who would be permitted to eat candy had to be communists and moved on to inspect the library for books that might be unacceptable. After a day of such oddments, the Legion "liberated" Mosinee and a good time was had by all at a community bonfire in which communist literature was burned. The consensus among born-again townspeople seemed to be that potato soup wasn't very good and that there was no place like home.

There was a certain self-doubt in the American people in those days. Those doubts had their genesis in the kind of war Korea was. After college students scrambled for and received precious deferments, the Government found nearly seven million other young men, many of them only in their late teens and early twenties, to roust the bandits, and off they went. If General MacArthur had been able to keep his promise and have all of them "home by Christmas," perhaps it could have been another "splendid little war," just as the Spanish-American War had been, fifty-two years before.

But that was not to be. The North Koreans beat the green American troops in initial battles, frequently surprising them in ambushes. Then in the autumn, with the war not yet half a year old, the Chinese committed 100,000 of their troops to the fray. The punitive expedition that Truman called a "bandit raid" grew very large indeed, but Truman had neither the desire nor the mandate to mobilize the manpower that could begin to cope with such a foe, if, indeed, it were possible. Times were good; Americans were in no mood to engage in another major war, especially if it turned out to be World War III.

Washington quickly realized that the best course was to end the war where it was. If the U.S. soldiers were not clear why they were in Korea, the picture was no clearer in Washington. General MacArthur did not agree with Truman's policy, resisted it, and publicly disassociated himself from it, for which Truman relieved him of his command. By 1951, the United States, China, and North Korea were engaged in peace talks that would drag on for two years. Men on both sides died as hard-nosed functionaries yammered on, looking for a way to save face. There had been no victory and now there was no peace, neither for Truman nor for the soldiers who had been sent to Korea. There was also no truce.

A major question was what would happen to the prisoners of war. The South Koreans held 106,376 Chinese and North Koreans; the communists were thought to be holding only about 10,000 Americans and South Koreans. To the best of anyone's knowledge, virtually all of the Americans wanted to return home. But among the Chinese and North Korean prisoners, only around 31,000 indicated that they wanted to be repatriated—less than a third of those held. For the communists, the prospect of losing so many soldiers through defection was not only embarrassing, it was unacceptable. For the Americans, the notion of returning to the communists soldiers who wanted something else was equally distasteful.

At first, the result was simply stalemate. But the communists quickly realized that they needed a propaganda offensive. That offensive rested squarely upon what can only be described as cruel and unusual punishment—both physical and mental—inflicted by the North Koreans and Chinese on captured Americans. Examples of this that reached the American public included forced marches, in which prisoners were abandoned to die when they got dysentery and could not keep up; lack of food; lack of heat; lack of latrine privileges; lack of humanity. Men were punched, kicked, and bayonetted while in prison; they were clubbed with rifle butts; their wounds and frostbite went mostly unattended. On one occasion, Marines were reportedly herded into a cave and killed by grenades thrown in after them. The State Department took the reports seriously and assured the public that evidence was being collected for the formal mounting of charges of war crimes.

The communists wanted to force the Americans to admit to self-incriminating slogans which would obfuscate the problem of the communist prisoners who did not want to go home. Better still, from the communist perspective, was that by using force as an inducement, they might persuade Americans at least to appear to be cool toward repatriation.

In this mean spirit, the communists manhandled Colonel Frank C. Schwable, chief of staff of a Marine air wing, whom they captured, starved, and forced to spend the winter in a hole with a blanket. They even denied him the right to urinate in the common latrine with other humans, and so he lay in his own waste. His "confession," obtained in 1953, was made public in an America obsessed with the idea that Americans were somehow losing their moral purpose and their sense of themselves to the wily communists, whom they perceived as proselytizing new faithful. The obsession was not accurate, but there was enough truth in it to give the lies it spawned credibility, for a while.

For example, some soldiers, abused and in poor condition, did agree to attend classes in which the Chinese lectured them on communism. The motives for attending such seminars included the Americans' fear of reprisal if they did not attend, boredom with doing absolutely nothing, and even the chance to sit in a warm room for a while. Whatever the reason, other soldiers took offense at it and ventilated their anger once they got home. "We called them pinkies or rats," reported Private First Class Lester Todd of Lincoln, Nebraska. "They were the fellows who had fallen for communism and wanted to continue to study it."

Private Todd's impressions may not have been very accurate—few, if any, American prisoners of the Korean War were indisputably and permanently converted to communism—but that did not make the offence of listening to lectures on communism any less real for him or for the millions of people who would soon accept such descriptions as great American truths. The scapegoating of American soldiers was not done in any consistent way. Veterans had their defenders, and some ably defended themselves. But by the end of the decade their reputation would be damaged.

The process started quietly enough. At first, there were only a few stories in the national press. An early one came in the April 4, 1953, issue of *The New York Times,* which cited "authoritative studies" to suggest that "Communist 'brainwashers' may have so twisted the minds of some American soldiers captured in Korea that after the Korean war ends they will publicly declare they do not want to come home."

Within a week, the Defense Department was the source for another story advising the public that some soldiers who served in Korea "appear to have succumbed to the relentless Communist pressures, repetitious arguments, distorted and selected information and various inducements to accept . . . Communist propaganda." The Defense Department, having raised an unpleasant possibility, seemed conciliatory. "Such captive soldiers cannot be condemned for cooperating with the Communists, at least outwardly, for the alternative may appear to be torture or death—or both." Government officials were sympathetic. Senator Styles Bridges, Republican of New Hampshire, said the atrocity reports were "sadly and unfortunately correct."

These sentiments seemed reasonable to a people who had always thought of themselves as well-intentioned. If everyone knew that torture and coercion were the order of the day, no one would expect any soldier to subject himself to it. Indeed, statements gained through coercion could themselves be the targets for an effective propaganda counterattack, which would be formidable if conducted by Americans, the grand masters of public relations. Chinese and North Korean cruelty would be seen for what it was.

Unfortunately, reassuring statements such as those issued by the Pentagon early in the spring of 1953 would soon become rare. And the masters of public relations would turn their art on their own kind.

The North began to release prisoners of war in 1953. They looked wan and vulnerable and they said almost nothing as they stepped down from ambulances, dressed in the blue greatcoats and tennis shoes that were the unlikely standard communist issue. Some were described as having "tears of joy" in their eyes; others "wore thin smiles." But they were hardly possessed of the ebullience that Americans liked to see in their homecoming soldiers.

The soldiers who were sickest were presumably the first to be released by the communists. Among these were Private Carl W. Kirtchenhausen of New York City, who suffered badly frostbitten feet and offered no smiles to anyone upon his deliverance. No sooner did his name come over the wires than reporters began to converge on his Upper Manhattan neighborhood. They wanted to learn more about the "confession" he was said to have given the communists while in captivity, in which he talked about "war propaganda put out by the forces of Wall Street."

Kirtchenhausen's neighbors, at first jubilant to hear that "Carl has been freed," quickly learned that they would have to defend him to inquiring reporters. They explained to the reporters that Carl was a Jew who fled Nazi Germany with his father before World War II. He certainly appreciated what individual freedom was, they said, and there was nothing about him to suggest that he was predisposed to disloyalty. "He was never like that at all," his former landlady insisted. "All that communist talk—they must have made him write it."

The next day, another group of thirty-five was released by the North, and again, they seemed unusually quiet to the Army people who received them. General Mark Clark, the United Nations commander, greeted each one personally and gave each a letter. "Because of the heavy personal sacrifices you have made in our great cause, we are humble in your presence," Clark said. He knew well what the Chinese and North Koreans had done to the Americans, and so he added, "I am confident you will never have reason to doubt that those sacrifices have our respect and gratitude." He was wrong. The newly freed Americans would soon have every reason to doubt.

It would have been reasonable to expect the Government to protect the identities of soldiers who were suspected of having been tainted by communist brainwashing—at least until a thorough effort was made to find out the truth of it. But the Government did no such thing. Nor did it make much effort to check the mental state of the newly freed men before making public statements about their loyalty. The Army's top psychiatrist recommended that homecoming soldiers need only be treated as though they had "just been around the corner to the drugstore," but that would hardly be possible for Americans trying to understand the press statements emanating from the Pentagon. The Government told the press that "twenty-two United States prisoners of war from Korea designated by the Air Force as victims of Communist propaganda" would be landing at Travis Air Force Base.

The Air Force piously said it would be a mistake to release the names of the twenty-two, because "to mark them now would be to mark them for life." But one of the names was leaked to reporters, as wiser heads in the Government surely knew it would be. The press, carried away by its own need to compete with itself, made the man's identity public. He was Paul Schnur, strangely identified as the son of a "retired leftist" (whatever that meant) who managed apartment houses for a former Progressive Party candidate for President. The elder Schnur was also described as the head of the San Francisco chapter of the Committee to Save the Rosenbergs. All but lost in the disclosure was that Paul Schnur had only recently received something that seemed to underscore his loyalty—a Bronze Star for bravery in battle.

The soldiers who returned with him were furious to learn that, whether by design or not, they were now all suspect. The Army ordered a tactical retreat. "Nobody in the Army has said any of these men were sold on communism while a prisoner of war," said Major James Campbell, the public information officer at Valley Forge Hospital. He added that the early reports of questionable behavior were based on a "limited and inconclusive study" that could turn out to be wrong "when the boys get their feet on the ground."

Even in retreating, the Army thus suggested that its suspicions were based on questionable things the men had done or said, not on any hasty conclusions or inappropriate behavior on the part of the Army. In any event, the Army gave all the returnees big breakfasts. And if the returnees were not as happy as some thought they should have been, perhaps it was because while in communist hands, three of them had developed tuberculosis.

Major Campbell tried to express for reporters the feeling of the freed Americans as he perceived them. "How would you feel," he asked them, "if you fought for your country and were captured and wounded and then flew 10,000 miles to a hospital to find you were being labeled a possible communist?" If the major had reflected just a little bit more, he might not have said that, since it was the higher officials in his own Army who were largely responsible for the early insidious smearing.

Ten of the newly freed soldiers were permitted to face assorted reporters and cameramen themselves less than two days after their release. The press, representing the public interest, wanted to know if the men who had gone to war had returned with Marxist tendencies. Reporters asked indelicate questions.

The soldiers were livid, "bitter beyond expression," and "insulted" that anyone, be he reporter or John Q. Public, would suggest they had communist tendencies. The communists "tried to show us that they had something," said Private First Class Rogers Herndon, "but they had nothing compared to what we have in the United States." A few of the soldiers acknowledged that, under duress, they had lent their names to some creative communist propaganda, and one soldier had no hesitation in telling reporters that after his right arm was amputated and his captors had threatened to kill him, he had admitted to the communist charge that the Americans had conducted germ warfare.

The Army then admitted it hadn't the vaguest notion of whether any of the Americans had accepted communism. After weeks of telling Americans that American prisoners of war had betrayed their country, the Army announced it would conduct a study to see if what it had charged was really true. *The New York Times,* which had been dutifully carrying the Army's characterizations for weeks, stepped back from the issue and addressed the Army sternly in an editorial, calling the press conference held by the soldiers "ill-advised" and saying that "it would be extremely unfair . . . to accuse these men of disloyalty until they had had sufficient time to recover. . . ."

The Army was not nearly as understanding as the editorial wanted it to be. Having painted the soldiers red, it assiduously pursued its efforts to find the evidence to prove it. More soldiers came home; by July of 1953, the communists had released 4,428 Americans. Few were listed as "missing." In August, the Government could report that 40 percent of all those held—2,730 men—had died in communist prisons. The Army charges began to look quite suspect.

As more men returned home and went public with the experiences they had while in the control of the North Koreans and Chinese, the brutality that had been inflicted upon them became more apparent. There was no reason for them to remain silent now. They told of a soldier who had been starved, then gagged and chained to a post in the summer sun until he died. And Lieutenant Colonel Thomas Harrison described kinds of torture utilizing water that were uncomfortably reminiscent of what the Americans had done during the Philippine Insurrection a half-century earlier. "They would bend

my head back, put a towel over my face and pour water over the towel,''
Harrison said. ''I could not breathe. That went on for hour after hour, day
after day.''

The soldiers were forthcoming; the public's compassion for them was
much harder to find. The stories were met with ''a muttered curse, a shrug
and the helpless question, 'Well, what did you expect.' '' Said a veteran of
World War II, ''I get the feeling I've read it all before.'' To which another
added, ''I think the American people have lost their capacity to be
shocked. . . .'' Americans were more concerned, it seemed, with the fact
that the war ended without having been won. Most of them did not
understand that the war was unwon by design and had nothing to do with the
quality of our soldiers.

That confusion was enough for the junior senator from Wisconsin, Joseph
R. McCarthy, and into the breach he went. McCarthy, a man who had spent
World War II as a paper-shuffler but who had somehow convinced most
people that he had been a fearless tail-gunner, was regarded as more than
qualified to talk about the question of uprightness among soldiers. ''We can
and must recapture our national honor,'' he said in a speech to the Marine
Corps League. ''. . . If we refuse to do so, the conquerer's boot will walk
across the land. . . .''

The Army was nowhere near completing its ballyhooed study. Indeed, it
had not yet even started it. But for reasons best known to the military,
perhaps rooted in the tactical mistakes committed by the high-ranking
officers who planned U.S. moves, the Army was not averse to leaking
private reports of one sort or another to newsmen, repeating earlier
convictions that ''some of the returning American prisoners . . . are now out
and out communists and fellow travelers.'' Two hundred Americans were
reported to have decided not to return to their loved ones at home but would
instead remain with their captors. Ultimately, only twenty-one Americans
would decline repatriation. But the Army's exaggerations would continue to
occupy a more conspicuous place in the American perception of the war.

When the press considered the twenty-one, it found all of them other than
the storied, conventional, easy-to-like, white-picket-fence lads who had
glistened so during the two world wars. And so the press played up the fact
that by the national standards, these latest soldiers were not typical Americans
and so, perhaps, the national character should not be seen in such a sorry light.
Defector Andrew Fortuna of Detroit, an Italian-American, had an alcoholic
mother, a father who had deserted her, and a brother who was an accused
felon. Fortuna also had a Japanese wife but the son she gave him died of polio

before his assignment to Korea. The two Bronze Stars he earned fighting in Korea did not cause the Army to be more lenient with him.

Another defector also had a foreign overlay. Albert Belhomme had actually been born in Belgium, his mother had been interned at a Nazi labor camp, and although he had wanted to be an officer his lack of American citizenship made that impossible. The absence of a happy American childhood and some disappointments as an adult thus explained to some the defection of Belhomme. And then there was William White, a twenty-three-year-old black whose parents had been divorced and who had been raised by his grandparents.

None of the above or their colleagues was the boy next door for most Americans, and so when the Army discharged all of them dishonorably, it made sense to the country. The Army also started formal court-martial proceedings against some other former prisoners who had signed "germ warfare" and other nasty propaganda slogans that had been devised by the Chinese and the North Koreans. It was clear that the Defense Department, which had now skillfully shifted the public's attention away from the civilians and high-ranking officers who had planned the unvictorious war to the combat troops who had fought it, sensed that there might be some value in making an example out of them.

The scenario was not so different from the infamous decision by the French in World War I to blame their Army's poor showing against the Germans on cowardly troops and to select three of many and kill them at a well-attended public execution. Before the decade of the fifties was over, the French incident, novelized twenty-two years earlier by Humphrey Cobb, would be transformed into a powerful motion picture called *Paths of Glory*.

The movie, the work of Kirk Douglas and Stanley Kubrick, was praised for its courage in providing a pungent reminder of the universality in the art of scapegoating. *Paths of Glory* was released in the afterglow of the McCarthy era and on the shank of the Government's drive to blame soldiers for not winning the Korean War. Praiseworthy as it was, Hollywood confined itself to making a statement about the French in World War I—not the American Army after Korea. Indeed, with the exception of a courageous few, nobody directly questioned the current scapegoating, certainly not in any serious, sustained way that might cause the Army to think twice about what it was doing. The analogy between past and present was clear enough, though. Like the French of nearly forty years before, the U.S. Government was supporting the creation of a view of soldiers that was as distorted as it was disrespectful. The country was running on slogans. Representative Robert Sikes, Democrat of Florida, said he supported the Army in going ahead with the courts-martial, which he thought would be a just response against "turncoat G.I.'s who played the Red's tune while they were captive."

Few preached the virtues of moderation. President Eisenhower, whatever his limitations, was never regarded as a mean or petty person, either as a general or as a politician. But he was not quick to challenge the validity of what the Army was doing. Instead, he only preached the virtues of forgiveness for any and all soldiers who had flirted with communism and exhorted everyone to take to heart the Biblical lesson of the Prodigal Son. If anything, his approach gave credibility to the Army's activities, even though there were few prodigal veterans who needed forgiveness. Eisenhower said he was sure, however, that the Army would not punish a soldier who had made a simple mistake. The soldier in question, Corporal Edward Dickenson of Crackers Neck, Virginia, was accused of communicating and currying favor with his captors "to the detriment" of his fellow prisoners.

As Americans began to feel that the veteran of Korea was somehow "different" in his character than all other U.S. soldiers who had served before him, the veterans began to believe it about themselves. They could see it around them—these men were not of the same stuff, they thought, as those who had fought World War II a decade before. A less generous G.I. Bill of Rights was there for the taking, but the veterans of Korea seemed as apathetic about it as the public was about them. The apathy was seen as "one of the major contributing factors to the failure of our Korean veterans to take advantage of the benefits that are available to them."

The press, which can only reflect the reality of those it talks to, began to write about the Korean veteran as a being apart. The reporters who prided themselves on their streetwise ability to ferret out the truth from bull-throwing politicos, started to pick up the deadly slogans of the scapegoaters. The Korean veteran "is a different breed from his older brother who came back from World War II," opined a writer for *The New York Times Magazine,* "the product of special times and of a very special war. . . . The new veterans are disquieting machine-like products of their special times. . . . There seems to be an almost robot-like disinterest about him that is in disturbing contrast to the assertive individualism of the World War II soldier. . . ."

Were they really different, after all? Or was it that society also saw others among its components that way? College students of the same generation, for example, were irked when they were described as indifferent to the political process. Before the decade was out, the nation would wonder at a whole generation, beaten, lost, and seemingly adrift in its alleged rootless indifference, exemplified by the likes of writer Jack Kerouac and actor James Dean.

Whether it was really true or not, it created a happy hunting ground for Joseph McCarthy, the senator who was giving his name to one of the dirtier pieces of American history. He attracted considerable attention when, in 1954, he went red-hunting in the Army, which, he assured his many admirers and constituents, was not only inept at war, but hiding communists in its olive-drab shrubs. The full fury of McCarthy, no small thing, descended on a hapless Army dentist named Irving Peress, who was ultimately cashiered after he took the Fifth Amendment, rather than answer McCarthy's questions about his past activities—which McCarthy claimed included recruiting soldiers into the Communist Party.

McCarthy also had strong words for General Ralph Zwicker, who ran Fort Monmouth, New Jersey, the camp in which McCarthy suspected Peress had been hiding communists. "You are a disgrace to the uniform," McCarthy told him. The Army tepidly responded by accusing McCarthy and his aide, Roy Cohn, of trying to get preferential treatment for their friend G. David Schine. If the Army knew that McCarthy had exaggerated his own World War II efforts, there was no hint of it in the exchange.

As the veterans of Korea came under suspicion, the veterans of World War I and II who dominated the membership rolls of the American Legion and other veterans' organizations came to think of themselves as the arbiters of loyalty. One obvious place to look for seditious material was books, and so the Legion intensified its traditional interest in what was being published, much to the dismay of librarians, who feared the Legion's criticism. But in the view of many veterans, there was no better place to take loyalty soundings than in that haven for eccentrics called Hollywood.

The Legion denied that it ever tried to create a blacklist, but before the decade was over, it would stalk hundreds of writers, actors, directors, and others in the film industry, seeking to determine if they had links to communism. The film studios hardly acquitted themselves with dignity, readily initiating loyalty screening programs before they really determined if the Legion's suspicions were accurate. Among the Legion's targets in those days were not only people who had made substantial contributions to American cinema, but people who had nothing to do with communism. "This is not witch-hunting or vigilanteeism as our critics may charge," the Legion maintained. "This is a presentation of facts."

The Legion's forays against artists and writers would, at the very least, underscore the divergence between American intellectuals and the two million veterans who belonged to the Legion. Some liberals came to equate Legion policy with the stance of all veterans, not just those who were members. In point of fact, lots of people outside of the Legion engaged in red-baiting and although the Legion may have been more intimidating than most, because of its size, it had no monopoly on the excesses of the 1950s.

The Legion remained firm, consistently supporting the red-hunting efforts of the House Un-American Activities Committee and J. Edgar Hoover's FBI. And after HUAC ceased to exist, many Legionnaires saw no reason to doubt the rightness of their cause. "Frequently, bitter criticism has showered not only congressional committees but the Legion because of its support of these agencies and its pronouncements," author Raymond Moley, Jr., would write in *The American Legion Story* in 1966, looking back on the turbulence that had, by then, been overtaken by more serious concerns. "Leading congressional figures in investigations have been subjected to abuse by the press, radio and television, on campuses and street corners, in the pulpit and Congress, and in academic and artistic circles. . . . In part, the outcry against congressional investigations of communism has been due to a liberalism which mistakes the acceptance of subversion as a manifestation of mere dissent. But a considerable part of the criticism has been inspired by communists and their fellow travelers."

Whether any good at all came out of the Legion's efforts to find communists in Hollywood in the 1950s is a question that veterans themselves would not agree on. What is clear is that the American Legion's militancy against communism all but totally eclipsed its traditional stand against the extremes of the right. The Legion had passed resolutions against fascism in 1935, 1937, 1938, 1939, 1940, 1941, 1942, and 1943. Its stance against fascism was such that the Legion noted in 1938, "The communists have called the Legion a fascist outfit, and now we find the German-American Bund charging us with giving up the Reds." Not many Legionnaires seemed to remember that in the 1950s. Nor did very many of its moderate critics, veteran and nonveteran, who became even more disaffected from it.

McCarthy's effectiveness would wax and wane before the decade was half over, especially after the debacle of the televised Army-McCarthy hearings in 1954, his censure by his fellow senators, and the unrelenting disapproval of President Eisenhower, who refused to have anything to do with him. But the Army apparently remained chastened and began to purge its ranks of various people—not because they did anything wrong in the Army, but because of what they might have done before. Some courts were disdainful of the practice and said that the less-than-honorable discharges the Army was issuing to certain individuals violated civil liberties. "It would seem basic that a soldier has a right to an honorable discharge if his military record merits it," said one judge, "and that he cannot be held to answer . . . for matters extraneous to his record."

The Army, its determination to ferret out political undesirables undiminished, then required inductees to take loyalty oaths and retained a strong interest not only in the new soldier's political past but also that of his parents. That led to some bizarre happenings. In the case of Norman Pierre Gaston, the Coast Guard at first refused to let him become an officer because his mother, although not a communist, was said to hold memberships in groups that the Coast Guard felt might be subversive. Mrs. Gaston came to her son's aid, telling the Coast Guard that she had, in fact, joined some groups without knowing precisely what they did. The Coast Guard finally permitted young Gaston to be an ensign, ruling that "because his relationship to his mother had not been close . . . no improper influence exists." Whatever her politics and whatever the groups she had joined, Mrs. Gaston said later she was very happy that Norman made ensign.

The Veterans Administration was not about to be outdone by Senator McCarthy, the FBI, the Army, and all the other groups and agencies dedicated to fighting the communist menace. The fact that a man had risked his life for his country, suffered wounds in battle, or perhaps even lost parts of his body by no means proved that he was loyal to the United States beyond the shadow of a VA doubt. Relying on a 1943 law that gave it the power to rescind VA benefits to anyone guilty of mutiny, treason, or sabotage, the VA set up a special committee on waivers and forfeitures. The committee moved with urgency against what were perhaps some of the least likely seditionists that America had ever seen—the former soldiers who had won its wars. But the VA outdid itself when it moved against James Kutcher.

In 1943, while serving as a rifleman near San Pietro, Italy, Kutcher was hit in a mortar explosion and lost both legs at the knees. He somehow survived, and after much hospitalization he returned to his hometown of Newark, New Jersey, three years later and took a job as a clerk with the Veterans Administration at a salary of $38 a week. Two years passed without incident. In 1948, his boss at the VA informed him that he was to be fired because he had been "disloyal to the United States."

Kutcher was rather astonished to hear it. He had never made any secret of his politics; his politics needed understanding. Kutcher believed in radical socialism, but hardly the kind the Soviet Union had any use for. He was a believer in the principles of Leon Trotsky, who had been expelled from the Communist Party because of his steadfast opposition to Joseph Stalin—the very same Stalin that the Americans, now in the throes of the Cold War, found so tiresome.

Kutcher wrote back to the VA with the obvious response. When he was drafted, nobody seemed to care about what he had done in 1938, and when his legs were blown off, nobody had asked him about his loyalty. Why would anyone care now? Kutcher could not understand why anybody would even notice him. He was not a party leader and he had always thought of himself as the kind of person who would get his name in the newspapers twice—once at birth, and once on the obituary page.

No sooner had the VA moved against Kutcher than the Newark Housing Authority, another agency determined not to brook anti-Americanism in its facilities, notified him that he and his parents would be evicted from their public housing project. He was unfit as a tenant, said the Housing Authority, because of his membership in the Socialist Party. The VA next suspended issuance of Kutcher's monthly $329 disability check, again because he was a Trotskyite. It notified him of its decision shortly before Christmas of 1955. Kutcher began to wonder, only half in jest, if the VA might now demand return of the artificial legs and canes the Government had issued him earlier.

Up until now, the VA had never even conducted a hearing to determine if the information it had about Kutcher was correct. But Kutcher retained the services of Joseph Rauh, a noted civil liberties lawyer and founder of the Americans for Democratic Action. Kutcher's predicament was also called to the attention of journalist Murray Kempton. These two all by themselves could see to it that the VA felt the sting of public disapproval. The rest of the press joined in and the VA was catapulted out of its stealth and into the limelight.

Soon a hearing was scheduled, with the VA saying that it had decided to do so out of "a sense of fair play and a desire to prevent hardship." The VA also explained why Kutcher's benefits had been suspended. It was because somehow the VA had learned that in 1951, Kutcher had attended a kind of summer camp for Trotskyites at which he said he rather liked the idea of workers and owners sharing in the wealth. He also reportedly said he did not think much of the situation in the United States, where cheaters and crooks "oppress the working class." In short, Kutcher was criticizing his Government—a right he had gone to war to protect.

The VA found these sentiments intolerable, and it was even further vexed when it heard that while at the camp, Kutcher also advocated the overthrow of the Government. Whatever the truth of it, Kutcher had now become the very first veteran whose benefits were suspended because of his asserted communism—even though he had neither been tried nor found guilty of violating the Smith Act, which made it unlawful to either teach or advocate the violent overthrow of Government.

The promised hearing took place, and from the instant that the doors of the hearing room swung open, it was clear that the Veterans Administration would be in trouble. In hobbled the forty-three-year-old Kutcher on the two canes he needed to remain ambulatory, seating himself at one end of an enormous table as cameras clicked away and television cameras recorded all that transpired, including Kutcher's denial that he had ever advocated the violent overthrow of anything, except, perhaps, the Third Reich. There was also the formidable presence of attorney Rauh, who asked the obvious questions that would put any true Constitutionalist to shame: Was the Government accusing Kutcher of treason? If it was, where was the case? Where were the witnesses and the evidence? And if there were no witnesses and there was no evidence, then, it seemed to Rauh, the VA was trying to "censor the pensioner's right to speak." And that Rauh was not about to permit.

To the surprise of nobody, the hand that turned the benefits off was required to turn them back on two weeks later. And the Veterans Administration assured everyone that there was nobody else like Kutcher out there, denied his due because of the misplaced zeal of the bureaucrats.

Maybe the VA had to pay this legless former soldier a disability pension, but it did not have to employ him, and so the agency continued to be as mean as it was mindless, refusing to return his job to him. This, too, ended in defeat for the agency, which was ordered to reinstate him by a Federal court six months later. But the dismissal occurred in 1948 and reinstatement was not bestowed until 1956. So, even though the Veterans Administration was required to pay him for the seven years of time lost, Kutcher had to struggle through some hard times—the price he paid for criticizing the Government for which he had fought so well. He remained with the VA until 1972, when he retired.

Meantime, the matter of all those allegedly disloyal soldiers who had defected to the North Koreans and Chinese remained open and undecided. Something of a public relations campaign was under way by mid-decade, with the Marines decorating those who had been prisoners and who had refused to "bear false witness against their country." No less than the Secretary of the Navy attended the event, and he praised the four officers and the master sergeant for electing "stern duty" over "flaccid collaboration." A New York Times reporter who witnessed it called it "an unusual investiture ceremony," which was really an "implied rebuke to those United States prisoners who signed germ warfare confessions and in other ways did the bidding of their captors."

The Marines' ceremony was held in January of 1954. Perhaps if the Marines had known what the Defense Department was learning about the conduct of the war just ended, they would have been more conciliatory toward the former captives, most of whom had been in the Army. It was not for another twenty months that Defense made its findings public, but when they came, they were in sharp contrast to the poor image of the American soldier that had been projected by certain people in the Army. In short, Defense said that there had been "misconceptions" about those taken prisoner in Korea. Contrary to the rumors most Americans had heard, only a "few of the men became sincere converts to communism. . . . The percentage seems to have been infinitesimal."

The Defense Department made it clear that these conclusions were not merely the impressions of the civilians who actually conducted the study, but were based upon hard facts. Of the 4,428 men who had by then been returned to the Americans, only 565 were questioned at all about their conduct as prisoners. Of these, all but 192 were immediately cleared of even the suggestion of wrongdoing. Of the 192, only one was eventually reprimanded, while two more were given restricted assignments, ones which were not sensitive nor requiring of a great deal of trust. Six more were tried and convicted of violating military conduct. But in the months to come, dozens of other cases among the 192 were dropped for lack of evidence.

The report thus strongly suggested that the previous reports of widespread wrongdoing had been grossly overstated and that there was really nothing more to say about the subject. But the Army apparently did not agree. Some former prisoners found that they could not get benefits. For the period of their incarceration they were supposed to receive $2.50 a day, but because of the allegations that had been made about their conduct—allegations that had never been proved or even tried and which were now being abandoned by the Defense Department—they were denied their due. It was as though the Army did not believe the Defense Department. To make matters worse, the Army required former prisoners of war to appear at public hearings to deny that they had ever been collaborators. And when those who were suspect wanted to see what evidence the Army had compiled against them, the Army declared the files to be secret.

So, the stage was set. The Government had gotten itself into a war it could not and did not win; high Army officials had not exactly distinguished themselves as military tacticians; and now ordinary soldiers were apparently going to be blamed for a loss entirely outside their control and stereotyped for motives they never had in the first place. *Paths of Glory,* which was in the process of being produced for the cinema, had its counterpart in contemporary American life. The score was written and orchestrated, the players were ready if reluctant. All it needed was a conductor.

22

The Scapegoaters

... let him go for a scapegoat into the wilderness.
—Leviticus 16:10

The Army could not have picked a better officer than Major (soon to be promoted) William Erwin Mayer to guide the nation on the course that it had decided was right and proper. From the Army's point of view, the Americans who had been held prisoner had exhibited a weakness that was nothing short of psychopathological. Mayer could certainly lay claim to being knowledgeable about psychopathology. He was a doctor, a graduate of the Northwestern University Medical School who had spurned the enticements and riches offered in the civilian sector and had instead consecrated his knowledge of psychiatry to the military.

The Army needed a medical judge of sorts whose own record would remain unstained by any of the blemishes that compromised the soldiers he was going to evaluate, no matter how intensely the Army's critics might scrutinize that record. Mayer seemed to fill the bill there, too. He was a patriot of such mettle that even Senator McCarthy at the peak of his powers could not have smeared him, the recipient of a coveted Bronze Star—the very same award won by some of the combat soldiers who were now under suspicion of being soft on communism.

Most important of all, the Army needed a master communicator, someone whose commentary would be listened to, a credible, clear-eyed seer whose pronouncements on the real meaning of what had happened in those prison camps would be listened to by ordinary Americans. It was clearly important that Americans continue to trust the civilian authority that got the nation into the war and the generals who had run it; they had to be told categorically that the wrongs committed by U.S. soldiers reflected badly not just on the Army and on the Government, but on the totality of American society. The Army's weakness was everybody's weakness, the Army believed. Again, the man of the hour was Mayer, an eloquent speaker who zealously believed in the vision of the Army and was now prepared to nurture the service as it had nurtured him. He was not about to be sidetracked by the moderation of the findings of the Department of Defense. He had other things to say, and he said them, in forceful speeches that he began to deliver all over the country.

Based on his own independent review of the facts, Mayer made a declaration that must have astonished the people who had worked so diligently to understand what really happened and who then put together the Defense Department's study. Mayer's message essentially was that *fully one-third of all the Americans captured in Korea gave in when the communists subjected them to brainwashing*. They gave in, he said, without threats of physical injury or actual torture. And who was to blame for this sorry state of affairs? American society, according to Mayer. "The behavior of too many of our soldiers in prison fell far short of the historical standards of honor, character, loyalty, courage and personal integrity," he told the country. The one-third at whom he directed his ire were either communists, collaborators, or both, insisted the major, adding that nothing like this had ever before happened in American history.

Mayer's appraisal was stark, harsh, and possessed of the unequivocality that the Army had always prized, on the battlefield and off. He said of the soldiers allegedly included in the one-third who had given in to communist brainwashing that not only did they not try to escape from the permanent communist prison camps, but they lost their will to live and died of their weakness, suffering from no particular disease other than their own lack of gumption. As for all those who died in communist hands, Mayer said that it was as much the failure of American prisoners to care for their own wounded, not just communist atrocities.

No such criticism had ever before been made by Americans about their own soldiers. Indeed, one would have to look hard to find that sort of rhetoric in any nation's military history. Even the French during World War I never suggested that their soldiers in German hands died because they lacked the moral conviction to continue breathing. But Mayer went even further. The record, he said, appeared "to raise serious questions about American character, and about the education of Americans." From Mayer's perspective, our schools and colleges were producing more "passive, dependent individuals who died early, and often, apparently, needlessly."

The solution to all those weak, passive men, Mayer said, was to develop new techniques for understanding the communists.

In a country so predisposed to endless moralizing and self-examination, Mayer quickly became the messiah of condemnation, and, given the gravity of his grim message and the importance assigned to it by the Army, there was nothing more important for him to do than spread the bad tidings about the Americans who had gone to Korea. Mayer hit the lecture circuit, and at one point he was delivering his vision to two groups of Americans a week. He seemed in perpetual motion, visiting not only churches, schools, and civic groups, but also chapters of that ultimate repository of passionate patriotism, the John Birch Society. Wherever he went, he was well received. When, for example, he spoke at the University of Colorado, someone who tried to challenge his condemnation of Korean War soldiers was forced to sit down by the derisive laughter of most others, who chose to believe Mayer and not the Department of Defense.

There were some who could not attend his lectures, but that did not mean they would not hear his message. Around 600,000 copies of his discourse were made—500,000 of them printed, another 100,000 committed to sound tapes. He became an "authority" on the prisoners.

Whether it was truly authoritative or not, there were groups around the country who took Mayer's message very much to heart and who got into the spirit of spreading his word. For example, Harding College in Searcy, Arkansas, an institution dedicated to the study of scripture, developed a kit for those who might want to help Mayer disperse his message. For a mere $29.95, anyone could purchase the kit, which included Mayer's speech and exhibits, and deliver the speech in his absence. Such a message needed a visual approach, too, and a film was based on the essence of his speech. The actor selected to give the narration was Ronald Reagan.

Thus the Korean War became not only the first war that America failed to win decisively but also the first war in which the abuse of prisoners was "blamed on the prisoners themselves and not on the enemy."

Mayer's clarion signals were also spread at times by established writers who embraced uncritically what he had to say. His words had power and persuasiveness; his message was heard and listened to in all parts of the land. And the suspicions about returning POWs were so strong in some quarters that when they returned home, the Army began to keep dossiers (the Army called them "files") on 3,323 men whose loyalty to the Government the Army had questions about. Of these, 1,644 were still in uniform, and another 1,679 had been discharged as of the spring of 1954. The Army sent these files to FBI offices closest to where the returning veterans lived, "for the simple reason that all prisoners had been exposed to Communist propaganda.'' Asian communism carried all the contagion of Asian flu, it seemed.

Not just the Army sat in judgment; the rest of America did, too. Perhaps it could not have been otherwise, given the urgency of Mayer's communication and the credibility assigned to it. Educators, writers, politicians, civic leaders, various Government officials, and many who were active participants in American intellectual life were moved by Mayer's rhetoric and convinced that his passionate denunciations were on target. These people were not necessarily either bad or uncharitable. Mostly, they were like gulls who had flown off course, into an Army gunnery range.

Professor Anthony T. Bouscaren of Marquette University felt that there was a "glaring weak link in American education which is helping the Communist realms win World War III.'' And Dr. Max Rafferty, then a school superintendent in California whose far-right convictions were destined to shape and run the educational system in that state, lamented the decline of what he called a "vanishing species—the American patriot.'' In the patriot's place, Rafferty complained, were a generation of young people who were "booted, sideburned, ducktailed, unwashed, leather-jacketed slobs.'' Rafferty railed against "all the phony sophisticates who clutter up our colleges against ROTC and parade in support of Fidel Castro.''

Betty Friedan, the writer, saw in the prisoners models of a new kind of American male who had been made passive by his mother, and who was "apathetic, dependent, infantile, purposeless . . . shockingly non-human,'' which she found "strangely reminiscent'' of the familiar '' 'feminine' personality as defined by the mystique.'' Senator Strom Thurmond was of the opinion that if our young men had really understood communism, not so many of them would have "succumbed to communist brainwashing.'' He took uncritically unto himself some of the bulk of the fanciful material used by Mayer and asserted flat out that 38 percent of POWs collaborated in some way and not one was able to escape from an enemy camp.

J. Edgar Hoover, whose operatives were ever busy keeping track of veterans suspected of having been tainted by communism, found that he had something in common with Betty Friedan. He complained of the "softness'' of American young people, which was unacceptable to him in view of "communist subversion and defiance of the law.'' William Buckley's *National Review* struck a similar note when it asked, also in apparent acceptance of what Mayer had charged, "What are we going to do about those of our fellow citizens who persisted in a course of collaboration with the enemy who has sworn to bury us?''

Admiral Hyman Rickover thought about future generations of soldiers who might be subjected to communist brainwashing and sensed that we had to improve the quality of our men through our educational system. In his view, the communists found it "relatively easy . . . to confuse our men" because the men had not been properly schooled in the strengths of democracy and were thus no match for communist ideologues. Rickover, like Thurmond, also accepted Mayer's dim view of the troops and said that "almost one-third committed what is technically called an act of treason." Mayer's calculations were apparently the source for everybody else's. It remained unclear, however, why Thurmond would use a figure of 38 percent and Rickover would use "almost one-third."

Even Dr. Benjamin Spock, everybody's favorite commonsense pediatrician, asked, "Are American youth underdisciplined, overcoddled?" and took Mayer's pronouncements as gospel. But unlike most others, he refused to accept the totality of Mayer's indictment of American society and his own instincts as a humanist saved him from excess. "I suspect," Spock wrote, "that an extremely potent factor in the lowered morale in the Korean war was the natural letdown after World War II, in the American people's spirit of devotion to the common cause. . . ." Of those who accepted Mayer, Spock came closer than any of the others to suggesting that the troops did not have a very clear idea of what they were supposed to be doing in Korea.

The war according to Mayer even permeated that preparer of good citizens, the Boy Scouts. When the editors of *Scouting* magazine heard his theme, they said it was just one more good reason why scouting should be taught to all young Americans.

What was unusual was that liberals and conservatives both agreed that there was proof positive of a general moral breakdown evidenced by the alleged failure of the young POW soldiers to resist the communists. There was no debate; the charges about the POWs were taken as fact. Those writers and thinkers who otherwise lived by their ability to pierce sham and phony arguments—and who so frequently jousted with each other—seemed uncharacteristically accepting of what they had been told. They were willing to embrace the worst judgment about a supposedly helpless group of young people. The Korean War POW thus became a pure symbol; he passed from propaganda to historical myth in a matter of a few years. And in the years to come, nobody could rescue him from the place of dishonor to which he had been consigned by Mayer.

Only a few scholars even bothered to try. Only a few had the courage to poke at the pseudofacts that they believed were the basis of Mayer's judgments. Of these, Albert Biderman spoke out most forcefully. Biderman, educated at New York University and the University of Chicago, was a sociologist by training and a cautious man by instinct. He was surely in as strong a position as Mayer to evaluate the behavior of the American prisoners. He had been in the Army during World War II, where he was assigned to the Psychological Division of Allied Headquarters. He had also been involved in the repatriation of American prisoners of war after Korea. He found it difficult to square his own perceptions with those he heard attributed to Mayer. And now, as Mayer's words became widely accepted as truth, both in and out of Government, Biderman, a civilian employee of the Air Force, found himself wondering just how true they really were.

He looked again at the Air Force POWs and studied his way through their records. If any military or civilian authority had seen disloyalty in these men, it surely would have appeared in such records, which were the same kinds of records to which Mayer had access. But Biderman was unable to find the disloyalty, unable to substantiate even a small part of what had seemed so clear to Mayer. He made his initial findings known at a meeting of the American Sociological Society in 1957.

Such a meeting was appropriate enough for an unassuming academic whose forte was determining and evaluating facts, not necessarily spreading the word among the masses; it hardly provided him with the kind of forum already enjoyed by Mayer's propositions. Biderman then broadened his inquiry to prisoners who had not been in the Air Force; he sifted through the same records that had been available to Mayer. The result was one of the strangest intellectual conflicts in military history. For where Mayer found perfidy, Biderman found fidelity; where Mayer saw weakness, Biderman found strength; where the critics who had been so quick to accept Mayer found something new and disturbing about Americans, Biderman found much that was old and reassuring. The differences were not just stark, they were frightening. For why should there be any discrepancy at all in a situation that had already been sketched with such naked contempt? These were the nub of Biderman's findings:

• The Americans captured in Korea upheld the military and moral standards at least as well as others had done in previous wars. Critics of the soldiers of the Korean War failed to adequately assess the "extremes of deprivation by the soldiers."

• Mayer's assertion that Americans passively remained in captivity without trying to escape was inaccurate. There were many escapes from the temporary camps that the communists had established near the combat lines. Moreover, even when taken well away from combat deep into communist territory, Americans tried to escape, even though they knew that it would be impossible for most of them to blend into the Asian population as so many of their World War II counterparts had blended in with the Europeans.

• The suggestion that Americans died because of their own weakness or negligence was simply not true. The reports from imprisoned military physicians, who saw firsthand what was going on, said clearly that Americans died because of untended wounds, frostbite, dysentery, pneumonia, and other conditions totally beyond the control of those imprisoned. Those who lacked the spunk to survive were few and played no greater role than had similar young men in other wars.

• The generally accepted fact that twenty-one Americans chose not to return home was insignificant not only compared to desertion rates in other wars, but also tiny compared to the fact that 88,000 of the Chinese and North Korean prisoners refused to be repatriated—much more than half of all the communist troops who fell into American hands.

Others who bothered to look more closely at Mayer's original message joined in the refutation. "In the current mood of self-criticism which has swept our country," said a group of American intellectuals in a statement, "there has been an unfortunate tendency to seek evidence for moral failure in U.S. society. . . ." The group, which included Lucien Pye, political scientist at the Massachusetts Institute of Technology, condemned the "use of incomplete data" to present a distorted picture of the U.S. soldier and his country. But they were only eggheads in a country that did not trust eggheads. It was as though they had not spoken at all.

"It is ironic," Biderman wrote, "that the legend that painted the American soldier so ingloriously should have been spread so eagerly by military men." He developed a book out of his findings, *March to Calumny*, which was published by Macmillan in 1963. The book earned him a Ph.D. from the University of Chicago. Despite its positive reviews, its calm, incisive message lacked the drama of Mayer's original accusation and it was neither timely enough nor pungent enough to refinish the tarnished image of the Korean War soldier. Curiously, no groups with national clout clamored to hear Biderman's rebuttal; the John Birch Society did not publicly welcome the news that our soldiers were not traitors and weaklings after all; no fundamentalist Bible school committed itself to spreading this scholarly account of Korean-era soldiering.

And twenty-five years after it was over, Biderman, by then a research professor at American University, would still not understand why the nation had turned on its own soldiers as it did. "There were terrible unspoken truths; there were grave injustices done to people," he would say. But why, he would be asked, were Americans so ready to accept the assertion that their country had gone to hell?

Part of it, he would reply, was Mayer's abilities as "a natural-born showman" who was superb at "artful manipulation"; part of it was Mayer's ability to "play with themes that had independent strength in the media. . . . The press and the people are consistently ready to believe what is not so in the face of repeated contrary evidence." Biderman would hasten to add that he never felt Mayer was disingenuous in what he preached; only that Mayer was dead wrong.

But the Army was convinced of the rightness of Mayer's message even before he delivered it, and many Americans came to agree with him after they heard it. If the communists were growing stronger and Americans weaker, perhaps stern measures could be justified in the Army, steps that might truly test the character and resolve of the soldier and his ability to withstand new technologies for mind-bending that might be introduced in the future. The Chinese had used starvation, water torture, and neglect; perhaps tomorrow's enemies would use drugs, the Army thought.

The military solution to this nonexistent problem in the 1950s was to secretly give powerful hallucinogens such as LSD to soldiers without telling them and getting their permission in advance. Many of those who were given LSD had horrible reactions to it and complained, after discharge from the Army, that their lives had been ruined by it.

For example, James Stanley, a black who had been a young master sergeant in 1958 and who was given LSD without his knowledge, immediately experienced strong hallucinations and a loss of memory. His personality changed; he began to assault his family. Under the power of his fists, his marriage fell apart. Few juries would have denied benefits in cases like Stanley's. But no jury could hear the case to its conclusion because the Supreme Court ruled almost thirty years after Stanley was given the drug that soldiers had no Constitutional right to sue their own Government for damages caused by such an episode. The Court agreed with the Government's recommendation that Stanley apply to the Veterans Administration for benefits, however unpromising it might seem.

Justices Sandra Day O'Connor and William Brennan dissented from the majority opinion. Justice O'Connor wrote that the conduct of the military in the Stanley case "was so far beyond the bounds of human decency that as a matter of law it simply cannot be considered a part of the military mission." To Justice Brennan, Stanley and thousands like him had been treated "as though they were laboratory animals."

The LSD test was not the only one to which soldiers would be put after Korea and for which they would suffer as veterans. Many thousands of men were exposed to radiation from nuclear tests conducted by the United States. Their number was enormous: The Government admitted that between 1945 and 1963, some 250,000 soldiers were ordered to witness the tests at fairly close range, but were not told by their superiors of the nature of the risks. All they were told was to cover their eyes. They did, and those who were facing the blast could, at the instant of detonation, see the bones of their forearms through their eyelids and the flesh of their hands.

No protective clothing was issued to the men who came to be known as "atomic soldiers," although the Government apparently had the wisdom to issue such clothing to the civilians who worked for Government agencies, who also witnessed the blasts. No reputable scientist ever suggested that massive doses of radiation were good for anyone, and, indeed, the Army did not say it was testing to determine the effects of radiation on humans. That would have been damnably silly, given what had happened to those near the explosions at Hiroshima and Nagasaki. The Army said instead that it wanted to determine what a nuclear blast would do to them psychologically.

"The psychological implications of atomic weapons used close to our own front lines are unknown," said Colonel H. McK. Roper, whose decision it was to send soldiers to the vulnerable positions they occupied on the Nevada desert when the bombs were detonated. The Army employed press agentry to clarify its motives and asked a series of questions in a 1957 handout designed to give press and public an enhanced view of what it called a "pioneer mission":

> Can a highly trained soldier think clearly and perform the duties of his fighting mission efficiently in the shadow of a nuclear bomb's mushroom cloud?
>
> Two minutes after a blast with an explosive force of over 20,000 tons of TNT, will his hands tremble as he kneels to field-strip and reassemble his rifle?
>
> Will he obey promptly the orders of his commanding officer, or will he falter as a choking dust cloud whirls around him?
>
> Will he move quickly to clear a mine field, or will he "gawk" at the eerie "snow cap" above his head?

The release proudly added, "For the first time since man has learned to split the atom, the United States Army is prepared to find the answers to these and other unknowns concerning human health behavior in nuclear warfare." The Army's use of language, emphasizing such images as trembling hands, faltering enlisted men, and gawking greenhorns, was indisputably the result of its mindset after Korea—a mindset based on its own hyperbole. The question the Army did not ask and clearly was not prepared to answer was what it would do for the soldiers who were exposed to radiation and then developed cancer. For years, the Government would simply deny claims made by veterans who said they got cancer because of radiation exposure, unless they could somehow prove that their cancer came from military service and not some other source. Not until May of 1988—more than three decades later—would the President sign legislation designed to make it easier for some of the veterans suffering from certain kinds of cancer. However, victims of other kinds of cancer among veterans who were exposed to radiation during World War II and after would remain unaided by the 1988 law.

Mayer, who gained considerable fame after beginning his odyssey through the ugly twilight of the Korean War, went on to bigger and better assignments. In the early 1960s, Senator John Stennis of Mississippi and Senator Strom Thurmond of South Carolina, both conservative Democrats, said they wanted to look into reports that President John F. Kennedy's Administration was "muzzling" members of the military who were outspoken critics of communism. An investigating committee took the project on, and Mayer was the star witness.

Although his testimony was given after Biderman had publicly raised serious and substantive questions about the negative things that had been said about Korean War soldiers, Mayer did not even acknowledge the existence of any of them. He spoke of the "apparent ease with which Americans were managed and controlled, the naiveté with which they responded to communist overtures, the fantastic number of deaths among U.S. prisoners in Korea, and the other problems that were so dramatically evident among the men that came back to us." He did not flinch from saying, once again, that the nation that had spawned such soldiers suffered from a "character damage which can be the seed of our own destruction."

Mayer also said that an original report he wrote right after the war had been suppressed by his superiors in Government—he didn't say which ones—because "the American public was not ready." It remained unclear, then, who had given him the permission he needed to make all his later allegations and under what circumstances the go-ahead was given.

Biderman's thesis was ignored by the Stennis-Thurmond committee, but some enlightenment was shown by another witness, retired General Samuel Lyman Atwood Marshall. The general, who had served in World War II and Korea, appeared with credentials that were unimpeachable; like Mayer and some of the suspect veterans, he was also a holder of the Bronze Star, among other awards for valor. Marshall enjoyed an enhanced sense of history and had, in fact, been a combat historian in the Pacific during World War II. He had written a number of books, including *Pork Chop Hill*. Sophisticated in the use of words, he made it clear that he was not about to be misled by flimsy propaganda, no matter who presented it or how artfully it might be served. He delivered his testimony without direct reference to Mayer or to any of the writers who embraced Mayer's indictment:

> A great nation may not be told "You are weak. Your young people were proved unfit for war. There is no hope for you but to start anew," without blighting its own power while renouncing pretension to greatness. Yet words of this kind have been spoken and reiterated ever since the Korean conflict. . . . This is a perversion of history, and I deny emphatically that the record has any such sinister significance.
>
> Certainly many were derelict without excuse, craven with reason. But it is less tolerable and a crime against ourselves that, because a relatively few under trial were found grievously wanting, all who suffered with them should be slandered, the great Army for which they fought should be besmirched and we should be asked to look askance at a whole generation of young Americans.

And yet, the generation *was* besmirched. For three and a half decades after the end of the Korean War, Washington remained without any monument to honor the memory of those who served in Korea. The men who fought that war bitterly complained among themselves and called themselves forgotten soldiers. Nobody listened to them. Not until America began to realize the magnitude of the mistakes it had made in Vietnam would it be able to put Korea in perspective.

If harsh and unjust criticism of the Korean War soldiers was called into question, the critics who issued it were not. They did very well indeed. When Mayer's collaborator-in-film ascended to the Presidency of the United States, Mayer would be summoned to Washington. There he would use his estimable talents to become Assistant Secretary of Defense for Health Affairs.

The people who were very young in the decade of the 1950s, the ones who Mayer had warned would be too soft to turn back the communist menace, would now become his responsibility, of sorts. For these were the very same people who were asked to fight in Vietnam. In Southeast Asia, America would give itself yet another chance to scapegoat good young men and women who had nothing to do with either the design of the war or its outcome.

EIGHT
The Vietnam War and the Agent Orange Affair

"WE HAVE NO EVIDENCE OF ILL EFFECTS—
WE HAVE NO EVIDENCE OF ILL EFFECTS—
THIS IS A RECORDING——"

23
The Red Carpet
Leads to Rejection

How can the Administration just look on the bright
side of things?
—Bobby Muller, founder, Vietnam Veterans of
America, 1978

Vietnam was a war as odd as it was brutal. To fight it, the United States had
assigned not mature men from all walks of life with a clear sense of purpose,
but teenagers from the have-little classes who were as much confused by the
conflict as they were motivated by a desire to serve their country. Their
average age was just over nineteen, at least seven years younger than their
celebrated counterparts of World War II and younger even than those who
had fought in Korea. They volunteered and were conscripted to serve their
country just as their forebears had been, but their confusion at what then
happened to them was understandable. These American youths had not been
dispatched to Vietnam to crush a despised Hitlerian tyrant or even a
wayward autocrat of King George's stripe, possessed of more power than
acuity. Instead, the United States had gone after Ho Chi Minh, an aged
socialist who had been our staunch ally during World War II, a charismatic
leader who had stubbornly resisted not only the Japanese imperialists but the
French colonialists and the Chinese communists, too, clinging to his dream
that Vietnam should be run by the Vietnamese. It was a dream not so
different from that of Emilio Aguinaldo, who had led his people in revolt
against the United States at the turn of the century in the nasty little war
known as the Philippine Insurrection. From his World War II days, Ho had
come rather to admire the Americans. But the leaders of the United States
never reciprocated; they were as unknowing about his culture, communism,

and ferocious nationalism as they were uncaring about his sensibilities and determination. "The Americans are much stronger than the French," a disappointed Ho observed in 1962, "though they know us less well."

The confusion of the American soldier sent to Vietnam grew only worse if he thought about his enemy's size and power. The United States had pitted itself not against an organized national madness comparable to Nazi Germany nor even against a force comparable to Kaiser Wilhelm's eager and able minions of World War I. At first, North Vietnam hardly seemed an enemy worthy of the most formidable military power on earth. It possessed only one-tenth of America's population, one-sixtieth of its landmass, one twenty-fifth of its railroads, and one thirty-fourth of its gross national product. During the course of the war, the United States punished this Lilliputian adversary by dumping 6.8 million tons of bombs on it, fully three and a half times the tonnage it had used to demolish the dreaded Nazis. To this it had added at least twelve million gallons of Agent Orange, the Pentagon's catchword for a powerful chemical defoliant sprayed in Vietnam to deprive an elusive enemy of both his hiding places and his crops.

Aside from the loss of life, nobody was quite sure what Vietnam had cost the Americans. There were estimates that the war had required anywhere from $140 billion (a conservative Pentagon estimate) to $676 billion, the estimate of a doctoral candidate who wrote a piece for *The Progressive*. These figures did not include the $233 billion that the Government estimated it would have to pay to its own veterans in benefits, a figure that was developed well before the suspected health effects of Agent Orange became a known problem. From 1964 to 1972, the formal period of America's warmaking in Vietnam, there was, apparently, little concern with either the human or financial costs. "There are many . . . prices we pay for the war in South Vietnam . . . but in my opinion one of them is not strain on our economy," Defense Secretary Robert McNamara confidently told Senate committees in January of 1967. Secretary McNamara's depreciated appraisal of the cost of the war in Southeast Asia was consistent with President Lyndon Johnson's apparent desire that the American public not be concerned about such trifles. The civilian economy was booming; Americans were satisfying their senses with imported wine, imported cars, imported anything. The needs of their social consciences were filled by the President's vision for a Great Society, in which poverty and ignorance would be displaced by plenty and enlightenment. Mr. Johnson and his advisers agreed that there was no reason to dampen the ardor of the 1960s with special taxes or depressing talk about wage and price controls or other painful disincentives to the inflation that had begun. And so, it was business as usual.

At first, the Vietnam War appeared in American living rooms as flickering inserts into nightly television news programs, provoking little more interest than a rerun of an old John Wayne movie. Each day, aluminum cans of 16-millimeter film, sealed with masking tape, would be shipped by correspondents in Southeast Asia to network offices in New York, where the associate producers of news shows ordered their film editors to take cuts of a minute or two from them. In dark, windowless, aggressively air-conditioned rooms, writers watched thousands of feet of such silent film, timed it on network-issued stopwatches, and quickly wrote brief introductions to the correspondent on the scene or little scripts that covered visual material not contained in the correspondent's narrative. Executive producers, always worried whether they could fill up newly created half-hour network slots with something that was visually exciting, began to count on such fare.

For network news, the Vietnam War became a convenience, the sort of TV staple that tenement fires already were for local news. There were interminable fires, violent explosions, weary young men bearing arms in the jungle, smoke billowing skyward, huts made of mud and straw, forbearing, hollow-eyed civilians staring into the camera, imploring a nation in their fragility and agony. It was something to look at, and all of it was easily banished with a turn of the channel selector. The networks aired it all dutifully and, for the most part, without ever questioning the war itself. Writers and producers saw so much of it that they succumbed to processing the footage, rather than trying to understand it. Thus, in the middle 1960s, as TV news came into its own and the power of newspapers declined, the Vietnam War was conducted largely without disclosure or explanation from the medium of choice. Part of the reason was that television was not yet confident enough to put a war in perspective, even though its own Edward R. Murrow had done that well and memorably, two wars earlier. Most of it was the ultimate expression of American journalism's shallowness, its predisposition, despite its much-trumpeted muckraking, to content itself with reporting what Government officials said they were doing.

It did not matter whether the journalists were broadcasters or creatures of print. Practitioners in the print media, nervously assuring themselves that there would always be serious readers, were no better in telling readers what was really going on or in questioning policies that had been adopted. The Pentagon Papers, which detailed the expense and bad judgment that accompanied America's involvement in Vietnam, after all, came to light only after the damage was done and in spite of Government efforts to suppress publication. The enormity of the tragedy was muted and trivialized, and it seemed remote to the numbed people back home who were enjoying life. At least, it did until later in the decade when students, confronting their own mortality, began actively and openly to protest the war. For too long a time, Americans, especially those who were not of draft age or who had deferments, did not seem to comprehend or care that this nation was in the process of losing more than 58,000 of its best young men to mortal combat or to the accidents that are combat's backwater, aspects of a war that had no clear purpose. Another 270,000 would be wounded. If war contained great truths, they had not been revealed to the soldiers who fought in Vietnam, and before it would end, around half a million of them would receive less than honorable discharges. About 15,000 women served in Vietnam, too, in civilian and military capacities. Nine of them were killed and some five hundred also received the stigmatizing discharges that were less than honorable. As for South Vietnam, it lost 183,000 soldiers and more than 400,000 civilians. If the North and South are taken as a whole, the country lost an estimated 1.3 million civilians and 400,000 troops. There were another three million wounded. It would be impossible to assign a realistic cash value to the utter devastation inflicted by the United States on Vietnam and its people.

A war that contained so much bad judgment in its conception, initiation, and financing was bound to go wrong in its execution. If the United States was unable to understand the motives of Ho Chi Minh, its soldiers could be expected to have some of the same problems, for some of the same reasons, with the Vietnamese people. And so, as did their forebears during the Philippine Insurrection, the Americans found that they could not tell friend from foe; there was no front and the enemy seemed to be everywhere. Many soldiers felt this, but none more acutely than William Laws Calley.

If Calley wasn't exactly the boy next door, he came a lot closer to it than the blacks, Mexican-Americans, and Puerto Ricans whose presence seemed to dominate so many rifle companies. Calley was white, born in 1943, the son of a Navy man who went on to become a rather successful purveyor of tractors and bulldozers. He grew up in Miami, Florida, and, in typical old-fashioned American style, liked girls, jokes, short haircuts, stylish clothes, horsing around, hanging out, drinking beer with his buddies, and the sports car races at Sebring. He had even owned a 1959 cream-colored Chevy with a blue stripe and, as a youngster, had been able to vacation at a country cottage his family kept in North Carolina. His friends were "clean-cut" and "fairly popular" and found him "always ready to laugh . . . he'd come up with things . . . to make people laugh." Calley was also typical of a certain kind of American student. He compiled an average record in high school but dropped out of Palm Beach Junior College after posting an academic record of two Cs, one D, and four Fs. He even engaged in that traditional American pastime of working on the railroad, briefly becoming a nonunion worker for the strikebound Florida East Coast Railway. Whatever Calley was, he wasn't crazy, and the Army, if not the railroad, thought he had potential.

Early on the morning of March 16, 1968, William Calley, by then twenty-five years old and happy to be a first lieutenant in the U.S. Army, found himself as the leader of a platoon of Charlie Company in a hamlet called My Lai 4, part of the Son My village in Quang Ngai Province, on the northeastern coast of South Vietnam. The soldiers, part of the Americal Division, had been led to believe they would meet the formidable 48th Vietcong Battalion there. They attacked My Lai with vigor, but found no enemy troops—only civilians. The civilians may well have thought more of Ho Chi Minh than of Lyndon Baines Johnson, but they had no guns or weapons of any kind and they did nothing to provoke the Americans. Nevertheless, for the next few hours the men of Charlie Company succumbed to their confusion and frustration and the rage that happens in war, sometimes, when men have no true sense of purpose. The soldiers under Calley and other officers killed 347 of those civilians: children, including toddlers; their mothers; and men and women far too old to fight or to hurt anyone. Huge holes were blown into bodies of the Vietnamese, limbs were cut off or shot off, heads were exploded. At one point, civilians were herded into a ditch and murdered by the Americans under Calley. Some of the younger women were raped or gang-raped before they were murdered. One rapist shoved the muzzle of his M-16 rifle into the vagina of his victim and pulled the trigger. Calley's 1st Platoon alone was responsible for roughly a third of the casualties. After the Americans finished their killing, they burned My Lai to the ground, destroyed its livestock and foodstuffs, then deliberately ruined its drinking-water supply.

Certain aspects of the incident at My Lai were witnessed not just by the soldiers who were there, but by Major-General Samuel W. Koster, Colonel Oran K. Henderson, and other high-ranking officers, who viewed the scene from their helicopters. At that point, General Koster, who had had a distinguished career in the military, was close to becoming superintendent of the United States Military Academy at West Point, from which he had been graduated in 1942. He was thus a commander who presumably possessed an enhanced sense of what is appropriate in time of war, and what is regarded as savagely uncivilized behavior. Even if General Koster had flown too high to see the bodies of the dead civilians, he would have had a difficult time not seeing Vietnamese homes on fire. Such arson contravened the policy of his own division. Whatever he saw, he did not move to intervene, nor did any of his fellow officers. Despite widespread knowledge of the tragedy among quite a number of high-ranking officers, the public had no inkling of what had happened. Those who participated in the massacre did not reveal what they really did. Senior officers who knew of it remained silent. The Army issued false and misleading press releases about the incident. The result was that what happened at My Lai as well as at other hamlets in Vietnam (killings of civilians also occurred elsewhere) did not start to come to public attention for more than a year and a half.

A formal inquiry was conducted under the leadership of Lieutenant General William R. Peers; its business was not formally completed until September 2, 1972. In the interim, all the soldiers who fought in Vietnam became the objects of scorn. They were despised on the college campuses they turned to after their discharges; they were shunned by veterans of World War II, who saw them as losers. As had happened in other times and other places, one soldier was selected to bear the weight of belated national disgust, and it was Calley. He became the butcher of a butchering war, the personification of a generation of young men curiously adjudged both barbaric and weak by the society that had so thoughtlessly sent them into battle. The definition of William Calley became the definition of every soldier.

What America quickly forgot or failed to acknowledge in the first place was that the sins of Calley and the others at My Lai were exposed not by righteous civilians in Government nor even by senior officers motivated by the lofty ideals and traditions articulated in the service academies. My Lai, or "Pinkville" as the soldiers called it, was dragged into the public spotlight by Ronald L. Ridenhour, a mere specialist fourth class who had served as a door gunner on an observation helicopter. Like the enlisted men who had defied peer pressure and revealed wrongdoing in the Philippines in the early 1900s, Ridenhour did not flinch from his responsibility as he saw it. He was nowhere near My Lai when the massacre occurred, but in the weeks that followed, he heard about it from other enlisted men.

"The guys I talked to didn't want to believe that they had taken part in this thing," Ridenhour would later tell a reporter. "I really don't know why it didn't bother them more. But that's something that everybody should be asking at this point." Hardly anybody was asking the question at that point, such was the effect of Vietnam on the American conscience. For if one asked questions, one would be inexorably led to the conclusion that the war had been a terrible mistake, and that the leaders Americans had trusted to be competent and well informed were neither. If Ridenhour shared in the national confusion caused by the war, as he had every right to, he nevertheless retained his grasp of the ideals that most Americans believed were part of their ethos. He began to ask his friends "how to handle this thing." Most advised him not to handle it at all and to forget he had ever heard about Pinkville. But he could not and would not forget.

It was in March of 1969 that he began writing lengthy, detailed letters—to President Richard M. Nixon, Defense Secretary Melvin Laird, Senators Edward M. Kennedy and George S. McGovern, and "at least 20 other members of Congress." His letter said, in part:

> Exactly what did, in fact, occur in the village of "Pinkville" in March, 1968 I do not know for *certain,* but I am convinced it was something very black indeed. I remain irrevocably persuaded that if you and I do truly believe in the principles of justice and the equality of every man, however humble, before the law, that form the very backbone this country is founded on, then we must press forward a widespread and public investigation of this matter with all our combined efforts. I think it was Winston Churchill who once said "A country without a conscience is a country without a soul, and a country without a soul is a country that cannot survive." . . . I have considered sending this to newspapers, magazines, and broadcasting companies, but I somehow feel that investigation and action by the Congress of the United States is the appropriate procedure, and as a conscientious citizen I have no desire to further besmirch the image of the American serviceman in the eyes of the world.

Ridenhour's efforts were reinforced independently by a Washington-based reporter, Seymour Hersh. If the insistent Ridenhour was the opposite of Calley, then Hersh was the antithesis of the passive journalists who had reported the war by rewriting Government press releases. Hersh knew that it never had been adequate merely to report what the Government said it was doing, either in Vietnam or anyplace else. His widely published stories about My Lai shocked and shamed a nation.

Calley was court-martialed, charged with the murder of 109 men, women, and children. At least twenty-four other Army personnel were also charged with a variety of offenses and crimes. General Koster, Brigadier General George H. Young, and Colonel Henderson were charged with misconduct or similar offenses; Calley, Captains Eugene M. Kotouc and Ernest L. Medina, and First Lieutenant Thomas K. Willingham were among thirteen men charged with major crimes against humanity as defined by the law of war. Charges were dismissed against all but Calley, although Koster was reduced to brigadier general and relieved of his Distinguished Service

Medal. He quit the Army soon thereafter. Young, who was censured and also relieved of his Distinguished Service Medal, left the Army, too. Henderson left the Army as well, but retained his interest in command when he became director of civil defense in Pennsylvania.

Calley was thus perceived as a scapegoat by many, and when he was sentenced to life imprisonment, after his conviction for murdering twenty-two civilians, there were demands from some interests for a reduction in sentence. And so it was reduced, from life to twenty years, then to ten years, then to parole after serving only three years under house arrest at Fort Benning, Georgia. Some Americans felt the reduction was justified, for it was widely known that Calley was not the only soldier to behave barbarically; others were of the same persuasion and nothing happened to them. After his release, Calley became a jewelry salesman in a store in Columbus, Georgia. Americans apparently would hold no ill feelings about him; the store's customers would soon tell visiting newsmen that Calley was the most popular salesman there.

The delay in finding out about My Lai and the public perception of the dismissal of charges against those who were involved might have presaged a frosty welcome for the first American prisoners to be released from North Vietnamese prisons. But that was decidedly not the case. The Vietnam homecoming did not begin as it would end. In 1973, when the first two American prisoners of war were released, they returned not to the recrimination and ill will they would come to know a few years later, but literally to a red carpet, spread for them upon the runway at Honolulu. If the military leadership was upset over the lack of victory or embarrassed over the tragedy of Calley and his kind, there was no hint of disappointment in the official embrace of the two pilots, who were treated not only to beer, banana splits, and a movie, but also to a shopping trip to the PX and the offer of the use of a Ford car at no cost for the next year. The wholesome, thoroughly American nature of the welcome had something of 1945 about it. The Defense Department organized what it called "Operation Homecoming" much better than it had the conduct of the late war, and Captain Brian Woods, one of the two freed pilots, was so impressed with all the hoopla that he said, "I'm feeling on top of the world."

Other Vietnam veterans, who had been given something less than the red carpet treatment, watched all of this with more than a little wonderment. As many as 100,000 of them were addicted to opiates or alcohol, of whom at least 80,000 were receiving no treatment at all. It was not the first time that American soldiers had problems with drug addiction. It had happened in the years after the Civil War, when morphine was poured into the wounds of men in great pain. Now more than one drug was being used to dull the senses of young men who were afflicted with a different kind of pain, and it was put in their bodies not by doctors, but by the soldiers themselves. They would be criticized for their drug use by the society that had sent them to war, and they would be accused by some of spreading drug addiction when they returned home. In truth, the nation's susceptibility to mind-altering substances was well established long before Vietnam became a burden to its conscience and its pride.

Drugs were frequently mentioned as a reason for the high unemployment among the veterans of Vietnam. But the truth was that jobs were hard to get even for veterans who had no drug problem, veterans unwelcomed by a people who did not want to be reminded of the war. Perhaps 250,000 Vietnam veterans between the ages of twenty and twenty-nine were unable to find work. Newspaper and magazine articles were beginning to take note of their anguish, distance, and seeming disaffection, although science had not yet named the condition. The nomenclature of PTSD, post-traumatic stress disorder, was yet to be devised by scientists who would soon reach the conclusion that somehow such homely phrases as "shell shock" and "combat fatigue," which had been used in World War I and World War II to describe the effect of the totality of war on the minds of men, were no longer appropriate. After all, not all the disaffected veterans had been shocked by shells or worn out by combat. The creation of a more appropriate lexicon was clearly in order.

New wages were also in order, lower wages that reflected Government's belated acknowledgment that it had conducted a costly war without benefit of special taxes to pay for it. The result of that awakening was that more stringent fiscal management was ordered for the soldiers who had survived the free-spending combat that took place during the Johnson and Nixon Administrations. When the fathers and uncles of Vietnam veterans came home from World War II, the G.I. Bill had paid all tuition and given veterans $75 a month, in a time when $75 a month could pay the rent and then some. Now, in a period of considerable inflation, the veterans were to get $200, which was to pay for higher tuition *and* the cost of staying alive. Some of the veterans thought that was not a very fair arrangement. The Defense Department's red carpet had been rolled up and stored away.

Richard M. Nixon was not in a particularly charitable mood in 1973 and '74, and that was understandable. His administration and his very political future were engulfed by the Watergate scandal; his acting FBI director had made an unconvincing effort to explain to Congress how and why FBI Watergate files had turned up in the White House; and the press was trying to determine what Nixon's relationship was to Robert Vesco, an elusive and mysterious international finagler and Nixon benefactor who seemed to feel that life on a Caribbean island was preferable to returning to Washington to answer all those unfelicitous questions. Nixon, seemingly anxious to demonstrate his fiscal virtue, now that his political frailty had been exposed, vetoed a VA health care bill that would have given the agency more doctors. He favored a cut in vocational rehabilitation funds for veterans and now impounded extra money that Congress, in a flash of conscience, had wanted to add to the veterans' educational stipend. Yet, Nixon insisted that "in every area of Government concern we are now doing more than we have ever done" to help veterans.

Perhaps the President, with all of his personal problems, could not have noticed the difficulty the veterans were in. But it was noticed by other public officials of lesser rank. In New York City, for example, Eleanor Holmes Norton, who ran the Human Rights Commission, found that four thousand Vietnam-era veterans were on relief and that they received "seriously inadequate" care by other agencies of Government. Like the Vietnam veterans themselves, Mrs. Norton said she was unable to square the Defense Department's welcome for the first prisoners of war—most of them "high-ranking, well-educated white officers"—with what was happening to the "far more numerous, low-ranking foot soldiers who are disproportion-ately poor, black or brown, and as ill-educated when they returned from the service as when they went in."

The straits of blacks were, indeed, desperate. There had been well-publicized racial tensions in the military, and there were strong suggestions that some commanders invariably placed the burden of guilt on blacks, rather than look upon racism as a problem that had to be resolved among all racial and ethnic groups. The Navy discharged thousands of men it regarded as "misfits and malcontents"—many of them black—with the result that some blacks who had served in Vietnam and wanted to reenlist found themselves out of the service. To make matters worse, their exit certificates—frequently general discharges under honorable conditions—carried code numbers which were interpreted by civilian employers to mean that the black sailors in question were unsuitable for work. It only exacerbated chronic unemployment problems among young blacks.

Mrs. Norton held hearings on the special unemployment problems of Vietnam veterans, black and white alike, and was told by Tim Vacaire, one of the veteran witnesses, "We don't want a handout. We just want a chance." The proceedings may have been well-intentioned, but veterans were already tired of such things. Fourteen disrupted Mrs. Norton's hearings by burning their discharge certificates. "We have no use for them," one angry veteran explained.

Efforts were made, after a fashion, to recapture the scene that had appeared so warming in Honolulu. In New York, there was a parade for veterans one Saturday afternoon arranged by the "Home with Honor Committee." It was, quite possibly, not the best time to have a parade in Lower Manhattan, at least not if the motive was to permit office workers to shower the soldiers with attention and confetti. The financial institutions were mostly closed. There was very little confetti, and the crowd of 100,000 along Broadway was hardly noticeable. In most other cities there were no parades at all.

A year after the veterans returned home, two of them summed up what they thought the peace meant: "Peace for the ordinary serviceman who has not dined at the White House has involved waiting in an unemployment line; a runaround from public agencies while trying to get a job; getting into and paying for school; and avoiding the war news in the newspapers." They had other things to avoid, too, mostly the baleful stares of their fellow citizens.

The Agent Orange issue had not yet surfaced, but already the veterans found that they were less than happy with the VA, including the man Nixon had named to run it, Donald Johnson, who had been national commander of the American Legion. The confrontation politics that had been used by war protesters in the 1960s were now the province of veterans who wanted the world to know their feelings. More than a dozen protesting veterans occupied a VA office in Los Angeles and demanded to talk to Johnson directly. He complied, but attended the meeting in the company of two armed guards, even though most of the protesters were paraplegics who could not have gotten out of their wheelchairs, however angry they might have been. The guards seemed a bit unnecessary; Johnson was, after all, six foot five and had been a sergeant who commanded respect, even among the able-bodied.

What was wrong with the VA? Congressman Olin Teague, a Democrat from Texas, accused the President of using it as a "dumping ground" to provide jobs for the people who had worked for CREEP, the Committee to Re-Elect the President. And Senator Alan Cranston claimed that Johnson gave jobs to his neighbors and that VA workers had been under some pressure to purchase raffle tickets for $100 each to win a "free" seat at a $1,000-a-plate dinner designed to raise money to finance Nixon's reelection campaign. If true, it would have violated the Federal law prohibiting the solicitation of campaign funds from Federal workers. The charges were not pursued; Johnson resigned, thereby making an investigation unnecessary.

It wasn't just the VA. For the veterans of Vietnam, it was the whole country. In a survey conducted by Daniel Yankelovich, 37 percent of the Vietnam veterans in school who were questioned said they would rather live in a country other than the United States. The confrontations continued, and as they unfolded, the divisions between American society and its ex-soldiers as exemplified in the Bonus March of 1932 seemed not so remote. Police in Washington clubbed a dozen Vietnam veterans on Independence Day when they attempted to cross a police line to picket the Capitol. Four others decided to occupy and hold the elevator at the Washington Monument. There was trouble at the White House, too: Five veterans determined to talk directly to Nixon barricaded themselves in a men's room there, quite possibly in the belief that this might be an appropriate setting for such a meeting. They spent two hours so confined, but got to talk only to one of Nixon's aides. Nixon, now facing the possibility of impeachment, had pressing business elsewhere.

As the Nixon era expired, a replacement was found for Johnson at the VA, after an exhaustive search turned up qualified people who wanted no part of it. The man who finally agreed to be Johnson's successor, Richard Roudebush, got no respect from the veterans. A few weeks after he took office, two men and a woman went to his office in downtown Washington and nailed his door shut, forcing him to discuss his proposed cutbacks in educational benefits. The talk ended and the three were promptly arrested. "They gave me the hammer as a souvenir," Roudebush said.

Gerald Ford replaced Nixon, and generosity marked his tenure—he was especially generous to Nixon, whose sins he neatly and promptly pardoned. He was less than generous to the veterans, however, and vetoed a proposed increase of 20 percent in their educational benefits, in order to promote "budgetary restraint." Congress overrode his veto.

The condition of Vietnam veterans was quite wretched by the time Jimmy Carter replaced Ford, but his Veterans Administrator, Max Cleland, challenged reporters to give him six months on the job. The challenge did not redound to Cleland's credit. If the Republicans had been transparently indifferent to the plight of the returned soldiers, the Democrats, it seemed to veterans, were better only in their piety, not their performance. For those veterans who thought their problems had been caused by the indifference of Republicans, the failure of the Carter Administration to do any better became almost too much to bear.

"I remember joining the Marines and standing in my dress whites and hearing the Star-Spangled Banner and crying like a baby," said Bobby Muller, a critic of the lack of Government action who was founder of the

Vietnam Veterans of America. "Nineteen sixty-seven. I cried out of pride."
But eleven years later, Muller could only condemn the "empty promises"
of the Carter Administration. Muller, who returned from the war paralyzed
from the waist down, had seen the VA in action in years of rehabilitation.

Max Cleland was also seriously disabled from his war wounds, but this
gave him no special credibility with Muller, who found Cleland's support of
Carter's performance insupportable. In what appeared to Muller to be an
effort to be positive, Cleland had noted that 80 percent of the veterans had
already adjusted, leaving only a "hard core" of 20 percent who seemed
unable to adjust. *Only 20 percent.*

"How can the Administration just look on the bright side of things?"
Muller asked.

24
When Not to Know
Means Not to Pay

"Oliver Twist has asked for more!"
—Bumble in Charles Dickens' *Oliver Twist*

After two hundred years of what it regarded as service to its warriors, the Government of the United States apparently found itself in the late 1970s with the nagging feeling that perhaps it had been too openhanded. In the years following the Vietnam War, the VA's budget had swelled, with its 240,000 employees determining how to allocate $15 billion to veterans and their dependents and how to run the largest health care system in the nation, which included 172 hospitals, 117 nursing homes, and 230 outpatient clinics. The VA's total budget of $27 billion also included what it cost to maintain 111 national cemeteries. And so, as the problems of the unlamented war rankled, some officeholders in the Veterans Administration came to feel that they had to teach themselves not to treat former soldiers with quite so much magnanimity.

J. C. Peckarsky was one such mainstay of Government. He had joined the VA in 1946 and by the late 1970s had risen through the interminable ranks of beadledom to become director of the agency's Compensation and Pension Service, the subdivision that asked the ultimate question: To pay or not to pay? "Part of my job," he told a reporter early in 1979, his voice etched with regret, "is to say no."

By that time, the 28th of March, 1979, hundreds of veterans of Vietnam had inquired, complained, and even filed papers describing strange and ugly things that they said were wrong with them. Peckarsky's desktop contained hillocks of their missives. They complained of cancer and deformed children or children born dead. They complained of miscarriages, loss of sex drive, and low sperm counts. They complained of strange aches and weaknesses all over the body, weird lumps in their flesh that would appear, festering sores that would not heal, ugly things that doctors would tell them were precancerous, but with no explanation of where they came from.

The veterans said they were sick, even to the point of being disabled, all because of their asserted exposure to a mysterious chemical cocktail—a cocktail they claimed to have ingested or absorbed without knowing it, a decade or so before. It was called Agent Orange. It was only supposed to have defoliated jungles and croplands to deny cover and food to the communists. But now, six years after U.S. troops had been ordered home from Vietnam, the veterans were beginning to think it had dealt them as much a mortal blow as it had the vegetation.

Peckarsky, an engaging man with an easy smile whose friends all called him Charlie, checked his files to see what, if anything, there was to all the talk about Agent Orange, or whatever the veterans called it. In his view, the veterans filing claims had either been misled about Agent Orange or were deliberately lying about it in order to get something for nothing.

"Absolutely nobody had an Agent Orange disability," Peckarsky declared, peering into a bunch of files and delivering his considered judgment on what it all meant. He wasn't entirely sure how many Agent Orange claims had been filed around the country—it took time for all of them to work their way through the VA's intake system, and there were probably thousands of them—but he did know how many had reached him for final review as of that day: 434.

Of all these, only one man claimed to have suffered from chloracne—a special kind of skin rash associated with exposure to chlorinated compounds. It was unclear whether the rash signaled anything else. Nor was it by any means certain that chloracne was the invariable harbinger of serious illness. But the Veterans Administration was of the feeling that anyone who claimed to have been doused with Agent Orange, or exposed to it through drifting wind or water, should not be permitted to pursue his claim successfully without a documented case of chloracne, which might or might not last a long time. "We think it was Agent Orange," Peckarsky said of the lone chloracne victim whose claim he honored. He explained that "when in doubt, we favor the veteran." Peckarsky added that the "rash is gone but the claimant has been awarded a 10 percent disability. That works out to $44 a month."

And so, without benefit of even a scrap of the science of epidemiology— without clinically and statistically comparing veterans who may have been

exposed to those known not to have been exposed—without really doing
anything at all, the Veterans Administration had concluded there was no
Agent Orange problem. The whole thing was a figment of the imagination
of veterans, it said. "It's only natural," Peckarsky remarked, "for them to
look for something to hang their ailments on."

Peckarsky, who thought he was being quite charitable to approve payment
to even the one case, said he could pretty much discount the Agent Orange
business because there had not been more claims. If there were real health
problems with Vietnam veterans, he figured there would be much more than
434 claims. This number was a "drop in the bucket," Peckarsky said. Such
was the state of the scientific method at the VA. For Charles Peckarsky and
his colleagues in the Veterans Administration, it was a matter of doing the
right thing and not letting the fleeceable United States Government be taken
advantage of.

A few months before, the Associated Press had carried a story out of
Washington quoting Dr. Lyndon E. Lee of the VA as saying that tiny traces
of a contaminant in Agent Orange called dioxin had been found in the fatty
tissues of ten veterans. The amount ranged, Lee said, from three parts per
trillion to fifty-seven parts per trillion. To those whose knowledge of dioxin
was modest, it seemed like practically nothing and Lee had said he was
"attaching no interpretation to it."

That was in December of 1978. Now, three months later, Peckarsky was
still trying to answer questions about dioxin. Actually, there were many
dioxins. The one that was of special interest to Vietnam veterans was
something called 2,3,7,8 tetrachlorodibenzo-para-dioxin, or TCDD. It was
an unavoidable contaminant in the manufacture of Agent Orange. TCDD did
nothing to kill plants; men thought it could kill them or perhaps render them
incapable of fathering a normal child.

Peckarsky felt that the veterans did not know whereof they spoke. "I
don't know of anything in the literature that says exposure to dioxin by the
male can cause birth defects in a subsequently conceived son or daughter,"
he said. "The preponderance of literature seems to be against it." There was
no doubt that there were a lot of questions remaining unanswered about
dioxin. But there was hardly reason to dismiss a finding of from three to
fifty-seven parts per trillion in the body fat of a few Vietnam veterans.

Peckarsky did not mention and may not have been familiar with the work
of Dr. James Allen, then a professor of pathology at the University of
Wisconsin Medical School, who had been studying the properties of dioxin
for twenty years. Allen had conducted experiments with laboratory rats and
found that dioxin produced malignant tumors in them in levels as low as 500

parts per trillion. He said he thought dioxin was "a million times more toxic than PCBs," another toxic substance he had researched. Nor did Peckarsky seem to be aware of the concerns of Dr. Matthew Meselson of Harvard, who said he thought that dioxin was perhaps "the most powerful carcinogen known. Nobody argues about the toxicity of this poison."

Meselson was wrong. The Veterans Administration was about to argue a great deal about the toxicity of this poison. The issue was not whether the findings of these early researchers and others would be proved right or wrong; science is such that facts and perceptions of them are changed all the time, although TCDD would remain feared as one of chemistry's most potent cancer-causing agents, at least ten thousand times more likely to cause cancer than PCBs. The issue in 1979 was whether the VA knew of the concerns in science about dioxin and was the agency open to suggestions that dioxin was, indeed, dangerous and that the Government should be actively working to determine if any of those suggestions had merit.

But the Government was not doing this. Indeed, one of Peckarsky's friends and colleagues was, in his public statements, creating a scientific thicket more formidable than any of the jungles that the Air Force had tried to defoliate. Dr. Paul A. L. Haber, the VA's assistant chief medical director and the man in change of all doctors, nurses, therapists, and dieticians, said that the VA would be pleased to treat victims of Agent Orange if only the Government had knowledge of clearly defined symptoms. The Government was not going to make awards if symptoms remained vague. But that sort of information could only be gained by a massive Government study. And such a study had not been undertaken.

And so Paul Haber did not know. It was as though Franz Kafka had written *Catch-22* rather than Joseph Heller. Kafka, after all, had worked for a Government agency that dispensed benefits to soldiers in Austria after World War I. "All the studies you read about concern rats, mice, baboons, but nothing about men," Haber said. That was an unusual position for Haber to take. In a single sentence, he cast serious doubt on science's traditional belief that findings of carcinogenicity in animal studies were presumptive evidence of possible problems for humans. If animal studies yielded no clues that humans could profit from, animal studies would be inane and quite useless. Programs of experiments with animals would be ripe for abandonment, as pleaded for by animal rights activists for years. And chemicals might then be regarded as somehow having the Constitutional right to be regarded as innocent until proven guilty, a disturbing notion, since men and women and children would have to get sick or even die in order to make the case against the chemicals.

As the Veterans Administration in Washington strove not to give the store away, one of its employees in Chicago had quite another goal, a goal that would soon get her into trouble. Her name was Maude deVictor, and she had none of the power of either Peckarsky or Haber. She was only what the VA called a veterans benefits counselor. She sat in an office of the VA in Chicago and dispensed advice to veterans of any war who needed it.

If veterans had been asked to rank on a scale of one to ten the dedication and forthrightness of functionaries within the labyrinthine bowels of the Veterans Administration, Maude deVictor would have received a grade of at least nine and a half. She had no illusions about the quality of service that the VA dispensed, but the veterans said she tried to be consistently compassionate, friendly, interested—qualities they did not always find in abundance at VA offices.

She was hardly in a position to make trouble for the United States Government. As a person who was trying to build a career in the bureaucracy, she did not want to make trouble. She was trying to recover from cancer. She was black. She had come from modest circumstances. She had been in the Navy between 1959 and 1961, and she knew what she was supposed to be doing. But she could not accept institutional dishonesty.

One day in 1977, deVictor had heard a story of strange symptoms from Ethel Owens, whose husband, Charles, was dying in a Chicago hospital. Owens, who had been in robust health before he went to Vietnam, was always ailing after he came home. He then developed lung cancer; his weight dropped from 170 to 100 pounds and his eyes changed color. Before he died, he told his wife he was sure he had been made ill by "those chemicals in Vietnam."

The VA's Washington office, to which deVictor sent Owens' file, rejected the suggestion that his cancer was related to any defoliant used in Vietnam. The VA said there was no "true incident of significant exposure to herbicides recorded" in his records. The VA did find some evidence that Owens had problems with his lungs while he was in Vietnam, and so Mrs. Owens ultimately received his death benefits. But the VA did not ascribe his declining health to Agent Orange. The VA's central office in Washington took a bit of extra time to return the Owens file to Chicago because Mrs. Owens had referred to some medical articles that VA officials had never seen and they wanted to make copies for their investigation. The VA seemed to know less about the problem as described in the scientific literature than some of the veterans.

In the weeks to come, deVictor heard more stories not unlike Owens', with some veterans strongly suspecting that they had been adversely affected by the chemicals that had been sprayed on them and around them during their tours of Vietnam. She thought she should begin to acquire at least enough information to inform her superiors of what was going on. She called the Dow Chemical Company and other chemical companies to find out more about the herbicides used; she consulted chemists and biologists. She made 387 telephone calls in October of 1977 alone to collect information on Agent Orange. She got maps of Vietnam and started to ask veterans with complaints where they had served. Then she endeavored to find out where Agent Orange had been sprayed, to see if there was a correlation. Her naiveté was such that she was sure that once the Veterans Administration learned of the problem, it would want to help.

One of the people deVictor spoke to was Alvin L. Young, at that time a captain in the Air Force. Young, who held a doctorate in agronomy, had a Strangelovian association with Agent Orange; he had helped design the spray nozzles for the planes that let loose deadly gray spindrifts over doomed canopied forests, and he was so taken with the chemical that he actually kept a vial of it on his desk. Logically enough, he was known to his friends as "Dr. Orange." DeVictor had a lengthy telephone conversation with Young and kept notes on what she heard him say. Her notes indicate she heard him liken Agent Orange to thalidomide and say that the military was watching the course of Agent Orange claims "with extreme concern, in the event that favorable decisions . . . should open the way to possible litigation."

Young would later dispute deVictor's version of the call. He acknowledged she did call him and that they did discuss the Owens case, but not that he had ever intimated that the Government might be more concerned with the prospect of litigation than with the welfare of the people who had fought the war. For its part, the VA at first said that deVictor's memo of the call was real enough, but later, Veterans Administrator Max Cleland claimed deVictor said she did not write the memo, which was at variance with what deVictor told others.

In any event, the VA did not respond the way she thought it would or should. Her boss asked her for a report on what she had been doing and why she had been doing it. When he told her to stop, she began to talk to a local television news reporter in Chicago, Bill Kurtis. The result was a show aired there on March 23, 1978, called "Agent Orange—Vietnam's Deadly Fog." It was not definitive but it was provocative.

Dr. Barry Commoner, the environmentalist, was interviewed on the show and said that it was quite possible that the TCDD contained in Agent Orange might well be stored in fatty tissue and cause ill health years later. His comments caused angst within the Chicago VA. Vern Rogers, the agency's local spokesman, quickly furthered its policy of denial and said that there was "absolutely no evidence" that Agent Orange had killed anybody.

In Washington, where Government had always been timid about banning chemicals, even after the Toxic Substances Control Act was passed in 1976, an initiative began to ban the herbicide 2,4,5-T. Agent Orange was made of a 50-50 mix of the butyl esters of two phenoxy herbicides, 2,4-D and 2,4,5-T. The latter was the one adjudged to have the dioxin contamination, and it was the latter that became the target of the Environmental Protection Agency.

The Veterans Administration decided that the Chicago television show was "entirely one-sided." VA's top management decided the controversy was a manufactured one—all without trying to determine whether there really was merit in what the veterans were claiming. At this point, the Agent Orange issue had still not touched a vast number of veterans; it had not yet become defined on nightly news reports or in national publications. But veterans were nevertheless showing up at VA hospitals, and the VA did not know what to do with them. Its response was to intensify the policy of denial already begun.

Dr. Gerrit Schepers of the VA's Washington office wanted to take some of the steam out of Barry Commoner's assertion that TCDD might be stored in the body's fatty tissue. Schepers was no dioxin researcher, but after he hurriedly consulted the literature he could find on the subject, he concluded that Commoner's theory was "implausible." He told his colleagues in the VA that Agent Orange claimants ought to be treated courteously, but if they had "no symptoms or signs," they should be offered "simple reassurance"—not the VA's money. "All VA personnel should avoid premature commitment to any diagnosis of defoliant poisoning," he said. And he made it clear that the VA would not look kindly upon any counselor who acted as Maude deVictor did. He urged the staff to call Washington for "technical guidance" if anybody had an Agent Orange problem.

As for deVictor, she was in an unhappy situation with her superiors in Chicago. They were vexed that she had gone to the press. She was transferred from her counseling job because, she was told, she had expressed her concern about the non-ionizing radiation given off by her video display terminal. She would ultimately put her career plans aside and leave the VA.

Quickly, the Veterans Administration concluded that it needed consultants to help evaluate what the veterans were claiming. It invited an unlikely pair of advisers to attend a meeting that was to be held in Paul Haber's office on

July 7, 1978: Dr. Ben B. Holder and Dr. Walter Melvin. Holder was medical director of the Dow Chemical Company, the major manufacturer of Agent Orange, a company that had a financial and ego stake in both 2,4-D and 2,4,5-T, which it marketed as weed killers to civilians. Melvin, who was a former scientific director for the Air Force, was now a professor at Colorado State University. No other outside consultants came to the meeting; there were also no veterans present.

To the surprise of nobody who attended the closed meeting, Holder said that the phenoxy herbicides were safe and that a "consensus of world experts" agreed that there would be no later health problems from Agent Orange unless the claimant first contracted chloracne. He did not name the people involved in this consensus, nor was he reported to have said that there were a goodly number of scientists who were worried about the long-term effects of herbicides and pesticides in general, and Agent Orange in particular.

In the give-and-take of the meeting, the EPA representative said that studies suggested that dioxin was a health hazard. But Melvin interrupted him right there, saying that just as many people said that dioxin was not a major problem. And before the meeting broke up, one of the participants, Dr. Lawrence Hobson, referred to Barry Commoner as a "populist scientific spokesman." The VA did not exactly knock itself out trying to find people better informed or more objective about dioxin and its profound ability to cause cancer in experimental animals. Indeed, the agency found itself so enthusiastic about Melvin's view of the world that it asked him to do a study for the VA—on reported industrial disasters elsewhere involving dioxin.

Schepers became the first person to head the VA's Agent Orange Policy Group. Since the group wanted to look at dioxin accidents in private industry and had already adopted a certain approach to making its determinations, he was a logical choice for the job. He had previously worked as a researcher for the Monsanto Chemical Company and said he thought he would "still have entrée there because of prior friendly associations." He had previously also worked for DuPont and before that had been a health official with the Bureau of Mines in South Africa, his native country.

Schepers would find a colleague with a similar background and point of view in Lawrence Hobson, who had taken such a dim view of Barry Commoner and who would now be assistant director of the VA's Special Office for Agent Orange. Prior to joining the VA in the 1970s, Hobson had been medical research director for a division of the Olin Mathieson Chemical Corporation, which, like Dow, DuPont, and Monsanto, was a major manufacturer of chemicals. Nor was Hobson unfamiliar with chemical warfare—during World War II, he was chief of the Medical Research Laboratory of the Government's Chemical Warfare Service.

So, the VA began its quest for more knowledge about Agent Orange and dioxin, but its quest was not marked with distinction. Two months after it began its special meetings, it was accused of violating a Federal law which requires that when outside advisers are involved, the meetings must be public and the advice sought from such sources must be balanced. The VA then decided to let members of "interested veterans' groups" attend the meetings.

That did not mean that the VA planned to reach out to veterans in general and invite them to determine if any health problems they had might be attributable to Agent Orange. On the contrary, the VA decided not to conduct an outreach program of any kind and would look at soldiers only if they brought themselves to hospitals and offered "acceptable evidence of long-term human herbicide toxicity." So, the same die was cast again: Vietnam's soldiers would be treated for Agent Orange if that was clearly the cause of their illnesses, but the Government which sent them to war would do nothing to define the cause.

Indeed, the Government seemed to harbor the apprehension that soldiers were bad for the chemical business. In the fall of 1978, Alvin Young and three others were the authors of a book published by the Surgeon General of the Air Force. The book grew out of an Air Force directive to produce a kind of position paper on the health effects of Agent Orange. If one presumed the Air Force's interest in retaining some small shard of objectivity, the book seemed to start oddly: "The use of herbicides in support of tactical military operations in South Vietnam . . . has had (and continues to have) a negative impact on the use of pesticides by numerous facets of our society."

The VA soon began to cite the book as an authoritative and scientifically objective summary on Agent Orange. And the Department of Defense was so happy with it that it told Congressional investigators that the book "supports the . . . [DOD] position presented in testimony that there is little or no relationship between many alleged symptoms and past exposure to . . . Agent Orange." The Defense Department had convinced itself that Agent Orange harmed nothing but plants and, so as not to burden the taxpayers unduly with something unnecessary, decided not to conduct a health study of veterans to see if they were suffering any ill effects.

Publicly, the Government took the high road. Jimmy Carter, then President, had a strong and abiding interest in human rights, and there was no reason to believe that he was more interested in their absence in Argentina or South Africa than in the war-caused suffering that might be occurring in his own country. "No steps we can take can undo all the damage done by war. . . . What we can do is to acknowledge our debt to those who sacrificed so much when their country asked service of them, and to repay that debt fully, gladly, and with a deep sense of respect," President Carter said. But it was not going to happen that way during the moral Carter years, any more than it had during the less moral years of the Harding Administration. Within the bowels of the enormous bureaucracy, a monster agency that ostensibly had been established to help veterans, assiduous steps were being taken to do everything but acknowledge the nation's debt to servicemen and servicewomen, especially if that meant spending money on an Agent Orange study.

Since the Agent Orange controversy seemed to have surfaced first in Chicago, it was only fitting that the Chicago VA would put it in a reassuring if somewhat slippery perspective for the rest of the functionaries. Vern Rogers, the VA's local publicity man, who had already announced to the world that there wasn't anything to worry about, now felt confident enough to produce an "Agent Orange Perspective" for his fellow employees in the Great Lakes region. He prepared his perspective in time for the New Year, and on January 2, 1979, he blamed the Agent Orange controversy on the media. He described a "usual scenario" so that VA workers would not be hoodwinked by veterans: "A Vietnam veteran calls the media to report he thinks he has a disease as a result of his exposure to 'agent orange,' and an 'investigative reporter' calls the hospital."

There was nothing more to it than that, he said, and he advised his fellow public information workers to simply quote Veterans Administrator Max Cleland if asked what the agency was doing: "VA is now involved in the most thorough professional examination of the effects of exposure to herbicides in Vietnam," and "to date there is no demonstrated association between exposure and disease." In fact, neither the VA nor any other part of Government was involved in a thorough examination of much of anything relative to the question at hand.

As press agentry wove its unvirtuous magic in Chicago, a former soldier in New York State was coming to the conclusion that veterans would not get a fair shake from the VA or any other Government agency unless they forced the issue in court. His name was Paul Reutershan, he was twenty-seven years old, and he worked for the Long Island Rail Road as a conductor. Reutershan had enlisted in the Army at seventeen and became a crew chief on a resupply helicopter in Vietnam. Frequently that helicopter would fly through what Reutershan would later recall as the fog of Agent Orange. When, in 1977, he was told that he had abdominal cancer he was quite astonished; he had never smoked nor drank, and he thought he had always taken care of himself. He began to search his mind for a cause, even though some of his friends told him that one cannot always find a specific cause for cancer. Reutershan had what his doctors diagnosed as a persistent case of chloracne on his back, and he called it to the attention of a local office of the Veterans Administration.

Even with its emphasis on chloracne, the VA denied him benefits. As far as VA doctors were concerned, the chloracne was a sign but not a conclusive one, and they informed Reutershan that he could not receive any payment for alleged sickness caused by Agent Orange until scientific research proved conclusively that the defoliant had, in fact, caused his cancer.

Reutershan grew angry that the Government wasn't doing anything to shed some light on the question and angrier still at statements like the ones issued by Vern Rogers that, in fact, the trouble was all the invention of journalists.

By 1978, Paul Reutershan was both angry and dying. "I got killed in Vietnam and didn't know it," he said to his mother. His intellect told him that he had very little time left to live, but he confided to his sister, Jan Dziedzic, that he was determined to live anyway and "complete this mission." The mission was both a $10 million lawsuit that he filed against the Dow Chemical Company and the creation of a struggling organization called Agent Orange Victims International, to which he invited other veterans with problems not unlike his own. When Reutershan lay dying in Norwalk (Connecticut) Hospital in December of 1978, he made one of his close friends, Frank McCarthy, promise that the lawsuit would not die as well. "No way," McCarthy told him.

Reutershan knew that whoever tried to lead Vietnam veterans would have to be as stubborn as he was resourceful. He knew that the veterans were confused about what had happened to them, angry at what they felt was their betrayal by a nation that no longer cared about them, and divided among themselves as to precisely what to do. His selection of McCarthy, rather than somebody else, to make the case against Agent Orange was not made lightly. McCarthy, thirty-five years old, a veteran of seven years in the infantry, was not a man to take responsibility lightly.

In Vietnam in 1966, while driving a jeep armed with a machine gun, McCarthy found his platoon pinned down by small arms and mortar fire. He opened fire, and although wounded himself, kept the enemy at bay, and was credited with preventing the Vietcong from destroying the platoon. In the citation that accompanied his Bronze Star, McCarthy was commended for his "outstanding display of aggressiveness, devotion to duty and personal bravery in keeping with the finest traditions of the military service and reflects great credit upon himself, the First Infantry Division and the United States Army.''

McCarthy was no less determined to distinguish himself in what he saw as a mighty struggle to make the Agent Orange case for the men and women with whom he had served. He was bitter about Reutershan's death, about the illness he could see in veterans he knew, about the Government's seeming indifference about doing anything at all for veterans of Vietnam. He borrowed $13,000 from a bank; his ex-wife pledged $20,000 in stock to guarantee his note, and, with the help of his old Army buddies, he proceeded to set up ten chapters of Agent Orange Victims International—in Boston; Kansas City, Kansas; New York City; Orlando, Florida; Glendale, Arizona; Mohegan Lake, New York; Beaver Falls, Washington; Catano, Puerto Rico; and Honolulu. He spent over $30,000 for the establishment of chapters between June of 1978 and August of 1979.

With much of the Veterans Administration acting as though nothing was wrong, McCarthy, aided for the most part by no more than two volunteers, was taking about 175 calls a day at his apartment on West 13th Street in New York's Greenwich Village. With each new call, he sent out a medical questionnaire and urged the veterans that no matter how they had been treated in the past, they should return to their local VA chapter and undergo whatever tests the VA was willing to give. After fourteen months of operation, McCarthy had files on 1,500 veterans and had logged in 7,296 calls. "My office is pathetic," he told a visitor in 1979. "We are totally swamped. We shouldn't exist and we don't want to. But we have to do this because no one else is doing the job."

"When I got the award," McCarthy said of his Bronze Star, "I felt pride and honor. Now, I see it as an honor bestowed on me by the men I served with. I still care about the U.S. Army. I went there with the ideals of John Kennedy. It upsets me that the Government thinks of me as a radical. I think of my Government as a monstrous bureaucracy, and what they are doing to veterans is criminal neglect bordering on atrocities. The Government needs revision; the bureaucrats are only out to benefit themselves."

McCarthy joined forces with lawyer Victor Yannacone, and before 1979 was out, the Reutershan-inspired lawsuit was combined with others in a class action against the five makers of Agent Orange.

The VA and Dow versus the Christians

[Environmentalists] have learned the trick of Hitler-type propaganda ... if you lie often enough people will begin to believe it.
—Earl B. Barnes, chairman of the Dow Chemical Company, speaking about some of the company's Christian shareholders, 1980

The Dow Chemical Company wisely took the Agent Orange matter much more seriously than did the United States Government. It had to; unlike the Government, it could be sued by angry veterans. Outwardly, Dow was telling reporters that there was nothing wrong with the suspect component in Agent Orange, the dioxin-contaminated herbicide trichlorophenoxyacetic acid, or 2,4,5-T. But internally, Dow's executives and its insurance carrier were quite concerned about what it would all mean for the future. If even a small part of what the veterans' complaints were attributable to was something made by the chemical industry, the liability questions could be of such a magnitude as to put the company's well-being very much in doubt.

Such a scenario was not out of the question. For nearly two decades, environmentalists and occupational health specialists had been complaining of a chemical industry that was largely unregulated, an industry that devised and marketed over one thousand new chemical compounds each year—without adequate pretesting, without knowing what the long-term effects might be, and without really knowing what the effects of last year's or last decade's chemicals might be.

By 1979, the concerns that had been the province of a small group of rather sophisticated, well-educated people were now squarely within the vision of many Americans. Environmentalism was no longer seen as quite the elitist activity it had been at the start of the decade. There was growing resentment over mistakes made by the chemical industry in the past; there was newfound compassion for the soldiers who had fought and lost an unpopular war. Matters were only complicated by revelations that had been made about an accident in 1976 at a chemical plant in Seveso, in northern Italy, which had released dioxin into the environment. Reports of ill health resulting from the accident were still in dispute. But there was little disagreement that the Italian Government, in an unattractively harmonious relationship with industry, had handled the matter badly and without making full disclosure. It had only fueled public apprehension. Three years later, wrangling over 2,4,5-T was clearly made worse by what had happened in Italy.

Dow, which had a leadership role in the industry, tried to assure those who bothered to ask that 2,4,5-T was venerable and trustworthy. The compound in question, Dow said, grew out of work done for the best of reasons in the late 1930s at the Boyce-Thompson Institute for Plant Research, then in Yonkers, New York, by P. W. Zimmerman and A. E. Hitchcock. They called it not a defoliant but a "plant growth regulator."

And so there was innocence in its early nomenclature, if not its side effects. Regulating the growth of plants certainly sounded high-minded enough, and it was seen as one of those boons to agriculture with which the chemical industry has always liked to identify itself. But the innocence did not last. No sooner had the idea for 2,4,5-T emerged from Boyce-Thompson than it was noticed by the Army, which was doing research in the possibilities of chemical warfare at a site in Frederick, Maryland. The strategic side of 2,4,5-T was appreciated, but World War II ended without the Government making use of the unpleasant side of the plant growth regulator. At least, it was nothing the Government ever talked about.

After the war, herbicides were a mainstay of the "Green Revolution." They were an answer, if only a temporary one, to those who claimed the world's population had grown too large and that the planet would not be able to support humankind without forever being stalked by famine. Herbicides efficiently killed weeds, and so wherever they were used, yields rose dramatically. By 1961, however, they were already suspect. Rachel Carson, in her acclaimed *Silent Spring,* sensed trouble coming from 2,4,5-T and other herbicides. She complained of chemical proponents who, without enough forethought, had urged the world to "beat its plowshares into sprayguns" and who muscled aside criticism as "the baseless imaginings of pessimists."

The industry wasn't quite as sure about 2,4,5-T as its public indifference to critics suggested. In early spring of 1965, four chemical companies arranged a closed meeting at Dow headquarters in Midland, Michigan. According to notes and memoranda written by some of those who attended the meeting, Dow disclosed the results of a study that showed that the dioxin contaminant in 2,4,5-T caused liver damage in rabbits, but said it did not want the results released to the public, because the situation might "explode" and cause more regulation for the chemical industry.

Dow successfully marketed 2,4,5-T for civilian use under the brand name Silvex, but by 1979 was desperately fighting a proposed Federal ban on the product. EPA scientists suspected that dioxin was harming humans as it did those laboratory rabbits, and neither Dow nor any other company was able to remove the TCDD contaminant. Dow was selling around seven million pounds of Silvex annually, most of it for consumption in the United States. From Silvex, the company realized around $12 million in gross sales; everything else it produced gave it a gross, in 1978, of over $6 billion. That meant that 2,4,5-T represented only two-tenths of 1 percent of Dow's profit sheet, hardly anything for Dow's accountants to get excited about. "We are not in this battle to defend one of the crown jewels," said Gary Jones, a perturbed Dow publicity executive.

But in reality, Dow saw the struggle as one with much broader, more serious implications than might be suggested by the ledgers. A lack of confidence in phenoxy herbicides could easily lead to weakening in the markets for all manner of chemical compounds designed to kill insects and unwanted plants. Dow thus tried very hard to convince the public that 2,4,5-T was a chemical benefactor that had gotten a bad name only because of the war.

"Two-four-five-T has been used for over thirty years, and there is not one single documented case of human injury," said Tim Scott, a Dow public relations man and one of Jones' aides. "It is one of the most documented chemicals in the world." As for the veterans, Dow was sorry, but the Agent Orange controversy had to do more with the unpopularity of the Vietnam War than it did with chemistry, at least from Dow's point of view. "The chemical was mostly the victim of Vietnamese propagandists, or whatever you want to call them, doctors, saying, 'Hey, we got a lot of problems here in Vietnam and we think it is because of Agent Orange,' " opined Jones.

If this was the coda of the age of unshakable faith in chemicals, Dow was up to a little bravura concertizing. But privately, away from its slick and effective public relations apparatus, the language was used in quite a different way. "Dow is very concerned over this litigation," its insurance company, the Fireman's Fund, said in an interoffice memorandum that was never meant for the public's eyes. Dow's litigation strategy was to defend itself against the veterans "on a low dose and lack of exposure basis," even though nobody had any real idea of what a "low dose" of anything as lethal as dioxin might be. Like its insured, the Fireman's Fund was sensitive to the public relations aspect of the thing. Its memo said, "The complexities of chemistry, coupled with our country's post Vietnam guilt and the emotional issues of cancer and birth defects, make these cases potentially very difficult to defend. The likelihood of adverse media exposure combined with these other factors could predetermine Dow's guilt."

As the class action against Dow neared, the company was afraid that Victor Yannacone, one of Long Island's more effusive lawyers, would turn the case into a "media event" and was further apprehensive because the case was being presided over by "a very liberal black judge," Robert Lee Carter. Judge Carter was apparently suspect not just because he had been associated with Thurgood Marshall in the *Brown* v. *Board of Education* school desegregation case in 1954, nor even because he had later become general counsel for the National Association for the Advancement of Colored People, but because he had been a second lieutenant in the Army Air Corps in World War II and may have felt sympathy for the suffering of those who had served in Vietnam. The company breathed easier when it succeeded in having the case transferred to "a very conservative judge named Pratt." Federal Judge George Pratt, manning his bench on Long Island, would handle the case for several years before his elevation to the Federal Court of Appeals.

If Dow was worried, so was the Fireman's Fund. Someone from the insurance company met with Don Frayer, Dow's dynamic claims manager and one of its key people on the Agent Orange controversy. According to a Fireman's Fund internal memo, Frayer assured them that Agent Orange had "caused no problems to Vietnam veterans." But they were chilled when he told them it was "possible that some liver problems and some minor neurological problems are caused by dioxins."

During 1979, Dow fretted more about adverse media publicity than it did about the dioxin problem. Indeed, according to its own internal insurance memoranda, there were people within the company who thought it best to remain silent, or run the risk of having the media sully the name of Dow more than they had already. With all of its fights with environmentalists and for all the times it had been singled out by antiwar protesters, Dow was nevertheless one of the better-run companies in a poorly regulated industry; the company was stung by what it perceived to be an image that was needlessly negative.

At least a part of Dow's role as the target for veterans was that even if veterans knew that Agent Orange had been formulated by the Defense Department, they were largely powerless to litigate against the Government. U.S. courts had ruled consistently that soldiers could not sue the Government for the injuries suffered in war. Wars had always been places where people got hurt. But nations had always been entities whose rulers never wanted to admit they had done anything wrong—the doctrine which since the Middle Ages had been commonly expressed in the phrase "The king can do no wrong." With no king available, the veterans might have sued the king's principal court jester, the Veterans Administration. Even this avenue was closed to them, however, because Federal law clearly prohibited veterans from suing the VA directly for denial of a claim. The soldiers had to settle for a secondary target, the king's provider. In this case, it was the chemical companies that had made Agent Orange.

Victor Yannacone, who had been part of the successful drive to get DDT banned in the early 1970s, was sure that he had a strong case. By the middle of 1979, he had organized the veterans he represented into twelve classes of victims, ranging from men with cancers and precursors of cancer, through chloracne, deformed or retarded children, and some with psychological problems. He suspected there were probably thirty subclasses. In those days, the phrase "post-traumatic stress syndrome" was not heard, but Yannacone thought much of what came to bear that label stemmed from exposure to the dioxin within Agent Orange.

From Yannacone's and McCarthy's point of view, there really was no alternative to going ahead with the lawsuit. "I thought that the EPA and the FDA would protect us," Yannacone said. "But not only have they not done what they said they would do, they are not even trying to do something. They have misled us." Yannacone was not terribly impressed that the Federal EPA had just ordered an emergency suspension of 2,4,5-T for most civilian uses in the United States. For him, it was too little, too late, and it did nothing to solve the problems of the veterans already exposed.

Yannacone's feelings about the strength of his own case were destined to encounter strong criticism by veterans in the months and years ahead. But his perceptions about Government's lack of good intentions would remain unchallengeable. Just ten days after the EPA's ban against 2,4,5-T went into effect, a meeting was conducted by VA officials in which they repeated the belief they had held from the beginning—that the "relationships between herbicide exposure and adverse health effects are purely hypothetical.'' The VA was hostile to the EPA ban because the ban could ''generate outside pressure for the VA to accept the postulated toxic effects of herbicides without further studies''—studies which the Veterans Administration had no intention of doing.

When Mrs. Richard Lutz, the mother of a Vietnam veteran, wrote to President Carter expressing her concern about her son's health because of his exposure to Agent Orange, she got a reply from Deputy Assistant Secretary of Defense George Marianthel that was as incredible as it was predictable, given what the Government had done so far. Marianthel told her that while the Government was sympathetic, ''We do not believe that a study of the health of our Vietnam veterans would add to the knowledge of the long-term health effects'' of Agent Orange. He also told her that it might be better to study the dioxin-poisoned survivors of the industrial explosion at Seveso, Italy, and that the symptoms complained of by veterans ''are almost certainly due'' to some cause other than Agent Orange. His source for this declaration was the book written by Alvin Young and published by the Air Force Surgeon General.

The Veterans Administration and the Defense Department had thus sustained a consistent course of denial, even though there was no scientific basis for taking such a hard-line position. But the position had momentum, and neither agency wanted to face the prospect of willingly paying many billions of dollars to men who suffered so profoundly from the aftereffects of war, whatever the precise cause.

The VA and Defense would soon mount a successful offensive to convince the public and the press alike that the veterans were ill-informed and not to be believed. In truth, the Government deliberately avoided informing both the public and itself, then hid behind non-science to accuse the soldiers of not being scientific. Much of the worst of what it did was hidden from the press, which had somehow never engaged in much hard reporting at the Veterans Administration.

And so it was as logical for the Defense Department to tell Congress that it was ''extremely doubtful that a retrospective epidemiological study'' of Vietnam veterans would prove anything, one way or the other, as it was for the Veterans Administration to instruct all of its medical centers in the black but necessary art of obfuscation. ''It is to be emphasized,'' said the VA to its far-flung facilities, ''that at this time the VA medical centers will refrain from efforts to induce veterans who are not currently part of their patient population to undergo an examination for the possible health-related effects of herbicides.''

On Memorial Day weekend of 1979, *The New York Times* published a series of three articles which attempted to examine the complaints of some veterans and the responses of Government. After it started to run, Veterans Administrator Max Cleland announced that, after due consideration, the Air Force would conduct a health study of the more than twelve hundred pilots and chemical handlers who had been associated with Operation Ranch Hand. That was the folksy name given to the unit responsible for spraying the herbicides, formerly known as Operation Hades.

It was an unusual development. The VA was presumably in business to protect the interests of all veterans and therefore would have been expected to insist on a broad-based study over which it would retain control. This was not broad-based, and the Air Force had already suggested that any exposure of ground troops to Agent Orange would be very small compared to exposure of Air Force people. And the VA, which had already done so much to get the Government out of any situation in which it might have to indemnify Agent Orange victims, continued to insist that all it wanted was the facts. "We have no desire at all to cover up or hide behind bureaucracy to negate any possible relationship between illness and Agent Orange," said the VA's Paul Haber.

The VA was curiously passive about what was widely seen as a usurpation of its role. Veterans Administrator Max Cleland said that the VA had played "no formal role in the decision-making" that led to the Ranch Hand study, and the Air Force made it clear that the study was under its control, not the VA's.

From the beginning of its study, through its use of language and the way it framed the problem before it, the Air Force marked itself as something other than an unbiased observer, just as the Veterans Administration had already done. For example, in minimizing the possible effect of Agent Orange on ground troops, the Air Force insisted that infantry did not enter sprayed areas until at least a month or even six weeks after spraying was completed. Veterans like Frank McCarthy were not amused by that assertion. The Congress did not know what to make of it until it later found records making it clear that Marines had entered sprayed areas on the very day that they were sprayed. The controller general of the General Accounting Office issued a report saying that, quite simply, the Air Force's contention was "inaccurate."

That the Air Force was trying to frame a study while succumbing to fanciful notions of its own invention caused some to wonder about what the value of the Ranch Hand study would really be. The National Academy of Sciences reviewed the "protocol" for Ranch Hand—the statement that set out the objectives and parameters of the study—and found it flawed. The NAS said that such a protocol "probably would not identify adverse health effects." The NAS also felt that the Air Force wasn't looking at enough people and suggested that it was inappropriate for an agency to study itself in the face of claims for compensation.

Quite a few members of Congress agreed, and some were especially concerned about what they perceived as the cavalier attitude toward ground troops of the Army and Marines. One congressman, David Bonior of Michigan, told his colleagues that VA policy on the issue was "hasty and ill-conceived" and that studying only those who had participated in Operation Ranch Hand was like "examining the crew of the *Enola Gay* instead of the exposed victims of the atomic bomb."

The criticism was especially hard for Alvin Young to take, since he had created the protocol and said he had spent a year doing it. Quite possibly the criticism should have been stronger, since Young had only recently served as an expert witness for the Department of Agriculture in its efforts to oppose the EPA decision to ban 2,4,5-T. At a time when he was supposed to be designing a study to determine whether Agent Orange may have harmed our troops, he was actively working as a witness before an EPA hearing officer to promote use of the suspect herbicide, 2,4,5-T, for civilian use. His role was unknown to the general public, to veterans, and perhaps even to the National Academy of Sciences.

In his testimony for the Department of Agriculture, Young quickly dispelled any notion that he could not be objective on questions raised about herbicides or, indeed, that there should be any questions. To hear him tell it, herbicides were almost good for you.

> When I first got into the herbicide business, which was in 1960, we weren't concerned about toxicity. . . . My heavens, we didn't consider the phenoxy herbicides toxic. We sprayed each other. We used to play it as a game, and we would go to our supervisor and say, are these things toxic and the answer was always, oh, no, no, no. Herbicides are not toxic. And as you read the old manuals . . . indeed you find exactly that. These materials are not toxic. . . . They were considered to be safe and that's why we used them in Vietnam. . . .

Young went so far as to testify that on the basis of the studies he had done with animals, he took "great comfort" in knowing that he had been "significantly exposed" to the phenoxy herbicides. Although they loved him at the Agriculture Department, Young's show got only mixed reviews at the Senate Veterans Affairs Committee, where one staff member called him a "glorified weed-killer" who was "not qualified to discuss the health effects of exposure to Agent Orange."

The Government's inability to respond to a problem as they had expected angered and disappointed veterans. Their ire left Gerrit Schepers unperturbed at his perch as head of the VA's Agent Orange Policy Group. "Some people are always dissatisfied," he said. At the upper reaches of the Veterans Administration itself, Paul Haber remained committed to the proposition that Agent Orange was harmless to humans until the veterans somehow proved it otherwise. He said he found nothing unusual about their complaints. "I've heard about veterans complaining of numbness and tingling and paralysis for as long as I've been at the VA," he said.

The liberals who normally supported social legislation were strangely silent; the veterans seemed to have no advocates with any power. Late in 1979, Robert Muller, the articulate and outspoken head of the Vietnam Veterans of America, wondered where all the enlightened antiwar people had gone. "I can't find them," he complained. "I'd like to take a full page ad in the newspapers and say, 'Dear Liberals: For years your slogan was Bring the Boys Home. Well, we're home. Now where are you?' "

By the end of the year Muller had some idea of where they were. Congress mustered up the courage to order the VA to do the epidemiological study it had not wanted to do, and Senator Alan Cranston, who had been the bill's shepherd, said it would be "inexcusable" if the cause of illness among Vietnam veterans escaped detection "because the matter was inadequately studied."

But ordering the VA to do something and getting it done satisfactorily were quite different matters. Largely because of the way it had broadcast its lack of objectivity, the VA was mandated to hire qualified outside people to do the study. Within the agency, those who worried about its squandering money fretted. J. C. Peckarsky, who really had taught himself how to say no, estimated that if the Government started paying Agent Orange claims, there would be "at least" 600,000 applicants. And up in Buffalo, one of the VA's doctors was feeling sympathy for the Dow Chemical Company. Dr. Israel Alvarez, who was in charge of the Agent Orange program there, wrote a solicitous letter to the company and asked for health studies that, he had learned, Dow would be conducting on soldiers exposed to the chemical. He thought the Dow data would be "extremely helpful" to him to "keep the issue in the right proportion. . . ." He complained that Buffalo's veterans were "militant" (due to the influence of the Love Canal controversy, he thought), and assured Dow, "We have kept the issue under control." Dow was very pleased with his letter and wrote him back, ". . . we think your collective efforts are being generally under-recognized."

Dow was not nearly so pleased with its critics. When five Roman Catholic and three Protestant groups representing Dow shareholders chided the company for not taking a morally defensible position, Dow's chairman, Earl B. Barnes, said they had "learned the trick of Hitler-type propaganda. . . . If you lie often enough people will begin to believe it." He accused the groups of not being truthful and said their "only interest" in the Agent Orange issue was to "do away with agricultural chemicals."

26
Avoid Politicians and Lawyers and Get a Good PR Man

> The committee expressed support for the view that
> excessive workloads and anxiety would be created if
> President Reagan went on television inviting any
> Vietnam veteran who is worried about Agent Orange
> to report to a VA hospital for an examination.
> —Minutes of internal meeting, VA Agent Orange
> Policy Committee, January 28, 1981

As Dow went about the unlikely task of attributing Hitlerian methods to its Christian stockholders, the VA began to cast about for outside contractors to supply it with clues on 2,4,5-T—clues that the VA was unable to provide for itself. That task was just as unlikely, since it involved finding somebody who knew something about the chemistry of herbicides but who still claimed to retain some objectivity about the subject. At least, the veterans hoped that the VA would look upon the search for an expert in such a manner.

On the basis of some research that had come across somebody's desk, the VA first sought out the expertise of Dr. Terry Lavy of the University of Arkansas. It asked him to do a book on the effect of herbicides on humans. Was he objective? To some, he seemed to be something of an advocate. Among other things, Lavy had worked for the National Forest Products Association in its fight against the proposed ban on 2,4,5-T. His book commission was awarded without competitive bidding. The monograph, *Human Exposure to Phenoxy Herbicides,* would emerge four years later. Behind its purple cover (showing a helicopter spraying something and five men carrying spray equipment on their backs), it contained a most unusual acknowledgment. For in it, Lavy thanked the National Forest Products

Association, among others, for having "supported much of the research reported." Some found it unsettling to be told that a strong advocate for herbicide and pesticide use had helped bankroll a Government-supervised study that was supposed to be looking for objective answers. For commercial reasons, the association had already endeavored to show, with Lavy's help, that its chemical use had harmed the health of no one.

Within the citations, the monograph also mentioned work that had been done for the National Agricultural Chemicals Association, hardly nonpartisan in the debate about herbicide and pesticide use. Lavy further expressed his thanks to Alvin Young, who, he said, was "instrumental in arranging that this monograph be written." Lavy's work became the document that the VA would send, free of charge, to anyone who inquired about the health effects of Agent Orange. He agreed that the dioxin contaminant in Agent Orange was "undoubtedly one of the most toxic synthetic materials," but contended that basically the furor about Agent Orange had all been caused by the media. And as far as Lavy was concerned, nobody had proved that either Agent Orange or dioxin had really done anything harmful to anyone.

But long before Lavy's book was available for stockpiling by the VA, more clues were needed about Agent Orange, as were more players. The VA left it to its own Dr. Lawrence Hobson to prepare a proposal that would solicit bids from those who might be interested in creating a protocol for the Agent Orange study that the VA had been ordered to do by Congress. Hobson's choices were not easy to make and even harder to understand. In a deposition given later but never made public, he said that the VA sought a scientist with "political sensitivity" who could realize the "political implications of the questions . . . who is able to be objective in the face of political pressure." He added, "We definitely don't want an investigator who is going to contribute to any kind of political strife or socio-economic strife either inadvertently or intentionally."

Hobson was asked in the deposition if a scientist would be regarded as less than objective if he had ever worked for a maker of Agent Orange. "Not unless they had publicized their results and their opinion," he replied.

After further dallying, the VA decided that the man to do the needed work would be Dr. Gary Spivey, a professor of public health at the University of California, Los Angeles. Alas, he was not to prove quite the unimpeachable source that the VA presumably wanted him to be. No sooner did he begin working on the design of the study than he was invited to speak before the California Assembly, on a proposed bill for veterans who thought they might be affected by Agent Orange. Basically, the California bill was to provide an outreach program so that veterans could learn about the ill effects that might follow exposure to Agent Orange.

Spivey attacked the bill. There was a certain lack of detachment in his words when he told the Assembly, "The fear which is generated by the current publicity is very likely to be the most serious consequence of the use of Agent Orange." His indiscretion received national publicity and the veterans were furious.

Jon Furst, a veteran and one of the leaders in the Agent Orange controversy, snapped that Spivey's testimony sounded "more like the words of a scientist who has answered the questions without looking at the facts." And Senator Alan Cranston, who had originally sponsored the measure empowering the VA to do the study, was again dismayed, although seemingly powerless to change the situation. Spivey, he said, "seriously compromised his personal credibility and therefore his effectiveness. . . ." For reasons that remained opaque, Spivey was permitted to design the study anyhow, but it was clear that nobody, not even the people in the Veterans Administration who had hired him, would be able to take his work seriously.

Such theater deserved more production. Act Two starred the Veterans Administrator, Max Cleland. He had only recently assured Congress that veterans with Agent Orange complaints would receive good hospital care—even if nobody in his agency understood the problem or had the slightest idea of what constituted good care under the circumstances. But then Cleland disclosed that in order to check on the quality of service being provided by his own agency, he had posed as a veteran who was sick and in need of aid and telephoned VA hospitals with questions about Agent Orange. Asking questions of the VA was something Cleland certainly knew how to do. He understood the system; he had been wounded in Vietnam, lost both his legs and an arm, and experienced hospitalization in VA facilities.

Cleland admitted publicly that nobody knew what he was talking about when he called around asking about Agent Orange, even though nearly two years had passed since the first claims had been filed with the agency. His telephone calls and subsequent disclosures puzzled many veterans. They knew that he knew the VA had failed to develop a cogent health care policy on the Agent Orange issue. They knew it because the VA had already conducted an in-house survey, sending questionnaires to hundreds of veterans treated at VA hospitals around the country. The survey, which Cleland had seen, showed that in a "majority of cases a VA physician did not discuss the results of the examination with the veteran" who had been complaining of Agent Orange. And so why should a Veterans Administrator with his estimable intelligence and sophistication have to resort to making those investigative telephone calls? The veterans who had not understood why they were in Vietnam now found that they could not understand Cleland, either, even though he was a man they were predisposed to like.

Individual complaints were common, but perhaps the essence of the mean spirit that Government had exhibited toward veterans earlier in the century was best expressed, during the post-Vietnam years, in the case of a man who went to a VA hospital to get what he thought would be an "Agent Orange health test"—only to be told by the VA doctor that he was "simply trying to get more money from the VA."

The complaints of veterans about the VA did not remain simply the unsubstantiated grousing that the rest of society found so easy to ignore. What they described was "generally confirmed" by investigators for the General Accounting Office, Congress's investigative arm. The GAO also criticized VA record-keeping as containing errors and omissions, not the least of which was the fact that the VA had decided not to keep the addresses of veterans in its Agent Orange registry, a very strange way to monitor the effects of war on soldiers, since it was sure to render them invisible to Government in short order.

The people who thought they were sick from Agent Orange decidedly did not get the idea from the VA that Government wanted them to come forward so that it could help them. For example, some decent and caring people within the VA thought it might be right and proper to put taped television spots on television stations all over the country, informing veterans that a pamphlet was available on Agent Orange. Cleland was willing to do the spots himself. But it never happened. A high-level policy group within the VA rejected the idea. The reason given: "It was believed that the impact would be a negative one, creating an interest and concern in areas of the country where there currently is none."

Inevitably, the Agent Orange affair became the stuff of empty political gestures, one of them by Ronald Reagan. Mr. Reagan conducted his election campaign against Jimmy Carter by skillfully projecting an image of old-fashioned honor, old-fashioned patriotism, and a respect for the armed forces and all they represented. Such patriotic fervor had not been seen in Washington since the days of World War II.

Two weeks before his lopsided victory over Carter, Reagan's staff issued a position paper in his name which called for Agent Orange remedies in much stronger terms than veterans had ever heard the Democrats use. According to the position paper, Reagan said there ought to be "temporary" medical care while the issue was being studied, and added: "This is the least we owe vets who may be suffering irreparable damage due to a government sponsored program.'' And yet another position paper issued by the Reagan-Bush camp called on Government not only to step up its investigation of Agent Orange, but also to ''provide adequate compensation for veterans who were harmed.'' But within two weeks after Reagan's swarming inauguration, the VA provided the Reagan transition team with a position that effectively would reduce Government responsibility—a move that the Reagan Administration embraced. The VA's Agent Orange Advisory Committee informed Reagan's people in the last week of January 1981 that ''excessive workloads [for the VA's workers] and anxiety would be created if President Reagan went on television inviting any Vietnam veteran who is worried about Agent Orange to report to a VA hospital for an examination.''

In any event, after the Reagan Administration was in place with its enormous mandate, the VA began more openly to treat Vietnam veterans as adversaries and seemed to feel confident about doing so. As this process unfolded in its guileful way, the President was seen on national television welcoming home the fifty-two Americans who had been held captive by Iran for 444 days. He gave the captives the spirited greeting they deserved, which was rather what the Vietnam veterans had hoped they would get when they came home. The veterans noticed the contrast between what the President was doing in 1981 and what the Government had done for their homecoming.

''All I could see,'' said John DiFusco, who had served in the Air Force, ''were the 55,000 who died in Vietnam. It's just once again that great feeling of being left out.'' Another veteran, Roger Melton, who worked as a therapist with some of his former service cohorts, said, ''It's almost as if the nation has been waiting for something to happen ever since the shame and disgrace of Vietnam.''

Enter David Stockman. The President had embarked on a massive spending program the likes of which had never before been seen in the United States—much of it going for the hardware of the new toys of the Defense Department, a commodity which is never bought cheaply. Stockman, as Reagan's director of the Office of Management and Budget, knew the nation would have to pay for defense spending; there was no tradition for short-changing defense contractors. He also knew that in order to keep any semblance of fiscal responsibility, the country would have to scrimp on many other things—among them, the claims of citizens who said they had been damaged by exposure to toxic chemicals.

Americans probably once believed DuPont's old motto of the 1940s, ''Better Things for Better Living Through Chemistry,'' but that was now giving way to the frightening disclosures about the Love Canal and other chemical disgraces; fears about past exposure to asbestos in the air and PCBs in seafood and drinking water; frustration at Government for its inability to regulate the shipment of chemicals; and anger at industry for its equal inability to safely dispose of chemical wastes. From Stockman's point of view, the veterans who claimed that they had been damaged by Agent Orange were special trouble for the Reagan Administration. If they were successful in their claims, the financial burden on the Government would be so great that it was certain the President would have to curtail spending in areas deemed more important. Even if they were unsuccessful, they represented a special political problem.

The Government's feelings were made clear in an undated memorandum written in the Office of Management and Budget that was not intended for public consumption. It described the "incipient movement towards federally financed toxic substances compensation" as posing "political difficulties of the highest order—because it involves the political cost of resisting popular proposals now in order to avoid potentially heavy costs in the more distant future." OMB foresaw "major battles" in the Congress because of Agent Orange and called toxic substances compensation "one of the most politically sensitive issues of the 1980s." OMB wanted to create a Cabinet-level working group to resist proposals for compensation, to keep them from becoming law. The Reagan Administration, which had courted veterans as one of its ploys to obtain power, was now quietly undermining one of its own publicly announced approaches to social policy.

The Administration was supported zealously by groups on the far right who shared its desire not to spend money on such things as payments to veterans who thought they were suffering from Agent Orange sickness. For example, on March 29, 1981, *The New York Times* printed an article which asserted that an unpublished report prepared by the House Subcommittee on Oversight and Investigations had accused both the VA and the Department of Defense of failing to deal properly with Agent Orange. Dow Chemical and President Carter's Agent Orange panel were also charged with complicity in the failure.

The *Times* article said that the subcommittee's criticism had been prepared prior to the Presidential election of 1980, but released after the election. There was apparently a feeling within the subcommittee that the criticism should not be made public, since the subcommittee itself had gained eight new members, who might not feel as strongly about the situation as had the former members.

The Veterans Administration was especially incensed at one section of the subcommittee report contained in the *Times* story, which quoted the report as saying that the VA had relied on "inaccurate and incomplete information" when it denied Agent Orange claims. The Defense Department was also criticized for not taking precautions "to prevent exposure of servicemen" and Dow was excoriated because it had allegedly failed to notify Government of its "awareness of the toxicity of Agent Orange."

No sooner had the *Times* published its story than the reporter who wrote it received a telephone call from Reed Irvine, the frequently blustery chairman of Accuracy in Media, a self-proclaimed watchdog group which, according to Irvine, was established to "combat media inaccuracy and distortion." Irvine demanded of the reporter where he had obtained the draft report. The reporter declined to tell him.

Irvine then demanded to come into the *Times* office and see the reporter personally so that, among other things, he and the reporter could discuss what might and might not be in the reporter's notes. The reporter turned him down on this offer, too. Irvine said that he had received "complaints" about the article, but when the reporter asked who had made the complaints, Irvine declined to say, telling the reporter that he had a right to protect his sources. The reporter replied that he had a right to know who his accusers were, and the telephone conversation then became rather acrimonious, before ending abruptly.

Various key editors at the *Times* and the paper's publisher then received quite a number of letters from Irvine and his associates. Irvine claimed that he had talked with Mark Raabe, then staff director of the subcommittee responsible for the controversial report that the *Times* had published. He quoted Raabe as saying that the *Times* account was not "balanced." He also charged that the *Times* had created a "gross distortion" of reality by calling the committee's "draft" an "unpublished staff report."

The incident was but an early example of the problems of inaccuracy that would plague Accuracy in Media in the 1980s. A day or so after it received Irvine's complaint, the *Times* was sent copies of a letter that Raabe had sent to Irvine. Rather than corroborate Irvine, Raabe accused Accuracy in Media of misquoting him and, worse, said that when he and Irvine spoke, they had never even discussed the issue of "balance" in the *Times* account. Worst of all, perhaps, was that Raabe informed Accuracy in Media that it had misspelled his name. Asked about all this months later, Irvine said he had not seen Raabe's letter. Both the reporter and the *Times* were attacked in the April 1981 edition of Accuracy in Media's *AIM Report*. The *AIM Report* charged that the *Times* had a "long record of misinforming its readers" and called the reporter's Agent Orange accounts a collection of "horror stories" that had spread "fear and suspicion" among the veterans who read them.

That Accuracy in Media's journalism was, to say the least, under something of a cloud did not seem to matter to Vern Rogers, who had been the VA's public relations man in Chicago when the Agent Orange issue first surfaced. A month after the *AIM Report* launched its attack, Rogers issued a memorandum to all VA facilities in the Great Lakes region not only praising the discredited story but also distributing it to all the VA offices within his purview. Moreover, once the *AIM Report* became known to Dr. Donald Custis, the chief medical director of the VA, it got circulation beyond anything Irvine could have hoped for. Custis ordered that it be sent to all VA offices. Custis wrote a memorandum of his own, in which he expressed the hope that "future media coverage of the herbicide issue will be more responsible than past accounts. . . ." He carefully noted that "it would be inappropriate for us to disseminate this report through an overt, official campaign."

Lest anyone think that the VA was about to interfere with the veterans who were struggling to have the Agent Orange problem defined, Custis added in his memo, "I would like to caution you against any action or initiative which might suggest to veterans that the VA has diminished its commitment to a thorough and responsible pursuit of knowledge and understanding of the many facets of this still perplexing issue."

In its "responsible pursuit of knowledge and understanding," the VA then hired Alvin Young. "Dr. Orange" had completed his work for the Air Force's Ranch Hand study and was looking around for something that would give him a sense of purpose, as the Air Force had. He told the VA that he had a "strong conviction" about working there and Dr. Barclay Shepard, head of the VA's Agent Orange office, noted it "would have a considerable potential for the enhancement of his military career."

Once aboard, Young, by now promoted to major, lost no time in tilling the creativity apparent in the Agent Orange book he had turned out so quickly the year before for the Air Force, to the immense satisfaction of his superiors. For his encore, he created a new report called "Agent Orange at the Crossroads of Science and Social Concern." The man whom the EPA had sought to disqualify as an expert witness, who had testified in the 1970s in civilian lawsuits against banning 2,4,5-T, was now the VA's voice of authority on Agent Orange.

In his book, Young spoke out on why he thought all the fuss persisted about it. It was absolutely nothing, he concluded. There were no scientific data to support the notion that Agent Orange had hurt anybody, and so it had to be that "social, political and legal concerns continue to drive the controversy.'' When he pressed the point further, he sounded curiously like Reed Irvine, because in his view, much of the problem was generated by and reposed within the press.

Young presented the scenario as he saw it: The press gives ''intense sympathetic coverage'' to veterans, who tended to ''confuse or misunderstand'' the issues, because the press ''usually contains many inaccuracies and reflects a highly emotional orientation.'' The press, he said further, insisted on its ill-considered habit to ''criticize, exaggerate and emotionalize'' the use of herbicides. He likened the fuss over Agent Orange to that other celebrated controversy over the Love Canal, where, in Young's view, nothing had really happened to make people sick.

It wasn't just the print media that was causing the trouble. Television, Young said, was vexing because on the subject of toxic chemicals, especially Agent Orange, it was ''overloaded with interviews with emotional laymen whose uneducated opinion . . . induced a similar emotional response in the viewer.'' Equally guilty, in Young's view, were well-meaning officials of local, state and perhaps even Federal government who were ''rarely knowledgeable'' about chemistry and so tended to bollix up things. Last but not least in Young's scenario were just ordinary citizens, who filed all manner of lawsuits and made a lot of trouble for the dedicated people trying to run the country, not because they wanted justice, but because they were selfishly obsessed with a need ''to verify the concern of the individual.''

For Young, the decision to halt the spraying of Agent Orange had been due not to a real health problem, but rather to the ''strong anti-Vietnam sentiment among members of the press and the general public.'' The claims of veterans, he said, might be due to the ''afflictions of aging and attendant psycho-social aberrations,'' and he repeated his hope, first voiced in the work he did for the Air Force, that the ''emotional role played by the national news media'' would not lead to restrictions on the use of beneficial herbicides in American agriculture.

Young then asked two rhetorical questions which clearly showed that he had adjusted quickly to the philosophy governing his new employer, the Veterans Administration. First, ''Are a few Vietnam veterans simply unable or unwilling to adjust to the larger society for no other reason than social or economic status?'' And second, ''Are they [the veterans] driven by an incentive on the one hand, to seek public recognition for their sacrifices and, on the other hand, to acquire financial compensation during economically depressed times?''

It may have seemed to anyone familiar with the working of Young's mind, and the high esteem in which he was held at the VA, that the agency was mired in the preconceived ideas it had already expressed. But Robert Nimmo, the Reagan appointee who had replaced Cleland as Veterans Administrator, told a meeting of the VA Advisory Committee on Agent Orange that nothing could be further from the truth. "We have no independent position on Agent Orange any more than we do on any other medical or scientific subject," he said.

By this time, veterans were demonstrating in various places around the country, and held a sit-in in the VA offices in Los Angeles to protest the treatment of the soldiers who had served in Vietnam, a ploy that was not destined to win them very much. Even as they demonstrated, Gary Spivey ended his labor in the same city, creating the protocol that the VA had paid him for, the guide that was supposed to establish sound parameters for a study of Agent Orange. It was sent to independent reviewers for their response. If they approved it, the scope of the study would be set and the work could begin. But the language of the reviewers was not kind.

One said that Spivey's effort "is clearly not a detailed plan which will allow the VA to proceed with the conduct of the study," and another complained, "Only the barest traces of substance are permitted by the author to leak out beneath a dense fog of concealment." A third reviewer said that the protocol seemed to have been written in a "conspiratorial atmosphere." It was not an auspicious debut for Spivey's work.

One of the more nagging problems with the protocol was the shroud thrown around it by the VA and by Spivey. For example, which alleged health effects were to be studied? Nobody would say. Even the scientists who reviewed the protocol really hadn't the slightest idea of what Spivey and the VA wanted the study to do, which may account for their restraint.

But the VA had a reason for the secrecy, which it was willing to make public. Spivey said he believed that if veterans found out which health problems were going to be studied, they would lie, and claim they were afflicted with whatever was being studied, thereby making a travesty of a serious scientific effort. Other scientists weren't sure they understood what Spivey was talking about. Disclosure of objectives in the occupational health studies of shipyard workers and people exposed to vinyl chloride had not thrown those studies off, nor did disclosure seem to undermine scientists at the American Cancer Society, who regularly informed the public of precisely what they were doing. One eminent reviewer, Dr. David Erickson of the Centers for Disease Control in Atlanta, said that for Spivey to suggest that claimants would conspire to conjure up certain illnesses was "insulting to veterans."

The veterans were, in fact, insulted. The Senate Veteran Affairs Committee found it necessary to hold hearings on Spivey's protocol. The senators had many questions for Spivey, but he was not to appear. No excuse for his absence was ever given publicly. But committee staffers said that they gave thought to issuing a subpoena for him. They didn't, and Spivey's dean showed up in his stead.

Veterans Administrator Nimmo appeared before the committee without pressure but may have wished that, like Spivey, he had made other plans. The senators were trying to understand what the veterans had not been able to understand: what impact, if any, Agent Orange had on human health, why nobody seemed to know anything about it, and how much it would cost in damages if science established that Agent Orange was as harmful as the veterans suspected it was. "We are dancing around the issue as to whether Agent Orange has caused this chamber of horrors," said Senator Arlen Specter, a Pennsylvania Republican, "because if it is decided that Agent Orange has caused it, there is going to be a very [big] impact on cost."

Nimmo then admitted that if Agent Orange was culpable, "We would be looking at costs of hundreds of millions of dollars per year into the middle of the next century." Clearly, the Government had been giving considerable thought to money. And with good reason. The Secretary of Health and Human Services, Richard Schweiker, said his staff had found evidence that "a greater number of persons than previously thought may have been exposed to" Agent Orange. "When I got this job in July," Schweiker said at a news conference, "I don't think anybody quite foresaw that we would be dumping chemicals on our people. I'll be quite honest with you. I don't think anybody foresaw that. Yet obviously, the Vietnam veterans have been saying something like that for some time."

A few more statements like that and the Government would have been paying claims. Fortunately for Government, a Health and Human Services scientist quickly pointed out, only four days after Schweiker's press conference, that in any study of ground troops "it may be difficult or probably impossible to define the exposure of each individual. . . ."

In its ungraceful ballet around the issue of Agent Orange, the Veterans Administration was alienating some of the groups with which it had traditionally enjoyed good relations, among them the largest veterans' organization in the nation, the American Legion. In 1981, most of the Legion's membership was of the World War II era, and some Vietnam veterans complained that the Legion was not as sensitive to their situation as it might have been, just as veterans of World War II were not convinced that those of the Great War understood them. But the Legion was, in fact, sensitive to what the Veterans Administration was doing. And the Legion-naires did not like the unilluminated doings that they were told about in Washington. No veterans' organization is overabundant in research scientists. But it did not take a research scientist to tell the Legion that the Agent Orange question was not being handled as well as it should have been. Over the year preceding, Legion representatives had tried, without success, to induce the VA to be more forthcoming. Then, in September of 1981, the Legion held its annual convention and passed a resolution noting that it had "continually called on the VA" to take "a more objective approach" to the Agent Orange question. The Legion said that the results of a study by some independent scientific group would be "more readily acceptable to Vietnam veterans who were exposed and their families."

It was one of those all-too-rare moments in American life when liberals, conservatives, and moderates could all agree that something was terribly wrong. The chairman of the House Veterans Committee, Congressman G. V. ("Sonny") Montgomery, normally a faithful supporter of the VA, felt compelled to write Nimmo, requesting that the study be transferred to the Centers for Disease Control (CDC), a Government scientific research agency in Atlanta, Georgia. Senator Alan Cranston joined in the request. "I do not know of one person in a responsible position in the Congress, the Executive Branch or the veterans organizations who favors the VA conducting the study," Cranston told Nimmo by letter.

The VA complied and when the scientists from CDC met with the weary and beleaguered Spivey to get his thoughts about the study, he was filled with advice, especially advice that was of a nonscientific nature. Someone in the CDC group kept notes of the conversation with Spivey. According to those notes, he made the following recommendations: "keep politicians and lawyers at bay"; "retain general legal counsel when dealing with VA and DOD" (Department of Defense); "get money in hand from VA before proceeding"; and, perhaps most important of all, "get a public relations person."

An official of CDC, who asked that his name not be used, later confided that the agency was not terribly happy about being given the study to do, and that it preferred to prevent new health problems from developing rather than solve old ones. He predicted that the CDC would give the Agent Orange study a "lower priority" than an effort that might prevent a disease from spreading.

The VA may have had its problems with Agent Orange, but that did not mean officials of the agency could not partake of the chocolate mousse of life in Washington. Administrator Nimmo spent $58,200 to refurbish his office and then, in a grand gesture that only underscored the VA's unique tradition for generosity, dispatched the furniture he had used to the office of his daughter, who worked in the Department of Commerce.

When he was not concerned with interior decoration, Nimmo continued to work as hard at his job as he ever did. When he was invited to speak at an American Legion convention in Hawaii, he arrived four days early, apparently so that he would have ample time to ponder the great issues of the day before speaking to assembled Legionnaires, who remained just as puzzled about the VA's Agent Orange activities as they had been when Nimmo began his tenure.

His seriousness of purpose was not always appreciated. The fact that he used a military aircraft to go to Reno for another speech and that, in contravention of advice from a VA lawyer, he used a Government chauffeur to drive him to and from work in a new Buick Electra did not sit well with his critics. The result was that a Congressional report came out on Nimmo, one which investigative wags took to calling the "Nimmo limo" report.

All the criticism clearly wearied him. In November of 1982, when the Vietnam Veterans Memorial was dedicated on the Mall, just a few blocks from his office, Nimmo failed to attend. That prompted even more criticism (Lou Cannon of *The Washington Post* called it Nimmo's "last act" of contempt). But Nimmo's supporters were quick to point out that Nimmo's fellow Californian, the President, did not attend either. Nimmo left office soon thereafter.

The President, easily as busy as Nimmo, had an excuse for not being there. When asked why he was absent from the first major gesture to heal the wounds of Vietnam, one paid for by veterans without the help of Government, Mr. Reagan said, "I can't tell until somebody tells me. I never know where I'm going."

With the VA seemingly unwilling or unable to do anything, a few congressmen began to think about the possibility of passing a law that would provide some payment to veterans exposed to Agent Orange. Nothing had yet been proved about what had happened in Vietnam, but there was enough information about Agent Orange's TCDD contaminant in the scientific literature to suggest that the veterans' fears were not rooted in irrationality. Congressman Thomas Daschle of South Dakota wanted a measure that would make the presumption that three disorders were caused by Agent Orange: cancer of soft-tissue organs, such as the lungs; porphyria cutanea tarda, a rare affliction of the liver; and chloracne. A serious case of dioxin contamination at Times Beach, Missouri, gave the bill some impetus, especially when the Government offered to buy out all 2,400 residents at a cost of $33 million. Health officials felt the town could no longer be safely inhabited. Daschle said that he did not see how the Government could move to protect civilians in Times Beach but continue to do nothing for veterans. Both the American Legion and the Veterans of Foreign Wars agreed with him and endorsed his proposed compensation bill.

That was enough to send Alvin Young into action. Within days after the American Legion and VFW issued their approvals of Daschle's bill, "Dr. Orange" appeared on *Nightline,* a late-night television program on the American Broadcasting Company. Young was dressed in civilian clothes. He was not identified as an Air Force major. No mention was made of the book he had written for the Air Force. Nothing was said about the National Academy of Sciences' criticism of the protocol he had designed for the Ranch Hand study. Nor was the audience told that Young had been an expert witness for the Department of Agriculture against the ban of 2,4,5-T and that he had long been an outspoken proponent of herbicide use. He was not identified as an employee of the Veterans Administration, nor was the public aware of the report he had done for the Air Force, "Agent Orange at the Crossroads. . . ." He was identified only as a VA "consultant," and the audience that night had no other context by which to judge him. Appearing with him in a debate situation was Dr. Samuel Epstein, author of *The Politics of Cancer* and a professor at the School of Public Health, University of Illinois.

Consistent with his advocacy of herbicides, Young assured the audience that nobody had ever died from dioxin exposure, adding, in what may have been one of the more remarkable scientific analyses ever presented on television, "I think there's a tremendous amount of emotion associated with dioxin. It's much like radiation: when you can't see it, there's a great deal of fear." In order to make clear that veterans had nothing to fear from Agent Orange, Young later created a slide show. On the very first slide, he showed an apple and orange, apparently to make the point that whatever liabilities might be assigned to the dioxin at Times Beach, it had absolutely nothing to do with the exact same substance if contained in Agent Orange.

Daschle's bill failed, because within the Government there was a strong feeling that the veterans had not proved their case with the certainty demanded by science. The American philosophy was harsh when compared to that of Australia, where its Government had to decide the same issue. Benefits were awarded there, after the Australians became aware that some Swedish studies raised the "possibility" that Agent Orange caused cancer. In Australia, it was up to the Government to prove beyond a reasonable doubt that a veteran's injury was *not* related to military service—precisely the opposite of the American position.

But were the U.S. veterans on the weak ground that Young, the VA, and others suggested? At one point in the agony of the American debate, Dr. Vernon Houk of the Centers for Disease Control testified before Congress that Federal health agencies believed that there was, in fact, an association between exposure to dioxin and the development of soft-tissue sarcoma in humans. Dr. Barclay Shepard, head of the VA's Agent Orange office, was on hand for Houk's testimony, and when he heard it, he leaned over and whispered to a colleague, "Somebody's gonna have to take him on."

Veterans were dispirited. "How much more evidence is needed before some of this doubt may be resolved in favor of veterans?" asked James Currieo, who testified for Daschle's bill for the Veterans of Foreign Wars. Nobody could say, but to hear the VA tell it, the Government's silence was for the good of the people. The new Veterans Administrator, Harry Walters, said that passage of the bill would "needlessly alarm millions of veterans and the population as a whole."

And so Daschle's bill died. In the Senate, Alan Cranston said that Congress could not make decisions properly where there were "fundamental differences of opinion between scientists." Despite his often-stated frustrations with the VA, Cranston said he continued to believe that the VA was the proper agency to make the ultimate decision on compensation.

As the VA delivered the *coup de grâce,* Dorothy Starbuck, the chief of the VA Benefits Program, told congressmen, "I would like to emphasize that the potential cost of paying compensation based on Agent Orange disabilities played no part in our deliberations on this measure."

When Ms. Starbuck made that lofty assertion, she must not have known about the calculations that were being made in her own agency. In one such record, the VA's general counsel, John Murphy, wrote a memorandum to his counterpart at the Office of Management and Budget, Michael Horowitz, and it was filled with lots of references to money. Murphy estimated that if the bill were passed, it would cost about $35 million a year for each year that it remained operative. "We estimate," said a handwritten note attached to Murphy's memo, "that 350,000 to 400,000 [troops] were in areas where spraying operations occurred." Murphy's memo was completed just four weeks after Starbuck's congressional testimony.

27
The White House Suppresses a Report

How can they stand this ostracism from the Army, Navy, Air Force and Marine Corps they were proud to serve and served so well?
—Major-General John E. Murray (U.S. Army, retired), October 12, 1987

If we don't take care of our veterans and reservists— who will fight the next war?
—Lieutenant Colonel Richard Christian (U.S. Army, retired), October 12, 1987

Agent Orange wasn't the only veterans' problem facing the Government. As the Vietnam veterans grew angrier about what they saw as their mistreatment and more frustrated about their inability to obtain help from the Veterans Administration, a smaller number of nearly forgotten men who had served thirty years earlier pressed claims of their own. In the late 1940s and 1950s, nearly a quarter of a million soldiers had been assigned to witness America's aboveground nuclear testing program. Thirty years later, beset with leukemia and other health problems associated with exposure to high doses of radiation, the "atomic veterans" wanted some sort of compensation.

Although almost all reputable scientists agreed that excessive exposure to radiation caused cancer, the Veterans Administration, apparently more concerned about the cost of the care than the justice of it, was either unable or unwilling to develop a cohesive policy for dealing with men who claimed they had been damaged by the atomic bomb. Some of them, convinced that they would never get a sympathetic hearing from the VA, turned in desperation to lawyers. But they quickly learned that they would be unable to pursue the Government outside of the VA route unless they successfully challenged the Civil War–era law that prevented them from paying a lawyer more than $10 for representation.

They found a friend in Gordon Erspamer, a San Francisco lawyer who took the case for no fee at all. Erspamer first moved to determine what the consequences were, if any, of not having a lawyer in dealing with the Government. Did the lack hurt the chances of the former soldiers to prove that their illnesses were, in fact, related to the atomic radiation to which they had been exposed? He found that since lawyers were unavailable for almost all of the cases appealed through the VA system, veterans frequently failed to produce evidence as required, with the result that the VA would simply terminate their cases on procedural grounds. Although the Government did not want veterans to have lawyers, it expected them to present evidence in the persuasive way that a good lawyer would. Only 1.2 percent of veterans who filed claims with the VA requested hearings that they were entitled to, as provided by law.

In responding to Erspamer, the VA insisted that veterans did not really need lawyers and that the system could be used by laymen. The VA had been set up to help veterans, the VA said, and the adversarial relationships that almost certainly would be created by lawyers were at odds with the tradition of the agency. Nobody said anything about the fact that the VA itself employed more than eight hundred lawyers to represent Government interests in handling claims against it and that one VA employee testified that veterans "would be better off having attorneys represent them. . . . They would possibly get a fairer shake."

Atomic veterans who dealt nonadversarially with the VA in San Francisco had fared badly; the VA had not even bothered to ask for an expert medical opinion on what radiation might have done to those who witnessed the nuclear tests. However, the Federal District Court in San Francisco was sympathetic to the veterans and sustained them in their contention that the old $10 limit on lawyers was unconstitutional. But when the VA appealed the case to the United States Supreme Court, a majority of the justices sided with the VA, not the veterans. William Rehnquist, then an associate justice and writing for the majority, said that Congress had been perfectly within its rights to pass the original legislation. He said that the VA system should continue as it was—"informal and nonadversarial"—and not be buffeted by lawyers, who would only "complicate" things. Associate Justice Paul Stevens wrote the minority's dissenting opinion. He declared that any citizen's right "to consult an independent lawyer and to retain that lawyer to speak on his or her behalf is an aspect of liberty that is priceless."

In rejecting the soldiers, the Supreme Court did them one small favor: It sent the case back to District Court for trial, essentially to give the veterans a chance to prove that in complicated cases such as this one, they had been denied due process by not having a lawyer in the first place. The radiation case involved complicated legal and scientific concepts—hardly the place for novices. (The need for a trial would be eliminated in November of 1988, when the $10 limit would end with the President's signing a law that would enable veterans to hire lawyers and pay them a fee that was not "excessive or unreasonable." The measure, which had strong backing in Congress, would also give veterans the right to a court appeal if they felt the VA denied them benefits they were owed. But even in making this unprecedented concession, there would be questions remaining. Veterans were not to take their appeals to the same courts as other citizens, but to an entirely new creation called the U.S. Court of Veterans Appeals. It was to have a curious feature: unlike the courts, whose judges are supposed to be appointed on the basis of their presumed judicial competence, the selection of judges for the veterans court would have to be politically balanced, with no more than half the judges of the same political party. Veterans wondered whether it would dispense justice or politics.)

Meanwhile, the Vietnam veterans, far more numerous and therefore more powerful than those filing the radiation claims, continued to press the Agent Orange issue. But Government officials apparently sensed that they were in a strong position to take the offensive and put the issue to rest once and for all. One way to mount that offensive was to use a collection of shabby Government paperwork called the Agent Orange Registry, which had been established by the VA to record all the health problems of veterans who came to VA hospitals to complain of symptoms said to be caused by Agent Orange. The man elected to exploit the issue was that resolute fan of herbicide use, Major/Dr. Alvin Young, who spoke to a meeting of the American Chemical Society in Washington.

The value of the registry had always been dubious at best; it was never a meticulously kept document. But that did not seem to bother anyone, because the agency had promised congressmen that the document would never be used to make conclusions about the health of veterans. The VA originally said it needed the registry only as a crude device to keep track of the kinds of health problems the veterans complained about. Congress, once all of the record-keeping errors and other mistakes were known, came to regard it as something not to be taken very seriously. But Young took it very seriously. He surprised those who knew what was really in the registry when he said that it contained some significant truths about the health effects of Agent Orange heretofore unknown to the American public.

Young's presentation to the Chemical Society was enhanced by a briefing he gave to the press. It was taken by the media as disclosure of something rather important. So when Young said that the Agent Orange registry did "not support the thesis that there [are] any unusual long-term health problems" associated with herbicide use in Vietnam, both *The Washington Post* and United Press International clambered to report his comments as a "major Agent Orange study"—a study that found that the herbicide had harmed nobody. *The New York Times* referred to the registry as a "medical study of 85,000 veterans." In fact, there had been no study at all, major, medical, or otherwise.

Senator Cranston saw the ploy for what it was and wrote a long letter to the VA, in which he expressed his "great disappointment" at Young's maneuvers and complained that the agency had once again sent out "misleading information" on Agent Orange. Cranston's letter received no attention from the press that had made so much out of what Young had to say.

It was not enough to transform an unkempt collection of names and symptoms into a study; the "findings" announced by Young would be even more newsworthy if they were corroborated by something else. The VA hoped that corroboration would be supplied by the old Air Force "Ranch Hand" study, which had set out to determine if pilots and herbicide handlers who had sprayed Agent Orange—"Operation Ranch Hand"—were suffering or at risk of suffering from particular medical problems. By late 1983, much of the press and the public had forgotten the warnings issued by the National Academy of Sciences about the inherent limitations of the Ranch Hand approach. The NAS had said in 1980, when the Ranch Hand study was getting started, that the Air Force was not investigating enough people to reach statistically significant conclusions. No important conclusions could be drawn from it as a result, the NAS said.

As it turned out, the Ranch Hand study offered not soothing corroboration for the VA's scientists and budgeteers, but suggestions that the former grunts might have been right, after all. It showed, among other things, that Ranch Hand pilots had higher than normal rates of skin cancer, liver disorders, and circulatory problems. It also showed that Ranch Hand families were beset by elevated rates of birth defects, infant mortality, and various rashes and things described as "birth marks." The report further said, however, that there was "insufficient evidence" to link any of the named health problems to Agent Orange.

Given all of that, the Government needed public relations. Air Force

Major-General Murphy A. Chesney certainly accentuated the positive when he said that the Ranch Hand study would be "reassuring" to Vietnam veterans. "These men are not dying off like flies," said Chesney, who was a member of the Ranch Hand study group. He added that as far as he was concerned, spraying Agent Orange in the jungles and fields of Vietnam had been "the right thing to do." He claimed that it "saved thousands of lives" and that if the United States found itself with a similar combat problem, "we've seen nothing that would keep us from using it again." But Dr. Richard Albanese, a civilian doctor who had served with Chesney on the panel, was less sure about Agent Orange. "A degree of concern is warranted," he said. "One can't have a sense that one should stop worrying about this."

Charles E. Thalken, an Air Force lieutenant colonel who had authored the Agent Orange book in 1978 with Young, the very same book that the Government considered so definitive, wasn't worrying at all. At the very time Albanese was issuing words of caution, Thalken was in Canada testifying as an expert witness for the forestry industry, which was opposing lawsuits brought by farmers, fishermen, and Indians who wanted no more 2,4,5-T sprayed near their homes. "Spraying," Thalken said, "imposes absolutely no danger to the bioenvironment." Later asked about his appearance, the Air Force said Thalken was testifying not as a spokesman for the Air Force but "in a private capacity as a consultant."

The Government thus held its own. A few months later, the chemical industry simply paid for peace with the veterans by offering $180 million to settle the class-action lawsuit they had brought against the companies which had made Agent Orange. The amount was acceptable to the veterans in the lawsuit—if not to veterans generally—and in a statement accompanying the settlement, Federal Judge Jack Weinstein said the money would be earmarked for an interest-bearing account that would benefit the claimants and their families. But the end of the lawsuit was more celebrated within industry than among the claimants. Chemical stocks rose in value, and some chemical makers said privately they would have been willing to pay much more.

Among some of the veterans, especially those who had elected not to participate in the lawsuit, there was much unhappiness. The sum of $180 million sounded like a lot, but divided among all those who believed that Agent Orange had hurt them, it seemed modest. Still, it was much more than the veterans had received from Government.

"It's a hell of a good start," said George Ewalt, Jr., one of the original plaintiffs, "better than anything we've had in the past fifteen years."

Whether it was the start or the finish was a reasonable question. Victor

Yannacone, a lawyer for the veterans who had been unceremoniously ousted during the lawsuit by his co-counsel, said he hoped that President Reagan "directs the Veterans Administration to honor the claims of the Vietnam combat veteran and recognizes that chemical bullets are just as deadly as lead bullets. . . ." The President did not order anything like the directive described by Yannacone.

In making the settlement, the chemical companies had denied they were guilty of anything, which meant that as far as they were concerned, 2,4-D and 2,4,5-T remained benign chemical compounds. The chemicals had not been proved guilty; therefore they remained innocent, in the eyes of their creators.

Judge Weinstein had quickly approved the settlement. He was not very happy with the case presented by veterans. He said that they did not have enough evidence to prove that Agent Orange had done anything except kill plants and that, as a result, the settlement was fair. In truth, the evidence assembled by the former soldiers and their lawyers would not have been impressive to any seasoned jurist. It was difficult to see how there could have been anything but skimpy evidence, since there had been an abysmal lack of cooperation given the veterans by the Government that had sent them into battle.

If Weinstein was not happy with the lack of substance in the veterans' case, he made it clear that he was by no means suggesting that their claims had been without merit; he felt that they should have been treated more compassionately. "Many do deserve better of their country," he said in his approval of the settlement. "Had this court the power to rectify past wrong-doings—actual or perceived—it would do so. But no single litigation can lift all of the plaintiffs' burdens. The Legislative and Executive branches of Government—state and Federal—and the Veterans Administration, as well as our many private and quasi-public medical and social agencies, are far more capable than this court of shaping the larger remedies and emotional compensation people seek." Kenneth Feinberg, who had assisted Weinstein, said, "Unless the Congress provides a comprehensive program, anything the court succeeds in doing will be a Band-Aid."

Whatever it was, the settlement took much of the steam out of the veterans' drive to win compensation from Government for the damage they suspected had been done to them by chemicals in Vietnam. In an editorial, *The New York Times* strongly suggested the veterans and their lawyers had pressured the chemical companies. The "vexed case of Agent Orange has been laid almost to rest," sighed the *Times*. Veterans dissatisfied with the size and structure of the settlement disagreed. They later pursued the case, but the settlement was upheld by the U.S. Court of Appeals in New York.

Of course, Agent Orange could not have been laid to rest just then. For there was still the matter of a Congressionally mandated health study of the soldiers who had served in Vietnam. There were still a few members of the Senate and House who wondered precisely what had happened to combat troops and what the Government's proper role should be in helping them.

From the beginning, Government had consistently raised the objection that it would be difficult, if not impossible, to measure the exposure of individual soldiers to Agent Orange because of the chaos of war. How could one prove beyond a doubt that a particular soldier was in an area when Agent Orange was sprayed, since the war in question had been unpredictable, filled with unexpected and random movements by all concerned?

But the Centers for Disease Control seemed to feel that this was a problem that could be solved. At least, this is what the CDC said when it got control of the study from the VA. "We view as the only remaining factors that will prevent the successful completion of this study to be the degree of participation among the selected veterans and the nonavailability of neces- sary resources," said a confident Dr. Vernon Houk, the CDC's top person assigned to the Agent Orange study. It was understandable that Houk and his colleagues would want the CDC to appear competent to do that which people at the VA had claimed could not be done—determine if soldiers had been, in fact, exposed to the chemical.

At the time CDC scientists accepted that responsibility, they were part of an agency in difficulty. For years, its scientists had been justifiably proud of the work they did in monitoring and investigating some of the nation's major health problems. CDC scientists used to like to tell visitors to Atlanta that working there was not like working for the Government at all—they felt independent and free to pursue their investigations with the freedom needed by responsible scientists everywhere. But then the CDC became a target for President Reagan's budget-cutters, at least in part because some powerful people in Government did not approve of the work it had done in connection with the Love Canal incident, but in greater part because Reagan's aides knew that the President was determined to spend enormous sums of money on Star Wars and other new hardware favored by the Pentagon. They were less interested in spending money to protect the public's health.

There were able people within CDC who were determined that it not die. The Agent Orange issue was seen by some of these people as giving the agency a new reason for existing.

For Houk to express so much optimism over a task that some in Government felt was nearly impossible was unusual for a scientist of his rank. But it was good news to people in the Congress who wanted the issue resolved. Success had to be just around the corner, they thought. There was no question that the veterans would cooperate—a respectable study was what they had been asking for—and Congress would provide the resources, a whopping $60 million in public funds to the CDC, before it was over. With the nation trying to spend its way out of yet another problem, the Agent Orange affair looked as if it might have a positive ending after all. CDC would save the veterans—and, the Fates willing, Agent Orange would save the CDC.

But how to begin? How could the CDC possibly make good on Houk's evaluation of the ease of the investigation it was about to undertake? The painfully difficult task of collecting the records which would show where troops had been in Vietnam fell to a retired Army lieutenant colonel named Richard Christian. He hoped his work would enable the Government to match troop movements with Agent Orange sorties. As a civilian, he was director of the Pentagon's Environmental Support Group. He would become the Government's most knowledgeable man on Agent Orange records.

Christian viewed the task as an enormous job of detective work, and as he proceeded with it, he was not unlike that master sleuth of television a few years earlier, Lieutenant Colombo. Cigar-chomping, direct, and plain-spoken, Christian had always brought a certain unassuming intensity to all the jobs he had had in the military. He had been connected with the Army all his adult life, having served as an enlisted man in Korea, where he was wounded while leading a bayonet charge against an enemy position. For his efforts he had received a Purple Heart, a battlefield promotion to sergeant first class, and a Combat Infantry Badge; he had survived twenty-one days of sustained armed combat. He was intensely sympathetic to the soldiers of Vietnam, and he thought he had the expertise to help them, gained in years of administrative work for the Army both in Europe and in Vietnam, prior to his retirement in 1973.

Christian told the Pentagon that it would take anywhere from $26 million to $55 million to do the job. He assembled a staff that, at its peak, numbered fifty-five people, and he went about trying to locate and organize a tangle of documents. In St. Louis, he and his people ferreted through the service records of no fewer than ten million service folk, looking for ones that would be useful to the CDC. He found still other files in Suitland, Maryland, and he sought detailed information on the course of the war itself at the Army War College in Carlisle, Pennsylvania. Once he had it all collected, he found himself with a veritable mountain of Government paper—forty thousand boxes of records, each weighing around forty pounds. In short, he was in possession of eight hundred tons of names, numbers, movements, advances, retreats, sorties, rescues, and bivouacs. It was nothing less than the paper agony of America's saddest, most pointless war.

The evidence of such a calamity was frustrating to behold. It was difficult to determine from the records where individual soldiers might have been on any given day. There were daily journals that indicated where they were *supposed* to be—but Vietnam had been a war in which almost nobody was ever where he was supposed to be.

The second part of the equation—if there was to be an equation—would be to discover precisely where Agent Orange had been sprayed. Determining exposure to the stuff would be equally maddening. Would epidemiologists try to include only those soldiers who were almost under a spray zone, or would they include others who were miles away and who might be just as seriously affected because of wind currents? If so, how many miles away? Could anyone state a "safe" distance? And what effect, if any, would the herbicide have had on drinking water available to combat troops in areas remote from spray zones?

Christian realized early on that there would be unsettling gaps in information. There were good records on Operation Ranch Hand, which had sprayed large areas with fixed-wing aircraft. But there also had been spraying that nobody had any record of. Soldiers had been asked to spray around the perimeters of base camps from herbicide cans that they carried on their backs. Helicopters had also done some unrecorded spraying, as had huge portable spraying machines and trucks that were specially adapted for that purpose. As far as Christian could tell, the written records of these work details had vanished, if, indeed, anyone had bothered to write them down in the first place. "Combat records," Christian would later recall, "were never made for any epidemiological study and anyone who thought so was out of his mind."

The combat records weren't just on paper. There was film as well, and what Christian found there bothered him. When the Air Force had described Operation Ranch Hand, it described situations wherein planes had been flying directly behind one another with windows open and Agent Orange spray everywhere. But when Christian studied the films, he saw planes flying at different altitudes, out of each other's spray lines, with windows closed. He regarded the Air Force's assurances that the Ranch Hand pilots and crew members had been heavily exposed without ill effect as simply the Government's "party line."

If Christian was depressed by the films and engulfed by the paperwork, he also found that work with the Centers for Disease Control was not nearly as stimulating and ordered as he had hoped it would be. In fact, on occasion, he found it highly unpleasant, especially when he later came to believe that the CDC was out to make him "the scapegoat" for its inability to deliver on its promise of a study. During the period he was trying to fathom the spraying records, Christian saw four directors of the CDC's Agent Orange study come and go. From his perspective, the once-formidable research group was showing the classic telltale signs of an agency that lacked the commitment, both scientific and political, to finish what it had started.

Christian apparently wasn't alone in this view. Helen Gelband, the Agent Orange specialist of the Congressional Office of Technology Assessment, let slip to a Congressional subcommittee that "we have not had a great deal of communication from CDC, and it has been sometimes difficult to find the right person to talk to." When Christian was asked to testify before the same group, he complained about the confusion at the CDC. "Time tables and numbers of subjects and disqualification factors repeatedly changed over the ensuing months," he told the subcommittee. From what Christian could gather, CDC scientists could not agree on a set of assumptions that would constitute "an exposure model crucial to the study." In other words, the scientists could not tell him what might constitute exposure to Agent Orange. If the CDC scientists could not tell him what they wanted, he thought, then how could he do his job properly?

CDC scientists decided at one point that they could do a better job than Christian. They went ahead and started to analyze for themselves records on troop movements to determine who might have been exposed to Agent Orange. Their efforts were, to say the least, a bit flawed. According to a Defense Department internal document prepared by Christian's associates, the CDC developed numbers based not on American troop locations, but on those of the enemy, which researchers had factored in by mistake. Further, their analysis "was written by individuals with no military experience and no background in tracking combat infantry units," and they also failed to check out their findings.

That was in early 1985. By the end of the year, having then spent almost all of the money appropriated, the CDC had convinced itself that the study it had assured everyone it could certainly do might not be possible after all. And who was to blame? The CDC criticized the "poor quality" of data it had gotten from Christian and said that his shortcomings "might compromise the credibility of the study." Even more nettlesome to Christian was the CDC's suggestion—made directly to the White House science panel studying Agent Orange—that he had held back and not given them all that he might have. The charge was made in an unsigned thirty-six-page document written in the usual Government bureaucratese. But on page 20, buried within dense scientific jargon, was what Christian saw as nothing less than a personal attack on his character and professional integrity: ''We suspected we were not receiving all possible information,'' said the CDC. Christian could neither forget nor forgive the CDC for this. He and the CDC were clearly on two different bumbledom express trains that were on a collision course. The wreck would occur in the White House.

Not the least bit abashed over having confused American and Vietcong troop movements, the CDC now moved to take over the entire records process from Christian, if permitted. If the CDC could not get its way, it suggested, it might not be able to do the study, and the Government would have only Richard Christian to blame. An irritated Christian wrote to the CDC's Vernon Houk, explained that he only did what he was asked to do, and demanded of Houk, why didn't CDC ''admit this was of their own doing?'' As far as Christian was concerned, if there was failure now, it was the CDC's fault—after all, they were the scientists. He said he would refuse to surrender his records job to CDC. ''We have gone the extra mile all along. . . . We want to see the study through for the sake of our Nation's Vietnam veterans,'' he wrote Houk.

This lack of rapport did not escape the vigilance of Alvin Young, who by then had become a part of the White House Office of Science and Technology, and was head of a subgroup there charged with responsibility for coming up with a resolution to the Agent Orange issue. On December 24, 1985, Young summoned Christian to the White House and told him what was in his Christmas stocking: His work would be subjected to ''peer review.'' Christian wondered what that meant. ''Peer review'' was a term normally used by scientists who were evaluating other scientists. From Christian's perspective, Young was not really asking for peer review. He was looking for a way to effect damage control on an issue that could be politically harmful to President Reagan, to many other politicians, and to the CDC itself.

By early 1986, Christian's relationship with the Centers for Disease Control was almost nonexistent. On Capitol Hill, members of Congress concerned with what was happening to Vietnam veterans heard reports about fierce infighting between Christian and people at the CDC. That was absolutely not where the Agent Orange effort was supposed to be. As a result, Alan Cranston and Senator Frank Murkowski, a Republican of Alaska, both members of the Senate Veterans Affairs Committee, wrote to President Reagan and to Otis Bowen, the Secretary of Health and Human Services, to complain about what they saw as a disaster in the making.

Cranston and Murkowski told Bowen that they understood there was "a nearly complete breakdown in the relationship" between Christian's people and those of the CDC. When they wrote to Reagan, they enclosed a copy of the letter they sent to Bowen and requested the President to "take the steps necessary to resolve the persistent, very counterproductive conflicts within the Executive Branch . . . that are significantly impeding effective work toward carrying out the study." The press either was not alerted to their letters or did not think enough of them to give them any public notice. Nobody inquired into the background to find out why they were written.

It wasn't really clear if the President heeded the senators' request. What was clear was that Major Young, working in the White House, moved quickly to investigate Christian. The two people selected to review his work were John Hatcher, an archivist for the Army, and retired Army Major-General John E. Murray. They were not asked to look at anything the CDC had done; it seemed to be assumed by the White House that whatever the problem was, Christian had to be the one culpable.

Indeed, when Young called Murray, Young emphasized that he had suspicions about Christian. As Murray later remembered it, Young told him to determine if Christian "was providing all he had to CDC." With that thought in mind, Murray—who had always had high regard for Young and regarded him as a colleague—began to study the fruits of Christian's tumultuous labor.

Murray seemed to be the sort of officer who would not be hostile to the Government's position that soldiers had not been damaged by Agent Orange. He had been, after all, an important part of management. He had devoted his life to the Army, which had rewarded him with considerable responsibility (he was the country's last defense attaché in Vietnam), and he believed that the war had not been a mistake. He had a reputation for being tough and smart; he was not a man who would jump to conclusions—and certainly would not be expected to take strong issue with Young.

In May, after five months of hard work, Murray reported his findings. They were a pleasant surprise to Christian, a prickly pear to Young. If Christian had been correct in his suspicions that his superiors and associates in Government were out to get him, they certainly could not do it now, for Murray's findings were hardly in keeping with the White House's preconceived ideas. He said that Christian's work was "of inestimable worth" and was "an excellent model of the careful performance of dull toil." The accolades were contained within a formidable document entitled "Report to the White House Agent Orange Working Group Science Subpanel on Exposure Assessment." It carried the letterhead of the Executive Office of the President and was the first report on Agent Orange ever written at so high a level in Government.

Murray and Young did not disagree on everything. Indeed, Young could take some comfort in Murray's assurance that the evidence at hand did not support a cause-and-effect relationship between the health problems of veterans and Agent Orange. But he could take no comfort at all in Murray's recommended way out of the Agent Orange mess, which was that the Government simply make a payment to Vietnam veterans for their "loss of grievance." The formula to be used for paying, Murray suggested, would be based on careful estimates of what it would cost the Government to continue with its Agent Orange study "or its possible options that promise disappointment." Murray filed his report not only with Young, which is what he was expected to do, but also with Caspar Weinberger, the Secretary of Defense, and with the Chairman of the Joint Chiefs of Staff and assorted other top officials.

Nobody at the White House thought that Murray would have the audacity to write to people outside of the immediate chain of command that had hired him. Donald Newman, the Under Secretary of Health and Human Services, was upset because the general had not observed Government protocol as Newman understood it. And so he made his own use of White House stationery when he quickly wrote a protest to Weinberger, charging that the "release of General Murray's report . . . is a serious breach of protocol. . . . In addition, in my opinion, [it] will seriously undercut the validity of our position." He did not say what that "position" was. It seemed clear, however, that he was referring to the Government's strongly held but obfuscated opinion that Vietnam veterans claiming sickness from Agent Orange should not be paid. Newman added that "the report contains opinions and conclusions which go far beyond his mandate for the study, the premature release of which could cause embarrassment to the Government." Newman concluded, "My purpose in writing you is to alert you to the situation and preclude premature release or discussion of this sensitive report."

Newman's letter never became public. Nor did Murray's report, which he later charged was deliberately suppressed by the White House. Murray became angry when his report was simply never released and, in fact, he called it a "concentrated cover-up." The more he thought of Newman and Newman's concerns about protocol—which had nothing to do with the suffering of Vietnam veterans—the angrier did he become. Unfortunately, the media did not know of his feelings. "There has been a waste of six years in the epidemiological study that cost the taxpayer at least $60 million,"

Murray fumed in a letter to Christian. Murray called the caper "a cat and mouse political tease." He accused the Centers for Disease Control of creating "make-work jobs" which accomplished nothing and diverted money that could have gone to help the veterans.

Murray was not alone in his exasperation with the study's lack of resolution. "We have waited for seven years," said Congressman Daschle, "and it has made a mockery out of this whole process." Neither Daschle nor his colleagues knew a thing about Murray's report, which was in the process of being forgotten by the Government that had commissioned it.

If Murray's report was deemed unfit for public consumption, the Government could make no use of whatever efforts were expended by John Hatcher, the other "peer" reviewer retained by Alvin Young. On October 2, 1987, Hatcher pleaded guilty to charges that he solicited and accepted a "sexual bribe" from an employee of the Army—in return for placing the employee in an intern program. When he was sentenced to six months in prison by U.S. District Judge Albert V. Bryan, Jr., in Alexandria, Virginia (where the Pentagon is), it cast a shadow on his work. Hatcher, who had resigned his civilian job with the Army in August of 1987, was ordered to undergo psychiatric treatment during his jail term.

If the Centers for Disease Control could not produce a study that would say with precision what Agent Orange might or might not have done to American troops, the scientists there were by no means denying that those troops were in difficulty. In February of 1987, the CDC reported preliminary results of a study which found that within five years after war's end, Vietnam veterans were dying at a rate that was 45 percent higher than those who had served during the same period but not in Vietnam. Vietnam veterans also had a 72 percent higher suicide rate than the same group, and a high incidence of "violent deaths," which included homicides, suicides, motor vehicle accidents, and accidental poisonings. Many of the deaths in this category were caused by drug overdoses. The CDC found it plausible to attribute this to the "unique environment and experience of serving in Vietnam and returning to an unsupportive and sometimes hostile climate in the United States." But the CDC said that veterans of World War II and Korea had exhibited similar problems of post-traumatic stress and suggested that it might be "due to unusual stresses endured while stationed in a hostile fire zone."

And so the Government's effort to learn the truth about Agent Orange had deteriorated into a mess that was bursting with conflicts of interest borne by men who had no business participating in what was supposed to have been an objective study, but which never had a chance. Great sums of money had been spent, politicians and soldiers had written letters, and the interests of the chemical industry and agribusiness had been served. But as the CDC study wound down, the soldiers knew no more than they had when they came home from the war.

Because the Government had betrayed so much bias against compensating Vietnam veterans, and because the quality of its science was so wanting, the American Legion decided to do a scientific study of its own and commissioned two prominent chemists and epidemiologists: Dr. Steven S. Stellman of the American Cancer Society, and his wife, Dr. Jeanne M. Stellman of the Columbia University School of Public Health. They were joined by John F. Sommer of the Legion's Washington office. For the Legion, whose World War II–era majority had always tried to find the positive side of most Government decisions, it was a most unusual step to take.

The Stellmans designed questionnaires seeking such information as the history of diagnosed illnesses, medical symptoms, and reproductive outcomes and sent them to thousands of American Legionnaires who had served during the Vietnam War, of whom 6,810 responded. Forty percent of those were veterans of service in Vietnam; the rest had served elsewhere during the same time.

Some of the most important information developed by the Stellmans and Sommer came in the final stage of their study, in which they found that among Vietnam veterans exposed to Agent Orange, there were significantly more cases of noncancerous fatty tumors, adult acne, skin rash with blisters, and increased sensitivity of eyes to light. Those exposed to the herbicide also showed significantly more instances of feeling faint, fatigue or physical depression, body aches, and colds. The researchers also found that the wives of veterans who had been exposed to Agent Orange suffered from a significantly higher than normal rate of miscarriages, a rate as high as that of women who smoked during pregnancy.

The Stellmans were confident that they were now able to demonstrate meaningful exposure to Agent Orange, so that the different health problems between exposed and nonexposed veterans could be indicated. "We never know quantitatively how much people were exposed to," said Steven Stellman. "But there is nothing wrong with doing health studies based upon less than perfect quantification of exposure, if you know the limitations of your study and you explain how these limitations affect your findings."

At the Veterans Administration, which consistently had denied the existence of any scientific information linking Agent Orange with health problems, functionaries were probably surprised at findings in one of their own studies. For in the summer of 1987, the VA inadvertently revealed the results of a study it had been sitting on, inexplicably, for six months. It was the largest study of deaths among Vietnam veterans ever conducted by the VA, involving the VA's examination of more than 52,000 death records, and it concluded that Marine ground troops who had served in Vietnam had died of lung cancer and cancers of the lymph system at a greater rate than Marines who saw no service in Vietnam. It further found that Marines who served in Vietnam had died at a 110 percent higher rate of non-Hodgkins lymphoma than would be expected in such a group. Non-Hodgkins lymphoma had often been cited in the scientific literature as related to exposure to herbicides like Agent Orange. Although the VA said it did not look for the causes of the cancers it discovered, it noted, surprisingly, that "exposure to Agent Orange may be suspected."

At first mention of the study's existence, the VA's Lawrence Hobson downplayed its significance. "I wouldn't say it's terribly worrisome," he said. "If I were a Vietnam veteran, I don't think I'd be the least bit disturbed about it." Alvin Young, the man who said he knew herbicides were safe because his bosses had told him so, issued a statement from his office in the White House suggesting that the VA study was invalid. "The numbers are small; it just doesn't add up," he said. He called the findings a "statistical fluke."

The White House and the VA expertly played down their own science, but Congressman Lane Evans, one of the Vietnam-era veterans serving in the House, countered that "the evidence is there that something is wrong for Vietnam veterans." In fact, the evidence was abundant. In another phase of their study for the Legion, the Stellmans had looked at how veterans of Vietnam were behaving as civilians and how they were faring. They found a wide range of adverse effects in these men. Those who had seen high levels of combat were clearly at greater risk for bad marriages, and were less happy and less satisfied with their lives. They also showed higher levels of anxiety, irritation, and feelings of helplessness and were more prone to use prescription drugs, alcohol, and tobacco. Earning power was significantly less for these soldiers than for those who had not gone to war in Southeast Asia.

There was scant indication that any Government scientist was the least bit interested in what the Stellmans said they had found, or even in those few Government admissions indicating that all was not as splendid as the likes of Hobson and Young had suggested. But one glimmer came in the spring of 1988. Its source was one of the Air Force's civilian consultants, Dr. Richard Albanese. In 1984, Albanese had not joined with his Air Force colleagues who held that the Ranch Hand study ought to be "reassuring" to ground troops worried about their exposure to Agent Orange. He adopted a far more independent and objective posture and continued to review data in the years following, even though his Air Force associates were saying publicly that there was really nothing to be concerned about. What he found was something to be very concerned about and should have been disturbing to any reasonable person trying honestly to determine what, if anything, had happened to the health of the Vietnam veterans. Albanese reported that in five of eleven health areas studied in 1984, he found real, not imaginary health problems. Among his findings: increased levels of cancer and defects among infants fathered by soldiers who had served in Vietnam.

There was a mini-stir in Washington. Senator Tom Daschle dryly noted that what the Air Force had found "reassuring" now appeared to be "seriously flawed." Albanese's candor had no immediate effect on the position the Government had been taking all along, while the CDC continued to insist to Congress that the Agent Orange study could not be done, because "for most of the ground troops, the exposure was not significant," according to Vernon Houk. But the CDC could not say what constituted insignificant exposure to such powerful stuff. Nobody could, because the research had not been done and the research money had now been frittered away.

There were scientists who felt that Houk was hiding behind science, not using it to search out the truth. Dr. Peter Kahn of Rutgers University, a scientist for the New Jersey Agent Orange Commission, was doing his own study on the effects of herbicides on veterans. He said that the CDC's method for selecting which troops were exposed was "guaranteed to get a large group of unexposed people." Kahn felt that the whole CDC–Agent Orange effort was being conducted "to give the appearance of doing a large, carefully engineered study," while it knew that this approach would yield no finding and no result. He acknowledged his belief that most ground troops in Vietnam had probably not been heavily exposed to Agent Orange but that there were "more creative ways to do a valid study." In other words, if CDC did not look, it would not find.

The CDC's murky Agent Orange science grew even cloudier early in 1988 when it released an oddment called the "Vietnam Experience Study." This study, much of it conducted on the telephone, had been designed a few years earlier. Its purpose had never been to plumb the depths of the Agent Orange question, nor even to wade through its shallows. Rather, it was supposed simply to survey the overall health problems of Vietnam veterans and compare them with those of former soldiers who had not served in Vietnam. Indeed, the Vietnam Experience Study had been envisioned originally by CDC scientists as what it would do *instead* of a study of the health effects of Agent Orange.

That fact was neatly ignored in early May, when the Government released the study and claimed it showed that the physical health of veterans who served in Vietnam was not significantly different from that of soldiers stationed elsewhere. The report, based in part on telephone interviews with 7,924 former soldiers who had served in Vietnam and another 7,364 who had served in West Germany, South Korea, and elsewhere during the same time period, was presented to the Senate Veterans Affairs Committee. The study added, however, that those who had served in Vietnam did tend to have more psychological problems and an unexplained loss in hearing and also suffered from more depression, more drug abuse, and a kind of hepatitis said to be common in Southeast Asia.

To its credit, the CDC did not claim that the study said anything definitive or even significant about any effects that might have been caused by Agent Orange. Scientists in Atlanta, remembering the CDC's older tradition of honesty and responsibility, knew better than that. But the Veterans Administration apparently felt no need to be restrained or careful or even ethical. Stretching for conclusions that were neither stated nor even hinted at by the CDC, Thomas Harvey, the VA's chief deputy, said the study exonerated Government from Agent Orange liability. Even better, from the VA's point of view, was Harvey's feeling that the study might well be used to defeat any proposed legislation to compensate veterans who suspected their health had suffered because of exposure to the defoliant. Such legislation, Harvey said, was "bad policy, bad politics and bad science" and it was "based on frustration." There were veterans who smiled when they heard that. Whatever the VA's expertise, it certainly knew about bad policy, bad politics, and bad science.

A few weeks passed, during which time President Reagan underscored a reluctant Government's much-belated concern for those cancer-ridden veterans who still survived their exposure to nuclear explosions during World War II and after. He signed legislation which would make it easier for some, but not all of them, to get disability benefits.

But then, as Memorial Day 1988 approached and some Americans prepared to watch yet another network television movie about the healing of the Vietnam veteran, the CDC released a new study which, it said, did deal with the Agent Orange question. This one showed that the soldiers who had sprayed the chemical in Vietnam retained excessively high levels of dioxin in their blood. Since dioxin was widely regarded as one of the most potent cancer-causing molecules on earth, veterans were understandably interested in what the high levels might mean for the future. The CDC couldn't say, and the VA people who were so interested in the Vietnam Experience Study inexplicably indicated absolutely no interest in this one.

Perhaps that was because VA employees were so terribly busy. The public didn't know it, but the VA had been routinely awarding cash bonuses of up to $5,000 to those of its professional staff who could decide the highest number of disability appeals. The bonuses were based on a quota system for lawyers and doctors who labored in the Board of Veterans Appeals, one of the groups established within the agency. The cherished values of Hippocrates and Solon were nowhere to be found in this little enterprise. Bonuses were given not for how assiduous Government doctors were in using their art to diagnose illness, nor for how astute Government lawyers were in insisting that the interests of justice be served for the survivors of America's wars. The bonus system was based only on how many of the cases they could process each week. And those eligible for bonuses were hardly out-at-the-elbows workers: The regular salaries of these professionals ranged from $52,000 to $62,000 a year. Lawyers and doctors were getting what the bonus marchers of 1932 could not get. The practice was discovered by the Vietnam Veterans of America, which publicly charged that this "assembly line" justice and medicine deprived veterans of their right to a fair hearing and was probably unconstitutional.

The criticism was rejected by Kenneth Eaton, chairman of the Board of Veterans Appeals. He told the Senate Veterans Affairs Committee that the perks were an "important management tool." But what had seemed right and proper to Eaton was just the opposite to a former member of the board, Daniel J. B. Bierman. He testified before the same committee that quotas and bonuses were at the heart of the "evilness of a system that promotes shoddy treatment of the cases by encouraging incomplete review."

There were more than a few in the Senate and elsewhere who wondered just how much time the VA spent on the case of each veteran who pressed a claim. Since the bonuses were significant, it seemed reasonable to believe they were envisioned to shorten lengthy and complex deliberations. But such was not the case. Bierman testified that the average time spent on each case was 7.8 minutes. The disclosure of bonus payments to lawyers and doctors offended even those who did not want to pay the true wages of war, with the result that such payments were suspended. Even in ending them, Eaton defended what the VA had done and said that the criticism had been merely the result of a "misunderstanding" and a "problem of perception."

As all of this went on, President Reagan plumped to have the VA elevated to a Cabinet-level agency. The media tended to see Reagan's suggestion as evidence that Government was more interested in the problems of veterans than before. Those active in the causes of veterans saw it otherwise, as a bureaucracy moving closer to the White House, not to its own constituents. In any event, a Department of Veterans Affairs, its chief to be of cabinet rank, was created in October of 1988. President Reagan signed the law on the fifth anniversary of the American invasion of Granada. Even its supporters and those who felt that former soldiers had not always received the attention they deserved wondered how or if the new, loftier agency's mission would change. "What we're going to do with it, God only knows," said Cooper T. Holt, executive director of the Veterans of Foreign Wars.

Some veterans were also disheartened by their suspicions that the VA was available to offer special help to congressmen who wanted to do favors for certain of their constituents, without overhauling the agency to benefit all former soldiers. Their suspicions were only intensified when, in 1988, the Vietnam Veterans of America discovered that Chairman Eaton had drawn up a list of favored members of Congress and had sent it to the sixty-five members who constituted the Board of Veterans Appeals. These favored congressmen were said to have been given special rights of review in any case in which they had expressed an interest. Mike Leaveck of the Vietnam Veterans of America called it a "special signature list" which included the top leaders of both houses.

It was not clear precisely what the VA expected of members of Congress it regarded as favored. Veterans noticed, however, that key members of Congress were opposed to the move to authorize court review of VA decisions.

And so the Agent Orange case began to wind down. The last legal challenge to the settlement with the chemical companies was swept aside in mid-1988, and nobody expected that the veterans would ever be in a position to press for justice against the Government itself. The veterans who had participated in the class-action lawsuit might expect to get around $5,700— not very much, considering what they had gone through and the real questions that remained about their health in future years.

The veterans had thus truly been outmaneuvered and defeated, much more decisively than they had ever been as soldiers. The Government had not wanted to pay, and so it would not pay; the obfuscators had pulled off a scam and succeeded in convincing much of the public and the media that there had not been all that much exposure to Agent Orange.

In a real sense, it never mattered whether there was massive exposure or not. There was massive exposure to a foul war; nobody disputed that. And what was abundantly clear was that war, any war, does a great deal of damage to the soldiers who fight it, whether the specific source of the damage is identifiable or not. The most important question was not whether Agent Orange caused illness to the troops who were exposed to it, but whether a nation of what Lyndon Johnson had called "reasonable men," a nation that had always prided itself on its morality and its fairness and its inherent goodness, would meet its commitments to the people it had sent to war—and not just to the war in Vietnam.

For two hundred years, the Government of the United States has largely failed to do this. If American political leaders met those commitments to their own people, American concerns about human rights in other countries would never ring hollow, and there might be more consistency in the media's obsessive, intrusive concerns about personal morality, including the rectitude of national figures. If there was a personal moral issue to be reported to the people, there was surely a greater national moral question in what happened to the soldiers who suffered from exposure to war.

The question was clear enough. How would the Government of the United States answer it? Perhaps the answer came one day, not very long ago, when a telephone call was made to an office in the Veterans Administration. This was the office where all the planning was to be done about pursuing the Agent Orange issue. The caller wanted to know what the VA planned to do about the study that showed the Marines were getting cancer, and what did the VA think about the CDC's decision not to pursue the Agent Orange study any further. "No one has been in charge of that office for several months," replied the VA employee who answered the telephone. "I can't say when or if anyone will be hired for that job."

And so it seemed that nothing had really changed.

Epilogue

Volume by exciting volume, you'll splash through the
tangled jungle, humpin' the boonies with the men of
the First Cav. Slide behind the controls of an F-4
Phantom rifling through Hanoi's deadly air defenses.... Every volume packed with searing combat
action ...
—From a brochure for Time-Life Books advertising
Combat Photographer, 1986

A man and a woman appear to have taken their lives
and the lives of their three children to publicize the
couple's belief that Vietnam veterans and their families are ill-treated.
—Report in *The New York Times,* March 7, 1986

The past is history now. We don't worry about that.
—General William Westmoreland (U.S. Army,
retired), 1980

The tragedy of Agent Orange was not unique. The Yankee frugality whose
virtues were extolled by successful and secure eighteenth-century clergymen
(and by clever politicians ever since) proved to be a stronger tradition than
the American sense of fairness. If the soldiers of Vietnam thought there had
never been a group of veterans so ignored, abused, and betrayed, it was not
because they tried to rewrite history, but because they knew so little about
it. Even though Daniel Shays raised issues that many Americans might feel
are central to their identity as a free people, as individualists who will not
tolerate the abuse of Government, he remains only a minor rebel in a
footnote to most American history books. Historians have reassessed the

strengths and weaknesses of early Federalism many times, but Shays' movement, his purpose, and the nature of unjust and failed policies that he and his friends could not accept have never received an adequate explanation outside of a select group of scholars. The problems that veterans have faced after most wars have been largely ignored by most political and social histories. When veterans in postwar periods are mentioned, it is usually in terms of their "readjustment," a bureaucratic word that apparently refers to their capacity not to ask anybody for anything.

If Government zealots finessed Vietnam veterans out of the honest scientific research and medical attention they needed and deserved, it was no worse than what their predecessors had done to the Spanish-American War soldiers who were shipped from Cuba to Montauk and left at the tip of Long Island to die in the summer of 1898. If VA doctors, doctors' helpers, and assorted red-tapists and obfuscators seemed to be premature in their conclusion that the toxic chemicals used in Vietnam hurt nothing but tropical plants, they were no more untimely than Surgeon General Sternberg had been eight decades earlier, when he decided, just as precipitously, that soldiers returning from Cuba suffered from only "mild" fevers that would soon go away.

The post-Vietnam period generally is often thought of as being somehow fundamentally "different" from other postwar periods in American history. It was rather different in the degree of national divisiveness it caused. Perhaps only during and after the Civil War itself were Americans so unable to agree on what the bloodshed was for. But Vietnam was not so different in the uncaring attitude demonstrated by the Government toward veterans. Most Americans had difficulty in seeing this because their impressions of postwar America were formed by vivid (if not totally accurate) memories of the good years following the end of World War II. The soldiers of World War II came home as unquestioned heroes after a struggle that the overwhelming majority of Americans saw as just and right against one of history's great villains. Such years had a poignancy and power that quite overshadowed the tepid welcomes given later to the combat veterans of the stalemate that was Korea, whose resolve, patriotism, and very manhood had been unjustly besmirched. Americans have always wanted to believe in their own decency and good intentions. The veterans of Vietnam were very much a part of that tradition. They, too, chose to believe that the post–World War II welcome home was the normative thing—not the vilification and false information spread after Korea. In truth, it was the years following World War II that had a stronger claim to being regarded as "different." Those good years were planned for and nurtured by a society for which the aimlessness of the Great Depression was too recent a memory; too unsettling in its implications for the future of America to even contemplate a return to. For Government, paying the wages of war seemed reasonable in 1945—its soldiers had conquered unquestioned evil and they represented all walks and classes of American life.

Government found those same wages very high in 1978, when the Agent Orange issue began to emerge. The middle-aged, undertutored functionaries for whom the Depression and its anguish were not relevant memories easily talked themselves into believing—with some gentle nudges from a friendly chemical industry—that herbicides were harmless to humans. The nature of the enemy in Vietnam, the humiliation of defeat, the way the U.S. war effort was conducted, and the way it was perceived by many Americans were also bound not to create a popular feeling that debts to soldiers should be paid. This judgment had nothing to do with the soldiers who fought the Vietnam War, but with the powerful civilians and high-ranking military advisers who got America into it. Soldiers only bore most of the cost of the mistake.

The other major reason why Vietnam seemed an aberration to most Americans was that strong questioning positions were taken later by those who actually fought the war. Soldiers who continued to think that the war had been a good idea blamed themselves for the lack of a definable victory. Soldiers who realized that the war had been a horrible mistake became conscience-stricken over the less than heroic way some had conducted themselves against a maddening, implacable foe and the Vietnamese civilians, who were always suspected of being hostile, whether they were or not. This was not an aberration at all, for there were striking parallels between the public anguish of the Vietnam veterans and the aftermath of the Philippine Insurrection, during which it was the soldiers themselves who made public disclosure of atrocities committed in the supposed interests of the United States. Indeed, the soldiers who served in the Philippines accomplished more than did an unaggressive press in calling certain unfortunate aspects of military behavior to the attention of the American people. Seventy years later, there was hardly anybody left who could remember the Philippine Insurrection. If someone had remembered, it would have made the 1970s easier for the soldiers coming home from Vietnam. Civilians might not have been so quick to judge; veterans could have found comfort in the knowledge that somebody had gone through it before.

After Vietnam, American soldiers at first blamed themselves for not winning, even though civilian and military leaders knew very well that they could not have won. Whether through incompetence or by design, it was convenient for Washington to permit the anguish of the grunts to continue; it made it that much more difficult for veterans to press any claims they might have against Agent Orange, an issue the Government feared, perhaps even more than it did the claims that arose from those who witnessed the nuclear tests. Their popular image to the contrary, veterans historically were always reluctant to ask for help, even when the leaders of veterans' organizations suggested that some benefits were due. For the past two hundred years, many veterans have insisted that nothing special for them was required after wars and have even been critical of those who needed help. Vietnam was no exception, and the burden of guilt caused by the nature of the Vietnam experience only intensified this reluctance. That, too, played into the hands of Government. In the way it handled the Agent Orange question, Washington saw to it that the pain of it was inflicted on the veterans and nobody else, especially the military and civil leaders who had led the nation to believe that Vietnam was crucial to the interests of American security.

"There is no new thing under the sun," Solomon told us in Ecclesiastes. It was certainly true in the years after Vietnam. There was nothing new and nothing different at all, except, perhaps, for flights of fancy that had their origin deep in the bowels of the Government agency ostensibly established to serve the needs of veterans. In 1979, as the Agent Orange controversy grew untended within Government warrens and the soldiers who fought in Vietnam remained largely ignored, the Veterans Administration celebrated the half-century of its existence by creating its own history, which bore the unlikely title "Fifty Fabulous Years." On page 104 of what only seemed to be an interminable manuscript, Veterans Administrator Max Cleland was quoted as saying that he was "personally committed to seeing that the VA makes a total effort to resolve the questions currently surrounding the after effects of the usage of Agent Orange. . . ." In the very next paragraph, "Fifty Fabulous Years" also noted that the VA had under study the claims made by 229 veterans who had been exposed to radiation as witnesses to nuclear tests between the end of World War II and 1963. "Results of . . . tests are being awaited," said "Fifty Fabulous Years," hopefully. Unfortunately, there was no cause for hope; the radiation issue would be mishandled in much the same way as the Agent Orange issue. The manuscript said that the "real story" of the VA lay "in its dedicated employees" whose "object is to implement the VA's mission, and for fifty years, VA employees have been doing just that."

The VA's mission—not its stated mission but its real one, nevertheless—is to limit the liability of Government for the wages of war. It has paid out millions in pensions and benefits that it could not have avoided; it has also squandered huge sums of money and has evaded responsibility for certain brutal effects of modern warfare. Its consistent intent to limit liability should be seen clearly. Its "mission" and its means of accomplishing it are really no loftier than those of its predecessor agencies, which were marked not just by inactivity, indifference, and waste but by scandal and corruption throughout American history.

No modern Veterans Administrator is thought to have misbehaved quite the way Charles Forbes did in 1924. But in the years of the Agent Orange controversy, VA workers were accused of graft and of accepting some $750,000 in cash and gifts from Smith, Kline & French, a pharmaceuticals maker. At least thirty-three VA doctors had their licenses suspended, revoked, or restricted because their competence and professionalism were seriously in doubt and they were regarded as a possible "threat to patient care." More often the VA's sin has been within the tradition not of old-fashioned money-filching corruption, but rather of timeless bumbledom and small-mindedness, as when, in 1985, it reportedly curtailed the $78.75-a-month pension of a World War I veteran because the VA's staff believed that the interest he received on the cash he had saved caused him to have an annual income that was over the VA limit by $436.20. Was it even possible that the press reports and complaints of veterans' groups about this case could be true? This veteran was hardly a likely target for the full fury of self-righteous Government; he was a pensioner of modest means— who was ninety-six years old! As part of the VA busied itself wasting time and money in the petty pursuit of checking out the $436.20, another devoted itself to so massively bungling the administration of veterans' hospitals that the General Accounting Office told Congress billions could be saved if only the VA could curb unnecessary admissions and excessively long stays in its facilities.

Even with all the consciousness-raising of the last few years in films and novels, the plight of too many veterans who fought the Vietnam War remains desperate. They are poorer, sicker, less employable, less resilient, and more pessimistic than are their peers who did not go to war. In this, they are not so different from veterans of either the post–Civil War or post–World War I periods. They are different only from the veterans of the one great war whose aftermath they either know or have been told about, World War II—veterans who received uncharacteristically warm support from American society.

The Administrations of Presidents Nixon, Ford, Carter, and Reagan were less than eager to pay the human cost of the mistake in Vietnam that had been malfinanced by the Administration of President Johnson, brutally prolonged by President Nixon and his advisers, and underanticipated by the Administrations of Presidents Eisenhower and Kennedy. But surely, they were no more uncaring than was Governor Bowdoin's administration in 1787, so ham-handed that it drove brave and loyal Massachusetts veterans of the Revolution into armed agitation. It was bad enough when civilian warmakers looked around for somebody to blame and accused the Vietnam veterans of having been poor soldiers, just as they had accused their Korean-era predecessors. But bad as that was, Korea and Vietnam veterans were not accused of inciting rebellion and they were not chased from their homes by an army bought and paid for by merchant princes of Boston or anywhere else. Only the men who served under Daniel Shays had that dubious distinction. If the bureaucrats who populated Washington after the Vietnam War seemed predisposed to ignore the anguish of veterans who had seen too much and done too much in a conflict that accomplished little more than push the American republic closer to financial ruin, it was no more unresponsive than were the successive Federal governments in the years after World War I, which so ignored veterans that they became the forgotten men of the Roaring Twenties and the most deprived and despised have-nots of all those who emerged when the twenties ceased to roar, and the bonus marchers were literally driven out of Washington by the same Army they had served so well.

Nor were combat troops the only people forgotten by Government. In the years after Vietnam, women who had served there as nurses and in other capacities attempted to remind society that their service deserved some recognition. Fully 15,000 American women worked in Vietnam, many of them in civilian capacities, serving with the United Service Organizations or the Red Cross. Whether military or civilian, they had a legitimate interest in the Agent Orange question and pressed the Government to help them determine if they had developed health problems because of their exposure to the herbicide. They were successful neither in learning more about their health problems nor in receiving official acknowledgment of their service. They were not very happy when, in October of 1987, the Federal Commission on Fine Arts rejected a proposal to add the figure of a woman to the Vietnam Veterans Memorial in Washington. Members of the commission said that they regarded the memorial as "complete" and that the addition of the statue of a woman "would open the doors to others seeking added representation for their ethnic group or military specialty."

The commission "insulted the women of America," said Stephen Young, vice-president of the Vietnam Women's Memorial Project, shortly after the vote was taken. "What they said is, 'We're basically going to be insensitive to women.' That's what men have done for a long time." To which Diane Carlson Evans, a founder of the Vietnam Women's Memorial Project, added, "And thus we continue to stereotype the American soldier as male."

It is pointless to argue if the angry children of the 1960s were more used, abused, and put upon than had been the despised Irish Catholic conscripts of the 1860s, the Italians and other immigrants of the early twentieth century, or the blacks who served with such valor at almost any time in American history. As veterans, all were subjected to Government policies that can only be thought of as mean-spirited.

The failure of Government to treat soldiers and veterans equitably after Vietnam was a failure of memory. Most of us were not aware of the wages of war that had not been paid in the past, and so we were more willing, as a people, to tolerate Government's shoddy behavior. We tended to regard it as something that had not happened before and probably would not happen again. We thus behaved as our forebears did after our other wars, for they did not remember either. It is unseemly for people so proud of their heritage to be so unaware of the dark side of it, the side that holds not our dignity, our sense of honor, and our generosity, but our greed, lack of compassion, and shortsightedness.

The years after the Vietnam War were not so different, but in their response to the war and what happened to them, the soldiers who suffered those years *are* different from those who came before them. Their uniqueness is important to the future of this country. For the first time in American history, the soldiers who fought for us are now our teachers. Unlike any other warriors of any other age, they are telling us about their war and their anguish and how they sense their own Government betrayed them. The passage of time has not dimmed their recollection of what happened, and they do not glamorize Vietnam. They are trying to tell us the truth as they see it and feel it, and they do it more effectively than could any historian or journalist or social critic. They speak bluntly, these soldiers who fought in Vietnam. Sometimes they abrade us with their anger and their insistence. But when they tell us what really happened to them, they return to us the memory we lost, the memory that has failed us so often during the past two centuries. These veterans have thus taken upon themselves the responsibility to instruct us. Their lessons are too important for us not to listen; they are master teachers.

A people who could remember, old or young, would be an extraordinary people. Such people would really know what it means to go to war. They would not be so easily influenced by slogans and uniforms and Post Office art and violence-glorifying war movies. If we were to listen well to our own soldiers of Vietnam, and we remembered, then would our young know what to expect if they were ever asked to fight another war. If those who would bear the principal burden of war know what to expect of it, know what to ask of those who run our country, then Government might be forced, at last, to accept full responsibility for all the decisions that modern warfare requires— be it the use of nuclear weapons, herbicides, or new approaches to killing that our technology may develop in the future. A Government forced to take full responsibility for its own violence might not be so quick to make war or even threaten to make war. Such a Government might begin to study the art of diplomacy more seriously than heretofore. It might reconsider the value of negotiations, might think more realistically about what constitutes the ''enemy'' and whether those regarded as unfriendly pose any threat at all to national security. If we were a people who remembered and we required such honesty from Government, we would not be simply a nation indivisible. We would be a most formidable people; we would be indestructible.

Acknowledgments

We must make clear that although we were determined to put the experience of the Vietnam veterans in the perspective it deserves, it was not our original intent to assume the burden of researching ten postwar periods and more than two hundred years of American history in order to achieve our goal.

Our interest in the subject began with what we knew generally about the fates of Americans who had returned home after service in Vietnam, especially how they had been treated when they asked their Government to help them determine if Agent Orange had been the cause of some of their health problems. Through good fortune, and with the help of some honest people in and out of Washington, we gained special knowledge about the shameful role of Government, information unknown even to many of the veterans who suspected the worst. The facts we uncovered were extraordinary and disturbing by themselves, but we felt that we had to put them in a context broader than that offered only by the years that followed Vietnam or by the spectacle of former soldiers being denied their due by wrongheaded bureaucrats. The issues dividing soldiers, veterans, and society are more complex than that, too thorny to be understood by the study of the aftermath of our war or Government's mishandling of a single issue. We felt that, at minimum, we owed a deeper, more penetrating look at the condition of soldiers after wars to the men and women who served in Vietnam, who thought that the shabby treatment they were getting had no precedent in history.

As we began our work, we limited ourselves to the postwar periods of the twentieth century and thought that perhaps they might provide us with the perspective we sought. The further we went back in time, the more rewarding did our adventure become. At another point, we thought of starting our book with the years following the Civil War. Not until we discussed our feelings fully with Fred Hills, our editor at Simon and Schuster, did we broaden our approach to its present dimensions. He convinced us that the most meaningful book of all would result if we went all the way back to the end of the Revolution and started our work there. He thus provided us with the spur we needed, and this book in its present form would not have been written without his vision and encouragement. We must also thank Burton Beals of Simon and Schuster, who always gave us careful and thoughtful suggestions; and our agent, Carl Brandt, whose candid observations about our work and whose steadfast confidence in us was of great value as we pursued an arduous, exciting task.

This book was researched with the help of librarians and other researchers at the following institutions: Vassar College, Poughkeepsie, New York; Jones Library and Amherst College, Amherst, Massachusetts; Dartmouth College, Hanover, New Hampshire; the United States Military Academy at West Point, New York; the Library of Congress, Washington, D.C.; the Newburgh Free Library and Washington's Headquarters, Newburgh, New York; U.S. Military History Institute, Army War College, Carlisle Barracks, Pennsylvania; the New York Public Library, Columbia University, Barnard College, Union Theological Seminary, and New York University, New York City; Georgetown University and American University, Washington, D.C.; Boston Public Library, Boston, Massachusetts; the Free Library of Philadelphia, Philadelphia, Pennsylvania; Adriance Library, Poughkeepsie, New York; Temple Hill and the New Windsor Cantonment, New Windsor, New York; Knox Headquarters, Vails Gate, New York; Brown University, Providence, Rhode Island; Forbes Library, Northampton, Massachusetts; Rutgers University, New Brunswick, New Jersey; and the American Antiquarian Society, Worcester, Massachusetts.

We are grateful to the scholars who wrote books over the years which dealt with the problems of veterans. We consulted hundreds of their contributions, created over the past two centuries, and we found them helpful. But there were not nearly as many books as we would have liked that dealt substantively with what happened to soldiers after wars. Thus, we found much of our information not in books but in newspapers, broadsheets, pamphlets, tracts, and periodicals of every stripe and political hue. Our consciences would surely be impaled if we did not pause to thank all those responsible—dreamers, philosophers, poets, polemicists, academics, scientists, publicists, lyricists, political activists, assorted revisionists, revolutionaries, Government functionaries, establishment regulars, and journalists, amateur and professional—for their musings about the way it was and the way it is. They stimulated us and provoked us and told us much about the passions and prejudices of times past. The fact that many of those responsible for articles and verse are unknown to us or that a number of their publications have sadly expired does not lessen our debt to them and our respect for their pungency as contributors to the historical record, although it does not necessarily signal our agreement with their point of view (eighteenth-century newspaper coverage of Shays' Rebellion, for example). Among the publications we relied on for quotes or for background were: *New-York Morning Post; New York Daily Advertiser; Massachusetts Centinel; Essex Journal and New Hampshire Packet; New York Tribune; New York Herald; New York Herald Tribune; Army and Navy Journal; Social*

Service Review; Leslie's Illustrated Newspaper; Chicago Tribune; Mississippi Valley Historical Review; William and Mary Quarterly; American Historical Review; National Advocate; General Advertiser; Niles Register; Military Affairs; New York State Journal of Medicine; Harper's; The Nation; The Washington Post; The New York Times; National Tribune; Schoharie County Historical Review; Mississippi Valley Historical Review; The Forum; Confederate Veteran; East-Hampton (L.I.) Star; New York World; New York Journal; New York American; New York World-Telegram; New York Daily News; Kingston, New York, *Evening Post; American Journal of Psychology; Liberty; The Saturday Evening Post; North American Review; The Messenger; The Crisis; The New Republic; Independent and Weekly Review; Boston Evening Transcript; Boston Herald; Collier's; New York Evening Post; The Century; The American Mercury; Forbes; The Wall Street Journal; Washington Evening Star; The Atlantic; Time; Newsweek; U.S. News & World Report; Saturday Review of Literature; Philadelphia Bulletin; Philadelphia Inquirer; Minerva; Cosmopolitan; Reader's Digest; AVC Bulletin; Communist Daily Worker; American Legion Magazine; Milwaukee Journal; Catholic World; National Review; McCall's; The Ladies' Home Journal; Scouting; Harvard Business Review; The New Yorker; Science; The Progressive; Detroit Free Press; Poughkeepsie New Yorker; Chemical & Engineering News; Life;* and *Journal of the American Medical Association.* Other sources of information included WNET, New York; CBS News, NBC News, ABC News, The Associated Press, United Press, United Press International, and Hearst's old International News Service.

We also want to thank the attorneys and staff of the former National Veterans Law Center in Washington, D.C., especially David Addlestone, Elliot Milstein, Bart Stichman, Ron Simon, Keith Snyder, Lew Golinker, and Georgynne Johnson. Also, James Dean, 1986–87 national commander of the American Legion; Robert Spanogle, the Legion's national adjutant; and John F. Sommer, Jr., deputy director of the Legion's National Affairs and Rehabilitation Commission; Dr. Jeanne M. Stellman and Dr. Steven D. Stellman, authors of a study of Vietnam veterans commissioned by the Legion; and June A. Willenz, executive director of the American Veterans Committee, Washington, D.C., and an authority on the role of women in the military.

Also providing scholarly thinking, research, help, tips, and favors, as well as encouragement, during the many years of this project were Gerald F. Keith, great-great-great-grandson of Daniel Shays, Caledonia, New York; Peggy Hepler and Barbara Jenkins of the Pelham (Massachusetts) Historical Commission; Nancy S. MacKechnie, Katharine A. Waugh, and Esther Williams, Vassar Library; Martha Noblick and Dan Lombardo, Jones

Library; D'Ann Campbell, Dean of Women's Affairs, Indiana University, Bloomington, Indiana; Alan Aimone and Georgianna Watson, West Point; John Slonaker, U.S. Military History Institute; Joseph Ellis, Dean of the Faculty, Mount Holyoke College; Prof. Robert Gross, Amherst College; Prof. Michael Zuckerman, University of Pennsylvania; Linda Grant DePauw, editor of *Minerva,* a quarterly report on women and the military; the U.S. Horse Cavalry Association, Fort Bliss, Texas; Veterans of the Abraham Lincoln Brigade, New York City; National Council of Churches Veterans Project, New York City; Veterans of the A.E.F. Siberia, Los Angeles, California; Vietnam Veterans of America, Washington, D.C.; National Association of Radiation Survivors, Los Angeles; Swords to Plowshares, Los Angeles; Robert S. Robe, president of the Scipio Society of Naval and Military History, Oyster Bay, New York; James Halpin and the staff of the Newburgh Free Library; Tom Hughes and Melvin Johnson, Washington's Headquarters, Newburgh; Fred Knubel, Columbia University; Dr. Marvin Wachman, chancellor of Temple University and former professor of history at Colgate University; James Leach, Colgate University; Frank McCarthy, president of Vietnam Veterans Agent Orange Victims, Stamford, Connecticut; and Earle Kittleman of the National Park Service, United States Department of the Interior.

Also, Philip D. Tobin, Roy Watanabe, Barry Lipton, Lewis A. Head, David O. Tyson, Louise Ransom, Gordon Erspamer, Dr. Hank Vyner, Robert Scrivner, Mab Salinger Gray, Bea Gross, F. Robert Kniffin, Howard Gordon, Marjorie S. Mueller, Lisa Denby, Elizabeth H. Shepard, William Serrin, Lou Sorrin, Bob Duncan, Mike Detmold, John Terzano, Louise Halper, Dean Phillips, John Smitherman, Nancy Loring, Anne R. Bloom, Meredith Platt, Edward J. Silberfarb, Derek Morgan, Vic Schwarz, Richard DeKay, Lewis H. Milford, and Emöke de Papp Severo.

Our gratitude goes to the many law students at American University who represented the rights of veterans. Their experiences helped us better understand the problems of those who have fought our wars. We would finally like to express our appreciation to many others we have not identified, either by design or by inadvertence, who gave us information and leads over the years on Government policies toward veterans.

R.S.
L.M.

Personal note: To Sara, who held our life together. To Tressa, for the future.—L.M.

Notes

CHAPTER 1

page
21   "Let the public only comply . . .": Letter, Henry Knox to Major General Benjamin Lincoln, Secretary of War, March 3, 1783, quoted in Francis S. Drake, *Life and Correspondence of Henry Knox, Major General in the American Revolutionary Army* (Boston: S. G. Drake, 1873), p. 79.

21   They included Eliphalet Allen . . . : Eliphalet Allen, Jeremiah Klumph, Jehu Grant, William Finnie, William Drew, John L. Schermerhorn, and Cornelius Sauquayonk were among those who applied for pensions, disability payments, or grants of land after the war. Their names were taken from U.S. Government records. See Chapter 7 of this book for accounts of what happened to these and other petitioners.

22   New Englanders like Luke Day . . . : Luke Day, Elijah Day, French, Fisk, Jewett, Wells, Drury, Parker, Murray, and Shays all participated in what is now called Shays' Rebellion, in western Massachusetts, 1786–87. See Chapter 5 of this book.

23   Counterfeit or real . . . : Eric P. Newman, *The Early Paper Money of America* (Racine, Wis.: Whitman, 1967).

23   "If anything can be done . . .": John Wingate Thornton, *The Pulpit of the American Revolution* (Boston: Gould & Lincoln; New York: Sheldon, 1860), p. 393. The Reverend Mr. Howard delivered his sermon on May 31, 1780, before the Council and the House of Representatives of the State of Massachusetts Bay.

23   "We are ardently pursuing . . .": Ibid., p. 519. The Reverend Mr. Stiles delivered his sermon on May 8, 1783, to Connecticut Governor Jonathan Trumbull and others at Hartford. His remarks were secular and quite impassioned. He complained that American commerce had been "monopolized" by Great Britain, then went on, in the style of the day, to articulate the pain that Anglo-Saxon Americans felt in breaking ties with England. "O England! how did I once love thee! how did I once boast of springing from thy bowels. . . . But now farewell—a long farewell—to all this greatness! . . . Blush, O Britain, for the stain of your national glory!" Stiles saluted the Army, the Navy, America's allies, and many of those who served prominently in the Revolution, including Lafayette, Steuben, Benjamin Lincoln, Greene, Chastelleux, Putnam, Warren, Mercer, Montgomery, DeKalb, and Pulaski. Of George Washington, he said, "How do I love thy name!"

page

23   The preachers might be talking about the merchant princes . . . : Sidney I. Pomerantz, *New York: An American City, 1783–1803* (New York: Columbia University Press, 1938), p. 159.

23   Or perhaps they were referring to land speculators . . . : Ibid., p. 179, fn.

24   "mortification" etc.: John C. Fitzpatrick, ed., *The Writings of George Washington* (Washington, D.C.: U.S. Government Printing Office, 1931–44), Vol. 26, p. 227. This was contained in a letter dated October 2, 1782.

24   "Stockjobbing, dissipation, luxury . . .": Ibid., Vol. 8, p. 119.

24   "pitiful and forlorn" etc.: Joseph Plumb Martin, *Being a Narrative of Some of the Adventures, Dangers and Sufferings of a Revolutionary Soldier. Interspersed with Anecdotes of Incidents That Occurred Within His Own Observation*, republished under the title *Private Yankee Doodle*, ed. George F. Scheer (Boston: Little, Brown, 1962), pp. 279–87. The book was first published in 1830, when Martin was seventy years old.

24   "Some of them had not a Shoe . . .": Jeremiah Greenman, *Diary of a Common Soldier in the American Revolution, 1775–1783*, republished (DeKalb, Ill.: Northern Illinois University Press, 1978), p. 270. Greenman served as a sergeant, then became regimental adjutant for Rhode Island troops.

24   "are imitating the Britons . . .": Charles Warren, *Samuel Adams and the Sans Souci Club in 1785* (Massachusetts Historical Society, May 1927), p. 320.

24   "rattling through our paved streets" etc.: Ibid., p. 321, quoting the *Boston Gazette*, January 24, 1785.

25   Major William Ballard . . . : Sidney Kaplan, "Veteran Officers and Politics in Massachusetts, 1783–1787," *William and Mary Quarterly*, Vol. 9 (1957), pp. 46–47.

25   In the spring of 1782 . . . : *The Journal of Lt. William Feltman, 1781–82* (Philadelphia: Historical Society of Pennsylvania, H. C. Baird, 1853; reprint, Arno Press/New York Times, 1969).

25   "I intend to pay it when it is due . . .": Josiah Quincy, ed., *The Journals of Major Samuel Shaw* (Boston: Crosby & Nichols, 1847), p. 98.

25   "Let us look upon freedom . . .": Thornton, p. 319. The Reverend Mr. West's sermon was delivered on May 29, 1776.

26   There were few, if any, official welcomes: Kaplan, pp. 36–37.

26   "Close on the eve of an approaching winter . . .": *New York Packet*, December 16, 1784. Watson's account of the occupation thus appeared nearly a year after Evacuation Day, November 25, 1783.

26   Nearly a quarter of New York's settled area . . . : Pomerantz, pp. 19–21, 298.

27   . . . some of them not paid in four years . . . : Minor Myers, Jr., *Liberty Without Anarchy* (Charlottesville: University Press of Virginia, 1983), p. 7. In their letters and comments, soldiers gave varying accounts of how often they had been paid. No soldier was happy with the quality of the money he received.

27   "pies, tarts, cakes, puddings . . .": The *New-York Morning Post* and other newspapers carried similar advertisements repeatedly in the years following the war's end. Most of these items were advertised in the *Post* on November 7, 1783, the same issue that carried Washington's Farewell Orders to the Armies of the United States, announced from his headquarters at Newburgh five days earlier.

27   Buyers with acceptable currency . . . : *New-York Morning Post*, various editions, autumn 1783.

28   "restore the credit . . .": *New-York Morning Post*, December 16, 1785, for this precise advertisement. But the book was available in New York City before the date of the ad. That

the British would permit publication of such a book and so praise it as they were losing their fight with the colonies underscored their general lack of commitment to winning the war.

CHAPTER 2

29   Notable among them was George Washington . . . : Minor Myers, Jr., *Liberty Without Anarchy* (Charlottesville: University Press of Virginia, 1983), p. 6. There were also troops in the south, in Albany, and in Pompton, New Jersey. The cavalry was in Connecticut.

29   "consider all your officers . . .": *Advice to Officers of the British Army* (London: Berry and Rogers, 1782), p. 91. The book was only 96 pages long and roughly as tall as a mass-market paperback, and was thus easily carried in a soldier's knapsack.

30   . . . an eleven-room fieldstone house . . . : The information on Washington's Newburgh headquarters was supplied by Tom Hughes, site manager, and Melvin Johnson, who is in charge of research. According to them, the army rented Jonathan Hasbrouck's house for a total of £59.13.0 for the whole sixteen months.

30   He worked in the Hasbrouck house . . . : The precise number of Washington's headquarters is a matter of some disagreement, but clearly he moved around a great deal and before coming to Newburgh spent very short periods of time in places known as his headquarters.

30   . . . more than he could bear: James Thomas Flexner, *George Washington in the American Revolution* (Boston: Little, Brown, 1968), shows more than one example of this. Washington's military demeanor, probably as imposing as anyone's in American history, succumbed to his "civilian" side frequently. One such occasion occurred in the spring of 1783 when George Bennet, an Englishman taken off a British ship that was commandeered in New York harbor, was brought before Washington. To Bennet's astonishment, Washington first asked him to have a glass of wine, then invited him to stay for dinner with Martha and some officers. "Mrs. W. was as plain, easy and affable as he was," Bennet fondly wrote his mother. Bennet also noted that Washington wore "an old blue coat and britches . . . seemingly of the same age & without any lace upon them." He also reported that the Washingtons ate well but "plain." Bennet's letter is in John C. Fitzpatrick, ed., *The Writings of George Washington* (Washington, D.C.: U.S. Government Printing Office, 1931–44), Vol. 26, p. 321, fn.

30   "I must confess . . .": Fitzpatrick, Vol. 26, p. 235.

30   "Enemy posts have been strengthened": Ibid., p. 251.

30   "as wild an idea as ever controverted common sense": Samuel Eliot Morison and Henry Steele Commager, *The Growth of the American Republic* (London and New York: Oxford University Press, 1951), Vol. 1, p. 201.

30   The king, mindful . . . : Ibid., p. 204.

31   "God save greate Washington . . .": *Tallmadge Orderly Books,* 1780–1785 (Albany: State University of New York, 1932), p. 651. This version of "God Save the King" was heard frequently among troops in New York State.

32   "ne'er-do-wells, drifters . . .": Ronald Hoffman et al., *Arms and Independence: The Military Character of the American Revolution* (Charlottesville: University of Virginia Press, 1984), p. 124.

32   "What think you of a soldier . . .": "A New Song, Written by a Soldier," author and date unknown. From *The Diary of the American Revolution,* the Harris Collection, Brown University, as compiled by Frank Moore (New York: Washington Square Press, 1967), p. 481.

32   "give a great disgust to the people": W. C. Ford, ed., *The Writings of George Washington* (New York and London: Putnam, 1890), Vol. 6, p. 385.

page

32   "no day nor scarce an hour passed . . .": Ibid., p. 262.

32   "like a careful physician . . .": Gary Wills, *Cincinnatus: George Washington and the Enlightenment* (Garden City, N.Y.: Doubleday, 1984), p. 6.

33   "dangerous . . . the nursery of vice . . ." etc.: Richard H. Kohn, *Eagle and Sword: The Beginnings of the Military Establishment in America* (New York: Free Press, 1975), p. 81.

33   . . . the states contributed around $500,000 a year . . . : Morison and Commager, Vol. 1, p. 272.

34   . . . maintenance of Army horses . . . Congress had to purchase . . . : Wayne Carp, *To Starve an Army* (Chapel Hill: University of North Carolina Press, 1984), p. 7.

34   The brutal truth was . . . : Morison and Commager, Vol. 1, p. 208.

34   "The present war being over . . .": John Wingate Thornton, *The Pulpit of the American Revolution* (Boston: Gould & Lincoln; New York: Sheldon, 1860), pp. 426–27.

35   "To the Betrayed Inhabitants . . ." etc.: Roger J. Champagne, *Alexander McDougall and the American Revolution in New York* (Schenectady and New York: Union College Press, 1975), p. 10.

35   "resign the rights . . .": Ibid., p. 19.

35   "Is it not enough . . .": Ibid., p. 24.

36   Many soldiers, desperate for cash . . . : Ibid., p. 183.

36   "in the most express . . ." etc.: Kohn, p. 20.

36   "It would be criminal . . .": Champagne, p. 186, quoting W. C. Ford, ed., *Journals of the Continental Congress, 1784–1789,* (Washington, D.C., 1904–37).

36   "until certain funds . . .": William T. Hutchinson and William M. E. Rachal, eds., *The Papers of James Madison* (Chicago: University of Chicago Press, 1969), Vol. 6, pp. 16, 18, "Notes on Debates," January 6, 7, 1783.

36   "The Army, as usual, are without pay . . .": Fitzpatrick, Vol. 26, p. 27.

37   "smiled at the disclosure" etc.: Hutchinson and Rachal, Vol. 6, p. 143.

37   "the difficulty will be . . ." etc.: Harold C. Syrett and Jacob E. Cooke, eds., *Papers of Alexander Hamilton* (New York: Columbia University Press, 1962), Vol. 3, pp. 253–55.

37   "Faith has its limits . . .": *Journals of the Continental Congress,* Vol. 24, pp. 295–97. See also Benson J. Lossing, *Pictorial Field-Book of the Revolution* (New York: Harper, 1859; reprint, Rutland, Vt.: Charles E. Tuttle, 1972), p. 674.

37   "Gentlemen, you must pardon me . . ." etc.: This version of what Washington said is based on an entry made by a witness to the meeting, Major Samuel Shaw, and appears in Josiah Quincy ed., *The Journals of Major Samuel Shaw,* (Boston: Crosby & Nichols, 1847), p. 104. A similar, but not identical, account of what Washington said may also be found in a letter written by David Cobb, a member of Washington's staff, to former Quartermaster General Timothy Pickering in 1825, which is contained in Charles W. Upham, *The Life of Timothy Pickering* (Boston: Little, Brown, 1873), p. 431. According to Cobb, Washington said, "Gentlemen, you will permit me to put on my spectacles, for I have not only grown gray, but almost blind in the service of my country." Cobb's account, however, was written when he was seventy-seven years old and the incident was forty-two years behind him.

CHAPTER 3

39   "Patriots and heroes . . .": Samuel Adams, as quoted in Sidney Kaplan, "Veteran Officers and Politics in Massachusetts, 1783–1787," *William and Mary Quarterly,* Vol. 9 (1957), p. 38.

page

39   . . . Frog's Neck . . . . : Now called Throgs Neck, and sometimes Throgg's Neck; it is that point in the Bronx where the East River meets Long Island Sound.

39   "They talked of antient history . . .": Julian P. Boyd, ed., *The Papers of Thomas Jefferson* (Princeton, N.J.: Princeton University Press, 1955), Diary for March 12, 1783, as reported in Minor Myers, Jr., *Liberty Without Anarchy* (Charlottesville: University Press of Virginia, 1983), p. 16. The tavern's name and its precise location are lost, although it must have been a decent enough place. According to Jefferson, Adams' best recollection was that the other diners there that evening included Generals Washington, Lee, and Parsons. There was no indication that Washington or any of the other generals heard the remark about the ribbon for Knox's hat.

40   The Society of the Cincinnati: The society maintains its headquarters at 2118 Massachusetts Avenue, NW, Washington, D.C.

41   . . . an untimely death from swallowing a chicken bone . . . : Noah Brooks, *Henry Knox, A Soldier of the Revolution* (New York: Putnam, 1900; reprint, New York: Da Capo, 1974), p. 256.

41   Knox . . . weighed 280 pounds: For reasons not entirely clear, Knox and eleven other officers were weighed at West Point close to the end of the war. Knox proved to be the heaviest of Washington's generals. Washington himself weighed 209 pounds. See Brooks, p. 265. William Sullivan, in his *Familiar Letters on Public Characters and Events from 1783 to 1815* (Boston: Russell Odiorne & Metcalfe, 1834), p. 100, described Knox as "a large full man above the middle stature; his lower limbs a very little outward, so that in walking his feet were nearly parallel. His hair was short in front, standing up, and powdered and queued. His forehead was low; his face, large and full below; his eyes, rather small, gray and brilliant. The expression on his face altogether was a very fine one. When moving along the street, he had an air of grandeur and self-complacency, but it wounded no man's self love." Brooks says that on another occasion, Knox was sent by Washington to a Congressional committee to report on the condition of the men at Valley Forge: "One Congressman, willing to show his wit and sarcasm, said that he had never seen a fatter man than General Knox nor a better dressed man than his associate." Knox seems to have been able to maintain a certain eating style, even through the lean times of the war.

41   "to represent the suffering condition of the troops": Francis S. Drake, *Life and Correspondence of Henry Knox, Major General in the American Revolutionary Army* (Boston: S. G. Drake, 1873), p. 64.

41   . . . New York City—evacuated officially that same day . . . . : The last of the British were actually out by December 5, and there were times when the Americans thought they would never leave. Sidney I. Pomerantz, *New York: An American City, 1783–1803* (New York: Columbia University Press, 1938), p. 17.

41   . . . Knox was given the conspicuous honor . . . : James Thacher, M.D., *Military Journal of the American Revolution* (Hartford: Hurlburt, Williams, 1862), p. 346.

41   "a dedicated bibliophile . . .": During his life, Knox accumulated 1,585 volumes, of which 364 were in French. See Drake.

42   "young lady of high intellectual endowments . . ." etc.: Otis' observations and predictions on the courtship of Lucy Flucker are contained in Brooks, p. 13.

42   "high-toned" etc.: Ibid., p. 13.

42   "What news? . . .": Ibid., p. 24.

43   "a fashionable morning lounge": Drake, p. 12.

43   . . . Thomas Longman, who was his supplier: At the time of his death in 1806, Knox still owed Longman money. The war had been ruinous for the book business.

page

44   "The great and chief end . . .": John Locke, *Two Treatises of Government,* as quoted in Massimo Salvadori, *Locke and Liberty* (London: Pall Mall Press, 1959), p. 171.

44   "our entire want of clothing": Brooks, p. 113.

45   "Order of Liberty": Myers, p. 17. Myers reports he saw not the *Gazette* itself but a photocopy of a manuscript said to be a copy of the Order of Liberty report. It makes no mention of Knox, nor is the Order of Liberty alluded to in Knox's own papers.

46   . . . Knox had created eight pages . . . : Ibid., p. 17. Myers says that the alternative proposal sprouted in officers close to General Gates, among them Captain Christopher Richmond, who had been associated with Major Armstrong's anonymous letters as a copyist. Others among this group were undoubtedly the same men who actively participated in what came to be called the Newburgh Conspiracy.

46   . . . mechanism for making possible the coup . . . : Baron von Steuben called himself "president" in the society's organizational phase and was so regarded by members, but Washington's presidency afterward is traditionally regarded as the first.

46   The critics included . . . : See Garry Wills, *Cincinnatus: George Washington and the Enlightenment* (Garden City, N.Y.: Doubleday, 1984), p. 141 (for Jefferson); North Callahan, *Henry Knox: General Washington's General* (New York: Rinehart, 1958), p. 215 (for Franklin); Edgar Erskine Hume, "Early Opposition to the Cincinnati," *Americana,* (1936), Vol. 30, p. 608 (for Jay and Adams). See also John C. Miller, *Alexander Hamilton: Portrait in Paradox* (New York: Harper, 1959), p. 146.

46   . . . Lucius Quinctius Cincinnatus . . . : In some sources, the name is given as Lucius *Quintius* Cincinnatus.

46   He resisted efforts in Rome . . . : This description of Cincinnatus comes from Livy's *History of Rome,* which combined fact with legend.

46   "It having pleased the Supreme Governor . . .": From an 1896 reprint of the founding papers of the Society of the Cincinnati, printed for the New York State Society of the Cincinnati. There are other versions of the founding papers in existence.

47   "Many of the younger Class . . .": Mrs. Warren is quoted in Marcus Cunliffe, *Soldiers and Civilians: The Martial Spirit in America* (Boston: Little, Brown, 1968), p. 41.

47   "planted in a fiery, hot ambition . . ." etc.: From a pamphlet called "Considerations on the Order or Society of the Cincinnati," written by Aedanus Burke in 1783 [New York Public Library].

48   "Squire Burke . . .": *Connecticut Courant,* January 13, 1784, as quoted in Louie M. Miner, *Our Rude Forefathers: American Political Verse, 1783–1788* (Cedar Rapids, Iowa: Torch Press, 1937), p. 91.

48   "Your pernicious designs . . .": Kaplan, p. 38.

48   "absolutely and purely to avoid . . ." etc.: Myers, p. 28.

48   "The Society shall have an Order . . ." etc.: Society of the Cincinnati founding papers, p. 9.

49   "most amazingly embarrassed" etc.: James Thomas Flexner, *George Washington in the American Revolution* (Boston: Little, Brown, 1968), p. 513.

49   Of the 442 officers of the Massachusetts Line . . . : Kaplan, p. 47. Kaplan based his reporting of numerical conclusions on the *Proceedings of the General Society of the Cincinnati,* 1784–85.

CHAPTER 4

52   "Col. Humphreys who lately arrived from France . . .": *New York Daily Advertiser,* May 31, 1786. The *Advertiser* probably was referring to Lieutenant Colonel David Humphreys,

page

former aide-de-camp to Washington, who later became an aide to Thomas Jefferson when Jefferson was minister to France. One of Jefferson's more pleasant tasks in Paris was to find French artisans who could create designs for the medals Congress wanted to give its heroes, and Humphreys assisted him.

52   One of the swords to Marinus Willet . . . : Ibid.

52   "high sense Congress entertain . . .": *Massachusetts Centinel,* January 24, 1787.

53   "Still the wretched creditor . . .": Ibid., p. 3.

53   Men of means, like Bowdoin . . . : David P. Szatmary, *Shays' Rebellion: The Making of an Agrarian Revolution* (Amherst: University of Massachusetts Press, 1980), p. 46.

53   Friends and acquaintances of the governor's . . . : Richard B. Morris, ed., *The Era of the American Revolution* (New York: Columbia University Press, 1939), p. 390, fn.

54   "repeatedly called upon . . .": *New York Daily Advertiser,* June 7, 1786, p. 2.

54   Before the war, the Massachusetts debt was only £100,000 . . . : George Richards Minot, *The History of the Insurrections in Massachusetts in the Year Seventeen Eighty-six and the Rebellion Consequent Thereon* (Boston: James W. Burditt, 1810), pp. 1–2.

54   In 1784, the Massachusetts legislature decided . . . : Ibid., p. 8.

54   "relapsed into the voluptuousness" etc.: Ibid., p. 11.

54   Governor Bowdoin understood such people: Morris, p. 390, n. 99; see also Sidney Kaplan, "Veteran Officers and Politics in Massachusetts, 1783–1787," *William and Mary Quarterly,* Vol. 9 (1957), p. 50. Kaplan says that most members of the Court were speculators in Federal securities.

55   "It soon became a common observation . . .": Minot, p. 18.

57   In 1786, [Pelham] contained . . . : These data were compiled by the Pelham Historical Society and presented in an exhibit in Pelham commemorating the two hundredth anniversary of Shays' Rebellion, October 1986.

58   . . . the two were "smoked" overnight . . . : According to the records of the Pelham Historical Society.

58   After the war, Pelham's farmers . . . : Richard D. Brown, "Shays' Rebellion and Its Aftermath: A View from Springfield, Massachusetts, 1787," *William and Mary Quarterly,* Vol. 40 (1983), p. 598.

58   "How they will be hindered from resisting illegal force . . .": John Locke, *The Second Treatise of Civil Government* (London: Pall Mall Press, 1959), Chapter 23, p. 104.

59   . . . at least five hundred farms were seized . . . : Szatmary, pp. 33, 38.

60   "with military parade": Ibid., p. 66.

60   Quickly, the names of the leaders . . . : C. O. Parmenter, *History of Pelham, Massachusetts, from 1736 to 1898* (Amherst, Mass.: Carpenter & Morehouse, 1898), p. 375.

60   Instead, he sold it: Nobody knows to whom Shays sold the Lafayette sword or what happened to it subsequently. The sale is mentioned by Judge Hinckley, March 1834, as quoted in Gregory H. Nobles and Herbert L. Zarov, eds., "Selected Papers from the Sylvester Judd Manuscript," filed with the Forbes Library, Northampton, Massachusetts. The fate of the sword has been of some interest over the years, especially to Shays' descendants. His great-great-great-grandson Gerald F. Keith of Caledonia, New York, said in a June 1986 interview with Richard Severo that there is no oral tradition in the family as to what happened to the sword.

60   "This excited the indignation . . .": Ibid.

61   . . . likable, down-to-earth . . . : Long after his problems with Massachusetts were over, and Shays was living on his Revolutionary pension in upstate New York, he met Millard Fillmore, who was then a New York State assemblyman. Fillmore described Shays as a

page

"short, stout, talkative old gentleman with a sprightly manner." See "Bicentennial Narratives" (unpublished collection prepared for the 200th anniversary of Shays' Rebellion by the Pelham Historical Commission, 1986). It seems improbable that a sprightly Shays as an old man of modest means would have been something less than he was as a young and vigorous farmer.

61   One was Oliver Clapp . . . : Oliver Clapp's tavern is described at some length in Carpenter and Morehouse, *The History of the Town of Amherst, Massachusetts* (Amherst, Mass.: Carpenter & Morehouse, 1896), p. 136. The authors said they got the description of Clapp's place from Charles Clapp, one of Oliver's descendants.

61   . . . William Conkey . . . : Conkey's place is also described in ibid., pp. 134–35.

62   "savage beasts of prey": Parmenter, p. 370. The description of lawyers was contained in a list of grievances sent by Thomas Grover, one of Shays' cohorts, to the *Hampshire Herald* on December 7, 1786. This was still during the period when farmers were petitioning the General Court for some relief. The General Court paid them no mind. Historian Michael Zuckerman of the University of Pennsylvania has noted that the elite of Boston were "indisposed toward the mantle of the Revolution" and were both "heedless" and "insensitive" to "the inflamed sensibilities of their fellow citizens." Zuckerman outlined his thoughts at a meeting of Shays scholars at Deerfield, Massachusetts, on November 15, 1986.

63   Like Shays, most of these men . . . : Kaplan, p. 51.

63   "particularly odious . . ." etc.: *Massachusetts Centinel*, July 14, 1787.

63   "May the enemies of *public faith* . . .": Kaplan, p. 48, quoting the *Independent Chronicle*, July 6, 1786.

63   "public faith . . ." etc.: Ibid., p. 50.

63   "a spirit of discontent . . ." etc.: *Massachusetts Centinel*, January 17, 1787. Bowdoin issued the speech "to the good people of Massachusetts" on January 12.

CHAPTER 5

64   "By the malign influence . . .": David P. Szatmary, *Shays' Rebellion: The Making of an Agrarian Revolution* (Amherst: University of Massachusetts Press, 1980), p. 56.

64   "In former days my name was Shays . . .": "The Confession of Captain Shays," an old song, as quoted in C. O. Parmenter, *History of Pelham, Massachusetts, from 1736 to 1898* (Amherst, Mass.: Carpenter & Morehouse, 1898), p. 399. It was written by Gordon Burrows in 1793, six years after the end of Shays' Rebellion. It was sung then and it was sung at the centennial of Shays' Rebellion, by the choir of the Olivet Church in Springfield.

65   "How Long will ye . . .": *Massachusetts Centinel*, January 13, 1787, p. 1.

66   "the infamous and ignorant leader . . ." etc.: Ibid., January 17, 1787, p. 2. It is entirely possible that the unidentified New Yorker was not a New Yorker at all, but Benjamin Russell himself, using his newspaper to further the interests of the merchants and speculators of Boston who were his friends and supporters. But it was the fashion in those days to print letters from unidentified readers, and so the New Yorker was probably taken as such by Russell's readers.

66   "traiterous opposition" etc.: Paul Marsella, "Propaganda Trends in the *Essex Journal and New Hampshire Packet*," *Essex Institute Historical Collections*, 114, No. 3 (July 1978), pp. 164–75.

66   "it is dangerous even to be silent": Sullivan to Rufus King, as quoted in Szatmary, p. 88.

page

66   "HUZZA my joe-bunkers! . . .": *Massachusetts Centinel,* July 11, 1787.

67   "Behold a country void of rule or law . . .": As quoted in Louie M. Miner, *Our Rude Forefathers: American Political Verse, 1783–1788* (Cedar Rapids, Iowa: Torch Press, 1937), p. 157.

67   Bowdoin then suggested that Massachusetts create . . . : Szatmary, pp. 82, 84–87.

67   But who would the other soldiers for such an army be?: Ibid., p. 86.

68   His name was Prince Hall . . . : See Charles H. Wesley, *Prince Hall: Life and Legacy* (Washington, D.C.: United Supreme Council, Southern Jurisdiction, Prince Hall Affiliation, and Philadelphia: Afro-American Historical and Cultural Museum, 1977), esp. p. 27.

68   . . . five thousand African-Americans lived in Massachusetts . . . : The authors are indebted to Prof. Sidney Kaplan of the University of Massachusetts for his insights on the blacks of Massachusetts, which he presented in November 1986 to a conference on Shays' Rebellion at Deerfield, Massachusetts. The conference was arranged by Prof. Robert Gross of Amherst College and sponsored by the college in cooperation with Historic Deerfield.

68   . . . he would not be permitted to bear arms . . . : Laws discriminating against the right of blacks to bear arms had been on the books since 1639, when the first such law was enacted in Virginia. See Jack D. Foner, *Blacks and the Military in American History* (New York: Praeger, 1974).

69   "To His Excellency, James Bowdoin . . .": As reported in Wesley, pp. 42–43.

70   The conversation [between Shays and Putnam]: As reported in Parmenter, pp. 395–97.

72   "small bodies of men . . .": *Massachusetts Centinal,* January 24, 1787.

72   The arsenal, stocked with seven thousand muskets . . . : Szatmary, p. 99.

72   "Unwilling to be any way accessary . . .": As printed by the *Massachusetts Centinel,* January 27, 1787.

72   The confrontation between Shays' men . . . : The account and quotations are from Joseph P. Warren, ed., "Documents Relating to Shays' Rebellion," *American Historical Review,* Vol. II, October 1896–July 1897, pp. 693–94.

73   "made a little shew of force . . .": Ibid., p. 695.

73   "the state of our finances . . .": Ibid., p. 696.

73   Luke Day permitted Ensign Richard Edwards . . . : *Massachusetts Centinel,* January 31, 1787.

73   "Although stone blind . . .": Ibid., February 10, 1787.

74   The letter from the insurgents . . . : Parmenter, pp. 380–82.

75   "open, unnatural unprovoked and wicked rebellion": *Massachusetts Centinel,* February 7, 1787.

75   "Will you now tamely suffer . . .": Ibid., February 28, 1787.

76   "Where is Shays? . . .": Ibid., July 7, 1787.

77   "The spirit of resistance . . .": Paul L. Ford, ed., *The Writings of Thomas Jefferson* (New York: Putnam, 1894), pp. 369–70.

77   "The expedition under General Lincoln . . .": Julian P. Boyd, ed., *The Papers of Thomas Jefferson* (Princeton, N.J.: Princeton University Press, 1955), Vol. 11, p. 222.

77   "I own I am not a friend . . .": Ibid., Vol. 12, p. 442.

78   In 1799, Shays and his son were sued . . . : Interview, Gerald Keith, great-great-great-grandson of Daniel Shays, by Richard Severo, June 20, 1986.

78   "Short, stout, talkative . . ." etc.: "Bicentennial Narratives" (unpublished collection prepared for the 200th anniversary of Shays' Rebellion by the Pelham Historical Commission, 1986).

page

79   . . . the Quabbin water delivery system leaks . . . : "Boston Delays Water Diversion Plan," *New York Times,* November 16, 1986. The leaky pipes are managed by the Massachusetts Water Resources Authority.

79   "Insurgents all what will ye say? . . .": *Massachusetts Centinel,* January 17, 1787.

CHAPTER 6

83   The Treasury had taken in $24.5 million . . . : The state of the U.S. Treasury was alluded to by President Monroe in his Annual Message, *Annals of Congress,* 15th Congress, 1st session, 1817, p. 15.

83   "No trousers and no coats": J. C. A. Stagg, *Mr. Madison's War* (Princeton, N.J.: Princeton University Press, 1983), p. 173.

84   "profaneness, blasphemy, debauchery" etc.: Brown Emerson, *The Causes and Effects of War* (Salem, Mass.: 1812), p. 12, as quoted in Peter Karsten, *Soldiers and Society: The Effects of Military Service and War on American Life* (Westport, Conn.: Greenwood Press, 1978), p. 26.

84   . . . ruination of . . . one of Dolley Madison's . . . dinner parties . . . : Dolley Madison's dinner party and her resourcefulness in saving the silverware is described in Andrew Tully, *When They Burned the White House* (New York: Simon & Schuster, 1961), p. 170. Mrs. Madison's banquet had been planned for forty people and the British found the meat left on the spit "a little too well done." Tully reports that in the kitchen the British found joints of lamb, squab, roasted and broiled chickens, "a wonderfully salty Virginia ham which had been sliced paper thin, a great pot of tripe, plates of nuts and apples, and pots of honey to go with the great chunks of bread the men had for themselves."

84   . . . stunning victory in the Battle of New Orleans . . . . : See especially Robert V. Remini, *Andrew Jackson and the Course of American Empire, 1767–1821* (New York: Harper & Row, 1977), pp. 285–86. See also Samuel Eliot Morison and Henry Steele Commager, *The Growth of the American Republic* (London and New York: Oxford University Press, 1951), pp. 425–26. The Treaty of Ghent had been signed on Christmas Eve, two weeks before the Battle of New Orleans on January 8, 1815, but there was no way such news could have reached New Orleans in time.

84   By 1817, the Americans and the British had begun to tolerate . . . . : In his speech, Monroe alluded to the ways in which both sides had worked to improve relations. President's Annual Message, 1817, p. 11.

85   "a wild wilderness": Mrs. Adams made that observation in 1800 when she went to Washington to visit her husband. A year later, Thomas Jefferson called it "Mayfair in the mud." By Monroe's time the city had changed, but it would be years before it would become the creation that L'Enfant had envisioned. For Mrs. Adams' quote, see James Sterling Young, *The Washington Community, 1800–1828* (New York: Columbia University Press, 1966), p. 3.

85   "At no period of our political existence . . ." etc.: All of these thoughts are found in Monroe's President's Annual Message, 1817.

86   . . . Meriwether Lewis and William Clark . . . . : See Richard Neuberger, *The Lewis and Clark Expedition* (New York: Random House, 1951), pp. 3–10; and Samuel Eliot Morison et al., *A Concise History of the American Republic* (New York: Oxford University Press, 1983), Vol. 1, p. 150.

page
86   "the firm establishment of the American character": James MacGregor Burns, *The Vineyard of Liberty: An American Experiment* (New York: Knopf, 1981), p. 237.

86   "Cold and unfeeling must be that man . . ." etc.: The *National Advocate*'s editorial was reprinted in the *General Advertiser*, February 17, 1815.

87   "like sweet poison on the taste . . .": Senator Macon's comments are contained in *Annuals of Congress*, 15th Congress, 1st session, 1817, p. 158.

87   . . . Joseph Bloomfield of New Jersey introduced them . . . : See ibid., pp. 491ff.

88   "through hurry, I suppose . . .": The apparent shortchanging of George Washington is mentioned in James Thomas Flexner, *George Washington in the American Revolution (1775–1783)* (Boston: Little, Brown, 1968), pp. 517, 518, 495. Washington never directly accused the Government of cheating him, but his wording of the explanation of the shortfall was surely written with the belief that it, like everything else concerning his service to America, would one day be in the public domain. Flexner reports that Washington billed the Congress for his services on July 1, 1783. The total was £8,422.16.4 of which £3,387.4.4 was for eight years of household expenses and £1,982.10.0 was for "secret intelligence."

88   "Let not the soldier . . ." etc.: The remarks of Congressmen Holmes, Colston, Harrison, and Southard and Senator Smith can be found in *Annals of Congress*, 15th Congress, 1st session, 1817, pp. 494ff.

90   "see the warworn soldier of the Revolution . . ." etc.: The comments of Senators Morril and Macon can be found in ibid., January 1818, pp. 151ff.

91   "the number of applicants for pensions . . .": The *Intelligencer*'s observation was reprinted in *Niles Register*, Vol. 15, September 19, 1818, p. 63.

91   . . . fire in the War Office . . . : Mentioned in ibid., p. 64.

91   "permanent asylum . . .": Ibid.

91   Not until 1851 . . . : In 1859, it was called the Soldiers Home. See Robert H. Wiebe, *The Opening of American Society* (New York: Knopf, 1984), p. 70.

91   "had almost been wholly perverted . . .": "Pensions and Pensioners," *Niles Register*, October 19, 1819.

91   "persons supposed . . ." etc.: Ibid.

91   "played the reveille . . .": Ibid.

92   "scythe of retrenchment": Charles F. Adams, ed., *Memoirs of John Quincy Adams* (Philadelphia: Lippincott, 1874–77), Vol. 5, pp. 314–15.

92   . . . fell from 18,800 . . . : Report of the Secretary of War, *American State Papers* (Washington: Gales & Seaton, 1832–61), Vol. 1, Class IX, *Claims*, 17th Congress, 2nd session, p. 885.

92   "mere sunshine and holiday soldiers . . .": Thomas H. Benton, ed., *Reports of the Debates in Congress* (New York: D. Appleton, 1829), Vol. 10, pp. 547–55.

92   "into the moral and political effect of the pension laws . . ." etc.: *Register of Debates in Congress*, Gales & Seaton, Vol. 10, Part 2, Dec. 27, 1833, pp. 2245–46.

93   "As a trading people" etc.: Charles Dickens, *American Notes*, from *The Works of Charles Dickens* (New York and Boston: Books, Inc., undated), Chapter 18, pp. 218–19.

93   "A wide variety of swindles . . .": Karen Halttunen, *Confidence Men and Painted Women: A Study of Middle Class Culture in America, 1830–1870* (New Haven, Conn.: Yale University Press, 1982), p. 7.

93   "magnificent fraud . . ." etc.: *Niles Register*, October 18, 1834.

page
93   The House Committee on Revolutionary Pensions said . . .: The report of the committee
        is dated January 8, 1834, and may be found in the minutes of the 23rd Congress, 2nd
        session, pp. 2ff.

CHAPTER 7

95   [John Paulding's claim]: *American State Papers* (Washington: Gales & Seaton, 1834),
        Vol. 1, Class IX, *Claims,* 14th Congress, 2nd session, p. 500.
96   [Ruth Roberts' claim]: Ibid., 1st Congress, 2nd session, p. 5.
96   [Jeremiah Ryan's claim made during the 1st Congress, 2nd session]: Ibid., p. 8.
97   [William Mumford's claim]: Ibid., p. 7.
97   [Hamilton's decision on the North Carolina officers]: Ibid., p. 9.
97   [Knox on half pay for artillery officers]: Ibid.
97   [Baron von Steuben's claim]: Ibid., pp. 5–16.
101   [Elizabeth Hamilton's 1816 claim]: Ibid., 11th Congress, 2nd session; 14th congress, 1st
        session, pp. 370–71, 467.
101   [Tom Paine's claim]: Ibid., 10th Congress, 2nd session, pp. 366–68.
102   [Jacob A. Young's claim]: This was among those published by the Government in 1852
        as *Rejected or Suspended War Pensions,* republished in 1969 (Baltimore: Genealogical
        Publishing Company), p. 105.
102   [Cornelius Sauquayonk]: Ibid., p. 101.
102   [Aaron Keeler]: Ibid., p. 98.
102   [John L. Schermerhorn]: Ibid., p. 102.
103   [Thomas Miller]: Ibid., p. 58
103   [James Nonemacher]: Ibid., p. 211.
103   [William Brown, John Grant, Jeremiah Khemph, and William Drew]: Ibid., p. 94.
103   [Eliphalet Allen and Jesse Miles]: Ibid., p. 93.
104   [Catharine Beatty]: Ibid., p. 197.
104   [Polly Davidson and Abiah Bumpas]: Ibid., p. 58.
104   [Joseph Wescott]: *American State Papers,* Class IX, *Claims,* 14th Congress, 2nd session,
        p. 499.
104   [John A. Thomas]: Ibid., p. 488.
105   [Basil Shaw]: Ibid., 15th Congress, 1st session, p. 548.
105   [Archibald Hamilton]: Ibid., p. 584.

CHAPTER 8

107   "Now these men have tasted the idleness . . .": Theodore Parker, *A Sermon on the
        Mexican War* (Boston: Coolidge & Wiley, 1848), p. 43.
107   "great reliance is not placed . . .": Lieutenant George B. McClellan in letter to his sister,
        May 1846. In George W. Smith and Charles Judah, *Chronicles of the Gringos* (Albuquer-
        que: University of New Mexico Press, 1968), p. 25.
108   "newly arrived immigrants . . .": Surgeon General's Office, *Statistical Report on the
        Sickness and Mortality in the Army of the United States . . . from January 1839 to January
        1855,* 34th Congress, 1st session, Senate Executive Document no. 96, serial 827,
        Washington, 1856, p. 625, as quoted in Francis Paul Prucha, *Broadax and Bayonet: The
        Role of the United States Army in the Development of the Northwest 1815–1860* (Madison:
        State Historical Society of Wisconsin, 1953), p. 41.

page

109   "All classes of labourers . . .": Prucha, p. 37.

109   "nine-tenths enlisted . . .": Ibid., p. 37.

109   The Rev. Lyman Beecher . . . : Ray Allen Billington, *The Protestant Crusade, 1800–1860: A Study of the Origins of American Nativism* (New York: MacMillan, 1938), pp. 70–71.

109   "convert the Papists to Christianity": Ibid., pp. 97–102.

110   . . . anti-Catholic incidents in New York, Philadelphia . . . : Carlton Beals, *Brass Knuckle Crusade* (New York: Hastings House, 1960), pp. 4, 11, 121.

110   The incidents were too violent . . . : Billington, p. 225.

111   "feels that the country has placed him on a seal of abasement . . .": Prucha, p. 38.

111   "will elevate the moral condition . . .": *Enlistment of Boys in the Army,* 26th Congress, 2nd session, House Report no. 125, serial 388.

111   In the 1830s, 540,000 immigrants . . . : Paul Boyer, *Urban Masses and Moral Order in America 1820–1920* (Cambridge: Harvard University Press, 1978), p. 76.

112   "of turbulent character and intemperate habits": Prucha, p. 39.

112   . . . peacetime desertions . . . : Ibid., p. 39.

112   . . . the lore of John Riley . . . September 4, 1845: Richard B. McCornack, "The San Patricio Deserters in the Mexican War," *The Americas,* Vol. 8 (July 1951–April 1952), pp. 137–39.

112   . . . included a recruiting station in New York City . . . : Edward M. Coffman, *The Old Army: A Portrait of the American Army in Peacetime, 1784–1898* (New York: Oxford University Press, 1986), p. 180.

112   . . . Riley asked for permission to attend Mass . . . : Fairfax Downey, "The Tragic Story of the San Patricio Battalion," *American Heritage,* Vol. 6, No. 4, (June 1955), p. 20.

112   "What a mercy it is . . ." etc.: Milton P. Braman, *A Discourse Delivered Before the Governor* (Danvers, Mass.: Dutton & Wentworth, 1847), p. 20.

113   . . . Batallón San Patricio . . . : Edward S. Wallace, "The Battalion of St. Patrick in the Mexican War," *Military Affairs,* Vol. 14 (1950), p. 85.

113   . . . Matthew Doyle, Patrick Mahoney . . . : The names are compiled in Dennis J. Wynn, *The San Patricio Soldiers* (El Paso: Texas Western Press, 1984), pp. 42–43.

114   . . . St. Patrick, the harp of Erin . . . : McCornack, p. 134.

114   "Can you fight by the side . . .": Wallace, p. 87.

114   . . . there probably weren't more than two hundred: Ibid.

114   Fourteen percent of all desertions . . . : Thomas Irey, "Soldiering, Suffering and Dying," in Odie B. Frank and Joseph A. Stout, Jr., eds., *The Mexican War* (Chicago: Sage, 1973), p. 117.

115   "Bring the damned son of a bitch out! . . .": Wynn, p. 14.

116   "a gross refinement of the cruelty . . .": George Ballentine, *Autobiography of an English Soldier in the United States Army* (London: Hurst & Blackett, 1853), Vol. 2, p. 245.

117   "Why should they not? . . .": Parker, p. 29.

117   "Government is at best but an expedient . . .": Henry David Thoreau, "Civil Disobedience," in *The Works of Henry David Thoreau* (New York: Crown Avenel, 1981), p. 416. The essay was originally entitled "Resistance to Civil Government" and was not published until the war was over.

117   "Law never made men a whit more just . . .": Ibid., p. 418.

117   The Mexican War saw 1,500 Americans die . . . : Irey, p. 110.

117   . . . 160-acre land grants . . . : Smith and Judah, p. 457.

117   Hawthorne's . . . biography of Pierce . . .: See Nathaniel Hawthorne, *Life of Franklin Pierce* (Boston: Ticknor and Fields, 1852).

CHAPTER 9

page
121   "If I were younger . . .": Hawthorne to Ticknor, May 26, 1861. The letter is quoted in
       one of the most understanding accounts of Hawthorne's attitudes, Randall Stewart,
       Hawthorne and the Civil War, University of North Carolina Studies in Philology, No. 34
       (Chapel Hill: January 1937), p. 91.
121   "I regret . . . I am too old . . .": Hawthorne to Bridge, May 26, 1861, ibid.
121   "If last evening's news . . .": Hawthorne to Lowell, July 23, 1861, ibid., p. 92.
122   "In times of revolution . . .": Nathaniel Hawthorne, *Septimius Felton or the Elixir of Life*
       (Boston: Houghton, Osgood, 1879).
123   "Will the time ever come again in America . . ." etc.: Nathaniel Hawthorne, "Chiefly
       About War-Matters by a Peaceable Man," *Atlantic Monthly*, Vol. 10 (1862), pp. 45ff.
124   "oppressed by the ebb . . ." etc.: Mary R. Dearing, *Veterans in Politics: The Story of the
       G.A.R.* (Baton Rouge: Louisiana State University Press, 1952), p. 1.
124   "have been fulfilled . . .": Hawthorne's views on slavery are contained in his campaign
       biography, *Life of Franklin Pierce* (Boston: Ticknor and Fields, 1852).
124   "I felt most kindly . . .": Hawthorne, "War-Matters," p. 48.
124   "If compelled to choose . . .": Julian Hawthorne, *Nathaniel Hawthorne and His Wife*
       (Boston: James R. Osgood, 1884), Vol. 2, p. 271.
124   "amputation seems the better plan . . .": Stewart, p. 97.
125   "when the soldiers returned . . .": Hawthorne's fears about homecoming veterans were
       relayed by his wife, Sophia, to Henry Bright after Hawthorne's death. See Sir Wemyss Reid,
       ed., *Life, Letters and Friendships of Richard Monckton Milnes* (London: 1890), Vol. 2, p.
       242.
125   . . . James T. Fields, actually purged . . . : Stewart, p. 96. See also comment in Alfred
       Kazin, *The American Procession* (New York: Knopf, 1984), p. 73. In the material that
       Fields chose not to use, Hawthorne used these words, among others, to describe Abraham
       Lincoln: ". . . about the homeliest man I ever saw, yet by no means repulsive or
       disagreeable. . . . There is no describing his lengthy awkwardness, nor the uncouthness of
       his movement. . . . [His] whole physiognomy is as coarse a one as you would meet
       anywhere. . . . A great deal of native sense; no bookish cultivation, no refinement. . . . on
       the whole I liked this sallow, queer sagacious visage. . . ." After Fields removed the
       material he thought so objectionable, Hawthorne told him, "What a terrible thing it is to try
       to let off a little bit of truth into this miserable humbug of a world! Upon my honor, the
       omitted part seems to me to have a historical value." See Randall Stewart, *Nathaniel
       Hawthorne: A Biograhy*, (New Haven: Yale University Press, 1948), pp. 226–28.
126   "Brown represented . . .": Kazin, p. 80.
126   "James Russell Lowell mused . . . Robert C. Winthrop feared . . . Dwight Moody . . .
       feared . . . : Dixon Wecter, *When Johnny Comes Marching Home* (Boston: Houghton
       Mifflin, 1944; reprint, Westport, Conn.: Greenwood Press, 1970), pp. 230–31. Wecter says
       a "moral collapse" was feared when the soldiers returned home.
126   ". . . the beautiful young men . . .": Whitman included this in a letter to his close friend
       William D. O'Connor in 1865, in an effort to explain his cycle of war poems *Drum-Taps*,
       which he felt succeeded in conveying "the pending action of this Time & Land we swim
       in." See Kazin, p. 118.
126   "Our land and history . . .": Walter Lowenfels, ed., *Walt Whitman's Civil War* (New
       York: Knopf, 1960), p. 320.
126   "The real war will never get in the books. . . .": Walt Whitman, *Specimen Days*,
       republished (Boston: Godine, 1971), p. 60.

page

127   "concussion of young men on each other": Kazin, p. 118.

127   "were of more significance . . .": Lowenfels, p. 292.

127   But in Robert E. Lee . . . : The comparison of Lee to Vercingetorix and Hektor is not an unreasonable one. Vercingetorix, as leader of the Gauls, attacked Caesar, defeating him at Gergovia in 52 B.C. He was ultimately defeated by Caesar. But in his *Commentaries* (Book 7) Caesar refers to his foe as "a young man of the highest power" who fought not for himself but for the "common liberty" of his people. As for the doomed Hektor, he probably remains the most beloved and compelling fictional soldier, not just in Homer's *Iliad,* but in all the literature of antiquity. His mother begs him not to fight the invincible Achilles: "Do not go out as champion against him, o hard one. . . . the running dogs will feed on you." As Achilles chased Hektor ignominiously around the walls of Troy, even Zeus was heard to say, "Ah me, this is a man beloved whom now my eyes watch being chased around the wall; my heart is mourning for Hektor . . ." See the Richmond Lattimore translation (Chicago: University of Chicago Press, 1951), Book 22.

127   . . . libations at Liberty Garden . . . : *New York Herald,* August 27, 1865.

127   "a magnificent sight . . .": Whitman, *Specimen Days,* p. 44.

128   "The only national debt . . .": The *New York Tribune* carried a description of the grand review of the armies on May 24–25, 1865. *The New York Times* was equally competitive and thorough in its coverage. "Every circumstance has combined to make [the parade] a complete success," the *Times* correspondent reported. The *Times* stories also ran on May 24–25.

128   "the gallant conquerers . . ." etc.: *New York Herald,* May 24, 1865.

128   . . . all-black 52nd Pennsylvania Regiment . . . : The return of this all-black regiment was reported by the *New York Herald* on May 24, 1865. The reception blacks received depended on where the homes they returned to were. Black Union soldiers whose homes were in the South or in border states like Kentucky were given hostile greetings by defeated Confederates. See Chapter 11 of this book for more details; see also Ira Berlin, Joseph P. Reidy, and Leslie S. Rowlands, eds., *The Black Military Experience, Freedom—A Documentary History of Emancipation, 1861–1867* (Cambridge and New York: Cambridge University Press, 1982), which is based on documents in the National Archives of the United States.

128   . . . the foot soldiers who had done Caesar's bidding . . . : In Roman times, soldiering was an accepted way of achieving some upward mobility, and the power of soldiers was well respected. Octavian forgave them taxes, Augustus gave them land, and Juvenal gave them satire:

> Who can count up the rewards of a successful Army career? If you do well during your service the sky's the limit, there's nothing you can't hope for.
>
> Find me a lucky star to watch over my enlistment and I'd join up myself, walk in through those barrack gates as a humble recruit. . . .
>
> Let us consider first, then, the benefits common to all Military men. Not least is the fact that no civilian would dare to give you a thrashing—and if beaten up himself he'll keep quiet about it, he'd never dare show any magistrate his knocked out teeth. . . .
>
> . . . Easier find a witness to perjure himself against a civilian than one who'll tell the truth if the truth's against a soldier's honor. . . .
>
> —Juvenal, Satire XVI, as quoted in Michael Grant, *The Army of the Caesars* (New York: Scribners, 1974), p. xxv.

129   "one vast central hospital": Justin Kaplan, *Life of Walt Whitman* (New York: Bantam, 1982), p. 26.

129   "Wanted—by A YOUNG MAN WHO SERVED . . .": *New York Herald,* August 5, 1865.
129   "not to slump . . ." etc.: *Army and Navy Journal,* quoted in Wecter, p. 188.
130   "The soldier is made . . .": Reported in ibid. Ware wrote his ideas for the American Unitarian Society.
130   "pass coldly by . . .": Reported in ibid., p. 189.
130   "are numbered by the thousands . . .": Fenton's concerns were reported in the *New York Herald,* December 4 and 13, 1865.
130   "blacklegs, burglars . . .": *Chicago Tribune,* quoted in Wecter, pp. 150–51.
131   "for an hour drop . . .": Quoted in Dearing, p. 55.
131   The corpses lay exposed and rotting . . . : This aspect of Antietam is mentioned in Paul H. Buck, *The Road to Reunion* (Boston: Little, Brown, 1937), p. 15.
131   But it was Memorial Day . . . : Memorial Day, or Decoration Day, as it was also known, grew out of a practice of placing flowers on the graves of Confederate soldiers. Nobody is sure when or where the practice began, but the date of May 30 is traced to the day in 1865 when James Redpath, a freed slave, led a group of black schoolchildren to a grave for Union soldiers in Charleston, South Carolina. The event attracted national attention. See Buck, p.116.
131   "to throw flowers on Confederate graves . . .": *New York Herald,* May 30, 1869. The Grand Army's position was prepared by an unidentified correspondent in Washington.
132   "Is this really true?" etc.: Ibid., May 31 and June 1, 1869.
133   "It is clear that the soldier element . . ." etc.: *Army and Navy Journal,* October 30, 1869, p. 157.
133   "The Government is slow to move . . ." etc.: As might be expected, the *Army and Navy Journal* covered Meade's speech, which was given at the Philadelphia Academy of Music on October 22, 1865. The *Journal* reported it in its issue of October 28, 1865, p. 154. Meade spoke of the "great debt . . . our Union has yet to pay." He was unusually candid, and he was more vocal in his caring about veterans-become-civilians than most Union officers of high rank.
134   "should be consigned . . ." etc.: *Army and Navy Journal,* January 13, 1866, p. 331.
134   . . . exhuming the remains . . . : See *Harper's Weekly,* December 31, 1871.
135   "sturdy common sense" etc.: Allan Nevins, *The War for the Union,* Vol. 1, *The Improvised War, 1861–1862* (New York: Scribner's, 1959), p. 416.
135   The Sanitary Commission "excogitated" three guiding principles . . . : U.S. Sanitary Commission, *A Report to the Secretary of War* (Washington, D.C.: McGill & Witherow, 1861), p. 182.
135   "secret school": Robert Penn Warren used the phrase in *The Legacy of the Civil War* (Cambridge: Harvard University Press, 1983), p. 46.
136   They were entitled to $75 . . . : Edward T. Devine, D. Kinley, eds., "Disabled Soldiers and Sailors—Pensions and Training," in *Preliminary Economic Studies of the War* (New York: Carnegie Endowment for Peace, 1919), p. 47.
136   "LEGS AND ARMS . . .": *Army and Navy Journal,* December 23, 1865. The *Journal* frequently contained ads from the makers and vendors of artificial limbs.
136   . . . an obscure young man named Horatio Alger . . . : He was neither a Hawthorne nor a Longfellow, but Alger wrote more than one hundred novels that rivaled or bested them for sales if not literary merit. There were no best-seller lists as such in those days, but had there been, Alger would have been listed almost constantly. His first novel was *Ragged Dick,* published in Boston in 1867 by Loring.

page

136   "I would have felt better . . .": This soldier's complaint may be found in Peter Karsten, *Soldiers and Society: The Effects of Military Service and War on American Life,* (Westport, Conn.: Greenwood Press, 1978), pp. 245–46.

137   "If there had been a single . . .": Ibid., p. 258.

137   "no vacancies exist": Wecter, p. 186.

137   "They strive to conceal . . .": *Soldier's Friend,* November 1865, quoted in Wecter, pp. 183–84.

137   "There is no disguising . . .": *Soldier's Friend,* June 1866, quoted in Wecter, p. 184.

137   "When peace came . . .": Carl R. Fish, *The Civil Service and the Patronage* (Cambridge: Harvard University Press, 1920), quoted in Wecter, p. 186.

137   Morphine . . . was injected . . . : The use of injectable morphine on Civil War soldiers is mentioned in Michael Baden, "Narcotic Abuse—a Medical Examiner's View," *New York State Journal of Medicine,* Vol. 72, No. 7 (April 1, 1972), and in *Legal Medicine Annual,* 1971, published by Appleton-Century-Crofts. Baden later served as chief medical examiner of New York.

138   . . . morphine was simply dusted on the wounds: See David Courtwright, "Opiate Addiction as a Consequence of Civil War," *Civil War History,* Vol. 24, (June 1978), p. 101.

138   "including powdered opium . . .": Ibid., p. 111.

138   "I confess, the more I learn . . .": Joseph Janvier Woodward, *Medical and Surgical History of the War of the Rebellion* (Washington, D.C.: U.S. Government Printing Office, 1870–88), Vol. 1, Part 2, p. 750.

138   "population's rurality and tendency to brood . . .": H. Wayne Morgan, ed. *Yesterday's Addicts: American Society and Drug Abuse, 1865–1920* (Norman: University of Oklahoma Press, 1974), p. 11. Morgan quotes an authority of the day as warning, "America is a nation of drug takers. Nowhere else shall we find such extensive, gorgeous, and richly supplied chemical establishments as here; nowhere else is there such a general patronage of such establishments" (p. 8). Clearly, America's drug ambience was not caused by its soldiers.

138   It was a time when morphine derivatives . . . : John S. Haller, Jr., and Robin M. Haller, *The Physician and Sexuality in Victorian America* (Urbana: University of Illinois Press, 1974), pp. 279–80.

138   "Veteran soldiers, as a class . . .": Courtwright, p. 103.

139   . . . something of a crime wave . . . : The crime wave, if that is what it was, is examined in Edith Abbott, "Civil War and the Crime Wave of 1865–70," *Social Service Review,* Vol. 1 (1925), pp. 212–34.

139   "had been more or less incapacitated . . .": Ibid., pp. 233–34; and see also "American Prisons," *North American Review,* October 1866, p. 383–412.

139   "the rapid development of crime . . ." etc.: Abbott, p. 227.

140   "Absence from home . . .": Wecter, p. 233. The word "jayhawking" came into use near the end of the war. It originally referred only to irregular soldiers who fought in eastern Kansas, but later was used to refer to all soldiers who were raiding guerrillas.

140   "to enlist in the army . . .": Wecter, p. 232, quoting E. C. Wines and T. W. Dwight, *Report on the Prisons and Reformatories of the U.S. And Canada* (Albany: 1867), and *Report on the License Law for the Commonwealth of Massachusetts,* Senate, No. 200, p. 34.

140   "since the close of the war . . .": Quoted in Abbott, p. 225.

140   "We do not want your lives . . .": Wecter, p. 231.

141   "with arms in their hands . . .": Abbott, p. 223.

page
141   "Now that our prisons . . .": *North American Review,* January 1866, p. 235.
141   "At this moment . . .": *Leslie's Illustrated Newspaper,* October 7, 1865, p. 39.

CHAPTER 10

143   "Better to have 500 maimed veterans . . .": As reported in Sophonisba P. Breckinridge, *Public Welfare Administration in the United States: Select Documents* (Chicago: University of Chicago Press, 1938), pp. 305–9.
144   "the atheistic roar of riot": Herman Melville, "House Top," in his collection of poems *Battle Pieces,* quoted in Alfred Kazin, *The American Procession* (New York: Knopf, 1984), p. 152.
144   "The paucity of news . . .": M. A. DeWolfe Howe, ed., *Home Letters of General Sherman* (New York: Scribner's, 1909), p. 295. Sherman was a Democrat who steadfastly supported Lincoln.
145   "very strange movement" etc.: *New York World,* February 16, 1863. Generals George B. McClellan, Henry W. Halleck, and Don Carlos Buell had top Union commands and were all Democrats.
145   "He never manifested the simple courage . . .": Howe, p. 315.
145   [McClellan's] emergence as a candidate . . . : See Samuel Eliot Morison and Henry Steele Commager, *The Growth of the American Republic* (London and New York: Oxford University Press, 1951), Vol. 1, pp. 679, 693, 695.
146   "justice, humanity, liberty . . ." etc.: Ibid., pp. 701, 732.
146   Of the twenty-five states . . . : The fourteen states which had enabling legislation for the election of 1864 were Iowa, Minnesota, Missouri, Vermont, Ohio, Kansas, Maine, Pennsylvania, Connecticut, New Hampshire, Maryland, Michigan, New York, and West Virginia.
147   "Indiana is the only important State . . .": John G. Nicolay and John Hay, eds., *Abraham Lincoln: Complete Works* (New York: Century, 1894), Vol. 2, pp. 577–78.
148   ". . . when men get home . . . Our armies vanish . . .": Howe, pp. 289, 315.
148   "Indiana troops seemed to be rather sickly": Abraham P. Andrew to his sister, October 23, 1864. Abraham P. Andrew III, *Some Civil War Letters* (Gloucester, Mass.: privately printed, 1925), quoted in Mary R. Dearing, *Veterans in Politics: The Story of the G.A.R.* (Baton Rouge: Louisiana State University Press, 1952), p. 36.
148   The furloughs or sick leaves . . . : Dearing, p. 38.
149   "Yesterday little endorsements . . .": Nicolay and Hay, pp. 374–75.
149   "Old Abe was up here a few days ago . . .": *Felix Brannigan Letters, 1861–63 and Undated,* quoted in Dearing, p. 16.
151   "with a view to enlisting the sympathy . . ." etc.: *New York Tribune,* August 11 and 21, 1865.
151   "for mutual confidence and mutual help": *Army and Navy Journal,* April 28, 1866.
152   "while soldiers and sailors in union . . .": Ibid., p. 578.
152   The *Chicago Times* . . . : See *Chicago Times,* August 25, 1866.
152   . . . Dr. Benjamin Stephenson . . . : See Mary Harriet Stephenson, *A Memoir of Dr. Stephenson* (Springfield, Ill.: 1894), p. 41 [New York Public Library]. Miss Stephenson's biography of her father is understandably adulatory, but in revealing some of his letters, she provides strong evidence of the G.A.R.'s earliest-known intentions.
153   "whatever views we may have as an order . . .": Ibid., p. 52.
153   "she was ignorant . . .": Ibid., p. 56.
153   "can't even get employment as a day-laborer . . ." etc.: Ibid., p. 52.

page
153   "The order is destined to be . . .": Ibid., p. 50.

154   "remember, ever, that Traitors . . ." etc.: Ritual of the Grand Army of the Republic as published in 1875 by Ezra Cook in Chicago. Cook published the secrets because, he said, "No Christian can fail to see that such obligations are at war with the fundamental principles of Christianity," and he further accused the G.A.R. of discriminating against veterans "who conscientiously refuse to join the order." The ritual is on file at the New York Public Library.

154   "The order is growing with superhuman strides in the East . . ." etc.: Stephenson, p. 49.

155   "we shall generate a faction . . .": *Boston Advertiser,* September 8, 1865.

155   "There is, indeed, danger . . .": Breckinridge, p. 308.

156   "to prove that the threats . . .": *New York Tribune,* November 16, 1866, p. 4.

157   "Let us be calm. . . .": Ibid.

157   "We had much rather raise corn . . .": Quoted in William A. Russ, Jr., "Was There a Danger of a Second Civil War During Reconstruction?" *Mississippi Valley Historical Review,* Vol. 25 (June 1938–March 1939), pp. 39–58.

157   "No thinking man . . .": Quoted in ibid., p. 44. Thomas wrote this letter on September 18, 1867.

158   "National anniversaries . . .": *New York Times,* editorial, May 31, 1869, p. 4.

158   . . . Arlington Heights Churchyard: This incident is covered in Chapter 9.

158   "Shall the Hatchet Ever Be Buried?" etc.: *New York Times,* June 3, 1869, p. 4.

CHAPTER 11

160   "Soldiers, I tell you . . .": Ira Berlin, Joseph P. Reidy, and Leslie S. Rowlands, eds., *The Black Military Experience, Freedom—A Documentary History of Emancipation, Series II* (Cambridge and New York: Cambridge University Press, 1982), p. 785.

160   "I am about to be mustered out . . .": Ibid., p. 796.

161   "swelled with idiots, . . .": "The Doctors and the Soldiers," *Harper's Weekly,* editorial, January 21, 1865, p. 35.

161   "of the villainous distemper . . ." etc.: *New York Times,* January 2, 1865. Lincoln apparently did not feel that the *Times'* reporting of what might be wrong with his army hurt him or his administration or in any way damaged national prestige or national security. Of the *Times* itself, Lincoln wrote that it was "always true to the Union, and therefore should be treated as well as any." This despite his lean popularity in the North and the draining effect that combat losses were thought to have among his constituents. See John G. Nicolay and John Hay, eds., *Abraham Lincoln: Complete Works* (New York: Century, 1894), Vol. 2, p. 525.

162   "There is a scheme on foot . . .": *Nation,* editorial, January 25, 1866, p. 97. *The Nation* had started publication in July 1865.

162   "a good number of sleeping rooms . . .": *Harper's Weekly,* July 22, 1865.

163   "A number of discharged soldiers . . .": *Army and Navy Journal,* March 12, 1870, p. 469.

163   . . . 200,000 who were black: Jack D. Foner, *Blacks and the Military in American History* (New York: Praeger, 1975), p. 45. Foner estimated there were 186,000 black soldiers serving in sixteen all-black regiments. But there were many others who served the Army as laborers, cooks, servants, and teamsters. Foner reported that black soldiers fought in 449 engagements, of which thirty-nine were "major," and sixteen black soldiers won the Congressional Medal of Honor for their service during the war.

page
164   . . . Ku Klux Klan . . . : See J. C. Lester and D. L. Wilson, *The KKK: Its Origin, Growth and Disbandment* (St. Clair Shores, Mich.: Scholarly Press, 1972, reprint of 1905 edition); also Thomas B. Alexander, "Kukluxism in Tennessee, 1865–1869," *Tennessee Historical Quarterly,* Vol. 8, No. 3 (1949), pp. 195–219.

165   . . . $10 a month and $3 for clothing . . . : Jay David and Elaine Crane, eds., *The Black Soldier: From the American Revolution to Vietnam* (New York: Morrow, 1971), p. 88. It was not until June 15, 1864, that Congress enacted legislation to achieve parity between soldiers of both races. It was then also that bounties for blacks were approved. Soldiers of both races were offered official inducements of $100 for one-year enlistments and $300 for three-year enlistments. Some soldiers, if Timesman Hamilton (see *New York Times,* January 2, 1865, p. 221) was accurate in his reporting, received more.

165   "The Negro gave one in three of his number . . .": *New York Tribune,* December 26, 1865. Horace Greeley's newspaper thus paid tribute to the blacks as the Ku Klux Klan was undergoing formation in Tennessee.

165   . . . 38,000 black troops had lost their lives . . . : Foner, p. 48.

165   "fraud and most flagrant rascality . . .": Racism in the Grand Army's Southern departments is documented in Wallace E. Davies, "The Problem of Race Segregation in the Grand Army of the Republic," *Journal of Southern History,* Vol. 13, No. 3 (August 1947), pp. 354–72.

166   "we live in a country . . .": G.A.R. *Journal,* Proceedings of the 25th National Encampment, 1891.

167   "When I enlisted in April . . .": Ibid., 21st National Encampment, 1887.

167   "rather shake hands . . .": Ibid.

167   "I have plowed many a day beside a nigger boy . . .": Ibid., 25th National Encampment, 1891.

167   "should these races . . .": *New York Herald,* August 10, 1891.

167   "In the South . . .": *New York Tribune,* August 10, 1891.

168   "As a Massachusetts woman . . ." etc.: WRC *Journal* for the 15th National Convention of 1897, pp. 322–23, as quoted in Davies, p. 368.

168   But Henry O. Flipper . . . : Flipper's story is in Edward M. Coffman, *The Old Army: A Portrait of the American Army in Peacetime, 1784–1898* (New York: Oxford University Press, 1986), pp. 226–29. Coffman, a professor of history at the University of Wisconsin, noted that generals tended to view blacks as problems. Coffman writes that President Grant told a general in Louisiana after the Civil War not to permit discharged black soldiers to purchase their rifles. As in wars past, white Americans feared black soldiers and thought that the blacks who fought for them would become their violent enemies later on.

CHAPTER 12

170   "what would be required . . .": William H. Glasson, *Federal Military Pensions in the United States* (New York: Oxford University Press, 1918), p. 162.

170   . . . as much as $150 million . . . : Ibid., p. 163.

170   . . . *Washington Post,* which defended . . . : The *Post*'s support and its markedly different approach to the whole question, compared to most other newspapers, is evident in articles that were published January 21, 23, 24, 27, and 28, 1879.

170   "That act was required . . ." etc.: Hayes to William Henry Smith, December 14, 1881, quoted in Charles R. Williams, *Life of Rutherford Burchard Hayes* (New York: Houghton Mifflin, 1914), Vol. 2, p. 338.

page

171   . . . six-sevenths of matters pending . . . : Glasson, p. 166, n. 1.

171   Both laws loomed . . . : Ibid., p. 166.

171   "I would promptly repeal . . ." etc.: Ibid., p. 177.

171   "I believe that the mass of the soldiers . . .": Ibid.

172   . . . *National Tribune* . . . : Donald L. McMurry, "The Bureau of Pensions During the Administration of President Harrison," *Mississippi Valley Historical Review*, Vol. 13 (June 1926–March 1927), pp. 343ff.

172   . . . number of claims rapidly . . . : *House Reports*, 387, 189, and 386, 46th Congress, 3rd session, as reported in Glasson, p. 166, n. 1.

172   The Union Army had used about 2.25 million . . . : *The Historical Development of Veterans Benefits in the United States,* Staff Report No. 1, prepared by the Congressional Committee on Veterans Affairs, released May 9, 1956. Data compiled by the Veterans Administration do not totally agree with those of the Congress. The VA issued a fact sheet entitled "America's Wars" in January of 1987 indicating that deaths among Union soldiers "in service" totaled 364,000. The VA estimated that nearly 500,000 Union and Confederate soldiers were killed in the Civil War, thereby making it costlier in terms of lives than any other in American history. World War II, the next-bloodiest, cost America 406,000 lives, out of a total of 16,535,000 who participated.

172   . . . no more than 61,000 . . . : The G.A.R. membership in 1880 was 60,678, according to Donald L. McMurry, "The Political Significance of the Pension Question, 1885–1897," *Mississippi Valley Historical Review*, Vol. 9 (June 1922–March 1923), p. 23.

173   The Pension Building was, and remains . . . : *Washington Post*, October 24, 1985. The building is now the National Building Museum, dedicated to papers and exhibits of the nation's architectural and building arts. The pension clerks moved out in 1926. In the years following its abandonment as a pension distribution center, it was used by the General Accounting Office, the Civil Service Commission, and Washington's city courts. At one point, there was talk of knocking it down, and it was saved, urns and all, through the efforts of many, not the least of whom was Wolf von Eckhardt, *The Washington Post's* former architecture critic and urban affairs specialist.

174   "Gentlemen like Mr. Warner must be taught . . .": *Congressional Record,* 49th Congress, 1st session, pp. 2045–46, quoted in McMurry, p. 23.

175   Cleveland signed 1,453 such bills . . . : Samuel Eliot Morison and Henry Steele Commager, *The Growth of the American Republic* (London and New York: Oxford University Press, 1951), Vol. 2, p. 228.

175   "They have vetoed . . ." etc.: *National Tribune,* November 8, 1888.

176   . . . James Tanner: See James E. Smith, *The Career of Corporal James Tanner* (Washington: W. H. Lowdermilk, 1892), p. 183.

176   [Tanner] was pressed into service . . . : Arthur H. Van Voris, "Corporal James Tanner, 1844–1927—Eye Witnesses at Lincoln's Death Bed," *Schoharie County Historical Review*, Fall–Winter 1967, *passim*. Van Voris based his article on papers written by Tanner.

177   "All over the land . . .": Tanner made the speech to the New York Department of the G.A.R., January 23, 1878. As reported in Mary R. Dearing, *Veterans in Politics: The Story of the G.A.R.* (Baton Rouge: Louisiana State University Press, 1952), pp. 217–18.

177   "plastered Indiana with promises": McMurry, "Pension Question," p. 30.

178   "Be liberal with the boys": McMurry, "Bureau of Pensions," p. 346. The nature of Harrison's mandate to Tanner was the subject of much speculation in the press.

178   "I will drive a six-mule team . . .": It certainly sounds like Tanner's rhetoric and is reported in Glasson, p. 226.

178   "and reissue them . . . 'God help the surplus' ": Smith, p. 209.

page

179   "This is a greater amount . . ." etc.: "The New Pension Building," *Nation*, editorial, May 30, 1889, pp. 438–39.

179   "The Regular expenditures of the Pension Bureau now far exceed the total cost of the whole Federal Government . . .": As reported in *The Nation*, ibid., p. 438.

179   "He would apparently like to pension . . .": As reported in ibid., p. 439.

179   "In encouraging this order . . .": As reported in ibid.

180   "Flood's brain was blown . . ." etc.: Ibid., July 25, 1889, p. 64, as quoted in McMurry, "Bureau of Pensions," p. 349.

180   "We of the North had the coffers . . .": See Smith, pp. 194, 208, for Tanner's concerns.

180   "Tanner's worst enemy . . .": Merrill was quoted in *Public Opinion*, Vol. 8, (September 21, 1889), p. 486; and *The New York Times*, October 31, 1888.

180   "I hold it to be a hideous wrong . . .": As reported in McMurry, "Pension Question," pp. 34–35.

181   "bounden duty of this great Republic . . .": Smith, p. 207.

181   "The difference which exists . . .": Ibid., p. 209.

181   "I beg to renew . . .": Ibid., p. 210.

182   "If he had been a man . . .": *Boston Globe*, September 14, 1889.

182   How close did Tanner really come . . . : McMurry, "Bureau of Pensions," p. 360.

182   . . . Dependent Pension Act of 1890: *Historical Development of Veterans Benefits in the United States*, p. 17.

183   "These wholesale pension schemes . . .": "An Unpleasant Contrast," *Nation*, editorial, May 15, 1890, p. 386.

183   "The hero covered with honorable wounds . . ." etc.: William M. Sloane, "Pensions and Socialism," *Century*, June 1891, pp. 185, 188.

183   "Savagery" etc.: Bell Irvin Wiley, *The Life of Billy Yank: The Common Soldier of the Union* (Indianapolis: Bobbs-Merrill, 1952), p. 347, as reported in Richard Slotkin, *The Fatal Environment* (New York: Atheneum, 1985), p. 305.

183   By the end of 1893, one million Union veterans . . . : M. B. Morton, "Federal and Confederate Pensions Contrasted," *Forum*, September 1893, pp. 73–74.

184   "Seven National Soldiers' Homes . . .": Ibid., p. 73.

184   "In works or active beneficence . . .": Robert H. Bremner, *The Public Good: Philanthropy and Welfare in the Civil War Era* (New York: Knopf, 1980), pp. 208–09.

184   "It is a lamentable sight . . .": *Richmond Dispatch*, quoted in *Confederate Veteran*, January 1893, p. 9.

184   "Did loyal citizens volunteer . . ." etc.: Allen R. Foote, "Degradation by Pensions: The Protest of Loyal Volunteers," *Forum*, December 1891, p. 29.

184   But up North, it was as though these sentiments . . . : Francis E. Leupp, "Defects in Our Pension System," *Forum*, March 1901–August 1901, p. 674.

185   . . . Noah L. Farnham Post . . . : Details of the Farnham Revolt were taken from "Complete History of the Farnham Post Revolt," *Forum*, December 1891, pp. 534–40; and Wallace E. Davies, "The Problem of Race Segregation in the Grand Army of the Republic," *Journal of Southern History*, Vol. 13, No. 3 (August 1947).

CHAPTER 13

190   "out of fashion" etc.: Julius J. Mark, ed., *The Holmes Reader* (New York: Oceana, 1955), p. 148.

page

190   "splendid little war . . .": John Hay made the observation in a letter to Theodore Roosevelt, dated July 27, 1898. See Stuart Creighton Miller, *Benevolent Assimilation* (New Haven, Conn.: Yale University Press, 1982), p. 12.

191   [The New York press during the Spanish-American War]: Joseph Wissan, *The Cuban Crisis as Reflected in the New York Press* (New York: Columbia University Press, 1934), pp. 24–32, as quoted in W. A. Swanberg, *Citizen Hearst* (New York: Scribner's, 1961), p. 116.

192   "Sending the *Maine* to Havana . . .": Walter Karp, *The Politics of War: The Story of the Two Wars Which Altered Forever the Political Life of the American Republic (1890–1920)* (New York: Harper & Row, 1979) p. 87.

192   . . . uniforms and ammunition were sidetracked . . . . : The delay was reported by General Nelson Miles, commander of the Army, and reported in T. Harry Williams, *The History of American Wars* (New York: Knopf, 1981), p. 322.

193   "will simply involve the destruction of thousands" etc.: *New York Times*, August 5, 1898, p. 7.

193   . . . would not permit female nurses . . . to attend troops in the field: "I do not approve of having female nurses with troops in the field or in camps of instruction," said Sternberg in a letter to the chief surgeon of the Fifth Army Corps. As reported in ibid., August 4, 1898.

194   . . . Koch . . . Le Reviere . . . Denner . . . : *New York Herald*, August 1, 1898.

194   "than the inadequacy of proper food . . .": *New York Times*, August 1, 1898.

194   "There was no food . . .": *New York Tribune*, August 1, 1898.

194   "many of the men were actually worse . . ." etc.: The officer and Mr. McMillan were quoted in ibid.

194   He waited a full three days . . . : Ibid.

195   "Thank God we are going to New York!" *New York Times*, August 1, 1898.

195   Dr. Alvah H. Doty . . . : Ibid.

195   . . . Sternberg said that whatever was wrong . . . : Ibid., August 3, 1898, p. 2.

195   "The men are worn out . . ." etc.: *New York Herald*, August 4, 1898.

195   "Don't be alarmed . . .": Ibid.

196   "At the time they left Santiago . . .": *New York Times*, August 3, 1898.

197   "Men who go to war . . .": The Boise *Sentinel*'s editorial was carried in ibid., August 2, 1898.

197   . . . Captain Risk was at fault . . . : *New York Herald*, August 4, 1897.

197   "It is Alger and not Pitt . . .": *New York Times*, August 4, 1898.

198   "keep lawns mowed . . .": *East-Hampton Star*, June 3, 1898.

198   "damn": Newton's fine was recorded in the *New York Herald* of August 18, 1898; the deliberations of the New York Board of Aldermen had been reported the day before.

198   "a little whale oil . . ." etc.: Betsey Beanstalk's opinions were carried in the *East-Hampton Star*, June 3, 1898.

199   His plans for Montauk were being revealed . . . : *New York Times*, August 6, 1898.

199   "I think I could believe that the disease . . . is homesickness": Ibid.

199   . . . wells should be dug . . . : *New York Tribune*, August 12, 1898.

200   . . . were taking water from a stagnant pond: *New York Evening Journal*, September 2, 1898.

200   "Contract physicians are not depriving themselves . . .": *New York Herald*, August 23, 1898.

200   "nursery of typhoid": *New York Times*, August 6, 1898.

201   "it is feared that there will be a deplorable . . .": Ibid., August 7, 1898.

page
201   "was of the opinion that in most cases the change . . .": Ibid., August 9, 1898. The description of conditions on the *Grande Duchesse* was contained in *American Legion Magazine*, July 1938, p. 3.

202   "Orders have been issued without regard . . .": *New York Times*, August 10, 1898.

202   "were sent before the camp was in shape . . .": Ibid., August 12, 1898.

202   "Strike the cymbals! . . ." etc.: *East-Hampton Star*, August 12, 1898.

202   "The fears of the people in the villages . . .": Ibid.

202   "There must be a screw loose . . .": Ibid., August 26, 1898.

203   "These starving men . . .": Miss Chadwick's letter was reprinted in *The New York Times*, August 27, 1898; it was this sort of thing that helped alert the general public to what was going on in Camp Wikoff.

203   . . . hardtack . . . filled with worms: Margaret Leech, *In the Days of McKinley* (New York: Harper, 1959), p. 300.

203   . . . 54,860 gallons of milk . . . etc.: The list of food sent to Wikoff was included by Alger in his book *The Spanish American War* (New York: Harper, 1901; reprint, Freeport, N.Y.: Books for Libraries Press, 1971), p. 427. The book was essentially Alger's defense of his administration during and after the war. It was dedicated "to the American Soldier and Sailor."

204   . . . he threatened to declare Wikoff quarantined . . . : *New York Herald*, August 17, 1898.

204   "disgracefully healthy . . . bully fight": *New York Times*, August 16, 1898.

204   "bully time": *New York Tribune*, August 16, 1898.

204   Roosevelt was promptly given leave . . . : Ibid., August 20, 1898.

204   "death-like pallor": Ibid., August 17, 1898.

204   . . . three Rough Riders spent the night in a police station . . . : *New York World*, August 26, 1898.

204   . . . Lieutenant William Tiffany . . . : *New York Herald*, August 26, 1898.

205   "I shall . . . stay one, two or three days . . .": Ibid., August 23, 1898.

206   Alger toured the camp . . . : Alger's appraisal was reported in *The New York Times*, August 26, 1898.

206   "All the time I was with him I did not see him . . .": *New York Herald*, August 25, 1898.

206   . . . hanging around the luncheon counter . . . : *New York World*, August 23, 1898.

206   Alger snapped, "None": *New York Times*, August 27, 1898.

206   "record of Camp Wikoff conclusively proves . . .": Alger, p. 438.

206   "The *New York Journal* was responsible . . .": Corporal Stanton testified before the War Investigation Commission, and his testimony was quoted in ibid., p. 438.

207   . . . Edward Findlay . . . : Findlay's plight was reported in the *New York Herald*, August 4, 1898.

207   "What kindness of heart is that . . .": *New York Times*, September 6, 1898.

207   "Shrunken and ghastly white . . .": Ibid., September 3, 1898.

208   "Well boys, how are you?": Ibid.

208   "twenty-five dozen suits of underwear . . .": Ibid., August 30, 1898.

208   "pathetic . . . emaciated . . .": Ibid.

208   . . . so many were dying so quickly . . . : *New York Herald*, August 23, 1898.

208   "Where will our patriots be found . . .": *New York Times*, August 30, 1898.

209   . . . wagered 50 cents on who would die . . . : Ibid., September 10, 1898.

209   "The whole trouble has been in the volunteer troops . . .": Ibid., September 12, 1898.

209   "and if they are not well cared for . . .": Ibid., September 22, 1898.

209   "baneful and pernicious": Alger's words, in Alger, p. 446.

page

210   "Soldiers do not like sympathy . . .": Quoted in ibid.

210   . . . James Fitch . . . "malarial poisoning . . .": Files courtesy of Department of the Army, U.S. Military History Collection, Carlisle Barracks, Pennsylvania.

CHAPTER 14

212   "They have become suspicious . . .": Mark Twain, "To the Person Sitting in Darkness," in *The Portable Mark Twain* (New York: Viking, 1946), p. 599.

212   "as invaders or conquerors . . .": Stuart Creighton Miller, *Benevolent Assimilation* (New Haven, Conn.: Yale University Press, 1982), p. 25, quoting Charles S. Olcott, *William McKinley* (Boston and New York: Houghton Mifflin, 1917), Vol. 2, pp. 110–11.

212   . . . insurgents reportedly "mutilated" etc.: U.S. Congress, 57th Congress, Senate Document 213, p. 9.

212   "treacherous and cruel . . ." etc.: Ibid., p. 8.

213   "I want no prisoners . . ." etc.: Ibid., p. 9.

213   . . . ten years of age: Miller, p. 220.

213   "Even the women carried arms": Senate Document 213, p. 12.

214   "very low in intelligence" etc.: Ibid., p. 8.

214   "did not efficiently respond": Ibid., p. 6.

214   "You are as fine a group of soldiers . . .": Miller, p. 226.

214   "repair to his home": Senate Document 213, p. 6.

214   "In this instance there was no overwhelming necessity . . .": Ibid., p. 46.

215   . . . Preston Brown . . . : Ibid., pp. 49ff. *"No sabe"* were the words attributed to the luckless Filipino in American records. The phrase was one the Americans used widely to describe the misunderstandings that frequently occurred between them and the Filipinos.

215   . . . Edwin F. Glenn . . . : Ibid., pp. 17ff.

215   . . . Julien E. Gaujot . . . : Ibid., pp. 28ff.

216   . . . James A. Ryan . . . : Ibid., pp. 63ff.

216   . . . Cornelius M. Brownell . . . : Ibid., p. 85.

217   "We burned hundreds of houses . . .": *Soldiers' Letters* (Boston: Anti-Imperialist League, 1899), p. 10. [New York Public Library]

217   "We bombarded a place called Malabon . . .": Ibid., p. 12.

217   "Talk about Spanish cruelty . . .": Ibid., p. 16.

218   People in Meadville, Pennsylvania . . . : Stuart C. Miller, "Our Mylai of 1900: Americans in the Philippine Insurrection," *Transaction*, Vol. 7, No. 11 (September 1970), p. 22.

218   "I am not afraid . . .": *Soldiers' Letters*, p. 2.

218   "I deprecate this war . . .": Ibid.

218   "forged or distorted documents . . .": *New York Times*, July 11, 1899, p. 6.

218   "With the danger from the invasion of the Chinese laborers . . .": *Congressional Record*, 55th Congress, 3rd session, [House], January 6, 1899, p. 449. Swanson went on to become a U.S. Senator and in 1933 would be appointed Secretary of the Navy by President Franklin Roosevelt.

219   "Without any prejudice, express or implied . . .": *New York Times*, February 26, 1902, p. 8.

219   "We can lick them . . .": *Soldiers' Letters*, p. 5.

219   "We have been in this nigger-fighting . . .": Ibid., p. 11.

219   "The weather is intensely hot . . .": Ibid., p. 13.

page
220   "I am probably growing hard-hearted . . .": Ibid., p. 15. Barnes' letter was published in the Kingston, New York, *Evening Post* on May 8, 1899.
220   "I have not had any fighting . . ." etc.: Willard B. Gatewood, Jr., *Smoked Yankees and the Struggle for Empire: Letters from Negro Soldiers, 1898–1902* (Urbana: University of Illinois Press, 1971), p. 257.
220   "All this never would have occurred . . .": Ibid., p. 279.
220   "We are now arrayed . . .": Ibid., p. 248.
221   "I confess to pleasure in hearing . . .": A. F. Beringause, *Brooks Adams: A Biography* (New York: Knopf, 1955), p. 166. See also Samuel Eliot Morison, Frederick Merk, and Frank Friedel, *Dissent in Three American Wars* (Cambridge: Harvard University Press, 1970), p. 77. Holmes made the comment in the summer of 1898.
221   "these soldiers are our own . . .": *Congressional Record* (Senate), 57th Congress, 1st session, 1902, 35, Part 5:5032ff. Lodge made the speech on May 5, 1902.
221   "I have never met a Filipino who was not a musician . . .": U.S. Congress, 57th Congress, Senate Document 331, Part 1, p. 99.
221   "I think I may say that we have had chiefly in mind . . .": Ibid., p. 64.
221   "that system of warfare . . ." etc.: Ibid., p. 72.
222   "Superior race" etc.: Ibid., pp. 77–78.
222   [General Hughes] was asked . . . about the burning of towns . . . : Ibid., p. 647.
223   "I never heard anything about it" etc.: Ibid., pp. 654, 655.
223   "To boast of what they had done"; "an exaggeration": Ibid., Part 2, p. 951.
224   . . . Charles Riley . . . : Ibid., pp. 1527–30.
226   "We have crushed a deceived and confiding people . . .": Twain, pp. 611–12.

CHAPTER 15

231   "If the time has come for Negroes and dagoes . . .": Arthur E. Barbeau and Florette Henri, *The Unknown Soldiers: Black American Troops in World War I* (Philadelphia: Temple University Press, 1974), p. 173.
231   . . . Prince Hall . . . : See Chapter 5 of this book for the story of Prince Hall.
232   . . . the Irish and the German Catholics . . . : See Chapter 8 of this book.
232   The Navy took only 5,328 of them . . . : Robert H. Ferrell, *Woodrow Wilson and World War I, 1917–1921* (New York: Harper & Row, 1985), p. 213.
232   "Our country has been invaded . . ." etc.: For Jackson-Claiborne correspondence see Spencer Basset, ed., *Correspondence of Andrew Jackson* (Washington, D.C.: Carnegie Institution, 1927), Vol. 2, pp. 56, 57, 59, 76, 87.
233   "keep to yourself your opinions . . .": Robert V. Remini, *Andrew Jackson and the Course of American Empire, 1767–1821* (New York: Harper & Row, 1977), Vol. 1, p. 254.
233   "noble enthusiasm" etc.: Basset, p. 119.
233   "As fighting troops the Negro . . .": Barbeau and Henri, pp. 127–28.
233   "tuberculosis, old fractures . . .": Ibid., pp. 55, 143–44.
233   "standardizing the mind is as futile . . ." : Daniel J. Kevles, "Testing the Army's Intelligence: Psychologists and the Military in World War I," *Journal of American History*, Vol. 55, No. 3 (December 1968), p. 571.
233   "Psychology has achieved a position . . .": Ibid., p. 566.
234   The worst scores for Northern whites and blacks alike . . . : Ashley Montagu, "Intelligence of Northern Negroes and Southern Whites in the First World War," *American Journal of Psychology*, Vol. 58, (April 1945), pp. 161–88. See also Ferrell, pp. 20, 212.

page

234   The blacks constituted only 9 percent . . . : Jack Foner, *Blacks in the Military* (New York: Praeger, 1974), pp. 110–11.

234   . . . uniforms of vintage . . . : Ibid., p. 119.

234   "The country is alarmed . . .": "The Rioting of Negro Soldiers," *Messenger,* editorial, Vol. 1, No. 2, November 1917, p. 6.

235   "The men will not be permitted . . .": Barbeau and Henri, p. 165. Greer's order was issued December 6, 1918.

235   "The Italians are not a sensitive people . . .": Reilly to Farley, March 4, 1917. From the archives of the Roman Catholic Archdiocese of New York, as reported in S. M. Tomasi and M. H. Engel, *The Italian Experience in the United States* (New York: Center for Migration Studies, 1970), p. 167.

236   "The Slavic and Latin countries . . ." Arthur Sweeny, "Mental Tests for Immigrants," *North American Review,* Vol. 215 (May 1922), pp. 600–612, as quoted in Salvatore J. LaGumina, ed., *Wop!* (San Francisco: Straight Arrow, 1973), pp. 195–96.

236   "Steerage passengers from a Naples boat . . .": Quoted in LaGumina, p. 184.

236   They were the victims of violence . . . : Data on the Italians may be found in Tomasi and Engel, pp. 48, 49.

236   A mob invaded an Italian neighborhood . . . : See *The New York Times,* August 8, 1920.

236   "They did not belong to the Church . . .": Thomas F. Coakley, D.D., "Is Peter's Bark Leaking?" *America,* Vol. 11, No. 5 (May 16, 1914). Father Coakley was trying to reassure Catholic readers who were concerned about what was then perceived as a diminution of their number and influence in the United States. He did this by explaining that it had never been realistic to count the "several millions of immigrants from Southern Europe" in the first place "for the simple reason that they did not belong to the Church in a real sense when they landed on our shores." Such concerns about the perceived lack of religiosity among Italians persisted for many years, and often it was attributed to what was believed by some as the Italian's intellectual inability to understand Catholicism or much of anything else.

237   "mongrelizing good old American stock": As reported in Richard Gambino, *Blood of My Blood* (New York: Anchor Books, 1974), p. 123.

237   The lynchings continued unabated . . . : *New York Times,* September 1, 1919.

238   "We are not asking favors . . .": Letter to *Brooklyn Eagle,* as published in *Crisis,* Vol. 18, No. 1 (May 1919), the "Looking Glass" section, p. 29. Filton added, "We have helped to gain the Victory for Democracy and we must share in the fruits."

238   "We helped carry 'Democracy . . .' ": Letter to *Brooklyn Standard Union,* published in *Crisis,* ibid., p. 29. Carpenter added, "I do not believe that my men returning home from France are seeking to make trouble anywhere. But I do believe that never again will they without a struggle, submit to the indignities under which they have suffered since birth."

238   "We are cowards and jackasses . . ." etc.: W.E.B. Du Bois, "Returning Soldiers," *Crisis,* ibid., p. 14.

238   "It organizes industry to cheat us . . .": Ibid.

239   Du Bois took it upon himself to write to the twenty-one French mayors . . . : Ibid., p. 12.

239   Some French restaurants . . . : William N. Colson, "Propaganda and the American Negro Soldiers," *Messenger,* July 1919, p. 24.

239   "To try to explain the theory of prohibition . . .": C. T. Crowell, "How Prohibition Works," *Independent and Weekly Review,* January 14, 1922, as quoted in LaGumina, p. 197.

239   . . . robberies and burglaries were fewer in the twenties . . . : Geoffrey Perrett, *America in the Twenties* (New York: Simon & Schuster, 1982), p. 398.

page
239   "If newspaper accounts of the 'crime wave' . . .": "The Permanent Crime Wave," *New Republic,* editorial, January 5, 1921, p. 156.

240   . . . Arthur Conan Doyle . . . : Perrett, p. 397.

240   . . . 25 percent of all prisoners . . . : Fred G. Holmes, "Making Criminals out of Soldiers," *The Nation,* July 22, 1925, pp. 114–16.

240   . . . beautiful to see a soldier "throw away his life": Julius J. Mark, ed., *The Holmes Reader* (New York: Oceana, 1915), p. 148.

241   "Karl Marx was right . . .": "Returning Soldiers," *Messenger,* unsigned editorial, March 1919, pp. 5–6. See also article by W.E.B. Du Bois, *Crisis,* Vol. 17, No. 5 (March 1919), pp. 218–23.

241   "hungry soldiers roam the streets . . .": "Unemployment and Unrest," *Messenger,* unsigned editorial, May–June 1919, p. 9. See also article by W.E.B. Du Bois, *Crisis,* Vol. 18, No. 2 (June 1919), pp. 63–87.

241   "The Negroes' greatest opportunity . . .": See William N. Colson, "Propaganda and the American Negro Soldier," *Messenger,* July 1919, p. 24; "An Analysis of Negro Patriotism," Ibid., August 1919, pp. 23–25.

242   . . . 600,000 soldiers . . .: U.S. Bureau of Labor Statistics, *Bulletin,* Vol. 352 (May 1924), as reported in Robert K. Murray, *Red Scare* (New York: McGraw-Hill, 1964), pp. 6–7, 9, 16.

243   "It is unfortunate to put the American Legion . . .": *New York Times,* April 9, 1919.

243   "mobbish" etc.: William N. Colson, "Confederate-Americanism," *Messenger,* Vol. 2, No. 2 (February 1920), p. 9.

243   "simply another Ku Klux Klan but national in scope": "The American Legion—Our National Ku Klux Klan," editorial, Ibid., p. 4.

244   . . . the student body of Harvard . . . : *Boston Evening Transcript,* September 9, 1919, p. 1.

244   ". . . what a power this organization can exert . . .": *New York World* as reported in *Literary Digest,* September 27, 1919, p. 10.

244   "What I say is that I am innocent . . .": *The Sacco and Vanzetti Case: Transcript of the Record of the Trial of Nicola Sacco and Bartolomeo Vanzetti in the Courts of Massachusetts and Subsequent Proceedings, 1920–27* (New York: Holt, 1929), Vol. 5, pp. 4896–4904.

245   The all-black 369th Infantry . . . : C. Eric Lincoln, *The Negro Pilgrimage in America* (New York: Bantam, 1967), pp. 90–91.

245   [Mothers and widows of black soldiers segregated]: See articles written by William A. Du Puy, *New York Times,* February 23, May 30, and July 11, 1930.

CHAPTER 16

247   "We could clean up enough . . .": *Hearings Before the Select Committee on Investigation of Veterans' Bureau,* U.S. Senate, 67th Congress, pursuant to Senate Resolution 466, October 22 to November 7, 1923, (Washington, D.C.: Government Printing Office, 1923). Forbes is said to have made a number of statements similar to this. See pp. 231, 255, 256.

247   . . . he appointed Colonel Charles R. Forbes . . . : *New York Times,* February 16, 1923.

247   . . . he was born in Scotland, but some insisted it was Wales . . . : Charles Merz, "The Betrayal of Our War Veterans," *Century,* August 1924, p. 435.

247   Columbia, M.I.T., and the Cooper Institute . . . : See cross-examination of Forbes in Senate *Hearings,* p. 1049. See also *New York Times,* April 11, 1952.

page
248   . . . drummer boy . . . he deserted just two months after . . . : M. R. Werner, *Privileged Characters* (New York: Robert McBride, 1935), p. 195.

248   "Willie off the pickle boat": Merz, p. 435.

248   . . . winning a Croix de Guerre . . . : Ibid., p. 436.

248   . . . $9,050,000 for the creation of hospitals . . . : Ibid.

249   . . . annual operating budget of more than $450 million . . . : Bruce Bliven, "Charlie, Ned and Warren," *New Republic,* May 28, 1924, p. 9.

249   . . . thirty thousand largely indifferent bureaucrats . . . : Werner, p. 195.

249   . . . the bureau had only about 24,000 . . . : Harold A. Littledale, article, *New York Evening Post,* February 16, 1920.

249   The case of Joseph Furphy . . . : Ibid.

249   The bureau smacked of corruption: Ibid.

250   . . . Charles Cramer . . . : Werner, pp. 203, 225.

250   . . . only 200 beds . . . : Senate *Hearings,* pp. 1062–63.

250   . . . since Jay Gould and Jim Fiske . . . : In 1869, Gould and Fisk nearly cornered the gold market because of Grant's inability to see them as rascals. See Samuel Eliot Morison and Henry Steele Commager, *The Growth of the American Republic* (London and New York: Oxford University Press, 1951), Vol. 2, pp. 66, 67.

250   Mortimer and his wife maintained an apartment . . . : Senate *Hearings,* p. 197.

250   She was a close friend of Mrs. Herbert Votaw's . . . : Werner, p. 196.

250   The Wardman Park did not exactly exude . . . : Ibid., p. 203.

251   . . . for it was Mortimer who paid the bills: Mortimer became the Government's star witness against Forbes. See Senate *Hearings,* pp. 196ff.

251   . . . inexplicably jumped into Hayden Lake . . . : Ibid., p. 241.

251   . . . Mortimer . . . delivered a $5,000 "loan" . . . : Ibid., p. 214.

251   But he was a most knowledgeable errand boy: Ibid., pp. 226–27.

251   . . . his wife and Forbes shooting craps on a bed . . . : Ibid., p. 1393.

251   . . . most unusual veterans' hospital . . . : Merz, p. 438.

252   [Forbes' purchases of floor wax and soap]: Senate *Hearings,* p. 778.

252   The unlawful drinking parties . . . : Ibid., p. 204.

252   . . . polished off a bottle of gin . . . : Werner, p. 221.

252   . . . 67,000 quarts of bourbon, rye, and gin . . . : Senate *Hearings,* p. 249.

252   . . . the largess in Perryville . . . : Ibid., p. 620.

253   . . . the Thompson-Kelly Co. . . . : This was a company in Boston having essentially the same ownership as Thompson-Black. Other companies in which J. W. Thompson had an interest were Alzina Construction of Springfield, Illinois, and Pontiac Construction of Detroit. Mortimer represented all of them at various times. See ibid., *passim.*

253   "You are missing the *real old* times" etc.: Werner, p. 224.

254   A young man named Tulladge . . . : Ibid., p. 223. See also Senate *Hearings,* p. 1029. In various documents, the name is also spelled "Tullidge."

254   Cramer . . . shot himself in the head: Werner, p. 225.

254   "I now deny generally . . .": Senate *Hearings,* direct examination of Forbes, p. 912.

255   . . . 200,000 pieces of mail . . . : Ibid., p. 917.

255   . . . drinking party at the Ritz-Carlton . . . : Ibid., p. 1010.

255   . . . naughty party at the Traymore Hotel . . . : Ibid., p. 1107.

255   . . . secret meeting in the Wardman . . . : Ibid., p. 1012.

255   . . . a $5,000 loan . . . : Ibid., p. 1014. A writer for *The Nation* called all of this an "orgy of corruption and inefficiency." See Arthur Warner, "The Betrayal of Our War Veterans," *The Nation,* March 5, 1924, pp. 249–50.

page

255   What about all the drinking . . . : Senate *Hearings,* p. 1018.

255   Charles R. Forbes, Charles F. Forbes . . . : Ibid., p. 1100.

255   . . . while in Spokane . . . : Ibid., p. 1021.

256   . . . the 67,000 quarts of liquor . . . : Ibid., p. 249.

256   . . . all the education . . . : Ibid., p. 1019.

256   . . . a secret code . . . : Ibid.

256   . . . Mortimer found Forbes and Mortimer's wife . . . : Ibid., p. 1067.

256   "It might have been a little indiscreet": Ibid., p. 1131.

256   "Didn't construct any": Ibid., p. 1062.

257   Charles Forbes was eventually tried . . . : Robert K. Murray, *The Harding Era* (Minneapolis: University of Minnesota Press, 1969), p. 461.

257   "a crook and a fixer": Werner, pp. 227, 228.

257   No sooner had his bootlegging charge been dropped . . . : Ibid., p. 228.

CHAPTER 17

258   "thousands of worthy claims . . ." etc.: Senate Report 103, 68th Congress, 1st session, Part 2, 1924, p. 26. This was based on the Senate's investigation of Forbes.

258   "complete indifference on the part of examiners . . .": Ibid. For a review of how the Veterans Administration handled the Agent Orange claims, see the last four chapters of this book.

259   "Neither Congress nor the people . . ." etc.: Ibid., p. 27.

259   "Congress little realizes . . .": William Edler, "Making a Wreck of the Veteran," *American Mercury,* July 1925, p. 257.

259   . . . 49,000 claims allowed for diseases . . . : Senate Report 103, p. 41.

260   "liquidation of genteel culture": As reported in William E. Leuchtenburg, *The Perils of Prosperity* (Chicago: University of Chicago Press, 1958), p. 144.

260   "clean straight game" etc.: Harold Seymour, *Baseball: The Golden Age* (New York: Oxford University Press, 1971), as quoted in Burl Noggle, *Into the Twenties* (Urbana: University of Illinois Press, 1974), p. 170.

260   . . . Jack Dempsey . . . : Roger Daniels, *The Bonus March* (Westport, Conn.: Greenwood, 1971), p. 38.

261   "renewed inflation, increased commodity prices . . .": Ibid., p. 28.

261   "he would hang himself by appearing in his own defense": Robert K. Murray, *The Harding Era* (Minneapolis: University of Minnesota Press, 1969), pp. 180–81.

261   . . . deficit of $650 million . . . : Daniels, p. 38.

261   "disaster to the nation's finances" Murray, p. 187.

262   . . . the President's legacy . . . : Arthur M. Schlesinger, Jr., *The Age of Roosevelt,* Vol. 2, *The Crisis of the Old Order* (Boston: Houghton Mifflin, 1957), p. 50.

262   "business activity, full employment and agricultural revival": *New York Times,* March 18, 1924.

262   "mercenaries out of our patriotic boys": Daniels, p. 36.

262   And Pierre S. du Pont . . . : In the May 1, 1927, issue of *Forbes* magazine, the du Ponts were described as "rapidly becoming the most influential and powerful family in U.S. industry. Their wealth, while not yet equaling that of the Rockefellers and Fords, probably ranks with that of George F. Baker and Andrew Mellon . . ." The item was reprinted in the August 10, 1987, issue of *Forbes,* p. 139.

262   "the most favored class in the United States": Daniels, p. 36.

262   The American Legion found it was no easy going . . . : *New York Times,* March 23, 1924.
262   "We performed splendidly . . .": Ibid.
263   "no longer consistently square their ideals . . .": Ibid.
263   "service they rendered was of such a nature . . ." etc.: Daniels, pp. 37, 39.

CHAPTER 18

264   "We ain't gonna ever get a bonus . . .": Unidentified bonus marcher as he marched into Washington in May of 1932. As quoted in Walter W. Waters [as told to William C. White], *B.E.F.: The Whole Story of The Bonus Army* (New York: John Day, 1935), p. 64.
264   . . . there were more than 32,000 patients . . . : *New York Times,* January 23, 1931.
265   "materially assist in the relief . . .": Ibid., January 26, 1931, p. 1.
265   Investment Bankers of America . . . Charles E. Mitchell . . . : Ibid.
266   They would be expected to pay interest . . . : Ibid., February 10, 1931.
266   "Inquiry indicates . . . that the number of veterans in need . . .": Ibid., February 27, 1931, p. 15.
266   "has refused to turn his hand . . ." etc.: Ibid.
266   Walter W. Waters . . . "no occupation or profession to resume": Waters, pp. 4–6. See also Donald J. Lisio, *The President and Protest* (Columbia: University of Missouri Press, 1974), pp. 65–66. On the question of whether he was a superintendent or just a worker, see also Roger Daniels, *The Bonus March* (Westport, Conn.: Greenwood, 1971), pp. 77–78.
267   "Newspapers, which can always be picked out of trash cans . . ." etc.: Waters, p. 9.
268   . . . 300 men all volunteered to give blood . . . : Ibid., pp. 26, 27.
268   "I don't know when we'll get to Washington . . .": Daniels, p. 80.
268   Indeed, about 1,000 soldiers had preceded him . . . : *Washington Evening Star,* July 29, 1932.
269   . . . Pelham Glassford . . . : Daniels, pp. 89–91.
270   "could not recognize the invasion . . .": Ibid., p. 91.
270   "borrowed drum corps": Waters, p. 85.
270   "a cross between a Congo village . . ." etc.: Ibid., p. 106.
270   The men would frequently be seen with empty bean cans . . . : Ibid., p. 84.
271   . . . met with a group of Boy Scouts . . . : Ibid., p. 82.
271   "If the farmers of this nation . . .": Johnson's thoughts were contained in a letter written later, as reported in Daniels, p. 120.
271   "double-crossed the nation": *Washington Post,* June 3 and 7, 1932, as quoted in Lisio, p. 103.
271   "Until very recently the average American . . .": Waters, p. 90.
272   "I hope that rumor is not true . . .": Daniels, p. 137.
272   "except the communist camp . . ." etc.: *Washington Evening Star,* July 25, 1932.
272   Hoover hung back . . . : *New York Times,* July 28, 1932.
273   "You and your bonus army . . .": Waters, p. 193.
273   "The first bloodshed by the Bonus Army . . .": Conrad A. Lanza, Assistant Chief of Staff, G-2, to Assistant Chief of Staff, G-2, II Corps, July 5, 1932, War Department, Office of the Adjutant General, RG 94, NA, as reported in Lisio, p. 155.
273   . . . James O. Harbord told the "first annual meeting" . . . : *Washington Evening Star,* July 26, 1932.
273   "the real design of those . . .": Ibid., editorial page.

page

273   . . . a "radical" group . . . : Ibid., July 27, 1932.

274   . . . Glassford . . . had his badge ripped off: Ibid., July 28, 1932.

274   The task fell to General Douglas MacArthur . . . : Lisio, pp. 196–225.

274   . . . Joe Angelo . . . : *New York Times,* July 30, 1932.

275   Among them would be a book salesman . . . : Daniels, p. 177.

275   . . . sang "My Country 'Tis of Thee": *Washington Evening Star,* July 28, 1932.

275   "The misguided men . . .": *New York Times,* July 29, 1932.

275   . . . 94 percent of those who had made the Bonus March . . . : William Manchester,
American Caesar (Boston: Little, Brown, 1978; reprint, New York: Dell, 1979), p. 164.

275   "Railroads are not permitted . . .": *Washington Evening Star,* July 29, 1932.

275   MacArthur was declared the "man of the hour". . . : Manchester, pp. 165–66.

276   "You cowards . . .": *Washington Evening Star,* July 29, 1932.

276   "unwarranted and un-American" etc.: Ibid.

276   "Government cannot be coerced by mob rule": *New York Times,* July 30, 1932.

276   McCloskey had come to Anacostia . . . : Daniels, pp. 182–85.

277   "mainly of Communists and other disorderly persons": *New York Times,* July 30, 1932.

277   "are not veterans, many are communists . . .": *Washington Evening Star,* July 29, 1932.

277   "molded, outwardly at least . . .": *New York Times,* August 1, 1932, p. 3.

278   "Hoover had to defame the poor idiots he had gassed": H. L. Mencken, "Animadversions
on the Campaign," *American Mercury,* November 1932, p. 382.

278   "Whether these men are really communists . . .": *New York Herald Tribune,* as quoted
in *Washington Evening Star* in a wrap-up of press comment, July 29, 1932.

278   "The obvious duty of the authorities . . .": *Plain Dealer,* as quoted in *Washington
Evening Star,* July 29, 1932.

278   "At a time when grubs of revolution . . .": *Memphis Evening Appeal,* as quoted in
Washington Evening Star, July 29, 1932.

278   "The end of tolerant dealing . . .": *Washington Evening Star,* July 30, 1932.

279   "No person because he wore a uniform . . .": Daniels, p. 227.

279   . . . MacArthur hired Waters . . . : *New York Herald Tribune,* January 22, 1935. The
Tribune ran two photographs of Waters, one as he was detained by police during the Bonus
March, the other at his desk in the War Department, where the mail and record chief was
shown giving him a large stack of papers.

CHAPTER 19

283   There were more than sixteen million of them . . . : Veterans Administration fact sheet,
issued by its Office of Public and Consumer Affairs, Washington, D.C., January 1987.

283   . . . roughly a third were women . . . : Richard Polenberg, *War and Society* (Philadelphia: Lippincott, 1972), p. 146.

284   "the Depression Psychosis": He noted the syndrome during the war and recalled it later
in John Kenneth Galbraith, *American Capitalism: The Concept of Countervailing Power*
(Boston: Houghton Mifflin, 1952; reprint, Armonk, N.Y.: M. E. Sharpe, 1980), p. 65.

284   The Department of Labor . . . predicted . . . : Geoffrey Perrett, *Days of Sadness, Years
of Triumph* (New York: Coward, McCann & Geoghegan, 1973), p. 337.

284   "Pearl Harbor of Peace" etc.: *New Republic,* August 2, 1943, p. 139, in the column
"Washington Notes" by "TRB," who in those years was Walter Lippmann.

page
284   And a poll by George Gallup's . . . : Davis R. B. Ross, *Preparing for Ulysses: Politics and Veterans During World War II* (New York: Columbia University Press, 1969), pp. 35, 36.

284   . . . a Government survey indicated . . . : Samuel A. Stouffer et al., *The American Soldier: Combat and Its Aftermath* (Princeton, N.J.: Princeton University Press, 1949), Vol. 2, p. 598.

285   "a shout in his heart" etc.: Stuart Chase, "Financing America's Future: Demobilization Day—A Preview," *The Nation,* October 2, 1943, p. 371.

285   Peace yielded . . . a sustained boom . . . : There are a number of sources documenting the state of the American economy after the war. See especially *The Economic Report of the President,* January 8, 1947, p. 1; *The Midyear Economic Report of the President,* July 30, 1948, pp. 1, 4; *The Economic Report of the President,* January 1949, pp. 1–3; Francis H. Heller, *Economics of the Truman Administration* (Lawrence: Regents Press of Kansas, 1981); *Historical Satistics of the United States* (Washington, 1976), Part 1, p. 135; Part 2, p. 1145.

285   . . . George C. Marshall . . . began to consider . . . : Joseph C. Goulden, *The Best Years* (New York: Atheneum, 1976), p. 19.

286   "Dr. New Deal" etc.: Polenberg, p. 73.

286   "the daily fare of ad writers . . .": R. M. MacIver in "Concerning the Peace" [review of Rudolph Flesch's *Toward an Abiding Peace*] *The Nation,* August 21, 1943, p. 218.

287   Rankin . . . thought of veterans' benefits . . . : Russell Whelan, "Rankin of Mississippi," *American Mercury,* July 1944, p. 31.

287   "I would rather send my child . . .": United States House of Representatives, Committee on World War Veterans' Legislation, G.I. Bill hearings, 78th Congress, 2nd session, Hearings on H.R. 3817 and S. 1767 (the "G.I. Bill"), February 24, 1944, pp. 162–63, as quoted in Ross, p. 108.

287   "We have 50,000 negroes in the service . . .": Ibid.

287   "While concentrating on military victory, we are not neglecting . . .": Samuel I. Rosenman, *The Public Papers and Addresses of Franklin D. Roosevelt* (New York: Random House, 1938), Vol. 12, item 83, as quoted in Ross, p. 64.

287   The following October, Roosevelt presented . . . : Ross, p. 92.

288   Congressmen . . . would be more inclined to make concessions . . . : John Morton Blum, *V Was for Victory* (New York: Harcourt, Brace, Jovanovich, 1976), p. 248.

288   "Colleges . . . will find themselves converted . . .": Robert M. Hutchins, "The Threat to American Education," *Collier's,* December 30, 1944, pp. 20–21.

288   "All of us are concentrating now . . .": *New York Times,* November 24, 1943.

288   "I finally decided that this is no time . . .": Ross, p. 53.

288   "Progressives should understand . . .": Polenberg, p. 76, quoting *Journals of David Lilienthal* (New York: Harper & Row, 1964), Vol. 1., p. 43.

289   "Liberals meet in Washington these days . . ." Polenberg, p. 73.

289   . . . Harry W. Colmery . . . : Goulden, p. 56.

289   Roosevelt signed it into law . . . : *New York Times,* June 23, 1944.

290   Between 1945 and '46, college enrollment . . . : Benjamin Cushing Bowker, *Out of Uniform* (New York: W. W. Norton, 1946), p. 234.

290   "will never again permit the callous indifference . . .": *New York Times,* April 8, 1945.

290   "take command over this country . . ." etc.: Bernard Iddings Bell, "The Church and the Veteran," *Atlantic,* December 1944, pp. 64–68.

291   "will surely bring a slump in morals . . ." etc.: J. Gordon Chamberlin, *The Church and Demobilization* (New York: Whitmore & Stone, 1945), pp. 12–14.

page

291   "our gravest social problem" etc.: Willard Waller, *The Veteran Comes Back* (New York: Dryden, 1944), p. 14.

291   "Our traditional policy has been to neglect . . .": Ibid., p. 15.

292   "If the Presidential election were being held at this time . . .": Gallup poll, as published in *New York Times,* December 5, 1943, p. 48.

292   "containing political argument . . .": *Time,* July 10, 1944.

292   . . . banned *The Republic* of Plato . . . : Ibid. See also *New York Times,* December 3, 1943.

292   "A civilian can be licked into shape . . .": Dixon Wecter, *When Johnny Comes Marching Home* (Boston: Houghton Mifflin, 1944; reprint, Westport, Conn.: Greenwood Press, 1970), p. 5.

292   "combine the worst vices . . ." etc.: Dixon Wecter, "Root, Hog or Die," *Saturday Review of Literature,* September 16, 1944, p. 30.

292   "friendly, generous, easy-going . . .": Wecter, *When Johnny,* p. 558.

292   "the author of the only competing book . . ." etc.: Willard Waller, "'Mr. Waller Protests," *Saturday Review of Literature,* December 9, 1944, pp. 19–20.

293   "our energies, our great affection . . ." etc.: *New York Times,* November 4, 1943.

293   . . . Boeing laid off 21,200 . . . : Goulden, p. 91.

293   . . . factories making armaments lost nearly 300,000 . . . income of the average worker had doubled since 1939 . . . : Perrett, pp. 399, 400, 401.

294   The wealthiest 5 percent of American society . . . : Polenberg, p. 94.

294   "reputation for being big-hearted" etc.: *New York Times,* January 9, 1944.

294   [Hoffman quoted; Atlantic Elevator Company]: J. Donald Kingsley, "Veterans, Unions and Jobs," *New Republic,* October 23, 1944, p. 513, and November 13, 1944, p. 621.

294   *Wall Street Journal* story . . . : Blum, p. 223.

294   "pay union dues . . .": Ibid., October 23, 1944, p. 513.

295   "must have the free right . . ." etc.: Herbert Hoover, "When the Soldiers Come Home," *Collier's,* February 5, 1944, p. 42.

295   "the public is turning again . . .": Frederick C. Crawford, "A Better America Through Freedom of Enterprise," in *A Better America* (New York: National Association of Manufacturers, 1944), quoted in Polenberg, p. 90.

295   "Plans are far advanced for a big business drive . . .": *New Republic,* October 23, 1944, p. 513.

295   "If we give special status to veterans today . . .": *New York Times,* April 7, 1945, p. 18.

295   The *Philadelphia Bulletin* conducted a survey . . . : Goulden, p. 53.

CHAPTER 20

298   "In most cases women cannot . . .": Lynda M. Van Devanter, testifying before the U.S. Senate Committee on Veterans Affairs, March 10, 1983, as reported in *Minerva,* Vol. 1, No. 3 (Winter 1983), p. 75.

298   Doris "Dorie" Miller was not exactly . . . : Jack D. Foner, *Blacks and the Military in American History* (New York: Praeger, 1974), pp. 172–73, 241. See also Geoffrey Perrett, *Days of Sadness, Years of Triumph* (New York: Coward, McCann & Geoghegan, 1973), p. 317.

300   Women had served . . . as nurses in the Revolution . . . : June A. Willenz, *Women Veterans* (New York: Continuum, 1983), p. 10.

page

300   . . . around four hundred of them . . . : Brenda Denzler, "Acceptance and Avoidance: The Woman Vietnam Vet," *Minerva,* Vol. 5, No. 2 (Summer 1987), p. 83.

300   Their status remained unclear . . . : Willenz, p. 15.

301   "Hello Girls": Stacey Fletcher, "Farewell—Adieu: Posthumous Encomium for a 'Hello Girl,' " *Minerva,* Vol. 5, No. 3 (Fall 1987), p. 111.

301   "The corps shall not be a part of the army . . .": Willenz, p. 171.

302   It took the Government more than thirty years . . . : N.Y.S. Assembly Subcommittee on Women Veterans, "Women Are Veterans Too! A Report on the 1986 New York State Assembly Hearings on Women Veterans," as published in *Minerva,* Vol. 5, No. 3 (Fall 1987).

302   Among them were the WASPs . . . : Yvonne C. Pateman, "W.A.S.P. Struggle for Militarization," *Minerva,* Vol. 2, No. 2 (Summer 1984), p. 1.

302   The Government said that the WASPs . . . : Willenz, pp. 26, 177.

302   Not until 1977 did the WASPs . . . : Ibid., p. 179.

303   . . . although there were at least 1.2 million women . . . gynecologists . . . : Ibid., p. 184.

303   "In most cases, women cannot receive gynecological care . . ." etc.: Van Devanter, testimony, p. 76.

303   . . . one study of two hundred women . . . : D'Ann Campbell, "Life Cycles and Turning Points: Wacs, Waves and Nurses of World War II," paper, Department of History, Indiana University, presented at American Historical Association Convention, December 30, 1985.

303   WAVES . . . and SPARS . . . : WAVES stood for Women Accepted for Volunteer Emergency Service; SPARS was a contraction of "Semper Paratus—Always Ready," the Coast Guard's Latin-to-English motto.

304   "an old-line bureaucrat . . .": "Baruch Report (cont'd)," *New Republic,* editorial, March 6, 1944, p. 304.

304   "makes the job a cruel joke": I. F. Stone, "Millionaires' Beveridge Plan," *Nation,* March 25, 1944, pp. 354–55.

304   "enmeshed in red tape": *Washington Post,* December 16, 1944.

304   "suffering needlessly . . .": Albert Q. Maisel, in *Cosmopolitan,* March and April 1945; see also *Reader's Digest,* April 1945.

305   "I would much rather be on Iwo Jima Island . . .": *New York Times,* March 25, 1945.

305   Hines . . . testified . . . : *New York Times,* March 25, 1945.

306   "As a World War I soldier. . .": *Washington Post,* June 8, 1944.

306   "I don't think there's any job in the country . . .": Omar N. Bradley and Clay Blair, *A General's Life: An Autobiography by the General of the Army* (New York: Simon & Schuster, 1983), p. 446.

306   . . . twenty million . . . Fully 43 percent . . . : Ibid., p. 447.

306   "We've got to look on veterans as individual problems . . .": "Veterans' New Dealer," *Collier's,* November 24, 1945, p. 24.

307   "medical old-fogyism": *Newsweek,* June 18, 1945, p. 35.

307   "rammed 630 bills through Congress . . .": Jack A. Underhill, "The Veterans Administration and the American Legion (1945–1947)," unpublished M.A. thesis, Columbia University, 1959.

307   "to the point where they might be changed . . ." etc.: Ibid., p. 22.

308   "tragic breakdown" etc.: *New York Times,* February 2, 1946.

308   "It sounds like communism to me": Underhill, p. 32.

308   "ranting of Rankin . . .": Ibid.

page

308   Stelle charged that . . . between 300,000 and 500,000 veterans . . . : *New York Times,* February 2, 1946.

308   "to the hilt": Underhill, p. 33. See also *New York Times,* February 2, 1946.

309   "Well, I never lost *my* temper": *New York Times,* February 2, 1946.

310   "We need a new organization . . ." Quoted in Charles G. Bolte, *The New Veteran* (New York: Reynal & Hitchcock, 1945), p. 74.

310   "The American Legion in my mind . . .": quoted in Ibid., p. 80.

310   ". . . we had an uncertain world . . .": Ibid., p. 81.

310   "We look forward to becoming civilians . . ." etc.: Ibid., pp. 96, 107.

311   "communist influences" etc.: *New York Times,* May 11, 1946.

311   Westbrook Pegler . . . Bill Mauldin . . . Franklin D. Roosevelt, Jr. . . . : *AVC Bulletin,* March 1, 1946.

312   "loud speakers for the Communist Party . . .": *New York Times,* August 22, 1948.

312   "I think the AVC can be a key organization . . ." *AVC Bulletin,* February 15, 1946.

312   "seemed to be to grab everything . . .": Bill Mauldin, "Poppa Knows Best," *Atlantic Monthly,* April 1947, p. 29.

313   "guilty of perjury . . .": *AVC Bulletin,* August 1948.

313   . . . Hiss-Chambers case . . . : *New York Times,* August 8, 1948, pp. 1, 5.

314   "The planning committee's contention . . .": *Communist Daily Worker,* August 10, 1948.

314   . . . the Legion's official position against Nazism and fascism . . . : The American Legion's position against right-wing extremism was contained in Resolution 205 passed in its 17th annual convention held in St. Louis, Missouri, September 23–26, 1935. The resolution as passed said: *"Resolved:* That the American Legion continue its active opposition to the advocacy in America of nazi-ism, fascism, communism, or any other isms that are contrary to the fundamental principles of democracy, as established under the Constitution of the United States of America." Similar anti-fascist resolutions were passed in 1937, 1938, 1939, 1940, 1941, 1942, and 1943. The Legion noted in 1938, "The Communists have called the Legion a Fascist outfit, and now we find the German-American Bund charging us with giving up the Reds." (Resolutions courtesy of the American Legion.)

CHAPTER 21

317   "How would you feel if you fought for your country . . .": *New York Times,* May 3, 1953.

317   . . . Joseph R. McCarthy and Robert A. Taft . . . : For McCarthy, see David M. Oshinsky, *A Conspiracy So Immense: The World of Joe McCarthy* (New York: Free Press, 1983), pp. 108, 109. For Taft, see Burton I. Kaufman, *The Korean War: Challenges in Crisis, Credibility and Command* (Philadelphia: Temple University Press, 1986), p. 35.

317   . . . Richard Nixon . . . : See especially *New York Times,* August 26, 1952.

317   . . . Lewis B. Hershey . . . : John E. Wiltz, "The Korean War and American Society," in Francis H. Heller, ed., *The Korean War: A 25 Year Perspective* (Lawrence: Regents Press of Kansas, 1977), p. 112. See also Joseph C. Goulden, *Korea: The Untold Story of the War* (New York: McGraw-Hill, 1982), p. 135.

317   . . . John F. Kennedy . . . : Kaufman, p. 35.

317   . . . the American Legion . . . : *New York Times,* August 26, 1952. The Legion asked for a Federal investigation to determine if the ACLU might be "properly classified as a communist or communist-front organization."

page

317   . . . Douglas MacArthur . . . : Goulden, p. 53.

318   . . . the State of Indiana . . . : Oshinsky, p. 140.

318   . . . the State of Ohio . . . : Ibid.

318   . . . Legionnaires went to Mosinee . . . : *Milwaukee Journal,* May 2, 1950, as quoted in ibid.

320   . . . cruel and unusual punishment . . . : For an authoritative account of this aspect of the Korean War, see Goulden, esp. pp. 558, 594, 603, and *passim.*

321   "We called them pinkies . . .": *New York Times,* April 27, 1953.

321   "appear to have succumbed . . .": Ibid., April 13, 1953.

321   "Such captive soldiers cannot be condemned . . .": Fact sheet, U.S. Department of Defense, as reported in ibid.

321   "sadly and unfortunately correct": Ibid., April 23, 1953.

322   "tears of joy" etc.: Ibid., April 20, 1953.

322   . . . Karl W. Kirtchenhausen . . . : Ibid.

322   The next day, another group of 35 were released . . . : Ibid., April 21, 1953.

323   "twenty-two United States prisoners of war . . .": Ibid., May 2, 1953.

324   "bitter beyond expression" etc.: Ibid., May 4, 1953.

324   The Army then admitted . . . : Ibid.

324   "it would be extremely unfair . . .": Ibid., May 10, 1953.

325   "They would bend my head back . . .": Ibid., August 6, 1953.

325   "a muttered curse . . ." etc.: *Newsweek,* August 17, 1953, p. 21.

325   "We can and we must recapture . . .": *New York Times,* August 21, 1953.

325   "some of the returning American prisoners . . . are . . . communists . . .": *Newsweek,* August 17, 1953, p. 21.

326   . . . *Paths of Glory:* See review, *New York Times,* December 26, 1957.

327   "turncoat G.I.'s . . .": Ibid., January 26, 1954.

327   Eisenhower said . . . the Army would not punish a soldier . . . : Ibid., January 28, 1954.

327   "one of the major contributing factors . . .": Ibid., September 27, 1953.

327   The Korean veteran "is a different breed . . .": *New York Times Magazine,* August 9, 1953.

328   . . . Irving Peress . . . : Oshinksy, p. 364.

328   . . . Ralph Zwicker . . . : *New York Times,* February 21, 1954.

328   "This is not witch-hunting . . .": Ibid., April 29, 1953; and *New Republic,* July 14, 1952. See also Victor Navasky, *Naming Names* (New York: Viking, 1980).

329   "Frequently, bitter criticism has showed . . .": Raymond Moley, Jr., *The American Legion Story* (New York: Duell, Sloan & Pearce/Meredith Press, 1966), pp. 359–60.

329   . . . resolutions against fascism in 1935 . . . : The American Legion's 1935 resolution was passed in its 17th annual convention held in St. Louis, Missouri, September 23–26, 1935. The resolution as passed said: "*Resolved*: That the American Legion continue its active opposition to the advocacy in America of nazi-ism, fascism, communism, or any other isms that are contrary to the fundamental principles of democracy, as established under the Constitution of the United States of America." This resolution and others were provided courtesy of John F. Sommer, Jr., Deputy Director, National Veterans Affairs and Rehabilitation Commission, American Legion, Washington, D.C.

329   . . . unrelenting disapproval of President Eisenhower . . . : Oshinsky, p. 496.

329   "It would seem basic . . .": *New York Times,* November 22, 1955.

330   . . . Norman Pierre Gaston . . . : Ibid., September 13, 1955.

330   . . . James Kutcher: See James Kutcher, *The Case of the Legless Veteran* (New York: Monad Press, 1973).

page
331   . . . Joseph Rauh . . . Murray Kempton . . . "a sense of fair play . . ." etc.: *New York Times,* December 24 and 31, 1955.
332   "bear false witness . . ." etc.: Ibid., January 12, 1954.
333   "few of the men became sincere converts . . .": Ibid., August 18, 1955.
333   . . . the Army required former prisoners of war to appear . . . : Ibid., December 16, 1955.

CHAPTER 22

334   . . . William Erwin Mayer . . . : *U.S. News and World Report,* February 24, 1956, p. 56.
335   "to raise serious questions about American character . . .": Ibid.
335   "passive, dependent individuals . . .": Ibid., p. 61.
336   "blamed on the prisoners themselves . . .": John Greenway, "The Colonel's Korean 'Turncoats,' " *Nation,* November 10, 1962, pp. 302–5.
337   "for the simple reason that all prisoners . . .": Eugene Kinkead, *In Every War but One* (New York: Norton, 1959), p. 64.
337   "glaring weak link in American education . . .": Anthony T. Bouscaren, "Korea, Test of American Education," *Catholic World,* Vol. 183, (April 1956), p. 24.
337   "vanishing species—the American patriot" etc.: Max Rafferty, "What's Happening to Patriotism?", *Reader's Digest,* Vol. 79, (October 1961), p. 108.
337   "apathetic, dependent . . ." etc.: Betty Friedan, *The Feminine Mystique* (New York: Dell, 1963), pp. 203, 296.
337   "succumbed to communist brainwashing": Strom Thurmond, "The Choice Is Ours, the Will to Win," *Vital Speeches of the Day,* 1962, p. 344.
337   "softness" etc.: J. Edgar Hoover, "Perpetuation of Our American Heritage: Revitalize the Outlook of Our Youth," Ibid., 1957, p. 747.
337   "What are we going to do . . .": *National Review,* editorial, July 17, 1962, p. 8.
338   "relatively easy . . . to confuse our men" etc.: Hyman G. Rickover, "Democracy: The Subject Our Schools Don't Teach," *McCall's,* March 1962, p. 124.
338   "Are American youth underdisciplined, overcoddled?" etc.: Benjamin Spock, "Are We Bringing Up Our Children Too 'Soft' for the Stern Realities They Must Face?", *Ladies' Home Journal,* September 1960, p. 20.
338   . . . just one more good reason why scouting . . . : Rex Lucas, "Personally Speaking," *Scouting,* January 1965, p. 3.
339   [Biderman's conclusions]: Albert Biderman, "Dangers of Negative Patriotism," *Harvard Business Review,* Vol. 40 (1962), p. 93.
340   Others who bothered . . . joined in the refutation: Ibid.
340   "There were terrible unspoken truths . . ." etc.: Interview, Albert Biderman, by Lewis Milford, November 1987.
341   . . . James Stanley . . . : *United States* v. *Stanley,* 55 Law Week 5101, June 25, 1987.
342   . . . see the bones of their forearms . . . : T. Saffer and O. Kelly, *Countdown Zero* (New York: Putnam, 1982). See esp. the firsthand accounts pp. 43, 75, 152.
342   "The psychological implications of atomic weapons . . .": Howard L. Rosenberg, *Atomic Soldiers* (Boston: Beacon Press, 1980), p. 38.
342   The Army employed press agentry . . . : *Effect of Radiation on Human Health, Health Effects of Ionizing Radiation: Hearings Before the Subcommittee on Health and the Environment of the Committee on Interstate and Foreign Commerce,* House of Representatives, 95th Congress, 2nd session 1978, p. 62.

page
343   "apparent ease with which Americans were managed . . ." etc.: *Military and Cold War Education and Speech Review Policies: Hearings Before the Special Preparedness Subcommittee of the Committee on Armed Services,* United States Senate, 87th Congress, 2nd session, Part 1, 1962.

343   "the American public was not ready": Ibid.

344   "A great nation may not be told . . .": Ibid.

CHAPTER 23

347   Their average age was just over nineteen . . . : Loren Baritz, *Backfire* (New York: Morrow, 1985), pp. 276, 277.

347   It was a dream not so different from that of Emilio Aguinaldo . . . : There are striking parallels between the Vietnam War and the Philippine Insurrection. Please see Chapter 14 of this book.

348   "The Americans are much stronger than the French . . .": Bernard B. Fall, *Viet-Nam Witness* (New York: Praeger, 1966), p. 105.

348   . . . nobody was quite sure what Vietnam had cost the Americans: Robert W. Stevens, *Vain Hopes, Grim Realities* (New York: New Viewpoints, 1976), pp. 4, 164. The doctoral candidate was Tom Riddell, and his piece for *The Progressive* was published in October 1963, pp. 33–37. He was working on his doctorate at American University.

348   These figures did not include the $233 billion . . . : Stevens, p. 170.

348   "There are many . . . prices we pay . . .": Quoted in ibid., pp. 10–11. See also Lawrence M. Baskir and William Straus, *Chance and Circumstance* (New York: Knopf, 1978), p. 8.

348   . . . that the American public not be concerned . . . : Lyndon Johnson seemed to feel that he could pursue the war and his social programs without damage to the economy. Some scholars have since argued that the economy of the country was not really strained. Robert Stevens argues that damage was done. For the view which supports the assertion that there was no damage, see J. F. Walter and H. G. Valter, Jr., "Princess and the Pea; or the Alleged Vietnam War Origins of the Current Inflation," *Journal of Economic Issues,* Vol. 16, (June 1982), pp. 597–608.

349   Each day, aluminum cans of 16-millimeter film . . . : That was precisely the scene at CBS News in New York, but it was not very different at the other two major networks.

349   . . . Edward R. Murrow . . . : His sense of history and of journalism's role is no myth, even though a generation of Americans cannot remember his work. The quality of his work may be found in the collection *In Search of Light: The Broadcasts of Edward R. Murrow, 1938–1961* (New York: Knopf, 1967), edited by Edward Bliss, Jr., long an editor at CBS News.

350   . . . losing more than 58,000 . . . : Baskir and Straus, p. 5. Baskir and Straus reported that 56,000 were lost. That figure rose to more than 58,000 in the decade after their 1978 book was published, as war service–connected injuries finally took their toll. The number is expected to increase in future years, according to the Vietnam Veterans of America. Michael Leaveck, VVA, interview by Lewis Milford, September 1988.

350   If Calley wasn't exactly the boy next door . . . : David Nelson of the *Miami Herald* profiled Calley in 1969. For the version of the profile on which the account here is based, see *New York Post,* December 6, 1969, p. 26.

351   . . . briefly becoming a nonunion worker . . . : Calley started out as a switchman and quickly became a conductor. His career was cut short in 1964 when he was arrested and

page

accused of permitting a forty-seven-car freight train to block traffic during rush hour. See ibid.

351   [My Lai massacre]: See Seymour M. Hersh, *Cover-Up* (New York: Random House, 1972), p. 4; and Lieutenant General William R. Peers, *The My Lai Inquiry* (New York: Norton, 1979), pp. 175, 179.

351   . . . aspects of the innocent at My Lai were witnessed . . . : Peers, p. 179.

352   My Lai . . . was dragged into the public spotlight . . . : Ibid., pp. 4–7; see also Christopher Lydon, "Pinkville Gadfly," a "Man in the News" feature, *New York Times,* November 29, 1969, p. 14. There were other enlisted men and officers who behaved as Calley did, but there were also many other soldiers who felt as Ridenhour did and who refused to commit crimes against civilians. One of them, Michael Bernhardt, was the subject of an article by Joseph Lelyveld in *The New York Times Magazine* on December 16, 1979. As compelling as Lelyveld's story was, Calley was the name most Americans remembered when they thought about the soldiers who fought the war.

353   Calley was court-martialed . . . became a jewelry salesman . . . : Peers, pp. 221–27; also Albin Krebs, "Notes on People," *New York Times,* July 29, 1977; and "Follow-Up on the News," Ibid., July 10, 1983.

354   . . . beer, banana splits, and a movie . . . : *New York Times,* February 14, 1973.

355   The nomenclature of PSTD . . . : *Graduate Center News Report,* City University of New York, Vol. 16, November 1, 1985.

355   Richard M. Nixon was not in a . . . charitable mood . . . : *New York Times,* February 15, March 1, and April 1, 1973.

356   The navy discharged . . . "misfits and malcontents": Jack D. Foner, *Blacks and the Military in American History* (New York: Praeger, 1974), p. 258. Foner fully documents many of the problems blacks had while in service.

356   "We don't want a handout . . ." etc.: *New York Times,* March 5, 1973, p. 17.

357   "Peace for the ordinary serviceman . . .": Ibid., March 29, 1974, p. 35.

357   . . . Johnson . . . attended the meeting . . . : Ibid., April 14, 1975.

357   . . . raffle tickets for $100 each . . . : See Ibid., April 23, 1974, and April 24, 1974, p. 26.

358   In a survey conducted by Daniel Yankelovich . . . : Richard Severo, ibid., May 22, 1974, p. 86.

358   Five veterans . . . barricaded themselves in a men's room . . . : See ibid., July 4, 1974.

358   . . . an exhaustive search turned up qualified people . . . : One of those who turned it down was Admiral Elmo Zumwalt, Jr., who commanded naval forces in Vietnam from 1968 to 1970, then served as Chief of Naval Operations. While in command, Admiral Zumwalt ordered that Agent Orange be sprayed in the Mekong Delta to expose Vietcong positions. He would later become convinced that his son, a Navy lieutenant, junior grade, got lymphatic cancer as a result of exposure to Agent Orange. His son, Elmo Zumwalt 3rd, who served on a patrol boat in the area ordered sprayed by his father, said that although he could not prove conclusively that all of his medical problems came from his exposure to Agent Orange, he was certain Agent Orange was the source. He also suspected that his son, Elmo R. Zumwalt 4th, who had a congenital dysfunction that confused his physical senses, suffered indirectly from the exposure to Agent Orange. Elmo Zumwalt 3rd died of cancer on August 14, 1988. Admiral Zumwalt said that even if he had known in advance that Agent Orange would cause its alleged health problems, he would have ordered that it be used, because he believed it reduced American casualties. His son supported the admiral's decision. Admiral Zumwalt's feelings and those of his son were the subject of a book, *My Father, My Son,* written by them with John Pekkanen (New York: Macmillan, 1986), and an article in *The New York Times*

Magazine of August 24, 1986. The obituary from the Associated Press announcing the younger Zumwalt's death was published in *The New York Times* on August 14, 1988.

358   "They gave me the hammer . . .": *New York Times,* August 29, 1974.

358   "I remember joining the Marines . . ." etc.: Ibid., November 15, 1978.

359   "How can the Administration just look on the bright side . . .": Ibid.

CHAPTER 24

360   "Part of my job is to say no": Interview, J. C. Peckarsky, by Richard Severo, at Veterans Administration Headquarters, Washington, D.C., March 28, 1979.

361   "Absolutely nobody had an Agent Orange disability": Ibid.

361   "We think it was Agent Orange" etc.: Ibid.

362   "It's only natural . . .": Ibid.

362   "attaching no interpretation to it": Item from Associated Press as published in *New York Times,* December 13, 1979.

362   "I don't know of anything in the literature . . .": Peckarsky interview.

363   "a million times more toxic than PCBs": Richard Severo, "2 Crippled Lives Mirror Dispute on Herbicides," *New York Times,* May 27, 1979. James Allen was one of the most respected pioneers in dioxin research, which grew out of his work in defining the toxicity of polychlorinated biphenyls, or PCBs. However, his credibility came under attack later in 1979, when he admitted that he had misused $892 in Federal research funds during 1978 and 1979 in order to take two ski trips. The misappropriation was called to the attention of Senator William Proxmire, Democrat of Wisconsin, by Kathryn Anderson, a disgruntled former associate of Allen's at the University of Wisconsin. The quality of Allen's research was never impugned. But the shadow of the misappropriation was used by certain chemical companies in an effort to undermine his personal and professional credibility. He resigned from the university in 1980. For the Allen story, see *Wisconsin State Journal,* October 19 and November 28, 1979, and January 19, 1980.

363   "the most powerful carcinogen known . . .": Severo, "2 Crippled Lives."

363   . . . although TCDD would remain feared . . . : Philip Shabecoff, "Estimate of Risk of Dioxin Is Cut in Cancer Study," *New York Times,* December 9, 1987. Even though the United States Environmental Protection Agency concluded that dioxin was only one-sixteenth as potent a carcinogen as had been estimated two years earlier, EPA said dioxin was nevertheless ten thousand times more likely to cause cancer than PCBs. Experiments in the 1970s at the Centers for Disease Control in Atlanta by Dr. Renate Kimbrough showed that PCBs caused cancer in laboratory animals at levels of one hundred parts per million. See Robert H. Boyle, *Malignant Neglect* (New York: Knopf, 1979), pp. 76, 77. R. J. Kociba, a chemist employed by the Dow Chemical Company, a maker of Agent Orange, developed data in the 1970s to suggest that dioxin was merely a thousand times more potent a carcinogen than polychlorinated biphenyls (PCBs). He has noted liver and lung cancer in laboratory animals at one hundred parts per trillion and has found precancerous hepatocellular nodules at ten parts per million. Thus, even the most conservative estimates underscore dioxin's power as a carcinogen.

363   "All the studies you read about concern rats . . .": Interview, Dr. Paul A. L. Haber, by Richard Severo, at Veterans Administration Headquarters, Washington, D.C., March 29, 1979.

364   One day in 1977, deVictor . . . : Interview, Maude deVictor, by Richard Severo, Chicago, Illinois, March 17, 1979. For Owens' story, see *Boulder Daily News,* August 7,

page

1978, p. 1; Howard Kohn, *Rolling Stone,* August 24, 1978, p. 31; *Chicago Sun Times,* March 23, 1979, p. 6.

365   She made 387 telephone calls . . . : DeVictor interview.

365   One of the people . . . was Captain Alvin L. Young . . . : United States Government Memorandum, October 12, 1977, obtained through the Freedom of Information Act (FOIA) by Lewis Milford; and March 17, 1979 interview by Richard Severo.

365   . . . he kept a vial of it on his desk: *Washington Post,* October 26, 1983, p. 25.

365   . . . deVictor's memo of the call was real enough . . . : *Plain Dealer,* March 19, 1980.

365   . . . Cleland claimed deVictor said she did not write the memo . . . : Letter, Cleland to Congressman Stark (FOIA, Milford).

365   . . . which was at variance with what deVictor told others: DeVictor interview.

366   Vern Rogers . . . "absolutely no evidence": *Chicago Sun-Times,* March 23, 1978, p. 6.

366   Agent Orange was made of a 50-50 mix . . . : Interview, J. H. Davidson, technical adviser, Dow Chemical, by Richard Severo, Midland, Michigan, March 22, 1979. According to Davidson, the formulation for Agent Orange came not out of the chemical industry but out of talks between the Department of Defense and the Department of Agriculture.

366   . . . and it was the latter that became the target . . . : E.P.A. Rebuttable Presumption Against Registration and Continued Registration of Pesticide Products Containing 2,4,5-T, *Federal Register,* Vol. 43, No. 78 (April 21, 1978).

366   "entirely one-sided": Minutes of meeting between VA and its herbicide consultants, April 12, 1978 (FOIA, Milford).

366   Dr. Gerritt Schepers . . . "implausible" etc.: Memorandum, May 18, 1978, for VA personnel from Gerritt Schepers on the subject "Potential Exposures of Veterans to Chemical Defoliants during the Vietnam War" (FOIA, Milford).

366   As for deVictor . . . : DeVictor interview.

367   "consensus of world experts" etc.: Minutes of the Ad Hoc Advisory Committee on Herbicides, July 7, 1978 (FOIA, Milford).

367   . . . it asked him to a study for the VA . . . : Minutes of meeting, VA Steering Committee on the Toxic Effects of Herbicides (FOIA, Milford).

367   "still have entrée there . . .": VA Memo of Telephone Contact, April 2, 1979 (FOIA, Milford).

367   . . . Lawrence Hobson . . . : Lawrence Hobson's résumé was obtained by FOIA, Milford. Also, Hobson Deposition, June 20, 1980, *National Veterans Task Force on Agent Orange* v. *Cleland,* No. 80-1162, Federal District Court for the District of Columbia, courtesy National Veterans Law Center.

368   So, the VA began its quest . . . accused of violating a Federal law . . . : Minutes of VA Steering Committee meeting, September 8, 1975 (FOIA, Milford).

368   "The use of herbicides in support . . .": Alvin Young et al., "The Toxicology, Environmental Fate and Human Risk of Herbicide Orange and its Associated Dioxin, USAF Occupational and Environmental Health Laboratory Technical Report," A.F. Surgeon General, issued October 1978.

368   "supports the . . . [DOD] position . . .": Assistant Secretary of Defense Richard Danzig to General Accounting Office, February 8, 1979, contained in Report of Controller General: *Health Effects of Exposure to Herbicide Orange in South Vietnam Should be Resolved,* April 6, 1979, pp. 32–33.

368   The Defense Department had convinced itself . . . : Testimony to Congressional investigators in August 1978. See also report from General Accounting Office to Rep. Ralph H. Metcalfe, August 16, 1978.

page

369   "No steps we can take can undo all the damage . . .": Presidential Review Memorandum on Vietnam-era Veterans, October 10, 1978, p. 10.

369   "A Vietnam veteran calls the media . . ." etc.: VA's "For Your Information Bulletin," January 2, 1979 (FOIA, Milford).

369   . . . Paul Reutershan . . . : See Richard Severo, "Vietnam Veteran's Family Vows to Continue His Fight," *New York Times,* December 19, 1978.

371   Frank McCarthy . . . "My office is pathetic" etc.: Interview, Frank McCarthy, by Richard Severo, February 15, 1979, and on other dates that year.

CHAPTER 25

372   "[Environmentalists] have learned the trick of Hitler . . .": Richard Severo, "Eight Religious Orders Join to Begin Stockholder Drive Against Dow Herbicide," *New York Times,* February 17, 1980. The action against Dow was coordinated by the Interfaith Center on Corporate Responsibility, a coalition of religious investors in American corporations. The stockholders were upset at Mr. Barnes' comparison of them with Hitler.

373   . . . Seveso, northern Italy . . . : Public concern was heightened with reports on the accident by Thomas Whiteside for *The New Yorker.* His research on the accident was published as *The Pendulum and the Toxic Cloud: The Course of Dioxin Contamination* (New Haven, Conn.: Yale University Press, 1979).

373   The compound in question, Dow said . . . : Interview, Gary Jones, public affairs manager, Dow Chemical Co., by Richard Severo, March 22, 1979.

373   "beat its plowshares into sprayguns" etc.: Rachel Carson, *Silent Spring* (Boston: Houghton Mifflin, 1962), p. 75.

374   Dow disclosed the results of a study . . . : David Burnham, "1965 Memos Show Dow's Anxiety on Dioxin," *New York Times,* April 19, 1983. The article also quoted Paul F. Oreffice, president of Dow, as saying, "There is absolutely no evidence of dioxin doing any damage to humans except for something called chloracne." Oreffice made the statement in March of that year on NBC's *Today* show.

374   Dow was selling around seven million pounds of Silvex annually . . . : Interview, Tim Scott, public relations, Dow Chemical Co., in Midland, Michigan, by Richard Severo, March 22, 1979.

374   "We are not in this battle to defend one of the crown jewels": Jones interview.

374   "2,3,5-T has been used for over thirty years . . .": Scott interview.

374   "The chemical was mostly the victim . . .": Jones interview.

375   "Dow is very concerned . . ." etc.: Interoffice memorandum, Fireman's Fund Insurance Companies, April 30, 1979.

375   "a very liberal black judge": Memorandum, Fireman's Fund Insurance Companies, June 19, 1979.

375   Judge Carter was apparently suspect . . . : Second Circuit *Redbook,* Federal Bar Council, 1984, p. 124.

375   "caused no problems to Vietnam veterans": Fireman's Fund memo, June 19, 1979.

376   "I thought that the EPA . . .": Interview, Victor Yannacone, by Richard Severo, Copiague, Long Island, New York, March 6, 1979.

377   "relationships between herbicide exposure . . ." etc.: Minutes of Meeting, VA Steering Committee on Toxic Effects of Herbicides, March 7, 1979, obtained through the Freedom of Information Act (FOIA) by Lewis Milford.

page

377   "We do not believe that a study . . ." etc.: Marianthel, to Lutz, April 4, 1979 (FOIA, Milford).

377   "extremely doubtful . . .": Defense Department to General Accounting Office, February 8, 1979 (FOIA, Milford).

377   "It is to be emphasized . . .": VA Circular to Medical Centers and Other Facilities, April 19, 1979 (FOIA, Milford).

378   . . . *The New York Times* published a series of three articles . . . : The articles, by Richard Severo, ran on May 27, 28 and 29, 1979.

378   The Air Force had already suggested that any exposure . . . : *Washington Post,* June 5, 1979.

378   "We have no desire . . .": *New York Times,* June 5, 1979.

378   "no formal role in the decision-making": Cleland to Lewis Milford, August 2, 1979.

378   "inaccurate": Report of the Controller General: *U.S. Ground Troops in South Vietnam Were in Areas Sprayed with Herbicide Orange,* November 26, 1979.

379   "probably would not identify adverse health effects": National Research Council of the National Academy of Sciences, "Review of the U.S. Air Force Protocol", May 6, 1980.

379   "hasty and ill-conceived" etc.: Congressman David Bonior, in a prepared statement submitted to the Senate Veterans Affairs Committee on September 10, 1980. The committee was holding oversight hearings on Agent Orange.

379   . . . spent a year doing it. . . . "When I first got into the herbicide . . ." etc.: Transcript of Testimony of Dr. Alvin Young, *EPA Suspension Hearings on 2,4,5-T,* July 22, 1980, pp. 9937, 10,014, 10,034.

380   ". . . glorified weed killer . . . Not qualified . . .": *Washington Post,* October 26, 1983.

380   "Some people are always dissatisfied": Constance Holden, "Agent Orange Furor Continues to Build," *Science,* Vol. 205, August 24, 1979, p. 772.

380   "I've heard about veterans complaining . . .": Ibid.

380   "I can't find them . . .": Quoted by Colman McCarthy, *Washington Post,* October 30, 1979.

380   "at least" 600,000 applicants: Tod Ensign and Michael Uhl, *Progressive,* December 1979, p. 11.

381   "extremely helpful" etc.; ". . . we think your collective efforts . . .": Alvarez to Dow Chemical, December 12, 1980; Dow Chemical to Alvarez, January 8, 1981 (FOIA, Milford).

381   "learned the trick . . ." etc.: *New York Times,* February 17, 1980.

CHAPTER 26

382   "The committee expressed support . . .": Minutes of Internal Meeting, VA Agent Orange Policy Committee, January 28, 1981, obtained through the Freedom of Information Act (FOIA) by Lewis Milford.

382   . . . Dr. Terry Lavy . . . : Dow Chemical USA to Richard Wasserstrom, National Forest Products Association, February 5, 1979 (FOIA, Milford); Dr. Lawrence Hobson of the VA to Lewis Milford, June 13, 1983.

383   "supported much of the research reported" etc.: See T. L. Lavy and VA Agent Orange Projects Office, *Human Exposure to Phenoxy Herbicides,* VA Monograph, May 1987.

383   "political sensitivity" etc.: Lawrence Hobson Deposition, June 20, 1980, *National Veterans Task Force on Agent Orange* v. *Max Cleland,* No. 80–1162, D.D.C., p. 52.

page
383   . . . a proposed bill for veterans . . . : It was California Assembly Bill No. 14, of December 1, 1980.

384   "more like the words of a scientist . . ." *New York Times,* August 11, 1981.

384   "seriously compromised his personal credibility . . .": Cranston to Agent Orange Working Group (FOIA, Milford).

384   Act Two starred . . . Cleland: *Detroit Free Press,* May 9, 1980.

384   "majority of cases a VA physician . . .": Dr. Donald Custis, Chief Medical Director, to directors of all VA facilities, February 11, 1981 (FOIA, Milford).

385   "simply trying to get more money . . .": Congressman David Bonior, prepared statement submitted to the House Subcommittee on Medical Facilities and Benefits on July 17, 1980. The veteran in question was one of Bonior's constituents.

385   "It was believed that the impact . . ." Agent Orange Policy Coordinating Committee statement, June 18, 1980 (FOIA, Milford).

385   "This is the least we owe vets . . ."; "provide adequate compensation . . .": Position Paper on Veterans Affairs, issued by a group calling itself Veterans for Republicans. The Reagan-Bush pamphlet also issued was entitled "Veterans, the Time Is Now."

386   "excessive workloads . . .": Minutes of Internal Meeting, Veterans Administration Agent Orange Policy Committee, January 28, 1981 (FOIA, Milford).

386   "All I could see . . .": Kathleen Hendrix, "Viet Vets React to the Hostages," *Los Angeles Times,* reprinted in *Congressional Record,* 97th Congress, 1st session, 127, part 22: 1194–96.

386   "It's almost as if the nation . . ." *Congressional Record,* February 6, 1981.

387   "incipient movement towards federally financed . . ." etc.: Memorandum, Office of Management and Budget, on toxic substances compensation, undated (FOIA, Milford).

388   "inaccurate and incomplete information" etc.: Richard Severo, *New York Times,* March 29, 1981.

388   "combat media inaccuracy . . ." etc.: Telephone conversation, Reed Irvine and Richard Severo, March 1981. The discussion was lively.

389   . . . Rogers issued a memorandum . . . : VA Memorandum from Vern Rogers to all directors of VA Installations in the Great Lakes Region (FOIA, Milford).

389   "future media coverage . . .": Lewis Milford, "Orange Journalism" *Progressive,* August 1981, p. 35.

389   "I would like to caution you . . .: Dr. Donald Custis, memorandum to VA offices, June 9, 1981, as reported in ibid.

389   "strong conviction" . . ."would have a considerable potential . . .": Memorandum, Dr. Barclay Shepard to Dr. Donald Custis, February 26, 1981 (FOIA, Milford).

390   "afflictions of aging and attendant psycho-social aberrations" etc.: Alvin Young, "Agent Orange at the Crossroads of Science and Social Concern" 1981 (FOIA, Milford).

391   "is clearly not a detailed plan . . ." etc.: The reservations were contained in a memorandum sent by Dr. Richard Hodder to the Special Assistant to the Chief Medical Director of the VA, November 6, 1981 (FOIA, Milford).

391   But the VA had a reason for the secrecy . . . : Spivey's reasoning was contained in a Draft VA Epidemiology Protocol, dated August 6, 1981 (FOIA, Milford).

392   "We are dancing around the issue . . ." etc.: United States Senate, *Oversight on Issues Related to Agent Orange and Other Herbicides,* 97th Congress, 1st session, November 18, 1981.

392   "a greater number of persons than previously thought . . ." etc.: Richard Schweiker, transcript of press conference, September 21, 1981 (FOIA, Milford).

page

392   "it may be difficult or probably impossible . . .": Memorandum, Dr. Patricia Honchar to officials within Health and Human Services, September 14, 1981 (FOIA, Milford).

393   "continually called on the VA" etc.: American Legion Resolution #387, September 3, 1981.

393   . . . requesting that the study be transferred . . . : Montgomery to Nimmo, September 27, 1982 (FOIA, Milford).

393   "I do not know of one person . . .": Cranston to Nimmo, October 7, 1982 (FOIA, Milford).

393   "keep politicians and lawyers at bay" etc.: The typewritten notes of November 5, 1982, giving Spivey's sentiments, were obtained through FOIA (Milford).

393   . . . $58,200 to refurbish his office . . . : *Report of the Controller General of the U.S.: Office Refurbishing, Use of a Government Vehicle and Driver, and Out of Town Travel by the Former Administrator of Veterans Affairs*, January 18, 1983.

394   . . . he arrived four days early . . . : Ibid.

394   . . . he used a Government chauffeur . . . : Ibid.

394   "last act" of contempt: Lou Cannon, *Washington Post*, November 15, 1982, p. 3.

394   "I can't tell until . . .": Ibid.

394   . . . Times Beach, Missouri . . . : See article by Richard Severo, *New York Times*, February 20, 1982. See also *Washington Post*, February 23, 1983.

395   "I think there's a tremendous amount of emotion . . .": Transcript, "How Dangerous Is Dioxin?" *ABC News Nightline*, March 15, 1983.

395   . . . Australians became aware that some Swedish studies . . . : See Australian Repatriation and Review Tribunal Decision and Reasons, No. N81/1810, January 5, 1982.

396   Dr. Vernon Houk . . . testified . . . : *Hearings on the Status of Federally Conducted Agent Orange Studies*, House Subcommittee on Oversight and Investigations, Committee on Veterans Affairs, 98th Congress, 1st session, May 3, 1983, p. 15.

396   "Somebody's gonna have to take him on": Lewis Milford was sitting directly behind Dr. Shepard during the hearings and heard him make the comment.

396   "I would like to emphasize . . .": Dorothy Starbuck, testimony, House Veterans Affairs Committee, April 27, 1983 (FOIA, Milford).

396   "We estimate that 350,000 to 400,000 [troops] . . .": Memorandum, Murphy to Horowtiz, May 23, 1983 (FOIA, Milford).

CHAPTER 27

397   "How can they stand this ostracism . . .": Interview, Major General John E. Murray, U.S. Army, retired, by Richard Severo and Lewis Milford, Washington D.C., October 12, 1987.

397   "If we don't take care of our veterans . . .": Interview, Lieutenant Colonel Richard Christian, U.S. Army, retired, by Richard Severo and Lewis Milford, Alexandria, Virginia, October 12, 1987.

398   Erspamer first moved to determine . . . : Appellees' Motion to Affirm filed in U.S. Supreme Court in *Walters* v. *National Association of Radiation Survivors*, No. 84–571, October term, 1984.

398   "would be better off having attorneys represent them . . .": Ibid., p. 17.

398   . . . the VA had not even bothered to ask . . . : Ibid., p. 18.

398   . . . Rehnquist . . . Stevens . . . : The majority and minority opinions may be found in *Walters* v. *National Association of Radiation Survivors*, 87 L. Ed. 220, United States Supreme Court, 1985.

399   The need for a trial . . . : see Veterans' Judicial Review Act, 38 U.S.C., sect. 101 et seq., November 18, 1988.

400   "major Agent Orange study": *Washington Post*, August 30, 1983.

400   "medical study of 85,000 veterans": *New York Times*, September 4, 1983.

400   "great disappointment" etc.: Cranston to the VA's chief medical director, Donald L. Custis, September 26, 1983, obtained through the Freedom of Information Act (FOIA) by Lewis Milford.

400   . . . the Ranch Hand study offered not soothing corroboration . . . : Air Force Health Study, Project Ranch Hand II, *Baseline Morbidity Study Results*, February 24, 1984.

401   . . . Chesney . . . "reassuring" etc.: *Washington Post*, February 25, 1984.

401   "A degree of concern . . .": Richard Albanese, ibid.

401   "Spraying imposes absolutely no danger . . .": Thalken gave testimony on spraying to the Supreme Court of Nova Scotia in *Victoria Palmer et al.* v. *Nova Scotia Forest Industries*. His testimony was cited in the judge's opinion of September 15, 1983. Based on his and other testimony, the people who wanted a ban on herbicide spraying lost.

401   "in a private capacity as a consultant": Colonel Johan Bayer of the Air Force in a letter to Lewis Milford, October 12, 1983.

401   "It's a hell of a good start . . .": *New York Times*, May 10, 1984.

402   "directs the Veterans Administration to honor . . .": Ibid., May 8, 1984.

402   Judge Weinstein had quickly approved . . . : In Re Agent Orange Product Liability Litigation, 597 F. Supp. 740, Eastern District of New York, 1984.

402   "Many do deserve better . . .": *Newsweek*, January 21, 1985, p. 68.

402   "unless the congress provides . . .": Ibid.

402   "vexed case of Agent Orange . . .": *New York Times*, September 4, 1986.

403   "We view as the only remaining factors . . .": Vernon Houk, Confidential Memorandum of March 5, 1982, to James Stockdale, chairman of Agent Orange Working Group (FOIA, Milford).

405   "Combat records were never made for any epidemiological study . . .": Christian interview.

406   . . . out to make him "the scapegoat": Ibid.

406   "we have not had a great deal of communication . . .": Helen Gelband, *Hearings Before the Subcommittee on Hospitals and Health Care of the House Veterans Affairs Committee*, House of Representatives, 99th Congress, 2nd session, July 31, 1986, p. 43.

406   "Time tables and numbers of subjects . . .": Richard Christian, *Hearings Before the Subcommittee on Hospitals . . .* p. 89.

406   "an exposure model crucial to the study": Ibid., p. 90.

406   "was written by individuals . . .": Internal Memorandum of Department of Defense, dated May 23, 1986. Obtained from Government sources.

406   "poor quality" etc.: All the quotations herein are from *Exposure Assessment for the Agent Orange Study, Interim Report No. 2*, November 18, 1985. Obtained from Government sources.

407   "admit this was of their own doing?" etc.: Christian to Houk, December 4, 1985 [obtained from private source].

408   "a nearly complete breakdown . . ." etc.: The letters were sent on January 10, 1986 (FOIA, Milford.) Murkowski was chairman of the committee.

408   "was providing all he had to CDC": Murray interview.

page
408   "of inestimable worth" etc.: Major General John E. Murray, U.S. Army, retired, "Report to the White House Agent Orange Working Group Science Subpanel on Exposure Assessment," Executive Office of the President, Office of Science and Technology Policy, May 27, 1986, pp. 45, 49, 50. Never made public.

409   "release of General Murray's report . . ." etc.: Memorandum from Donald Newman to Caspar Weinberger, May 28, 1986, which was never made public.

409   "There has been a waste . . ." etc.: Murray to Christian, December 19, 1986 [obtained from private source].

410   "We have waited for seven years . . .": Congressman Daschle, *Hearings Before the Subcommittee on Hospitals . . .* p. 44.

410   . . . Hatcher . . . accepted a "sexual bribe": *Washington Post,* October 3, 1987.

410   "unique environment and experience . . ." etc.: Staff report, Vietnam Experience Study, "Postservice Mortality Among Vietnam Veterans," *Journal of the American Medical Association,* February 13, 1987, pp. 790, 795.

411   Some of the most important information developed by the Stellmans . . . : Steven D. Stellman, Jeanne M. Stellman, and John F. Sommer, "Combat and Herbicide Exposures in Vietnam Among a Sample of American Legionnaires," and interviews by Richard Severo and Lewis Milford at various times in 1988.

412   [The VA study] concluded that Marine ground troops . . . : Patricia Breslin et al., "Proportionate Mortality Study of Army and Marine Corps Veterans of the Vietnam War," Veterans Administration, undated, released in the summer of 1987.

412   Non-Hodgkins lymphoma has often been cited . . . : Such a study by the National Cancer Institute was reported in *Journal of the American Medical Association,* September 1986.

412   "I wouldn't say it's terribly worrisome. . . .": *New York Times,* September 1, 1987.

412   "The numbers are small . . ." etc.: Young's observation was carried by The Associated Press on September 14, 1987, and appeared in many papers around the country the next day.

412   "the evidence is there . . .": Ibid.

412   . . . higher levels of depression, anxiety, irritation . . . : Steven D. Stellman et al., "Social and Behavioral Consequences of the Vietnam Experience Among American Legionnaires," undated, commissioned by the American Legion, work completed in 1987. See Matthew "Study Links Tumors to Agent Orange Exposure": *Philadelphia Inquirer,* November 11, 1987, p. 1.

413   "for most of the ground troops . . .": *New York Times,* September 1, 1987.

413   "guaranteed to get a large group of unexposed people" etc.: Dr. Peter Kahn, interview, by Lewis Milford, November 1987.

413   "Vietnam Experience Study": Made public early in May 1988.

414   "bad policy, bad politics and bad science" etc.: for Thomas Harvey's views see *New York Times,* May 13, 1988.

414   . . . high levels of dioxin in their blood: Ibid., May 27, 1988.

415   "important management tool": Ibid., June 10, 1988.

415   "evilness of a system . . ." Ibid.

416   "What we're going to do with it . . .": *New York Times,* October 26, 1988.

416   . . . a list of favored members of Congress . . . : Ben Franklin, *New York Times,* May 8, 1988.

EPILOGUE

419   "Volume by exciting volume . . .": *Combat Photographer* was the first book in "The Vietnam Experience," a series of books promised by Time-Life. It was offered with an

page

"authentic 1968 Battlemap" of Vietnam, Laos, and Cambodia that would be the reader's to keep "just for agreeing to examine [the] introductory volume."

419   "A man and a woman appear to have taken their lives . . .": Gene I. Maeroff, *New York Times,* March 7, 1986.

419   "The past is history now. We don't worry about that": Westmoreland made the observation at a parade honoring Vietnam veterans. It was reported in the Newark, New Jersey, *Star-Ledger,* June 14, 1980.

422   . . . veterans historically were always reluctant to ask for help . . . : A recent example of this was found in an Op Ed piece written by Joseph R. Kurtz, Jr., which was published in *The New York Times* on March 10, 1986. In it, Kurtz, a Vietnam veteran identified as being the owner of an advertising and public relations firm, conceded that many went through "mental and physical anguish" but that the Vietnam war "has become a cop-out." Vietnam, he said, "has become an excuse for veterans' undirected lives." For one of the better pieces on the subject, see Peter Marin, "Coming to Terms with Vietnam," *Harper's,* December 1980, p. 50.

422   "Fifty Fabulous Years" . . . interminable . . . : The manuscript totaled only 107 pages but seemed much longer.

423   . . . VA workers were accused of graft . . . : *New York Times,* August 17, 1985.

423   At least thirty-three VA doctors had their licenses suspended . . . : Ibid., August 20, 1985.

423   . . . curtailed the $78.75-a-month pension . . . : Newburgh, New York, *Evening News,* editorial, June 9, 1985.

423   . . . the General Accounting Office told Congress . . . : *New York Times,* August 11, 1985. The Agent Orange issue had virtually nothing to do with the alleged waste. The GAO cited the VA's practice of admitting the patient, then waiting days before scheduled surgery was actually performed. From the GAO's assessment, it would appear that the VA was not doing a very good job even with the ordinary health problems suffered by veterans, let alone things like Agent Orange.

424   "insulted the women of America" etc.; "And thus we continue . . .": "Commission Vetoes Vietnam Women's Statue," *Washington Post,* October 23, 1987. See also Letter to the Editor from Barbara L. Shay dated October 28, 1987, *New York Times,* November 11, 1987. For women who asked for a study on Agent Orange, see *New York Times,* November 10, 1985.

Index

AVC. *See* American Veterans Committee

Accuracy in Media, 388; report of, 388–389

Adams, Abigail, 85, 440n

Adams, John, 39, 43, 46, 435n

Adams, Samuel, 24, 53, 75

Advice to the Officers of the British Army, 28, 29–30, 432–33n

African Lodge of Freemasons, 69–70

Agent Orange: and cancer, 362–63, 376, 394–96, 400, 412, 413, 471n; content of, 362, 366, 372, 472n; definition, 348; effects, 365, 368, 392, 411, 470n; formulation for, 366, 472n; increasing concern about, 364–66, 393; spraying of, 348, 376, 390, 401, 470n. *See also* dioxin

Agent Orange controversy: blamed on media and the war, 369, 370, 374, 383, 390; investigation of, 15; public silence on, 380. *See also* Veterans Administration and Agent Orange

Agent Orange victims: action by, 370, 399; disability benefits for, 414; government's refusal of compensation, 370, 409, 411, 416, 419; proposed payment for, 394; suit against chemical industry, 370, 371, 375, 401–3, 473n

Agent Orange Victims International, 370, 371

Aguinaldo, Emilio, 212, 218, 347

Air Force study on Agent Orange. *See* Operation Ranch Hand

Albanese, Richard, 401, 412–13

Alger, Horatio, 136, 151, 160, 200, 446n

Alger, Russell A., 196, 203, 454n; investigation of, 209; pressure for dismissal, 207; review of Camp Wikoff, 205–6

Allen, Edgar, 167

Allen, Eliphalet, 103

Allen, James, 362–63, 471n

Alvarez, Israel, 380

America: eighteenth-century, 43; after Korean War, 318, 337; nativism, 110-111, 218; need for self-definition, 110; in 1920s, 260; and its veterans, 417, 425–26; post-Vietnam period, 420, 423, 425

American: attitudes on poverty, 90; barbarity, 217; character, loss of, 13, 17–18, 425; colonists, 32–33, 44; conflict between generosity and costs, 88, 90, 261; gifts to charity, 184; nationalistic groups, 242; patriotism, 191, 220, 241, 242, 263; work ethic, 135, 136, 150–51, 160, 212

American Cancer Society, 391, 411

American Civil Liberties Union (ACLU), 317, 466n

American Legion, 18; anticommunism, 265, 271, 308, 314, 317, 318–19, 328–29, 466n; antifascist position, 314, 329, 466n, 467n; and bonus marchers, 276, 279; ideology, 243, 265, 310; opposition to blacks and labor, 243–44; political clout of, 307; press support of, 244; support for veteran's programs, 261, 262–263, 265, 289, 295; and the VA, 307–9, 392–93, 395; and other veterans' groups, 308–11

American Veterans Committee (AVC), 303; founding, 309–10; ideals and purpose, 310–11, 312; linked to communism, 311–18; membership, 311, 312; trial of communist member, 313–14

Americans
and the British: in Boston, 43; after War of 1812, 84; British views of Americans, 55–56, 431n
and Filipinos, 212–14, 218–19, 222–223, 455n
and Vietnam, 347–48

Americans for Democratic Action, 331

Amherst College, 79

Anderson, Sherwood, 277

Andrews, Lincoln, 262, 263

Anti-Imperialist League, 217, 220, 221

antiwar sentiments and organizations, 112–13, 117, 217, 220, 221, 242, 380

armed forces: blacks accepted in, 299–300; racism in, 356; women in,

300–303. *See also* Air Force; Army;
Marines; soldiers
Armstrong, John, 37
Army
American: blacks in, 232–33, 234;
Catholics in, 111, 113; in Civil War;
125; deserters, 112, 114–17, 118;
immigrants in, 109, 111, 237, 244;
life in, 107–8, 125; makeup, 108–9;
minorities in, 350; regulars, 192,
205; role of, 108; in Vietnam,
125, 344, 347, 348; women in,
300–301
Confederate: meager pensions, 183–84;
soldiers'graves, 131–32, 134; veterans, 164, 180, 183
Continental (Revolutionary), 29, 433n;
deprivations of, 35, 36, 40–41, 44,
84; financing of, 34, 36; life in, 23–
24; pay for, 35–36, 41; during war,
25, 39
after Korean War: loyalty oaths, 330;
LSD experiments on soldiers, 341–
342; McCarthy's investigations of,
328, 329; and POWs, 322, 324–26,
334–38; soldiers exposed to radiation, 342–43
Union: blacks in, 128, 163–65, 168,
449n; and politics, 146–49, 153,
154, 174, 448n; public perceptions
of, 161–62
Army Reorganization Act, 301
Arrears Act, 171
Attucks, Crispus, 69

B.E.F. *See* Bonus March
Ballentine, George, 116
Barnes, Earl B., 381
Barnes, Julius H., 262
Barton, Clara, 195, 300
Bascomb, Joseph, 25
Battalion of St. Patrick, 113–16, 118
Beanstalk, Betsey, 198
Beatty, Catharine, 104
Beck, James B., 171
Beecher, Henry Ward, 180
Beecher, Lyman, 109
Belhomme, Albert, 326
Bell, Bernard Iddings, 290
Bellows, Henry W., 134, 135
Bennett, James Gordon, 132
Beveridge, Albert J., 225
Biderman, Albert, 338–40, 343; *March
to Calumny*, 340
Bierman, Daniel J. B., 415
Binet, Alfred, 233

Black Shame, 235
blacks: demands for rights, 238, 241,
299; discrimination and violence
against, 68, 164–65, 168, 220, 222,
231, 233–35, 237–38, 245, 299,
439n; as distinguished and willing
soldiers, 220, 231, 234, 245; during and after Civil War, 124, 128,
131, 168; negative attitudes toward,
132, 167, 219–20, 287, 450n; rejection of, for military service, 231,
232, 234; in Revolutionary Army,
68–70, 439n; testing of, 233–34; in
Union Army, 128, 163–65, 168,
449n; in War of 1812, 232–33; in
World War I, 231–35. *See also* veterans, black; women
Blackwell, Dr. Elizabeth, 300
Blaine, John James, 240
Blair, Montgomery, 148
Bliss, George, 137
Bloomfield, Joseph, 87, 91
Bolte, Charles G., 309–10
Bonior, David, 379, 474n
Bonus Bill (1920s), 261–63
Bonus Loan Bill, 266
Bonus March (called B.E.F): beginnings
of, 267–69; camp of, 270, 275; criticism of, 267–68, 273, 276; demonstrations by, 268, 270, 271, 272;
ended by Federal troops, 274; as
forgotten, 279, 286; government
opposition to, 270–73, 277–78;
moved to Johnstown, Pa., 276–77;
participants, 269, 272, 275; rumored
links with communism, 267–68,
271–74, 277, 278; second,
278–79
bonuses for veterans, history: in 1920s,
261–63; in 1930s, 265; cut in 1933,
278; passed in 1934, 279
Boston, 84; British in, 43; as early government seat, 9, 10; "London Book
Store" in, 43–44; rich society of,
10, 12, 24, 54, 67, 74, 438n
Massacre, 33, 44, 69
Tea Party, 44
Bouldin, Thomas T., 92
Bouscaren, Anthony T., 337
Bowdoin, James, 52–54, 59; and Shays'
Rebellion, 62, 63, 67–73, 75, 77,
231
Boy Scouts of America, 242, 338
Boyce-Thompson Institute, 373
Bradley, Omar N., as VA director, 306–
309

Braman, Milton, 112–13, 117
Brennan, William, 341
Bridges, Styles, 321
British: and American currency, 56, 57; aristocratic thinking, 42–44; and colonial economics, 41, 44; views of Americans, 55–56, 431n; views on the Revolution, 28, 30, 432–33n; after War of 1812, 84–85
British Army, 435n; blacks in, 68; vs. colonists, 33; as formidable enemy, 29, 31; makeup, 30–31, 32; satire of, 28, 29
Brown, John, 126
Brown, Preston, 215
Brownell, Cornelius M., 216–17
Buckley, William, 337
Bullock, Alexander Hamilton, 134
Bumpas, Abiah, 104
Burke, Aedanus, 47–48
Burrows, Julius Caesar, 225

CDC. *See* Centers for Disease Control
Caesar, Julius, 127, 128, 445n
Caldwell, Bill, 310
Calhoun, John C., 92
Calley, William Laws: description of, 350–51, 469–70n; My Lai incident, 351–52, 470n; punishment for, 353, 354; as scapegoat, 352, 354
Camp Wikoff (at Montauk Point, L.I.), 197, 200; Army's incompetence concerning, 199, 200, 207; death and corpses at, 208, 209; dismantling of, 209; furloughs issued from, 206, 208; help of local residents, 203, 204; lack of water, food, and shelter, 199–200, 201, 203, 205, 454n; newspaper coverage of, 198, 200, 206, 207; spread of typhoid, 201, 204
Campbell, James, 323
Cannon, Lou, 394
Carpenter, W. S., 238, 457n
Carson, Rachel, *Silent Spring*, 373
Carter, Jimmy, 385; and Agent Orange problem, 368–69, 387; lack of action for veterans, 358–59
Carter, Robert Lee, 375
Castle, Frederick A., 201
Catholics: in the Army, 111, 115; Irish, 110, 111; against Italians, 235, 236, 457n; as Mexican War issue, 113–115, prejudice against, 109–110, 113, 115, 129; Protestants against, 109–110, 111

Centers for Disease Control (CDC), studies by
    on Agent Orange for VA, 393, 396, 403; complexity, 403–5; failure, 406–10, 413; investigation of, 407–410; preliminary results, 410
    on dioxin, 414–15
    "Vietnam Experience Study," 413–14, 415
Chaffee, Adna R., 209–10
Chaloner, Sergeant, 73
Chamberlin, J. Gordon, 291
Chase, Stuart, 285
chemical contamination: citizens' claims of, 386–87, 394–95, 401; herbicides, 373–74, 377, 379–80, 390, 395, 477n; Love Canal, 380, 387, 390; plant accident in Italy, 373; in Times Beach, 394–95
chemical industry: class action suit against, 370, 371, 375, 401, 416, 473n; companies, 367; denial of toxicity of products, 374, 388, 402, 473n; environmental concerns, 373; unregulated by government, 366, 372. *See also* Dow Chemical Company
Chesney, Murphy A., 401
Childs, Marquis, 304
Chinese Exclusion Act (1882), 218
Christian, Richard, and Agent Orange study: collecting of material, 404–5; conflict with CDC, 405–8; investigation of, 407, 408
Cincinnatus, Lucius Quinctius, 46
Civil War, 135; battles, 131, 145; government following, 133, 136, 163; literary views of, 121–28, 144; loss of life, 172; national social problems following, 137–42; North-South conflicts following, 131–32, 134, 158–59, 166; perceptions of, 149–50; and politics, 144–50. *See also* Army, Confederate; Army, Union; veterans
Claiborne, William C. C., 232–33
Clapp, Oliver, 61, 62, 438n
Clark, Mark, 322
Clay, Henry, 86
Cleland, Max: and VA failure on Agent Orange issue, 378, 384; as VA head, 358, 359, 365, 391, 422
Cleveland, Grover, 174, 175, 177, 191
Coffman, Edward M., 450n
Colmery, Harry W., 289, 307
Colson, William, 241, 243

Colston, Edward, 88, 89
Colyer, Vincent, 162–63
Commoner, Barry, 365, 367
communism: American Legion vs., 265,
    271, 308, 314, 317, 318–19, 328–
    329, 466n; AVC linked to, 311–14;
    Bonus March linked to, 267–68,
    271–74, 277, 278; fear of, 241, 242,
    287, 317; government hunting for,
    328, 329, 334, 336–37; and Korean
    War, 320–27, 331; national concern
    over, 311–14, 317–18. *See also*
    American Legion; Army
Concho, 194–95
Congress, 353; and Agent Orange issue,
    380, 393, 394–95, 403, 407, 413;
    failure to pay veterans, 36–38, 51;
    investigation of Philippine Insurrec-
    tion, 221–26; and veterans' benefits,
    33, 45, 87–91, 103, 170–71, 175,
    182–85, 261–63, 271, 358, 399. *See
    also* legislation
    General Accounting Office (GAO): on
        Operation Ranch Hand, 378; on VA,
        385, 423, 479n
    House committees on pensions and
        claims, 93, 94, 96, 101, 105, 174
    Oversight and Investigations, Subcom-
        mittee on (House), 387–88
    Un-American Activities Committee
        (House), 313, 329
    Veterans Affairs, Committee on
        (Senate), 303, 392, 404, 414
    Veterans Committee (House), 393
Conkey, William, 11, 79; tavern of, 61–
    62, 74
Cook, Ezra, 449n
Coolidge, Calvin, and bonus bill, 263
Coxey, Jacob S., protest by, 268
Cramer, Charles, 250, 254
Cranston, Alan, 357; faith in VA, 396;
    and VA study on Agent Orange,
    380, 384, 393, 400, 407–8
Crim, John W. H., 257
crime: big money and, 175, 239, 260;
    Prohibition and, 239, 252, 257; after
    Revolution, 27; veterans linked to,
    139–41, 239–40; waves, 139, 239–
    240
Cuba: campaign against, 190, 192, 211;
    diseases of, 192–93. *See also*
    Spanish-American War
Cuban evacuation disaster, 193–210;
    blame placed on soldiers and press,
    196, 206, 209–10; conditions on the
    evacuation ships, 194–95, 197; in-

vestigation of, 196–97; questions
    about, 208–9; seriousness of sol-
    diers' illnesses, 193–94; War De-
    partment's denial of responsibility,
    196, 197, 199, 206, 208, 209–10.
    See also Camp Wikoff
Currieo, James, 396
Curtis, Charles, 272, 275–76
Custis, Donald, 389
Cutler, Enos, 112

DOD. *See* Department of Defense *under*
    Government agencies
Darling, Flora Adams, 208
Daschle, Thomas, 410, 413; Agent Or-
    ange bill, 394–95, 396
Daugherty, Harry Micajah, 250, 257
Daughters' Auxiliary League, 208
Davenport, William, 112
Davidson, Polly, 104
Davis, Jefferson, 132, 144; funeral of,
    166
Day, Elijah, 63
Day, Luke, 59, 60, 63, 72, 73
de la Peña, Augustine, 216–17
Deegan, William F., 246
Delano, Frederic A., 288
Dempsey, Jack, 260
Dependent Pension Act (1890), 182–85
Depression: bonus question, 265; "psy-
    chosis," 284, 294–95; and veterans,
    264, 267
Deutsch, Albert, 305
deVictor, Maude, 364–66
Dickens, Charles, 93
Dickenson, Edward, 327
DiFusco, John, 386
dioxin: civilian contamination by, 394–
    395; description of, 362, 373; re-
    search on, 362–63, 414–15, 471n;
    toxicity of, 362–63, 396, 471n. *See
    also* Agent Orange; 2,4,5-T
Disabled American Veterans, 254, 276,
    309
Disqualification Act, 75
Dodge Commission, 209–10
Dodge, Grenville M., 209
Doty, Alvah H., 195
Dow Chemical Company, 365; chemical
    toxicity concerns, 372, 373, 374;
    class action lawsuit against, 370,
    371, 375, 401, 473n; critics of, 381,
    387–88; fear over media publicity,
    375–76; as manufacturer of Agent
    Orange, 367; research by, 380–81,
    471n

Doyle, Arthur Conan, 240
drug abuse problems: after Civil War,
    137–39, 354–55, 447n; link with
    wars, 138–39; after Vietnam, 354
Du Bois, W.E.B., 231; and black social
    concerns, 241; champion of black
    soldiers, 234, 238–39, 299
Dubois, Fred T., 222
Dudley, W. W., 174
du Pont, Pierre S., 262; family, 460n
DuPont Company, 262, 386
Durham, Knowlton, 263

EPA. *See* Environmental Protection
    Agency
    under Government agencies
Eagen, Charles E., 203
Eastman, George, 262
Eaton, Kenneth, 415, 416
Eaton, Secretary of War, 111
Eckhardt, Wolf von, 451n
Eisenhower, Dwight D., 312, 327, 329;
    and Bonus March, 274, 275; popu-
    larity of, 306, 308
Elder, William, 259
Eliot, Charles William, 180–81
Ellis, Joseph, 17–18
Emerson, Brown, 84
Epstein, Samuel, 395
Erb, Frank M., 219
Erickson, David, 391
Erspamer, Gordon, 398
Evans, Lane, 412
Ewalt, George, Jr., 401

farmers: in debt, 59–62; protests by, 14,
    49–50, 59–60, 75, 77; as veterans,
    21, 58; yeomen, 55, 56
Faust, Joseph, 223
Feinberg, Kenneth, 402
Felder, Thomas B., 257
Feltman, William, 25
Fenton, Reuben E., 130
Fields, James T., 125
Fillmore, Millard, 78, 437–38n
Filton, Paul, 238
financial crises: "Black Friday" panic
    (1869), 175; Panic of 1819, 85, 91,
    92; Panic of 1873, 175, 184. *See
    also* Depression
Finn, John J., 185
Finnie, William, 100–101
Fireman's Fund, 375
Fitch, James, 210
Flesch, Rudolph, *Towards an Abiding
    Peace*, 286

Flipper, Henry O., 168
Flood, Thomas S., 180
Flucker, Lucy, 41–44, 54
Flucker, Thomas, 42
Foner, Jack D., 449n
Foote, Allen R., 184, 185
Forbes, Charles R., appointment by Har-
    ding, 247–48, 249–50; as corrupt
    official, 251–54, 257, 304, 308,
    423; investigation of, 254–57, 258;
    in retirement, 257
Ford, Gerald, 358
Fortuna, Andrew, 325
Franklin, Benjamin, 46
Frayer, Don, 375
Freedom of Information Act (FOIA), 15;
    government information obtained
    through, 472n, 473n, 474n, 475n,
    476n, 477n
Friedan, Betty, 337
Furnham, E. D., 217
Furphy, Joseph, 249
Furst, Jon, 384

GAO. *See* General Accounting Office
    under Congress
G.A.R. *See* Grand Army of the Republic
G. I. Bill, 16, 22; American Legion and,
    289, 307; after Korean War, 327;
    provisions and effects, 289, 290,
    355; Roosevelt's plans for, 287–89;
    after Vietnam, 356; and women, 302
Galbraith, John Kenneth, 284
Gates, John, 313–14
Gaujot, Julien E., 215–16
Gearhart, Bertrand W., 286
Gelband, Helen, 406
Glassford, Pelham, and Bonus March,
    269–70, 272, 274
Glenn, Edwin F., 215
Goff, John W., 233
Government: corruption in, 249–57, 260;
    ineptitude, 249, 250; failure to help
    veterans, 15, 16, 96–97, 100–106,
    133–34, 417; failure to pay soldiers,
    29–30, 37–38, 88, 206, 260, 263;
    fear of veteran costs, 88, 90, 103;
    manipulation of, 175; power to be-
    stow honor, 51–52; protests against,
    12, 13, 14; spending, but not on
    veterans, 386, 403; treatment of
    women, 300–303; veterans' message
    to, 425–426
after Revolution: attitude toward vete-
    rans, 35; currency of, 54–56; as
    debtor, 34; half-pay for officers, 31–

33; issue of pay for Army, 27, 29–30, 35, 36–38, 47, 54, 432n; national tax plan, 33–34, 36; need for credit, 34, 53

after War of 1812: financial situation, 83, 85, 92; pension system, effects of, 91–94; rejection of veterans' claims, 96–97, 100–106; rejection of war widows' claims, 101, 103–4; veterans' benefits, 86–91, 92

after Cuban invasion: investigation of War Department, 209–10; and pension claims, 205, 210. *See also* Camp Wikoff; Cuban evacuation disaster

after World War I, 260; plan for veterans, 247; proposed bonus, 261–63; rapid discharge of soldiers, 242; sponsored trip for veterans' wives and widows, 245–6

after World War II: peace planning by, 285–86; services for veterans, 288–290, 304–8

after Korean War: attempts to find a scapegoat, 317–18, 326, 333; hunting for communists, 318–19, 328–331, 334; soldiers used for experiments, 341–44. *See also* prisoners of war

after Vietnam War, and Agent Orange: blame for controversy on media, 369, 370, 383, 390; criminal neglect of veterans' problems, 368, 371; failure to deal with issue, 358–59, 384, 385, 394, 399–400, 410, 417; fears about costs, 369, 377, 380, 387, 392, 396, 397; flawed and biased research, 368, 382–84; policy on chemical research and use, 366–369, 377, 378–79, 389; policy of denial and concealment, 377, 380, 395, 396, 412, 414; refusal to honor victims' claims, 370, 409, 411, 416, 419. *See also* Agent Orange; Veterans Administration and Agent Orange

Government agencies
Defense Department: accusations against POWs, 321; criticism by House subcommittee, 387, 388; denial of Agent Orange problem, 368, 377; investigation of Korean War, 332–33, 335; and Operation Ranch Hand, 378; welcome for Vietnam veterans, 354, 355, 356

Department of Health and Human Services, 392, 407

Department of Veterans Affairs, creation of, 416–17

Environmental Protection Agency (EPA), 366, 367; and class action suit, 376; and dioxin, 374; hearings on herbicides, 379–80; suspension of 2,4,5-T, 376–77, 379, 389, 395

Federal Bureau of Investigation (FBI), 329, 336, 337

Federal Bureau for Vocational Rehabilitation, 249–50

Federal Commission on Fine Arts, 424–25

Office of Management and Budget (OMB), 386, 387, 396

Pension Bureau, 171; claims to, 172; liberality of, 178–82, 182–83; political side of, 174, 177

Pension Office, 93, 94

Supreme Court: and "atomic veterans," 398–99; and LSD exposure, 341

U.S. Court of Veteran Appeals, 399

U.S. Sanitary Commission, 134–35, 155

Veterans' Bureau, 248; corruption in, 251–54; investigation of, 254–57; costs and effects of waste and graft, 257, 258–59; public silence about, 259

War Department, 193, 196–99, 206, 208, 209–10; description of, 196

See also Centers for Disease Control; Congress; Veterans Administration

Grand Army of the Republic, 157, 191, 243; and black soldiers, 165–68, 450n; and Confederate graves, 131–132, 158; founding and purpose of, 152–53; growth, 154, 174–75; organization, 153–54, 156, 449n; pension policy, 175, 177, 179, 185; power of, 152, 156, 172, 174–76, 185; revolt of Farnham Post, 185; Women's Relief Corps, 168

Grande Duchesse, 201

Grant, Madison, *The Passing of a Great Race*, 237

Grant, Ulysses S., 127, 132, 133; as President, 157, 250, 459n

Gray, Jacob, 166

Greeley, Horace, 151, 152, 156–57

Greene, Nathaniel, 25

Greenman, Jeremiah, 24, 432n

Haber, Paul A. L., 363, 364, 366, 378, 380

Hall, Prince, 68, 69–70, 231

Hamilton, Alexander, 36–37; and nationalist cause, 33, 34; as Secretary of the Treasury, 97–100

Hamilton, Archibald W., 105–6

Hamilton, Elizabeth, 101

Hamilton, J. R., 161–62

Hancock, John, 75

Harbord, James O., 273

Harding, Warren G., 247, 248, 253, 261
Administration, 247, 248, 304; corruption in, 249, 250, 254, 257, 261–262, 278

Harney, William Selby, 115–16

Harper, James, 110

Harrison, Benjamin, 166, 175, 178, 181–182; and pensions, 177–78, 451n

Harrison, Gilbert, 309–10, 311

Harrison, Thomas, 324

Harrison, William Henry, 89

Harvard University students: in army to quell Shays' Rebellion, 67; in patrols against Irish Catholics, 110; as strikebreaking volunteers, 243–44

Harvey, Thomas, 414

Hasbrouck, Jonathan, house of, 30, 433n

Hatcher, John, 408, 410

Hawley, Joseph, 171, 172

Hawthorne, Nathaniel: and the Civil War, 121–22, 144, 444n; enthusiasm for Mexican War, 117–18; on Lincoln, 125, 444n; "Chiefly About War-Matters," 122–25

Hayes, Rutherford B., 170–71, 172

Hayne, Robert, 92

Hearst, William Randolph, 190, 191

Heath, William, 48

Hektor, 127, 445n

Henderson, Oran K., 351, 353–54

Herndon, Rogers, 324

Hersh, Seymour, 353

Hershey, Lewis B., 317

Heyl, Charles H., 197

Hinckley, Judge, 60, 61

Hines, Frank T., 304–6, 307, 309

Hiss-Chambers case, 313

Ho Chi Minh, 347, 351; and Americans, 347–48, 350

Hobson, Lawrence, 367, 368, 383, 412

Hoffman, Paul G., 294

Holder, Ben B., 367

Hollingsworth, Oscar, 276

Hollywood, anticommunist witchhunt in, 328–29

Holmes, Oliver Wendell, Jr., on advantages of war, 190, 192, 221–222, 227, 240–41

Holt, Cooper T., 416

Hoover, Herbert, 266, 294–95; and Bonus March, 267, 268, 270–71, 272, 274, 277; criticism of, 276, 277; loss of election, 278
Administration, and Bonus March, 270–72; criticism of, 277; press support of, 278; report, 277–78

Hoover, J. Edgar, 329, 337

Houk, Vernon, 396, 403, 407, 413

Hovey, Alvin P., 177

Howard, Simeon, 23

Hughes, Robert P., 222, 223

Human Rights Commission, 356

Humphreys, David, 52, 436–37n

Hurley, Patrick J., 267, 270, 273

Hutchins, Robert M., 288, 290

immigrants: in the Army, 109, 111, 237, 244; discrimination against, 235–37, 242, 244, 457n; fear of, 218–19; prejudices against, 125–26; U.S. as nation of, 218

Indians: Army forays against, 92, 192; as enemies, 133; relations with, 85; in wars against British, 102

Ingalls, John J., 170

Irish: in Battalion of St. Patrick, 113, 114; Catholics, 110–11, 115, 235; as immigrants, 111, 219

Irvine, Reed, 388, 390

Italians: discrimination and violence against, 235–37, 242, 244, 457n; service in World War I, 237, 244; views of, 235–7, 457n

Jackson, Andrew: and enlisting black volunteers, 232–33; as President, 92; as war hero, 84

jawhawking, 140, 447n

Jefferson, Thomas, 39, 46, 77, 79, 86, 143, 435n, 437n, 440n

Jenkins, Barbara, 13, 14, 17

Jews, fear of, 287; seen as radicals, 242

John Birch Society, 336, 340

Johnson, Adam, 79

Johnson, Andrew, 127, 131, 152, 157

Johnson, Donald, 357

Johnson, Hiram, 271

Johnson, Lyndon Baines, 351; and cost of Vietnam, 348, 355, 469n

Jones, Gary, 374

Jordan, David Starr, 237

Kahn, Peter, 413
Kaplan, Sidney, 439n
Kazin, Alfred, 126
Keeler, Aaron, 102
Kempton, Murray, 331
Kennedy, John F., 317; Administration,
     Senate investigation of, 343
Kirtchenhausen, Carl W., 322
Knox, Henry, 189: bookstore of, 42, 43–
     44, 435n; description, 40, 41, 435n;
     recognition for veterans, attempts,
     35, 39–40, 45–50, 52, 435n; as Sec-
     retary of War, 53, 69, 96–97; and
     Shays' Rebellion, 67, 69; specula-
     tion by, 53–54
Kociba, R. J., 471n
Korean War: blame for, 317; Chinese in,
     319, 341; economic stimulus of,
     285; "lost generation" psychology,
     327, 337, 344; psychodrama follow-
     ing, 317, 318–19, 326–27, 340–41;
     soldiers as scapegoats, 318, 326,
     333, 335, 338, 343. See also Army;
     Government; prisoners of war; veter-
     ans
Koster, Samuel W., 351–52, 353–54
Ku Klux Klan, 164, 165; lynchings by,
     237–38, 245
Kurtis, Bill, 365
Kurtz, Joseph R., Jr., 479n
Kutcher, James, vs. the VA, 330–33

labor movement: Legion opposed to, 243;
     unions, 243, 293, 295; and World
     War II veterans, 293–95
Lafayette, Marquis de, 60, 62, 111
LaGuardia, Fiorello, 294
Landreau, Norman, 276
Lavy, Terry, Human Exposure to Phe-
     noxy Herbicides, 382–83
lawyers: for "atomic veterans," 397–98;
     and Civil War veterans' claims, 170,
     171; vs. farmer-veterans, 62, 438n;
     and VA, 393, 398; veterans' ability
     to hire, 398–99
Leaveck, Mike, 416
Lee, Lyndon E., 362
Lee, Mary, 134
Lee, Robert E., 127, 134, 145, 445n
legislation concerning veterans: for bo-
     nuses, 261–63, 266, 279; for pen-
     sions, 87–91, 170–71, 172, 182–85;
     selective service, 285, 293, 299; for
     victims of cancer, 343. See also
     G. I. Bill
Lemon, George E., 172, 175, 182

L'Enfant, Pierre Charles, 49, 85, 127,
     173, 440n
Lesser, A. Monae, 194
Lewis and Clark expedition, 86
Lilienthal, David, 288–89
Lincoln, Abraham: concern for veterans,
     136, 137, 148; death, 166, 176;
     Hawthorne's description of, 125,
     444n; and the New York Times, 161,
     449n; plans for peace, 152, 153; as
     politician, 144, 147, 148–49; as
     President, 144, 145, 164; writers'
     support of, 126
Lincoln, Benjamin, 67, 73, 74
Lindley, Ernest K., 307
Locke, John, Two Treatises on Govern-
     ment, 44, 58–59
Lodge, Henry Cabot, 221, 222
"London Book Store," 42, 43–44, 435n
Longman, Thomas, 43, 435n
Louisiana Purchase, 85
Lowell, James Russell, 126
Lutz, Mrs. Richard, 377

MacArthur, Arthur, 226
MacArthur, Douglas, 279, 306; and Ko-
     rean War, 317–18, 319; and removal
     of bonus marchers, 274–78
McCarthy, Frank, 370–71, 376, 378
McCarthy, Joseph R., 317, 325; red-
     hunting in Army, 328, 329, 334
McCarty, Lucius, 238
McClellan, George B., 145, 148, 149
McCloskey, Eddie, 276
McDougall, Alexander, 35–57
MacIver, R. M., 286
McKinley, William, 190, 191; as Presi-
     dent, 192, 196, 212; review of
     Camp Wikoff, 207–8, 209
MacLeish, Archibald, 289
McMillan, Samuel, 194
McNamara, Robert, 348
Macon, Nathaniel, 87, 90
Madison, Dolley, 84, 440n
Madison, James, 37, 77
Maisel, Albert Q., 304–5
Marianthel, George, 377
Marines: at Arlington Cemetery, 132,
     158; and blacks, 231, 234, 299; and
     bonus marchers, 272; ceremony for
     "loyal" POWs, 332–33; exposed to
     Agent Orange, 378, 412; women in,
     301
Marshall, George C., 285–86
Marshall, Samuel Lyman Atwood, 343–
     344; Pork Chop Hill, 344

Martin, Joseph Plumb, 24, 432n
Marx, Karl, 241, 271
Massachusetts: Board of State Charities, 155–56; and the Constitution, 76–77; debtors' protests in, 59–61; repressive measures against dissent, 69, 75; Revolution veterans in, 49–50, 52, 59–62; speculation in, 54–55; tax policies, 54, 57–58; yeomen, 55, 56, 59. *See also* Boston; Pelham; Quabbin Reservoir; Shays' Rebellion
Massachusetts Centinel: and paper money, 53, 55, 56, 438n; on Shays' Rebellion, 63, 65–66, 71, 73–74, 76, 79
Mauldin, Bill, 311, 312
Mayer, William Erwin: findings of, 335–336; judgments disputed, 338–41; as POW authority, 336–38; post in Reagan Administration, 344; qualifications as Army investigator, 334–35; as witness in House, 343
Meade, George G., 133–34, 446n
Meigs, Montgomery C., 172–73, 174
Mellon, Andrew, 261, 262
Melton, Roger, 386
Melville, Herman, 144
Melvin, Walter, 367
Memorial Day: after Civil War, 131–32, 158–59; as official holiday, 158; origin of, 446n
Mencken, H. L., 278
merchants: bounty in New York, 27; and the British, 43–44, 55–56; failure to support soldiers, 35–36; financing to quell Shays' Rebellion, 67; need for hard currency, 53
Merrill, George S., 180
Meselson, Matthew, 363
Mexican War: and Catholic issue, 113–115, consequences of, 117–18; gains, 112; government treatment of deserters, 114–17, 118; popularity, 112; veterans, 117
Michea, Anthony, 217
Miles, Jesse, 103
Milford, Lewis: information on Agent Orange, 472n, 473n, 474n, 475n, 476n, 477n; interviews by, 469n, 476n, 478n
Militia Act, 69
Miller, Doris ("Dorie"), 298–99
Miller, Thomas, 103
Mitchell, Charles, 265

Moley, Raymond, Jr., *The American Legion Story*, 329
Monk, Maria, 109–10
Monroe, James, 83: 1817 message to Congress, 83, 85; and veterans' benefits, 85, 86–91
Montauk Point, L.I. *See* Camp Wikoff
Montgomery, G. V., 393
Moody, Dwight, 126
Morgan, H. Wayne, 447n
Morril, David L., 90
Morris, Robert, 33, 34, 36
Morris, W. C., 137
Mortimer, Elias H., 250; and Forbes, 251–52, 254; government appointment, 257
Morton, Oliver P., 147, 150, 156
Muller, Robert (Bobby), 358–59, 380
Mumford, William, 97, 100
Murkowski, Frank, 407–8
Murphy, John, 396
Murray, John E., "Report to the White House . . . ," 408–9, 410, 478n
Murrow, Edward R., 349, 469n
Myers, Minor, Jr., 436n
My Lai incident, 351–52, 354

NAACP. *See* National Association for the Advancement of Colored People
National Academy of Sciences (NAS), and Ranch Hand study, 378, 379, 395, 400
National Agricultural Chemicals Association, 383
National Association for the Advancement of Colored People (NAACP), 243, 245–46, 375
National Forest Products Association, 382–83
Neal, Moses Leavitt, 66–67
Nevins, Allan, 135
New Republic: on crime, 239–40; and unemployment fears, 284, 295; on the VA, 304, 305
New York City: after Revolution, 26–28, 41; and the *Concho*, 195; homeless and ill veterans in, 130, 204, 207; naval review and parades in, 127, 208, 235, 357, 445n; Tories in, 31
New York Herald, 158; and blacks, 132, 167, 445n; on Camp Wikoff, 200, 205, 206; on Civil War soldiers and veterans, 128, 129, 144, 148, 158; and Spanish-American War, 191, 195

New York Times, 158, 161–62, 294, 445n, 479n; on Agent Orange, 378, 387–89, 400, 402, 475n, 476n; and bonus marchers, 275, 277; denial of crimes in Philippines, 218; on immigrants, 219; on Korean War veterans, 327; on POWs, 321, 324, 332; and Spanish-American War, 191; on the VA, 305, 309

New York Tribune: and blacks, 165, 167, 450n; on Civil War veterans, 151, 152, 156; on pensions, 170; and Spanish-American War, 191, 194

Newburgh (N.Y.): Conspiracy, 37–38, 45–46, 47, 436n; Washington's headquarters in, 30, 36, 37

Newman, Donald, 409

news media: Agent Orange controversy blamed on, 369, 370, 383, 390; government and, 377; perceptions of American journalists, 65; Vietnam coverage, 349–50, 353, 377. *See also* newspapers and periodicals; television

newspapers: and the American Legion, 244; and blacks, 132, 167; and the Bonus March, 276, 278, 279; on Camp Wikoff, 198, 200, 201, 205–208, 454n; and Civil War soldiers and veterans, 128, 129, 161–62, 169–70, 450n; criticism of, 64–65, 144, 388–89; and Cuban evacuation disaster, 196–97, 206, 209–10; distribution curtailed during Civil War, 144–145; and Shays' Rebellion, 63–67, 169; and Spanish-American War, 190–91, 215

newspapers and periodicals: *American Protestant Vindicator*, 109; *Army and Navy Journal*, 129, 133, 136, 151, 163, 446n; *Atlantic Monthly*, 122, 124, 125; *Boston Globe*, 182; *Chicago Times*, 152; *Chicago Tribune*, 130; *Cincinnati Inquirer*, 311; *Cleveland Plain Dealer*, 278; *Commonweal*, 271; *Communist Daily Worker*, 313, 314; *Crisis*, 231, 239, 241; *East-Hampton Star*, 198, 202; *Essex Journal and New Hampshire Packet*, 66; *Forum*, 183–85; *Hampshire Chronicle*, 66; *Harper's Weekly*, 161, 162; *Intelligencer*, 91; *Journal*, 190; *Journal and Messenger*, 157; *Leslie's Illustrated Newspaper*, 141; *Memphis Evening Appeal*, 278; *Messenger*, 234–35, 241, 243; *Nation*, 162, 163, 179, 183; *National Advocate*, 86; *National Review*, 337; *National Tribune*, 172, 175; *New York Daily Advertiser*, 52, 436n; *New York Herald Tribune*, 278, 309, 462n; *New York Journal*, 206; *New-York Morning Post*, 432n; *New York World*, 144, 145, 148, 244; *Niles Register*, 91, 93; *North American Review*, 140, 141; *PM*, 305, 311; *Philadelphia Bulletin*, 179–80, 295; *Philadelphia Press*, 179; *Richmond Dispatch*, 184; *Saturday Review of Literature*, 292; *Soldier's Friend*, 130, 137; *Wall Street Journal*, 263, 294; *Washington Evening Star*, 273, 278; *Washington Post*, 170, 271, 400, 450n; *World*, 190. *See also* *Massachusetts Centinel*; *New Republic*; *New York Herald*; *New York Times*; *New York Tribune*

Nimmo, Robert, as VA head, 391–94

Nixon, Richard M., 317; appointees, 357; as President, 353; problems for administration, 355–56, 358; and veterans, 355, 356

Nonemacher, James, 103

Northcott, R. S., 167

Norton, Eleanor Holmes, 356–57

O'Connor, Sandra Day, 341

Oglesby, Richard James, 130

Olmstead, Frederick Law, 134–35

Olson, Martin P., 219

O'Malley, Charles M., 112

Operation Ranch Hand, 378–79, 389, 390, 395, 405; book based on, 368, 377, 401; criticism of, 378–79, 400; findings, 400–401; questioned, 412–413

"Order of Liberty," 45, 436n

Otis, E. S., 212

Otis, Harrison Gray, 42, 67

Owens, Charles and Ethel, 364, 365

POWs. *See* prisoners of war

Pace, John, 272

Paine, Tom, 101–2

Parker, Theodore, 117

Parsons, Eli, 75

Paths of Glory, 326, 333

Patman, Wright, 266, 272

Patterson, Robert, 311

Patterson, Thomas M., 222

Patton, George S., 274

Paulding, John, 95–96
Peckarsky, J. C., 360–64, 380
Peers, William R., 352
Pegler, Westbrook, 311
Pelham (Mass.), 11, 74, 79; economic
    problems, 57–58; Historical Com-
    mission, 12, 13, 437n, 438n; and
    Revolutionary politics, 57–58;
    Shays' farm, 61, 78
Pension Building, 172–74, 451n
pensions for veterans
    in 1818: debates over, 88–91; legisla-
    tion, effects of, 91–93; proposed by
    Monroe, 85, 86–88; swindles, 93–
    94
    in 1832, 103
    after Civil War, 170–73, 175–86; gov-
    ernment promises of, 160–65, 175
    after Spanish-American War, 205, 210
Pentagon Papers, 349
Peress, Irving, 328
Pershing, John J., 233, 243, 301
Philbin, Philip J., 305
Philippine Insurrection: Army assessment
    of, 222–26; compared to Vietnam
    War, 191, 221, 347, 350, 421; as
    guerrilla war, 212–13, 222; incidents
    of torture and abuse, 215–18, 455n;
    length of, 190, 221; opposition to,
    215, 217–19, 221, 226; as racist,
    216, 219–20, 222–23; Samar inci-
    dent, 213–15; Senate investigation of
    soldiers, 221–26; sentences for
    atrocities, 215–18, 223
Philippine Islands, 211; American con-
    tempt and fear of Filipinos, 212–14,
    218–19, 222–23, 455n; dislike of
    Americans, 212; soldiers in, 212–13.
    See also Philippine Insurrection
Pickering, Timothy, 45, 48
Pierce, Franklin, 117, 118, 124
Pinchot, Gifford, 277
political parties, 111
    Communist, 242, 313–14, 328. See
    also communism
    Democratic: and the Civil War, 143,
    145, 448n; and soldiers' vote, 292
    Know-Nothing, 111
    Republican, 143, 152; and Civil War,
    144; Radical, 144, 154, 156, 157;
    and soldiers' votes, 147–49, 174,
    292; and Spanish-American War,
    191–92, 196
    Socialist, 331
    Socialist Labor, 242
politics: and the G.A.R., 153, 156, 165,
    174, 175, 177, 179; and the mili-
    tary, 144; and the press, 144; Revo-
    lutionary, 57–58; and soldiers'
    votes, 146–49, 153, 174, 175, 292,
    448n; and the Spanish-American
    War, 191
Polk, James, 112
post-traumatic stress disorder, 355, 376,
    410
poverty: government policy toward, 86–
    87, 89; judgments on, 90; soldiers
    and, 24–27, 83–84, 86–87, 184,
    240, 241; veterans and, 18, 26, 27,
    129–131, 204, 207, 267, 356–57,
    423
Pratt, George, 375
prisons: for debtors, 59, 61, 65; pleas for
    reform of, 141; veterans in, 139–41,
    240–41
prisoners of war (Korean War POWs):
    accused of communist sympathies,
    321–24; accused defectors among,
    325–26; Army dossiers on, 336–37;
    Army investigations of, 324–25,
    334–38; behavior blamed on society,
    335; defenders of, 338–41, 343–45;
    judged, 336–38, 341; release of,
    322, 324; torture and abuse of, 320,
    324–325
Protestant Reformation Society, 109
Protestants, against Catholics, 109–11
Pulitzer, Joseph, 190, 191
Putnam, Rufus, 62; conversation with
    Shays, 70–71
Pye, Lucien, 340

Quabbin Reservoir, 10, 13, 17, 78–79,
    440n

Raabe, Mark, 388
racism: Germans' use of, 235; homecom-
    ing black soldiers attacked, 237–38;
    in Philippine Insurrection, 216, 219–
    220, 222–23; in the military, 356.
    See also blacks
radicalism: fear of, 242, 330; Jews and,
    242, 287. See also communism
Rafferty, Max, 337
Ramage, William J., 166–67
Randolph, A. Philip, 238, 299
Rankin, John E.: opposition to social pro-
    grams for veterans, 286–87, 289;
    prejudices, 287, 305, 308, 311
Rauh, Joseph, 331, 332
Raum, Green B., 182
Rayburn, Sam, 294

Reagan, Ronald, 336, 344; and AVC, 312; election promises of, 385–86; and Vietnam Veterans Memorial, 394
  Administration: corruption in, 410, 415; curtailment of veterans' benefits, 18; lack of action on Agent Orange, 385–87, 402, 409; spending in, 386, 393–94, 403; VA made cabinet-level agency, 415–16
Reb, Johnny, 127, 183
Red Cross, 193, 195, 196
Reed, Mrs. Harriet, 168
Reeve, Felix A., 218
Rehnquist, William, 398
Reilly, B. J., 235
Represas, George, 272
Reutershan, Paul, 370, 371
Revolutionary War: battles, 39; consequences, 54–55; elite society after, 12, 24, 54, 74, 438n; financial problems following, 22–25, 34–38, 53–57, 67; inducements to volunteers, 25, 31; meaning of, 9, 12, 40, 44, 74; *See also* Army, Continental; Government; veterans
Ricardo, David, 56
Rickover, Hyman, 337–38
Riddell, Tom, 348, 469n
Ridenhour, Ronald L., 352–53, 470n
Riley, Bennet, 115
Riley, Charles, 224–26
Riley, John, 112–16, 118
Riot Act, 69
Risk, Samuel, 194, 195, 197
Rogers, Edith Nourse, 289
Rogers, Vern, 366, 369, 370, 389
Roosevelt, Franklin Delano, 275–76, 286; cuts to veterans, 278, 279; death of, 305–6; peace planning, 285–86; and soldiers' votes, 292; and veterans' concerns, 287–89, 304
Roosevelt, Franklin D., Jr., 311
Roosevelt, Theodore, 193, 200; description of, 199, 204; as President, 214
Root, Elihu, 214; report on military atrocities in Philippines, 223
Roper, H. McK., 342
Ross, Edward, 236
Roudebush, Richard, 358
Rough Riders, 193, 204
Russell, Benjamin, 65, 66, 79, 438n
Rutledge, William, 153
Ryan, James A., 216
Ryan, Jeremiah, 96

Sacco and Vanzetti, 244
Saddler, M. W., 220
Santa Anna, Antonio de, 114–16
Santiago, 197
Sauquayonk, Cornelius, 102
Schepers, Gerrit, 366, 367, 380
Schermerhorn, John L., 102
Schnur, Paul, 323
Schwable, Frank C., 320
Schweiker, Richard, 392
Scott, Tim, 374
Scott, Winfield, 114–17
Selective Service Act (1940), 285, 293
Selective Service System, 299, 317
Severo, Richard: interviews by, 471n, 472n, 473n, 476n, 478n; *New York Times* articles by, 378, 387–89, 475n, 476n; on Vietnam veterans, 470n
Shafter, William R., 193, 194
Shays, Daniel, 9, 10, 12, 419; description of, 60, 61, 62, 78, 437–438n; honorary sword, 60, 62, 437n; ideals of, 60, 79, 92; judgments against, 76; protest of, 69–71, 74; subsequent to rebellion, 77, 79.
Shays' Rebellion: actual confrontation, 72–73; aftermath, 74–76, 79, 438n; army to quell, 10, 63, 67–68, 70, 72–76; background, 59–62, 64; commemoration of, 11, 13–14, 17, 437n; and newspapers, 63–67, 169; participants in, 21, 62–63, 431n; perceptions of, 10, 12, 76, 77, 79
Shepard, Barclay, 396
Shepard, William, 72, 73, 75
Sherman, William Tecumseh, 144, 145, 173-74; and soldiers' voting, 147–48
Sikes, Robert, 326
Singing Boys in Blue, 156
Skelton, Keith D., 310
slavery: attitudes about, 124, 125; black fear of, 231; mixed feelings over, 132
Sloan, John H., 195
Sloane, William M., 183
Smith, Adam, 56
Smith, Jacob H., 211, 212, 213–14
Smith, Jess, 250
Smith, William, 89, 90
Snow, Walter, 216
Society of the Cincinnati, 40, 46, 52–54, 60, 62, 63, 436n; criticism of, 46, 47–50; founding language, 46–47, 48–49, 436n

soldiers: Army experiments on, 341–42, 397; Army's judgment of, 318, 335, 336; blamed for their problems, 196, 209–10, 318; discrimination against, 136–37, 141; and drug addiction, 137–39; 354–55, 447n; expectations of, 95, 128; impoverished, 24–27, 65, 83–84; life, 23–24, 108, 125; in literature, 126–27, 444n, 445n; pay for, 29–30, 37–38, 88, 206, 260, 263, 432n; perceived as revolutionaries, 37–38, 60, 65, 66, 156–57, 271, 274; racism of, 218–20; role of, 128, 189, 227, 445n; support for, 134, 221; victims of fraud, 93–94, 130; views of, 84, 88–90, 95, 108, 117, 129–30, 133–37, 140–41, 341, 344; votes of, 146–49, 153, 174, 175, 292, 448n; war crimes committed by, 215–16, 221, 223–226, 351–52. *See also* prisoners of war

Soldiers' and Sailors' Home, 133–34
Sommer, John F., 411–12
Southard, Samuel L., 89
Spanish: colonialism, 190, 212, 222; shock over American barbarism, 217; treatment of Filipinos, 220
Spanish-American War, Cuban campaign, 190, 211; end of, 192–93, lack of preparedness for, 191, 192; press support of, 190–91, 215. *See also* Government; Philippine Insurrection
Specter, Arlen, 392
speculation: in Boston, 54–55, 438n; in land, 36, 54; with soldiers' certificates, 36, 53; in stock, 262; among wealthy, 53–54, 437n
Spivey, Gary, and Agent Orange study, 383–84, 391–93
Spock, Benjamin, 338
Stanley, James, 341
Stanton, Edward G., 206
Stanton, Edwin M., 147, 176
Starbuck, Dorothy, 396
Starr, Louis E., 311
Stelle, John, 307–9
Stellman, Jeanne M. and Steven S., 411–412
Stennis, John, 343
Stephenson, Benjamin, 152–54, 156, 165
Sternberg, George Miller, 193, 195, 199, 201, 208, 420, 453n
Steuben, Baron von, 45, 48, 52, 111; pension for, 97–100
Stevens, Paul, 398

Stevens, Robert W., 469n
Stevenson, Henry, Jr., 276
Stewart, Paul, 294, 295
Stiles, Ezra, 23, 34, 431n
Stockman, David, 386, 387
Stone, Francis, 74
Stone, I. F., 304
Sullivan, James, 66, 69
Summerhays, John W., 197
Swanson, Claude A., 218–19, 455n

Taft, Robert A., 312, 317
Taft, William Howard, 221–23, 248, 260
Tanner, James, 174; career of, 176–77; criticism of, 179–82; and veterans' pensions, 177–78, 451n
Taylor, John Thomas, 266, 307
Teague, Olin, 357
television: and Agent Orange issue, 365, 390, 395; homecoming of Iran hostages on, 386; Vietnam War on, 349–50
Temple, Robert, 93
Thalken, Charles E., 401, 477n
Thomas, Bissell, 223
Thomas, John A., 104–5
Thompson, J. W.: companies of, 250, 251, 253, 459n; trial of, 257
Thoreau, Henry David, 117, 125–26, 443n
Thurmond, Strom, 337, 338, 343
Todd, Jane H., 131
Todd, Lester, 321
Toxic Substances Control Act, 366
Treaty: of Ghent, 84, 440n; of Paris, 29
Truman, Harry S., 290, 312; and Korean War, 317–19; and the VA, 306, 308
Twain, Mark, 127, 212, 226–27
2,4,5-T (trichlorophenoxyacetic acid), 372; banned by EPA, 376–77, 379, 389, 395; dangers of, 374; development and uses of, 373, 374; VA study of, 382–83. *See also* Agent Orange; dioxin

unemployment: after Civil War, 129–31, 132, 150; during Depression, 265; fear of, after World War II, 284–85, 294–95; after Revolutionary War, 22; for Vietnam veterans, 355
United States government. *See* Government

VA. *See* Veterans Administration
VFW. *See* Veterans of Foreign Wars
Vacaire, Tim, 356

Vallandigham, Clement L., 145–46

Van Devanter, Lynda M., 303

Vercingetorix, 127, 445n

Vesco, Robert, 356

veterans: adjustment problems, 52, 132; anticommunism of, 328, 329; as citizens, 150; as dissidents, 9, 12, 35, 358; government pledges to help, 156, 358, 385–86; and history, 297, 420, 423, 426; homecomings, 26, 117, 127, 128; homes and hospitals for, 91, 133–34, 162, 180; lack of information on, 15; lack of public acceptance for, 23, 26, 132, 358, 387; lawsuits against government forbidden for, 341, 376; linked to social problems, 137–42, 240–42, 354; numbers of, 14–15; poverty of, 18, 26, 27, 129–31, 204, 207, 267, 356–357, 423; protests by, 13, 14, 37, 151, 268, 279, 370; rejection of claims by government, 96–97, 100–106; victims of government corruption and neglect, 35, 358–59, 423–24; viewed as mercenary, 16, 35, 160, 184, 261. *See also* farmers; soldiers; women

"atomic": failure of VA toward, 397–399, 422; lack of legal redress, 341, 398–99; as victims of experiments, 342–43

black: abuse or neglect of, 17, 128, 163–64, 445n; bounties for, 163–65, 450n; and G.A.R., 165–68; of Vietnam War, 356; violence against, 238

Civil War: advice for, 129–30; benefits for, 128–29, 135–36; desperate straits of, 129–31; discrimination against, 132, 141, 150, 161; drug addiction and crime problems, 137–141; expectations of, 128; government pledge to help, 156; neglect of, 135, 136–38, 150–51, 154, 159; organizing of, 151, 152–55; parades for, 127–29, 208, 235, 357, 445n; pensions for, 170–73, 175–76; problems with officers, 132–33; promised bounties for, 160–65

Korean War: attacked by McCarthy, 328; bitterness among, 344; defenders of, 321; seen as different, 327

Revolutionary War, 21, 431n; adjustment problems of, 52; benefits for, 85–86, 90–92; events to honor, 51–52; lack of sympathy for, 23, 26; land for, 45; money problems of, 22–27, 35–36, 56–63, 432n; protests by, 37; thoughts on recognition for, 39, 45, 47, 48. *See also* Shays' Rebellion; Society of the Cincinnati

Spanish-American War: camp hospital for, 197–204; death from diseases, 194–95; evacuation from Cuba, 193–97; in New York City, 204, 207; safeguards on pension claims, 205, 210; serious diseases of, 190–191, 193–95, 199

Vietnam War: anguish of, 18, 370, 386, 421, 425, 479n; deaths among, study of, 412; demonstrations by, 356–57, 358, 391; in desperate straits, 356–57, 423; drug abuse, 354–55; government philosophy toward, 390, 391, 395; health problems, 410–12, 414; homecoming for, 357, 386; memorial for, 394, 424; proposed outreach programs for, 383–84; red carpet treatment for, 354, 355, 356; unemployment, 355, 356. *See also* Agent Orange; Veterans Administration and Agent Orange

War of 1812, 86, 87

World War I: in "crime wave," 239–240; Government neglect of, 258–260, 279; made to feel guilty, 255, 262; programs for, 247–50; radicalism among, 242. *See also* Bonus March; bonuses for veterans

World War II: as different, 297, 423; and G. I. Bill, 289–90; Government planning for, 285; public wanting bonus for, 295–96; seen as social problem, 290–92, 293; work for, 294–96

Veterans Administration: and Bonus March, 272, 275; on cabinet level, 415–16; conflict with American Legion, 307–9; corruption and inefficiency in, 357, 410, 415, 423; criticism and protests against, 304–305, 357, 358; employees' bonus system, 415; history, "Fifty Fabulous Years," 422; huge budget of, 360; medical services, 303, 304–6; real mission of, 422–23; red-hunting by, 330–32; revamping of, 306–7; weak leadership, 304, 358, 393–94. *See also* Veterans Bureau

Veterans Administration and Agent Orange
Agent Orange special groups and offices, 367–68, 387, 391, 396
Agent Orange Registry, 399–400
Chicago office, 364–66, 369
Congressionally mandated health study, 380, 383; criticism of, 387–88, 392–393; investigation of, 407, 408–10; protocol for, 383–84, 391–93. *See also* Centers for Disease Control
lack of action, 258, 358–59, 394; policy of denial, 361–64, 366, 367, 369, 377, 380, 389–91, 392, 396, 411, 414
professed lack of knowledge, 363, 364
studies, 366–68, 380, 389–91
See also Agent Orange; Operation Ranch Hand
Veterans of Foreign Wars (VFW), 311, 416; and Agent Orange controversy, 395, 396; and Bradley in VA, 308–9
veterans organizations, 309; and the American Legion, 308–9; formation of, 309–10; linked to communism, 311–14. *See also* American Legion; American Veterans Committee; Disabled American Veterans; Society of the Cincinnati; Veterans of Foreign Wars; Vietnam Veterans of America
Vickers, Arthur H., 218
Vietnam: civilians, atrocities committed against, 351–52, 354; destruction of, 349, 350, 352
Vietnam Veterans of America, 303, 359, 380, 415, 469n
Vietnam War: compared to Philippine Insurrection, 191, 221, 347, 350, 421; costs of, 348, 350, 469n; dead, monuments to, 18, 394, 424; devastating, 348, 350; evaluation of, 347, 352–53, 421; public indifference about, 349–50; reporting of, 349–50, 353, 377; soldiers in, 352, 470n; Time-Life series on, 419, 478–79n; as unpopular, 16, 416–17; young soldiers in, 344, 347, 348. *See also* Agent Orange; Government; veterans
Vietnam Women's Memorial Project, 424–25
Volstead Act, 239, 240, 252, 257

Wallace, Henry A., 293, 312
Waller, Littleton W. T., 213–15
Waller, Willard, 291, 292–93
Walters, Harry, 396

war(s): aftermath of, 15; commentary on, 126, 240–41; crimes, question of, 226–27; lack of concern over, 189–190; losses, 14, 451n; protests and questioning about, 217, 226; unpopular, 16, 319. *See also under names of wars*
War of 1812: aftermath of, 83–85; assessment of, 84, 86; blacks in, 232–33; national spirit following, 86; soldiers, poverty of, 83–84. *See also* Government; veterans
Wardman Park Hotel, 250, 251
Ware, John, 130
Warner, William, 174
Warren, Mrs. Mercy, 47
Warren, Robert Penn, 135
Washington (D.C.): Bonus March on, 267, 269–74; burning and rebuilding of, 84, 85; demonstrations in, 358; designs for, 49, 127, 172–73, 440n; early views of, 85, 440n; parades in, 127–28; Pension Palace in, 172–74, 451n; Vietnam Veterans Memorial in, 394, 424
Washington, George: as Army leader, 26, 29, 68, 95, 431n, 432n, 433n, 435n; concerns over Army pay, 36–38; at headquarters, 30, 36, 433n; and Knox, 40–41, 49; shortchanged by Government, 88, 441n; and Society of the Cincinnati, 49; and soldiers' poverty, 23–24; worries of, 29–33, 36
"water cure": in Philippine Insurrection, 215–16, 221, 223–26; in Korean War, 324–25
Waters, Walter W., 270–73; organization of Bonus March, 266–68, 274, 277; subsequent Government job, 279, 462n
Watson, Elkanah, 26, 432n
Watt, Robert J., 295
Webster, Noah, 48
Wecter, Dixon, 292–93
Weinberger, Caspar, 409
Weinstein, Jack, 401, 402
Welsh, Herbert, 221
Wescott, Joseph, 104
West, Samuel, 25, 432n
Whitman, Walt, on the Civil War, 126–127, 444n
Willenz, June A., 303
Willet, Marinus, 52, 54
Willits, Jeremiah, 139–40
Wilson, Woodrow, 233

Winthrop, Robert C., 126
women: black, discrimination against,
    168, 245–46; in G.A.R., 168; gov-
    ernment discrimination against, 300–
    303; in military service, World War
    I, 300–301, World War II, 301–4;
    nurses, 193, 300, 301, 453n; and the
    press, 156–57; of the Revolution,
    103–4; role in government-veteran
    issues, 14; in Vietnam War, 350,
    424–45; war widows, 101, 103–4,
    134, 245–46; in work force, 283–84
Women's Air Force Service Pilots, 302–3
Women's Army Auxiliary Corps, 301–2
Women's Relief Corps, 168
Woodward, Joseph Janvier, 138
World War I: blacks during and follow-
    ing, 231–35, 238; fear of radicalism
    and minorities, 242; military service
    of women in, 300, 301; social unrest
    following, 238–42. See also Govern-
    ment; veterans
World War II: costs of, 293; end of,
    296–97, 306; fear of Depression fol-
    lowing, 283–5; positive views of,

16, 283; women in military service,
    301–3. See also Government; veter-
    ans

Yankelovich, Daniel, 358
Yannacone, Victor, 371, 375, 376, 401–
    402
Yerkes, Robert M., 233–34
Young, Alvin L. ("Dr. Orange"), 365,
    383, 412; advocacy of herbicides,
    379–80, 389–90; 395; Air Force
    Ranch Hand study, 368, 377, 389;
    conflicting roles of, 379, 395; inves-
    tigation of Christian, 408–10; on
    Nightline, 395; on VA Registry,
    399–400; VA report, "Agent Orange
    at the Crossroads," 389–91
Young, Jacob A., 102
Young, S.B.M., 199, 200
Young, Stephen, 424

Zuckerman, Michael, 438n
Zumwalt, Elmo, Jr. and 3rd, 470n
Zwicker, Ralph, 328

ABOUT THE AUTHORS

RICHARD SEVERO is a prize-winning writer for *The New York Times*. His widely acclaimed biography *Lisa H.* was published in 1985. Severo has long combined his strong interest in science and the environment with a social conscience. He has written extensively about chemical contamination of the environment, especially by PCBs and dioxin, and about occupational health, genetic research, housing and civil rights, drug abuse, and about consequences associated with the handling of nuclear waste. He has been praised by veterans and scientists for his coverage of the Agent Orange affair. Severo has won such important national recognition as the George Polk Award for his investigation of milk adulteration in New York, as well as the Penney-Missouri and Mike Berger awards for reporting on urban social concerns. He has been nominated four times for the Pulitzer Prize. Prior to joining the *Times*, he wrote for *The Washington Post*, CBS News, the *New York Herald Tribune* and The Associated Press. His articles have appeared in several magazines, among them *The New Yorker, The New Republic,* and *The Reporter*. The author teaches at Vassar College and lives in Newburgh, New York.

LEWIS MILFORD is a lawyer who heads the Vermont office of the Conservation Law Foundation, a New England environmental organization which seeks to protect New England's natural resources. This is his first book. His interest in the problems of former veterans started many years ago, when he was a lawyer for the National Veterans Law Center in Washington, D.C. In this capacity for five years, he represented Vietnam veterans in Federal court and before Congress on many issues, including Agent Orange. He has testified before Congress on many occasions on issues affecting veterans. Born in Camden, New Jersey, he is a graduate of the Georgetown University Law Center and was on the law faculty at American University. He lives in Montpelier, Vermont.